D   DREAMS

THE   IN YOUR   DREAMS

Purchased with funds
provided by
Friends of the
Jacksonville Library

Books by Mary Summer Rain

Nonfiction
Spirit Song
Phoenix Rising
Dreamwalker
Phantoms Afoot
Earthway
Daybreak
Soul Sounds
Whispered Wisdom
Ancient Echoes
Bittersweet
*Mary Summer Rain's Guide to Dream
    Symbols*
The Visitation
Millennium Memories
Fireside
Eclipse
The Singing Web
Beyond Earthway
Trined In Twilight
Pinecones
Love Never Sleeps
Tao of Nature
Woodsmoke
*In Your Dreams—The Ultimate Dream
    Dictionary*

Children's
Mountains, Meadows and Moonbeams
Star Babies

Fiction
The Seventh Mesa
Ruby

Audio Books
Spirit Song
Phoenix Rising
Dreamwalker
Phantoms Afoot
The Visitation

MARY SUMMER RAIN

IN YOUR
DREAMS

THE ULTIMATE DREAM DICTIONARY

HAMPTON ROADS
PUBLISHING COMPANY, INC.

for the evolving human spirit

Cover design by Marjoram Productions
Cover digital imagery © 2004 PictureQuest/Rubberball

Hampton Roads Publishing Company, Inc.
1125 Stoney Ridge Road
Charlottesville, VA 22902

434-296-2772
fax: 434-296-5096
e-mail: hrpc@hrpub.com
www.hrpub.com

If you are unable to order this book from your local
bookseller, you may order directly from the publisher.
Call 1-800-766-8009, toll-free.

Library of Congress Cataloging-in-Publication Data

Summer Rain, Mary, 1945-
 In your dreams : the ultimate dream dictionary / Mary Summer Rain.
    p. cm.
 Summary: "The updated, revised, and expanded edition of *Mary Summer
Rain's Guide to Dream Symbols*. A quick reference book that explores the power of
dreams for personal transformation, the book supplies concise meanings for
more than 20,000 dream images"--Provided by publisher.
 ISBN 1-57174-433-9 (6 x 9 tp : alk. paper)
 1. Dreams--Dictionaries. 2. Dream interpretation--Dictionaries. 3.
Symbolism (Psychology)--Dictionaries. I. Summer Rain, Mary, 1945- Mary
Summer Rain on dreams. II. Title.
 BF1091.S818 2005
  154.6'3'03--dc22

                        2004023096

10 9 8 7 6 5 4 3
Printed on acid-free paper in Canada

Preface

Throughout the decade since I wrote my first dream dictionary, readership feedback has been eye-opening. Not only was the volume eagerly received, readers cried for more. They asked for a larger dream guide which included their own list of words that I had overlooked. And, as the years passed, the list of words people wanted interpretations for grew longer. Clearly, these lists proved that every single thing we encounter, see, experience, touch, or have even a rudimentary knowledge of can become critical elements appearing in dreams. No object, obviously, is too outlandish, rare, or ridiculous to include. "I dreamed of the Tinman in the *Wizard of Oz,*" one correspondent wrote. "What does the Tinman mean?" Therefore, dream interpretation books should fully embrace as many elements of our world as possible. Otherwise, the reference volume remains incomplete and falls short of adequately providing the questing dreamer with the required tools for arriving at insightful interpretations.

A well-rounded interpretation can't be gained if key pieces are missing from the puzzle. And some of a dream's most revealing elements are depicted on the smallest puzzle fragment. Every piece holds a clue. Every symbolic piece plays an integral part in serving the whole message. Every piece, no matter how small or insignificant it may initially appear, is in the dream for a purpose and requires our attention. Every piece refines the clarity of the dream's overall message.

Keeping the above facts in mind, and realizing that our world's vocabulary has grown by leaps and bounds with the technology explosion and other contributing factors such as recently popularized slang, I've included these new terms for the purpose of providing a more comprehensive volume of dream symbols. This, then, is a completely new volume which embraces a current view of our daily realm of experience. This, then, is warmly offered as a helpful tool for gleaning optimum insights found nowhere other than . . . in your dreams.

A

AARDVARK represents a tendency to hide from problems. Escapism. Denial.

ABACUS denotes a need to refigure an old situation or condition. A change in perspective may be indicated.

ABALONE symbolizes inherent beauty and value of spiritual gifts, talents, or knowledge.

ABANDON connotes that which has been left unattended or shed.

ABANDONMENT (of property) pertains to a giving up of one's interest in something.

ABBESS represents spiritual grace in leadership.

ABBEY symbolizes a need to regain one's spiritual sacredness toward beliefs.

ABBOT See abbess.

ABBREVIATIONS represent a need to cut short certain aspects in life. May come as an advisement to focus on the main issue instead of the smaller details that are inconsequential.

ABDICATE denotes a need to finally leave something alone. Or admit it's time to let another take over the reins of a situation.

ABDOMEN means to take heed of one's inner prompting.

ABDUCTEE (alien) denotes a feeling of helplessness. A situation one has no control over. May refer to a situation in which one is in over one's head, meaning one doesn't have the knowledge base or experience to deal with a situation.

ABDUCTION denotes the taking of something without the right of ownership. A type of takeover. Could also mean a manipulative or domineering nature.

ABERRATION See abnormality.

ABEYANCE indicates a need to keep one's distance.

ABHOR means a hidden aversion or a need to face a fear.

ABIDANCE (compliance) represents a warning to follow the letter and spirit of the law.

ABIDING (enduring) connotes a lasting situation. May be advising a greater level of acceptance.

ABILITIES See talents.

ABJURE See forswear.

ABNORMALITY represents a diversion from the norm. Not necessarily a negative symbol.

ABODE See house.

ABOLISH denotes a warning to get rid of something in one's life. May refer to an attitude, perspective, or relationship.

ABOLITIONIST will characterize a compassionate individual; empathy; one who abhors mistreatment of others and expends energy to prevent/stop it.

ABOMINABLE SNOWMAN represents spiritual concepts that are not readily accepted.

ABORIGINE means a back-to-basics simplicity is required. May indicate extraneous or inconsequential issues that are being given too much time or energy.

ABORTION symbolizes a voluntary separation from something; a conscious choice to distance oneself. This dreamscape symbol is rarely literal.

ABORTIONIST denotes one who instigates some type of separation; one who stops the progression of a new idea/plan/beginning.

ABOUT-FACE represents a sudden change in perspective, behavior, or attitude.

ABOVE (direction) means a higher level.

ABOVEBOARD means following the law or rules; honesty.

ABOVE GROUND represents conventional standards in society.

ABRACADABRA See charm.

ABRASIONS (skin) mean aspects causing friction in life. Could refer to an element causing surface irritations and may signify a caution not to make a bigger issue of them.

ABRIDGE symbolizes a need to curtail or shorten something. May also be pointing to one's habit of cluttering the issue with minor, insignificant details.

ABSCESSES connote aspects leading to negative conditions. Elements carrying the ability to exacerbate a situation.

ABSENT refers to a void in one's life.

ABSENTEE will be an individual who chooses not to participate in something; may point to a form of denial or unwillingness to face an element of reality.

ABSENTEE BALLOT signifies one's right to express an opinion.

ABSENTMINDED reflects a lack of awareness and/or focus.

ABSINTHE means a self-imposed bitterness in one's life.

ABSOLUTE ASSIGNMENT means the giving of something entirely over to another.

ABSOLUTE CONVEYANCE stands for the washing of one's hands of an issue; the giving of something without conditions or expectations.

ABSOLUTE OWNER signifies one owning all interests in something.

ABSOLUTE PITCH represents something perfectly matched; true alignment.

ABSOLUTION means the shedding of self-guilt, probably a false one. Could be pointing to a call for forgiveness or acceptance.

ABSORBENT signifies a need to take in something; a call for greater effort required for understanding.

ABSTINENCE suggests the need to stop doing something in life; self-control/self-denial.

ABSTRACT (art) symbolizes confusion; skewed thinking.

ABSTRACT (text) See summary.

ABSTRACTING JOURNAL refers to the main points of various, specific issues; highlights.

ABSTRACTING SERVICE denotes those who are experienced in perceiving the most important elements of an issue.

ABSTRACT NUMBER pertains to an unknown or undisclosed amount. Questionable quantity.

ABSTRACT OF TITLE warns one to double-check facts relating to the history or background of something.

ABSURDITY connotes an outrageous or ridiculous situation, belief, or perception.

ABUNDANCE is synonymous with enough or more than enough of something.

ABUSAGE points to the use of reasoning that fails to fit an issue.

ABUSE means the serious misuse of something in one's life. This may refer to a type of addiction, or treatment of others.

ABUTMENT advises the need to touch or get close.

ABYSS warns of a path to nowhere. May refer to a loss of will or purpose.

ABYSSINIAN (cat breed) represents honesty. This symbol suggests that the dreamer cherish her/his sense of individuality.

ACACIA (tree) stands for the complexity of an issue; a multifaceted element.

ACADEMY (educational) suggests more information or learning is required.

ACADEMY (military) refers to unyielding and/or strict indoctrination.

ACAROPHOBIA (fear of skin infestation) See fear.

ACCELERATION LANE stands for a time to keep pace with developing issues.

ACCELERATOR symbolizes rate of one's action taken; usually indicates a need to stop procrastinating.

ACCELERATOR (broken or missing) usually advises of a pause time needed. A time of nonaction is required before further advancing action is given to an issue.

ACCELERATOR CARD (computer) represents an increase in the speed of communication or the time it takes to gather information.

ACCENT (language) refers to a different way of saying something. An alternative way to express ideas, feelings, or perspectives.

ACCENT MARK reveals that more emphasis is needed. Advises that something isn't being given enough attention or importance.

ACCEPTANCE LETTER (received) denotes a go-ahead for one's plan. This go-ahead normally comes from one's conscience or Higher Self.

ACCEPTANCE SPEECH indicates one's need to acknowledge something. It can also point to a greater level of acceptance needed.

ACCESS connotes the way to or from something.

ACCESS CODE refers to the key to something.

ACCESSORY represents secondary or affecting aspects connected to a main issue.

ACCESSORY (to a crime) warns of an illegal, unethical, or immoral involvement with an instigator or perpetrator.

ACCESSORY (home decor) depicts the elements in one's life that contribute to personal perspectives.

ACCESSORY BUILDING stands for the important supportive and related elements to an issue. See barn, garage.

ACCESS RIGHTS (ingress and egress) connotes the rights to be involved in an issue.

ACCESS ROAD points the way; an indication that one's way or advancement isn't as blocked as previously thought.

ACCESS TIME points to a designated or proper time to do something.

ACCIDENT is a warning symbol that cautions one to be watchful. May also point to a guiltless act.

ACCIDENT ALERT means minor altercations that cause minimal damage.

ACCIDENT INSURANCE See insurance.

ACCIDENT PRONE represents a careless individual; advises the need for greater awareness and to remain focused on the moment.

ACCLIMATIZE indicates the need to accept situations, or take a wait-and-see position.

ACCOLADES come as praise.

ACCOMMODATION signifies compromise, perhaps a call to be more tolerant.

ACCOMPANIMENT refers to the need for symmetry in one's life, greater balance given to relationships.

ACCOMPLICE warns of a negative relationship.

ACCORDION means alignment with the truth.

ACCORDION PLEAT (fabric) suggests a flexible character; attitudes which have a give-and-take leeway, yet still maintain their basic elements.

ACCOSTED symbolizes a bold confrontation; forwardness of one's nature.

ACCOUNT represents the balance of payments (karma) in one's life.

ACCOUNTANT symbolizes the need to make a personal accounting. This may indicate a need for retrospection or rethinking.

ACCOUNT EXECUTIVE will normally refer to one's conscience and come to remind the dreamer to keep a check on integrity regarding behavior.

ACCOUNTS RECEIVABLES/PAYABLE come in dreams to remind us of our personal balance sheet and will reveal debts still owed and/or repayments received. These debts will be issues one still needs to resolve/rectify. The repayments will be those already taken care of.

ACCOUTERMENT connotes surrounding aspects of one's life that affect perspective.

ACCREDITATION signifies an accepted standard of readiness.

ACCRUAL warns of the need for further knowledge gained.

ACCUMULATION usually indicates excesses. It may denote an emotional build-up, or reveal one's extraneous elements connected to a specific issue.

ACCURSED (under a curse) denotes one's tendency toward suggestibility; gullibility; a false reason attributed to a situation or condition for the purpose of avoiding personal responsibility.

ACCUSATION signifies possible wrongdoing. Depending on the situation in the dreamer's real time life, this could be pointing to a false accusation.

ACE means a winning situation, an agreeable outcome.

ACE IN A HOLE symbolizes a hidden advantage.

ACERBIC warns the dreamer of a bitterness in one's life; a cynical nature.

ACETYLENE TANK advises of a good situation that has the potential to turn explosive.

ACETATE (fabric/film) symbolizes

strength gained from an outside source. This points to an element (or individual) which provides support or encouragement.

ACHES represent life pains one allows self to feel.

ACHIEVEMENT CERTIFICATE comes as a commendation from one's Higher Self.

ACHIEVEMENT TEST means a need to examine one's state of progression toward personal advancement.

ACHILLES (Greek mythology) warns one of one's weak points; can also indicate a lack of strength associated with specific aspects of a plan/idea which could ultimately turn out to be a recurring problem or area of concern.

ACID (chemical) signifies a burning situation or relationship; caustic behavior.

ACID (drug) denotes a desire to alter one's reality. A dependency on a shifted perspective in order to face reality. A belief in the false premise that one can't face reality without first altering it in some manner.

ACID DUST warns of a current atmosphere contaminated with harmful attitudes or ideas.

ACIDOPHILUS MILK signifies the need to digest information better.

ACID PH (reading) comes in dreams to advise one to soften behavior; will indicate a tendency toward acerbic communications, perhaps cynicism.

ACID RAIN warns of dangerous spiritual concepts.

ACID REFLUX (disease) refers to a need to slow the rate of ingestion. Points to a tendency toward taking things in too fast; gulping; a rushed intake. This may apply to food ingestion or be indicating a habit of mentally taking in information at too quick a pace.

ACID ROCK connotes negative influences.

ACID SOIL represents a hardness to one's basic, foundational attitudes/behavior.

ACID TEST symbolizes ultimate verification.

ACID TRIP indicates a willful desire to alter one's world view.

ACID WASHING refers to a lightening up needed.

ACKNOWLEDGMENT means some type of response is required. This may also reveal some type of denial is taking place.

ACME See summit.

ACNE signifies the need to remove negative aspects from one's life.

ACOLYTE warns of misplaced adoration of spiritual personalities.

ACORNS signify the source of one's strength. May also point to the beginning traits of an unyielding personality.

ACOUSTICAL (material) stands for an attempt to focus on every related aspect of an issue; a blocking out of unrelated elements.

ACOUSTICAL SURVEILLANCE See listening post.

ACOUSTIC FEEDBACK (thru microphone) advises of a need to listen to oneself. This symbol points to bad attitudes/behavior.

ACOUSTIC TORPEDO represents actions or intent to counter/nullify a specific falsehood.

ACOUSTICIAN means one who insists on being accurately heard.

ACQUAINTANCE refers to people in one's life who have the potential to affect changes.

ACQUAINTANCE RAPE warns of betrayal or dirty dealings performed by someone the dreamer knows fairly well.

ACQUIESCE connotes a giving-in situation; perhaps warning of the need to have more tolerance or acceptance.

ACQUISITION signifies something added to one's life; could point to a new perspective or a new relationship.

ACQUITTAL generally denotes innocence.

ACRE symbolizes the extent of one's spiritual aspects.

ACRID See bitter.

ACRIMONY See acerbic.

ACROBAT represents the contortions one goes through to gain a goal.

ACRONYM advises one to give greater attention and focus to the main elements of one's path.

ACROPHOBIA (fear of high places) See fear.

ACROSS A BOARD points to all-inclusiveness.

ACTING OUT stands for a desire to force the manifestations of desires or outcomes.

ACTION LINE (phone) signifies a direct line of communication; keeping a strong pulse in current action/situations in one's life.

ACTIVATED CHARCOAL denotes the need to better filter or analyze information.

ACTIVE DUTY comes to advise that the time has come to implement a plan/idea. It's time to get into the action.

ACTIVE LIST symbolizes one's readiness for action.

ACTIVIST signifies one who fights for one's beliefs.

ACTIVITIES AND POSITIONS of people in dreams are extremely important to take note of and recall. They shed invaluable insights on overall intent and serve to clarify other questionable symbols. See specific activities and positions.

ACT OF GOD represents unpreventable situations. It may also point to a situation of blame-shifting by placing responsibility on an untouchable, absent source.

ACT OF WAR won't usually be associated with a literal war between countries but will most often point to behavior inciting conflict.

ACTOR/ACTRESS warns of the need to stop acting. It could also signify an advisement to drop the false persona.

ACUPRESSURE See shiatsu.

ACUPUNCTURE denotes the need to give closer attention to specific aspects (points) of a situation which need addressing.

ACUTE-CARE (medical) signifies a need to take care of a temporary unhealthy situation. This could even refer to an attitude, manner of current behavior, or relationship.

ADAGIO (dance) reflects the need for trust regarding a partner/close associate.

ADAM (biblical) characterizes a weak personality; lack of self control; easily manipulated; fearful of reaching for more information/knowledge.

ADAMANT See stubborn.

ADAM'S APPLE symbolizes difficulty in swallowing foreign ideas; an inability to think outside the box.

ADAPTER signifies an ability to adapt to

changing situations. This symbol may be advising one to have more tolerance and acceptance.

ADDENDUM means something additional must be included in a situation or relationship. May reveal the presence of extenuating aspects associated with something.

ADDER (snake) refers to a venomous nature.

ADDICT symbolizes one who is not in control of one's life.

ADDING MACHINE represents the need to more accurately analyze one's situations and relationships; closer attention needed.

ADDITION (symbol) means one or more aspects need to be included in an issue.

ADDITION (to home) stands for a desire to expand and/or improve one's sense of security and comfort zone. May also refer to a deeper appreciation of those closest to one.

ADDITIVE designates something not of pure form. This symbol could also be pointing to a need to include surrounding factors when making decisions or formulating beliefs.

ADDLE See confusion.

ADDRESS represents an important place. An address can signify the pinpointing of a problem or source of answers.

ADDRESS BOOK refers to quality of friends and associates. Check its condition for greater clarity.

ADDRESSOGRAPH (machine) signifies indiscriminate sharing of information; arbitrary communication; lacking selectiveness in those one chooses to share with; broadcast information.

ADENOID symbolizes difficulty in speaking, of expressing oneself.

ADEPT denotes a proficiency.

ADHESION signifies a strong attachment. May point to a stuck condition.

ADHESIVE represents the need to connect with someone or bring a situation together.

ADHESIVE TAPE denotes the need to bring a connectedness into life. May indicate some type of scattered thoughts, perspective, or condition that requires a cohesiveness.

AD HOC symbolizes an active one mindedness; focused on one issue.

ADIRONDACK CHAIR refers to a respite time. May come as an advisement to take a break and enjoy the scenery.

ADIRONDACK MOUNTAINS mean a call back to nature, to the simple, basic things.

ADJOINING PROPERTIES stands for a connection or related association.

ADJOURN means a time-out needed, a respite required. A pause is required to step back from an issue.

ADJUDICATE advises of a need to make a legal or public statement; a personal type of disclosure.

ADJUSTING designates the need to make alterations, usually acceptance.

AD LIBS signify a call to stop making excuses in life.

ADMINISTRATIVE LEAVE comes to advise a need to take a break from planning, even thinking too much.

ADMINISTRATOR refers to someone who oversees a situation. May point to an individual who either should or shouldn't be in charge.

ADMIRAL signifies one who is in command, not necessarily properly so.

ADMIRALTY CLOTH (fabric) stands for maintaining control; keeping one's composure in the face of disappointment, surprises, or emergencies.

ADMIRATION cautions against excesses in this area. Recall who was giving or receiving the admiration.

ADMISSION TICKET connotes one's right to participate in something.

ADMONISHMENT is always a strong warning symbol.

ADOBE means a down-to-earth attitude or relationship. It may also point to the dreamer's most comfortable position on something.

ADOLESCENT denotes a juvenile outlook, belief, or perception.

ADONIS (Greek mythology) warns against self-love; may signify a false emphasis on external or surface characteristics.

ADOPTING connotes a taking in of something; an act of sheltering.

ADORATION is a warning symbol. Only the Divine is deserving enough to be adored.

ADORNMENT represents one's outward presentation of self, a public persona; an external enhancement.

ADRENAL GLANDS signify aspects affecting one's emotions.

ADRENALINE/EPINEPHRINE refers to situations or individuals who bring about high emotion. A passionate response or causal factor.

ADRIFT means spiritual drifting.

ADULT denotes a mature aspect.

ADULT EDUCATION suggests further information is needed regarding a particular issue.

ADULTERY warns against the taking of something that cannot be yours. This symbol tends to point to prevarications and betrayal.

ADVANCE (payment) symbolizes responsibility; trust and faith.

ADVANCE GUARD refers to the need to be watchful, to notice developing events.

ADVANCE PERSON signifies someone who has the ability to prepare the way.

ADVENT denotes beginning of something, the first signs of its entry into one's life.

ADVENTURER characterizes an individual who has a tendency to throw caution to the wind; someone who is often a thrill-seeker.

ADVENTUROUS suggests a need for caution.

ADVERSARY signifies an opposition aspect in one's life; may reveal the true nature of someone in the dreamer's life.

ADVERTISEMENT cautions one to look closer at a situation.

ADVERTISER is one who attempts to get people's attention.

ADVERTISING AGENCY See Madison Avenue.

ADVISING symbolizes action/counsel the dreamer should heed.

ADVISOR points to an individual who is capable of giving appropriate counsel.

ADVOCATE designates an action one should take.

ADWARE (Internet) See Pop-ups (Internet).

ADZ represents personal energy expended on required work. Advises against the taking of short-cuts and energy-saving methods.

AERATOR connotes a need for breathing room or less intense mental concentration applied to an issue.

AERIALIST cautions against compulsiveness in thought or convoluted thought patterns. This symbol may point to haughtiness.

AERIAL LADDER refers to the reaching for higher thought or loftier meanings to life.

AERIAL PHOTOGRAPH advises of one's need to broaden perspective; widen view to get an over-all, more comprehensive understanding.

AERIAL RAILWAY See cable car.

AERIE signifies high philosophical thought.

AEROBIC EXERCISE represents a caution against being over-emotional.

AERODYNAMIC (shape) means streamlined thought.

AERONAUTICS refer to one's energy applied to thought.

AERONEUROSIS warns of excessive thought given to an issue.

AEROPHOBIA (fear of drafts or airborne matter) signifies one's fear of expressing one's own opinion or thoughts. This dream element may also indicate a reluctance to be open to new ideas.

AEROSOL CANS warn of being under too much pressure.

AEROSPACE symbolizes thought.

AEROSPACE ENGINEERING signifies the manner in which one processes thoughts; may denote a reaching for loftier thinking.

AESOP will be one who speaks truth in a simplistic manner.

AESTHETICIAN is one who has mesmerizing speech, yet may not always speak the truth.

AFFAIR (love) symbolizes lack of loyalty; a deceptive nature.

AFFECTATIONS represent a false sense of self or the need to impress others.

AFFIDAVIT refers to proof, verification.

AFFILIATE will point to an individual, group, or perspective the dreamer shares an affinity with.

AFFINITY GROUP denotes a lack of individuality, an inability to stand alone for one's beliefs.

AFFIRMATION means confidence in one's belief system or perspective.

AFFIRMATIVE ACTION connotes equality; action taken or required to effect a more balanced or positive change.

AFFLICTION represents aspects in one's life that one allows to cause negative effects.

AFFLUENT signifies earthly wealth.

AFFORDABLE indicates an element that's well within one's reach to obtain/attain without expending much energy.

AFGHAN See blanket.

AFGHAN (dog breed) infers an interfering or smothering friend or associate.

A-FRAME (house design) symbolizes one's lifestyle striving toward spiritual alignment.

AFRICA represents uncluttered thoughts and ideas.

AFRICANIZED BEE See killer bee.

AFRICAN VIOLET denotes purity of manner and thought; a gentle nature.

AFRO (hair style) alludes to confused or convoluted thought.

AFTERBIRTH refers to aspects leading up to the birth of an idea. May also be pointing to hindsight.

AFTERBURNER denotes more physical or mental energy required to avoid quitting before something is accomplished. An extra boost required.

AFTEREFFECT will point to a secondary reaction setting in after the first reaction has had time to settle.

AFTERGLOW signifies inner light. May refer to residual good feelings or a knowing of something's rightness.

AFTER-GROWTH See second growth.

AFTER-HOURS represents the need for additional work applied to a life aspect.

AFTERIMAGE symbolizes the lingering impressions one is left with.

AFTERLIFE connotes a reassurance that no situation is hopeless, that there's light at the end of the tunnel. It reveals the uplifting fact that one can get past current problems.

AFTERMATH usually means the consequences of something and comes as a premonition type of symbol.

AFTERNOON designates a more relaxed time to accomplish something.

AFTERPAINS symbolize the need to let go of a hurtful aspect.

AFTER-SHAVE represents the need to soothe an abrasive situation or relationship.

AFTERSHOCK signifies negative effects remaining after an event; ramifications.

AFTERTASTE denotes secondary thoughts on an issue.

AFTERTHOUGHT symbolizes the need to thoroughly discuss something and think it through before leaving the issue.

AFTERWORD See epilogue.

AGATE designates multiple talents.

AGAVE signifies one's diversity.

AGENCY denotes a controlling center of operation.

AGENDA cautions one to give more serious attention to responsibility.

AGENT refers to a middleman who is not necessary; one who represents self as a facilitator. Usually points to one having a personal agenda or ulterior motive.

AGENT ORANGE represents an extremely destructive aspect in one's life; this being one that may appear beneficial at first but will later leave negative effects behind.

AGE OF AQUARIUS means a time of great change and major shifts in societal thought.

AGE OF CONSENT warns of being old enough to know better or take responsibility for one's actions; time to be culpable.

AGE OF REASON means old enough to understand.

AGERATUM (botanical) signifies a fragile personality; emotional sensitivity.

AGE SPOTS (on hands) suggest knowledge gained through experience.

AGGRANDIZE is a serious caution against boastfulness. May be stressing a warning against placing an ideal or individual on a pedestal.

AGGRAVATE warns of a life aspect that is capable of making situations worse. Could be referring to an attitude, plan, perspective, or an individual in the dreamer's life.

AGGREGATE defines a need to consider the whole rather than focusing on the separate parts.

AGGRESSOR designates individuals who may turn on one.

AGILITY signifies one's talent to persevere.

AGING denotes the passing of time in the dreamer's life; maturity. May refer to a new stage of mellowness, acceptance.

AGITATION symbolizes aspects which cause mental or emotional disturbances.

AGNOSTIC cautions against the tendency to demand proof of everything.

AGONY signifies the need to stop dwelling on the past. Greater level of acceptance needed.

AGOUTI connotes an introverted personality.

AGREEMENT represents an aspect that must be resolved.

AGRICIDE represents an intentionally destructive nature.

AGRICULTURAL DISTRICTING stands for a long-term interest or life goal geared toward nurturing an ideal and seeing it successfully manifest.

AGRICULTURE symbolizes one's interest in seeing things come to fruition.

AGROCHEMICAL denotes aspects in one's life that appear to improve situations, yet may prove to be detrimental in the end.

AGROUND designates an off-course spiritual situation.

AID signifies assistance.

AIDE denotes someone capable of giving assistance.

AIDE-DE-CAMP symbolizes one's need to be more regimented and efficient.

AIDS (disease) represents fear of expressing intimate feelings; may also reveal bad blood indicating bad intentions.

AIKIDO See martial arts.

AILMENT signifies aspects in one's life that could be detrimental.

AIM reflects a personal goal, purpose, or chosen course in life.

AIMLESS warns against having no ambition or direction in life. Could also be warning against having no opinion or perspective on an issue.

AIR always symbolizes one's mental/emotional state.

AIR ALERT warns of an attack on one's attitudes, perspectives, plans, or beliefs.

AIR BAG (vehicle) denotes the need to protect one's thoughts and/or emotions.

AIR BASE connotes the mind and its condition in respect to one's thought patterns and process. The basis of one's attitudes and perspectives.

AIR BED comes as an advisement to sleep on it; more thought-time is required before a decision should be made.

AIRBORNE refers to the act of thinking.

AIRBRUSH warns against touching up, changing one's basic ideas to please others.

AIR CARGO symbolizes the transporting of one individual's thoughts to another; the burden of communicating something.

AIR CASTLE means daydreaming; unrealistic ideas.

AIR CLEANER naturally stands for a need to clean (clear) the air. This symbol indicates the current presence of a misunderstanding or bad feelings.

AIR CONDITIONER represents cool or cold attitudes; insensitivity. May indicate a call to cool down a hot temper or angry attitude.

AIRCRAFT See airplane.

AIRCRAFT CARRIER symbolizes a caution for the dreamer to cease letting one's thoughts and opinions ride on those of others.

AIR CUSHION represents a time for deep thinking; a time to postpone a decision for the purpose of giving more thought to the issue; reserving a conclusion.

AIRDROP connotes the dropping of ideas. This symbol could come as an advisement to drop false or damaging perspectives and attitudes.

AIREDALE TERRIER (dog breed) denotes a frivolous nature. This suggests that one needs to get focused and be more serious.

AIRFARE stands for the personal cost of thinking a certain way, following a specific philosophy.

AIRFIELDS represent how an individual takes off with new ideas and plans. Could also point out how an attitude or idea was presented (landed).

AIR FILTER refers to the need to filter new ideas instead of letting them flood in and overwhelm. May also be indicating the opposite, that some issues are being altered by being run through one's personal perspective instead of being looked at in their entirety.

AIRFLOW signifies free-flowing thought patterns. Recall what the air was flowing through. Was it clear or blocked?

AIR FORCE represents forced thought or opinions on another; regimentation of thought.

AIR FORCE ONE suggests an overriding attitude or ideology. Someone's opinion or way of thinking that will end up superseding those of others.

AIR FREIGHT means excessive thought, bulk mental weight.

AIR FRESHENER refers to a need to refresh an issue by revisiting it.

AIR GAUGE comes in dreams to recommend one check the atmosphere (mood) of a situation or relationship for building/deflating pressure.

AIR GUN signifies explosive thoughts, ideas. This symbol carries a polarity interpretation. A negative meaning would be acting on sudden ideas before they're thought out. A positive meaning would refer to epiphanies.

AIR HAMMER symbolizes nagging, harping, a repetitive commenting on the same issue.

AIR HEAD denotes one who cannot discern incoming information, an individual who fails to recognize the varying values of thoughts and ideas. Fragmented thought; inability to focus.

AIR HOLE refers to taking a breather in regard to hard thinking; leaving room to accommodate new ideas.

AIR HORN might stand for a sudden thought that grabs one like an epiphany or it can refer to a loud and clear communication.

AIR HOSE signifies a source of fresh ideas.

AIR LANE symbolizes one's lack of thought diversity and individuality. A thought pattern which remains within a singular, rigid pathway.

AIR LAYERING means to intermix the application of various thoughts. A blend of old ideas or concepts to create a new one.

AIRLESS represents a thoughtless personality; no creativity; no ingenuity; a rigid mind; stale ideas and/or perspectives.

AIRLIFT connotes renewed spark to old thoughts and ideas.

AIRLINER See airplane.

AIR LOCK signifies thoughts one shuts off from self. Self-imposed ignorance, or a refusal to be open to different perspectives.

AIRMAIL refers to one's acceptance of another's idea; an open mind.

AIRMAN represents one who is a concentrated thinker.

AIR MARSHAL signifies guarded thought; a diligent watch for negatives or misfit ideologies which may have the potential for adulterating one's philosophy.

AIR MATTRESS denotes the need to sleep on it.

AIRPLANE represents ideals, attitudes, and belief systems.

AIR PLANT typifies an intellectual; learning is a priority in life.

AIR POCKET symbolizes a temporary loss of ideas or new thoughts on an issue.

AIR POLLUTION reveals a dangerous atmosphere. The dreamer will be able to recognize this situation and relate it to a specific element, such as working environment, social life, or home life.

AIRPORT SECURITY refers to a careful watch on one's thoughts. Inspection of motives or attitudes may be required.

AIRPORT TERMINAL denotes one's abil-

ity to sort out thoughts and ideas. This represents choices of thought.

AIR PUMP refers to the ability to expand on thoughts; take ideas further. Serves to point to a situation, concept, or individual which acts as an impetus spurring one to greater thought.

AIR QUALITY (rating) won't necessarily point to physical health but rather the tone of the atmosphere surrounding a particular issue, situation, or relationship.

AIR RAID signifies a warning to stop allowing others to change your mind, attitudes, or thoughts on an issue.

AIR RAID SHELTER means defensiveness toward attitudes and perspectives; strength of convictions.

AIR RIFLE See air gun.

AIR SHAFT signifies the venting of one's thoughts/opinions.

AIR SHOW denotes an example being shown regarding the potential of one's thought process or reach for knowledge.

AIRSICKNESS symbolizes a fear of having or expressing one's unique or different ideas.

AIR SOCK See windsock.

AIRSPACE denotes the need to make time to think; contemplate.

AIR SPEED refers to rate of thought and how ideas are processed.

AIR STRIKE connotes a warning for the dreamer to protect self from harmful ideas or belief systems. Advises fearlessness toward pointing out a bad idea.

AIRSTRIP represents the manner in which one's ideas are expressed. Recall the physical condition of the dreamscape airstrip.

AIR TAXI (commuter plane) signifies short-term ideas that are quickly exchanged for others.

AIR TERRORISM warns against forced ideas or allowing others to change your mind. The act of controlling another's thoughts.

AIRTIGHT signifies solid ideals or thoughts on an issue; convictions.

AIRTIME symbolizes one's tendency (or opportunities) to broadcast personal thoughts, ideas, or beliefs.

AIR TRAFFIC CONTROLLER indicates the need to keep one's thoughts from crossing or mixing, creating confusion. The need to keep issues separate from one another.

AIR VENT refers to a venting of thoughts, attitudes. May indicate a reluctance to voice opinions that should be aired. Could be suggesting greater assertiveness.

AIR WALK signifies connecting thoughts. The ability to put ideas and concepts together.

AIRWAVES connote various levels of thought; also may refer to how the general public is thinking on a specific issue—popular opinion.

AIRWAY most often refers to inspiration. New life breathed into an idea or old thought. Was the dreamscape airway open or blocked?

AIRWORTHY means worthy ideas or thoughts.

AIRY-FAIRY (appearance/behavior) usually stands for a frivolous personality but can also refer to a highly optimistic individual.

AISLE represents a passageway, a way through something thought to be impassable.

AJAR indicates an out or opening left.

ALABAMA stands for a staunch defense of one's traditional beliefs.

ALABASTER refers to a hard coldness in attitude. May refer to a perspective generated from an aloof attitude. Can indicate a stubborn and unyielding attitude.

À LA CARTE symbolizes a caution to look at aspects individually instead of as a conglomerate whole.

ALADDIN symbolizes one's wishes for easy access to goals; an easy way out. Advises to get motivated, get moving to accomplish goals yourself instead of just sitting around wishing for things to happen or suddenly manifest.

ALADDIN'S LAMP represents having the source of great potential in one's hands but also needing the wisdom to use it properly.

ALAMO indicates a final confrontation.

ALAMODE (fabric) See silk.

ALARM CLOCK usually signifies that it's time to wake up! Change ways.

ALARMIST is one who exaggerates in the negative. One who incites worry or fear, envisioning only the worst.

ALARMS (security) represent a severe warning; take notice. May be pointing to an isolated individual, fearful of sharing perspectives with others.

ALARM SYSTEM denotes a need for higher awareness of one's environment or immediate surroundings. This symbol can also reveal one's self-devised shield around self. Perhaps a fear of letting anyone get to close. Perhaps a self-preservation perimeter.

ALARM SYSTEM (bank) refers to one's finances. Depending on surrounding dreamscape elements, this symbol comes as either a warning signal that brings attention to a developing financial problem, or it signifies successful financial safeguards that are in place.

ALARM SYSTEM (business) signifies safeguards one places on life dealings. This symbol won't exclusively be associated with the workaday aspect of one's life but is usually tied into one's philosophy of daily living and covers such elements as attitudes toward others, tolerance, acceptance, and unconditional goodness—how others are treated on a daily basis.

ALARM SYSTEM (home) relates to one's home life. Is the home a safe-haven? Or is it a place of continual unrest and discord?

ALARM SYSTEM (vehicle) directly pertains to one's physical body. Healthful manner of living or a physically destructive one. Was the alarm going off?

ALASKA indicates one's untapped natural talents.

ALASKA HIGHWAY signifies a rugged path with a road that isn't as rough as one anticipates.

ALASKAN MALAMUTE (dog breed) See malamute.

ALBACORE See tuna.

ALBATROSS denotes one's burdens, sometimes self-created.

ALBINO represents a lack of individuality; a fear of showing one's true colors. Can mean a tendency for noncommittal.

ALBUM (music) reveals the type of inspiration one connects with. What kind of music was the dreamscape album?

ALBUM (photo) indicates the value of family, friends, and life experiences.

ALCATRAZ See prison.

ALCHEMIST is one who attempts to force impossible results; improbable goals; unrealistic ideas or perspectives.

ALCOHOLIC is one who attempts to escape life's problems or past.

ALCOHOLIC BEVERAGE symbolizes a need to relax. Abuse denotes a need to face problems.

ALCOTT (Louisa May) portrays a desire to reform repressive attitudes and perceptions.

ALCOVE represents places of respite. It can also be pointing out an overlooked venue of solace.

ALDER (tree) denotes a need to appreciate life's happier moments.

ALDERPERSON See council person.

ALERT (signal) represents a warning, an advisement to be more aware.

ALEXANDRITE (gemstone) stands for mood fluctuations. This symbol will advise of a need to stabilize emotions.

ALFALFA denotes a need for nourishment.

ALGAE indicate basic life aspects that are spiritually nourishing.

ALGAE-EATER stands for spiritual discernment; a heightened recognition of spiritual opportunities and blessings.

ALGEBRA signifies one's beginning calculations and process of analyzation.

ALIAS indicates identification with more than one personality of self. The negative side to this symbol is a caution against trying to be someone you're not; a false public persona.

ALI BABA represents one who holds the key or answers.

ALIBI signifies guiltlessness.

ALICE IN WONDERLAND suggests an unrealistic life perspective; may possibly refer to an amazing phase of discovery.

ALIEN (earthly being) connotes that which is perceived as being foreign or unfamiliar.

ALIEN (other world being) represents the existence of a wider reality. An advisement to expand perspectives to those possibilities outside the box.

ALIENATION designates a separateness imposed. May be self-induced.

ALIGNMENT denotes the need to return to the course.

ALIMENTARY CANAL signifies a need to focus on one's priorities.

ALIMONY represents payments due. This may not always refer to financial issues. It may also point to a need to give more attention to one's life partner.

A-LIST pertains to those people thought to be a specific field's cream of the crop.

ALKALI indicates dangerous situations or relationships.

ALKALI FLATS See salt flats.

ALKALOID refers to the duality of possessing both positive and negative aspects.

ALLAY refers to a need to be rid of fears of problematical aspects to life.

ALLEGATION signifies unproven claims made.

ALLEGIANCE connotes support or loyalty, some of which is misplaced.

ALLEGORY reflects a parablelike message; deeper meaning.

ALLERGIST is one who finds the root cause of people's problems.

ALLERGY indicates negative aspects directly associated with relationships or belief systems.

ALLEVIATE constitutes a life element that serves to lessen intensity or severity.

ALLEY means the back way in or out of a situation. Another path providing entry or escape routes.

ALLEY CAT signifies a degenerate lifestyle or a hardscrabble existence; hard times.

ALL FOOLS' DAY See April Fools' Day.

ALLIANCE represents a partner or associate. Depending on surrounding dream details, this symbol may be suggesting an alliance be made or broken.

ALLIES refer to friendships that are loyal and true; relationships that can be counted on.

ALLIGATOR connotes spiritual aspects that are self-serving.

ALLIGATOR CLIP See roach clip.

ALL-NIGHTER infers greater effort or attention given to a particular issue; greater effort or thought needs to be given to it.

ALLOTMENT See ration.

ALLOWANCE refers to the need to make allowances in life; be more tolerant.

ALLOY connotes an aspect of one's life where an inferior element has been added.

ALL-POINTS BULLETIN comes as a warning call to be on one's toes, watchful for a negative element that's developing within one's immediate circle of friends and/or relations.

ALL-PURPOSE (product) will naturally point to an element in one's life that will serve multiple aspects.

ALL SAINTS' DAY appears in dreamscapes to remind us that goodness and perseverance, acceptance and tolerance, are qualities we all must strive to practice.

ALLSPICE won't normally refer to a literal spice but rather all elements of one's life should be spiced with acceptance for the things we can't do anything about and also use a smattering of a sense of humor sprinkled in our behavior.

ALL-STAR reflects an idea composed of the best elements.

ALL TERRAIN VEHICLE (ATV) symbolizes one's versatility; perseverance. May also be pointing out that there are ways to solve a problem that haven't been thought of.

ALLUDE See inference.

ALLURING symbolizes temptations; distracting characteristics. Something which diminishes focus on a goal or issue.

ALLUVIAL SOIL stands for an unstable foundation brought by skewed spiritual concepts.

ALL-WEATHER (clothing) signifies those qualities of attitude which serve us in all manner of situations. These would refer to acceptance, patience, a sense of humor, and tolerance.

ALMANAC cautions one to check facts. Further research is required.

ALMOND (nut/oil) represents the need to avoid stress and/or give more attention to one's physical condition.

ALMOND-EYED usually indicates a perceptive individual.

ALMS See donation.

ALOE VERA warns one to soothe a burning situation or desire.

ALONE signifies a situation that may be needed. A suggestion that solitude or quiet time may bring about emotional healing or mental clarity.

ALOOF connotes an arrogant personality.

ALPACA See llama.

ALPENGLOW indicates one's gentle nature.

ALPENHORN means a call to tranquility. This indicates one is experiencing a hectic lifestyle which requires periods of rejuvenation by way of solitude or respite.

ALPHA AND OMEGA define the most important aspect of an issue or concept. A clear view of the beginnings and endings.

ALPHABET suggests a need to return to some basic, foundational elements of an issue. This symbol will normally reveal the fact that one has taken ideas too far afield and has lost some of its elemental ideas.

ALPHABETICAL signifies order and priorities needed.

ALPHABET SOUP advises of a mix of ideas; an aspect that has become confused by bringing too many nonessential elements into it.

ALPINE See mountain.

ALPINE WILDFLOWERS represents choices/decisions made from a spiritual/moral/ethical foundation instead of from what the ego wants.

ALTAR denotes adoration. Watch this one.

ALTAR CLOTH will serve as a clarifying symbol for an altar. What's important here is to recall the condition, color, or designs of the cloth.

ALTAR RAIL represents respect for one's spiritual beliefs. Could also denote some type of barrier between a belief system and one's faith in same.

ALTERATIONS refer to changes required.

ALTERED STATE (mind/reality) will usually reveal a skewed perception but may also indicate a journey through any of the parallel dimensional aspects of true Reality.

ALTER EGO symbolizes a need to know the completeness of self.

ALTERNATING CURRENT (AC) connotes indecision; vacillation.

ALTERNATIVE ENERGY (usage) points to a more natural way of achieving a goal. See solar power.

ALTERNATIVE SCHOOL symbolizes free thought; thinking outside the box.

ALTERNATIVE SOCIETY refers to a large group of people who share a philosophy which varies from the general public's. This symbol may appear in a dream to underscore the fact that it's okay to think differently, you're not alone.

ALTERNATOR denotes the source of one's indecision.

ALTHEA (botanical) See hibiscus.

ALTIMETER cautions against one's changing emotions. May indicate a manic-depressive or a self-image which is growing loftier.

ALTITUDE SICKNESS symbolizes a high attitude, stance, or position that isn't yet deserved; aloofness; haughtiness. Can also refer to concepts one isn't ready to understand or accept.

ALTRUISM corresponds with empathy; selflessness.

ALUM (root) warns of a need to stop something in one's life; a need to staunch some type of behavior.

ALUMINUM signifies the need for reflection.

ALUMINUM FOIL connotes a warning regarding food one ingests. Perhaps a change in diet is required, or maybe a change in perspective (ideas).

ALYSSUM (flower) typifies inner balance and peace.

ALZHEIMER'S DISEASE is a suggestion to be more focused.

AMALGAM warns of an element in one's life that affects one's communication skills in a negative manner and could end up causing harm down the road.

AMALOGIST warns against making false relationships.

AMANITA symbolizes a dangerous situation or relationship.

AMARANTH indicates perseverance and inner strength.

AMARYLLIS constitutes a focused personality; well grounded.

AMATEUR NIGHT represents one's ability and willingness to hear out others.

AMAZEMENT refers to a revelation in one's life.

AMAZON (jungle) symbolizes confused or convoluted path.

AMAZON (river) warns of a spiritual path fraught with dangers.

AMAZONITE (gemstone) comes to represent a healing element in one's life.

AMBASSADOR refers to goodwill and helpfulness.

AMBER connotes resiliency and loyalty. May also denote preservation, which would mean that something in one's life needs to be treasured or always remembered.

AMBERGRIS will stand for the practice of infusing one's behavior with elements meant to divert or cover up true characteristics/attitude.

AMBER ALERT means acute watchfulness due to a situation in progress. Be on one's toes.

AMBIANCE indicates the type of one's surroundings. Ambiance is usually associated with pleasing decor or soothing surroundings; however, a dreamscape may point to one that needs altering.

AMBIDEXTROUS denotes one's ability to see all facets or perspectives of a situation.

AMBIGUITY symbolizes doubts.

AMBISEXUAL indicates a total lack of prejudice.

AMBITION represents the level of one's energy applied to goals.

AMBIVALENCE signifies a contrary personality; indecisiveness.

AMBLING means nonchalance or loss of clear direction or purpose. This symbol may also refer to a defeatist attitude.

AMBROSIA warns that the quick and most appealing solutions are not always the right ones.

AMBULANCE usually warns of a need for medical attention.

AMBULANCE CHASER means one who takes advantage of another's ill-fortune. A self-serving personality, one with ulterior motives.

AMBUSH connotes a deceitful situation or relationship; betrayal.

AMENABLE designates an agreeable personality.

AMENDMENT means additions or changes are required in one's life.

AMENDS cautions one to make reparation.

AMENITIES denote positive benefits to a situation, relationship, or decision.

AMERICA See North America; South America.

AMERICANA suggests a deep-seated sense of patriotism; a love of one's homeland.

AMERICAN DREAM refers to basic life goals or basic rights common to everyone. The good life that is without ties to country, nation, or ethnicity.

AMERICAN INDIAN characterizes the inherent human bond with nature.

AMERICA'S CUP (yacht race) indicates spiritual one-upmanship.

AMETHYST means spiritual inner beauty that shines forth.

AMIABLE defines an agreeable personality.

AMICABLE represents a good-natured individual. This may have a negative meaning in that one could be easily taken advantage of.

AMINO ACID symbolizes aspects in life that are needed but may be lacking.

AMISH signifies simplicity. May be a sign that something can be accomplished without complexity. Solutions may be found through simplifying matters.

AMMONIA warns of dangerous thoughts and points out the existence of a way to neutralize/cleanse them.

AMMONITE reflects an ability for intricate thought; high intelligence and great wisdom.

AMMUNITION signifies validations.

AMNESIA indicates forgetfulness, perhaps purposely; denial or escapism.

AMNESTY symbolizes absolute forgiveness or a new measure of acceptance through tolerance.

AMNESTY INTERNATIONAL points to energies expended toward the support of another's right to be an individual and have expressive rights.

AMNIOCENTESIS represents an inner knowing or precognition. May point to an ability to see though superficial presentations. A skill which allows one to get to the core of an issue.

AMNIOTIC FLUID refers to the safeguards in place to protect a new endeavor.

AMOEBA refers to the beginning formations of an idea, plan, or solution.

AMORPHOUS indicates an inability to bring thoughts together; indistinct thought; obscure perspective.

AMORTIZATION connotes a need to pace oneself. Could mean one who tends to lump problematical situations together and be overwhelmed; therefore, requiring clearer thinking to take one thing at a time.

AMOROUS suggests a desire for a greater measure of closeness.

AMPERE denotes a one-minded personality. This usually indicates narrow-mindedness.

AMPERSAND (& sign) will reveal the presence of a second (or more) individual or elements involved in an issue. This usually comes when an issue is perceived as standing alone or an individual believes she/he is a singular aspect of something.

AMPHETAMINE warns of one's lack of energy and/or awareness.

AMPHIBIAN denotes one who is spiritually grounded.

AMPHITHEATER indicates a clear view of events; a good comprehensive perspective.

AMPLIFIER cautions the dreamer to listen better. Something is being missed.

AMPUTATION strongly suggests the need to cut off something in life. Could point to a relationship, habit, addiction, etc.

AMPUTEE points to the wholeness of one's beingness comprised of heart and soul, emotions and thought.

AMUCK warns of a violent personality, perspective, or relationship.

AMULET See charm.

AMUSEMENT PARK refers to a thrill-seeking personality. Is suggestive of an advisement for one to recognize value in the simple things.

ANABIOTIC advises greater awareness.

ANACHRONISM points to something lacking chronology; will reveal the fact that something's out of order.

ANACONDA reveals an uptight personality; rigidness.

ANAGRAM signifies solutions available within the problem itself; a need to shift perception and look at something in a different light/way.

ANALGESIC reveals the fact that painless resolutions are possible. Refers to the existence of a life aspect which has the properties of a soothing balm.

ANALOGY reveals the type of one's relationships, perspectives, and/or behavior.

ANALYSIS suggests the need to carefully analyze something important.

ANALYST will reveal an individual who is skilled at unraveling confusing issues/situations.

ANARCHY warns of a lack of purpose or direction. May also indicate a need to rise up against adversity or injustice in one's life.

ANASAZI PEOPLE represents beginnings and a return to the Way.

ANATHEMA reveals an issue or individual to avoid.

ANATOMY (study of) signifies a need to look at all parts of a problem, relationship, or situation.

ANCESTOR refers to past relationships, not necessarily familial ones.

ANCESTOR WORSHIP comes in dreamscapes to remind us of the importance of learning from another's past experience or example.

ANCHOR warns one to get spiritually grounded. Depending on surrounding dreamscape factors, this symbol could also indicate a need to pull up the anchor and move away from a false conceptual belief system.

ANCHOR BOLT (structural) denotes a prevention of foundational movement; surety of one's foundational premises or beliefs.

ANCHORPERSON points to an individual who is capable of holding things together; one who serves as a grounding element.

ANCHOR TENANT signifies a main attraction; an element that will be the main draw.

ANCHOVY typifies a spiritual aspect that is not readily accepted; one that is initially distasteful and arbitrarily rejected.

ANCIENT connotes old and wise.

ANCIENT HISTORY suggests elements which are irrelevant to a current situation.

ANDALUSITE (gemstone) symbolizes depression. This symbol stands for a healing aspect that improves perspectives and raises one's general outlook.

ANDIRON symbolizes that which fires one into action. A life aspect that holds the fuel which, once ignited, flares up into action; the potential for action.

ANDROID signifies a mindless personality or one incapable of thinking for self. One who finds safety in routine, and fears variation from set ways.

ANECDOTE denotes the need to learn more of an issue before making a decision or final judgment.

ANEMIA indicates a lack of basic facts. May also be literal; a lack of basic nutrients.

ANEMONE (botanical) represents mental awareness/acuity.

ANESTHESIA warns of apathy.

ANESTHETIC (general) signifies one's *total* apathy.

ANESTHETIC (local) symbolizes one's *selective* apathy.

ANESTHETIST points to one who incites apathy in others.

ANEURYSM warns one to cease dwelling on emotional pain.

ANGEL represents spiritual messages. May come to reveal angelic qualities associated with someone the dreamer knows.

ANGEL DUST (drug) symbolizes dangerous practices.

ANGELFISH typifies the finer aspects of spiritual truths or a spiritual life.

ANGEL HAIR See fiber glass.

ANGEL FOOD CAKE signifies the ingestion of spiritual fluff.

ANGELICA (botanical) corresponds to insights.

ANGEL OF DEATH is most frequently a death premonition.

ANGER MANAGEMENT naturally is a strong advisement to get one's anger under control.

ANGINA warns of overdoing and voluntarily placing oneself in stressful situations.

ANGIOPLASTY comes in a dream to advise of a need to open up (unclog) an attitude or emotion that's preventing free-flow. This free-flow can be related to emotions, communication with another, a negative perspective, or nearly any other form of negativity one is harboring.

ANGLE IRON refers to support required.

ANGLER connotes one who fishes around instead of being direct.

ANGLEWORM refers to bait; incentives; lures.

ANGLING denotes a spiritual nonchalance.

ANGLOPHOBIA (fear of England/English) See fear.

ANGORA (fabric) represents a gentle and thoughtful personality.

ANGUISH warns of immersing self in painful memories.

ANIMA pertains to feminine aspects, the gentle elements of one's inner being; the positive aspects of character and behavior.

ANIMAL will be associated with personality/character qualities. See specific type.

ANIMAL BEHAVIORIST points to a need to better understand a friend.

ANIMAL CARETAKER refers to one's level and quality of compassion.

ANIMAL CONTROL (officer) points to an individual who can be depended on to keep her/his friends out of trouble.

ANIMAL CRACKER indicates a respect for life.

ANIMAL GROOMER See groomer (animal).

ANIMAL HOSPITAL implies a source of extreme compassion and/or aid.

ANIMAL HUSBANDRY connotes a nurturing nature.

ANIMALISM symbolizes misplaced spiritual beliefs.

ANIMAL MAGNETISM denotes one who inherently possesses a powerful personality that attracts the attention of others.

ANIMAL RIGHTS ACTIVIST characterizes a devotional concern for the welfare of one's friends.

ANIMAL SHELTER refers to quality of respect and care given to friends and close associates. Recall condition of the dreamscape shelter. Was it clean? Or filthy?

ANIMAL TRAINER signifies a manipulation of friends and relationships with others.

ANIMATION signifies one's immature outlook on life.

ANIMISM reflects the life force in all things; the fundamental essence.

ANIMUS infers the male aspects' harsher elements to one's character, the more aggressive elements.

ANISE corresponds to a strong personality trait that affects one's behavior.

ANKH typifies enduring peace and spiritual knowledge.

ANKLE denotes support of one's burdens in life.

ANKLE-DEEP suggests a considerable involvement in something.

ANKLET shows the condition or state of one's own self-support system.

ANNALS (historic) refer to lessons learned from the past.

ANNEX signifies the need to join something. Could be thoughts, relationships, etc.

ANNIE OAKLEY is one who is independent. Will point to a self-sufficient woman.

ANNIHILATE represents a need to get rid of an aspect in one's life.

ANNIVERSARY signifies important dates; a date to remember.

ANNIVERSARY RING See ring (jewelry).

ANNOTATION constitutes an explanation.

ANNOUNCEMENT connotes one's need to reveal something.

ANNOUNCER is someone who has a message. The words are usually for the dreamer alone. Recall what was being announced.

ANNOY See irritate.

ANNUAL (yearly) refers to one's tendency to repeat actions.

ANNUAL RING (of tree) typifies a warning sign to stop continually going in circles throughout life, or repeating the same mistakes.

ANNUITY represents good karma returning.

ANNULMENT signifies the breaking of a relationship.

ANNUNCIATION See announcement.

ANODE denotes one's level of energy, impetus, drive.

ANOINTING means a blessing; higher recognition.

ANOMALY refers to a deviation from the norm of one's path, belief system, or perception.

ANONYMOUS represents hidden intentions; or a wish to avoid recognition.

ANORAK emphasizes one's personal methods of overall protection; shielding measures.

ANOREXIA points to one's lack of motivation, direction, or purpose. This dreamscape symbol may also reveal one's false perceptions; obsessive in regarding a distorted perception of oneself.

ANSWERING MACHINE symbolizes one's preference for indirect communication. May indicate a fear of confrontation.

ANT denotes cooperation; goal oriented; mental focus.

ANTACID warns of stressful situations or relationships.

ANTE means putting your share of time or energy into something.

ANTEATER signifies a disruptive nature coupled with mental focus.

ANTECHAMBER See foyer.

ANTELOPE connotes a free-spirited personality.

ANTENNA suggests the need for clarity of thought and ideas. Requiring sharper perception.

ANTEROOM See foyer.

ANT FARM symbolizes an attempt to understand cooperative/joint efforts and what can be accomplished from them.

ANTHEM denotes loyalties and the expression of same.

ANTHILL represents order and/or cooperation toward the common good.

ANTHOLOGY indicates the variety of philosophies in which one believes.

ANTHONY (Susan B.) characterizes one who fights for one's rights, especially against gender-repressive abuses.

ANTHRACITE stands for a motivational aspect; encouragement; an inner drive not readily perceived by others.

ANTHRAX signifies the often fatal effects of being a follower rather than an original thinker.

ANTHROPOLOGIST is one who sparks past-life memories within the dreamer.

ANTHROPOLOGY denotes the benefits of learning from past experiences.

ANTIAIRCRAFT symbolizes the shooting down of one's thoughts or ideas.

ANTI-ANTIBODY warns of highly dangerous persons or relationships.

ANTIBALLISTIC MISSILE represents one's immunity to the destructive ideas and thoughts of others.

ANTIBIOTIC signifies one's need for increased defenses, protection.

ANTIBODY typifies one's personal defense mechanisms. May point to someone who has the potential of protecting the dreamer.

ANTICHRIST connotes an embodiment of negativity or evil.

ANTICIPATION reveals anxiety over future events.

ANTICOAGULANT warns the dreamer to keep things fluid and moving along.

ANTIDEPRESSANT (drug) points to a need to gain more acceptance and/or recognize one's many blessings.

ANTIDOTE means a solution. An aspect in one's life that has the capability of countering a negative element.

ANTIFREEZE cautions against allowing spiritual interest to freeze up.

ANTIGEN denotes destructive aspects.

ANTIGRAVITY refers to personal freedoms and rights.

ANTIHISTAMINE symbolizes aspects in one's life that allow breathing room and times of respite.

ANTI-INFLAMMATORY portrays a need to reduce stress in one's life. May point to someone who has the potential to keep relationships or situations from flaring up.

ANTIMONY stands for a multifaceted aspect.

ANTIPASTO represents variety, choices, and opportunities.

ANTIQUE corresponds to the value in old ideas or ways.

ANTIQUE DEALER points to one who seeks out and offers old ideas or ways to others.

ANTIQUE RING (jewelry) See ring (jewelry).

ANTIQUE SHOP points to where old tried-and-true ideas and ways can be found. But recall the condition of the dreamscape shop. If it was dusty, it means that antiquated thoughts or beliefs are being sold and represented as highly valuable.

ANTISEPTIC reveals a need to protect against a negative situation, relationship, or belief system.

ANTISOCIAL refers to an introverted personality.

ANTITANK typifies one's need for major defensive measures or protection against an aspect in life.

ANTITOXIN warns one to increase personal defenses against a specific danger in the dreamer's life. This symbol reveals the presence of a threat.

ANTLER alludes to one's personal defense mechanisms; a method of body language.

ANTONYM signifies opposition.

ANTSY typifies a restlessness; perhaps lacking acceptance.

ANUBIS warns one to pay more attention to the ramifications of actions.

ANVIL indicates a need to reconfigure a life aspect. May be associated with the dreamer or someone the dreamer is acquainted with.

ANXIETY represents worry. This is a caution to be more within the attitude of acceptance.

AORTA refers to aspects closest to the heart; highly emotional aspects.

APARTHEID denotes racial prejudice; intolerance; lack of acceptance.

APARTMENT indicates a personal need to be around others.

APATHY warns of being emotionally neutral and without compassion.

APE cautions against loss of individuality.

APERITIFS refer to the lack of good nutrition.

APERTURE (camera) symbolizes sight or awareness of one's perceptions.

APEX See summit.

APHID refers to a mentally or emotionally draining personality.

APHRODISIAC indicates ill-attained love; romantic coercion or manipulation.

APHRODITE (Greek deity) means one who uses love for various ends. Makes love into a self-serving tool.

APIARY refers to an industrious nature.

APOCALYPSE connotes a personal revelation; may possibly be associated with a personal conflict.

APOLLO (Greek mythology) refers to male inner beauty, which is often self-denied.

APOLOGY symbolizes an admission of guilt.

APOPLEXY warns of a self-induced inability or affliction, usually to avoid responsibility or gain sympathy.

APOSTLE means one who follows another's spiritual lead.

APOSTROPHE indicates an omission in life.

APOTHECARY See pharmacy.

APPALACHIAN TRAIL refers to a concerted effort to follow the natural way; simplicity.

APPALOOSA (horse breed) denotes inner strength.

APPARATUS See equipment.

APPARITION means an important message.

APPEAL refers to an effort to convince others to see things your way.

APPEASE suggests a compromise needed.

APPELLATE COURT is associated with the people who have the capability of altering your future course.

APPENDECTOMY indicates the need to remove an unnecessary element in one's life.

APPENDIX (listing) signifies the need to do further research.

APPETITE represents one's motivational state. Was the dreamscape appetite voracious or scant?

APPETITE SUPPRESSANT points to a voluntary control of one's desires; effort to take one day at a time.

APPETIZER signifies one's sources of personal motivation.

APPLAUSE means a personal commendation.

APPLAUSE SIGN reveals insincere expressions of appreciation; forced responses.

APPLE typifies good health.

APPLE BLOSSOM symbolizes mental health; rationale.

APPLE BUTTER suggests attention given to healthful elements; an awareness of the more beneficial life aspects.

APPLE CIDER See cider (apple).

APPLEJACK See alcoholic beverage.

APPLE PIE signifies aspects one most closely identifies with as representing hearth and home. This dreamscape element almost always comes as a call to never lose sight of the importance of those closest to us.

APPLESAUCE denotes a pleasant blending of ideals.

APPLIANCE See specific type.

APPLICATIONS refer to one's need to apply self.

APPLIQUÉ connotes a tendency to add to or decorate that which can stand on its own.

APPOINT represents a chosen position. May also represent an arrogant attitude.

APPOINTMENT signifies a need to communicate with another.

APPRAISAL represents an understanding of true value.

APPRAISER denotes one who can reveal the true value of something.

APPREHEND denotes a catching or taking hold of something important.

APPRENTICE symbolizes a need to learn from the bottom up; a need to gain basic and fundamental information or skill.

APPRISE See inform.

APPROVAL warns against one requiring this in order to feel self-worth or have faith in belief systems.

APRICOT (fruit/tree) stands for a healing force that comes from within.

APRIL denotes a time to begin expanding renewal efforts on one's path.

APRIL FOOLS' DAY reveals something foolish done by the dreamer or by an acquaintance of the dreamer.

APRON alludes to self-protective measures.

APRON STRING refers to fear or reluctance to let go of a protective situation or relationship. A connection restricting individuality or self-reliance.

APSE connotes the need to make more time for meditation and/or contemplation.

APTITUDE TEST refers to one's personal understanding of something.

AQUAMARINE (color/gemstone) pertains to the healing benefits of spiritual truths.

AQUANAUT is one who totally immerses self in a spiritual life; a cloistered nun, monk, or reclusive visionary.

AQUARIUM means spiritual arrogance; the confining of spiritual concepts as a possession.

AQUEDUCT represents a specific spiritual course.

ARABESQUE denotes balance.

ARABIAN (horse breed) signifies a noble character; integrity.

ARACHNID See spider.

ARACHNOPHOBIA See fear.

ARBITRATOR characterizes the need for some type of mediation in one's life, perhaps from an outside source to resolve one's own inner conflict over an issue.

ARBOR applies to the perceptible aura of highly spiritual individuals; surrounding self with spiritual ideals.

ARBOR DAY calls for an outward display of spiritual attitudes; a celebration of same.

ARBORETUM suggests the dreamer surround self with higher spiritual aspects.

ARBORVITAE (botanical) stands for the tree of life; comes as a symbol of motivational strength.

ARCADE alludes to games people play.

ARCANE pertains to the ability to understand complex concepts. Depending on surrounding dreamscape factors, this symbol may come as a caution to shed outdated thought.

ARCH portrays a gentle passing through openings in one's life. The ease of taking advantage of opportunities.

ARCHAEOLOGIST is one who ill-uses the past, such as exposing past transgressions of others. Someone in the dreamer's life who digs up the dirt on others.

ARCHEOLOGY (study of) represents a fascination with the past to the extent of ignoring the present. May also reveal an unhealthy penchant for gossip or exposing the dirt on others.

ARCHAIC exposes an outdated idea, belief system, or perspective.

ARCHANGEL portrays critical spiritual messages from the highest source.

ARCHER comes as a messenger.

ARCHERFISH stands for spiritual focus; a sharpened and defined spiritual direction.

ARCHETYPE characterizes a model individual or represents a person one wishes to emulate.

ARCHFIEND reveals a person in one's life who has great potential to cause harm or negativity.

ARCHIPELAGO signifies resting points along one's spiritual path.

ARCHITECT characterizes individuals who attempt to plan out their lives in great detail. One who attempts to create his own reality; a master manipulator to gain personal goals.

ARCHIVE a repository of past events. This symbol may be a call to remember one's past.

ARCH SUPPORT refers to perseverance, inner strength to keep going forward.

AREA CODE denotes a specific region important to the dreamer.

ARENA symbolizes one's circle of relationships or activities.

ARGONAUT (Greek mythology) reflects one on an adventurous quest.

ARGUING See fight.

ARGYLE (pattern) infers well-defined perspectives.

ARID implies a low level of spirituality.

ARISTOCRACY stands for arrogance.

ARITHMETIC See mathematics.

ARIZONA stands for the potential/power of inner strength.

ARK is synonymous with compassion and generosity.

ARKANSAS represents a tendency to have a difficult time understanding another's point of view; a type of stubbornness.

ARK OF THE COVENANT exemplifies our connective bond to the Divine.

ARLINGTON NATIONAL CEMETERY represents honor, respect for those who have given the ultimate for others.

ARM signifies personal work/efforts applied to one's purpose.

ARMADA pertains to a spiritually overbearing and manipulative personality.

ARMADILLO stands for one's personal defense mechanisms.

ARMAGEDDON alludes to a major conflict forthcoming (or expected) in one's life; may also refer to a great fear which is unwarranted.

ARMBAND represents an outward show of emotions or attitudes.

ARMCHAIR indicates a rest period.

ARMISTICE DAY constitutes a conflict resolution.

ARMOIRE alludes to hidden aspects of self.

ARMOR illustrates the dreamer's personal level of protection, self-preservation measures. Recall the armor's condition for greater clarity.

ARMORED CAR/TRUCK signifies one's emotional shield or untouchability.

ARMORED PERSONNEL CARRIER refers to an expectation of a forthcoming conflict and the defensive/offensive preparedness related to it.

ARMOR PIERCING (munitions) may stand for a chronically combative individual, but usually this symbol will refer to the big guns, meaning major power or proof backing one's attitudes or issues.

ARMOR PLATING represents defensiveness; may point to one's tendency to always be ready for a conflict.

ARMORY applies to perseverance and inner strength.

ARMREST suggests a time to put one's aggression and active conflict aside, let the resentment go and get on with life; a need for acceptance and forward movement.

ARMS CONTROL advises of a need to rein in one's determination to actively pursue or exacerbate a currently ongoing conflict.

ARMS-LENGTH suggests a need to distance oneself from a particular situation or issue.

ARMS RACE points to an escalating conflict/disagreement in one's life.

ARM-TWISTING characterizes a manipulative individual. It may point to a situation in which coercion is involved.

ARM WRESTLING indicates a challenge-loving individual.

ARMY pertains to one's personal capability to be assertive.

ARMY ANT exposes a strong opposition or force; a potential for destructiveness coming from a source thought to be too insignificant to give any credence.

ARMY BRAT represents experience in unpredictability; one who is capable of making quick adjustments to routine changes.

ARNICA (botanical) points to priorities and the need to get them straight.

AROMATHERAPY alludes to one's receptivity to surroundings.

ARRAIGNMENT is a call to explain one's actions; a time to face up to deed's or responsibilities.

ARREARS reflects an overdue communication; time to get caught up on something.

ARREST refers to being caught for negative behavior.

ARRHYTHMIA denotes an irregularity of one's emotions; emotional vacillation.

ARROGANCE signifies egotism.

ARROW pertains to a swiftly traveled course.

ARROWHEAD illustrates the beginning of one's course.

ARROWROOT defines an aspect that counters a harmful element in one's life.

ARROYO denotes dangerous probabilities that are currently present along one's path; the dips and low points which carry a high probability for trouble or difficulties.

ARSENAL See armory.

ARSENIC applies to poisonous aspects one voluntarily accepts in life.

ARSON stands for willful destruction done in one's life.

ARSON INVESTIGATOR means suspicion of wrongdoing. This will usually indicate a situation that sparks questionable elements.

ARSONIST is one who enjoys causing destruction.

ART usually signifies creativity or a personal type of imaginative expression.

ART DECO (pattern/style) symbolizes a nonconformist or nonconforming attitude, idea, or behavior.

ARTEMIS (Greek mythology) characterizes cleverness and resourcefulness.

ARTERY refers to aspects in life that emotionally affect us.

ARTESIAN WELL signifies free-flowing spirituality; spiritual behavior which is routinely given or expressed.

ART FILM represents experimental thought, often presented to make one think deeper on a particular issue.

ART GALLERY symbolizes the display or sharing of one's individualized expression. Also can point to what one admires in life.

ARTHRITIS reveals a hidden fear or retained life stressors.

ARTICHOKE is a warning against accepting half-truths; or immature concepts that are incomplete.

ARTICLE (written) signifies the need for further in-depth study.

ARTICULATE cautions one to fully express self.

ARTIFACT denotes validating aspects in one's life.

ARTIFICIAL signifies a lack of genuineness or credibility.

ARTIFICIAL COLORING reveals false perspectives, one's that are purposely displayed to the public.

ARTIFICIAL EYE See glass eye.

ARTIFICIAL FLAVOR reveals the presence of false attributes; imitation qualities.

ARTIFICIAL FLOWERS See silk flowers.

ARTIFICIAL HOUSEPLANTS See houseplant (artificial).

ARTIFICIAL INSEMINATION alludes to a way around barriers to produce the same goal or result.

ARTIFICIAL INTELLIGENCE warns of giving another too much power or control of one's life.

ARTIFICIAL LIMB See prosthesis.

ARTIFICIAL NAILS See false nails.

ARTIFICIAL RESPIRATION connotes an element in one's life that serves as a life-saving factor.

ARTIFICIAL SWEETENER points to an effort to be optimistic, yet isn't working well.

ARTIFICIAL TURF suggests one's affected traits/personality emulates another's.

ARTILLERY indicates one's level of mental acuity.

ARTILLERY RANGE means mental exercises. Any game, puzzle, etc. that is routinely utilized to keep one's mental faculties sharp.

ARTISAN represents personal expression; sense of freedom and individuality; creativity.

ARTIST signifies creativity and the expression of same.

ART NOUVEAU (decor/pattern) represents a flowing expression of individuality; the ease with which one displays her/his uniqueness.

ASBESTOS connotes the duality of one's personal choice of insulating method. This particular one, of course, can be self-destructive.

ASCENDING always indicates one's advancement; a rise to higher standards.

ASCETICISM symbolizes a life of self-denial, deferring to others.

ASCORBIC ACID relates to inner strength.

ASCOT suggests airs, outward affectations one puts on.

ASEXUAL applies to physical and emotional independence.

ASH signifies a de-emphasis of the physical aspects in deference to the higher spiritual ones. May also indicate a complete riddance of something from one's life.

ASH (tree/wood) stands for a de-emphasis on materialistic aspects.

ASHAMED calls for a personal examination of one's actions.

ASHCAN implies getting rid of one's materialistic trappings or extraneous life elements. This, of course, can also be pointing to belief systems, unrealistic goals, relationships, or business dealings.

ASHEN (complexion) warns of ill health or discovery of one's negative action.

ASHRAM cautions against spiritual reclusiveness.

ASHTRAY represents important reminders to leave the past behind and move forward.

ASH WEDNESDAY applies to penance; a reminder of our physical mortality.

ASKANCE (look) means disapproval or questioned behavior.

ASKEW refers to confusion in one's life. An off-balance perception or conclusion derived from incomplete information.

ASKING PRICE will stand for a negotiable issue, one having leeway.

ASP (snake) denotes a threatening relationship.

ASPARAGUS comes as a reminder of our current physical beginnings; youth.

ASPARAGUS FERN suggests a fragile-appearing nature, yet may not be literal.

ASPEN (tree/wood) points to a need to strengthen one's sensitivity; compassion.

ASPHALT denotes a serious separation from the grounding aspects in life.

ASPHYXIA means something is smothering the dreamer.

ASPIRANT applies to one seeking the highest level; actively reaching higher.

ASPIRATOR warns of a need to clear out a congested mind, situation, or relationship.

ASPIRIN signifies the need for respite.

ASSAILANT is one who can do harm in some way.

ASSASSIN pertains to an individual who could ruin one's life or reputation.

ASSAULT RIFLE denotes an aggressive personality, one always on the lookout and ready to pick a fight/argument.

ASSAY OFFICE depicts a need to reassess one's priorities.

ASSEMBLY LINE cautions against routine conformity in life. This may be associated with one's way of thinking.

ASSENT See agreement.

ASSERTIVENESS TRAINING implies the need to be more assertive. This dreamscape symbol usually represents an introverted or retiring personality. It's a call to stand up for oneself. Stop belittling oneself.

ASSESSED VALUE signifies one's individual perception of worth which may or may not be accurate.

ASSESSMENT stands for taking stock of various life aspects.

ASSESSOR will refer to an individual who claims to be an expert in determining the worth of another's talents/skills. This symbol may point to an overly critical personality.

ASSET represents all that has value in the dreamer's life.

ASSIGNMENT pertains to a message to continue one's work or along one's path. Be more responsible.

ASSIMILATE refers to the need to take in that which is important; to understand. It may also come as a caution to be a better listener.

ASSISTANT is one who helps. Does the dreamer need help with something? This dreamscape element may be pointing to stubbornness related to a false sense of independence.

ASSOCIATE characterizes partnerships; a working together.

ASSORTMENT (of almost anything) usually reveals available options.

ASSUMPTION cautions one to stick with the facts.

ASTER (botanical) stands for one's memories and the importance of certain past events.

ASTERISK stands for high importance; getting the dreamer's attention. Reveals the fact that there's more to something than meets the eye; extenuating conditions.

ASTEROID signifies minor events in one's life.

ASTHMA connotes more breathing room is required.

ASTIGMATISM symbolizes the lack of clear understanding; perception is skewed.

ASTRAL PLANE indicates a call to stay in the here and now.

ASTRINGENT signifies a severe or uptight personality. May also relate to a need to tighten up or calm one's ire.

ASTRODOME denotes hidden activities.

ASTROLOGER alludes to one who can pull many aspects together.

ASTROLOGICAL PLANTING TIME-TABLE represents an aspect in one's life that has the capability of providing the highest probability for a successful outcome.

ASTROLOGY (study of) denotes an attempt to better understand self and all surrounding elements of one's life; how they coalesce into one interdependent whole.

ASTRONAUT characterizes our ability to expand ourselves and traverse finer dimensions.

ASTRONOMER is one who intellectually focuses on humankind's ancient heritage as a basis for other life aspects. May refer to the act of delving into possibilities.

ASTRONOMICAL CLOCK comes in dreams to advise us to remember that we should let nature take its course; suggests greater acceptance for the passing of the natural phases of time.

ASTRONOMY (study of) signifies one's interest in humankind's ancient ancestry.

ASTROPHYSICS (study of) denotes an interest in the composition of certain knowns but has no vision toward what lies beyond.

ASYLUM warns of some type of craziness going on in one's life.

ASYMMETRICAL suggests a balance is required.

A-TEAM represents the power of spiritual forces.

ATHEIST connotes those who would destroy spiritual beliefs.

ATHENA (Greek mythology) characterizes one who applies personal integrity to problem resolution. May also represent wisdom and/or a just personality.

ATHENAEUM refers to further study, specifically through extensive reading.

ATHLETE signifies physical accomplishments.

ATHLETE'S FOOT cautions against giving priority to physical accomplishments rather than focusing on spiritual aspects.

ATHLETE'S HEART stands for compassion, generosity, tolerance; a big heart.

ATHLETIC SUPPORTER symbolizes the guarding of one's weak/vulnerable points.

ATLANTIS cautions against negative or wrong use of high knowledge/power/intelligence.

ATLAS indicates expanded world knowledge required. More information is needed. May also reveal that a situation in the dreamer's life carries the potential to have far-reaching ramifications.

ATMOSPHERIC PRESSURE reveals the amount of stress currently present within one's immediate surroundings; the amount of pressure one is under.

ATOLLS signify spiritual serenity through protection.

ATOM most often refers to the importance of the smallest aspects of one's life. A call to pay attention to details, the little things that are being overlooked.

ATOMIC BOMB exemplifies lack of compassion and a disregard for life. Also signifies the danger in ignoring the smaller details in one's life. Smaller elements don't mean they're unimportant or can't carry power.

ATOMIC CLOCK signifies perfect time. Usually comes as a dream element to remind us of the timing of things. It's important to not loose sight of the fact that there's a time for everything and, understanding that, we can gain a bit more acceptance/patience with the waiting.

ATOMIZER means a cover-up.

ATONEMENT infers reparation; reconciliation or contriteness.

ATRIUM depicts an openness of outwardly displayed attitudes and/or emotions.

ATROCITIES illustrate an absolute disregard for life.

ATROPHY warns of letting talents go unused.

ATTACHÉ is the front person for another's mission or purpose.

ATTACHÉ CASE stands for priority material regarding one's mission.

ATTACK refers to a specific conflict in one's life.

ATTENDANCE RECORD won't normally refer to one's physical presence but more likely be associated with mental focus.

ATTENDANT implies a personal helper.

ATTENTION DEFICIT DISORDER (ADD) symbolizes inattention and cautions one to begin focusing and concentrating more on an issue in one's life.

ATTIC pertains to the conscious mind.

ATTORNEY characterizes a need for complete honesty.

ATTORNEY GENERAL relates to a need to reassess major moves that are planned.

AUBURN (color) suggests a deeply impassioned sense of rationale; groundedness.

AUCTION warns one of always attempting to get the most out of relationships and situations. Giving the nod to the highest bidder; self-serving agendas.

AUCTIONEER is one who exaggerates value.

AUDIENCE exemplifies the ever-present watchers in one's life; the eyes on us.

AUDIO BOOK refers to bringing the written word to life; giving fuller and expanded meaning to what is written.

AUDIO CASSETTE represents alternative means of receiving messages.

AUDIOVISUALS signify the need to look at differing aspects of a situation or relationship in one's life.

AUDIT (tax) denotes suspected transgressions committed; a call to maintain honesty.

AUDITION cautions against trying to always be what others want you to be.

AUDITOR represents someone who checks up on another.

AUDITORIUM signifies a need for an audience.

AUGER cautions one to dig down for more information. May also point to the issue of one's emotions—to be more open and expressive.

AUGMENTATION means an exaggeration; something added to the original.

AUGUST (month) denotes a time to repair relationships; address closures.

AULD LANG SYNE connotes an overly reminiscent nature; a dwelling on the past.

AU NATUREL implies a tendency toward aspects that are natural; without trappings, decoration, or dressing. May also point to a lack of ulterior motives.

AUNT relates to a maternal-figure alternative.

AU PAIR will characterize a situation of barter; services exchanged for knowledge.

AURA portrays one's spiritual condition.

AURORA BOREALIS comes as a spiritual comfort or acknowledgment.

AUSPICIOUS stands for an upcoming situation, decision, or relationship being a favorable one; meaningful; a perfect time for something to happen.

AUSTERITY alludes to a disassociating type of personality; one who voluntarily withdraws from society and its trappings. May also refer to an individual who maintains an uncluttered perspective or spiritual belief.

AUSTRALIA suggests congeniality; friendships.

AUSTRALIAN SHEPHERD (dog breed) represents a friend who can help you keep it all together.

AUSTRALIAN SILKY TERRIER (dog breed) signifies a dependable friend who will be there for support in any situation.

AUSTRIA denotes an attention to detail; a tendency to strive for perfection.

AUTHENTICATE means verification.

AUTHOR(ESS) denotes originator; creativity; imagination.

AUTHORITY FIGURE most often refers to someone of greater experience, knowledge, or control. Oftentimes this symbol refers to one's own conscience or Higher Self.

AUTHORIZATION symbolizes permission granted; a legal right.

AUTISM indicates willful suppression of one's inner light and/or spiritual knowledge.

AUTOBAHN (Austria/Germany) stands for a lightning-fast pace. Depending on surrounding details, this could be either a positive or negative symbol.

AUTOBIOGRAPHY represents shared experiences; a willing opening up of oneself.

AUTOCLAVE See sterile.

AUTOCRAT indicates a warning against manipulating the lives of others.

AUTO-FOCUS indicates a continually clear perception regardless of one's distance from the subject/issue.

AUTOGRAPH relates to someone important to the dreamer. Can also refer to the act of leaving one's mark on another's life.

AUTO-HYPNOSIS denotes the need to go within to learn more about oneself; changes have to start with oneself, come from within.

AUTOMAT signifies quick fixes; shortcuts to accessibility.

AUTOMATED TELLER MACHINE (ATM) symbolizes fast cash. A source of solving short-term cash-flow situations. A temporary fix to a problem, a fix that usually demands repayment.

AUTOMATIC DOORS stand for current options that are wide open to take advantage of.

AUTOMATIC PILOT cautions against letting others lead your way or make your decisions.

AUTOMATIC WRITING usually refers to one's conscience; one's Higher Self.

AUTOMATION represents a loss of personal input. A shortcut way of doing things.

AUTO MECHANIC implies a need to seek a medical evaluation.

AUTOMOBILE corresponds to the physical body. Its components will be associated with various parts of the physical body.

AUTONOMY stands for one's independence and the freedom to express uniqueness.

AUTOPSY signifies a need to analyze a past action, relationship, or belief system; pick it apart piece by piece. Also denotes a need to get to the source of a problem or situation.

AUTO SHOW refers to a presentation of options available for one's lifestyle. This means elements such as diet, manner of living, behavior, and directional choices.

AUTOSUGGESTION stands for self-taught methods. May point to acceptance.

AUTUMN (season) means a time for reflection; a time to slow one's pace.

AUTUMN LEAVES indicate a time to slow down; an acceptance of a natural lull in advancements; a time for introspection before moving on.

AUXILIARY will refer to backup reserves. This symbol may be associated with a variety of personal elements in one's life. It may point to energy resources, or knowledge. It may indicate a reserve of faith one falls back on.

AVALANCHE denotes spiritual smothering; an overload of conceptual data intake.

AVALON cautions one against the tendency to have utopian dreams and unrealistic life goals.

AVANT-GARDE stands for the expression of one's character by way of attitudes, perception, or behavior which is unorthodox by the general public's standards.

AVATAR is synonymous with spiritual arrogance.

AVENGER symbolizes an activist on the side of spiritual, ethical, or humanitarian justice.

AVENTURINE (gemstone) stands for stubbornness. This symbol is calling for a better attitude of acceptance.

AVENUE represents a wide path ahead; possibly many distractions along the way.

AVERSION signifies one's distaste for one or more aspects entering or interfering with life.

AVIARY warns against confining one's spiritual talents or knowledge.

AVIATOR is one who holds to one's own ideals, beliefs, and attitudes.

AVIATOR GLASSES denote a shadowy single-vision; only one's personal viewpoint or perspective.

AVOCADO implies a soft-hearted personality with a tough skin. May also point to a need to lighten perspective toward a more optimistic attitude.

AVOIDANCE warns against running away from situations or relationships. Could also point to denial or apathy.

AWARD most often exemplifies commendations from higher sources; a recognition of personal achievements.

AWKWARD (gait) suggests a path one is uncomfortable with.

AWL pertains to the presence of deceit; situations or relationships that are full of holes.

AWNING symbolizes temporary spiritual shelter; a temporary spiritual respite.

AWOL may refer to a refusal to participate in something, but normally it's associated with a denial of some kind; a flight from responsibility or reality; an inability to face an issue and deal with it.

AX warns of trouble ahead along one's path; an abrupt ending in the offing.

AXIS connotes a central focal point which other aspects revolve around.

AXLE exemplifies a motivating force that supports one's actions.

AYERS ROCK alludes to the spiritually obvious; an aspect or even an individual who spiritually "stands out" in respect to her/his moral or ethical behavior.

AZALEA signifies hidden talents.

AZT may not mean the presence of AIDS. More likely, it will represent an effort made or some type of aid utilized for the purpose of maintaining a status quo position; a tool for holding one's own; prevention of a decline.

AZTECS portray ancient belief systems.

AZURE (color) denotes spiritual stretching in regard to thoughts extended past the knowns.

AZURITE denotes high spiritual capabilities.

B

BABBLING (brook) reveals incoherent or convoluted spiritual beliefs.

BABBLING (talk) warns of meaningless dialogue.

BABOON represents a tendency to imitate others; lacking individuality and its free-expression.

BABUSHKA implies a caution against keeping one's thoughts tightly under wraps instead of expressing them.

BABY relates to false innocence; immaturity or novice.

BABY BLUE (color) signifies a beginning development of spirituality, one's initial recognition of sensing an actual relationship with the Divine Essence.

BABY BLUES See postpartum depression.

BABY BONNET applies to a juvenile thought process.

BABY BOOK refers to a desire to remember all the phases of one's spiritual journey.

BABY BOOMER characterizes societal changes.

BABY CARRIAGE represents undeveloped ideas and concepts carried around.

BABY FOOD See Pablum.

BABY MONITOR signifies an ongoing personal supervision of a newly accepted philosophy.

BABY OIL suggests logic greased with immature reasoning.

BABY-PROOFED signifies a desire to protect one's blossoming spirituality or new path.

BABY'S BREATH (flower) connotes the breath of new life breathed into an aspect of life.

BABY SHOES signify baby steps one is taking along a path.

BABYSITTER characterizes a temporary nurturing and mothering condition.

BABY STEPS denote the tentative steps taken when beginning a new direction.

BABY TALK refers to a voluntary reversion to immature reasoning.

BABY TOOTH See milk tooth.

BACHELOR/BACHELORETTE portrays a reluctance to make relationship commitments.

BACHELOR'S BUTTON (flower) connotes self-sufficiency.

BACK (anatomy) refers to unseen or unanticipated events; surprises. May also point to a need to watch one's back, meaning either physical or situational aspects.

BACK (directional placement) symbolizes

background position; may caution one to either come forward or else stay in the background.

BACKACHE points to burdens carried, possibly in a silent manner which can frequently internalize emotional pain.

BACKBEND symbolizes energy expended to go the extra mile; going over and above what's necessary.

BACKBITE implies a vindictiveness.

BACKBOARD warns against a reluctance to seek emotional support or counsel. May reveal a need for assistance in strengthening perseverance.

BACKBONE pertains to strength of character. Recall the condition and alignment of these.

BACK BRACE denotes a need for self-protective measures in respect to one's efforts expended. This dreamscape symbol may be pointing to the existence of a possibly harmful situation needing a "strong back" (endurance).

BACK-BURN (fire fighting) means using the identical elements of a problem to solve it. A back-burn is the intentional lighting of a fire to burn back toward an approaching forest or grass fire. It meets fire with fire. As a dream symbol it suggests taking a head-on approach.

BACK BURNER means something being kept on hold; not a top priority at this time.

BACK COUNTRY alludes to simplicity. May also come as a sign pointing out the importance of something relevant in one's life that isn't readily visible or obvious.

BACKDOOR denotes a way out.

BACK DRAFT symbolizes a combustible situation nearing flashpoint that can come back at you.

BACKDROP warns against redesigning one's past or current reality.

BACKFIELD relates to a secondary position of support.

BACKFILL signifies a life element capable of filling a void in one's life.

BACKFIRE indicates repercussions; something not working out according to plans.

BACKFLASH represents a need to remember an element of one's past which will be relevant to today.

BACK FLIP See somersault.

BACK FLOW warns of a backlash; possible retaliation or a boomerang effect.

BACK FORTY (land) signifies opportunities for further cultivation (development).

BACKGAMMON applies to a noncommittal relationship.

BACKGROUND illustrates underlying aspects in one's life that more attention should be given to.

BACKGROUND MUSIC reveals an underlying mood or attitude.

BACKHAND represents a versatility in handling problems.

BACKHOE denotes a need to dig back for more information.

BACKLASH indicates a negative reaction.

BACK LIGHT signifies a false aura.

BACKLIST applies to something that endures.

BACKLOG relates to an aspect in life that's unfinished; something that requires attention.

BACK LOT reveals a contrived exterior persona.

BACKORDER signifies a wait for something one wants.

BACKPACK implies the basic necessities pertinent to one's life.

BACKPEDAL means a retreat; a going backward; a possible retraction required.

BACK PRESSURE denotes a restrained condition.

BACKREST depicts the necessary pauses along one's path.

BACK ROAD represents in-depth study. The symbol points to valuable information gained or needed by less obvious venues.

BACKROOM connotes hidden aspects.

BACK RUB represents care of one's burdens; an ability to take burdens on while pacing oneself.

BACK SCRATCHER stands for an opportunity to become involved in a mutually synergistic relationship. May point to an element one receives benefits or payback from.

BACK SEAT points to one's rightly designated position. This cautions against trying to always be in the driver's seat.

BACKSEAT DRIVER is one who gives orders and opinions without a right to them.

BACK SLAP usually refers to a congratulatory or friendly gesture.

BACKSLASH (on keyboard) stands for a break in a message or a separation between messages.

BACKSLIDING warns of a slipping back action; a loss of forward movement or progression.

BACKSPACING suggests the need to go back and discover something that was missed. A need to delete or correct something. Oftentimes, more frequently than realized, the spaces between events are full of lessons to be learned but not recognized as being such.

BACKSPIN applies to an emotional shock or revelation.

BACK SPLASH stands for an effort to keep spirituality from entering into issues that should remain separate.

BACKSTAB points to a vindictive personality; betrayal.

BACKSTAGE stands for one's private life, attitude, or that which one does not publicly display.

BACKSTAGE JOHNNY characterizes an intrusive personality; one who disrespects another's privacy.

BACKSTAIRS denotes hidden or secretive movements; alternative agendas.

BACKSTITCH cautions of the need to make amends from the past.

BACKSTOP symbolizes safeguards one creates for self.

BACK STREET usually infers the presence of clandestine behavior; private agendas.

BACKSTRETCH suggests a halfway point.

BACKSTROKE warns of a need to review; go back over spiritual concepts. This dreamscape symbol may also point to a need to turn around and look where one is spiritually headed. May caution against attempting to move forward while looking backward.

BACK TALK usually points to rudeness or impertinence, but may also signify a defense of one's opinion/behavior; standing up for oneself.

BACK-TO-BACK symbolizes the absence of a break between events or issues.

BACK-TO-BASICS denotes a need to return to the fundamentals.

BACKTRACK stresses the need to return to the beginning of a path.

BACKUP (computer) See Go-Back.

BACKUP (generator) connotes a high level of energy reserves.

BACKUP (gun) can refer to secondary protective measures. Also may warn of multiple life issues one is carrying around and stewing over.

BACKUP (offer) refers to a contingency plan; may also indicate a slim chance taken.

BACKUP (plan) denotes one's reserves; contingencies.

BACKWARD (direction) connotes a reverse in one's direction. May represent a need or caution.

BACKWASH refers to an aftermath in turmoil; spiritual truths coming back at a reluctant individual.

BACKWATER warns of stagnant spiritual belief systems.

BACKWEB refers to things hidden in the background.

BACKWOODS portray pure spiritual talents.

BACKYARD alludes to one's rightful territory, perhaps cautioning one against sticking one's nose into other people's business.

BACON symbolizes one's job; working.

BACTERIA denotes infectious situations or relationships; a warning symbol.

BAD BLOOD relates to animosities; bad relationships; grudges.

BAD BOY will reveal one who ignores convention or traditional behavior.

BAD BREATH See halitosis.

BAD EGG will be associated with a negative individual; one who isn't the least interested in reforming.

BADGE signifies identity; a need to be identified or recognized. Sometimes will also mean a commendation of some type.

BADGER stands for a nagging personality, usually one who interferes in another's life.

BADLANDS pertains to places one should not be. This may refer to geography, life situations, belief systems, or personal relationships.

BADMINTON denotes a back-and-forth situation or relationship. May also refer to one's own thought process; indecision; vacillation.

BAD MOUTH points to a disparaging, critical personality.

BAD NEWS most often comes as a revelation about something in one's awake-state life, or it's shown as a forewarning.

BAD RAP denotes the perception of negativity regarding an innocent element/individual.

BAFFLES signify a thwarted aspect in life. It cautions of the probability that something will not succeed.

BAG represents some type of interference in one's life.

BAGEL implies the ingestion or acceptance of a diversity of multi-cultural aspects.

BAGGAGE means excesses in one's life; a carrying of unnecessary aspects, possibly referring to attitudes, beliefs, material possessions, etc.

B

BAGGAGE HANDLER See porter.

BAGGER (at register counter) suggests someone who consolidates another's ideas, pulls them together.

BAGGY (clothing fit) usually indicates a relaxed personality; one having a fair amount of general acceptance.

BAG LADY characterizes priorities; giving attention to only those life aspects that are necessary basics; the needful things in life.

BAGMAN portrays debts or underhanded dealings.

BAGPIPE symbolizes an individual who consistently talks about nothing important; a gossip; one who talks to gain attention or hold the floor.

BAGUETTE (bread) pertains to life's basic necessities; the basics which sustain us.

BAGUETTE (gem shape) depicts a supporting aspect in one's life. This could refer to an individual, situation, or belief.

BAIL (bond) means a temporary reprieve.

BAIL (eject) warns against staying in a situation; it's literally time to bail out.

BAIL (water) cautions one to empty one's mind of damaging spiritual concepts.

BAILIFF characterizes one who maintains order.

BAILSMAN See bondsman.

BAIT denotes enticements. This is a warning dream symbol.

BAIT AND SWITCH cautions against being taken in through deceit or false promises; ulterior motives; unethical practices.

BAKE relates to something finished; bringing to fruition.

BAKE-OFF represents the best possible outcome.

BAKER signifies an expanding scope of one's spiritual understanding and personal application. One who has the capacity to bring something to fruition.

BAKER'S DOZEN means personal generosity; giving more than required; going the extra mile for others.

BAKERY most frequently stands for the ingestion of sweet and/or high-caloric foodstuffs. This is usually a warning symbol for the literal physical meaning. This dreamscape element may also refer to a source for generosity in one's life.

BAKE SALE represents efforts expended to help another.

BAKING POWDER signifies aspects in one's life that need to be blended or mixed with others.

BAKING SODA symbolizes a cleansing aspect in one's life.

BAKLAVA depicts those sweeter life aspects that come quite naturally.

BALANCE BEAM (gymnastic) reminds us to walk a balanced path. Usually points to a current situation of imbalance in the dreamer's life.

BALANCE OF POWER implies a need to share responsibility and control; each individual requires her/his own portion which is answerable for.

BALANCE OF TRADE pertains to our daily give-and-take equilibrium.

BALANCE SHEET refers to one's karmic record.

BALANCE WHEEL denotes a stabilizing aspect or influence.

BALCONY portrays perceptual clarity.

BALD (head) characterizes a thoughtless individual; one who rarely thinks for self or has original ideas.

BALE stands for a need to open up. This may refer to one's thoughts, emotions, or finances.

BALE HOOK (farm implement) represents an aid in handling heavy issues. This aid could be anything: understanding, acceptance, patience, etc.

BALEEN See whalebone.

BALKAN STATES suggest a sense of being overburdened.

BALL (child's) suggests simplicity, ease of communicating ideas.

BALL (gala) a celebrated event in one's life; verification of one's recent steps taken.

BALLAD relates to lessons learned.

BALL AND CHAIN naturally refers to a burden one carries; a weight.

BALLAST warns of a need to unload. This means one is carrying excessive weight in relation to emotional, mental, or spiritual aspects.

BALL BEARING connotes an easier, smoother method of operation.

BALL BOY comes to remind us of the little, everyday blessings of helpfulness we often overlook or never stop to appreciate.

BALL CLUB will represent those we show support to.

BALL COCK cautions against not taking personal responsibility in the regulation of one's spiritual quest for the truth.

BALLERINA portrays a woman who is a true lady; genteel thoughts, actions, and graceful manner (within and without).

BALLET represents a situation that has been engineered; players dancing through their parts; dancing through life with prearranged steps instead of letting the moment dictate movements.

BALLET SLIPPERS may indicate a lack of seriousness; dancing through life. Also may refer to the graceful manner one utilizes acceptance.

BALL GAME See specific type.

BALL GOWN reveals our right to celebrate recent steps or decisions in life. Recall the condition and style of gown to determine if the symbol points to a positive or negative meaning.

BALLISTICS usually refers to a test to prove guilt or innocence, but may also signify an extreme reaction to something as in *going ballistic.*

BALL LIGHTNING illustrates a concentrated effort to gain one's attention. This is directed toward the dreamer and comes as a warning signal.

BALL OF FIRE suggests a highly efficient and energetic individual.

BALL OF LIGHT exemplifies high spiritual illumination.

BALL OF TWINE alludes to the need to proceed cautiously. Closure for something can come easily if issues are handled slowly, otherwise, entanglements will result.

BALL OF WAX refers to a complete aspect of an issue encompassing all related elements.

BALLOON represents an exaggeration.

BALLOON FLOWER usually refers to inner joy. Depending on surrounding dreamscape aspects, this symbol may advise one to lessen the tendency to exaggerate.

BALLOON MORTGAGE depicts the ultimate payment of debts coming due. This usually relates to an emotional aspect in one's life—relationships. May also reveal an upcoming time when one must pay the piper.

BALLOT stands for freedom of speech; one's right to have a say, making of choices.

BALLPARK symbolizes one's recognition of limits; bounds.

BALLROOM represents the place or life arena in which we do our dancing. We shouldn't be doing fancy footwork anywhere in life. May also indicate a reason to celebrate recent decisions. Surrounding details of the ballroom's condition reveals which meaning applies.

BALM points to that which soothes in one's life.

BALMY reflects an enjoyable atmosphere that is free of difficulty; pleasant and uplifting; encouraging.

BALSAM (tree/wood) comes in dreams to point to spiritual tranquility.

BALSA WOOD applies to our innate personal talents. May refer to thoughts which make light of our burdens.

BAMBI characterizes true innocence; a naïveté.

BAMBOO connotes developing talents.

BAN pertains to lack of freedom and/or rights in one's life. May also point to something the dreamer needs to stop doing.

BANANA symbolizes inner goodness. Sometimes seen only after other aspects have been peeled away.

BANANA SPLIT denotes one's inner goodness that is frequently enhanced by other expressions of one's talents.

BAND (of people) signifies strength in numbers. Depending on the dreamer's specific life circumstances, this dreamscape symbol may point to a need to go it alone.

BAND (musical) depicts the beginning stage of being able to work together with others; cooperation; a synergistic association.

BANDAGE indicates a healing needed. It's time for an emotional wound to heal. May also point to a "temporary fix" requiring greater future attention.

BANDANNA means unclear thought; a tendency to cover same.

BANDBOX signifies the care one gives to important life aspects.

BANDICOOT implies small blessings.

BANDIT characterizes one who possesses that which has been ill-gotten; ulterior motives.

BANDLEADER portrays an individual who instigates a mood of cooperation among people. Depending on the dreamer's life situation, this symbol could also point to a negative attitude of arrogance or manipulation.

BANDOLEER illustrates a warrior type of personal preparedness; strong defenses.

BAND SAW alludes to cutting remarks or deeds in a relationship.

BAND SHELL signifies the opportunities to experience leisurely enjoyment along our life journey.

BANDSTAND refers to a tendency to be the center of attention.

BANDWAGON warns against the inclination to follow others or fad ideas. May point to a penchant for grandstanding or lobbying.

BANGLE (jewelry) suggests individuality and the feeling of freedom to express it.

BANISH symbolizes an exile type of situation or attitude. What does the dreamer want to get rid of for good? Is the dreamer behaving in a manner that banishes self from something?

BANISTER See handrail.

BANJO stands for gaiety; lightheartedness.

BANK (built up) implies a situation, concept, or relationship that requires additional supportive aspects be applied.

BANK (financial) pertains to that which one saves or values as being highly meaningful; personal riches.

BANK (land) See riverbank.

BANKBOOK suggests one's personal wealth. Is all the money hoarded or withdrawn to help others?

BANK CARD means an individual's right to aspects in life that would be considered personal assets.

BANK DEPOSIT signifies an effort to accumulate reserves. This can relate to any element in one's life and related dream details will clarify which was intended.

BANK DRAFT See certified check.

BANK EXAMINER usually comes in dreams to caution one against trying to fool oneself when it comes to one's behavioral balance sheet.

BANKROLL (money roll) portrays personal wealth. May indicate generosity depending on the surrounding dreamscape details.

BANKRUPT denotes one who is wealthy yet remains devoid of spiritual assets; a miser. May also indicate a literally penniless individual; apathy.

BANK STATEMENT suggests a reconciliation between how one *thinks* one is doing in life regarding behavior and how one is *actually* performing.

BANK TRANSACTIONS indicate how well riches (talents) are managed and utilized.

BANNER denotes a means of getting attention. Try to recall what the banner said to gain greater clarity.

BANNS (marriage) reveal an intent; an announcement.

BANQUET suggests a generous situation; sharing.

BANQUET ROOM stands for a place of sharing. The key here is to recall the room's condition, how it was decorated, and if it was full of people or empty.

BANSHEE warns of death. This may forewarn of a spiritual, emotional, or actual physical demise.

BANTER infers playful teasing yet usually exposes some type of hidden message.

BANYAN (tree) symbolizes strong roots/foundations.

BAPTISM connotes a spiritual birth; a rebirth; perhaps a return to innocence.

BAPTISM OF FIRE stands for experiencing an ordeal before one *thinks* one is ready.

BAR (candy) relates to taking the time to recognize and enjoy the sweet aspects of life.

BAR (energy) means a recognition of those life elements which are capable of boosting one's perseverance.

BAR (exclude) infers denial or exclusionary attitudes. Who was barred from what?

BAR (liquor) See tavern.

BARB implies hurting, sharp aspects in life.

BAR BACK characterizes one who can offer support.

BARBARIAN characterizes a severely unmannered individual; crude thought patterns; primitive behavior.

BARBECUE represents a burning thought or attitude that cooks and sizzles within the person.

BARBED WIRE connotes an individual's harmful attitude (tendency) to angrily cut self off from another; animosity; prickly barriers to a situation yet not impossible to get past.

BARBELL alludes to those life aspects that build strength; endurance-builders.

BARBER See beautician.

BARBERSHOP implies a need to trim or restyle one's thoughts, attitudes, or belief systems.

BARBIE DOLL refers to an unrealistic image to emulate.

BAR CHART symbolizes a quick gauge of how one is progressing.

BAR CODE relates to systematically hidden information; concealed costs of something.

BARD See storyteller.

BAREBACK (riding) exemplifies a free spirit; one going forward unrestrained; unfettered.

BARE BONES apply to essentials; bottom-line facts.

BAREFOOT characterizes an individual who walks a path with full knowledge of what each step means. Having total awareness while walking a path.

BAREHEADED signifies an expressive individual; honest; forthright.

BARE-KNUCKLE implies one who is vulnerable.

BARF BAG will be associated with an awareness of a potential for experiencing a highly disagreeable situation.

BARFLY characterizes a tendency to shrug responsibility; may point to apathy or despair.

BARGAIN will emphasize a good plan or course.

BARGAIN BASEMENT suggests a wealth of opportunities. Recall the type of items that were featured.

BARGAIN HUNTER is one who seeks the best course of action; identifying a solution having the least resistance or fewest number of problematical elements.

BARGAINING CHIP represents an inducement, an ace-in-the-hole.

BARGE pertains to a spiritually lethargic rate of progress; spiritually overburdened.

BAR HOPPING indicates a restlessness.

BARITE (gemstone) represents longevity. This symbol denotes intensified attitudes.

BARK (confection) See chocolate.

BARK (dog) represents a warning or greeting from a friend. Refer to dream details for clarity.

BARK (tree) applies to one's external presentation of strength. Was it rough (arrogant or aggressive), or smooth like a birch (quiet strength)?

BARKEEPER See bartender.

BARKER (fair) characterizes a loudmouth; one who usually has much to say about nothing; someone who has a tendency to love drawing attention to self.

BARLEY applies to essential elements in one's life.

BAR/BAT MITZVAH denotes the point of responsibility for self.

BARN connotes those life aspects which one shelters from others or keeps protected.

BARNACLE pertains to extraneous aspects that one allows to weigh down or impede progress.

BARN DANCE See hootenanny.

BARN OWL stands for intuitiveness.

BARNSTORMING See stunt flying.

BARN WOOD represents a well-weathered element, well-seasoned and experienced.

BARNYARD stands for down-home attitudes and/or relationships; an unaffected personality.

BAROMETER portrays the amount of pressure one is under.

BAROQUE (decor style) will usually point to an extravagant personality.

BARRACKS suggest a lack of individuality; self-repression.

BARRACUDA characterizes a lack of moral or ethical value; a vicious personality.

BARRED OWL stands for multifaceted aspects. This symbol will usually point to a need to clarify a complexity in one's life.

BARREL means abundance.

BARREL CHAIR applies to personal mass. This warns of the tendency to carry around more weight than necessary. May refer to various aspects in life, not merely body weight.

BARREL CHESTED denotes a giving personality.

BARREL RACING most often reveals a confident woman; one who isn't fearful of giving something her best effort.

BARREN implies a lack of new life or lack of new emotional, intellectual, or spiritual growth. May warn of an apathetic perspective.

BARRETTE signifies thoughts that are caught up or restrained.

BARRICADE means self-imposed blocks one places in the way of progress.

BARRIER exemplifies a temporary pause for the dreamer. This may refer to various life aspects and won't necessarily imply an insurmountable obstacle.

BARRIER REEF stands for a time of rest during one's spiritual quest.

BARRISTER See attorney.

BARRISTER BOOK CASE signifies a respect for knowledge.

BARROOM relates to a place where emotional support or sympathy can sometimes be received.

BARSTOOL See high chair.

BARTENDER is one who frequently serves potential advice to others or provides a sympathetic ear. May not always represent positive communication.

BARTER implies give and take; a sharing of talents.

BARTON (Clara) characterizes a great desire to provide others with basic comforts.

BASALT applies to an individual who has become hardened after a highly emotional life stage; verging on apathetic. Also may refer to the need to avoid diversionary side-roads while traveling one's path.

BASE refers to foundational elements or a secure position.

BASEBALL relates to winning through skill and speed. Not necessary a totally commendable symbol depending on what surrounding symbols show.

BASEBALL CAP usually points to a casual nature.

BASEBALL DIAMOND denotes one's tendency to follow the same pattern to achieve goals.

BASEBOARD alludes to finished ideas that conclude previous lines of thought and bring them together.

BASEBOARD HEAT pertains to a rising level of intensified emotions that has the potential of being costly.

BASE CAMP signifies our comfort zone—what we retreat to when rejuvenation or rest is required.

BASE COAT represents attention to foundational work which finishing work and detailed aspects will be built upon.

BASE HIT defines an action or a move that caused no negative ramifications.

BASE LEVEL cautions one to research spiritual concepts back to their beginnings.

BASELINE symbolizes a point at which to begin gauging progress or decline.

BASE LOAD will represent one's tolerable stress level.

BASEMENT stands for the subconscious mind.

BASENJI (dog breed) denotes a sensitive nature; strength through emotional sensitivity.

BASE PAY exemplifies required time and work; a tendency to avoid doing more than necessary. This dreamscape symbol means that more effort is required in order to receive additional benefits.

BASE PRICE will usually signify the very least amount of cost something will have

for us. This cost won't be monetary but rather an expending of emotional involvement or energies.

BASHFUL can frequently mean feelings of inferiority, but most often it's associated with a desire to remain out of the limelight; one not wanting acknowledgment or recognition.

BASIC TRAINING implies having the basics regarding something. This would infer further learning is required.

BASIL corresponds to a light flavoring or hint; a suggestion.

BASILICA warns against spiritual arrogance, believing one is more spiritually special or unique than another.

BASIN See sink.

BASK connotes voluntary absorption of something; a pleasurable time of rejoicing in happiness or well-being.

BASKET alludes to a need to gather more information.

BASKETBALL (ball or game) suggests an active situation where one needs to keep on one's toes and stay aware of what others are doing.

BASKET CASE signifies an emotionally confused individual.

BASKET WEAVE (pattern) denotes integrated ideas.

BASS (fish) applies to spiritual talents and the generous sharing of them.

BASS (tone) refers to depth of meaning or emotion.

BASS DRUM represents that which affects us most deeply on an emotional level.

BASSET HOUND (dog breed) symbolizes melancholy; sadness related to a friend.

BASSINET means spiritual respite; a need to rest along one's newly begun path.

BASSOON reflects deep thoughts; high philosophic contemplation.

BASSWOOD refers to fortified strength; determination.

BASTE (cook) cautions against allowing spiritual beliefs to dry up.

BASTE (sew) refers to a temporary pulling together of some aspect in the dreamer's life; a makeshift repair until further attention can be given.

BAT (animal) means the use of spiritual intuition in all aspects of life.

BAT (sport) relates to the condition and quality of one's progression.

BATBOY/GIRL is one who can supply another with the tools to further progress.

BATHHOUSE (pool) points to a serious need to cleanse some aspect in one's life.

BATHING signifies a lack of negatives in the dreamer's life; cleansing of negatives.

BATHING CAP warns against a reluctance to approach spiritual concepts. May reveal an actual situation of denial.

BATHING SUIT signifies a tendency to submerge self into spiritual concepts but not let it touch one; a spiritual distancing or reserve.

BATHMAT refers to spiritual protection; personal safeguards one uses against the possibility of slipping spiritually.

BATHOLITH applies to wisdom of the ancients.

BATHOMETER signifies an aspect that determines the depth of spiritual belief and/or application.

BATHOPHOBIA (fear of bathing) See fear.

BATHROBE symbolizes how relaxed or comfortable one is with one's personal spiritual beliefs. Recall condition and type of dreamscape robe for more definitive clarity.

BATHROOM means a cleansing is needed.

BATH SALTS bring a message to soften one's spiritual attitude.

BATHTUB suggests a spiritual submersion is required. This would imply an individual who is fearful or has a reluctance to really get into their beliefs.

BATH WATER pertains to the quality of one's spiritual beliefs. Check the condition of this water—its color, etc.

BATHYSPHERE alludes to a journey into the deeper aspects of spiritual concepts.

BATIK (pattern) cautions against a tendency toward selective beliefs.

BATMAN represents over-confidence.

BATON characterizes an arrogant or egotistical personality.

BATTALION denotes a great amount of force, people, support, or opposition. Surrounding dreamscape aspects will clarify this meaning.

BATTER (cooking) means condition and quality of something before it is ready to be finalized; type of preparation.

BATTER (sports) alludes to the one who scores or a main player.

BATTERING RAM connotes force applied. This is most frequently a warning against the necessity of applying force to achieve desired results. May point to coercion.

BATTERY (cell) depicts reserve energy. This cautions against using up most of one's energy before something is accomplished.

BATTERY (injury) reveals a harmful situation or individual.

BATTING AVERAGE reveals the state of one's progress.

BATTLE indicates a tough time ahead; a real struggle to reach a goal.

BATTLE-AX characterizes a stern and consistently angry personality.

BATTLE CRUISER denotes an ability to easily maneuver through spiritual conflict.

BATTLE CRY exemplifies a need to generate greater courage.

BATTLE FATIGUE seriously warns against continual struggles without taking the needed time to reflect, meditate, gain inner peace.

BATTLEFIELD points to the issue leading to conflict.

BATTLEMENT denotes the logic, reason, and foresight given when considering the possibility of a forthcoming conflict.

BATTLESHIP stands for a well-armed but cumbersome approach to a spiritual conflict.

BATTLE STATION will stand for one's perspective in an active disagreement or conflict.

BAUBLE reflects an unimportant element; insignificance.

BAWDRY exposes crudeness.

BAY (animal sound) See howling.

BAY (hold off) represents procrastination; an effort to extend the time when one must deal with something. May be pointing to denial, laziness, or irresponsibility.

BAY (water) reveals a sheltered, comfortable sense of spirituality.

BAY (window) denotes a greater view or wider perspective may be required.

BAYBERRY pertains to the reminiscing of times past.

BAY LEAF applies to a life aspect that enhances one's life.

BAYONET illustrates a threatening position or situation.

BAYOU portrays a spiritual situation where one has become complacent or sluggish in advancing or has willingly allowed aspects to stagnate.

BAZAAR alludes to the vast array of learning sources and opportunities available to us.

BAZOOKA signifies one's inner power; personal resources in respect to defending self against various threatening aspects in life.

BEACH refers to the transition stage of how well spiritual beliefs are applied to the physical (the living of them). Was the dreamscape beach rocky? Eroded? Covered with Red Tide? Smooth, fine sand? Was the sand white or black?

BEACH BAG stands for the elements of the spiritual beliefs we carry with us.

BEACH BALL refers to the lightheartedness of manifesting one's spirituality through daily behavior and interaction.

BEACH BUGGY See dune buggy.

BEACH BUM characterizes one who lives one's spiritual beliefs at all times; someone who literally walks her spiritual talk.

BEACHCOMBER exemplifies looking for spiritual rarities that one can treasure.

BEACH FLEA See sand flea.

BEACHFRONT (property) indicates an eye toward spirituality and the desire to live close to one's beliefs. This illustrates a spiritual priority.

BEACH GRASS means strong spiritual roots.

BEACHHEAD points to one's first priority for addressing issues needed to confront.

BEACH UMBRELLA signifies a good perspective of spiritual beliefs. One who is not enamored with nor blinded by the glare of outlandish claims.

BEACON means a source of enlightenment that will further spiritual development or understanding; a light to be guided by.

BEAD signifies a small matter of importance. Although small, it's not a trivial matter for the dreamer.

BEADWORK stands for taking deserved pride in one's work, skill, or accomplishments.

BEADY-EYED suggests a suspicious personality; envious or malicious.

BEAGLE (dog breed) refers to a sympathy-seeking friend.

BEAKER applies to some aspect in the dreamer's life that needs precision blending.

BEAM (facial expression) stands for inner joy; happiness.

BEAM (ray) symbolizes higher knowledge or intelligence.

BEAM (timber) indicates inner strength; a supportive ability.

BEAN represents one of many connecting elements; a portion.

BEANBAG pertains to the whole comprised of many equally important parts.

BEAN COUNTER characterizes someone who looks at all aspects of a relationship, situation, or problem.

BEANIE See skullcap.

BEANPOLE refers to unrecognized strength. This dreamscape symbol points to something very near the dreamer that has the potential of providing great inner strength but is overlooked because of its simplicity or commonness.

BEAN SPROUTS caution against ignoring the importance of each part or aspect of a situation.

BEANSTALK refers to the unique aspects of individuality, strength, and potential that touch our lives.

BEAR (animal) characterizes an overbearing personality, relationship, or situation; often points to the source of a dreamer's stress.

BEAR CLAW (actual or design) stands for a desire to maintain control of one's life.

BEARD symbolizes hidden physical aspects in one's life. May point to one's tendency toward duplicity by holding opposing philosophies—one for the public, one hidden.

BEARDED COLLIE (dog breed) signifies a friend having unusual/eccentric characteristics, yet can always be depended on to be there for you.

BEARDED LADY points to an anomaly in one's life; someone the dreamer needs to pay more attention to.

BEARD-TONGUE (botanical) points to one's sense of humor. This symbol indicates a need to uplift one's outlook on life.

BEAR HUG connotes the potential for a smothering or manipulative type of affection.

BEARING WALL stands for a main supportive element.

BEAR MARKET stands for a financial decline; a drain on (or waning of) one's energies or fortitude.

BÉARNAISE SAUCE relates to a beneficial added element in one's life.

BEARSKIN (blanket or rug) alludes to emotional warmth and security; an overbearing individual who has been neutralized.

BEAST corresponds to crude or unacceptable behavior.

BEATIFICATION cautions against elevating others.

BEATNIK See hippie.

BEAUTICIAN signifies individuals with a tendency or talent to alter the perspectives of others, easing them into a better sense of self.

BEAUTIFUL is, as always, in the discriminating eye of the beholder. Recall what was given this specific characteristic. Was it truly beautiful?

BEAUTIFUL PEOPLE come in dreams to warn against equating glamour or high-class social standing to a priority to strive for or envy.

BEAUTY MARK portrays the distinctive qualities one has; personal uniqueness.

BEAUTY PAGEANT pertains to misplaced perception of beauty; an overemphasis on the physical attributes of an individual, especially women.

BEAUTY SHOP illustrates an attempt to enhance appearances. May indicate the striving to maintain a false persona or raise one's self-esteem.

BEAUTY SCHOOL See cosmetology.

BEAUTY SLEEP won't literally equate to physical beauty but rather the beauty of pacing oneself for the purpose of expending energy on beautiful (selfless) acts.

BEAVER stands for the ability to recognize one's spiritual aspects at home while balancing and utilizing life's opportunities. This dreamscape element points to an ability (or need) to fully integrate all aspects of one's life.

BECKON almost always applies to a draw or inclination toward something.

BED cautions against overdoing; a need for rest.

BED AND BREAKFAST (B & B) stands for an easy or comfortable personality or situation; an individual who is at home anywhere. This dreamscape symbol also points to a home away from home and serves to underscore the fact that one doesn't have to be alone in life. On the same hand, this element identifies someone is open to the dreamer.

BED BOARD suggests a firm attitude or character.

BEDBUG warns of a negative aspect related to sleeping arrangements or sleep patterns. May be a life irritant causing excessive stress whereby sleep is disturbed.

BED CHECK indicates a need to make sure you're where you need to be as far as your own life progression toward goals. Doing what you know you're supposed to be doing; a continual monitoring.

BEDDING (clothes or linens) portrays a condition of rest.

BEDDING (plants) refers to a good and/or well-developed beginning of something.

BEDLAM means complete confusion. This may refer to a relationship, a situation, or a mental/emotional state.

BED OF NAILS refers to a hard and difficult life phase.

BED OF ROSES signifies a prime, most desirable situation.

BEDOUIN denotes spiritual separatism; keeping one's beliefs apart from the possibility of other concepts infiltrating them.

BEDPAN cautions against an inability to rest well; a tendency to bring work into times designated for rest.

BEDPOST symbolizes those aspects that support or lead to a resting period in one's life.

BED REST comes as a caution that one is working too hard and needs to take a break. This symbol may also point to a need to put something to bed and give it a rest.

BEDRIDDEN is a state of forced rest. This comes as a forewarning against working too hard.

BEDROCK stands for strong and enduring foundations.

BEDROLL represents an easy going personality. An ability to pace oneself and rest anywhere along the way.

BEDROOM signifies one's personal atmosphere or surrounding that induces rest periods.

BEDROOM COMMUNITY denotes a healthy separation between rest and work.

BEDROOM EYES exemplify a magnetic personality.

BEDSIDE MANNER illustrates one's level of sensitivity to others.

BEDSORE warns against not being motivated to work; lingering too long in a rest period.

BEDSPREAD portrays the type of rest one is receiving. Recall the color, design, and condition of the dreamscape spread. Was it a wild, geometric shape? Floral? In need of laundering? Torn? Was it the color of wake-up blaring red? Or a soothing color conducive to sleep?

BEDSPRING indicates the quality and/or variety of restful activities one utilizes.

BEDSTEAD refers to aspects that support one's state of rest; the qualitative value of such rest.

BEDTIME STORY pertains to restful and peaceful thoughts before retiring. It refers to those thoughts that are on the mind just before sleep takes over. This dreamscape element may be suggesting that less stressful thoughts be entertained before attempting to sleep.

BED WARMER suggests preparations for taking an intended respite from something.

BED-WETTING illustrates a tendency for self-induced rest interruption; an individual who can't allow time for solid rest.

BEE characterizes industrious and cooperative teamwork.

BEE (caught in hair) points to those elements in life that serve as motivators and facilitators which act as an impetus to take an immediate response and get going.

BEE BALM refers to an ability to ignore the small irritations in life.

BEECH (tree/wood) signifies lessons experienced; a need to increase one's level of acceptance/tolerance.

BEEF cautions one to ingest well-defined and developed concepts; a warning against the acceptance of raw aspects.

BEEFCAKE (male model) cautions against misplaced priorities related to one's personal value as an individual.

BEEHIVE means the center or focus of activity; main interest or point of attention.

BEEKEEPER characterizes hidden agendas; an individual who wants something in return; one who takes and takes. This may point to one who has an ulterior motives for caring.

BEELINE denotes an industrious nature; the shortest and most direct route; one who can spot the bottom-line and cut through the extraneous elements; an individual who gets right to the point.

BEE STING comes as a call to get moving; an advisement to get on one's way.

BEELZEBUB See devil.

BEEPER advises to stay in contact or keep communication links open.

BEER See alcoholic beverage.

BEER-BELLY (appearance) indicates overindulgence; lack of self-control.

BEESWAX refers to an industrious nature.

BEET reflects intensity, frequently indicates anger or deep embarrassment.

BEETLE signifies negative interferences in one's life.

BEGGING stands for desperation.

BEGINNER implies lack of experience or knowledge; perhaps immaturity as well, depending on surrounding dreamscape elements.

BEGONIA stands for balance.

BEHAVIORAL THERAPY suggests an attitude adjustment is needed; a change in how one behaves because of incorrect thought or perception.

BEHEAD infers the need to bring one's thinking back in line because of losing one's head over something; or it can mean that one is in serious trouble and is getting closer to the chopping block.

BEHEMOTH symbolizes an aspect in one's life that is mammoth; perhaps overwhelming; too big to handle alone.

BEHIND (directional position) relates to a lower level; or it may point to the proper position one should be taking.

BEHIND (losing ground) suggests a quickened pace is required to catch up with matters. Perhaps more knowledge needs to be gained.

BEHIND THE SCENES alludes to hidden aspects of what is seen or manifested in the open. May point to hidden agendas.

BEIGE (color) defines a neutral position; possible indecision; a blending into the background and not wishing to be noticed. Could indicate an introverted personality.

BEJEWELED means a self-aggrandizement; seeing self as brilliant and full of great worth.

BELATED reflects inefficiency; lacking attention to one's awareness level. Or it may remind us of something important that we forgot.

BELCH signifies a need to bring up and air negative attitudes that could eventually be harmful.

BELFRY warns of alarming relationships or situations; a call to take heed or attention.

BELGIUM represents hospitality; a willingness to help others.

BELL is a call for increased awareness. May indicate a call to duty or responsibility.

BELLADONNA (plant) implies an emotional settling is required; a calming.

BELLBOY/HOP characterizes personal assistance; possible servitude.

BELL BUOY serves as a spiritual marker that guides one through a safe passing.

BELLFLOWER (botanical) suggests a need to listen to one's inner voice/conscience.

BELL JAR alludes to narrow-mindedness.

BELLOWS indicate a requirement for more air; a need to remove self from some aspect in life that's suffocating.

BELL PULL denotes the knowledge and acceptance of possibly needing help through life.

BELL RINGER refers to someone trying to get the attention of others.

BELLS AND WHISTLES connote a life element that's full of extra benefits. Depending on the related dreamscape aspects, this symbol could also reveal a tendency to want more than is necessary.

BELLS OF IRELAND (flower) signify a reminder to utilize natural talents for acts of goodness.

BELLY See abdomen.

BELLYACHE See stomachache.

BELLY DANCE connotes a tendency to brag; to show off. May also point to enticements.

BELLY FLOP applies to unexpected or disappointing spiritual results.

BELLY LAUGH means great joy; hearty amusement.

BELLY-UP suggests a type of failure; or it could be indicating that now's the time to belly-up to the table and take responsibility or action.

BELOW (directional position) stands for under or may be revealing the correct positional placement of something.

BELOW DECK corresponds to a protected place.

BELOW THE BELT indicates retaliation and vindictiveness; unethical retribution.

BELT symbolizes self-created restraints.

BELTANE exemplifies a springlike time frame in one's life; a time of purification and renewal.

BELT BUCKLE defines the excuse for one's self-restraint.

BELT TIGHTENING points to severe self-restraint; self-denial. Sacrifices are needed.

BELTWAY stands for a way around something.

BELVEDERE See gazebo.

BENCH See specific type.

BENCHMARK depicts an ultimate example or sample of something.

BENCH PRESS refers to aspects in life that serve as strengtheners.

BENCH WARMER characterizes inaction, yet preparedness for action.

BENCH WARRANT seriously warns against wrongdoing.

BEND (in road) connotes a slight veering away from something; a minor shift in direction.

BEND (shape) See bent.

BENDER exposes a desire to escape reality; a call to take responsibility or expand one's capacity for acceptance, tolerance.

BENDS (decompression) warns of the ramifications of trying to advance too quickly.

BENEATH (directional position) usually reveals a hidden element not perceived.

BENEDICTION points to a spiritually sanctioned individual or deed.

BENEFACTRESS symbolizes the source or impetus that serves to provide ways to advance or succeed.

BENEFICIARY means recipient. Perhaps good fortune is in the offing; the one who benefits.

BENEFIT (event) alludes to receiving or giving help through the aid of others.

BENEFIT OF THE DOUBT connotes trust.

BENEVOLENCE defines generosity, yet may also indicate an ulterior motive.

BENIGN alludes to innocence; harmless; neutral.

BENNY See amphetamine.

BENT refers to an aspect in life that isn't straight (true or honest).

BENTWOOD implies a natural inclination.

BENZENE symbolizes one's control over highly flammable situations or relationships.

BEQUEST represents the act of giving.

BEREAVEMENT reveals a personal sorrow.

BERET pertains to a carefree, often eccentric, personality.

BERG See iceberg.

BERGAMOT (tree) refers to the healing life aspect in regard to recognizing the duality of one's personality. That which is sour can also be fragrant. This symbol points to a recognition of the up side to difficult situations.

BERIBERI characterizes a highly repulsive or extremely distasteful aspect that one tries to avoid getting close to.

BERLIN WALL signifies the destructiveness of building walls to separate/segregate peoples; emphasizes the rightness of tearing down those walls and becoming unified.

BERM indicates support; protective aspects.

BERMUDA TRIANGLE means spiritual fluctuations; vacillations.

BERNHARDT (Sarah) exposes overdramatized emotionality.

BERRY relates to those life aspects that are fruitful.

BERTH (anchorage) indicates a comfortable spiritual position.

BERTH (sleeping) refers to taking the time to rest while on a path's journey.

BERYL (gemstone) alludes to pure intentions; true life offerings that come our way.

BESIDE (directional placement) connotes an equal positioning aspect.

BESIEGED reflects an overwhelming situation.

BEST-CASE SCENARIO stands for the best one can expect.

BESTIARY denotes a high interest in animals and what can be learned from them.

BEST MAN characterizes male support in life.

BEST SELLER means that which is most popular; aspects having a great draw. This dreamscape element reveals a common interest held by a large group of people and can be a gauge for determining that group's level of spiritual, philosophical, or ethical advancement.

BET signifies chances taken; a willingness to second-guess outcomes; a tendency to dismiss or give weight to facts.

BETA BLOCKER stands for a need to be calm, not show inner nervousness.

BETEL NUT implies a mesmerized state of mind and that which causes it.

BETHLEHEM illustrates the beginnings of a new spiritual concept.

BETONY (plant) cautions one to take care of some type of wound. This may be an emotional injury.

BETRAYAL applies to untrustworthy relationships.

BETROTHAL refers to intentions toward making a long-term commitment; may point to a need to rethink the plan for a union.

BETWEEN (directional placement) stands for the middle position.

BEVELED signifies angles to an issue or situation that should be seen and taken into consideration.

BEVERAGE pertains to a life element that has the potential of fulfillment; quenching a thirst; satisfying an emptiness; refreshment.

BEVERLY HILLS corresponds with those who have the greatest responsibility and potential to help others; those with the means to help others.

BEWITCHED warns against allowing anyone to capture one's free will; a lack of individuality, thought, or control over one's life. This dreamscape element may also point to an unrealistic perspective; being overly enamored with something or someone.

BEZEL (jewelry) represents the foundational support/motivation for one's shining, gemlike elements of spiritual behavior.

BIANNUAL applies to something happening twice.

BIAS means a slanted perspective; a preferential attitude.

BIAS TAPE (sewing) stands for efforts put into making sure a plan doesn't unravel.

BIB warns against sloppy talk from sloppy thought; a call to halt gossip; cautions against thoughtless speech.

BIBLE portrays revised or altered words and concepts.

BIBLIOGRAPHY symbolizes literary works one should peruse; additional research needed.

BIBLIOPHOBIA (fear/distrust of books) See fear.

BICARBONATE OF SODA See baking soda.

BICHON FRISE (dog breed) represents a supportive friend.

BICKERING comes to point out inconsequential disagreements; nit-picking.

BICYCLE depicts mental, physical, or spiritual balance.

BICYCLE PATH denotes a well-balanced path. Recall its condition to make sure the path was smooth and clear of debris, otherwise it means an *unbalanced* path.

BIDDY (old) points to a fussy, nit-picking, crabby individual.

BIDET warns against incomplete hygiene.

BIER See coffin.

BIFOCALS indicate more than one perspective to any aspect; an ability to see both the surface and deeper levels.

BIGAMY illustrates a lack of commitment; a disregard for others; a tendency toward self-importance.

BIG BANG THEORY denotes explosive beginnings.

BIG-BONED stands for endurance; fortitude.

BIG BROTHER characterizes a hidden overseer in one's life. Usually reveals the fact that information thought to be private has been uncovered by another; being covertly watched.

BIG DIPPER reminds us that, although we strive to routinely perform small spiritual acts in our lives, they should be starred by a few larger ones as well.

BIG ENCHILADA characterizes one who is most important or holds the most power, a possibly inflated self-image.

BIGFOOT connotes aspects of reality that are not accepted.

BIG GUN suggests the most influential or powerful element or individual.

BIG HAIR See bouffant (hair style).

BIG HEAD stands for arrogance; egotism.

BIGHORN SHEEP denotes adaptability; awareness of one's options.

BIG LEAGUE pertains to highest level; aspects holding the power.

BIGMOUTH reveals a gossiper. Telling more than is necessary; boastfulness. May even point to a betrayer.

BIGOTRY means intolerance.

BIG SHOT characterizes someone of importance; influential. May be a misplaced attribute.

BIG SISTER (organization) stands for feminine guidance.

BIG STICK denotes threats or a threatening situation or relationship. Could be associated with someone who feels insecure without it.

BIG TICKET stands for costly in the way of energy or emotions expended.

BIG TOP (circus) points to the main event; where all the main action will take place.

BIG WHEEL refers to someone of influence, wealth, or power.

BIKE See specific type.

BIKER pertains to independence; a freewheeling personality.

BIKE LANE See bicycle path.

BIKINI symbolizes a lack of inhibitions.

BILE portrays aspects in one's life that are considered bitter.

BI-LEVEL indicates balance.

BILGE suggests a personal, spiritual transitional stage; spiritual watchfulness.

BILGE PUMP refers to watchfulness for skewed spiritual ideas in one's life; a readiness to maintain a pureness in personal spiritual beliefs.

BILGE WATER means negative or skewed spiritual concepts that need to be pumped out of one's belief system.

BILINGUAL connotes a talent for conceptual interpretation.

BILL stands for a debt that comes due. It may also may mean something that will end up needing recompense for.

BILLBOARD means a warning or reminder; an attention-getting attempt.

BILLET cautions one to make accommodations for those who would provide protection or help.

BILLFOLD See purse.

BILLIARD BALL pertains to an aspect of skill and/or ability to preplan.

BILLIARD TABLE See pool table.

BILLIARDS See pool (game).

BILLIARD STICK See cue stick.

BILLIONAIRE exemplifies great personal monetary wealth and the spiritual responsibility to help others.

BILL OF GOODS refers to dishonesty; a bad transaction.

BILL OF HEALTH characterizes one's state of health.

BILL OF LADING pertains to the manner in which one holds to promises; how we deliver and follow through.

BILL OF RIGHTS means one's right to have rights. This is an important dreamscape fragment. Everyone has basic rights.

BILL OF SALE represents a completed transaction in life.

BILLOW implies expansion of something related to the dreamer's life.

BILLY CLUB exemplifies force; a forceful nature; ill-used power.

BIMBO portrays misplaced priorities; having little interest in intellectual aspects; generally inept.

BINARY means dual purpose; two-fold.

BINARY STAR denotes wisdom shining forth from knowledge and reason.

BINDER (legal) stands for warranted promises or agreements.

BINDER (notebook) cautions one to retain that which has been learned or recorded.

BINDERY depicts a need to keep records, thoughts, concepts, or beliefs together. This would come as a warning against letting these aspects become scattered.

BINDWEED (plant) stands for tenacity; hanging on with all one's might.

BINGE signifies an overindulgence; an excessive personality. People can binge on things other than alcohol. A tirade or bouts of rage could be symbolized as binging; an obsession could be implied.

BINGO (game) cautions against a steady tendency toward expectation.

BINOCULARS imply a need for closer inspection; pay attention to that which is just beyond the obvious. There's more than what's right in front of you.

BIOFEEDBACK cautions one to listen to inner promptings more; emphasizes the strength of one's inherent inner power; the power of thought.

BIOGRAPHY implies depth of personality; more to an individual than on the surface.

BIOHAZARD warns of a high risk factor connected with an aspect of the dreamer's life.

BIOLOGICAL CLOCK always denotes physical age and the passing of time. This means one is getting older so it'd be wise to attend to priorities. Time is growing short.

BIOLOGICAL WEAPONS warn of an aggressively dangerous situation or individual in the dreamer's life; a contaminating element.

BIOLOGY (study of) connotes a personal interest in all living aspects of one's world. This would indicate a high respect for life.

BIONICS refer to the integration of conceptual and technical aspects; may relate to one who has the talent of visualizing great advances through inventive means.

BIOPSY indicates a need to look closer or examine something in the dreamer's life.

BIORHYTHM characterizes our vibratory and cyclical connectedness to earth and all life upon it.

BIOSPHERE signifies synergetic relationships; self-supporting.

BIOTELEMETRY portrays self-awareness; a heightened awareness of all aspects of self.

BIPARTISAN alludes to having two separate opinions or perspectives on the same issue. May indicate indecision.

BIPLANE implies the tendency to double-check one's thoughts; a habit of caring about the possibility of wrong thinking.

BIPOLAR denotes duality or the center between two extremes. May point to indecision.

BIPOLAR (disease) See manic-depressive.

BIRCH applies to an open and honest situation or atmosphere.

BIRD reflects personality characteristics. See specific type.

BIRD BAND represents a unique characteristic (usually perspective) which separates an individual from the crowd.

BIRDBATH suggests the need for emotional or character cleansing. There's something in one's personality that needs attention, improvement.

BIRDBRAIN connotes a lack of intelligence, reason, or logic; may refer to silliness or flightiness; a tendency to make light of serious matters.

BIRDCAGE stands for restrained thoughts; fear of extending one's thought process or doing further research. May also apply to emotional aspects.

BIRDCALL signifies a call to think more deeply and follow ideas and concepts as far as they can go.

BIRD DOG warns of a hounding being done.

BIRD FEEDER implies deeper understandings; a thought process that relates to the interconnectedness of all life.

BIRDHOUSE signifies noble and high ideals that are held to and take precedence (kept close to home).

BIRD NEST stands for ingrained character traits and thought processes. What was the condition of the dreamscape nest? If it was high up in the top of a tree, the symbol relates to one's thought process. If it was lower to ground, it relates to emotions.

BIRD OF PARADISE illustrates extravagant and elaborate thoughts. May point to thoughts of grandeur.

BIRD OF PREY See specific type.

BIRDSEED refers to research; the feeding of one's thoughts; a thought process that is nourished.

BIRD'S-EYE characterizes broad scope understanding; a comprehensive overview or perspective.

BIRD SHOT represents a negative element which is used to destroy another's unique attitude or perspective.

BIRDSONG is usually associated with a light heart; inner joy and acceptance.

BIRD WATCHER stands for watching one's thoughts, analyzing self and how conclusions are reached.

BIRTH always points to some type of new life; renewal; new beginnings.

BIRTH CANAL means the path to some type of rebirth; perhaps the way to a revelation.

BIRTH CERTIFICATE may denote a past-life identity which represents one's spiritual heritage, or it may come as a validation of new thought.

BIRTH CONTROL (methods) warn of a reluctance to change one's life or make new beginnings; a fear of veering off in a new direction; a reluctance to start over.

BIRTHDAY suggests a special reason to recall one's heritage (usually spiritual). May simply come as a reminder to celebrate one's recent steps toward new beginnings.

BIRTHDAY GIFT relates to a recognition of another's accomplishments or advances in life.

BIRTH DEFECT cautions one to watch out for some type of defect presenting itself along a new path taken.

BIRTHING CENTER reveals the atmosphere or surroundings that will provide opportunities for new beginnings.

BIRTHMARK advises one to accept imperfections.

BIRTH PANG signifies adjustments required along one's new path. No path is without obstacles or patches of rough road.

BIRTHRATE will point to one's rate of progression toward new beginnings.

BIRTHRIGHT underscores everyone's right to choose new beginnings.

BIRTHSTONE depicts a vibrationally aligned set of aspects that will best serve an individual.

BISCUIT See cracker.

BISECT suggests an importance to a middle position or path.

BISEXUAL (activity) signifies one who perceives all sides to an issue.

BISEXUAL (gender) See hermaphrodite.

BISHOP applies to spiritual arrogance.

BISMUTH symbolizes a multifaceted element.

BISON See buffalo.

BISQUE (china) stands for something left unfinished or needing refinement.

BISQUE (color) reflects a lack of ambition; loss of direction. May indicate neutrality.

BISQUE (soup) connotes a hearty constitution; a strong, earthy personality.

BISTRO represents an informal relationship or atmosphere.

BIT (tool) corresponds to an effective aid in accomplishing a goal.

BITEWING (dental x-ray) suggests a need to check one's language for negativity or harmful words.

BIT PART (in a play) reveals a small role one is playing or needs to play in a relationship or some type of situation.

BITTER denotes something that's distasteful; something painful or hard to take in life.

BITTERN (bird) suggests spiritual serenity; deep solace generated from one's spirituality.

BITTERNUT (tree) pertains to the unavoidable, naturally occurring events in life that are irritating, yet not lasting; life's more difficult lessons to work through.

BITTERROOT (plant) relates to continual blessings in life that may, initially, appear as negatives.

BITTERSWEET (plant) reminds us that beauty frequently follows our pains in life.

BIVOUAC applies to keeping oneself free and unencumbered while walking a new path.

BLACK (color) stands for mystery or negativity. Black will always accompany a premonition of a death.

BLACK-AND-BLUE alludes to relationships or situations that will end up harming the dreamer.

BLACK-AND-WHITE stands for clarity; clear perception; the facts.

BLACK-BAG points to ill-gotten riches. These riches could relate to aspects other than money.

BLACKBALL denotes negative choices or a shutting-out of something.

BLACK BEAR characterizes an extremely dangerous person closely associated with the dreamer.

BLACKBEARD See pirate.

BLACK BEAUTY See designer drug.

BLACK BELT symbolizes self-confidence in one's personal quality and strength of protection.

BLACKBERRY (fruit) represents fruitful aspects of life that manifest through one's personal nature; the fruits of a spiritual life.

BLACKBERRY (techno gadget) See PDA.

BLACKBIRD signifies an omen.

BLACKBOARD brings messages. What was written?

BLACKBOARD ERASER points to a willful denial of information; a refusal to look at facts or messages one doesn't want to hear or face.

BLACK BOOK denotes secrecy.

BLACK BORDER/EDGING (on letter) represents very bad news.

BLACK BOX (flight recorder) indicates a record of events; the recording of one's life; karmic record.

BLACK BREAD signifies an element which provides robust nourishment.

BLACK CHERRY represents an unusually sweet aspect; uniquely pleasing.

BLACK CLOTHING is a forewarning of death; may be physical, emotional, or spiritual.

BLACK COHOSH (plant) usually represents an element which brings about a balanced state in one's life.

BLACK DEATH means a fatal situation or relationship.

BLACK DIAMOND stands for ill-use of material wealth.

BLACK ENVELOPE usually portends a death of some type.

BLACK EYE (bruise) implies interfering actions. May point to a retribution.

BLACK EYE (iris color) suggests dark perceptions; a pessimistic view.

BLACK-EYED SUSAN connotes favorable results forthcoming.

BLACK FLAG See Jolly Roger; may also warn of a need to stop a type of behavior.

BLACK FOREST symbolizes an attitude of mystery behind spiritual gifts.

BLACK FOREST CAKE pertains to the richness of spiritual talents—the wealth of knowledge and potential; the dispelling of spiritual mysteries.

BLACK FROST warns of a destructive freezing of one's spiritual beliefs or the cessation of spiritual application in life.

BLACK GOLD See oil field.

BLACKGUARD alludes to an unprincipled individual; one who exhibits a vile, abusive manner.

BLACK HAT naturally stands for a negative personality; the bad guy.

BLACK HAW (tree) connotes the rewards resulting from acts of goodness/generosity.

BLACKHEAD indicates negative aspects that clog understandings; obstructions to clarity.

BLACK HEART will point to a malicious, vengeful individual.

BLACK HILLS means sacred aspects that need protection and reverence.

BLACK HILLS GOLD stands for sacred spiritual wealth.

BLACK HILLS GOLD (mined) refers to a defilement of sacred spiritual wealth.

BLACK HOLE pertains to depression; feeling of futility; a place of no return.

BLACK HUMOR reveals poor taste or an intent to shock.

BLACK ICE warns against spiritual concepts that are dangerous and difficult to perceive.

BLACKJACK (card game) suggests a tendency toward playing the odds; taking chances in life.

BLACKJACK (weapon) See billy club.

BLACK LIGHT alludes to lessons learned from negative experiences. Hidden aspects.

BLACKLIST means prejudice, censure.

BLACK LOCUST (tree) represents self-confidence; self-assuredness.

BLACK LUNG (disease) corresponds to the acceptance of dark thoughts and ideas.

BLACK MAGIC warns against obtaining personal goals through the use of negativity.

BLACKMAIL portrays a gross negative use of knowledge; betrayal.

BLACK MARKET applies to underhandedness in obtaining goals; ill-gotten objectives.

BLACK MASS denotes spiritual negativity; a destructive spiritual force.

BLACK MONEY represents hidden assets; secret wealth.

BLACK NIGHTSHADE (plant) illustrates the duality of nature. This may apply to human nature as well.

BLACK OAK denotes a strong negative aspect in one's life.

BLACK OLIVE suggests uniqueness; the more rare elements of life.

BLACK OPAL is associated with the more mysterious elements of reality; the unknowns which await discovery.

BLACK OPS signify covert or underlying agendas; secret activities.

BLACKOUT (consciousness) exemplifies selective memory.

BLACKOUT (electrical) warns against sporadic or selective perception.

BLACK PEPPER refers to aspects to which the dreamer has a strong adverse reaction.

BLACK POWDER stands for an element essential for an explosive situation to manifest.

BLACK SHEEP characterizes a personalized or unique path; one who dares to be different.

BLACKSMITH illustrates reformations or rejuvenations that will be solid and strong.

BLACK STRAP See molasses.

BLACK TIE alludes to an extremely formal personality; a stuffy attitude; aloofness.

BLACKTOP See asphalt.

BLACK WALNUT (tree/wood) signifies the fulfillment coming from extensive efforts expended; the fruits of one's labors.

BLACK WIDOW (spider) symbolizes an extremely dangerous individual or relationship in one's life.

BLADDER stands for an aspect in one's life that holds negatives within; warns of a need to release negative elements.

BLADE See knife.

BLAME reminds us to double-check our thoughts and actions. This may not apply directly to the dreamer but to another person associated with the dreamer.

BLANCH denotes shocking information.

BLAND alludes to neutrality or uninteresting aspects.

BLANK refers to lack of thought or ideas.

BLANK BOOK stands for a lack of ideas; no clue as to what's going on; no solutions.

BLANK CARTRIDGE suggests a lack of power or effectiveness.

BLANK CHECK stands for unlimited resources or opportunities.

BLANKET signifies a compassionate personality; one who provides solace and support.

BLANKET CHEST See cedar chest.

BLANKETFLOWER suggests an advisement to protect sensitivities.

BLANKET STITCH reflects an intent to finish or complete a project or goal.

BLANK EYES characterize apathy.

BLANK TAPE represents a lack of communication; nothing to hear, nothing to record.

BLANK WALL signifies the sense of having no ideas regarding how to proceed or having no idea what steps to take next; lacking a solution. Usually this phase is temporary.

BLARNEY STONE denotes a desire to be eloquent or persuasive.

BLASPHEMY pertains to contempt.

BLAST FURNACE warns of internalized negatives such as anger, hate, jealousy, guilt.

BLASTING CAPS/POWDER See dynamite.

BLAZE See fire.

BLAZER (jacket) signifies a casual attitude.

BLAZING STAR (flower) points to sudden insights; inspiration.

BLEACH cautions against a tendency to whitewash things so their negativity can't be seen; a habit of being overly optimistic; a desire to sterilize negative elements so they can be ignored or overlooked.

BLEACHER warns of complacency; a tendency to sit back and watch others do the work.

BLEARY-EYED connotes a need to pace one's intake of information; a call to rest; overworked.

BLEEDER See hemophilia.

BLEEDING indicates a loss of essential life elements; waning energy and motivation; a lessening of one's inner strength and power.

BLEEDING GUMS See gum disease.

BLEEDING HEART (botanical) characterizes a sympathetic personality.

BLEMISH illustrates an imperfection connected to an aspect of the dreamer's life.

BLENDER suggests mixing; cautions against a separatist attitude toward various life aspects.

BLESSED THISTLE denotes aspects pertaining to female assistance or support.

BLESSING portrays a recognition of sacredness.

BLIGHT (plants) refers to negative aspects that eat away at one's morals and ethics.

BLIGHT (urban) applies to negative elements that break down and erode advancement.

BLIMP illustrates cumbersome thoughts and ideas, overblown concepts; a cluttered thought process.

BLIND (awareness) points to an insular type of perception. One's view is designed for self-preservation.

BLIND (hunting) warns against a tendency to hide one's true intentions. May indicate underhandedness, vindictiveness, a hidden agenda, or ulterior motives.

BLIND (sightless) connotes self-induced lack of understanding; purposeful ignorance; denial.

BLIND (Venetian) indicates a habit of altering one's scope of perception; self-controlled views of life; choosing how much to see and understand.

BLIND ALLEY stands for futile efforts.

BLIND DATE exemplifies questionable relationships; a relationship full of unknowns.

BLINDER warns of apathy; self-generated ignorance; disinterest.

BLINDFOLD represents confusion; being misled.

BLINDMAN'S BLUFF (game) reflects grasping in the dark; attempting to proceed without adequate information or clear perception.

BLIND-SIDED cautions one to be more perceptive, more aware; the need to look at all angles; a surprise that comes because nobody was aware enough to perceive its first signs.

BLIND SPOT advises of an obstructed view or perception; a specific angle of perception that isn't a clear view.

BLINK implies inattention; a temporary loss of awareness. May also point to the act of backing down.

BLINKER (light) attempts to bring one to attention; a warning.

BLIP means a shift from the norm; a call to attention.

BLISTER stands for the burning effects of one's actions.

BLITZ illustrates an overwhelming aspect in one's life.

BLIZZARD warns of a spiritual suffocation; the intake of too many spiritual concepts too quickly.

BLOATED (appearance/feeling) warns

against excesses. May point to someone who's full of hot air.

BLOB stands for something that's undefined; nebulous; vague.

BLOCK (shape) represents an insensitive personality; unforgiving; opinionated.

BLOCK (toys) signify crude planning; simplistic activity.

BLOCKADE exemplifies those blocks in our life that are put in our path by others. These can be overcome.

BLOCK AND TACKLE stands for aspects that allow us to overcome obstacles in life.

BLOCKHEAD characterizes a narrow-minded individual; unable or unwilling to think outside the box.

BLOCKHOUSE applies to one's defenses.

BLOCK PARTY signifies a reminder to appreciate those around you.

BLOND (hair) refers to a sunny disposition; an optimist.

BLOOD pertains to those aspects that equate to one's life force or driving motivation.

BLOOD BANK applies to a reserve of perseverance.

BLOOD BROTHER portrays a deep-seated, bonded relationship.

BLOOD CLOT depicts a negative aspect that's blocking one's motivation. May also point to something that has the potential of blocking one's way.

BLOOD COUNT alludes to the need to review those aspects that motivate the dreamer. Perhaps some of these are not all positive ones.

BLOOD DONOR See donor (blood).

BLOODHOUND (dog breed) suggests a friend with acute deduction and perceptual abilities.

BLOODLESS warns against a lack of motivation; apathy; denial.

BLOODLETTING means misconceptions that lessen one's motivation; a draining of one's strength, perseverance, and/or determination.

BLOOD MEAL signifies a revitalizing element.

BLOODMOBILE will represent an opportunity to express/utilize one's goodness by helping others. In some dreamscapes, depending on the related elements, this symbol may indicate an aspect in one's life that has the potential to drain one's resources or energy.

BLOOD MONEY warns of goals gained at the cost of another; ill-gotten gains; the destruction of another.

BLOOD POISONING denotes dangerously negative motivations.

BLOOD PRESSURE alludes to one's motivational energy level and interest.

BLOOD RED See maroon.

BLOOD RELATION refers to individuals who are motivated by the same aspects as the dreamer.

BLOODROOT (plant) connotes negative motivations.

BLOOD SAUSAGE signifies the ingestion (acceptance of or connection to) a negative aspect.

BLOODSHOT (eyes) represents one who is confused regarding motivational factors.

BLOOD SPORT will reveal vindictiveness, maliciousness, or a dark draw toward ruthlessness.

BLOODSTAIN pertains to the effects of one's motivation; what one's actions leave behind due to their specific type of motivation.

BLOODSTONE stands for inherent fortitutde.

BLOODSTREAM portrays the motivating current that flows through one's life.

BLOODSUCKER characterizes one who diminishes the motivation of another; discouragement; negative attitudes; cynicism.

BLOOD TEST suggests one's motivation is in question.

BLOODTHIRSTY stands for vengeful motivation; out for blood.

BLOOD TRANSFUSION See transfusion.

BLOOD TYPING relates to a desire to stay true to one's motivational aspects.

BLOOMERS suggest old-fashioned ideas, usually related to a prudish type of attitude.

BLOOPER suggests that we laugh at our mistakes.

BLOSSOM represents the beautiful effect of right living; the bloom of achievement, unconditional goodness, and/or right choices.

BLOTTER (ink) refers to a need to clean up mistakes; admit to guilt; make amends.

BLOUSE represents a basic need; necessary aspect in one's life which often reflects one's level of emotional response —compassion vs. indifference, softhearted vs. dispassion.

BLOW DOWN (trees) signifies devastation left in the wake of an emotional conflict.

BLOW-DRYER cautions against letting viable thoughts and ideas dry-up.

BLOWFISH refers to a tendency to be preachy.

BLOW GUN See blowpipe.

BLOWHARD characterizes a gossip; a braggart.

BLOWHOLE denotes breathing room; aspects in life that give us a breather.

BLOWING A WHISTLE points to an informer; betrayal. See whistle-blower.

BLOWOUT illustrates an aspect that will cause temporary delays or setbacks; an overwhelming aspect.

BLOWPIPE cautions against a dangerous individual or situation.

BLOWTORCH relates to a need for the dreamer to make either connections or separations in life. Surrounding dream elements will clarify which interpretation the symbol is intending.

BLOWUP depicts emotional explosions or a failed endeavor.

BLUBBER (cry and mutter) refers to grief; could also point to self-pity.

BLUBBER (fat) symbolizes one's excesses; extraneous elements one needs to drop.

BLUE represents spirituality and spiritual aspects in life.

BLUE BABY connotes a new beginning that is struggling for air; a difficult start.

BLUEBEARD characterizes unspiritual behavior and lack of faith.

BLUEBELLS (flower) illustrates spiritual joy.

BLUEBERRY corresponds to the fruits of one's personal spirituality.

BLUEBIRD refers to spiritual joy and contentedness.

BLUE BLOOD normally signifies nobility, coming from a long line of socially prominent family members, but in dreams, this symbol will be associated with an individual's personal, singular quality of having a quiet, dignified wisdom.

BLUEBONNET (flower) stands for an aspect-aligned element.

BLUE BOOK symbolizes the value of various spiritual concepts.

BLUE BOX refers to unethical communications; stealthy dealings.

BLUE CHEESE stands for spiritual nourishment.

BLUE CHIP portrays preferred spiritual beliefs or behaviors. This may be a negative element if connected to fads or current popularity.

BLUE COLLAR signifies one who applies spiritual beliefs to daily life; the actual hands-on work of spiritual behavior.

BLUE FLAX (botanical) suggests tolerance.

BLUE FLU See sick-out.

BLUEGILL (fish) symbolizes spiritual joy; a heightened inner sense of spiritual warmth.

BLUEGRASS (music) signifies a down-home type of spirituality.

BLUE HEAVEN (drug, also blue angel or blue devil) warns of a need to escape responsibility/reality; possibly an aid meant to bolster one's desire for denial.

BLUE JAY See bluebird.

BLUE JEANS depict one who is comfortable and relaxed with one's spiritual beliefs.

BLUELINE (book production proof) comes to advise of a need to read things carefully. This will be associated with reading people and situations.

BLUE LIPS suggest an inability to express opinions, attitudes.

BLUE MOON implies rare and extremely valuable spiritual wisdom.

BLUENOSE characterizes moral arrogance; prudish attitudes.

BLUE PENCIL refers to a need to make some type of correction.

BLUE PLATE (special) refers to one's specific spiritual foundation, a special element of that foundation or belief system.

BLUEPRINT signifies spiritual planning.

BLUE RIBBON pertains to praise, recognition.

BLUES (music) cautions against spiritual melancholy; a need for balance between the lightness and beauty of spirituality and the heaviness of physical living.

BLUE SCREEN OF DEATH (computer) comes as a critical sign alerting one that all his/her efforts are about to be rendered invalid/ineffective.

BLUE-SKY LAW represents the preservation of one's efforts expended; a preventative against back-sliding.

BLUE SPRUCE connotes one's connectedness to spirituality through nature.

BLUESTOCKING refers to a woman with spiritual wisdom.

BLUE STREAK symbolizes spiritual swiftness; some spiritual aspect has come as a bolt of lightning; a quick spiritual awakening and response; a possible epiphany.

BLUE VELVET (designer drug) signifies a desire to shift away from reality; using a negative to manifest a negative; denial; escapism.

BLUE WHALE signifies spiritual generosity; one who has a spiritually magnanimous nature.

BLUFF (promontory) connotes a front associated with a bluffing situation or aspect.

BLUING warns against spiritual arrogance; pretending more spirituality than possessing.

BLUR denotes a need for more clear understanding; unclear perception.

BLURB (review) reflects one person's opinion.

BLURT (outburst) points to unauthorized announcement or revelation; possible betrayal.

BLUSH illustrates embarrassment.

BOA CONSTRICTOR means a smothering or constricting situation or relationship.

BOAR indicates a haughty personality; a bore to others.

BOARD (wood) may refer to some type of building element or a kind of stiffness in one's character, attitude, or perspective; unyielding.

BOARD AND BATTEN (construction) represents sturdy character foundations.

BOARDER (renter) refers to opportunities taken; temporary and short-term openings to utilize karma-balancing situations.

BOARD GAME will be associated with the games one plays in life, usually psychological ploys put into play with the interaction with others.

BOARDING PASS will signify one's right to make a particular journey or be active in a specific issue/relationship.

BOARDING SCHOOL is synonymous with the reality of life. We eat, sleep, and learn as we go.

BOARD OF EDUCATION refers to those who would confine the gaining of knowledge to specific realms of subject matters.

BOARD OF HEALTH signifies those who endeavor to maintain a state of healthfulness. This dream symbol will be related to those people who are associated with the dreamer; helpful individuals.

BOARDROOM portrays decision-making; the knowing of our Higher Self.

BOARDWALK cautions against a voluntary separation from one's spiritual aspects.

BOAST See brag.

BOAT represents a spiritual path and its quality. Recall the condition of the dreamscape boat to gain further clarity.

BOAT BUILDING See shipbuilding.

BOAT CAPTAIN stands for the one who spiritually leads. This should be none other than self following one's inner guidance.

BOATHOUSE corresponds with a spiritual home; the living of spiritual beliefs.

BOAT LIFT means spiritual compassion; a spiritual rescue endeavor.

BOAT PEOPLE characterize those wanting to be spiritually saved; spiritual freedom.

BOAT SHOW signifies the many types of options available for a personalized spiritual journey.

BOBBER (fishing) refers to that which maintains the level of one's spiritual search or inquiry; holding one's spirituality at a steady level rather than raising it up or down depending on one's current mood or attitude.

BOBBIN (sewing) pertains to order of one's priorities; maintaining a smooth and untangled manner of operating; a first-things-first attitude.

BOBBLE-HEAD (figure) represents indecision. The key here is to recall whose image was on the Bobble-head's face.

BOBBY PIN refers to keeping one's thoughts or attitudes in place instead of letting them become tangled or become wildly windblown.

BOBBY SOCKS imply an informal attitude; a casual personality.

BOBCAT See lion.

BOBOLINK (bird) represents joy.

BOBSLED denotes a spiritual path that's quickly sped over; a rush to a spiritual goal without gaining the riches and depth along the way.

BOBWHITE (bird) denotes secretiveness.

BOCK BEER symbolizes a strong constitution; strong beginnings.

BODEGA refers to sources of basic needs close to home. May be suggesting that the search for answers has been taken too far afield; answers are closer than one thought.

BODHISATTVA characterizes absolute selflessness.

BODY (unidentified) exemplifies outstanding aspects that require attention in one's life.

BODY ART symbolizes one's personal attitude or character traits. Body art in dreams can be an extremely revealing symbol.

BODY BAG depicts a failure to attend to important aspects in one's life.

BODY BUILDING applies to an attention

to one's weaknesses; a building-up of inner strength.

BODY COUNT won't relate to corpses but rather those who have been severely affected by the negative behavior of someone.

BODYGUARD connotes an awareness of one's protective aspects (tools) and the utilization of same.

BODY LANGUAGE indicates the nonverbal messages we send out and receive; unspoken communications; implied meanings; innuendos.

BODY ODOR stands for offensive behavior.

BODY PIERCING suggests a contrariness; boldness.

BODY SEARCH indicates a suspicion of concealment; possible dishonesty.

BODY SHOP suggests repair work needed. This will refer directly to some physical aspect in one's life. In some dreams, this symbol will point to cosmetic/plastic surgery and one's desire to alter oneself.

BODY SLAM represents a severe emotional blow/reaction.

BODY STOCKING/SUIT pertains to a second skin one wears; thick-skinned; possibly represents a fear of being hurt.

BODY SURFING symbolizes a willingness to get close to spiritual issues; an adventuresome spiritual attitude.

BOG illustrates something that bogs one down, keeps one from going forward in an unfettered manner.

BOGEYMAN characterizes those we fear in life.

BOHEMIAN refers to a free-thinking personality; one who is not afraid to live an unconventional lifestyle or have differing attitudes and/or perspectives.

BOIL (hot liquid) stands for an agitated or heated situation or attitude.

BOIL (skin) warns of suppressed emotions; an irritation remaining under the skin.

BOILER (furnace) exemplifies hot situations or relationships in one's life.

BOILERPLATE (contractual) represents certain elements which cannot be avoided.

BOILER ROOM pertains to one's surroundings that could lead to explosive encounters or outcomes.

BOILER ROOM (telemarketing) refers to high-pressured coercion.

BOILING POINT connotes the point at which a condition or relationship becomes explosive.

BOIL OVER signifies an element gone past tolerance.

BOLDFACE (type) means emphasis. This is a call to pay attention.

BOLOGNA alludes to a belief system derived from a variety of sources.

BOLO TIE relates to attitudes that are not consistent; a changeable personality.

BOLSTER (pillow) signifies a need for support; to be bolstered up.

BOLT denotes strength of connections. This may relate to relationships or ideas.

BOLT CUTTER alludes to cutting strong ties.

BOMB represents explosive situations or relationships; also disappointments; failures.

BOMB BAY (compartment) means aspects in one's life that are on the verge of exploding unless they are calmed or altered.

BOMBER (aircraft) characterizes an unpredictable individual or situation.

BOMBER JACKET suggests an untrustworthy character.

BOMBPROOF signifies a strong constitution; emotional strength.

BOMBSHELL depicts great disappointments; shocking news.

BOMB SHELTER illustrates fear of disappointments; a lack of faith.

BOMBSIGHT portrays destructive intentions.

BOMB-SNIFFING DOG signifies a friend who is devoted to keeping other friends on the right track and away from self-destructive behavior.

BOMB SQUAD points to those who are skilled/capable of disarming a potentially explosive situation.

BONANZA suggests a great find of some type; coming across something that has been searched for.

BONBON See candy.

BOND (fasten) signifies a connection in one's life.

BOND (monetary) applies to a need for security; some element of security in one's life.

BONDSMAN characterizes a trusted individual; one who provides temporary security.

BONE represents aspects in one's life that signify foundations. This could be attitudes, relationships, or belief systems.

BONE CHINA represents a fragile issue.

BONE MARROW pertains to the life of one's foundational beliefs.

BONE MARROW TRANSPLANT refers to a need for new life brought into one's foundational beliefs or attitudes.

BONE MEAL signifies a strengthening factor.

BONFIRE portrays one's inner fire; motivation.

BONG usually symbolizes an element that facilitates level-headedness; a tool that cools down a heated situation or makes something more palatable to accept. This won't necessarily be symbolically associated with drugs.

BONGO DRUMS stand for dual operations; the working together of two individuals or two elements to a single issue.

BONING KNIFE warns of a threatening aspect directed toward one's foundational attitudes or beliefs.

BONNET characterizes old-fashioned ideas; often a prudish or overly simplistic attitude. May also point to naïveté.

BONSAI stands for forced attitudes; thoughts or ideas that are not naturally come by; mental manipulation; coercion.

BONUS pertains to actions or decisions that will lead to the manifestation of greater benefits than first realized.

BONUS POINTS imply the accumulation of good karma.

BON VOYAGE stands for embarking on a spiritual journey that many support.

BOOBY (bird) signifies misconceptions; illogical reasoning.

BOOBY PRIZE refers to some benefit or reward forthcoming.

BOOBY TRAP symbolizes a rigged situation or relationship; ulterior motives; a set-up.

BOOK signifies knowledge and the need for same; further study needed.

BOOK BAG is associated with the knowledge we carry with us; suggests a need to not leave our intellect behind.

BOOK BINDING See bindery.

BOOK BURNING warns against censorship or an attempt to silence another's right to free speech/expression.

BOOKCASE denotes broad-scope knowledge and suggests a need to study a variety of volumes. Was the dreamscape bookcase empty or full?

BOOK CLUB pertains to a wide variety of writings on one subject; shared interests.

BOOK COVER/JACKET refers to first impressions and reminds one not to make them the sole source of one's opinion or assessment.

BOOKEND cautions one to stop studying a subject until deeper comprehension has been attained.

BOOKING See appointment.

BOOKING AGENT will relate to someone who takes care of logistics. In some dreams, this symbol may point to a manipulative individual.

BOOKKEEPER characterizes the Book of Life; one's karmic record; an accounting of one's behavior.

BOOK LIST will usually reveal material one should be aware of. In some dreams, depending on the related elements, this symbol might indicate someone attempting to manipulate what another is exposed to, or is trying to sway an attitude/perspective.

BOOK LOVER reveals one's particular type of interest. This symbol won't necessarily equate to a love of knowledge because what if the book lover's books were erotica? Recall if any titles or subject matter were displayed.

BOOKMAKER (bookie) indicates one who is seen as an instigator; negative influence.

BOOKMARK suggests a pause in studying or learning is needed. This would usually indicate a need for contemplation and assimilation of that already learned.

BOOKMOBILE connotes the learning of healing methods; physiological research; the reading of medical books.

BOOK OF THE DEAD appears in dreams to symbolize the fact that life goes on; a suggestion to have faith, fortitude.

BOOKPLATE warns against an arrogance of knowledge; an intellectual possessiveness or aloofness.

BOOK REVIEW pertains to a message from one's Higher Self in respect to the quality of material and personal relevance of a book title.

BOOKSELLER will refer to an individual who can offer a wealth of information/ knowledge.

BOOKSHELF See bookcase.

BOOKSTORE signifies research and a wealth of knowledge.

BOOK VALUE denotes the true value of something.

BOOKWORM warns against a tendency to accumulate knowledge without applying it; a habit of voraciously consuming information, yet doing nothing with it.

BOOM (economic flourish) portrays a productive path.

BOOM (sound) signifies a call for the dreamer to be more aware or to listen and pay greater attention to life.

BOOM BOX symbolizes arrogance; a craving for attention.

BOOMERANG cautions one to watch for aspects that will come back at or turn on self.

BOOMTOWN characterizes a productive life.

BOONDOCKS represents spiritual remoteness; spiritual apathy.

BOOSTER CABLE advises that helpful or supportive connections be made in one's life; points to a need to be re-energized; an impetus.

BOOSTER CHAIR alludes to a need to see better on an issue; better perspective is required.

BOOSTER SHOT warns against not following through with something; a need to be mindful of one's continual progress. May also indicate the need to re-energize an idea or plan, perhaps a relationship.

BOOT symbolizes the outward quality and style of one's path walk.

BOOT CAMP applies to getting the basics of something.

BOOTH connotes privacy; individuality.

BOOTIE (baby's) suggests immature steps taken; a new path entered with immature attitudes and expectations.

BOOTJACK relates to a time to pause along one's path.

BOOTLEG warns against attempting to accomplish or gain something through unethical or immoral means.

BOOTSTRAP refers to a path walked with strong determination; an aspect that serves as an impetus for perseverance.

BOOTY illustrates that which has been obtained or gained through stealth or manipulation.

BOOZE See alcoholic beverage.

BOOZE HOUND See alcoholic.

BOP (bebop music) suggests a break from the norm.

BORAX denotes a lack of quality.

BORDELLO See house of ill repute.

BORDER represents some aspect in one's life that represents a dividing line.

BORDER COLLIE (dog breed) signifies a friend who can help you keep it together.

BORDERLAND exemplifies a fringe area in one's life or beliefs.

BORDERLINE means a questionable aspect in one's life.

BORE (drill) implies perseverance; pushing forward.

BORE (dull) cautions against a lack of motivation; suggests the need to expand interests or be more expressive.

BOREAL (north) signifies a higher direction to one's path; elevated levels of study; higher attitudes and perspectives.

BOREHOLE alludes to a testing aspect in one's life that should be followed through with.

BORN-AGAIN usually signifies a renewed faith, not necessarily a religious one but simply a rekindled faith in something.

BOROUGH refers to a specific area of concern in one's life.

BORROW implies a temporary solution or situation.

BORROWED TIME warns against overdoing; trying to accomplish too much too fast.

BORZOI (dog breed) represents acute perception.

BOSS characterizes a higher authority, perhaps even one's Higher Self.

BOSTON TERRIER (dog breed) denotes a friend with aggressive defenses; distrust; suspicious nature.

BOTANICAL symbolizes the quality and quantity of how well one applies spirituality to daily life.

BOTANICAL GARDENS represents an ideal spiritual life; a life of applying beliefs in all aspects.

BOTANIST illustrates one who works hard at applying spirituality to daily life.

BOTANY (study of) portrays an individual who looks for ways to apply spiritual concepts to everyday living situations and relationships.

BOTOX (injections) cautions against a tendency toward altering one's true self. Indicates a desire to be something you're not; nonacceptance of one's natural beingness; pride. May warn of a poisonous aspect that one willingly invites.

BOTTLE warns against keeping something bottled up inside.

BOTTLEBRUSH advises one to keep clarity within self; a caution to clean out imperfect attitudes.

BOTTLED GAS See propane.

BOTTLED WATER (designer) signifies a tendency to follow trends. This symbol will point to falling for false claims.

BOTTLE-FEED means forced ideas, thoughts, or concepts.

BOTTLE GREEN (color) stands for weakening energies.

BOTTLENECK denotes complications; congested aspects; backed-up thoughts or plans.

BOTTLE OPENER represents the key for quenching a specific type of thirst. The clue to clarified meaning is to recall if a certain type of bottle was displayed.

BOTTLE WASHER won't ever be a demeaning symbol, rather it will indicate an individual who is capable of performing a multitude of tasks.

BOTTOM (directional placement) denotes foundation or beginning point.

BOTTOM DRAWER represents one's hopes, future goals.

BOTTOM FEEDER means one who tends to have poor spiritual ideals or belief systems; one whose spirituality is poorly nourished.

BOTTOM LAND represents a fertile element.

BOTTOMLESS signifies great depth to something or someone.

BOTTOM LINE signifies the point of something; the bare facts.

BOTTOM-UP stands for something begun by the common folk. This symbol equates to a grassroots movement or new attitude.

BOTULISM cautions against the severely damaging effects of negative thought and action.

BOUCLE (yarn type) pertains to a gentle, down-home individual who takes life in stride.

BOUDOIR See bedroom.

BOUFFANT (hair style) characterizes an egotistical personality; one whose ideas are blown up and inflated for the purpose of impressing others.

BOUGAINVILLEA portrays a bright spiritual life.

BOUGH connotes an opportunity to utilize one's spirituality.

BOUILLABAISSE illustrates spiritual diversity; a broad base of spiritual concepts from which one can learn.

BOUILLON (soup) stands for clarity in understanding.

BOUILLON CUBE pertains to aspects in one's life that bring clarity; clarity from a specific source.

BOULDER represents major problematical aspects in one's life.

BOULEVARD pertains to a wide and well-used path. This may not be the best course for the dreamer to travel.

BOUNCE indicates a suggestion to be more resilient.

BOUNCED MAIL (email) signifies a communication which has been rejected or returned unread.

BOUNCE LIGHT refers to an effort to soften the harshness of something.

BOUNCER characterizes one who keeps order and maintains a peaceful atmosphere.

BOUNDARY LINE defines the generally accepted playing field.

BOUNTY means a reward for something accomplished.

BOUNTY HUNTER symbolizes misplaced priorities; wrong motives; being in expectation of rewards for good deeds done.

BOUQUET (flower) illustrates a commendation from higher spiritual sources.

BOUQUET (scent) implies quality; positive or negative indications.

BOURBON See alcoholic beverage.

BOURBON STREET pertains to a person's tendency to not take life seriously; a somewhat hedonistic perspective.

BOURGEOIS exemplifies middle-class conventions and attitudes.

BOUT signifies a confrontation between rivals; a needed meeting to settle differences.

BOUTIQUE relates to specialty; specific aspects in life. What type of products were for sale in the dreamscape boutique? Recalling these will clarify the meaning.

BOUTONNIERE marks distinction; one singled out for a specific reason.

BOW (archery) stands for an aspect that helps to target a problem.

BOW (boat) denotes the leading aspect of one's spiritual search; that which is the forerunner of such a path.

BOW (fiddle/violin) symbolizes an essential element needed to convey or express something. May mean confidence, courage, etc.

BOW (greeting) illustrates an act of respect; concession.

BOW (ribbon) connotes finality; a finished aspect in one's life.

BOWED (shape) signifies a rounded aspect; gentleness.

BOWER See arbor.

BOWIE KNIFE See knife.

BOWL (sport) refers to obtaining goals through unethical means.

BOWL (utensil) indicates a need for containment regarding an aspect in the dreamer's life.

BOWLEGGED illustrates perseverance throughout one's life.

BOWLER (hat) suggests a man's tendency toward primness, social propriety.

BOWLING ALLEY denotes a condition or situation where one might be tempted to act in an unethical manner.

BOWLING BALL symbolizes the tool which one uses to act in an unethical manner. This would be a specific act or a statement voiced. May point to something that comes as a big surprise that bowls one over.

BOWSTRING (archery) connotes that which connects aspects pointing to a specific problem; surrounding elements that help to identify a problem.

BOWSTRING (truss) signifies an individualized means of support; unusual support aid.

BOW TIE alludes to a constrained personality; an individual who is frequently considered stuffy or straight-laced.

BOW WINDOW stands for extended perception; a good view.

BOX (container) warns of a boxed-in condition, situation, or relationship. Individuals can also box themselves in. May point to concepts and perspectives within the proverbial box and come as an advisement to think outside that box.

BOX (shape) represents a square thought process; not open-minded.

BOX (sport) portrays an argumentative personality.

BOX CAMERA suggests old-fashioned attitudes; out-of-date perspectives.

BOXCAR refers to extra aspects we carry around in life that are heavily weighted; negative memories; bad feelings retained.

BOX CUTTER refers to a dislike for being boxed in; also may point to an individual with a tendency to think outside the box.

BOX ELDER (tree) stands for fortitude; courage.

BOXER (dog breed) denotes protectiveness of a friend; may indicate a watchful or hesitant personality.

BOXER SHORTS exemplify sexist perspectives, a sexually domineering attitude.

BOXING GLOVE connotes a combative nature. Also may point to a tendency (or need) to box one's way out of something.

BOXING RING will indicate the arena (issue) of conflict.

BOX LUNCH applies to conservative attitudes; frugal.

BOX OFFICE implies that which attracts attention; a draw; popularity.

BOX SEAT means a high position; benefit of wealth or position.

BOX SPRING relates to quality of rest times; quality of relaxation and a pause from the daily grind of life.

BOX TOP represents something that needs opening in one's life. What kind of box is the dream presenting? Are there words on it?

BOX TURTLE denotes endurance.

BOXWOOD (tree) stands for a particularly strong natural skill/talent.

BOY characterizes beginning or foundational male perspectives.

BOYCOTT means a demonstrative protest; an active coercion.

BOYFRIEND symbolizes male relationships.

BOY SCOUT represents good deeds and the formation of basic life perspectives.

BOYSENBERRY relates to the fruits of enduring life struggles.

BOY WONDER depicts high accomplishments gained from an early recognition of opportunities.

BRACE means support. What is being braced? This answer will clearly define what needs support in the dreamer's life.

BRACELET connotes a subjugated situation or relationship.

BRACES (dental) are an indication that one's verbal tendencies require strengthening. This may be pointing to *stronger* words needed or it may infer a need for better *aligned* verbal expression (straight talk).

BRACKEN stands for a tangled and prickly path due to one's lack of spiritual application.

BRACKET represents an aspect that assists in supporting the personal weight of life problems and adversity.

BRAG exemplifies a lack of peace within self.

BRAID (hair) pertains to *twisted* thought patterns; confusion; convoluted thinking process; twisted perspectives.

BRAILLE advises of opportunities to see clearly; warns against a tendency to claim ignorance.

BRAIN pertains to one's thought process and quality of same.

BRAINCHILD characterizes the birth of a brilliant idea.

BRAIN CORAL connotes spiritual intelligence and/or high knowledge.

BRAIN DAMAGE applies to thought patterns or perspectives that are not correct; inability to correctly reason or perceive logically.

BRAIN DEAD portrays total apathy; may also come as a premonition of someone's physical demise.

BRAIN DISEASE points to a certain dysfunction in one's thinking or perspective.

BRAIN FEVER denotes a condition that inflames one's thoughts.

BRAINLESS means irrationality; unreasonable; illogical thought.

BRAIN-PICKING relates to in-depth contemplation and analysis. May indicate a need to bounce ideas off of someone trusted to be your sounding board.

BRAIN SCAN advises one to self-examine thought processes and paths of logic; a self-check of one's reasoning abilities or processes.

BRAINSTORMING means deep thought applied to problem-solving or inventiveness.

BRAIN SURGERY reveals a serious need for a dramatic change in thought, perspectives, or sense of reasoning.

BRAINTEASER (puzzle/riddle) signifies a problematical aspect in one's life that's extremely difficult to solve or resolve; calls for deeper analytical thought.

BRAIN TUMOR points to an inability to apply logic and reason to thought.

BRAINWASHING stands for a willful destruction of another's ideals, attitudes, or perspectives. May also point to a need to cleanse one's thought process.

BRAIN WAVE connotes mental impulses; inspiration; sudden ideas or epiphanies.

BRAKE warns of a need to halt something, or slow one's actions/movement.

BRAKE FLUID pertains to a life element utilized to control the pace of one's progression.

BRAKE LIGHT symbolizes one's intention to slow down.

BRAKE LINE pertains to the ability to control one's life pace; the *essential* element that maintains control of one's pace.

BRAKEMAN characterizes one's immediate support person; an individual who is at the ready to give assistance.

BRAKE PEDAL refers to aspects in one's life that allows a slower pace; that which brings about a slowing; the personal access to controlling one's pace.

BRAKE SHOES stand for the singular element in one's life which will stop one from progressing into a negative situation. Usually this element is related to self-control, will power, or other type of self-generated solution.

BRAMBLE See bracken.

BRANCH (office) refers to secondary sources other than the main one.

BRANCH (tree/shrub) See bough.

BRAND (cattle) denotes possession; the exclusive owner of something; originator; titleholder.

BRANDING IRON stands for possessiveness; personal identification of something.

BRAND NAME pertains to general knowledge; that which is generally recognizable.

BRANDY See alcoholic beverage.

BRASS points to a harsh, boisterous personality; unrefined. May also mean something that's changeable. Could indicate a life aspect that mellows over time.

BRASS KNUCKLES stand for a severely aggressive or argumentative nature with intent to cause harm; prepared for a fight.

BRASS RING symbolizes an aspect that suggests a strong possibility to have the ability to realize goals; something that may manifest one's dreams or goals; goals are in reach.

BRASS TACKS apply to the basic facts of an issue or situation; something of the utmost importance and its fundamentals.

BRAT signifies an ill-mannered, juvenile attitude.

BRAWL cautions against loss of temper; inability to settle differences in an intelligent and reasonable manner.

BREAD represents aspects that sustain us; the necessities in life.

BREAD AND BUTTER means one's livelihood; that which provides basic needs.

BREADBASKET denotes a source of those life aspects that contribute to the quality and dependability of our livelihood; that which holds elements of our sustenance.

BREADBOARD refers to life aspects that support one's livelihood.

BREADBOX portrays quantity of energy put into one's livelihood.

BREAD CRUMBS signify a minuscule amount of something.

BREAD LINE denotes a lack of necessities or livelihood elements. This may indicate one's basic moral, emotional, or spiritual aspects.

BREAD MACHINE reflects ease of making a living; that which comes easily to one.

BREAD MOLD suggests a possible need to change jobs or breathe freshness into the current one.

BREADSTICK represents the convenience or handy opportunities one often overlooks.

BREADWINNER characterizes one who supplies necessities; one who does the work.

BREAK (broken) points to the need to repair something in one's life. Surrounding dreamscape details should clarify what needs fixing.

BREAK (in text) indicates a need to pace the rate of one's informational intake.

BREAK (time-out) calls for a pause or rest from something.

BREAK DANCING refers to efforts expended on trying to become independent or to begin expressing one's own unique perspectives.

BREAKDOWN (emotional) implies a falling-apart situation or condition; stressed beyond endurance.

BREAKDOWN (vehicle) refers to a literal physical condition. Directly points to some type of physical illness.

BREAK-EVEN POINT suggests a time/phase when one's applied energies are about to pay off and show progression.

BREAKFAST connotes the quality of a new beginning.

BREAKFRONT (furniture) signifies a crack in one's presented veneer; a break in one's affected presentation.

BREAK IN See burglar.

BREAK-IN (phone operator) stands for an urgent message.

BREAK-IN (tame) refers to a need to become acclimated; tone down a wild idea or behavior.

BREAK-IN (wear down) advises one to reach a comfortable point or position; take the stiffness out of something; become more familiar and comfortable with something.

BREAKING POINT connotes a critical point where one either breaks away or is over-stressed by conditions.

BREAKOUT (escape) signifies a form of retreat or freedom; distancing from something; extraction of oneself from a negative element; perhaps overcoming something.

BREAKTHROUGH means a great advancement or realization has been accomplished.

BREAKUP illustrates the separation of a specific life aspect. This may be a promising dream symbol because it could point to a new freedom or independence.

BREAKWATER stands for a major spiritual barrier. This may be a temporary necessity.

BREAST relates to emotions, usually unexpressed sensitivity.

BREAST-BEATING denotes sorrow. This action may represent a desire to elicit sympathy from others.

BREAST-FEEDING usually refers to a nurturing nature; may also indicate immaturity and/or a fear of being independent.

BREAST IMPLANTS symbolizes one who needs to bolster self-image; a misplaced perception of personal worth. May also point to a need to increase one's nurturing nature.

BREASTPLATE warns of a fear of being hurt; indicates a lack of confidence in self or one's own defenses.

BREAST PUMP suggests a need to give nourishment to another.

BREAST STROKE suggests spirituality taken to heart.

BREATH exemplifies one's inner life-force.

BREATHING TUBE See artificial respiration.

BREATHLESS cautions the dreamer to slow down. One or more aspects in life are being rushed through.

BREATH MINT reveals a need to freshen one's inner drive; points to a staleness.

BREATH TEST points to adulterated speech. May mean prevarications, gossip, slanted facts, etc. A self-analysis is advised.

BREECH DELIVERY warns of a possible backward or upside down outcome to a developing relationship or situation.

BREECH OF CONTRACT will refer to a wrongdoing; going back on one's word.

BREEDER (of dogs) connotes an individual who maintains interest in something for the prime purpose of getting something back out of it; an ulterior motive for a quickly made friendship.

BREEDER REACTOR cautions against creating more than can be consumed or assimilated; excesses. May also warn of multiple ramifications associated with a plan or act.

BREEDING GROUND means a fertile condition or atmosphere; an atmosphere conducive to productivity or fruitfulness.

BREEZE implies low mental activity. This may not be a negative dream fragment.

BREEZEWAY denotes thoughts that connect main ideas to form more complex concepts; connective elements.

BREW (beer) See alcoholic beverage.

BREW (concoct) symbolizes a mix of various thoughts or ideas; long contemplation on innovative concepts; inventiveness.

BREWER'S YEAST represents the source of innovative thought; brilliant thought and ideas; the power behind something; impetus.

BREWMASTER is normally associated with one who is expert at providing the perfect form of stress-relieving sources unique to each individual. However, depending on the related elements of the dream, a brewmaster may also point to a routinely conniving person.

BRIAR See bracken.

BRIBE means ill-gotten favors, benefits, or goals.

BRIC-A-BRAC stands for the unnecessary aspects with which one clutters life.

BRICK signifies life's building blocks; one's personal foundational aspects that should be solid and strong.

BRICK CAVITY WALL denotes one's insular defenses.

BRICKLAYER characterizes one who works hard and diligently at insuring strong foundational values.

BRICK RED (color) indicates a lack of empowerment, motivation, or energy; a sickly type of perseverance.

BRIDAL VEIL may represent the presence of possible contradictions; can indicate the preservation of one's secret past.

BRIDAL WREATH (botanical) indicates a celebration of a new path/journey beginning.

BRIDE portrays a desire or need for a life partner.

BRIDEGROOM represents a desire or need for companion influences in life.

BRIDE PRICE pertains to an unnecessary payment extended for a personal relationship; a forced or bribe-generated relationship.

BRIDESMAID/BEST MAN characterizes a need for support in decision-making or support while making a life-altering choice.

BRIDGE (game) See card (playing).

BRIDGE (dental) implies half-truths spoken. May also indicate the need for more information regarding an issue.

BRIDGE (structure) always denotes some type of connective element.

BRIDGE CLOTH refers to preparations for a lighthearted debate or semi-conflict.

BRIDGE LOAN refers to a stop-gap plan; an interim move to take up the slack.

BRIDGE RING See ring (jewelry).

BRIDLE denotes a means of control.

BRIDLE PATH relates to a controlled life path; a path that is traveled at an easy pace.

BRIEF (legal) pertains to facts presented in a concise manner.

BRIEFING reveals a situation where one doesn't have all the facts. Signifies a need to be brought up to speed on an issue.

BRIEFCASE cautions one to have all facts together before making decisions or judgments.

BRIM depicts a full capacity; a life aspect that has been fully developed or explored. Was something in the dream full to the brim, or not?

BRIMSTONE relates to a passionately demonstrative attitude connected to a specific cause or issue.

BRINDLE (color) signifies congeniality; an open perspective.

BRINE portrays the preservation of spiritual concepts or truths.

BRINE SHRIMP represent individual spiritual concepts or beliefs.

BRINK symbolizes the point at which a major decision or action will occur.

BRIOCHE suggests light nourishment.

BRIQUETTE stands for that which serves as an impetus; life aspects that light a fire and serve as motivation.

BRISKET denotes emotionally warming feelings.

BRISTLECONE PINE (tree) reflects lessons in life; reminds us to learn from past mistakes.

BRITTANY SPANIEL (dog breed) denotes a compassionate friend; a sympathetic and sensitive nature.

BRITTLE reveals dryness. Portrays something that's unyielding; a lack of nourishment which may be mental, emotional, or spiritual.

BRITTLE (bones) suggests weakness in respect to fortitude/perseverance.

BRITTLE (confection) See peanut brittle.

BRITTLE STAR characterizes spiritual reaching; one's research that extends as far as it can be taken.

BROADBAND signifies a wide range of communication skills; an ability to communicate with others on any level; also communications made at a faster rate.

BROADCAST (airwaves) connotes the spreading of information. May infer gossip.

BROADCLOTH (fabric) represents a broad-scope perspective; open to alternatives or varying opinions.

BROAD JUMP See long jump.

BROADLOOM See broadcloth.

BROADSIDE indicates unexpected events; surprises in life that deeply affect us.

BROADSWORD See sword.

BROADWAY (NYC) cautions against a tendency toward theatrics; a habit of overdramatizing; exaggerations.

BROCADE (fabric) illustrates a way of life that's rich in compassion and possesses an emotional depth; a life of living spiritual beliefs.

BROCCOLI signifies multi-level talents and the utilization of same.

BROCHURE indicates a hyped aspect; something that's portrayed in a glossy presentation.

BROIL refers to heat from above; pressure from one's boss or Higher Self.

BROILER characterizes the aspect in one's life that has the capability of bringing pressure or heat.

BROKEN LIGHT BULB signifies a temporary lull in one's ability to see clearly; a short period of puzzlement or confusion.

BROKEN RECORD denotes repetition.

BROKEN WING represents a hampered ability to think clearly; a phase of delay in ability to lay plans.

BROKER See agent.

BROKERAGE stands for a precarious aspect in one's life. May refer to pending plans; also may point to the need to shop something around.

BRONCHITIS alludes to an inability to clearly process thoughts and ideas. May also reflect a congestion involving emotions.

BRONCO represents individuality and the freedom to express same.

BRONCOBUSTING infers a struggle for individuality. May also warn of a domineering personality.

BRONZE is suggestive of the beauty that comes from the blending of specific life elements.

BRONZE CASTING exemplifies the resulting product of blending specific life aspects; the touchable goal or creation.

BRONZE STAR portrays recognition for perseverance.

BROOCH (jewelry) connotes an attention-getting aspect or one who enjoys getting the attention of others.

BROOD (deep in thought) cautions against a tendency to dwell on specific aspects without productive results.

BROOD (many offspring) characterizes many new opportunities in the offing.

BROODER HOUSE symbolizes a wealth of new ideas; multiple plans for new beginnings.

BROOK See stream.

BROOM cautions one to look past the surface; sweep away surface debris to get a clearer perception of what's beneath.

BROOMSTICK refers to an aspect-in-hand that allows one to see past the surface.

BROOMSTICK SKIRT suggests strong opinions kept to oneself.

BROTH denotes clarity.

BROTHEL See house of ill repute.

BROTHER characterizes a close male associate in life; a male who is a close friend.

BROTHERHOOD signifies male camaraderie that has a deeply connecting aspect between members.

BROUGHAM See carriage.

BROW See forehead.

BROWBEAT points to forced beliefs or perspectives. May indicate a manipulative personality; coercion.

BROWN (color) symbolizes one's earthy aspects; life, attitude, and emotional side rather than anything spiritual.

BROWN BAGGING portrays a frugal nature.

BROWN BREAD typifies a down-home nature.

BROWNIE (fairy) See fairy.

BROWNIE (confection) pertains to those life aspects one views as personal treats.

BROWNIE (young Girl Scout) denotes the beginning development of ethics and feminine perspectives.

BROWNIE POINT cautions against the expectation of praise; doing good for the purpose of gaining praise or reward.

BROWN-NOSE points to a desire to impress people.

BROWNOUT warns against overwork; loss of one's former high energy level.

BROWN RICE relates to wholeness; acceptance of the whole rather than choosing easier, softer aspects.

BROWNSTONE commends one's tendency to give others space; an acceptance of another's totality.

BROWN SUGAR connotes a genuinely sweet personality; one whose true nature is without negative qualities.

BROWSE pertains to selectiveness; looking for specifics.

BROWSER (Internet) applies to one's personal way to access information.

BRUISE characterizes minor emotional or psychological injuries.

BRUNCH depicts a starting point that begins in the middle; suggests one go back to the beginning.

BRUNETTE (hair color) usually infers level-headedness; a down-to-earth attitude and generally optimistic perspective.

BRUNT denotes one's main burden or responsibility.

BRUSH See specific type. Generally warns of a tendency to brush things aside; a habit of avoiding priorities or serious aspects. May point to a need to straighten out some type of confusion.

BRUSH FIRE stands for a willful neglect or destruction of one's talents; a voluntary cessation of spiritual acts.

BRUSSELS SPROUTS indicate the little acts of goodness we do that nourish or encourage others.

BRUTUS (Marcus Junius) warns of the self-destructing power that vindictiveness carries.

BUBBLE connotes negative aspects in one's life; a possible indication of one's insulating efforts—keeping self in a bubble.

BUBBLE BATH warns against submerging oneself in negative situations, relationships, or beliefs.

BUBBLE GUM illustrates an arrogance in the face of negatives; a foolish attitude.

BUBBLE TOP signifies a fear of being injured in some way; lack of confidence in one's protective or defensive abilities. Goes back to feelings of vulnerability.

BUBBLE WRAP suggests a protective measure; something needs special handling.

BUBONIC PLAGUE pertains to highly contagious negative attitudes; demonstrates the speed and destructive force of following the crowd when the crowd is in serious error; a contaminant.

BUCCANEER characterizes those who may threaten or harm another's spiritual beliefs.

BUCK (kick) pertains to attempts to reject or refuse something; reluctance.

BUCK (male deer) See deer.

BUCK (money) See money.

BUCKBOARD signifies a rough ride along one's path, yet the rider persists without complaint.

BUCKET denotes the retention of important spiritual truths. Recall what condition the dreamscape bucket was in. The type of material it was made of should be added to the interpretation. Was it dented? Have a hole? All these factors give added dimension toward clarity.

BUCKET BRIGADE characterizes the sharing of spiritual truths toward a common goal, usually to extinguish a negative element.

BUCKET SEAT means self-confidence, individualism, or separatism; independence.

BUCK FEVER exposes that which destroys innocence; a passion to prove self; a destructive predatory nature.

BUCKING See buck (kick).

BUCKLE portrays determination.

BUCKSHOT pertains to solid facts of ammunition that backs up one's goal or claim.

BUCKSHOT (rubber) means ineffectiveness; a threat with no backing; a warning.

BUCKSKIN refers to a soft touch aspect to one's character.

BUCK TEETH typifies an outspoken individual; often one who speaks before thinking.

BUCKTHORN (tree) signifies a focus on one's goals; nearing achievement.

BUCOLIC (atmosphere) alludes to an extremely peaceful situation or relationship.

BUD (flower) indicates new beginnings.

BUD (fruit) means the beginnings of a fruitful endeavor.

BUDDHA characterizes highest spiritual attainment; enlightenment and the true wisdom that accompanies it.

BUDDY portrays a reluctance to be on one's own; a fear of solitude; lacking self-confidence or independence.

BUDDY SYSTEM symbolizes a companion needed for security purposes.

BUDGERIGAR See parakeet.

BUDGET cautions against the practice of disproportionate activities; suggests a need to prioritize; long-term foresight and planning.

BUD VASE signifies a personal pride and feeling of rightness in respect to one's new beginning.

BUD WORM is an extremely negative aspect that damages new beginnings.

BUFF (color) suggests gentleness; a passive nature.

BUFF (polish) represents the act of finishing something to the best of one's ability.

BUFFALO (bison) symbolizes gullibility. May also indicate perseverance.

BUFFALO HEART represents great inner strength; endurance through intense adversity.

BUFFALO ROBE denotes one's shield of inner strength.

BUFFALO WINGS relate to attempts to intermix specific aspects that do not blend or will not coalesce.

BUFFER ZONE signifies one's social distance or space separating self from others.

BUFFET See sideboard.

BUFFET (meal) symbolizes the wide variety of opportunities open to us.

BUFFING WHEEL stands for that which allows one to finalize goals.

BUFFOON See clown.

BUG See specific type. Generally portrays irritations in life. May have positive meaning when specific insects are shown.

BUG See listening device.

BUGABOO implies the subject of one's worst fear; a continual problem or irritation.

BUGBANE See black cohosh.

BUG-EYED connotes ignorant perception; amazement due to a lack of knowledge or understanding.

BUGGY suggests a simplistic plan for a phase of one's life journey.

BUG-JUICE signifies a fairly useless element in respect to expecting any benefits.

BUGLE is a call to action or attention.

BUILDING (act of) depicts the act of creating; active efforts.

BUILDING CODE represents limits/perimeters one sets for an intended plan.

BUILDING PERMIT denotes a final decision/verification to go ahead with a new plan.

BUILDINGS See specific type.

BUILDING SITE symbolizes the groundwork for a new plan.

BUILT-IN denotes instinctual behavior; inherent qualities or talents.

BUILT-UP signifies development, may pertain to self by way of implying one's boastfulness or egotistical nature.

BULB (flower) refers to an upcoming budding of talent or other aspect in one's life; first efforts applied toward the actualization of future plans.

BULB (light) applies to a new awareness; solutions; bright ideas. Unless the bulb was burnt out or broken, then the opposite meaning applies. If the dreamscape bulb was too big for the socket, then it points to grandiose ideas.

BULGE pertains to a need to release something, usually pressure. May refer to emotions that are building up inside.

BULGUR signifies strength of character; a strong constitution.

BULIMAREXIA (bulimia and anorexia) illustrates a lack of self-control; a love/hate attitude.

BULIMIA connotes an inability to voice or stand up for personal opinions. It means that one publicly agrees with popular opinion but secretly rejects them.

BULKHEAD symbolizes an aspect in life that serves as one's main support system.

BULK MAIL equates to wide disbursement.

BULK PURCHASE typifies a personal need for security; expresses a need to be well provisioned.

BULK RATE signifies a more cost-effective way of accomplishing something; a way to achieve a goal through the output of less energy.

BULL characterizes a tendency toward narrow-mindedness; self-possessed.

BULL BOAT refers to the avoidance of spiritual concepts due to primitive or outdated attitudes.

BULLDOG (dog breed) denotes a bullish associate or friend.

BULLDOZER illustrates a need for clear understanding; to clear away the rubble that covers the ground-level facts.

BULLET pertains to the negative aspects of self that could injure others.

BULLET CASING refers to spent or empty threats; emotional issues that have lost their explosive impact. May also indicate something carrying the potential for leading to an explosive event.

BULLETIN draws attention to something that should be known; news that affects the dreamer.

BULLETIN BOARD pertains to messages; news; communications.

BULLETPROOF VEST exemplifies an emotionally devoid personality; a fear of being affected or affecting others; a measure against being emotionally hurt.

BULLET TRAIN infers high-speed travel; advises one to slow down in order to absorb that which is presented along the way.

BULLFIGHT means hard-headedness; an inability to compromise.

BULLFROG connotes a need to give serious attention to spiritual matters.

BULLHEADED characterizes a stubborn nature; one rarely given to compromise. May point to narrow-mindedness.

BULLHORN advises one to voice personal attitudes or opinions; a need to express feelings.

BULLION See gold or silver.

BULL MARKET implies a solid or improving financial condition.

BULLNECKED reveals a stubborn personality; one who can be obnoxiously assertive through the tendency to feel superior due to a false self-image of super strength.

BULLPEN points to a situation where several individuals share a narrow-minded group attitude or opinion.

BULLPEN (baseball) represents one's backup resources; a source of reserve energy or support.

BULLRING stands for a manipulative situation or condition; a set-up.

BULL SESSION advises of the need to casually discuss something; air opinions and attitudes; express personal perspectives.

BULL'S-EYE confirms one's right course; on target.

BULLWHIP implies an aggressively bullish nature; unyielding; demanding. May infer coercion.

BULLY characterizes bullish behavior; outwardly demeaning to others; a sense of self-importance derived through intimidation.

BUM See tramp/hobo.

BUMBLEBEE characterizes one-mindedness; a focused mind; industrious.

BUMP (in road) points to small, temporary difficulties in one's path.

BUMPER pertains to one's tenacity; an ability to bounce back from problems or emotional injury; a self-protective measure.

BUMPER CAR alludes to a personal enjoyment of the game; a tendency toward conflict for the thrill of winning.

BUMPER GUARD suggests an acknowledgment of the possibility of missteps being taken along one's life journey and precautions taken to allow for them.

BUMPER STICKER connotes one who is openly opinionated. These are extremely revealing if they can be recalled accurately.

BUMPER-TO-BUMPER means little movement; a condition or situation that isn't going anywhere.

BUMPY (road) refers to a phase of one's path which presents temporary difficulties to override.

BUNDLE See package.

BUNDLING BOARD stands for a path shared with another, yet each remaining separate and free to have differing perspectives.

BUNDT CAKE/PAN signifies the little rewards in life that come in many forms and from various sources.

BUNGALOW See cottage.

BUNGEE CORD denotes secured defenses; backup safeguards applied when taking life chances.

BUNGEE JUMPING means false bravado; a show of bravery while knowing safeguards are in place.

BUNION refers to the bumps and pains received during one's walk through life.

BUNK BED relates to multilevel dreams; dreamscape fragments often have dual meanings for the dreamer.

BUNKER identifies one's lack of faith and/or self-confidence; a fear of one's life path.

BUNKHOUSE typifies the nature of one's casual relationships; a relationship that will have a short life span.

BUNNY See rabbit.

BUNSEN BURNER calls for a need for self-analysis or serious introspection.

BUOY (channel marker) is a directional marker for one's spiritual path.

BUOYANCY means spiritual resiliency.

BUR will indicate a troublesome irritation in one's life, one that can be easily removed if given a close enough look.

BUREAU (furniture) See dresser.

BUREAUCRAT refers to narrow-mindedness; focused on self-serving issues; centered on own agendas.

BURGER See hamburger.

BURGLAR characterizes an untrustworthy individual; underhandedness; ulterior motives; someone who will end up taking something.

BURGLAR ALARM stands for an awareness for certain negative eventualities and one's efforts to circumvent them.

BURIAL GROUND See graveyard.

BURIAL MOUND suggests a past difficulty that shouldn't be forgotten; a call to remember lessons learned from past experience.

BURIAL PLOT points to one's ultimate end. May refer to a failure of some type; an irreversible ending or finalization.

BURIED ALIVE signifies the smothering or covering-up of one's identity, plan, idea, or any other aspect directly associated with the dreamer.

BURIED TREASURE denotes true value that is rarely identified as such. An example would be spiritual generosity when one helps another without an expectation of payment. Unconditional goodness would be a buried treasure few perceive as having great value.

BURKA refers to a shield one uses to distance oneself from others. May indicate an introverted or reclusive personality. Could expose one who hides in a shell.

BURL (wood) is the inherent beauty of individuality; the creativity of each individual's unique talents.

BURLAP (fabric) symbolizes strength of character and an enduring constitution.

BURLESQUE means that something or someone is being mocked; a travesty.

BURMESE (cat breed) denotes an expressive individuality; outgoing.

BURN (clothing) connotes a ridding of one's outward affectations; a change in persona.

BURN (hair) indicates forgetfulness, perhaps due to a conscious desire to be rid of certain memories; the destruction of thoughts, perspectives, or attitudes.

BURN (incinerate) denotes a total destruction of something.

BURNED-OUT pertains to a state of exhaustion; being worn out. May indicate a sense of defeat.

BURNING BUSH generally means epiphanies, but may also reveal one' deepening attitude of apathy.

BURNOOSE represents an ability to control stress.

BURNT OFFERING signifies subjugation; attempts to appease or plead.

BURP infers some irregularity with an aspect in one's life. A life element causing irritation.

BURR points to a slight or temporary problem; minor irritation.

BURRO See donkey.

BURROW indicates trepidation; escapism; attempts to hide from something.

BURROWING OWL characterizes an ability to see through others; acute perception into other's psychological maneuvers.

BURSITIS represents a reluctance to act or go forward.

BURYING (act of) stands for cover-ups; secrets; hiding something. May also indicate intentions to forget and forgive, yet nothing worth burying can really ever be forgotten; can also mean denial.

BUS pertains to an aspect in one's life that serves to benefit many. May also refer to an overblown situation or even obesity, depending on surrounding dreamscape elements.

BUSBOY connotes one who is capable of repairing wrongs done; one who has the ability to clean up what others leave behind.

BUS DRIVER (public) exemplifies a caring and giving personality; one who has the potential to help or carry one for a ways.

BUS DRIVER (school) See school bus driver.

BUSH denotes fullness of spiritual/humanitarian acts. Was the dreamscape bush full or scrawny?

BUSH BABY symbolizes heightened awareness.

BUSHEL indicates a large quantity of something. What was in the bushel?

BUSH JACKET characterizes an adventurous nature.

BUSH LEAGUE See minor league.

BUSHMAN is one who immerses self in a spiritually humanitarian lifestyle; one who places importance on the basics.

BUSHMASTER (snake) denotes a dangerously manipulative personality.

BUSH PILOT typifies one who guides others to a spiritually interactive life; one who guides humanitarian causes.

BUSHWHACKER connotes an individual who is capable of making one's way through life's difficulties; also can denote one who ambushes others.

BUSINESS CARD represents an egotistical personality; a desire to be known and recognized. May serve to reveal someone's identity or purpose.

BUSINESS SUIT stands for an intent to be serious.

BUSING means a forced integration of ideas by another.

BUS STATION suggests a need to be helpful at a different location; implies assistance is needed somewhere else.

BUS STOP refers to an opportunity. What this opportunity is depends on the surrounding dreamscape elements. This may be an opportunity to make a choice in life.

BUST (sculpture) represents an individual or ideal that's important for the dreamer.

BUSTED See arrest.

BUSTIER pertains to a tendency to reveal more than is necessary, usually to one's detriment.

BUSTLE (skirt type) means social haughtiness; status conscious.

BUSYBODY stands for an interfering personality.

BUSY SEASON points to a phase of greatest activity.

BUSY SIGNAL denotes a wrong time to communicate with someone. This indicates a communication that wouldn't go well and suggests a later time to attempt the connection.

BUTANE represents thoughts that could be damaging depending how they are acted upon.

BUTCHER characterizes a scathing personality; one who focuses on the negative aspects of others; one who cuts apart ideas or plans.

BUTCHER BLOCK (table/pattern) denotes negative aspects of one's life that others can gossip about or use negatively.

BUTCHER KNIFE connotes a cutting-up or chopping-at situation; an aspect used to cut down someone or something.

BUTCHER PAPER suggests attempts at concealment.

BUTLER portrays an individual who is submissive to another; giving deference to another; a subservient nature.

BUTLER'S PANTRY refers to the comfort and convenience of being well prepared. May point to a personal abundance of subservient methods.

BUTTER points to the richness of a simple life and the unaffected perspectives that accompany it.

BUTTER-AND-EGGS (botanical) represents a sunny disposition; optimism.

BUTTERBALL portrays excessiveness; an extraneous aspect; overblown or fattened to extreme.

BUTTER CHURN connotes those aspects that create life's true and simple riches.

BUTTER COOKIE represents a touch of sweetness to something; an unexpected blessing or pleasing element.

BUTTER CREAM See butter cookie.

BUTTERCUP (flower) means life's real joys; inner happiness; laughter.

BUTTERFINGERS caution against letting things slip through your fingers; denotes a need to get a grasp on self, life, or some important aspect.

BUTTERFLY exemplifies renewal and rejuvenation. May refer to an ability to bounce back after specific setbacks or disappointments; an enlightened change in perspective or attitude.

BUTTERFLY EFFECT comes to remind us that everything we do in life has some type of ramification or effect left in its wake.

BUTTERFLY NET signifies one's intentions toward rejuvenating oneself; an intent to make self-improvements.

BUTTERFLY ROOF (construction type) signifies a backward way of thinking.

BUTTERMILK alludes to life's spiritually rich rewards.

BUTTERNUT (tree) points to one's receptivity to others; congeniality.

BUTTERSCOTCH (flavor) implies something that has a rich flavor to it, rich as in spiritually or heartily wholesome.

BUTTON advises of the need for some kind of physical connection or link-up needed.

BUTTON-DOWN refers to the need to secure something in one's life.

BUTTONHOLE represents the openings that life presents to us for opportunities.

BUY-BACK will denote a change of mind; getting something back which one lost or gave away.

BUY-DOWN signifies unloading a larger aspect in exchange for a smaller one. This is usually a positive dreamscape symbol.

BUYERS' MARKET pertains to the best time to take advantage of specific opportunities.

BUYOUT connotes an acquisition of the whole; obtaining something in its entirety; having it all. Who is doing the buyout in the dream? The dreamer, or someone else?

BUZZARD characterizes a gloating nature; one who stands in wait to pick over what's left.

BUZZER advises of a need to make communications in a discreet manner. This will directly refer to a specific aspect in the dreamer's life.

BUZZ SAW See circular saw.

BUZZ WORD warns against a desire to impress others; a need to bolster self-esteem and worth.

BYLINE denotes an acknowledgment; giving credit where credit is due.

BYPASS pertains to the avoidance of unnecessary aspects; going around something.

BY-PRODUCT illustrates that which all thoughts, words, and actions may cause. We don't always see the widespread effects of what we say and do in life.

BYSTANDER usually refers to apathy; one who watches yet does not act. In some dreamscapes, it may indicate a witness to something; a guiltless party; innocence. Or it may point to knowledge gained through observation.

BYWORD comes in dreams to emphasize a particular message. Recall what this byword was, how it was used, and by whom.

C

CAB See taxi.

CAB (of truck) indicates the controlling aspects of one's life.

CABAL refers to schemers that in some way affect the dreamer's life.

CABANA symbolizes a need for temporary shelter; to remove oneself from heated situations.

CABARET See bistro.

CABBAGE pertains to the rougher aspects directly affecting one's life.

CABBAGE ROSE comes to reveal and underscore one's deep affection/admiration.

CAB DRIVER See taxi driver.

CABERNET See wine.

CABIN denotes a life aligned with nature; an inner connection or inherent bond with nature.

CABIN BOY refers to a young individual who is capable of helping one along his/her spiritual journey.

CABIN CLASS represents middle of the road; an average rating.

CABIN CRUISER alludes to a spiritual cruising along one's spiritual path; a lack of spiritual seriousness.

CABINET portrays that which is kept from the public eye.

CABINETMAKER See carpenter.

CABIN FEVER signifies a desire to be close to nature without being vibrationally aligned; a forcing action applied to one's wants or goals.

CABLE stands for an aspect in life that serves as a strong support.

CABLE CAR connotes advancement generated by a strong supporting aspect in one's life. Can also refer to threatening thoughts.

CABLEGRAM will signify a spiritual message.

CABLE-KNIT (design) refers to interwoven ideas; thoughts that intertwine.

CABLE TELEVISION implies information obtained through the assistance of others.

CABOOSE means a finalization; the end of something.

CABSTAND exemplifies a waiting time. This usually refers to one's inability to advance on one's own.

CACHE symbolizes the high value of one's hidden talents. This is most often a warning to stop stashing away one's abilities.

CACTUS applies to spiritual beliefs that are protected.

CACTUS WREN denotes acting on one's awareness; responding to insights/feelings.

CADAVER most often denotes learning opportunities; a reminder of our mortality.

CADAVER DOG will usually point to a friend who cares about the dreamer's welfare.

CADDIE represents a follower and implies indecision or an inability to think for self. May also refer to a clinging type of personality.

CADDY suggests a need to keep something in it's proper place.

CADET characterizes the beginning stages of developing combative perspectives; one who can be perceived as a fledgling headed for a draw toward the military-machine attitude.

CADMIUM reflects an additional aspect to something, possibly an external facade of some type.

CAESAREAN SECTION reveals an immediate action needed to save a new beginning.

CAFETERIA represents a lack of choice; not realizing the wide scope of opportunities available.

CAFFEINE denotes motivational factors that serve as an impetus in life.

CAFTAN See burnoose.

CAGE pertains to an aspect that prevents the exercise of one's freedoms or rights. This may even refer to oneself.

CAGED BIRDS refer to suppressed emotions.

CAIMAN See alligator.

CAIRN illustrates markers along life's path. This serves as a guiding aspect.

CAJEPUT (tree) stands for motivation; encouragement to keep going.

CAKE pertains to a goal or that which is strived for.

CAKE PAN refers to that which assists in achieving goals; a foundational tool.

CAKEWALK signifies a sure thing; simple task to perform.

CALADIUM (plant) suggests a rich or bountiful natural talent.

CALAMARI warns against the mental intake of too many differing spiritual concepts at one time.

CALAMINE (lotion) represents a solution to a current life irritation.

CALCIFICATION suggests an unyielding viewpoint, grown hard through lack of a giving nature or experience.

CALCITE stands for misunderstandings; calls for situational clarity.

CALCIUM symbolizes those aspects in life that serve to strengthen us. A caution is indicated for dream symbols that portray an excess of calcium.

CALCULATOR pertains to complex thought patterns; intricate planning; detailed and analytic contemplation.

CALDERA represents a formerly hot issue or situation and the possibility of it reactivating in the future.

CALENDAR signifies time, a specific date. This dream fragment is usually presented as being important for the dreamer.

CALENDAR GIRL See pinup girl.

CALF (bovine) characterizes the beginnings of an end; a fatalistic aspect; something that will not manifest as planned.

CALIBRATE connotes a striving for perfection.

CALICO (pattern) means a natural gentleness; a lack of affectations.

CALICO CAT stands for a quiet independence; a tolerant attitude bordering on nonchalance, yet maintaining a strong loyalty to friends.

CALIFORNIA represents the hope/expectation related to one's personal dream.

CALIPER signifies a desire for perfection; accuracy. May come as an advisement to give greater attention to this.

CALISTHENICS mean preparedness; one's level of experience.

CALK See caulk.

CALL pertains to communication.

CALL BLOCKING signifies a desire to avoid talking to a specific individual.

CALL BOX suggests an immediate need to communicate something or get in touch with someone. The dreamer will know what this is referring to.

CALLER ID denotes selective communications. May indicate a reluctance to connect with certain people.

CALL FORWARDING symbolizes heightened attention given to communications; not wishing to miss any messages.

CALL GIRL implies a lack of self-respect; poor self-image; one who lacks individuality and requires the guidance and/or attention of others.

CALL GUIDE (911 operators) represents immediate availability for responsive advice.

CALLIGRAPHY refers to important messages.

CALL-IN (radio show) See talk radio.

CALLING CARD (printed) connotes one's intention or outward presentation to the public.

CALLING CARD (telephone) stands for communication preparedness; insuring one's ability to be able to reach others.

CALLIOPE indicates a whimsical personality; one who fails to take life seriously; optimism taken to the far extreme.

CALL SCREENING points to the option of choosing whose calls to accept or reject.

CALL SHEET symbolizes opportunities to take advantage of.

CALL SIGN pertains to one's chosen identity; that which one wants to be known by.

CALL TO ARMS stands for a time to move into action; to actively engage one's personal defenses.

CALLUS characterizes a hardened attitude or nature. May also indicate a need to protect oneself behind a hardened barrier.

CALL WAITING applies to a desire to accommodate others; wanting to be available for others.

CALORIE alludes to an aspect that helps keep a balance for the dreamer.

CALORIE CHART illustrates opportunity options for balance in life.

CALORIE COUNTING signifies an effort to bring greater balance into one's life.

CALUMET See peace pipe.

CALVARY exemplifies personal sacrifices that may not be needed.

CAMBRIDGE (Mass.) typifies the frequent negativity that may result from intelligence wrongly utilized.

CAMCORDER is a sign to remember some event in one's life. This infers important lessons to be learned.

CAMEL connotes tenacity and perseverance.

CAMELLIA stands for affected beauty and feigned innocence. This is a caution dream fragment that warns against a tendency toward pretense.

CAMELOT characterizes a paradiselike society; the earthly utopian concept.

CAMEL'S HAIR (fabric) indicates inner strength.

CAMEO signifies prominence; an aspect in one's life that's uniquely treasured or featured.

CAMEO APPEARANCE represents a dreamscape's "featured" individual whose symbology will be of personal importance to the dreamer.

CAMERA represents that which preserves the truth; the facts. This would be a caution for the dreamer to recall things factually.

CAMERA (hidden) generally points to a means of security, yet may also indicate a loss of privacy.

CAMERA CELL PHONE alludes to an opportunity to capture the moment. Depending on surrounding dreamscape elements, this symbol may point to unethical practices of invading the privacy of others.

CAMERA PERSON characterizes one who is focused on the truth or facts. May also reveal an interfering personality.

CAMERA SHOP portrays the many and varied methods of preserving the truth or collecting facts. Could also indicate the options available for those intending to interfere in another's life.

CAMISOLE depicts innocence.

CAMOUFLAGE means hidden aspects; pretense. May point to an introverted personality who wishes to blend into the background and not be noticed.

CAMPAIGN illustrates an attempt to expend energies into a cause or goal.

CAMPAIGN BUTTON signifies a show of one's attitude/opinion; may display a specific cause one has an affinity for.

CAMPAIGN FUND is associated with the energies/resources one reserves for a special cause or goal.

CAMPAIGN MANAGER will be associated with one who facilitates action and keeps the momentum going.

CAMP DAVID suggests a required pause needed in one's intellectual pursuits; a relief from responsibility.

CAMPER (person) characterizes someone who is on a short-term break from life's hectic pace.

CAMPER (RV) signifies that which is capable of providing temporary respite from stress.

CAMPFIRE denotes an inner tranquility; inner peacefulness with one's current place in life or along the path.

CAMP FIRE GIRLS represent an advisement for young people to be taught the value of keeping a balance between work and play—between the daily stressful work toward achieving goals and that of leisure creativity.

CAMPGROUND pertains to an understanding of life's frequent temporary conditions and/or situations; the need to balance stressful work with relaxation.

CAMPHOR OIL pertains to a relief of some type. This will usually refer to something that provides breathing room or eases some type of pain.

CAMPING refers to a temporary return to a calmer situational/emotional state. May be suggesting that more acceptance/tolerance would reduce current stress/anxiety.

CAMPING GEAR signifies the need to equip oneself with more tools to achieve a less stressful state of mind; gear up to gear down.

CAMP ROBBER See gray jay.

CAMPSTOOL implies situational ease; one is comfortable in most situations; adaptability.

CAMP STOVE denotes an emergency source of energy (heat/cooking); refers to an element of preparedness.

CAMPUS (university) connotes an attitude of camaraderie toward learning. May also indicate a caution against an attraction to learning *because* of the socializing.

CAN is a container; what the can contains determines the dream symbol's intent. See specific symbol entry words for a clearer meaning.

CANADA relates to a diversity of inherent talents.

CANADA GOOSE denotes inspiration.

CANAL denotes spiritual connections; most often means spirituality running through one's life.

CANAPÉ signifies attempts made; a time period of trying out various aspects; exploration; expanding one's experience.

CANARY exemplifies singing and may refer to a joyful emotion or possibly a gossip situation.

CANARY YELLOW usually stands for inner joy but, depending on the surrounding elements, this symbol may reveal gossip or betrayal.

CANCAN (dance) suggests unrestrained happiness.

CANCELLATION advises against going through with something.

CANCELLED CHECK represents verification; proof of what one expended in the form of energy or resources.

CANCER is a grave warning to watch for an extremely dangerous negative in one's life.

CANDELABRA signifies an enlightening source that reaches out to illumine multiple life aspects.

CANDID (behavior/speech) naturally points to honesty or the need for it.

CANDIDATE implies a situational position one is headed for.

CANDID CAMERA advises to remember that we're never alone, never unwatched.

CANDLE typifies that which can ignite our spiritual or natural talents/abilities. May indicate hope.

CANDLEHOLDER See candlestick.

CANDLELIGHT (ambient mood) signifies a warm, amiable state of being; contentedness.

CANDLE MAKING represents those activities that bring light and compassion to others. The one making the candle will be the person bringing that light and compassion.

CANDLEMAS DAY stresses the importance of hope, perseverance.

CANDLE SNUFFER means a tendency to reverse the effects of spiritual acts or "smother" the enlightening effects of another's spiritual deeds; cynicism; lack of hope.

CANDLESTICK connotes quality of one's spiritual perception and manner of reception; condition of an individual's inner state toward spiritual acceptance.

CANDLEWICK portrays the basis for one's moral, ethical, and spiritual motivation.

CANDY pertains to the sweet aspects of life; the joys and blessings.

CANDY APPLE signifies a negative element which neutralizes a positive one; nothing lost, nothing gained.

CANDY CANE points to the quality of familial relationships.

CANDY-GRAM denotes a pleasing message; a sign of a sweet relationship.

CANDY SHOP indicates the varied ways and methods that are available for experiencing life's small but meaningful joys.

CANDY STRIPER alludes to the attainment of inner joy through doing for others.

CANDYTUFT (flower) represents life's joyous, brighter moments.

CANDY WRAPPER represents recently experienced joys that shouldn't be so quickly forgotten.

CANE See walking stick.

CANE SUGAR See sugar.

CANISTER (for food) represents basic necessities; the main ingredients that can be built on.

CANKER SORE implies speech infected with a slant toward personal attitudes. May point to cynicism, intolerance, etc.

CANKERWORM refers to a destructive force in one's life which damages perspective and attitudes. This force is causing such negativity as cynicism, apathy, intolerance, etc.

CANNABIS See marijuana.

CANNERY means preservation. Usually advises the dreamer of a need to recall or retain the memory of an event for the purpose of learning from it.

CANNIBAL is a fatally destructive individual; one who has no ethics, morals, or spiritual behaviors.

CANNON represents explosive aspects to one's life. May even be one's own personality.

CANNONBALL denotes the act of outraged explosions; acting in an uncontrollable manner.

CANOE symbolizes a well-paced and tranquil method of traveling one's spiritual path.

CAN OF WORMS means troubling aspects; problems; an issue that will be troublesome if pursued.

CANOLA indicates proper and well-prepared plans; the right atmosphere for advancement.

CANONIZE signifies spiritual conclusions based on personally devised criteria.

CANON LAW stands for religion, not necessarily spiritual truths; pseudo-spirituality; spiritual laws set down by humans.

CAN OPENER means the act of remembering or utilizing important life aspects.

CANOPIC JAR See cannery.

CANOPY See awning.

CANTALOUPE pertains to good beginnings.

CANTEEN means spiritual reserves; spiritual beliefs that one can always fall back on and gain encouragement from.

CANTERBURY BELLS (flower) signify nostalgia.

CANTICLE denotes inner spiritual joy; a full heart.

CANTILEVER portrays an unrecognizable method for obtaining balance; a seemingly unlikely solution.

CANVAS (fabric) relates to a coarse yet strong personality.

CANVASS See survey (poll).

CANYON symbolizes the more troublesome times of one's life walk; the deeper, more shadowed paths we need to move through.

CAPACITOR See condenser.

CAPE (clothing) denotes temporary protective measures taken or required.

CAPE (shoreline) signifies a projection of the way one delves into spiritual aspects; living a spiritual life.

CAPE COD (architecture) represents a settled/comfortable feeling in regard to one's spirituality.

CAPER refers to those unnecessary aspects that an individual believes are important; a self-generated need for more and more interesting and exciting aspects.

CAPILLARY is a finely defined aspect to one's life.

CAPITAL GAIN represents an increase in return for personal efforts expended.

CAPITALIST is one who does good deeds for the sole purpose of personal gain.

CAPITAL LETTER marks an emphasis on something.

CAPITAL PUNISHMENT refers to an excessive retaliation; unjust judgment; vindictiveness.

CAPITOL defines the prime source of something.

CAPITOL HILL See Congress.

CAPITULATE means giving in; a surrender of some type. This dream symbol usually comes as an action advisement when a situation is futile.

CAPOTE See serape.

CAP PISTOL pertains to the tendency to make noise without having any supporting strength or backing; baseless verbiage; idle threats.

CAPPUCCINO connotes personal motivations enriched by generosity.

CAPSIZE means a spiritual reversal; an overturn.

CAPSTONE symbolizes the completion of one's purpose; finalization.

CAPSULE See pill.

CAPSULE (space) represents an exploration of the unknown with the intention of not being touched by it; a reserved interest.

CAPTAIN characterizes one who leads others. This may advise the dreamer to be captain of self.

CAPTAIN HOOK portrays a devious personality.

CAPTAIN'S CHAIR refers to a leadership position. Who was sitting in this chair? Was it empty?

CAPTAIN'S LOG signifies a recording of events. This may come as a suggestion to keep a daily journal.

CAPTION defines something; an explanation; further clarity.

CAPTIVE usually means unwillingness; a forced situation.

CAPTIVE AUDIENCE alludes to a mesmerized or enthralled group. What's important with this dreamscape symbol is to recall what or who was the powerful draw.

CAPUCHIN See monkey.

CAR equates to the quality of one's physical condition. This most often refers to one's personal physiological system.

CARAFE represents spiritual quality. What was the condition of the carafe? What did it contain?

CARAMEL denotes the little joys in life that are worked for and savored for a time.

CARAMEL APPLE refers to a benefit carrying an extra measure of bonus; a sweet deal.

CARAPACE signifies one's defenses; an ability to remain sensitive within a hardened society.

CARAVAN denotes a protected life path through a tight association with others of like mind. Depending on surrounding dreamscape elements, this may not be a positive symbol.

CARB-COUNTING refers to self-restraint.

CARB CRAZE See fad diet.

CARBINE See gun.

CARBOHYDRATES relate to an essential element for balance.

CAR BOMB points to a selectively destructive motivation.

CAR BOMBER characterizes one who is destructively vindictive.

CARBON denotes the harmful effects of negative actions.

CARBON-14 DATING indicates a need for a *generalized* verification.

CARBON COPY suggests duplication; a veering away from one's individuality.

CARBON MONOXIDE warns of a dangerous condition, situation, or relationship that appears innocent; danger from an unexpected and unsuspected source.

CARBON PAPER stands for a life aspect that entices one away from individuality.

This could be something like another's expression of ridicule, skepticism, etc.

CARBUNCLE denotes a currently festering negative aspect that can cause personal harm.

CARBURETOR represents the *proper mix* of elements needed to accomplish a goal or maintain a motivational force.

CARCASS represents lack of life; a death. The carcass of a dog means the death of a friendship.

CAR COAT suggests a readiness for a short journey; may point to a phase of temporary diversions from one's path/goal.

CARD (green) See green card.

CARD (greeting) reveals emotions and/or attitudes. Also see greeting card.

CARD (index) See index card.

CARD (playing) refers to insecurities.

CARD (to verify identity) means a verification of one's identity and right to participate in a specific activity or be in a certain place. This symbol may be a call to examine one's behavior in respect to being true to self—not pretending to be someone you're not. The symbol may also appear as a warning message to underscore the fact that someone is venturing into areas that are either not their concern or not within their right to be there.

CARDBOARD exemplifies insubstantial aspects in one's life; a superficial personality or relationship.

CARD CATALOG (library) alludes to order; an efficient and systematic way to maintain one's life.

CARD COUNTER (blackjack) will point to someone who achieves goals through negative means.

CAR DEALERSHIP pertains to the physical aspects in one's life. May represent a source for alternate courses in life.

CARD HOLDER connotes special treatment; a membership; belonging to a specific group. Can the dreamer recall what type of cards were in the holder? Sometimes this symbol can literally point the way for the dreamer by clearly showing who should be contacted.

CARDIAC ARREST warns of overexertion or overstressing self. May precede an unexpected event or bit of news.

CARDIAC MASSAGE illustrates a need to externalize emotions and attitudes.

CARDIAC MONITOR points to a current situation where one needs to monitor emotions or stressful situations.

CARDIGAN refers to an easy-going nature; maturity through experience.

CARDINAL (bird) portrays an aspect of high importance; a need to give one's attention to something.

CARDINAL (priest) See religious figure.

CARDINAL FLOWER signifies intense emotions.

CARDINAL POINT (one of the four directions) indicates one's directional priority. See specific direction.

CARDIOLOGIST suggests an individual who is capable of helping another through emotional difficulties/strains.

CARDIOPULMONARY RESUSCITATION (CPR) advises to reactivate an aspect in one's life that has been left behind or abandoned; an element representing a new lease on life.

CARD ROOM suggests a place of risk.

CARDSHARP/SHARK characterizes one with ulterior motives; having a hidden agenda; deviousness.

CARD SHOP cautions one to carefully choose how something is said; advises to search for the right words.

CARDSTOCK (paper) refers to an element meant to give greater endurance/strength to a communication/message.

CAREER DAY relates to the wide choices one has in life. May indicate a change in job.

CAREGIVER stands for one who cares for another. This may not always indicate a compassionate or loving personality.

CARESS typifies feelings of affection.

CARETAKER denotes some form of custodial position.

CARFARE implies a price for advancement; the need of another to help move one along a course or life path.

CARGO suggests aspects one views as personally important.

CARGO HOLD refers to a storage of cherished life aspects. This symbol may be pointing to memories or current elements in one's life.

CARGO PANTS represent preparedness for the unexpected.

CARHOP connotes those who make life a little easier or more convenient.

CARIBOU See reindeer.

CARICATURE warns of one's tendency to perceive others in a distorted manner; an exaggerated view of others; failing to look beyond the obvious surface features.

CARJACKER characterizes one who has no personal direction or motivation; one who solely depends on the efforts of others in order to move along one's path.

CARLSBAD CAVERNS depict the inherent beauty of natural talents and abilities when freely shared with others.

CARMINE (color) See maroon.

CARNAGE denotes dangerously negative aspects in one's life that have the capability of causing far-reaching destruction.

CARNATION applies to one who is socially correct; an individual who is overly concerned about social mores.

CARNEGIE HALL pertains to high attainment and the recognition of same.

CARNELIAN (gemstone) refers to false expressions; personality affectations.

CARNIVAL defines a whimsical atmosphere or condition; a situation lacking seriousness; verging on the ridiculous. May warn of a dangerous hoodwinking situation.

CARNIVORE implies a predatory nature.

CARNY (carnival worker) characterizes one who is out of touch with reality; unrealistic perceptions of life. May also indicate entrapment or a rigged situation.

CAROB identifies the substitutes that are available for us to utilize; alternatives. This applies to being innovative in respect to making do when first choices are not available.

CAROLER See Christmas carol.

CAROUSEL exemplifies a path that's going in circles and will prove to be unproductive.

CARP represents the act of nagging; nit-picking; belittling.

CARPAL TUNNEL SYNDROME warns of repetitiveness; suggests the use of alternatives.

CARPENTER characterizes one who has the ability to build on knowledge and talents to make constructive life contributions.

CARPENTER ANT indicates a destructive personality, one who tears down that which is being created or built upon.

CARPET pertains to underlying characteristics of an individual's path.

CARPETBAG typifies self-interest; self-gain. May also mean highest priorities.

CARPETBAGGER relates to one who takes advantage of another's misfortune. Depending on surrounding dream elements, a carpetbagger may also indicate one who has priorities straight.

CARPET BEETLE warns of destructive elements that are present on one's path; the existence of negative aspects that impair progress. This symbol may point to self-defeating action or thoughts.

CARPET PAD pertains to a life aspect which softens one's path.

CARPET SWEEPER represents an attempt to keep the underlying characteristics of one's path clear of surface negatives.

CARPET TACK signifies efforts expended on maintaining the integrity of one's path/journey.

CAR-POOL denotes attempts to conserve one's energy and resources. This doesn't mean to hold them back, just not expend them in unproductive manners.

CARPORT implies temporary shelter. This meaning will be clarified by surrounding dream symbols.

CAR RENTAL signifies an advancement along one's path through the assistance of another.

CARRIAGE means antiquated health practices; also may refer to a physiological system that's low on energy.

CARRIAGE TRADE portrays selective

relationships; a catering to wealthy, powerful, or influential individuals; elitist attitude.

CARRIER PIGEON See messenger.

CARRION illustrates the remains of a situation or relationship.

CARRION CROW typifies the feeding on remains. This is not necessarily a negative aspect depending on surrounding dream aspects. It could infer a cleaning up or utilization of what remains. May even come as an advisement to clean up after oneself, to tie up loose ends.

CARROT represents enticements; inducements.

CARRYING CHARGE relates to aspects in life that have a price; an extra price paid for what one wants or does.

CARRYON BAG points to attitudes or ideas one believes are essentials.

CARRYOUT refers to shortcuts.

CAR SEAT (child's) symbolizes an immature perspective; a path taken with juvenile attitudes.

CAR SHOW See auto show.

CARSICK indicates an inner recognition of a wrong path taken.

CART See wheelbarrow.

CART (shopping) See shopping cart.

CARTE BLANCHE stands for a no limit situation; ability or freedom to take things as far as one can.

CARTEL signifies a controlling group.

CARTILAGE implies tenacity; resilient personality.

CARTOGRAPHER illustrates farsightedness; an ability to map out one's own path.

CARTON refers to dual aspects; an aspect that contains a secondary element.

CARTOON can advise that one should use humor in life, or it may warn of a tendency toward avoiding reality.

CARTOUCHE connotes an important individual in one's life.

CARTRIDGE stands for the convenience of easy replacement; the ease by which something is utilized or replaced.

CARTRIDGE (ink) See ink cartridge.

CARTRIDGE CLIP (ammo) signifies one's preparedness to back up facts or means of defense.

CARTWHEEL refers to feelings of joy.

CARVE (wood) suggests the need to make one's own way; express greater individuality. Also see woodcarving.

CARVINGS (fine detail work) stand for fine details to which one needs to give attention.

CAR WASH denotes a need to clean up one's act.

CASANOVA (Giovanni Jacopo) characterizes a philanderer; a user; ulterior motives.

CASCADE See waterfall.

CASCARA SAGRADA warns of a serious need to get rid of wasteful aspects in one's life. These may refer to beliefs, attitudes, or certain situations.

CASE GOODS signify a need to keep something protected or advises of the wisdom of putting something away.

CASE HISTORY advises one to look into and know the background information on something important.

CASE LOAD implies an excessive backlog of work or information being processed.

CASEWORKER characterizes one who attempts to assist many others.

CASH pertains to genuineness; having the resources one claims to have.

CASH BOX refers to the safety of one's liquid assets. May indicate hoarding.

CASH COW suggests any element which provides ongoing benefits.

CASH CROP signifies one's personal efforts to support self; a successful means to an end.

CASH DISCOUNT stands for benefits gained by one's resourcefulness.

CASHIER (store) represents the piper who needs to be paid.

CASHIER'S CHECK alludes to guarantees; a secured aspect.

CASH MACHINE See automated teller machine (ATM).

CASHMERE (fabric) connotes a gentle nature.

CASH-OUT refers to a decision to reap immediate benefits from a positive aspect which could be held for a longer period of time.

CASH REGISTER symbolizes materialism.

CASINO See gambling casino.

CASKET exemplifies life's precariousness; a reminder of our mortality.

CASPER (ghost) characterizes the demystification of reality.

CASSANDRA (Greek mythology) pertains to skepticism; one whom others don't believe.

CASSEROLE typifies a situation or condition created by several aspects in one's life.

CASSETTE represents something the dreamer needs to hear.

CAST (bone) comes as a cautionary message; warns against going too fast; a headlong pace without looking.

CAST (fishing) refers to spiritual fishing; a reaching for some type of spiritual information.

CAST (of play/film) cautions one to take a better look at those involved in relationships or those with whom one is associated; people may not be the same as they present themselves. There may be some hidden role-playing going on.

CASTANET applies to inner delight after proving one right; personal gloating.

CASTAWAY denotes dependency on another's spiritual direction instead of being the captain of your own ship; being lost without the spiritual direction or leadership of another.

CASTE (system) pertains to segregation; a separatist; tendency to classify others according to personal perceptions; labeling others.

CASTE MARK will be directly associated with one's self-image, how one perceives oneself.

CASTER denotes a desire to protect something.

CASTING (ceramic) refers to a fragile formulation; a weak idea having temporary qualities and few lasting effects.

CASTING (fishing) denotes tentative attempts made; moves to test the waters.

CASTING (metal) refers to a strong formulation; a strong idea having lasting qualities and/or effects.

CASTING AGENCY implies the right person for the job. May indicate role-playing; someone who's not what they seem.

CAST IRON indicates strength; a strong constitution; perseverance.

CASTLE exemplifies one's perspective that lacks reality or clear vision.

CASTLE IN SAND See sand castle.

CASTLE IN THE SKY reveals unrealistic ideas or goals; impracticality.

CAST OFF (boat) means a beginning spiritual journey.

CASTOFF (discard) refers to that which one disregards; shedding one's relationships, attitudes, or beliefs.

CASTOR OIL advises of the need for a personal purification; a cleansing. This may refer to emotional, mental, or situational aspects.

CASTRATION suggests efforts expended to control one's wanderlust.

CASUAL WEAR suggests a relaxed attitude.

CAT (domestic/wild) pertains to one's quality or type of independence. See specific type such as cheetah, Cheshire, calico, etc.

CATACLYSM usually symbolizes the result of a particular event, relationship, behavior, or situation in one's awake-state life.

CATACOMB represents buried or hidden information. May point to buried memories.

CATALEPSY signifies deep-seated fears.

CATALOG illustrates the vast array of choices in life.

CATALPA (tree) points to a need to recognize or set better priorities.

CATALYST alludes to those individuals or situations that serve as motivational surges in life.

CATALYTIC CONVERTER advises us to make the most out of every situation or opportunity given us.

CATAMARAN portrays spiritual freedom; an unencumbered spiritual journey.

CATAMOUNT See lion.

CAT-AND-MOUSE implies games being played in one's life; trifling with one another.

CATAPULT refers to highly motivational aspects that serve to speed one forward or into action; an impetus.

CATARACT See waterfall.

CATARACT (of eye) denotes impaired perception; a clouded viewpoint.

CATASTROPHE denotes major events in one's life which may end in a devastating manner.

CATATONIA characterizes an autistic-type of perception; extreme apathy.

CAT BURGLAR portrays a devious personality; sneaky; activity done behind another's back; clandestine activities.

CATCALL means disrespect; uncouth expressions.

CATCH 22 typifies a situation that appears to have no outlet for advancement; an appearance of having no means of movement; a boxed-in situation.

CATCHWORD denotes ideas that are widely known. This symbol may come as a revelation for the dreamer depending on what was said by whom.

CATECHISM represents spiritual indoctrination.

CATEGORY denotes separatism; attitudes based on class or position.

CATER means the act of waiting on or serving another; subservience.

CATER-CORNERED See diagonal.

CATERPILLAR characterizes the transitional phases in life. May specifically point to a neophyte stage of development; a time for learning and absorbing before experiencing the bloom of awareness or enlightenment.

CAT-EYED (a human) reveals a talent for seeing through another's hidden personality or agenda; an ability to perceive what lies in the shadows and darker places of life.

CAT FIGHT means vicious disputes; uncontrolled disagreement.

CATFISH denotes a cattiness to one's spiritual belief; a pretentious or arrogant spiritual attitude.

CATHARSIS advises of the need to release emotions; a closure required.

CATHEDRAL connotes spiritual excesses; a grandiose spiritual attitude.

CATHETER applies to a need to empty out that which one is retaining; the need for routine self-analysis.

CATHODE GLOW STICK denotes a safety measure taken.

CATHOUSE See house of ill repute.

CATKIN (botanical) represents proof that one's idea is about to take hold.

CATNAP advises one to take a break; pause; short rest.

CATNIP signifies a mesmerized state; warns of a need to awaken to reality.

CAT SCAN advises one to look at all angles. This dream symbol would suggest that the dreamer is not seeing something in its totality.

CATSCRATCH DISEASE suggests a negative response to one's expression of independent behavior or thought.

CAT'S-EYE (gemstone) symbolizes a watcher in one's midst.

CATTAIL denotes the need to recognize life's little benefits that come our way; to appreciate the things we have.

CATTLE represent a lack of individuality and self-confidence.

CATTLE CALL illustrates a desire to alter self according to how others wish you to be.

CATTLE GUARD connotes the self-created limits and barriers one devises to prevent decision-making or exercising individuality.

CATTLE PROD signifies procrastination or a reluctance to be about one's business.

CATWALK exemplifies ways to get around things; alternate routes. May also point to having a better perspective of things; an over-all view.

CAUCUS stands for a specialized meeting of selected people. May come as a suggestion that a meeting of some type is needed.

CAULDRON warns of a brewing situation, condition, or relationship.

CAULIFLOWER alludes to bigness or generosity.

CAULIFLOWER EAR suggests the habit of listening to gossip.

CAULIFLOWER TUMOR See polyp (medical).

CAULK denotes the need to seal something in one's life; a promise; a conclusion.

CAUSEWAY signifies feeble or noncommitted attempts to delve into spiritual concepts.

CAUSTIC usually refers to behavior or speech which has the potential to burn oneself or another. This symbol might point to a plan, relationship, or situation which could end up burning the participant.

CAUTERIZE advises of the need to heal a wound; a closure is required.

CAUTION (sign) See road signs.

CAVALRY characterizes following orders and charging ahead with the crowd; a lack of individualized thought and reason.

CAVE signifies natural defenses; inherent knowledge.

CAVEAT EMPTOR advises one to know one's issues; do one's homework and be knowledgeable regarding a specific aspect.

CAVE DWELLER stands for one who lives by one's instincts.

CAVE-IN symbolizes a loss of instinctual reactions or knowledge; some aspect in life will not turn out as planned.

CAVERN alludes to nature's hidden aspects of the extended realities.

CAVIAR means spiritual arrogance; a spiritually egotistical individual.

CAVITY (tooth) warns against the speaking of infected words. This would indicate gossip, slander, false accusations, or a crass manner of speech.

CAYENNE PEPPER See red pepper.

CB (citizen's band radio) advises to keep communications open.

C-CLAMP applies to a need to hold something together until it can maintain its own position. This usually refers to a relationship.

CEASE FIRE obviously means to stop fighting or maintaining an on-going disagreement.

CEDAR illustrates a need for spiritual cleansing or energized protection of one's spiritual beliefs.

CEDAR CHEST reflects care given to the preservation of one's cherished memories.

CEDAR WAXWING (bird) suggests the importance of being a good listener. This dreamscape element points to a possible current habit of not truly listening to others.

CEILING usually means the top of something; one's limitation.

CEILING (high) signifies an analytical thought process.

CEILING (low) denotes a need to expand ideas or way of thinking.

CEILING FAN refers to a cooling period needed. A pause during one's advancement along one's path.

CELEBRATION means a reason for rejoicing. Surrounding dreamscape elements will help to clarify the intent here.

CELEBRITY relates to someone in the dreamer's life who stands out for some reason—or *should* stand out.

CELERY denotes difficulties that require acceptance.

CELESTIAL OBJECTS symbolize pure spiritual aspects. See specific terms.

CELESTITE (gemstone) points to fragility; a need to reinforce emotional sensitivity.

CELIBACY calls for some type of abstinence that's required for a time. This symbol certainly won't be exclusively associated with sex.

CELL (biological) relates to an inclusion of reality; an overall scope of reality; the wholeness of one's life experience.

CELL (enclosure) represents one's quantitative quality of experience. Recall how the cell was designed and/or decorated.

CELLAR indicates the deeper aspects of the subconscious where fears, bad memories, etc. are kept hidden away.

CELL DIVISION stands for an exponential growth/spreading of an element; multiple ramifications. This could refer to one's recent behavior.

CELL MATE characterizes one of like mind.

CELL MEMORY equates to fixed origin. This symbol stands for a pure element in one's life, one that can't be contaminated by surrounding aspects.

CELLO points to a tendency toward melancholia.

CELLULAR TELEPHONE symbolizes preparedness and/or efficiency.

CELLULITE cautions against the acceptance of extraneous aspects in life; excesses.

CELTIC (atmosphere) denotes a need to delve into the spirituality that relates to this ancient culture.

CELTIC CROSS signifies an esoteric spiritual aspect.

CEMENT means unresolved or inconclusive aspects in one's life and advises to get these settled; a need to finalize something.

CEMENT MIXER means that an aspect in life needing a resolution or conclusion will manifest in the dreamer's life.

CEMENT SHOES stand for something one needs to answer for; an extremely negative deed needs to be repaired or made amends for.

CEMETERY See graveyard.

CENSER (incense vessel) stands for that which creates an affected atmosphere.

CENSOR characterizes a manipulative personality; one who would have others view life according to the perspectives and attitudes of self; a fear of thinking outside the box.

CENSUS cautions of one's inability to exist anonymously.

CENTAUR (Greek mythology) depicts a balance of physical strength and intellectual capability.

CENTER (position placement) defines a position that offers the widest variety of choices.

CENTER FIELD indicates a position where one is able to maintain balance through an awareness of one's current placement in life.

CENTERFOLD (magazine) depicts a position of prominence for the purpose of gaining the widest range of exposure and attention.

CENTERPIECE signifies decorative appeal; attractiveness; that which creates an appealing atmosphere; the focus of attention.

CENTIPEDE suggests an ability or need to overcome life's little irritations.

CENTRAL BOOKING points to being caught for doing something negative.

CENTRAL CASTING indicates a source or pool of individuals one can choose from for the purpose of selecting a helper or aide who's fit for the project.

CENTRAL INTELLIGENCE AGENCY See CIA.

CENTRAL PARK (NY) portrays a means of respite within one's workday; may also refer to the positive and negative duality of life.

CENTRIFUGE cautions one against mixing separate life aspects; a need to keep ideas or concepts separate.

CENTURION characterizes one who is perpetually on guard.

CERAMIC connotes the aspects in life that have a tendency to be more fragile, such as one's emotional sensitivity.

CEREAL stands for the basic, foundational beginnings of something. Was that beginning a hot (enthusiastic) or cold (blasé) one?

CEREBRAL PALSY illustrates intellectual clarity accompanied by aspects that hamper physical action; an understanding of one's direction and path with some trouble with carrying it out.

CEREBRUM See brain.

CEREMONY implies a ritual; societal custom; specialized observance.

CEREMONY (secret) See secret ceremony.

CERTIFICATE suggests a commendation for accomplishments or an official seal of legality. See specific type such as marriage license, divorce and death certificate.

CERTIFIED CHECK means solid facts; guaranteed aspect.

CERTIFIED MAIL represents a need to make sure something is done or carried out; certain delivery or communication.

CERTIFIED NURSE ASSISTANT (CNA) stands for one who has knowledge of basic care-giving; a qualified basic care-giver.

CERTIFIED PUBLIC ACCOUNTANT (CPA) See accountant.

CERUSSITE (gemstone) stands for one who is easily manipulated.

CESSPOOL connotes humanity's most base aspects.

CHABLIS See wine.

CHACO CANYON portrays ancient wisdom; hidden human heritage.

CHAFF illustrates leftover, unusable aspects.

CHAFING DISH exemplifies an aspect that requires constant attention; a need to prevent some aspect from getting cold.

CHAIN means interconnected aspects; relevancy.

CHAIN GANG stands for individuals who are strongly connected by a shared negativity.

CHAIN LETTER symbolizes the strong possibility and probability for failure; attempting to achieve an end or goal that can only succeed through the actions of others.

CHAIN LINK FENCE is a dream fragment that refers to one's inner need to define ownership; possessiveness; marking personal perimeters.

CHAIN MAIL denotes a lack of confidence in one's own protection; personal fear of not being able to defend self.

CHAIN OF COMMAND refers to levels of authority. This dreamscape symbol usually comes when someone is going over another's head.

CHAIN REACTION exemplifies the vast effects caused by the spoken word and one's actions.

CHAIN SAW represents the utilization of natural aspects to cut through problematical elements in life.

CHAIN-SMOKING means an internalization of problems; high anxiety.

CHAIN STITCH (needlework) denotes a need to take one step at a time in respect to repairing past mistakes.

CHAIR signifies a short or temporary rest period may be needed.

CHAIR LIFT connotes a rising on the thoughts of others' unearned advancements through resting on laurels.

CHAIRPERSON characterizes organized leadership of a specialized aspect in one's life.

CHAISE LONGUE implies an attitude of nonchalance; indifference.

CHAKRA symbolizes inner resources; reserves of energy.

CHALET (architecture) pertains to a gentle personality; homey lifestyle.

CHALICE applies to one's spiritual aspects. This may not be a positive dream fragment, depending on the chalice's condition or color.

CHALK portrays subliminal or peripheral knowledge that may or may not be remembered.

CHALK ERASER See blackboard eraser.

CHALK LINE denotes level-headedness; straight and true.

CHALLENGER alludes to one-upmanship; one who strives to outdo others; one driven to continually prove his worth.

CHAMBER portrays a special room or place unique to the dreamer.

CHAMBER MUSIC represents a specialized audio unique to the dreamer; personalized sound that soothes or motivates.

CHAMBER OF COMMERCE alludes to business associates and manner of group operation. May indicate a need to find out more about a particular geographical region.

CHAMBER OF HORRORS points to one's subconscious fears; extreme anxiety.

CHAMBER POT connotes an aspect that is out of character, out of place in one's life.

CHAMBRAY (fabric) denotes a dual purpose; two-fold reason for doing something.

CHAMELEON may refer to indecision; a vacillation; aspects that keep reversing direction.

CHAMOIS (cloth) implies a soft nature.

CHAMOMILE stands for an easy-going personality; calm; difficult to rile.

CHAMP See champion.

CHAMPAGNE See alcoholic beverage.

CHAMPION characterizes proven abilities or talents.

CHAMPIONSHIP represents a final test/challenge.

CHANCE denotes the unexpected; that which comes our way.

CHANCELLOR portrays a ranking position; authoritarian aspect.

CHANDELIER exemplifies specialized light of ideas or thoughts that are outwardly displayed in a focused or attention-getting manner.

CHANGELING illustrates a state of evolution; a metamorphosis; transition.

CHANGE OF LIFE See menopause.

CHANGEOVER represents a state of conversion; change of thought or attitude.

CHANNEL (trench) pertains to a directed flow or worn path; a direction traveled by many in the past.

CHANNEL (TV/radio/scanner) represents choices for receiving incoming information.

CHANNEL BLOCKING (TV) stands for censorship, usually in relation to protecting someone from emotionally/morally damaging subject matters.

CHANNELER (psychic) characterizes one who listens for the guidance of others instead of self.

CHANNEL LOCKS refer to an aspect that contains several opportunities or useable options.

CHANNEL MARKER will come as a symbol that keeps one within the bounds of the right spiritual direction; a marker keeping one from straying from one's spiritual path.

CHANT denotes a means to inner light and/or knowing.

CHANTILLY LACE signifies a very special delicate touch to something.

CHAOS represents disorder of some kind; confusion.

CHAOS THEORY attempts an explanation of true Reality; a reminder of the interconnectedness of all things.

CHAPARRAL refers to an aspect that's capable of bringing about an emotional healing.

CHAPEL illustrates a temporary time of spiritual respite or peace.

CHAPERON characterizes one's Higher Self; higher guidance; one's conscience.

CHAPLAIN signifies someone who will listen; a nonjudgmental individual.

CHAPLIN (Charlie) illustrates the importance of humor in life.

CHAPPED LIPS refers to a need to soften one's language/manner of speaking. This usually points to unkind comments or cattiness.

CHAPPED SKIN implies an inability to accept differing ideas or attitudes of others.

CHAPS symbolize a need for temporary or short-term protection; a temporary situation exists for increased awareness, watchfulness.

CHAPTER (book) indicates a stage in life; a special period of time.

CHAR denotes emotional sensitivity.

CHARADES stand for an inability to verbalize thoughts or adequately express self.

CHARBROIL See barbecue.

CHARCOAL represents positive outcomes from negative aspects; the event of good effects generated from bad happenings.

CHARCOAL STARTER (fluid) signifies the motivational force needed/applied to begin the process of working toward a positive resolution/outcome.

CHARGE (accuse) implies a placing of blame; to implicate.

CHARGE (care) refers to an aspect one needs to take special care of; protective wardship; safe-keeping.

CHARGE (debt) pertains to the realization that payment for something will come due; a deferment of reciprocation for a time.

CHARGE (energize) illustrates a strong motivation; excitement.

CHARGE (race forward) means a committed intention backed by an urgency to carry it out. May point to impatience or impulsiveness.

CHARGE-BACK signifies a mistaken benefit, one which turns out to be a debit.

CHARGE CARD alludes to impatience; lack of priorities. May point to a situation where payback or a reciprocal response is delayed.

CHARIOT cautions one to slow down; a need to utilize reason before taking action.

CHARITY stands for opportunities.

CHARLATAN characterizes pretenses.

CHARM (object) exemplifies a lack of faith. May indicate a superstitious personality.

CHARMED LIFE indicates an appearance of good fortune.

CHARM SCHOOL See finishing school.

CHART defines specific course perceptions. These may show what the dreamer has planned out or may clarify what *should* be drawn up.

CHARTER (document) depicts a statement or record of one's purpose.

CHARTER (rent) See lease.

CHARTER MEMBER denotes one who participated in something's beginning stage of development.

CHARTREUSE portrays an inner joy through healing.

CHARWOMAN See servant.

CHASE symbolizes going after something; pursuit.

CHASM illustrates perceived difficulties; differences of opinion.

CHASTE refers to a modest personality; may mean humility.

CHASTITY BELT implies forced modesty or false humility.

CHAT suggests passing conversation; surface communication.

CHAT ROOM (Internet) comes as a reminder to communicate responsibly, even though it's done anonymously.

CHATEAU refers to extravagant goals.

CHATELAINE stands for a woman who is in control.

CHATTERBOX characterizes one who does little in-depth thinking; a gossip or someone who incessantly speaks of issues that are unimportant. May indicate one who rarely listens.

CHAUFFEUR infers a lack of self-motivation; taking a back seat and letting others do the driving (work).

CHAUVINIST denotes an attitude of superiority.

CHEAP designates something of low value; obtaining something without putting much effort or personal expense out.

CHEAPSKATE warns of a tendency to hoard abilities, knowledge, or one's personal humanitarian assets.

CHEAT SHEET indicates advancement through ill-gained means. Depending on the related dream elements, this symbol may also point to a need to remember something.

CHECK (bill) refers to one's valid debts.

CHECK (examine) connotes a need to substantiate something.

CHECK (mark) means aspects that need attending to.

CHECK (stop) cautions one to get something in check and under control; put a stop to something.

CHECKBOOK represents one's personal distribution of assets; where one utilizes abilities.

CHECKER See clerk.

CHECKER (flag) represents the attainment of a goal.

CHECKER (game piece) represents one aspect of a planned direction.

CHECKER (pattern) means continual duality expressed; an ability to see both sides of a situation.

CHECKERBOARD typifies the many decisions in life; planning; the wisdom of analyzing situations.

CHECKLIST advises increased awareness; attention given to details.

CHECKMATE signifies an unavoidable aspect in one's life; may indicate a defeat or a personal conquest, depending on the surrounding dreamscape symbols.

CHECKPOINT advises self-analysis or introspection.

CHECKROOM pertains to trust.

CHECKUP stands for some aspect in the dreamer's life that requires examining.

CHEEK implies audacity; impudence. May also denote strength.

CHEER connotes encouragement; that which spurs one on.

CHEERLEADER characterizes those who encourage us in life.

CHEESE signifies those life aspects that are complete, full.

CHEESECAKE (dessert) suggests a rich reward; well-deserved outcomes.

CHEESECAKE (photo) connotes misplaced priorities; enticement; the use of wrong methods for obtaining goals.

CHEESECLOTH (fabric) represents an aspect that contributes to and serves to maintain wholesome attitudes; the straining of information; refined analyzation.

CHEESE SPREAD denotes a false impression (assumption) that an element has a wholeness, completeness; an element that's a lesser substitute for something greater.

CHEETAH signifies swiftness; quick action.

CHEF characterizes the method and quality of food preparation. This may infer food for the mind or emotional fulfillment.

CHEF'S HAT applies to the action of cooking up something.

CHEF'S SALAD indicates a balanced blend; the combining of several aspects in the dreamer's life.

CHELATION THERAPY suggests the presence of poisons (negatives) in one's system and advises of taking measures to eliminate them.

CHEMICALS symbolize compound aspects, usually negative.

CHEMICAL ABUSE See substance abuse.

CHEMICAL WARFARE applies to a manner of conflict resolution that causes debilitating or fatal effects.

CHEMISE See camisole.

CHEMIST stands for one who utilizes a wide variety of aspects to create desired responses or goals.

CHEMISTRY (study of) portrays an interest in many life aspects and how they may or may not interrelate.

CHEMOTHERAPY pertains to the utilization of negatives to attempt positive outcomes.

CHENILLE (fabric) depicts old-fashioned ideas that remain valid throughout time.

CHER (singer) characterizes a resilient personality; enduring talent.

CHERNOBYL emphasizes the dangers of too little knowledge.

CHEROOT See cigar.

CHERRY (fruit/tree) typifies a sweet situation; prime aspects of something.

CHERRY (condition) stands for something in prime state.

CHERRY BLOSSOM signifies the sweetness of one's strong faith in oneself.

CHERRY BOMB indicates something or someone in life with the capability of making a lot of noise with little or no damage.

CHERRY PICKER (truck) signifies high-minded work; high level work to be done.

CHERRY TOMATO connotes those little often-overlooked aspects in life that present us with a convenience or ease.

CHERUB denotes young innocence; an angelic youthfulness. This won't necessarily point to a child but can be a descriptive symbol for an adult, as well.

CHESAPEAKE BAY refers to deeper spiritual conceptual connections.

CHESHIRE CAT characterizes cleverness; a sly watchfulness.

CHESS illustrates the intricacies of life; many moves are available, yet few right ones.

CHESSBOARD exemplifies the options which life presents to us; a situation with many options.

CHESS PIECE reveals which directional moves are open to us. See specific piece.

CHEST (anatomy) refers to our protected emotional center.

CHEST (cedar) See cedar chest.

CHEST (of drawers) See dresser.

CHEST (treasure) See treasure chest.

CHESTNUT stands for heartfelt feelings; warm emotions.

CHEST-THUMPING reveals an overblown self-image; a boastful personality.

CHEVAL (mirror) typifies the need to see the totality of self. This would infer aspects that are being denied.

CHEVRON (pattern) implies strong goals.

CHEW (dog treat) refers to a friend's deep thought. May point to a need to consult a friend or ask her opinion on something.

CHEW (masticate) suggests a need to give some deep thought to something.

CHEW (tobacco) symbolizes a habit of mentally dwelling on something too long.

CHIC (appearance) represents an overemphasis placed on appearances.

CHICKADEE signifies acceptance from a heightened level of fortitude.

CHICKEN denotes fear; a reluctance to face life.

CHICKEN (game with vehicle) denotes ultimate irresponsibility and disregard for others, not to mention self.

CHICKEN AND EGG(S) points to confusion; a need to get priorities in line; a reminder to figure out what comes first.

CHICKEN COOP signifies the self-confining aspects of insecurities.

CHICKEN FEED means an aspect of little value.

CHICKEN-HEARTED refers to a lack of courage.

CHICKEN LITTLE characterizes paranoia; unnecessary fear.

CHICKEN LIVER points to a reluctance

due to fears; possible inferiority complex or lack of faith/confidence in oneself.

CHICKEN POX warns of the negative effects caused by a lack of courage or faith.

CHICKEN WIRE portrays how we fence self in when there is a lack of courage, faith, or perseverance.

CHICKWEED comes as a reminder that there is value in something one has perceived as being valueless.

CHICORY alludes to an aspect that serves as a substitute for the ones we believe will strengthen and motivate us; an alternate source of courage.

CHIEF defines a prime aspect in one's life.

CHIFFON (fabric) signifies those aspects that are easily seen through.

CHIFFOROBE See dresser.

CHIGGER typifies aspects in life that are irritating; those aspects that get under one's skin.

CHIGNON implies knotted thoughts; a need to sort things out.

CHIHUAHUA (dog breed) advises to never underestimate the abilities or power of another.

CHILD ABUSE won't normally equate to literal child mistreatment but will be associated with some type of abusive behavior being done to destroy innocence, perhaps even to one's child within.

CHILDCARE stands for a need to recognize and care for one's inner child.

CHILD LABOR reveals energies expended toward an issue or idea that is still immature.

CHILDPROOF reminds us to attend to each advancing stage in life and not attempt things we're not well prepared to take on.

CHILDREN connote a stage of acceptance and innocence; a belief in possibilities and one's dreams.

CHILD RESTRAINT alludes to the importance of preserving certain childlike qualities such as trust.

CHILD'S PLAY defines an activity that's easy; simplistic. For some dreamers, depending on the related elements, this symbol may be a call to give your child within a little more freedom of expression.

CHILD SUPPORT will usually come as an advisement to give more credence and support to one's child within.

CHILI denotes situations or relationships that could develop into hot ones.

CHILI BEANS indicate aspects we add to already-heated situations.

CHILI CON CARNE reminds us that we have the ability to control the heat of a situation.

CHILI DOG pertains to one's preference for involvement in spiced-up or heated situations.

CHILI POWDER illustrates one's personal ability to maintain control of situations.

CHILL connotes a cooling-down aspect to a situation or relationship. May come as an advisement to stop being angry and give more thought to something.

CHILLER (book/film) See thriller.

CHILL FACTOR cautions one to be aware of additional cooling factors that may seriously affect a situation or relationship; aspects which add to an already chilled attitude.

CHILLY refers to cool or unfriendly attitudes.

CHIME denotes a call to listen; a calling to something in one's life.

CHIMERA characterizes self-delusion; something with no substance.

CHIMNEY pertains to emotional control.

CHIMNEY POT portrays an aspect that improves the outward flow of one's emotions; that which draws out feelings and emotional expression.

CHIMNEY SWEEP relates to the need to maintain a state of untainted attitudes. The symbol of a chimney sweep will point to someone who can expertly clear away tainted ideas.

CHIMNEY SWIFT (bird) suggests a recognition of home-life priorities. This refers to recognizing what's important and what's not in respect to home life relationships.

CHIMPANZEE See monkey.

CHINA See ceramic.

CHINA (country) suggests the duality of fragile treasures and multiple mass produced products. This refers to the fine, delicate elements in one's life being interspersed with the common, unremarkable aspects.

CHINABERRY (tree) indicates sensitivity to delicate situations.

CHINA DOLL represents a woman with seemingly fragile qualities.

CHINA SYNDROME is a symbol that seriously warns of the fatal effects caused by overheated and uncontrolled emotions; self-destruction.

CHINATOWN refers to the synergetic absorption of seemingly foreign aspects into one's belief system.

CHINCHILLA defines egotism; apathy toward others; a dangerous focus on self.

CHINESE LANTERN (flower) suggests that one's natural talents need to be opened up into the light of day. This advises one to be more useful to others.

CHINESE PUZZLE denotes confusion; difficulty in finding resolutions.

CHINK (gap) typifies faulty conclusions; a hole in one's perception or thought process.

CHINKING (gap filler) applies to aspects that serve to fill in the empty or missing elements in one's life; answers; those factors which make something solid or whole.

CHINO (fabric) signifies a readiness to expend energies.

CHINOOK WIND represents a factor that heartens one; encouragement; uplifting elements.

CHINTZ (fabric) defines an emotional or perceptual cover-up.

CHIPMUNK portrays hoarding; emotional reserves; the withholding of communication or expression.

CHIPPED BEEF stands for a tendency to criticize; a nagging personality.

CHIPPENDALE (dancer) exposes those who entice others toward negative or at least less-than-positive elements; questionable behavior; ulterior motives.

CHIPPENDALE (furniture) cautions one against forcing beliefs and perceptions on others.

CHIPPER (machine) See wood chipper.

CHIROPRACTIC ADJUSTMENT emphasizes a desire for inner balance and alignment to one's current path.

CHIROPRACTOR characterizes integrity; perseverance; advancement through one's own efforts; one who can help to keep others aligned.

CHISEL refers to advancement by way of self-discovery; perseverance. Represents a life tool to use for taking one thing at a time.

CHIVALROUS (behavior) denotes a high respect for others; respect for life; selfless; unconditional goodness.

CHIVE indicates positive factors we intentionally add to our life.

CHLORINE advises of a need to clean or purify specific aspects in one's life.

CHLOROFORM warns of a dangerous lack of awareness or attention to vitally important elements in one's life.

CHLOROPHYLL stands for the quality and level of one's personal healing ability.

CHOCK defines an aspect that prevents one from either backsliding or rushing headlong.

CHOCOLATE indicates questionable pleasures; temporary enjoyments that may bring negative effects later on.

CHOIR signifies a group expression; shared joys; a unified opinion.

CHOIR LOFT depicts spiritual joy.

CHOKE CHAIN (dog) See choke collar.

CHOKECHERRY (tree) exemplifies life aspects that bring sorrow. May point to spoken words that the speaker ends up wanting to take back.

CHOKE COLLAR warns of life factors that we allow to control us; manipulation.

CHOKE HOLD refers to dangerous situations or individuals in life that threaten advancement. These can be self-generated.

CHOKER (necklace) represents voluntary self-restraint; the act of holding self back.

CHOKING warns against attempting to swallow ideas one knows are wrong or one is not prepared to fully absorb.

CHOLERA means a lack of intestinal fortitude.

CHOLESTEROL stands for the positive/negative duality of many life aspects.

CHOPHOUSE See steakhouse.

CHOPPER (aircraft) See helicopter.

CHOPPER (bike) See motorcycle.

CHOPPING BLOCK represents a dangerous path or result.

CHOP SHOP emphasizes incorrect analyzation; improper dismantling of conceptual ideas; fragmented conclusions.

CHOPSTICKS imply the utilization of incorrect means to reach a specific end.

CHOP SUEY warns of one's tendency to mix concepts; a habit of getting things wrong; will advise one to listen harder, focus on the facts.

CHORD (music) refers to an aspect that has a specialized meaning for the dreamer.

CHORE denotes something needed to be accomplished.

CHOREOGRAPHER characterizes an individual who does the planning.

CHORUS (repeat verse) will come in a dreamscape as a strong emphasis. What message did the chorus convey?

CHORUS (singers) an idea or perception shared by many.

CHOW CHOW (dog breed) stands for a friend's inner strength; perseverance; drive.

CHOWDER (clam) See clam chowder.

CHOW HOUND denotes an insatiable appetite. This is usually associated with a seeker of knowledge who takes in things in a voracious manner, possibly without absorbing any of it.

CHRISTENING See baptism.

CHRISTMAS defines a major spiritual awakening.

CHRISTMAS CACTUS refers to a spiritual blooming; perhaps an epiphany of some kind.

CHRISTMAS CANDLE represents the light of one's spirituality. Was it burning? Was the wick broken or missing? How big was the candle?

CHRISTMAS CARD refers to spiritual greetings and messages.

CHRISTMAS CAROL indicates sharing of spiritual joys.

CHRISTMAS CENTERPIECE (floral) denotes spiritual talents and behavior.

CHRISTMAS CLUB cautions against the saving-up of spirituality for a special occasion.

CHRISTMAS FERN stands for spiritual growth. Recall its condition. Was it a sprout or full-grown?

CHRISTMAS GIFT points to spiritual giving, sharing.

CHRISTMAS LIGHTS relate to one's shining spiritual light. They weren't broken, were they?

CHRISTMAS ORNAMENTS show up in a dreamscape to reveal the fact that someone is decorating spiritual beliefs with clutter.

CHRISTMAS PUDDING See plum pudding.

CHRISTMAS STOCKING represents expectation of spiritual rewards.

CHRISTMAS TREE denotes extraneous, unrelated aspects attached to spiritual beliefs.

CHROME refers to an attraction to the shiny aspects in life; a draw toward outwardly affected elements.

CHROMOSOME advises one to know self.

CHRONICLE pertains to developmental stages leading up to the present; a need to research how something came about. This may be an advisement to keep a journal.

CHRYSALIS stands for developing spirituality.

CHRYSANTHEMUM pertains to the golden time of life; a time of respite and reflection; a restful time of introspection.

CHRYSOBERYL (gemstone) points to intellectual clarity.

CHRYSOTHERAPY represents an understanding of the healing qualities of natural aspects.

CHUCK (tool) See key.

CHUCK HOLE See pothole.

CHUCK WAGON signifies an aspect that serves to nourish us along our path; sustenance while journeying through life.

CHUGALUG warns against an impulsive intake of information without adequately understanding it.

CHUGGING (stilting steps) indicates determination; moving forward despite difficulties.

CHUM See friend.

CHUMP means a foolish person or one with a habit of being disinterested in things; someone never having an opinion.

CHUNNEL (English Channel tunnel) signifies a diversionary tactic to get around spiritual issues.

CHURCH indicates a type of spiritual connection and the quality of same. What was the church's condition? Size?

CHURCH BELLS refer to a call to spirituality. May advise the utilization of greater spiritual behavior.

CHURCH KEY See bottle opener.

CHURCH MOUSE characterizes a quiet spirituality; cherished spiritual beliefs.

CHURCHYARD defines spiritual inactivity; dormant spirituality; a seemingly dead spirituality.

CHURN (butter) applies to personal efforts applied to enrich one's path.

CHUTE See parachute.

CHUTE (utility slide) refers to a quick exit or end to something.

CHUTNEY signifies an interesting mix of multiple elements, often a rich and beneficial one.

CHUTZPAH portrays one who displays great nerve; gutsy.

CIA represents in-depth information. Depending on surrounding dreamscape factors, this may also reveal spying activity being done in the dreamer's life.

CIA AGENT characterizes one who knows all about something or has access to private information.

CIBORIUM connotes a high respect for one's spiritual beliefs.

CICADA denotes an obsession with self; always wanting to attract attention. May also indicate excessive verbiage; meaningless chatter.

CICHLID (fish) stands for spiritual companionship; an enhanced depth of spiritual camaraderie and support.

CIDER (apple) represents an aspect that contributes to one's time of respite or reflection.

CIDER PRESS reflects quality rest time; tranquility.

CIGAR denotes an absorption of specialized ideas or concepts.

CIGAR BOX alludes to the manner by which one holds specific ideas or concepts.

CIGARETTE pertains to an absorption of well-defined ideas.

CIGARETTE BUTT relates to ideas that have been used up; ideas that are old and no longer viable.

CIGARETTE CASE signifies the practice of holding onto certain ideas until one is ready to look at them.

CIGARETTE FILTER cautions against the acceptance of ideas only after they've been run through the filter of one's personal attitudes and perspectives.

CIGARETTE HOLDER warns against keeping a distance from well-defined ideas.

CIGAR TUBE denotes a desire to keep certain ideas fresh and new.

CINCH (belt) comes as an advisement to reserve one's opinion; tighten up on the tendency to overdo in the area of giving advice; restraint is indicated.

CINCO DE MAYO refers to freedom; independence; victory.

CINDER See ash.

CINDER BLOCK symbolizes lighter foundational elements that are just as effective as heavier ones.

CINDERELLA represents acceptance of one's situation; perseverance.

CINEMA See movie theater.

CINEMATOGRAPHER typifies one who is interested in recording life in its reality; one with an eye on recording events.

CINNABAR (color) refers to emotional expressiveness; a zest for life.

CINNAMON (color/spice) signifies an aspect that the dreamer perceives as being especially homey and companionable.

CINQUEFOIL (bush/flower) represents a bright viewpoint of life; living with a good sense of humor and general happiness.

CIPHER suggests a need to solve or resolve something; represents a key or solution.

CIRCLE (ceremonial) may expose the putting on or wearing of another's path through fantasized, self-created means for the purpose of self-aggrandizement.

CIRCLE (shape) implies completion. May also indicate an endless path; going in circles.

CIRCLEHEAD WINDOW See fan window.

CIRCUIT stands for a designated path; making the rounds.

CIRCUIT BOARD portrays an individualized thought process; how one perceives life, forms ideas, deduces and resolves problems.

CIRCUIT BREAKER warns of a possible situation of mental or emotional overload; defensive measures set in place to prevent oneself from becoming overly stressed or emotionally drained.

CIRCUIT RIDER (traveling cleric) advises one to utilize spirituality wherever one is.

CIRCUIT TESTER suggests a need for self-analysis; introspection.

CIRCULAR SAW expresses a need to quickly and cleanly cut through an aspect in one's life.

CIRCULAR WINDOW See fan window.

CIRCUMCISION calls for a need to excise an aspect in one's life.

CIRCUMNAVIGATE advises one of the need to go around something.

CIRCUMSTANTIAL EVIDENCE means a lack of solid proof.

CIRCUS indicates a laughable or ridiculous situation.

CIRRHOSIS warns of a situation filled with negatives; a negatively congested aspect.

CIST See coffin.

CISTERN refers to the spiritual aspects one holds within self.

CITADEL symbolizes the high point of one's life; the goal or purpose for which one strives.

CITATION (legal notice) stands for a commendation or reprimand from a higher authority.

CITIZEN implies a group or location with which one is connected.

CITIZEN'S ARREST indicates one's responsibility to take action against negative elements; points to activism.

CITRINE (color) refers to joyful spirituality.

CITRONELLA pertains to the act of conflict resolution by way of positive means; the avoidance of harmful solutions.

CITRUS (fruit) See specific type.

CITY stands for a group density; concentrated area saturated with multiple perspectives.

CITY CLERK will represent a record-keeper; an individual who can provide a wide variety of specific information.

CITY COUNCIL can sometimes equate to the limits/boundaries of one's plans or range of effectiveness, but most often a city council will symbolize one's own inner source of insights, conscience, and/or vision.

CITY DESK connotes a need to be informed of aspects surrounding oneself.

CITY EDITOR characterizes one who is kept abreast of aspects surrounding self.

CITY HALL represents a need to conduct self appropriately. Could also mean a difficult road ahead regarding a specific situation.

CITY MANAGER advises one to handle personal business instead of depending on others to manage it.

CITY PLANNING COMMISSION See city council.

CITY ROOM is associated with incoming information; news.

CITY SLICKER indicates an individual who expertly utilizes societal aspects but may be lacking in managing the more basic elements of life.

CIVET denotes a quick wit.

CIVIC CENTER will normally be associated with cultural aspects. This symbol will have a unique meaning for each dreamer depending on how elements in his/her life relate to a cultural aspect.

CIVICS (study of) connotes a desire to understand the workings of surrounding authoritative systems.

CIVIL DEFENSE portrays the protection of one's surrounding aspects. This applies to personal preparedness.

CIVIL DISOBEDIENCE symbolizes one's right to disagree with those in authority.

CIVIL ENGINEER denotes an individual who plans and creates amenities for others.

CIVILIAN exemplifies an individual who is not subject to the demands or wiles of others.

CIVIL LIBERTIES naturally represent the basic rights everyone has. This dream symbol may be associated with a right the dreamer is being denied or, perhaps, the dreamer is denying someone else a basic right.

CIVIL RIGHTS reminds us of our personal freedoms; the positive aspects of personal perspectives and private directional planning.

CIVIL SERVICE alludes to serving others; a selfless nature.

CIVIL WAR connotes an internal conflict within self regarding one's immediate surroundings.

CLAIM stands for possessiveness; a declaration of ownership.

CLAIM (insurance) See insurance claim.

CLAIM-JUMPER warns against forming friendships for ulterior motives.

CLAIMS ADJUSTER will be someone who has the talent for assessing situational damage and recommending solutions/recompense.

CLAIRAUDIENCE won't necessarily be associated to a psychic skill but rather come in a dream to advise of a need to listen to someone more closely.

CLAIRVOYANCE is a suggestion to pay closer attention to insights, hunches, inner feelings.

CLAMBAKE alludes to possible negative aspects to keeping silent about something.

CLAM CHOWDER signifies rich and valued spiritual concepts that are utilized.

CLAMMY cautions of unpleasant aspects in one's life; an uneasiness; apprehensiveness; nervousness.

CLAMP (artery bleeder) points to a warning regarding one's physical condition.

CLAMP (engine hose) refers to a need to seal off some type of destructive behavior.

CLAMP (utility tool) comes as an advisement to become more serious; clamp down and straighten up.

CLAMSHELL warns of broken promises or secrets told. May indicate betrayal.

CLAN refers to a tightly related group of people bonded by shared beliefs or perspectives.

CLAP See applause.

CLAPBOARD implies an overlapping of issues in one's life. This could suggest a need to separate out different aspects instead of creating a confusing situation.

CLARET See wine.

CLARINET symbolizes lyrical verbiage; enhanced statements.

CLASH (of colors) indicates a conflict; mixed issues; confused logic.

CLASP signifies a holding on to something; keep a connection going.

CLASS See category.

CLASS (educational) refers to issues or subjects one requires better understanding of.

CLASS ACT alludes to high quality; distinction.

CLASS ACTION means action taken on behalf of others; someone ready to fight for the rights of others.

CLASSIC pertains to a distinctive aspect that has endured through time.

CLASSICAL MUSIC applies to those aspects in our lives that we individually perceive as soothing.

CLASSIFICATION See category.

CLASSIFIED AD serves as a guide for the dreamer. This specific dream symbol will lead one to that which is sought or else will indicate that which one needs to give to others.

CLASSMATE characterizes those who walk the same path as the dreamer; those with like interests.

CLASSROOM indicates a learning atmosphere or source of information.

CLASSY (appearance) is often associated with a quiet dignity/wisdom.

CLATTER represents a great disturbance. Usually this will refer to one's vibrational field or personal aura.

CLAUSE (in document) comes to bring your attention to something important; a reminder.

CLAUSTROPHOBIA warns of being in a closed-in situation or relationship. This may also be self-generated. See fear.

CLAW (animal) cautions of an attitude that goes against nature; a clawing toward something; a struggle.

CLAW (fetish) indicates a desire to characteristically emulate or be protected by a specific characteristic.

CLAW HAMMER indicates the duality of one's ability to secure something in life or take it apart.

CLAY portrays a necessity to be resilient as one walks life's path.

CLAYMORE See sword.

CLAY PIGEON exemplifies a life aspect that serves to sharpen our responses and instincts. However, in some dreams this symbol may point to personal weakness—an inability to stand up for oneself; someone who is easily taken advantage of.

CLEAN (anything) means attentiveness.

CLEANING (act of) points to an attempt to clean up one's act; efforts to improve a situation.

CLEANING SERVICE stands for efforts expended for the purpose of cleaning up after others. This symbol won't usually refer to a literally cleaning but rather point to fixing/repairing other people's mistakes or handling damage control left in the wake of their actions.

CLEAN ROOM signifies any type of element/idea/situation in one's life that is without negative aspects.

CLEANSER connotes some type of cleansing is needed. This symbol will point to the tool one needs to achieve that end.

CLEAN-SHAVEN illustrates a desire to keep things out in the open; honesty; an aversion to hidden aspects.

CLEAN SWEEP stands for an action which covered every detail.

CLEARANCE (height) denotes the amount of room one has. This will be clarified by surrounding dreamscape elements.

CLEARANCE (sale) cautions of a last chance to accomplish something. May indicate a need to be rid of unnecessary attitudes or perspectives that clutter logic.

CLEAR-COAT will represent a final finish; implementing a protective element to a finalized issue.

CLEAR CUTTING comes in dreams as a symbol having the duality of two possible meanings pointing to either an advisement or a warning. The advisement would be to *rid* oneself of every aspect of a certain negative in one's life. The warning would be to *stop* eliminating every shred of a particular element. The dreamer will know what these elements are.

CLEAR-EYED symbolizes one who sees clearly; a lack of distortion.

CLEAR-HEADED represents an individual who reasons calmly without letting personal perspectives or extraneous factors interfere.

CLEARINGHOUSE indicates a need to sort out issues or feelings.

CLEAR LUMBER refers to building material without any flaws. This, of course, will equate to a plan, idea, or choice of path progression.

CLEAR SPAN (construction) points to something that needs no support; an aspect that can easily and safely stand on its own.

CLEAT advises of a need to get a better grip on one's path.

CLEAVAGE (a split) indicates a separation; a division.

CLEAVER symbolizes a life aspect that has the capability of severing something. The dreamer will know what this refers to.

CLEFT PALATE stands for untruths; unbalanced statements; the addition of personal input into alleged statements of fact.

CLEMATIS (botanical) exemplifies the beautiful and prolific effects of spiritual acts that endure or "cling" to others.

CLEMENCY alludes to unconditional forgiveness.

CLENCH depicts a need to grasp something; the act of holding on.

CLENCHED TEETH indicate controlled anger or the rising of same.

CLEOPATRA warns against the utilization of one's physical attributes as a means of manipulation; ulterior motives; a personal agenda.

CLERIC See religious figure.

CLERICAL COLLAR points to a tendency to present self in a spiritual light.

CLERK pertains to the selling of something; may infer the selling of self or one's personal perspectives.

CLICHÉ has a dual meaning. It may infer that one is too nonchalant or it may indicate that one has acceptance. Surrounding dreamscape factors will clarify this meaning. What did the cliché refer to?

CLICK means that something has finally been understood. This specific type of sound also accompanies certain actual psychic experiences, therefore, it may relate to this factor for the dreamer.

CLIENT characterizes an individual for whom one does a service; those one assists.

CLIFF signifies a situation that is on the edge in life; living on the edge.

CLIFF DWELLER denotes one who finds security by living on the edge; self-confidence; reliance on one's carved out position in life.

CLIFFHANGER exemplifies high anxiety; suspense; left on the edge while waiting for results or conclusions.

CLIFF'S NOTES suggest a lack of details.

CLIMATE gives clues to the general attitude or feeling of a dream, one of the overall elements. See specific type.

CLIMATE CONTROL means a conscious effort or desire to control one's surroundings.

CLIMATOLOGY (study of climate) represents an interest in understanding how surroundings affect events or people's reactions in life.

CLIMAX stands for the manifestation of long-sought goals; a dramatic or intense conclusion to something.

CLIMBING symbolizes an upward or forward striving.

CLIMBING ROSES stand for an enduring admiration/love.

CLINGING cautions of a need to let go of something or someone.

CLINIC (instructional) advises of the need to gain further information or knowledge about something.

CLINIC (medical) refers to a factor in life that has the capability of providing assistance for minor problems.

CLINICAL (explanation/description) means the basic facts of something.

CLINICIAN is one who has specific knowledge; a specialized teacher.

CLIP (clasp) infers the act of holding something together.

CLIP (cut off) pertains to a separation; severing; shortening or trimming.

CLIP (swindle) means the act of taking advantage of another; ulterior motives.

CLIP ART stands for the opportunity to take advantage of a variety of ways to express oneself.

CLIPBOARD portrays an orderly individual; efficiency; a tool to help one attend to details.

CLIPPER See ship.

CLIPPERS (hair) symbolize the trimming of life factors that affect one's attitude and perspective.

CLIPPERS (nails, dog) mean a need to trim down the riled attitude of a friend.

CLIPPERS (nails, person) indicate an attempt to control one's negative aspects such as anger, aggressiveness, impulsiveness, etc.

CLIPPING SERVICE represents an individual who will search out and collect all known information on a particular subject; someone to do one's research.

CLIQUE cautions against social arrogance or selectiveness.

CLOAK See serape, burnoose, burka. May also have the additional interpretation of inferring secretiveness.

CLOAK-AND-DAGGER signifies the act of leading on or may indicate intriguing aspects to a situation or relationship; sequential surprises.

CLOAKROOM stands for a specific life factor that is not what it seems; an aspect full of cover-ups or misrepresentations.

CLOCK always calls the dreamer's attention to a warning of time.

CLOCK MAKER characterizes an individual who sets limits; one who is highly efficient; one who motivates others.

CLOCK RADIO indicates an acceptance of one's responsibility.

CLOCK TOWER portrays a major sign that indicates the right time for major events to happen in one's life. Advises of the wisdom of accepting the concept that there's a right time for everything.

CLOCK-WATCHER connotes the wasting of time; one who ill-uses time. Suggests impatience, anxiety.

CLOCKWISE pertains to advancements.

CLOCKWORK advises of the proper workings of one's life; things are unfolding as they are meant to in a regular and normally expected manner.

CLOG (obstruction) warns of a life factor that needs immediate attention (clearing) before further advancement can occur.

CLOG (shoe) means that one's path is being traversed in a clumsy or difficult manner. This situation is correctable.

CLOGGING (type of dance) refers to a difficult path chosen.

CLOISONNÉ represents heavily layered and elaborately designed identity presentations; false appearances; a major problem with the acceptance of one's true self.

CLOISTER exemplifies the ability to obtain inner tranquility through one's spiritual beliefs. May also come as an advisement to get out there and make a difference.

CLONE cautions of the tendency toward the imitation of others.

CLOSE CALL implies a need to give closer attention to one's actions.

CLOSED suggests an attempt to approach a path or obtain knowledge for which one is not yet prepared to absorb.

CLOSED BOOK suggests a person, situation, or concept that cannot be understood; puzzling; too convoluted to analyze at this point.

CLOSED-CAPTIONED advises of one's options open for further understanding.

CLOSED CIRCUIT connotes one's free-flowing energies; energies that have no blockages; free-flowing current through the chakras.

CLOSED DOOR advises against attempting to enter regions one is not advanced enough to travel.

CLOSED SHOP See union.

CLOSED SIGN suggests denied access. May mean one is not ready to enter. Recall what sort of building or shop the sign was on. This will pinpoint what aspect the dreamer is being told she's not ready for.

CLOSE ENCOUNTER points to a personal experience that nearly happened.

CLOSE-FISTED warns against being greedy; stingy. May also allude to a need for anger management.

CLOSE-KNIT indicates strong bonds; solid ties with another.

CLOSE-MINDED warns against being opinionated or lacking the desire to intellectually seek an understanding of new theories.

CLOSE-MOUTHED relates to trustworthiness; integrity; loyalty.

CLOSE-OUT reveals the last of something; the final remnants.

CLOSE SHAVE See close call.

CLOSET stands for aspects of self that one keeps hidden. These may even be kept hidden from oneself—an attempt at denial.

CLOSE-UP (lens shot) portrays close inspection; analyzation.

CLOSING COSTS refer to the final efforts/resources needed to conclude an issue or reach a goal.

CLOSING DATE (mortgage loan) signifies a time to shoot for in regard to achieving something.

CLOSURE doesn't mean forgive and forget, it means gaining acceptance and moving on.

CLOT (blood) may indicate the beginnings of a healing or it may refer to a life factor that prevents advancement.

CLOTTING FACTOR relates to one's ability to heal after a hurtful or destructive event.

CLOTH See specific type.

CLOTHES BASKET See hamper.

CLOTHES HANGER is an advisement to let go of something one is clinging to or hanging on to; hang it up and move on.

CLOTHESHORSE characterizes an individual obsessed with appearances.

CLOTHESLINE emphasizes the need for increased awareness. In some dreams this symbol will suggest a need to air something, perhaps a grievance or grudge; get something out in the open.

CLOTHESPIN suggests an opportunity to air grievances or held back opinions.

CLOTHES RACK suggests choices for expressing oneself.

CLOTHING generally gives indications into one's personality or physical condition.

CLOUDS connote thought patterns; ability to analyze and reason.

CLOUDBURST pertains to sudden realizations; a pouring out of new and fresh ideas.

CLOUD NINE signifies a state of elation.

CLOUD SEEDING represents forced or planted ideas; coercive thought; manipulative statements.

CLOUDY (atmosphere) suggests a phase of unclear issues.

CLOVE (multisectioned bulb) stands for beginnings that have more than one generating aspect.

CLOVE (spice) connotes a life aspect that one utilizes to make specific factors more appealing.

CLOVE OIL stands for something that temporarily relieves emotional pain.

CLOVER represents spiritual abundance.

CLOVER LEAF (four leaves) See charm.

CLOVER LEAF (three leaves) See shamrock.

CLOWN characterizes one's foolish aspects.

CLOWN FISH portrays foolish factors connected to one's spiritual beliefs.

CLOWN SUIT illustrates immaturity; false or forced happiness.

CLUB (bat) indicates a bullish personality; manipulative; coercive.

CLUB (group) exemplifies those with a life perspective or interest.

CLUB CAR pertains to an expectation for preferential treatment.

CLUBFOOT connotes personalized difficulties traversing one's path. This will be meant for the dreamer to overcome.

CLUBHOUSE symbolizes a desire to belong; a personal need for acceptance.

CLUB SANDWICH refers to multilayered or multifaceted aspects to a concept, situation, or perception one holds.

CLUB SODA See soda water.

CLUE comes as hints from one's Higher Self or inner knowing.

CLUMSINESS represents inattention to details; a suggestion to sharpen one's awareness.

CLUNKER implies inefficient or inoperable life factors such as outdated and primitive beliefs that no longer apply in today's world.

CLUSTER connotes multiples of the same aspect, such as more than a couple adversaries or friends.

CLUSTER (stars) reveal that there's more than one opportunity or solution.

CLUSTER BOMB portrays a major outcome or effect that will create devastating effects on a wide variety of life aspects.

CLUTCH See clench.

CLUTCH (vehicle) denotes that which causes one to gear up or down; a motivational factor allowing control over the choice of which gear to use.

CLUTCH BAG/PURSE refers to aspects one holds close or dear.

CLUTTER defines a disorderly state. Usually refers to one's perspectives that need to be put in order.

COACH (conveyance) See carriage.

COACH (tutor) cautions us to use discernment when being advised or taught by another. May also point to manipulation.

COAGULATE See clot.

COAL portrays deep-seated negativity; undesirable attitudes; behavior covering the beauty of one's spirit within.

COAL BIN reveals hidden negatives one conceals.

COAL MINE advises one to dig down and bring out negative attitudes for the purpose of neutralizing them.

COAL OIL See kerosene.

COAL TAR illustrates that which we utilize for the purpose of insulating self from hurtful elements.

COAL TRAIN See train (coal).

CO-ANCHOR signifies a dual responsibility.

COARSE (texture) denotes harshness of character or behavior.

COAST See shore (land).

COASTER refers to protective measures; doing no damage.

COAST GUARD characterizes those who work to provide spiritual safety for others; one's advisors or spiritual guardians.

COAST GUARD CUTTER denotes a life aspect that provides spiritual emergency help.

COASTING warns of a downward path; sliding downward.

COASTLINE represents a position approaching spiritual involvement; the precursor stage to spiritual searching. What was the coastline's condition? Rocky and rough? Sandy and beachlike?

COAT represents one's exterior presentation to the world; how we want to be seen or what we use to conceal the real self.

COAT OF ARMS infers ancestral arrogance.

COAT ROOM See cloakroom.

COATTAIL warns of the desire to let others lead; cautions of the tendency to let others do the work in advance of self; advancing through the efforts of others instead of self.

CO-AUTHOR signifies a tandem idea or plan.

COB See corncob.

COBALT (blue) signifies behavior based on a rich spiritual base.

COBALT (green) suggests materialism; fiscal wealth.

COBBLER See shoemaker.

COBBLER (fruit dessert) symbolizes well-deserved rewards.

COBBLESTONE portrays a bumpy road that one chooses to take.

COBRA illustrates a threatened or dismayed individual. See snake.

COBWEB indicates sticky situations or relationships in which one gets caught because of not applying adequate reasoning; the trap one walks into.

COCAINE warns of an inability to cope with reality; a lack of taking responsibility; escapism. May also point to an elitist hypocrisy.

COCCYX BONE signifies one's base or foundational attitudes.

COCK See rooster.

COCKATIEL See parrot.

COCKATOO See parrot.

COCKCROW (dawn) connotes beginnings; a new day; a dawning aspect.

COCKED (position) indicates imbalance; a slanted aspect or perspective.

COCKER SPANIEL (dog breed) characterizes companionship; gentle associations. May have communication troubles.

COCKEYED alludes to foolishness; absurdity.

COCK FIGHT warns of a tendency to use others to resolve one's conflicts.

COCKLE symbolizes one's innermost feelings.

COCKLEBUR depicts emotional pain.

COCKLESHELL signifies the remains of one's emotional feelings; leftover feelings following an emotionally charged event.

COCKPIT pertains to mental or emotional control.

COCKROACH refers to major disruptions in one's emotional or physical life.

COCKSCOMB warns of egotistical attitudes.

COCKTAIL See alcoholic beverage.

COCKTAIL TABLE See coffee table.

COCKTAIL WAITRESS characterizes an individual who has the capability of easing one's problems. May also point to someone who aids another in avoiding reality.

COCOA portrays a life aspect that soothes.

COCOA BUTTER pertains to emotional healing.

COCONUT expresses the fact that strength and nourishment can result from life's more difficult lessons.

COCONUT MILK characterizes a life aspect that provides rich lessons or rewards.

COCONUT OIL signifies those factors in one's life that serve to soothe and soften the hurtful or difficult aspects of one's path.

COCOON connotes a stage of respite where one absorbs what has been learned before advancing to the next spiritual stage of gaining wisdom from that knowledge; a time of planning; the pause before action.

CODDLE warns of overindulgence; a lack of discipline.

CODE stands for specialized communication; hidden messages understood by a select group.

CODE BLUE warns of an extremely dangerous situation approaching.

CODE BOOK symbolizes an aspect that serves as the key to understanding something.

CODEINE represents those life factors that we believe help us get through the more difficult times.

CODE NAME refers to a secret identity.

CODE OF ETHICS suggests a specific standard of behavior.

CODE WORD See password.

CODEX suggests highly valuable information or knowledge.

CODFISH stands for spiritual arrogance; a sense of spiritual superiority.

CODGER portrays a disinterested or irascible elder.

CODICIL See addendum.

COD-LIVER OIL advises of a deficiency in one's life.

COEDUCATION symbolizes information that will benefit everyone.

COFFEE stands for persevering energy; that which enriches one's motivations.

COFFEE BEANS depict the freshness of renewed energy; sparked motivation.

COFFEE BREAK refers to a need to pause for the purpose of restoring one's energy.

COFFEE CAKE denotes nourishment through energizing pauses of respite.

COFFEE GROUNDS signify the negative aspects one leaves behind after being re-energized.

COFFEE KLATCH pertains to the emotional uplift brought by sharing restful energizing times with others.

COFFEE MILL refers to an aspect that has the capability of energizing one.

COFFEEPOT illustrates a brewing situation and may indicate a percolating condition within self that advises of a rest period.

COFFEE SHOP exemplifies a rest period and the need to choose a specific manner for same.

COFFEE TABLE typifies an offering of comfort extended to others.

COFFEE-TABLE BOOK applies to something we openly share with others.

COFFER See cache.

COFFIN may mean an emotionally comatose state of being, or it may actually come as a forewarning of a death.

COFFIN NAIL stands for any negative aspect in one's life that is serving as a serious detriment.

COG portrays a vitally important part of an aspect.

COG RAILWAY denotes that which provides movement for specific aspects in one's life.

COGWHEEL signifies an important aspect of one's life.

COHABITATION suggests a closeness to another; a bonded relationship.

COHORT See partner.

COIL may refer to the act of going in circles or it may warn of the dangerous situation of coiling up as an internal spring, indicating inner tension and stress.

COIN signifies the little rarely recognized opportunities that come our way.

COINCIDENCE connotes destined connections.

COIN COUNTER is a symbol that advises us to count our blessings.

COIN PURSE denotes a recognition and appreciation of one's gifts.

COIN SORTER suggests a need to differentiate the various values of multiple benefits/blessings which we're continually being touched by.

COIN WRAPPER represents the act of saving one's opportunities. This indicates appreciation of their value.

COITUS See intercourse (sexual).

COKE-HEAD characterizes total irresponsibility and a lack of interest in dealing with reality.

COLANDER See strainer.

COLD means a lack of warmth. Specific surrounding dreamscape symbols will clarify this reference.

COLD (illness) See head cold.

COLD-BLOODED signifies a lack of emotional response; an individual having absolutely no sensitivity; apathy.

COLD CALL stands for the sudden introduction of a completely new issue into one's life; an issue or situation that came without warning.

COLD CASE (file) means something in one's past that's been left unresolved.

COLD CASH refers to immediately available assets. These may be in the form of money, emotional support, virtues, means of assisting others, etc.

COLD CELLAR See root cellar.

COLD CREAM denotes a need for emotional softening.

COLD CUTS represents aspects that provide immediate nourishment.

COLD DUCK See alcoholic beverage.

COLD-EYED implies a lack of personal opinion or involvement.

COLD FEET portrays a lack of faith or courage; a giving in to one's fears.

COLD FISH characterizes one in the habit of not showing emotions.

COLD FRAME stands for tough love; holding back on emotional warmth or compassion for the purpose of strengthening another.

COLD FRONT means the approach of an unresponsive attitude.

COLD-HEARTED refers to a lack of warm emotional expression; apathy; insensitivity.

COLD PACK (canning) represents unbiased information gathered followed by proper emotional expressiveness.

COLD SHOULDER warns against judging others; calls for forgiveness and a resulting response of at least neutrality.

COLD SHOWER advises of a cooling-off period.

COLD SORE See canker sore.

COLD STORAGE portrays a protection of what one values.

COLD SWEAT indicates nervousness, fear, or anxiety.

COLD TURKEY stands for immediate and absolute withdrawal of something in one's life; complete abstinence and distance.

COLD WAR warns against maintaining deep animosities; continuing underlying negative feelings.

COLD WATER represents a diminishing value of spiritual elements; spiritual disagreements.

COLD WAVE typifies a time period of unemotional responses.

COLESLAW implies several factors contributing to the reason for one receiving neutral responses from others.

COLEUS refers to an acceptance of varied personalities of those with whom one is associated.

COLIC signifies life aspects that are not well accepted.

COLITIS warns of intolerance.

COLLAGE (art form) reminds us of life's diversity and the beauty of same. This dreamscape symbol usually calls for more acceptance on the dreamer's part.

COLLAGEN stands for the revitalizing and binding aspects in one's life.

COLLAPSE indicates failure; lack of support or strength.

COLLAR symbolizes an aspect that one considers burdensome; possible guilt.

COLLARD GREENS See kale.

COLLATE advises one to give detailed attention to the orderly integration of facts.

COLLATERAL signifies insurance against failure when taking risks.

COLLATERAL DAMAGE See road-kill.

COLLEAGUE See associate.

COLLECT stresses the need for gathering something of importance for the dreamer. This may refer to information, emotions, or even the collecting of self, indicating scattered emotions, thoughts, or beliefs.

COLLECTIBLE refers to highly valued aspects as viewed by the dreamer.

COLLECTIBLES stand for the wide variety of life elements that one can be particularly drawn to, have an affinity for.

COLLECTION denotes a personal possessiveness.

COLLECTION BOX See poor box.

COLLECTIVE CONSCIOUS reminds us of our inter-relatedness to all living things.

COLLECTOR connotes a specific interest (often kept hidden) and the strong attraction for all aspects of same. This can be a revealing dream if one recalls what was being collected.

COLLEGE implies higher learning.

COLLIE (dog breed) characterizes a faithful friend.

COLLISION pertains to a harmful or negative result.

COLLISION COURSE warns of a destructive relationship or dangerous perspective, emotional basis, or path.

COLLISION SHOP stands for a source one can go to for the purpose of repairing some type of damage done to a situation.

COLLOQUIALISM in dreams helps to narrow down meanings in the spoken language of other dream characters presented.

COLLUSION warns of deceitfulness or secretiveness; perhaps betrayal.

COLOGNE See perfume.

COLON (anatomy) stands for preparations or time frame preceding the act of shedding some excesses in one's life.

COLON (punctuation mark) is an indication that something will follow, usually an explanation.

COLONEL characterizes a highly regimented individual.

COLONIST characterizes perseverance; self-reliance; one who isn't hesitant to experience new ideas or adventures.

COLONNADE defines the way leading to something important for the dreamer.

COLONY connotes a group of like-minded individuals who desire to establish a location of camaraderie in relation to ideals.

COLOR aspects of dreams are extremely revealing. See specific color for interpretation.

COLORADO signifies the power of enduring fortitude.

COLORBLINDNESS emphasizes the fact that one views all aspects of life according to personal perspectives; opinionated.

COLOR-CODED indicates a need for proper identification or classification. This would imply that there is a problem with sorting out feelings or situations.

COLORFAST represents no chance for change; immutability.

COLOR FILTER means an altered or colored perspective.

COLOR GUARD signifies pride of heritage.

COLORING (activity) refers to an expression of one's personal opinion; may also pertain to a desire to change reality.

COLORING BOOK suggests an opportunity to express one's personal perspective; may indicate a desire to alter or *color* things according to one's viewpoint. Recall what images were in the book.

COLORIZATION (old films) stands for enhancement; enrichment without altering anything.

COLORLESS stands for neutral; having no personal animation or unique expressiveness.

COLOR PHASE (pelt/plumage) is associated with a particular phase one is in regarding attitudes affecting behavior.

COLOR SCHEME reveals a specific tone

of something. This can refer to clothing, one's home decor, or an entire atmosphere/scene of a dream.

COLOR WHEEL displays the many choices we have regarding our attitudes and their expressed behavior. Recall if any colors were highlighted. These would be sending an advisement message.

COLOSSUS portrays something of great size.

COLOSTOMY denotes the utilization of alternate means of shedding one's excesses or extraneous aspects; bypassing the normal means.

COLOSTRUM defines an aspect that richly nourishes and protects.

COLT stands for the freedoms of youth that maturity usually suppresses.

COLTSFOOT (botanical) suggests carefree footing and comes to advise one to pay closer attention to where one is going or how one is behaving.

COLUMBINE (flower) relates to inner peacefulness.

COLUMBUS (Christopher) characterizes misinterpretations; confusion; perceptual problems; possessiveness.

COLUMN See pile (post).

COMA means an unresponsive state. This does not infer a lack of awareness.

COMB pertains to a need to straighten out one's thoughts.

COMBAT warns against the wrong type of conflict resolution.

COMBAT FATIGUE exemplifies the self-destructive effects of conflict.

COMBAT FATIGUES indicate preparedness for conflict, ready for a fight.

COMBAT ZONE will be directly associated with a particular issue, relationship, or type of behavior that's involved in some form of conflict for the dreamer.

COMBINATION DOOR (glass/screen) refers to an open mind.

COMBINATION LOCK denotes the various methods of opening something up or solving problems.

COMBINE connotes a blending or mixing of something in the dreamer's life.

COMBINE (machine) stands for several tasks being handled by a single aspect or solution.

COMB-OVER (hair over baldness) refers to baseless opinions; thoughts brought in to hide the fact that one has no real thoughts or opinions on an issue.

COMBUSTION See flashpoint.

COMEDIAN characterizes an unrealistic perspective; one who makes a joke of everything.

COMET defines spiritual awakenings; enlightening insights.

COMFORTER See quilt.

COMFORT STATION signifies the resting points that are necessary along our path.

COMFREY defines self-healing capabilities; acceptance; tolerance.

COMIC BOOK connotes a manner of escape from life; unrealistic perceptions; a hesitancy to face reality.

COMIC RELIEF advises of a need to maintain a sense of humor throughout life.

COMING-OUT PARTY represents an exposure of a particular element of oneself, usually individuality; a shedding of inferiority feelings; the celebration of one's uniqueness.

COMMA (punctuation mark) symbolizes a separation of ideas and comes as a caution for the dreamer to avoid running concepts together.

COMMAND is an authoritative directive. The clue here will be whether or not the authority figure is a positive or negative one as perceived by the dreamer.

COMMANDER IN CHIEF pertains to an authority figure of the highest rank. For the dreamer, this may be in reference to an individual that is highly respected.

COMMANDO represents impulsiveness; knee-jerk reactions; a short-tempered personality; destructive resolutions.

COMMAND POST will most often indicate a center of authority or direction. Depending on related dreamscape elements, this symbol may be pointing to oneself and be an advisement to take control of one's own decision/direction.

COMMENCEMENT means the beginning stage of applying what has been learned.

COMMENDATION portrays approval.

COMMENTARY defines the opinion or perspective of another.

COMMERCIAL signifies an offered aspect; something being shown to the dreamer.

COMMERCIAL ART signifies benefits in reaching goals through using one's unique expression of creativity.

COMMISSARY See grocery market.

COMMISSION (assignment) depicts having the authority to do something; one's right to act or proceed.

COMMISSION (sales) points to rewards for energies expended.

COMMISSIONER will usually be associated with oneself, one's conscience.

COMMITMENT emphasizes a promise; a responsibility to carry something through.

COMMITTEE symbolizes a group chosen to perform a function. This would indicate a tone of authority or confirm rightness for the dreamer.

COMMON DENOMINATOR pertains to an aspect that is shared by others. May mean the simplest aspect; bottom line.

COMMON GROUND refers to a unifying factor.

COMMON-LAW MARRIAGE underscores the concept of living by the *spirit* of the law; arrangements agreed to without contractual formalities; having a mutual *understanding* of something.

COMMON WALL refers to a shared idea/philosophy, yet each person having her/his own unique perspectives of it.

COMMOTION denotes disruption.

COMMUNE (group) represents a living arrangement based on the utilization of talents and supplies that are provided by and for all participants; unconditional sharing.

COMMUNITY CENTER applies to the enjoyment of social contacts. May refer to a life element that is available to all.

COMMUNITY CHEST symbolizes one's reserves of generosity; one's ability to share or give to others.

COMMUNITY PROPERTY points to an idea/concept shared by many.

COMMUTER pertains to a vacillating period in one's life.

COMMUTER PLANE See air taxi.

COMPACT (makeup) designates the act of smoothing over or covering up one's perceived faults.

COMPACT (size) signifies something that's condensed; efficient; convenient.

COMPACT DISC (CD) symbolizes condensed information; acquiring a large block of knowledge in a short span of time.

COMPACTOR advises of a need to diminish the amount of one's wastefulness. May point to a need to make one's life less scattered. Or realize priorities.

COMPANION characterizes one with whom the dreamer closely associates.

COMPANION PLANTING denotes a mutually beneficial relationship.

COMPANY PERSON will be associated with watching one's own back; taking care of Number One by prioritizing a mutually beneficial loyalty rather than sacrificing that same faithfulness in lieu of loyalty to a friend.

COMPANY STORE signifies a continual energizing of one's expended efforts; getting a large return on what one puts out.

COMPANY TOWN portrays group dependency.

COMPARATIVE RELIGION (study of) denotes a desire to gain an awareness of all elements of an issue.

COMPARISON SHOPPING advises of a need to research something; don't accept the first presentation or offer of an aspect.

COMPASS connotes direction. This usually will point to a path different from the one the dreamer is walking or believes is right for her.

COMPENSATION depicts a return for something; amends; balance or counterbalance; may point to an unexpected benefit from having to accept an alternative.

COMPENSATORY DAMAGES will point to retribution; payback.

COMPETENCY HEARING usually stands for self-doubts, wondering if one is crazy for thinking a particular way or having an uncommon perspective.

COMPETITION will most often be associated with a goodwill or lighthearted type of rivalry, often oneself taking both challenger roles for the purpose of pushing limits or expectations.

COMPLACENT defines a lack of motivation yet may also indicate acceptance. Surrounding dreamscape symbols will clarify this intent.

COMPLAINT indicates an active objection to something.

COMPLAINT DEPARTMENT usually points to where one can go to get answers or resolutions.

COMPLEMENTARY will reveal an unexpected benefit.

COMPLETER SET (dinnerware, collectibles, etc.) denotes the whole of an issue. If one or more pieces were missing from this dreamscape element, then it means that one still doesn't have all the facts of associated aspects to an idea or situation.

COMPLETION DATE (construction) stands for the time allotted for the attainment of a goal. Also see closing date, deadline.

COMPLICATION means entanglement. This may even refer to one's own thought process.

COMPLIMENT refers to praise or encouragement from one's Higher Self.

COMPOSER (music) stands for one who creates a harmony or discord.

COMPOSITE CHARACTER (in story) depicts one possessing a wide variety of qualities and characteristics drawn from other individuals. May stand for a lack of individuality.

COMPOSITE PHOTOGRAPH will reveal one's multifaceted aspects.

COMPOSITE STORY represents a scenario comprised of elements taken from several other situations.

COMPOST See mulch.

COMPOTE suggests a mix of multiple benefits.

COMPRESS (bandage) advises of an urgent need to attend to an unhealthy situation; needing pressure (energy) put on something to staunch the outflow of information or ramifications; something requiring hot (energy output) or cool (acceptance) attention.

COMPRESSED AIR advises one to get more breathing room; move away from some life aspect that feels suffocating.

COMPRESSOR characterizes an individual or situation that brings about better understanding.

COMPROMISE stands for the need to make some concessions in life.

COMPULSION cautions one to gain better control over impulsiveness.

COMPUTER connotes a need for analyzation or better understanding.

COMPUTER DISC symbolizes a great amount of information. Recall what type of disc it was.

COMPUTER GRAPHICS symbolize the clarification of communication or an idea through the use of helpful visuals.

COMPUTER HACKER will reveal an individual who has an ulterior motive; a person who is unscrupulous and intrusive.

COMPUTER PIRATE refers to someone who steals; acquisition without ownership right.

COMPUTER PROGRAM indicates a life aspect that greatly shortens one's research time and provides extensive information.

COMPUTER PROGRAMMER characterizes an individual who believes in the ability to make reality coincide with personal perspectives, desires, or plans.

COMPUTER SPYWARE relates to a life aspect that serves as a tool for intrusiveness into one's life.

COMPUTER VIRUS pertains to disinformation willfully given. Also may point to a new problem with one's formerly accepted perceptions.

COMPUTER WORM refers to a negative element that affects several aspects of one's life.

COMRADE will be a close associate, one who shares like ideas, perspectives, and interests.

CONCEALMENT warns of a cover-up or the hiding of something.

CONCENTRATION CAMP can signify forced attitudes or it can come in a dream to advise of greater attention needed on an issue.

CONCERT (performance) represents a display of talent or knowledge.

CONCERT (synergy) advises of the benefits of a collaboration.

CONCESSIONAIRE characterizes one who associates with another for self-serving purposes.

CONCH (shell) represents spiritual aspects that are cherished.

CONCH BELT implies a desire to surround self with the more natural aspects of life.

CONCIERGE portrays an individual who serves to make life easier.

CONCLUSION directly relates to an ending.

CONCOCTION connotes a mix of personal perceptions.

CONCOURSE alludes to a passing stage or life situation.

CONCRETE See cement.

CONCUBINE implies feminine inferiority; chauvinism; subservience.

CONCUSSION defines a personally shocking event; mentally or emotionally shocking.

CONDEMNATION signifies absolute rejection of something. Who was doing the condemnation? About what?

CONDENSATION symbolizes life aspects that naturally generate spiritual effects or benefits.

CONDENSED MILK pertains to rich nourishment.

CONDENSER suggests a need to be more concise or look at the basic issue rather than its extraneous elements.

CONDIMENT connotes an additional aspect one interjects to life; a dressing or spicing of something.

CONDITIONAL USE PERMIT stands for one's right to temporarily display a variant form of behavior or have a specific type of attitude.

CONDITIONER (hair) denotes a desire to keep one's perspectives and thoughts well aligned with logic and reason.

CONDOM connotes the level of one's protective concerns.

CONDOMINIUM illustrates self-confidence and independence realized through the support of others.

CONDOR See vulture.

CONDUCTOR (music) connotes an individual who has the ability to bring harmony to a situation.

CONDUCTOR (transit) characterizes those who offer helpful guidance along one's path.

CONDUIT denotes that which conveys in a supporting, protective manner.

CONE (ice cream) See ice cream cone.

CONE (shape) suggests a need to pinpoint something; bring to a defined point or conclusion.

CONE (traffic) signifies a cautionary advisement; cautionary guidelines.

CONEHEAD portrays unrealistic perspectives. May point to an out of touch personality.

CONESTOGA WAGON See covered wagon.

CONEY ISLAND See amusement park; hot dog.

CONFECTION exemplifies an aspect perceived as sweet or desirable; little life aspects to which we treat ourselves.

CONFECTIONER will point to someone who has a tendency to be an optimist, brighten another's day.

CONFEDERATE (flag) signifies a strong reluctance to let go of things.

CONFEDERATE (soldier) characterizes Southern attitudes.

CONFERENCE indicates a situation requiring further discussion.

CONFERENCE CALL advises of a need to

communicate with several others on an important matter.

CONFERENCE ROOM points to a need for a face to face meeting.

CONFERENCE TABLE advises that it's time to put it all on the table.

CONFESSIONAL signals a need for honesty; suggests an untruth is preventing advancement and it's time to open up and let it all out.

CONFESSIONAL SEAL equates to confidentiality.

CONFETTI represents joyful celebration.

CONFIDANTE characterizes someone to whom you can openly talk; one who can be trusted with personal information.

CONFIDENCE GAME See swindler.

CONFIDENTIAL FILE illustrates multiple secrets or hidden aspects.

CONFIGURATION (shape) applies to a wide variety of life factors and has an even greater scope of interpretation. See specific shape.

CONFINEMENT advises of an inability to proceed; marks a time frame when a pause or delay is required. There is also another meaning for this symbol and that is a warning that one is confining oneself in some way, holding oneself back.

CONFIRMATION represents verification.

CONFISCATE implies a need to retrieve or seize something.

CONFLUENCE stands for the act of joining or coming together. This usually indicates a need for an agreement to take place.

CONFORMIST warns of a lack of individuality or thought.

CONFRONTATION may be giving advice to get something out in the open.

CONFUSION usually indicates mental turmoil.

CONGEAL means a coming together or nearing solidification.

CONGESTION (lung) See pneumonia.

CONGESTION (sinus) refers to a suffocating situation requiring clearing so one can breathe freely. Suggests a need to clear the air.

CONGESTION (traffic) See traffic jam.

CONGLOMERATE means the joining of several factors. The dreamer will understand what this means by including surrounding dreamscape elements.

CONGREGATION connotes a large group. This does not specifically infer a spiritual connection.

CONGRESS represents a meeting of several people or groups for the purpose of a specific communication. This typifies a need for resolving differences between more than two or three people.

CONIFER denotes everlasting beauty and benefits of spiritual behavior.

CONJOINED TWINS usually exposes a compatible individual. May also reveal someone who is totally dependent upon another; a lack of individuality.

CONJUNCTIVITIS warns of a major error in perception; strongly advises to clear up one's way of seeing things.

CONJURER characterizes an individual who has the capability to make things happen; someone who gets things done.

CONNECTICUT represents foundational morals/ethics.

CONNOISSEUR portrays an individual who has spent a great deal of time gaining full knowledge of something; an expert.

CONQUISTADOR connotes one who enjoys winning; having control over others.

CONSCIENTIOUS OBJECTOR pertains to an individual who stands up for personal beliefs; one who isn't reluctant to perform civil disobedience.

CONSECRATION defines a recognition of sacredness or spirituality.

CONSEQUENCE doesn't always infer negativity; it may only indicate the result of something else.

CONSERVATION EASEMENT See easement (conservation).

CONSERVATIONIST relates to one who places a high priority on the preservation of positive life aspects.

CONSERVATISM marks a tendency to avoid change; fear of something new or innovative.

CONSERVATORY represents a recognition of certain life benefits and efforts spent on preserving/nurturing them.

CONSIGNMENT stands for possible benefits gained from the actions of another.

CONSIGNMENT SHOP refers to a possible source from which to receive benefits.

CONSOLATION PRIZE portrays the fact that benefits are derived from the act of participation alone.

CONSOMMÉ exemplifies the rewards and benefits of clear perspectives; also see bouillon.

CONSPIRACY warns of dangerous planning.

CONSPIRATOR reveals one with ulterior motives and agendas.

CONSTABLE See sheriff.

CONSTELLATION comes in dreams to give recognition for spiritual behavior.

CONSTIPATION denotes an inability to express oneself; a repressive personality; possibly a manipulative relationship.

CONSTITUTION normally refers to perseverance; one's inner strength/fortitude; may also be associated with one's unique moral/ethical code.

CONSTRUCTION LOAN symbolizes the aid of someone who can help another obtain the necessary tools to begin a new path or set an idea in motion.

CONSTRUCTION PAPER illustrates a need to formulate a plan of agreement to build on.

CONSTRUCTION SITE signifies a time of building; constructive advancements.

CONSULATE represents a place of safety; where protection is provided.

CONSULTATION infers the need for advice.

CONSUMER ADVOCATE will point to someone who watches for negatives associated with a wide variety of life aspects. If the dreamscape consumer advocate was the dreamer, this symbol is pointing to oneself, the conscience.

CONSUMER PRICE INDEX refers to the increased cost of waiting to act on something—the additional price of indecision/procrastination.

CONTACT DERMATITIS advises one to avoid a life aspect that causes extreme irritation, stress, or anxiety.

CONTACTEE (alien) indicates an individual who is attuned to her/his Higher Self, is aware of insights and gut feelings.

CONTACT LENS See glasses.

CONTAGION warns of an extremely harmful influence.

CONTAGIOUS connotes a perception,

belief, or attitude that will quickly be accepted by others.

CONTAINER suggests a need for containment. What was in the container? This symbol may also point to a need to release something that has been contained far too long.

CONTAINMENT denotes a completely controlled situation; something that has no ability to spread or affect others. A resolution or solution has been found; something that's no longer a problem.

CONTAMINATION warns of the infiltration of an extremely corrupt or deadly facet into one's life. May also refer to a literal contamination of a perspective; a truth has been compromised with a false element.

CONTEMPLATION advises one to give deeper thought to something.

CONTEMPORARY (architecture/decor) refers to a bland personality with no display of personalized character.

CONTEMPT OF COURT stands for willful recklessness, obstinacy.

CONTEST represents a competitive situation.

CONTESTANT points to a competitive nature; a vying for position; a personality with a tendency to better others.

CONTINENT will point the dreamer to an important aspect that's personally pertinent. Clarity will come when the specific continent name or country is shown. For general interpretations, see specific continents.

CONTINENTAL BREAKFAST suggests a physiological need to lighten up one's routinely stressful mornings.

CONTINENTAL DIVIDE advises of a major division in one's life. This may be a serious disagreement in a relationship or it may even relate to a divisive element within self.

CONTINENTAL DRIFT suggests the possibility of a firm decision, perspective, or attitude shifting position.

CONTINENTAL SHELF pertains to underlying facets to something that creates supporting extensions; something backed by additional facts that have not yet surfaced.

CONTINGENCY means possible alternate plans.

CONTINGENCY FEE symbolizes a reward or benefit resulting from a successful outcome.

CONTINUITY denotes a state of absolute coherence; a perceptual manner that contains no distorting aspects.

CONTORTIONIST characterizes a manipulative personality. May point to an individual who has a tendency to distort things, make them more complicated than necessary.

CONTOUR MAP reveals the ups and downs of an intended path; takes the lay of the land into consideration.

CONTRABAND means the utilization or possession of negative aspects such as selfish motives, apathetic attitudes, etc.

CONTRACEPTIVE See birth control (methods).

CONTRACT portrays a bona fide agreement one must honor, even if the contract is with oneself in the way of a private resolution.

CONTRACT (on life) portrays an agreement about which one must make a choice. Whose life was the contract on? Yours? And who put the contract out?

CONTRACT LABOR represents paid help/assistance.

CONTRACTOR defines an individual who gains by doing your work. May also point to someone who is capable of materializing your plans.

CONTRADICTION alludes to discrepancies in one's life. This symbol cautions the dreamer to examine self and one's dealings.

CONTRAIL represents a spiritual effect generated by positive perspectives or attitudes.

CONTRAINDICATIONS are the possible negatives one may encounter by a certain behavior or chosen path.

CONTRIBUTION means one's personal input.

CONTROLLING INTEREST signifies the one with the greatest input and having the most to lose.

CONTROL PANEL usually comes in dreams to advise of a need to take control of one's life; displays the fact that the controls are right in front of one.

CONTROL ROOM will point to the source for pulling everything together and making things run smoothly.

CONTROL TOWER refers to a defined source of manipulative behavior.

CONTROVERSY applies to a difference of opinion. This may even imply a self-generated factor whereby an individual's actions don't match expressed attitudes.

CONVALESCENT HOME illustrates a situation or life aspect that will serve as a healing factor.

CONVENIENCE STORE exemplifies a tendency to take shortcuts; quick measures taken.

CONVENT pertains to voluntary spiritual isolation.

CONVENTION CENTER relates to the meeting of like-minded individuals for the purpose of sharing information and learning.

CONVERSATION PIECE symbolizes an aspect that draws attention or curiosity.

CONVERSION CHART (measurements) point to options having equal value.

CONVERT denotes a change in one's belief or attitude.

CONVERTIBLE implies a means of exchange; a life aspect that can be utilized in differing ways or forms.

CONVEYOR BELT signifies a means of communication or delivery.

CONVICT relates to an individual who has done wrong in the past. However, this does not infer that this person is still doing so.

CONVOLUTED (shape) symbolizes a twisted aspect that curls back on itself. This could refer to a thought process or an actual situation or relationship.

CONVOY indicates strong support; strength in numbers.

CONVULSION portrays a violently uncontrollable response; a strong knee-jerk reaction.

COOK (food preparation) connotes the act of planning; in the process of completing something.

COOK (gourmet) See chef.

COOK (person, drugs) points to one who concocts, manufactures negative elements.

COOK (person, food) characterizes one who is capable of giving sustenance to others.

COOK (short-order) See short-order cook.

COOKBOOK denotes the many opportunities and ways that serve to provide the formula to reach goals or help others.

COOKIE (confection) pertains to life's small rewards.

COOKIE (Internet) represents unrequested information or assistance; being bombarded by things we don't want to hear or aren't relevant.

COOKIE (tracking, Internet) reveals that information is being gathered about oneself; an invasion of privacy; your every move being monitored. The only positive aspect of this dreamscape symbol would be if this came as an advisement for self-examination, to take a good look at your own behavior.

COOKIE CUTTER stands for repetitiveness; a lack of variation, usually regarding thought.

COOKIE CUTTER (housing) indicates a desire to surround oneself with like-minded people who share your perspective and attitudes.

COOKIE JAR connotes that which one reaches for; goals and aspirations.

COOKIE SHEET refers to preparations for sharing a specific idea.

COOKING SCHOOL represents a means of becoming aware of the many ways one can help others in life.

COOK-OFF refers to competitive planning.

COOKOUT See barbecue.

COOKWARE See specific utensil.

COOL (temperature) signifies self-control. May indicate nonchalance.

COOLANT will represent as aspect that

serves as a settling-down or calming source for the dreamer.

COOLER is any factor that maintains a state of control or calm.

COOLING RACK comes to suggest a cooling-down period.

COOLING TOWER points to a need to temper one's spiritual zealot behavior.

COON See raccoon.

COONSKIN CAP represents a backward perspective or way of thinking.

COOP See cage.

COOPERATIVE (co-op/food) depicts a mutually beneficial relationship or situation.

COOPERATIVE (housing ownership) signifies a responsibility shared by others.

COORDINATES (map) will represent a goal; often points out that a substitute will not suffice in this case.

COOTIE See lice.

CO-PAYMENT symbolizes a shared expense/responsibility.

COPERNICUS stands for an unshakable faith in one's idea or belief.

COPIES connote multiples of the same thing. This usually denotes an advisement to repeat some positive aspect. May also point out redundancy.

COPILOT characterizes confidence; the supportive reserves that one has.

COPING SAW stands for tools used to plan and carve out one's personally designed path.

COPPER (color) represents intellectual brilliance coupled with an outgoing personality.

COPPER (metal) denotes a choice aspect

for one to utilize for the purpose of communicating something.

COPPERHEAD See viper.

COPPERSMITH characterizes an individual who inherently brings positive influences into the lives of others.

COPPER TUBING denotes a questionable life aspect.

COPPERWARE is a dream symbol that means a warning. The dreamer will understand this by combining surrounding dreamscape fragments.

COPPER WIRE portrays clear communications.

COPSE stands for one's personally inherent attributes that serve to benefit others.

COPULATION implies a temporary joint effort.

COPY relates to a duplicate or imitation.

COPYCAT cautions against imitating others. We can aspire to acquire virtuous qualities but we are each uniquely different and distinctly defined.

COPY EDITOR characterizes one who keeps elements of an issue from contradicting each other; one who keeps things straight, from becoming confusing; a fact-checker.

COPY GIRL signifies an assistant; one who is capable of transmitting communications.

COPYHOLDER represents the one who has the sole right to an idea.

COPY MACHINE denotes an opportunity to emulate another or obtain a personal imitation of something. All opportunities are not meant to equate to positive aspects.

COPYREADER See proofread.

COPYRIGHT points to the originator of something; right to sole ownership.

COPYWRITER can signify an individual who always knows what to say for any situation or it can be associated with exaggerations/enticements.

CORAL symbolizes one's spiritual attributes and/or talents.

CORAL (jewelry) indicates the visibility of one's spirituality; the outward expression of spiritual behavior.

CORALBEAN (tree) indicates the many elements to a complex aspect.

CORAL-BELLS (flower) point to one's blessings.

CORAL FISH stands for spiritual protectiveness; a tendency to guard beliefs from outside influences.

CORAL REEF represents the fragileness of maintaining a spiritual balance within a physical existence.

CORALROOT (flower) denotes the expression of spiritual behavior and the manifestation of their compassionate qualities.

CORAL SNAKE See snake.

CORD See rope.

CORD (electrical) connotes that which conducts energies; the connection between a source of power and the object of receivership.

CORDIAL See alcoholic drink.

CORDLESS pertains to one's inner reserves of energy.

CORDONED alludes to an attempt at protective measures. May also point to an attempt at distancing.

CORDUROY (fabric) implies a rugged personality; accepting of life's tougher experiences.

CORDWOOD defines one's level of preparedness.

CORE signifies a center point; beginnings; most emotionally sensitive or vulnerable aspect; one's most inner feelings. May also point to the bottom line cause or source.

CORE SAMPLE refers to an attempt to discover the cause of something.

CORIANDER signifies aspects unique to one's personality.

CORK (bark) stands for one's multilevel abilities.

CORK (float) pertains to a resilient nature.

CORK (stopper) refers to control; restraint.

CORK BOARD connotes acceptance; a venue of information or display.

CORKSCREW portrays deep involvement; may infer a twisted situation.

CORM refers to storage; preservation.

CORMORANT denotes spiritual nourishment after sorting out truths; generally points to a tendency to accept concepts without discrimination.

CORN typifies a nourishing aspect that comes from within self; a self-generating power source.

CORNBALL signifies uncommon, often criticized, ideas/behavior.

CORN BRAID See cornrow.

CORN BREAD represents nourishment through personal efforts.

CORN CHIP signifies the small benefits/ blessings we gain throughout daily life.

CORNCOB portrays personal effort.

CORNCOB PIPE connotes the reaping of benefits generated through one's personal efforts.

CORNCRIB symbolizes life aspects that serve to preserve the benefits of personal efforts.

CORN DOG pertains to the multiple benefits of one's efforts.

CORNEA stands for inherent or genetically inspired perceptions.

CORNER means a turning point in one's life; a different direction.

CORNERSTONE stands for concepts or beliefs that serve as one's foundation.

CORN-FED relates to inner strength; healthy perspectives.

CORN FIELD signifies an abundance of inner strength.

CORN FLAKES represents strongly motivated beginnings.

CORN FLOUR stands for the benefits of inner strength/fortitude; a natural acceptance and the benefits which grow from it.

CORNFLOWER (botanical) portrays the beauty of one's inner strength that results from self-reliance.

CORNFLOWER BLUE (color) usually signifies a gentleness, a dignity, to one's spirituality.

CORNHUSK refers to additional sources one can apply their talents and efforts through.

CORNHUSK DOLL signifies the end product of one's creative efforts.

CORNHUSKING denotes the actual work of one's personal efforts.

CORNICE symbolizes an elaborate concealment.

CORN KERNEL applies to the great significance of each small effort one makes.

CORNMEAL typifies the versatile benefits of personal effort.

CORN OIL defines the promise of beginning effort.

CORN PONE See corn bread.

CORNROW (hair style) characterizes the beauty of mental efforts applied to organized planning.

CORN SILK connotes the inner healing aspects of personal efforts.

CORN SNAKE denotes misplaced fears; fearing what we don't understand.

CORN STALK exemplifies the strengthening effects of hard work.

CORNSTARCH pertains to the personal enrichment one gains through personal efforts.

CORN SYRUP See sugar.

CORN TASSEL refers to the multiple energies associated with spiritual nourishment.

CORNUCOPIA symbolizes one's inherent spiritual aspects and the wide variety of benefits resulting from the utilization of same.

CORN WHISKEY See mash (drink).

CORONA See aura.

CORONATION defines recognition from higher sources.

CORONER See medical examiner.

CORONET See crown.

CORPORATE IMAGE stands for the type of image one desires to project in respect to appearances/status/behavior.

CORPORATE RESHUFFLE refers to a re-positioning of the main players.

CORPORATION signifies an organized group of individuals associated by a common interest.

CORPSE refers to an aspect in one's life that has no more viability; a dead issue.

CORRAL denotes personally controlled or confined aspects. May indicate a need for some type of containment.

CORRECTION FLUID/TAPE refers to efforts to correct one's mistakes.

CORRELATION symbolizes interconnecting aspects; a relationship between ideas.

CORRESPONDENCE SCHOOL emphasizes learning opportunities.

CORRESPONDENT refers to an individual who communicates with and for others. May indicate a source of information.

CORRESPONDENT (foreign) See foreign correspondent.

CORRIDOR indicates a passageway; the way between stages of life; connecting aspects.

CORROSION stands for the deterioration of something in one's life.

CORRUGATED refers to a time frame consisting of rough roads; difficulties ahead.

CORSAGE pertains to one's inner beauty that others perceive.

CORSET See girdle.

CORTEGE alludes to an individual's personal surround of associates or assistants.

CORTISONE typifies one's inherent aspects that have the capability to heal and restore.

COSIGN signifies an agreement to share responsibility.

COSMETICS denote those superficial

aspects one utilizes to improve appearances. This usually refers to appearances other than physical ones.

COSMETIC SURGERY represents an altered appearance; a changed self-image.

COSMETIC SURGERY SHOW refers to a display of the many ways one can alter oneself.

COSMETOLOGIST See beautician.

COSMETOLOGY (study of) stands for an interest in learning how to make others feel better about themselves, be helpful in raising their self-esteem.

COSMIC DUST represents the constant presence of spiritual forces in our lives, forces we're rarely aware of.

COSMIC NOISE pertains to the sounds within the silence; eternal vibratory frequency activity; subliminal suggestions our consciousness picks up.

COSMIC RAY signifies the intellectual dawning of a profound spiritual truth; epiphany.

COSMOLOGY (study of) connotes an emersion into spiritual aspects.

COSMOPOLITAN (appearance/character) signifies intellectual sophistication pertaining to worldwide cultures; an extensive intellectual base.

COSMOS means the higher spiritual realm.

COSMOS (flower) points to a suggestion to use more of one's goodness in a selfless manner.

CO-SPONSOR characterizes an associate supporter or provider.

COSSACK illustrates one who charges forth to action without having complete information.

CO-STAR pertains to a second individual in the limelight or in a position of centered attention.

COST-CUTTING stands for an attempt to preserve resources/energies.

COST OF LIVING will relate to that of the dreamer and usually refer to the personal cost of actions, thoughts, and motivations.

COSTUME represents characterization. This may indicate one's alter-ego or complete opposite personality. Could reveal one's true character, or attributes one wears as a costume for the public.

COSTUME JEWELRY suggests an alternate way to improve appearances; may also point to a tendency to add extraneous elements to an issue.

COSTUME SHOP stands for opportunities to understand others; choices to experience another's persona.

COT refers to short periods of rest or pauses.

COTILLION (formal ball) cautions against the need to be accepted or recognized in some manner.

COTSWOLD (architecture) represents a laid-back personality, one that reflects level-headedness and quiet logic.

COTTAGE signifies acceptance of self; one who is comfortable with just having basic needs met.

COTTAGE CHEESE implies wholesome perspectives and attitudes.

COTTAGE INDUSTRY means self-sufficiency; an inner contentedness through personal efforts applied.

COTTER PIN symbolizes simple solutions/tools for making connections and securing them.

COTTON connotes an unsophisticated self-image; a lack of expressive ego; a comfortable perspective of oneself.

COTTON BALL/BATTING suggests a softening of one's harsher character/behavioral traits.

COTTON CANDY refers to simple pleasures derived from life.

COTTON GIN pertains to unadulterated attitudes; pure thought.

COTTONMOUTH See water moccasin.

COTTON PICKING applies to the wholesomeness of honest, hard work.

COTTONSEED stands for foundational ideals that generate a positive self-image later in life.

COTTONSEED OIL typifies the richness of a wholesome life coupled with an accepting self-image.

COTTON SWAB denotes a cautious attitude.

COTTONTAIL See rabbit.

COTTONWOOD (tree) exemplifies the beauty of combining wholesome living with spirituality.

COUCH represents physical comfort; restfulness; leisure.

COUCH GRASS See quack grass.

COUCH POTATO cautions against laziness, physical and mental.

COUGAR characterizes the strength of quiet wisdom.

COUGH portrays a fear of disclosure; fear of the truth.

COUGH DROP/SYRUP indicates an aspect that soothes one's fears.

COUNCIL advises of the need to deliberate. This may even infer self-examination.

COUNCILPERSON exemplifies one who researches and decides something.

COUNSELOR stands for one who advises another.

COUNTING (act of) advises of a need to take stock of something; there is imperative reason to count blessings or opportunities.

COUNTDOWN cautions of a need to keep an eye on the time; warns of a situation where time may be running out.

COUNTENANCE relates to facial expressions and what can be read from them. See specific expressions.

COUNTER (response) usually refers to a compromise.

COUNTERATTACK indicates a retaliatory response.

COUNTERBALANCE connotes an action or response that offsets another or serves as a balancing factor.

COUNTERCLOCKWISE illustrates an aspect that goes against the grain; an unexpected event; a reversal; going backward.

COUNTERCULTURE defines something that is considered a turn from the norm; visible expressions of individuality that veer away from those shared by the majority.

COUNTERFEIT defines something misrepresented.

COUNTEROFFER refers to an active negotiation; a time of give and take.

COUNTERPART characterizes a clonelike aspect of something or someone; a complementing factor.

COUNTERPERSON See clerk.

COUNTERSPY See double agent.

COUNTER TOP denotes work convenience.

COUNTERWEIGHT represents an element that gives balance to an issue or situation.

COUNTING SHEEP stands for efforts put into gaining or forcing a relief from daily stress.

COUNTING TO TEN refers to an attempt to gain patience.

COUNTRY (decor) alludes to relaxed attitudes.

COUNTRY (foreign) will have a uniquely specific meaning for each dreamer.

COUNTRY-BRED stands for down-home common sense; a more pointed sense of real priorities.

COUNTRY CLUB represents social and recreational opportunities.

COUNTRY COUSIN advises of the many benefits and strengths that come from being honest and unsophisticated.

COUNTRY-DANCE represents the joys of being unaffected by negative worldly aspects.

COUNTRY FOLK signifies those who have a down-to-earth sense of priorities; knowledge of solid basics.

COUNTRY KITCHEN denotes a large heart; emotional largess.

COUNTRY MUSIC symbolizes one's specific manner of expressing emotions.

COUNTRY MUSIC AWARDS (CMA) refer to the rewards of simple joys.

COUNTRYSIDE stands for the beautiful aspects of innocence and simplicity; unsophisticated attitudes; an honest and down-home personality and perspective.

COUNTRY STORE See general store.

COUNTRYWOMAN characterizes a genteel individual with quiet dignity.

COUNTY pinpoints a specific message for each dreamer.

COUNTY FAIR connotes wholesome pride in one's hard work and the sharing of the resulting products.

COUNTY SEAT will refer to an aspect of legal offices and a specific connection the dreamer has for one of these.

COUP stands for a clever move; a strategic move that has been successfully executed; results from a masterful plan.

COUP DE GRÂCE signifies an aspect that brings about a finality; a fatal blow; an unexpected, shocking move.

COUP D'ÉTAT denotes an overthrow of authority; a revolt of some type.

COUPE (car style) implies a questionable situation; a situation with few exit possibilities.

COUPLING (tool) stands for connecting elements.

COUPON illustrates life aspects that save time, energy, or money.

COUP STICK stands for the resulting benefits of bravery and courage.

COURIER characterizes those who serve as messengers; one bringing a message.

COURSE (golf) See golf course.

COURSE (route) typifies a visual of one's personal path. This most often will refer to that which one is headed for.

COURT represents a venue/option for receiving a conflict resolution.

COURT CLERK characterizes one who keeps track of schedules and appointments. An orderly and efficient individual.

COURT COSTS signify the added costs (financial/emotional) of not being able to personally resolve conflicts.

COURTESY CAR represents benefits which bridge a temporary loss; a suitable temporary alternative.

COURTESY CARD signifies the little amenities in life; small conveniences.

COURTHOUSE refers to legal aspects.

COURT-MARTIAL alludes to an infraction of the set of rules by which one agreed to abide.

COURT ORDER symbolizes an imperative aspect in one's life; a must comply type of directive.

COURT REPORTER warns against repeating falsehoods; cautions one to get the facts right.

COURTROOM connotes an analytic atmosphere; a situation where one attempts to get at the truth.

COURTSHIP stands for a time of persuasion; a period when one tries to impress another.

COURTYARD exemplifies temporary pauses or times of relaxation.

COUSIN characterizes trace association or relationship.

COUSTEAU (Jacques) signifies an in-depth spiritual search.

COUTURE See fashion designer.

COVE portrays spiritual security; one's sense of one's spiritual belief's protective qualities.

COVEN refers to a spiritually related group of people.

COVENANT See agreement.

COVENANT (property) connotes restric-tions devised and upheld by another. Can indicate bounds and restrictions related to one's home aspects.

COVERALLS denote protective measures related to one's work.

COVER CHARGE implies a price for certain benefits enjoyed.

COVER CROP represents an aspect which preserves another; protection measures.

COVERED BRIDGE represents a connecting path that will be safe to travel upon.

COVERED WAGON stands for a path traveled with courage and self-reliance.

COVER GIRL indicates the tendency to believe one needs dramatic attention-getting aspects to be noticed.

COVER LETTER denotes an introduction or synopsis of a more detailed aspect.

COVER STORY pertains to major news or information.

COVER-UP portrays an attempt to hide something.

COW alludes to compassion and the expression of same.

COWARD won't necessarily be a demeaning characteristic but rather will reveal the necessity for gaining greater self-confidence and being less self-deprecating.

COWBANE (botanical) signifies warm social interactions; congeniality; a personable individual.

COWBELL calls for the expression of compassion.

COWBIRD implies a tendency to take advantage of others.

COWBOY/GIRL characterizes the sense of freedom in following one's personal path.

COWBOY/GIRL BOOTS represent precautionary measures taken to insure a reasonably safe course.

COWBOYS AND INDIANS (game) signifies an ongoing conflict (perhaps hidden) between two people of varying opinions/perspectives.

COWCATCHER illustrates an attempt to clear one's way as one's path is traveled.

COW COLLEGE connotes a learning stage that provides for personal growth.

COWFISH stands for spiritual generosity; spiritual largess.

COWHAND See cowboy/girl.

COWHIDE (fabric) applies to the power of compassion.

COWL pertains to protected thoughts; an enigmatic personality.

COWLICK portrays a perspective that is not in line with others one has.

COWORKER characterizes those associated with one's work. This work may be one's spiritual work or a personal situational relationship.

COW PIE refers to the signs of compassion that mark a trail.

COWSLIP (botanical) denotes steady emotions; serenity.

COW TOWN defines an unsophisticated setting or situation which relates best to the simple and down-home elements of life.

COYOTE signifies a preference for solitude. May indicate the trait of slyness.

CRAB denotes a negative personality or situation.

CRAB APPLE alludes to a tart personality; a cantankerous disposition.

CRABGRASS exemplifies a negative aspect that has infiltrated and spread through one's life and is difficult to excise. May point to a bad or irritating habit.

CRABS See sexual disease.

CRACK (attempt) advises one to proceed in spite of doubts or fear of failure.

CRACK (drug) See cocaine.

CRACK (expert) See expert.

CRACK (fissure) indicates an aspect in one's life that has an imperfection; may refer to one's belief system, personal perspectives, or even one's outward presentation.

CRACK (hairline break) reveals the beginning sign of a possible failure; a hint that a problem is developing.

CRACK (mental breakdown) See breakdown.

CRACK (sound) is a means of drawing attention to something the dreamer needs to be aware of.

CRACK (to solve) means a resolution is forthcoming.

CRACK BABY reveals a new plan/path having negative aspects associated with it right from the start.

CRACKER (food) denotes small benefits or considerations.

CRACKER (party favor) signifies inconsequential noise-making; an aspect that may appear serious yet proves to be innocuous.

CRACKER-BARREL connotes informal discussions and the need to continue these.

CRACKERJACK (expert) portrays one who has a talented ability for something specific.

CRACKER JACKS (snack) refer to the formation of an expertly devised, polished plan.

CRACK HOUSE stands for a highly dangerous situation or condition.

CRADLE represents immaturity, often a preferred state for the purpose of avoiding responsibility or culpability.

CRADLE BOARD illustrates a dependency on others.

CRAFT SHOW will reveal the wide variety of creative ways that are available for one to use as one's own unique form of expressiveness.

CRAFTSPEOPLE See artisan.

CRAG exemplifies major chances taken in life; major difficulties marking one's path.

CRAM warns against a tendency to take in too much information too fast.

CRAMP is a symbol that means restrictions.

CRANBERRY symbolizes one's natural talents.

CRANBERRY BOG connotes a nurturing of one's talents.

CRANBERRY SAUCE refers to the actual utilization of one's talents.

CRANE (bird) indicates inquisitiveness.

CRANE (machine) portrays a penchant for learning; continual reaching; extending of self.

CRANK refers to a life aspect that has the capability of providing a beginning or acting as an impetus.

CRANK (drug) See cocaine.

CRANKSHAFT denotes one aspect of several that serve to generate new starts.

CRANKY stands for bad-tempered; unpredictability.

CRANNY reminds us of space left in our lives for something; having an ability to accommodate.

CRAPE MYRTLE (botanical) denotes an even balance between mental and emotional elements; synergy.

CRAPS (dice game) warns against taking slim chances.

CRASH refers to a destructive aspect; serious consequences.

CRASH CART connotes last minute efforts to save some failing aspect in the dreamer's life.

CRASH COURSE advises of an urgent need to learn or understand something more fully. This will indicate a current situation of misunderstanding, assumption, or lack of complete information.

CRASH HELMET advises of a great need to protect one's thoughts. This may indicate the necessity of keeping thoughts to self.

CRASH LANDING depicts a sudden and unexpected conclusion to something that may or may not end up in total devastation.

CRASH PAD exemplifies preparations for the unexpected.

CRASH TEST refers to a need to reinforce one's defenses; may be suggesting that one not be so sensitive and stop taking things personally.

CRASH TRUCK pertains to the immediate action taken after an unexpected failure or great disappointment.

CRATE refers to one's desire to hide specific aspects of self.

CRATER See caldera.

CRAVAT applies to a desire to distinguish self from others.

CRAVE implies an inner weakness of some type.

CRAVEN See coward.

CRAWLING means a slow pace and may not infer a negative intent.

CRAWLSPACE denotes access to something; room for more research *beneath* an issue; the presence of aspects that aren't obvious.

CRAYFISH applies to a voluntary withdrawal from an agreed-upon event or responsibility.

CRAYON indicates an immaturity; undeveloped ideas.

CRAZY See insanity.

CRAZY QUILT (pattern) indicates confusion or may mean that something is comprised of an odd mixture of aspects.

CRAZYWEED stands for a life factor that causes emotional or mental confusion.

CREAKY stands for something that's outmoded or has been ignored for too long.

CREAM (color) represents gentle joy; an inner peacefulness and acceptance of life.

CREAM (dairy) portrays the quality of richness to one's life. This, of course, does not refer to monetary aspects.

CREAM CHEESE illustrates a smoothly consistent and wholesome life aspect.

CREAMER represents a life aspect that has the capability of providing deeper elements to one's life; deeper meaning; greater richness.

CREAMERY symbolizes the dreamer's wholesome aspects that blend to create a richly rewarding life.

CREAM PUFF advises of something in the dreamer's life that's still in excellent condition. This usually comes to bolster feelings of inferiority or counter feelings of inadequacy.

CREAM SODA illustrates a rewarding or beneficial aspect in one's life.

CREASE (in dress pants) denotes level of perfection. Is the crease ironed in or was it caused by wrinkles?

CRÈCHE serves as a reminder of spiritual responsibilities.

CREDENTIALS connotes experiential documentation; level of one's knowledge. This is usually a warning dream symbol that advises the dreamer to check someone's qualifications—even those of self.

CREDENZA symbolizes a superstitious nature; paranoia; a lack of trust.

CREDIT implies an assumption of one's good character; a certain level of confidence.

CREDIT BUREAU represents a record of one's life activities; frequently refers to the Book of Life or one's personal karmic record.

CREDIT CARD relates to a life aspect that allows one to obtain something in advance of one's readiness to reciprocate or pay back. This dreamscape symbol may also refer to the good points on one's karmic record—one's good credits.

CREDIT HOUR indicates learning or knowledge acquired or needed; may also be associated with the acknowledgment of efforts applied to a goal.

CREDIT LINE (of article) See byline.

CREDIT LINE (monetary) indicates the amount of leeway one has before it's time to answer for one's actions. This dream fragment can also refer to one's life span.

CREDITOR usually pertains to those to whom one owes a karmic debt.

CREDIT RATING signifies one's level of

trustworthiness and attention to personal responsibility.

CREDIT REPORT stands for an overview of how well one is managing one's affairs.

CREDIT RISK comes in a dream to reveal the level of one's integrity toward following through with responsibilities.

CREDIT SCORE refers to opinions based on personal perspectives. Usually points to opinionated, class distinction.

CREDIT UNION refers to an opportunity.

CREDITWORTHINESS underscores one's high trust and confidence, or lack of same.

CREED defines one's basic spiritual beliefs. Sometimes, may point to personal perspectives.

CREEK See stream.

CREEL signifies one's personal tools for a spiritual search or involvement; what one spiritually reaps. Was the creel full or empty? What condition was it in?

CREEPY (atmosphere/feeling) comes in a dream to advise one to sharpen awareness; be prepared to face the unexpected.

CREMATORIUM connotes a finality; an aspect conclusion; an absolute closure.

CRÈME DE LA CRÈME stands for the best manifestation of something; highest standard; most desired element.

CREOSOTE signifies a buildup of negative attitudes or perspectives.

CREPE (fabric) suggests a personality whose mental aberrations are easily perceived.

CREPE (pancake) pertains to fragile beginnings.

CREPE PAPER refers to temporary celebrations; short-lived joys.

CRESCENT (moon) See moon (crescent).

CRESCENT (shape) portrays bright beginnings or endings, depending on surrounding dreamscape factors.

CREST See ridge.

CREVICE applies to unexpected situations that make one's life path more difficult.

CREW refers to those who work together on a common project.

CREW CUT (hair style) represents short-sighted thinking/perspectives.

CREWELWORK (needlework) suggests an attention to details.

CRIB (infant) exemplifies immaturity; an inability (or refusal) to face reality.

CRIBBAGE pertains to some aspect in one's life that has been exposed.

CRIB DEATH (SIDS) represents a voluntary withdrawal from reality.

CRICKET (insect) indicates certain emotionally soothing aspects in life; good fortune.

CRIME (witness) See witness.

CRIME SCENE INVESTIGATOR characterizes one who is proficient and experienced at getting to the bottom of things.

CRIMINAL characterizes a law-breaker. This will usually refer to someone the dreamer knows in life.

CRIMINOLOGY (study of) refers to an individual interested in the ways people go wrong and possible reasons why.

CRIMP (tool) symbolizes an attempt to shorten or pinch something into a shorter time frame.

CRIMPED (hair style) refers to uptight perspectives. Can indicate a type A personality.

CRIMSON (color) suggests an old animosity; may refer to suppressed anger or resentment.

CRINGE denotes a personal reaction that may indicate revulsion, fear, disappointment, or dismay.

CRINOLINE (fabric) refers to a stiffness to one's underlying character; resentful acceptance.

CRIOSPHINX characterizes inner strength through belief in convictions.

CRIPPLED defines an impairment that will not halt advancement. May come as an advisement to stop believing one is somehow impaired.

CRISIS means an unexpected disturbing event that one must face and overcome.

CRISIS CENTER signifies a source for immediate help.

CRISIS MANAGEMENT comes to advise of a need to control one's reaction to stressors.

CRISP connotes an aspect that's fresh yet fragile at the same time.

CRISPER (fridge drawer) implies an attempt to preserve something; a desire to keep something new and fresh.

CRISSCROSS relates to a return to some aspect in one's life.

CRITIC characterizes one who has the habit of looking for another's faults; judgmental.

CRITICAL MASS warns of an attitude/behavior which is currently sustaining the momentum of a negative relationship/situation.

CRITIQUE stands for personal assessment; judging through one's personal perspectives.

CROAKING typifies a fear to speak. This usually refers to the voicing of truths that are preferably kept to oneself.

CROCHET (needlework) depicts personal acts done for others.

CROCKERY See earthenware.

CROCODILE connotes underlying negative spiritual aspects or forces.

CROCODILE TEARS characterize the expression of false emotions for the sake of obtaining sympathy or attention; insecurity.

CROCUS marks a change in one's direction or situation.

CROISSANT defines beginnings rich in spiritual factors.

CRONE See wise woman.

CRONIES represent those one is in cahoots with.

CROOKED (shape) denotes distortion which may indicate one's manner of thought process.

CROP (food) symbolizes an aspect of nourishment.

CROP (riding whip) represents impatience.

CROP (trim) portrays an aspect that has been shortened prematurely or one that should never have been altered.

CROP CIRCLE characterizes skepticism in the face of facts.

CROP DUSTING connotes wrong beginnings; applying preventive measures before a determination has been made to see if an issue/idea can strongly develop on its own.

CROPPED (hair style) usually points to individuality in respect to expressing one's unique thoughts/perspectives.

CROP ROTATION indicates a concern for another's welfare; keeping ideas fresh.

CROQUET (game) exemplifies vindictiveness that is hidden behind sophistication.

CROSS (crucifix) See crucifix.

CROSS (making sign of) exposes religious rather than spiritual faith.

CROSS (shape) portrays burdens.

CROSS BAR/BEAM illustrates a supporting aspect.

CROSSBILL (bird) denotes ingenuity.

CROSSBONES denote severe consequences; a deadly idea, attitude, behavior, or relationship.

CROSSBOW alludes to that which leads straight to one's goals.

CROSSBREED See hybrid.

CROSS-COUNTRY symbolizes a long journey traversed along untraveled paths. May indicate a new trail blazed.

CROSSCURRENT connotes conflicting perspectives, usually within self.

CROSS-DRESSING pertains to a desire to share or understand the condition or experiential aspects of another.

CROSS-EXAMINE indicates a need to double-check something; a need to look at something from a different angle.

CROSS-EYED infers a distorted perception.

CROSS FENCING represents the act of keeping issues separate from each other; an attempt to keep individual issues from affecting or contaminating one another.

CROSSFIRE warns of being caught in the middle of a situation or relationship.

CROSS HAIRS advise of a need to readjust or alter one's sights on something.

Suggests that one isn't seeing something quite accurately; one isn't focused on the true target.

CROSSHATCHED (pattern) suggests a well thought out idea; an analytical thought process.

CROSSING (street) indicates an altered direction or change in course.

CROSSING GUARD characterizes protective elements in one's life; someone who cares about the welfare of others.

CROSS-LEGGED stands for insecurities; a reluctance to share aspects of self.

CROSS MATCHING implies an attempt to seek compatibility. This may not refer to the obvious aspect of one's relationship with another but could be indicating the search for belief systems that feel right for self.

CROSSOVER pertains to appropriate crossing points along one's life path.

CROSS-REFERENCE advises of a need to check out some aspects to determine the facts.

CROSSROAD pertains to the time for making a major decision in life. This most often has to do with a change in direction; an opportunity for change.

CROSS SECTION advises of the wisdom of looking within something, usually self.

CROSS-STITCH alludes to precision and the need to give it attention.

CROSSWALK defines the safest route to take in life.

CROSSWAYS warns of a perspective or behavior that is counter-productive; it's more than misaligned, it's almost opposite from the truth of a matter.

CROSSWIND signifies life's unexpected aspects that can blow us off balance.

CROSSWORD PUZZLE denotes miscommunications; trouble communicating.

CROTCH (tree branch) infers a junction in one's path; a fork in the road.

CROUCHING symbolizes insecurities; poor self-image.

CROUPIER characterizes someone who urges another to take chances, or an individual who will benefit or lose by the chances you take.

CROUTON refers to hard choices.

CROW represents clear messages; straight talk; a messenger of the Higher Self.

CROWBAR indicates a forced aspect.

CROWD illustrates wide appeal; an attention-getting aspect.

CROWN warns against egotism or goals of grandeur.

CROWN JEWEL refers to one's greatest desire.

CROWN OF THORNS connotes self-sacrifice; perhaps a masochistic personality.

CROW'S NEST cautions one of the need for a better view of something; wider perspective required; greater wisdom.

CRUCIFIX is an outward sign that marks one's self-sacrifices; a desire to display one's personal pains.

CRUDE OIL refers to an unrefined and often rude personality.

CRUET represents specialized knowledge.

CRUISE (luxury trip) cautions against displaying spiritual affectations.

CRUISE CONTROL advises one to alter the speed by which one's path is taken. This usually refers to the need to slow down; pace oneself.

CRUISE MISSILE warns of the destructive power of uncontrolled thoughts.

CRUISER (cabin) denotes a spiritual journey lacking seriousness.

CRULLER (pastry) portrays an inflated and twisted perspective.

CRUMBLES (confection topping) suggests the importance of the smallest element of an aspect; no element of something going to waste.

CRUMBS pertains to aspects one isn't satisfied with.

CRUSADES imply negative spiritual activism.

CRUST alludes to the harder aspects of life that precede one's smoother and more palatable path.

CRUTCH warns against the use of others as excuses for not taking personal responsibility; a message to stand on your own feet and utilize inner strength.

CRYING pertains to the grief of regret or remorse.

CRYONICS is a strong warning against one's love of self and giving priority to one's physical essence.

CRYPT connotes hidden aspects; secrets.

CRYPTOGRAM defines secret communications; hidden intentions.

CRYPTOGRAPHY (study of) indicates a desire to understand esoteric matters and comprehend life's enigmatic aspects.

CRYSTAL (glassware) implies displayed sophistication; a touch of social arrogance.

CRYSTAL BALL cautions one against impatience to know the future and/or the utilization of unnecessary perceptive tools. May indicate a lack of faith; anxiety.

CRYSTALS (natural) relate to the clarity and depth of one's personal spiritual attunement.

CUBBYHOLE stands for the tendency to segregate people according to personal attitudes and judgments.

CUBE (shape) See square.

CUBICLE (work) suggests a need to keep one's head down and attend to one's own business. This symbol usually appears to dreamer's who tend to get into other people's business.

CUBIC ZIRCONIA denotes a lack of genuineness; an attempt at grandeur through imitation; misrepresentation.

CUBISM (art form) represents a rigid perception.

CUCKOO (bird) signifies manipulation.

CUCKOO CLOCK characterizes an extremely regimented personality; efficiently attentive to details.

CUCUMBER pertains to possible difficulties forthcoming.

CUE BALL refers to a beginning move.

CUE CARD defines an individual who rarely speaks for self.

CUE STICK alludes to the level of precision; a beginning move is made.

CUFF (end of shirt) refers to that which protects one's mobility and tenacity.

CUFF LINK represents an arrogance toward one's work.

CUL-DE-SAC connotes a need to backtrack; reverse one's path; nowhere to go but back the way one came.

CULL warns against a tendency to choose only the best of something.

CULT exemplifies a group of individuals who have specific beliefs that are considered aberrant or dangerous. This symbol usually comes as a warning message regarding some associates of the dreamer.

CULTIVATE defines a nurturing personality or life aspect.

CULTURAL CENTER refers to opportunities to learn more about others.

CULTURAL EXCHANGE signifies an attempt to understand those who we perceive as being different from ourselves.

CULTURED PEARL See pearl (cultured).

CULTURE SHOCK represents a need to return to reality and have the acceptance or inner strength to face problems.

CULVERT denotes the direction and manner in which one utilizes personal spiritual gifts.

CUNEIFORM (shape) alludes to an opening up aspect or result.

CUP symbolizes one's personal perspective on the quality and quantity of one's life situation. Was the cup decorated? What was it made of? Was it filled or empty? With what?

CUPBOARD represents personal life aspects that nourish one.

CUPCAKE signifies the generous giving of self.

CUPID characterizes love.

CUPOLA denotes mental extensions of thought that typify the activity of an analytic mind.

CURARE warns against continual states of stress; a need to relax.

CURATOR defines an individual who is devoted to the protection and preservation of intellectual pursuits and values.

CURB advises of a need to curb some aspect in the dreamer's life; a caution against excesses. This usually points to some type of negative behavior.

CURB SERVICE denotes convenience.

CURD connotes rich rewards and nourishment through self-effort.

CURDLE implies changes that may go bad.

CURE alludes to some type of healing or it may refer to the preservation of something.

CURE (harden/set) refers to the temporary state of fragility before something is finalized.

CURE-ALL warns of a misplaced belief/faith in something; equates to a false panacea.

CURETTE refers to a life aspect that has the capability to remove a negative factor from one's life.

CURFEW cautions against a prolonged activity; a time for everything; time management.

CURIE (Marie) characterizes the application of intelligence; the instigating force behind discovery.

CURIO exemplifies a life aspect that is of high interest to the dreamer.

CURIO CABINET denotes a collection of high interest issues. May indicate life puzzlements.

CURIO SHOP signifies a source providing many puzzling or interesting elements.

CURL (hair) pertains to an analytic thought process.

CURLER connotes one's attempt to figure something out.

CURLEW (bird) points to complex thought.

CURLICUE (design) suggests a flamboyant characteristic; extraneous flourish.

CURLING IRON cautions against forcing conclusions; making attempts to understand complicated or high-minded concepts.

CURLING STONE represents a weighty element that has been slid into an issue.

CURRANT refers to the little nourishing aspects that are abundant in our lives.

CURRENCY See money.

CURRENT (electrical flow) relates directly to one's personal energy circuitry and may be referring to physical, emotional, or mental energy.

CURRENT (present time) indicates the present and most often is an advisory message given for the purpose of bringing the dreamer back to the here-and-now.

CURRENT (water flow) portrays the rate of speed one travels along the spiritual path. This will clarify if it is too fast and dangerous or if there is a drag factor.

CURRICULUM will most often identify specific learning areas on which one should be focusing.

CURRYCOMB connotes the attention and control given to one's wilder aspects.

CURRY POWDER refers to a particular slant used to spice something up.

CURSE (spell) See spell.

CURSOR stands for a reminder for one to keep focused; stay aware and mentally attentive remain in the moment.

CURTAIN means privacy; the time separating daily activities; may refer to denials or secrecy.

CURTAIN CALL denotes appreciation for one's shared talents.

CURTSY See bow (greeting).

CURVE (shape) connotes a gentile veering of course.

CURVE BALL warns against having expectations; events or happenings that don't turn out as expected.

CUSHION denotes an aspect that softens or eases.

CUSP symbolizes crossroads or turning points in one's life.

CUSPIDOR See spittoon.

CUSS See swear (cuss).

CUSTARD alludes to the richly nourishing inner rewards of applying one's spirituality.

CUSTER (George) characterizes the karmic results of bigotry and racism.

CUSTODIAL RIGHTS refers to something one is solely responsible for.

CUSTODIAN pertains to individuals who are designated with the authority to be the Keepers, the Preservers of spiritual truths.

CUSTOM connotes traditionally accepted practices.

CUSTOM-BUILT indicates personalized attitudes; perception based on one's specialized database of knowledge.

CUSTOMER denotes one who has a right to receive service.

CUSTOMER SERVICE DESK implies a life aspect from which one can receive assistance or information.

CUSTOMS (border) exemplifies a check time in one's life; a point in time when one needs to inspect paths and the manner they are traveled.

CUT refers to the act of severing something.

CUT-AND-DRIED means having no questions about; an aspect that is clear and factual.

CUTAWAY (clothing style) denotes openness; nothing to hide; forthright.

CUTBACK advises one to ease up on something; lessen the amount of energy spent on an issue.

CUTESY (behavior) may simply equate to a lighthearted playfulness or it can point to a serious personality affectation.

CUT FLOWER See bouquet (flower).

CUT GLASS signifies a finely faceted aspect in one's life.

CUTLASS See sword.

CUTLERY refers to sharpness, acuteness.

CUTOFF (limit) denotes the need to detach self from a harmful element.

CUT-OFFS (clothing style) refer to the preservation of a partially worn but still useable aspect.

CUTOUT (die) See die cut (model).

CUTOUT (paper) represents an element in one's life that needs to be cut out or stopped.

CUT-RATE will normally equate to a good deal.

CUTTHROAT warns of a vicious personality; having no scruples.

CUTTING BOARD refers to an attempt to be precise when excising something from one's life, behavior, or plans.

CUTTING ROOM reveals selective perspectives or presentations; issues which one's personal viewpoint make subjective; lacking objectivity.

CUTTLEBONE advises of a need to sharpen one's speech for the purpose of bringing clarity.

CYANIDE stands for the dangerous ramifications of making financial gain a priority.

CYBER CAFÉ stands for an information-friendly atmosphere; opportunity for discovery.

CYBER CRIME refers to stealthy wrong-doing; negative behavior without witnesses; anonymous underhandedness.

CYBERSPACE verifies the idea that there is no true emptiness in life, that even the spaces are full. This dreamscape symbol comes to remind us that undreamed possibilities can, one day, change our entire preconceived concept of what reality consists of.

CYBER-SPEAK points to appropriate language/communications for specific subjects or issues.

CYBORG characterizes the natural blend of spirituality and physics that create reality.

CYCLAMEN (botanical) suggests a gentle, yet loyal personality trait; a stand-up quality.

CYCLONE See tornado.

CYCLOPS (Greek mythology) pertains to the lost aspects of reality; skepticism toward those ideas which one perceives as being far-reaching.

CYLINDRICAL (object) connotes a message for the dreamer. What color was it? Did it contain any writings?

CYMBALS are attention-getters; a call to listen; an advisement to be watchful and aware.

CYNIC defines a distrustful personality; skepticism. May point to a hopeless attitude.

CYPRESS (tree) stands for grief; a mourning time.

CYST denotes the presence of a destructive negative aspect that has taken hold. This may be a negative spiritual concept, a negative idea or attitude, or a harmful emotion.

CZECHOSLOVAKIA suggests strong traditions and a personal sense of noble heritage.

D

DABBLE represents a lack of seriousness. May indicate part-time interest in something.

DACHSHUND (dog breed) implies a caution against the tendency to make the physical aspects a priority; a high interest in materialism.

DADDY See father.

DADDY LONGLEGS refers to fears that are overcome; unwarranted fears and anxieties.

DAFFODIL portrays the bright prospects of new beginnings.

DAGGER signifies harmful aspects in one's life. Frequently this symbol indicates an associate or someone the dreamer knows.

DAGGER FERN See Christmas fern.

DAGUERREOTYPE advises of a special current meaning for past relationships; importance of old friends.

DAHLIA refers to opportunity.

DAILY DOUBLE represents a situation that has the capability of bringing multiple rewards or disappointments.

DAINTINESS (mannerism) suggests fragile sensitivities; a need to get one's hands dirty or toughen up.

DAIQUIRI See alcoholic beverage.

DAIRY alludes to nourishment.

DAIRY FARM refers to a major aspect of one's life serving as a source to nourish the perspectives of self and others.

DAISY illustrates happiness; a joyous attitude toward life.

DAISY CHAIN symbolizes exuberance.

DALMATIAN (dog breed) signifies a traveling companion; a friend having a protective nature.

DAM always means some type of spiritual block. Some aspect of one's spiritual belief or behavior is being held back.

DAMAGE CONTROL refers to the need to counter a negative.

DAMAGE DEPOSIT symbolizes the recognition of possibilities.

DAMASK (fabric) exemplifies a rich and full experience.

DAMASK ROSE suggests a dignified, genteel nature.

DAMP indicates the presence of an additional aspect to something in the dreamer's life.

DAMPER stands for a life factor that can be utilized to increase or decrease one's understanding, depending on how it is used.

DAMSELFISH suggests a deeply seated protective nature toward one's spirituality.

DANCE refers to a personal manner of expressing emotions.

DANCE CARD suggests opportunities for interaction. Recall if the card had only a few names on it or if it was full. Recalling specific names will hold meaning for the dreamer.

DANCE HALL pertains to an emotional outlet.

DANCE INSTRUCTOR characterizes those who have the capability to bring out another's emotions or self-expression.

DANCE WEAR connotes an outward desire to express one's emotions.

DANDELION means benefits that are not readily seen or realized.

DANDER (pet) pertains a friend's irritations that bring about mental or physical reactions.

DANDRUFF implies a need to shed misconceptions.

DANDY (appearance) warns against a preoccupation with one's appearance.

DANGER of any kind clearly means just that. The surrounding dreamscape elements will help to pinpoint the source.

DANISH (pastry) refers to a benefit that manifests almost immediately after a decision is made.

DAPPLED (pattern) signifies an attitude or perspective that is not consistent.

DARE refers to intimidations; challenges.

DAREDEVIL portrays an attitude of overconfidence; a disregard for obvious high risks; a tempt of fate.

DARK suggests something that is difficult to perceive; may refer to negativity; obscure or enigmatic.

DARK AGES (setting) See Middle Ages.

DARK HORSE alludes to an individual or situation that surprisingly overcame low expectations.

DARKROOM denotes a life aspect that has the capability of reversing negative factors in one's life.

DARNING NEEDLE symbolizes an opportunity to repair or make amends.

DART signifies events that we allow to impede our progress.

DART BOARD advises to continually vent negative emotions in a positive and nonharmful manner.

DARTH VADER characterizes an individual who misuses spirituality; may clearly refer to a spiritually dark individual.

DARWIN (Charles) alludes to evolution. This does not refer to biological aspects but rather emotional, perceptual, mental, or spiritual.

DASHBOARD pertains to protective measures.

DATA relates to information the dreamer needs.

DATABASE stands for one's personal scope of attained knowledge or information. This will not refer to the comprehension of same.

DATA PROCESSOR connotes the utilization of information, how one uses what one knows.

DATE (food) denotes versatility.

DATE (point in time) comes in dreams to pinpoint an important time frame for the dreamer.

DATE (time reservation) marks a need to give attention to an activity or meeting.

DATE BOOK represents a reminder for important scheduled events in one's life.

DATELINE pertains to time or place of origination; the source of something.

DATURA (plant) illustrates a life aspect that alters one's perspectives, reactions, or comprehension.

DAUGHTER characterizes a younger female individual toward whom one has a protective and nurturing relationship in life.

DAVENPORT See couch.

DAVY JONES'S LOCKER warns of a spiritual fatality; a spiritual path that is leading into dangerous ground.

DAWN indicates the light of new beginnings.

DAY (time) implies the time of light, activity, or progression.

DAY BED suggests the importance of pause times during one's day.

DAYBOOK advises of a need to be more time-efficient and attentive to one's responsibilities.

DAYBREAK See dawn.

DAY CAMP refers to the reservation of a portion of one's day for relaxation and mental rest.

DAY CARE alludes to the manner in which our routine responsibilities are managed.

DAYDREAM pertains to personal, private thoughts, often expressing unrealistic scenarios or desires. This may point to a veering from reality; escapism. On the other hand, this symbol can also refer to one's mental probing for possibilities existing outside the box.

DAY-GLO (colors) will come as attention-getting markers. Recall what was colored in such an outstanding way.

DAY JOB indicates one's source of sustenance, yet may not point to one's goal or source of satisfying benefits.

DAYLIGHT-SAVING TIME denotes an attempt to alter reality.

DAY LILY (botanical) denotes emotional sensitivity.

DAY ROOM signifies a pause from one's routine or regimentation.

DAYSTAR See morning star.

DAZED connotes a nonreceptive state of mind; unclear thought.

DAZZLED warns against being blinded by amazement; cautions against perceptual abnormalities; affected by seemingly spectacular aspects.

DEACON characterizes an individual who has been spiritually helpful in one's life.

DEAD means lifeless; an absolute conclusion; a final closing.

DEAD AIR indicates an interruption in communication or thought.

DEAD-AIR SPACE exemplifies a lack of fresh ideas; stale concepts or a stage of intellectual neutrality. May also point to some type of insular element.

DEADBEAT warns against personal apathy; emotionally unaffected.

DEAD BOLT implies attention to security. This may infer protection from others in respect to the exposure of one's hidden activities, thoughts, or perceptions; a desire to keep an aspect of one's life secure.

DEAD DROP refers to secrets; extremely private communications.

DEAD DUCK pertains to certain failure; death.

DEAD END (sign) See road signs.

DEADEYE denotes an expert level of attainment; one who always knows exactly what one is doing.

DEADFALL stands for unappreciated or unrecognized life aspects that serve to nourish. Points to positive aspects resulting from a seemingly negative event.

DEAD HEAT warns against obsessive competition.

DEAD HORSE stands for an advisement to accept an issue, leave it, and go forward; an aspect in one's life that can't be changed by putting more energy into it.

DEAD LETTER advises of failed communication attempts.

DEADLINE reminds us of the passing of time; may warn that time is running out. Often this symbol refers to the time restrictions one places on self.

DEADLOCK means an impasse; a no-win situation, plan, or relationship.

DEADLY NIGHTSHADE See belladonna.

DEADPAN (expression/response) portrays an individual who is expressionless; one who does not show emotion.

DEAD RINGER suggests a need to remember whatever has been presented as a double; this may also represent a déjà vu incidence.

DEAD SPOT connotes a mental block or lack of communication.

DEAD WEIGHT cautions of a need to unload the negative aspects one carries around that slow down or prevent advancement or growth.

DEADWOOD warns of a tendency to hold onto the negative emotional effects of past events; a need for closure.

DEAF usually refers to self-denial or a willful avoidance of the truth.

DEAL (distribute) means active sharing of something.

DEAL (transaction) refers to a specific condition or event in the dreamer's life.

DEAL-BREAKER points to asking too much in a negotiation; needing a more equitable compromise.

DEALER (card) refers to a questionable source; one who may be expert enough to manipulate outcomes.

DEALER (merchandise) characterizes one who is the source of something; one who can supply something to others.

DEALERSHIP connotes a specialized source; an outlet supplying the individualized needs of others.

DEAN characterizes intellectual authority or counsel.

DEAN'S LIST denotes intellectual accomplishments.

DEAR JOHN (letter) reveals a desire to end a relationship.

DEATH stands for termination; finality. May not specifically point to a physical death.

DEATHBED alludes to an approaching end or conclusion to something.

DEATH BENEFIT relates to life aspects associated with a finalization of something; aspects that result from a conclusion.

DEATHBLOW signifies a devastating event in one's life.

DEATH CERTIFICATE refers to proof that something is finalized and no further activity is possible.

DEATH DUTY See inheritance tax.

DEATH HOUSE See death row.

DEATH MASK may forewarn of an actual physical death but most often it relates to an extremely dangerous situation or relationship that has the strong potential to have devastating ramifications or conclusions if continued.

DEATH PENALTY means no opportunity for a second chance; no way out.

DEATH RATTLE forewarns one of approaching finality; a need to prepare for the worst.

DEATH ROW relates to the realization that one cannot hide or run from making retributions.

DEATH SENTENCE reveals a bad decision or intended behavioral move.

DEATHTRAP warns of an extremely dangerous life situation.

DEATH VALLEY pertains to a long-suffering stage in one's life.

DEATH WARRANT applies to a life aspect that will seal one's fate in an extremely negative manner. Who was signing the death warrant? Was it yourself?

DEATHWATCH symbolizes an irreversible situation that is heading toward devastation.

DEATH WISH warns against fatalism; self-destructive perspectives or actions.

DEBATE advises one to listen to the perspectives of others, not for the purpose of changing your mind, but to come to a greater understanding of another's point of view.

DEBAUCHERY warns against a tendency to focus on the physical aspects of life, especially the sensual pleasures.

DEBIT points to a deficiency in some area. Surrounding dreamscape elements will help to clarify the intent here.

DEBIT CARD refers to an easy access into debt. This may not be indicating finances but be pointing to some other type of indebtedness.

DEBONAIR (appearance) suggests an exterior presentation of classiness which may not be a true representation of oneself.

DEBONING KNIFE denotes an aspect in one's life that could remove one's support system; perhaps an attitude or decision.

DÉBRIDEMENT advises of a need to go into something and clean it up, excise the damaged elements. This would relate to a situation left unattended too long.

DEBRIEFING alludes to the wisdom of conducting frequent mental self-examinations. We learn from ourselves when we spend time double-checking our motives, responses, perspectives, and actions.

DEBRIS signifies a need to clean up the remaining aspects of past actions.

DEBT most often refers to a nonfinancial aspect in one's life. However, it can still relate to actual monetary conditions.

DEBT CONSOLIDATION represents an active interest and attempt to repay all debts; a desire to make retribution.

DEBT COUNSELING indicates an interest in getting assistance and advice for repaying one's debts. This may be pointing to life aspects other than financial.

DEBUT refers to the time to introduce something; time to bring something out into the open. This usually points to an attitude or some type of underlying conflict that has been brewing.

DEBUTANTE warns against the need for attention or to be recognized; also warns against making one's class or social position in life a priority.

DECAFFEINATED implies a lessening of one's motivation, energy, or interest.

DECAL may advise the dreamer to pay attention to what the dream decal represented as a personal message or it may indicate the dreamer's personal attitude about something. A decal symbol signifies the public expression of an attitude.

DECAPITATION warns of a situation where one figuratively loses one's head over something. This symbol calls for an immediate return to logic and reason.

DECATHLON represents the extent to which one goes for the purpose of accomplishing a goal.

DECAY illustrates a decomposing situation, relationship, or perspective; a rotten element that is long past having positive or productive capabilities.

DECELERATION refers to a slowing down action. May come as an actual advisement.

DECEMBER stands for a time of renewal and reflection.

DECENTRALIZATION calls for an admonition to stop being too focused, causing a myopic perspective. This dream symbol advises one to view things with a more opened eye, bringing a wider scope of information.

DECEPTION is a warning symbol. The word is self-explanatory. There is some type of deceiving going on in your life. The real clue here is: Who is doing it? Oneself?

DECIDUOUS defines an atmosphere of change, the inevitability of such; a changeable situation.

DECIMAL POINT symbolizes value.

DECISION denotes the need to give serious thought to something; time to stop vacillating or procrastinating.

DECK (boat) connotes deeper spiritual perspectives.

DECK (cards) implies game-playing in connection with one's interaction with others.

DECK (pack of drugs) cautions against the utilization of negative or altering aspects to accomplish something.

DECK (platform) represents improved perspectives; a better vantage point.

DECK CHAIR alludes to an acceptance of improved perspectives.

DECK HAND characterizes one who assists in bringing about one's spiritually enlightened perceptions.

DECK SHOES denote a self-styled spiritual insulation; a voluntary separation from spiritual issues or concepts.

DECODE(R) means comprehension; clarity of understanding.

DECOMPOSITION See decay.

DECOMPRESSION CHAMBER warns against the tendency to speed through high spiritual concepts without taking the time to thoroughly comprehend them; a fast spiritual retreat.

DECONGESTANT pertains to a need to clear emotional congestion within self.

DECOR See accessory (home decor).

DECORATE (act of) relates to special preparations. What is being decorated? How is it being done? With what type of items?

DECORATION DAY See Memorial Day.

DECOUPAGE exemplifies the addition of specialized aspects to something. May point to an overplay or overdone glossing of facts.

DECOY connotes imitation or diversion

in one's life. Could be pointing to ulterior motives and personal agendas.

DECREE signifies an authoritative statement; an order or advisement.

DECREPIT alludes to time-worn and will most often refer to the mental state of defeat or lost motivation.

DEDICATED LINE represents putting one's energy into a single goal/purpose.

DEDICATION symbolizes an expression of respect and honor.

DEED will underscore one's right to something.

DEEP implies a considerable distance and will be associated with surrounding dreamscape elements.

DEEP-DISH illustrates an aspect in one's life that took some doing to create.

DEEP FREEZER stands for a life aspect that has been set aside. Did the dreamscape reveal what was in the freezer?

DEEP FRYER connotes serious trouble.

DEEP POCKETS represent a current status of considerable wealth. This symbol may not point to financial aspects. It could refer to a wealth of knowledge, information, blessings, talents, etc.

DEEP-ROOTED refers to an attitude or perspective that has been held for a long while.

DEEP-SEA portrays higher spiritual philosophy.

DEEP-SIX exemplifies a total rejection of something due to spiritual beliefs.

DEEP SPACE stands for great extensions of thought; contemplation of philosophical possibilities; the serious consideration of the far reaches of physics; thinking outside the box.

DEEP WATER implies an in-depth spiritual search or path.

DEER applies to a tendency to be cautious; watchful; aware.

DEER FLY refers to the biting aspects in life that can cause temporary irritations if one isn't watchful and aware.

DEERSKIN connotes some type of attachment to nature.

DEFACE warns against vindictiveness; uncontrolled anger or retaliation.

DEFAME warns against gossip or maliciousness; advises forgiveness and closure.

DEFAULT stands for a life aspect one has failed to follow through with. Could indicate a falling back to old ways.

DEFEAT may apply to a winning situation or a losing one, depending on other aspects of the dream. Either way, it reminds one to act the same way—accepting without the expression of pride or jealousy.

DEFECTIVE illustrates a flawed aspect in one's life. Surrounding dreamscape factors will usually clarify this for the dreamer.

DEFENDANT most often characterizes an individual who has a need to explain self.

DEFENSE MECHANISM stands for psychological methods utilized to protect oneself from guilt, low self-esteem, conflict, shame, or other personally injurious feelings.

DEFERMENT suggests a postponement or permanent release from responsibility. In some cases, this symbol will point to procrastination.

DEFIBRILLATOR warns against stress and refers to a positive life aspect that will help one to accomplish this.

DEFICIENCY DISEASE See specific disease.

DEFICIT indicates an inadequate aspect in one's life. The dreamer will usually know what this aspect is.

DEFICIT SPENDING points to overwork; possibly putting the cart before the horse.

DEFINITION spelled out in a dream will clearly come as an important personal message for the dreamer. Pay close attention to these.

DEFLATION relates to a loss of motivation or a need to go back and begin something over again. May also advise of a need to place less importance on something.

DEFLECTOR corresponds with one's protective measures.

DEFOGGER advises of a need to improve perspectives.

DEFOLIANT See agent orange; preemergent treatment.

DEFORMITY (human physical) denotes an opportunity for growth.

DEFRAUD reveals ulterior motives; ill-gotten gains or method of achieving a goal.

DEFROCK cautions against doing something that isn't aligned with one's high ideals.

DEFROCKED signifies an attitude/perspective/behavior that's counter to one's professed belief.

DEFROST advises of a call to be less rigid; attain or express more understanding, compassion, or tolerance.

DEFUSE depicts a need to halt further progression toward an explosive situation, relationship, or belief.

DEGREASE exemplifies an action that caused friction.

DEHUMIDIFIER signifies a life aspect that is devoid of any associated spirituality; the act of removing spiritual aspects from a selected portion of one's life.

DEHYDRATION (of body) usually points to a spiritual need.

DEHYDRATION (of food) indicates foresight; preservation of blessings.

DÉJÀ VU pertains to the manifestation of past precognitive or dream experiences; a repeat experience.

DELAWARE signifies individualism; liberty.

DELAYED will usually be presented in a dream to remind us that timing is important and delays are sometimes for the best.

DELEGATE characterizes a representative individual; one who reflects a certain perspective, attitude, or belief system.

DELETE (computer command) reveals one's capability or option to rid self of something. Usually surrounding dreamscape elements will clarify what this is pointing to.

DELETION suggests a missing or removed aspect in one's life.

DELFT/DELFT BLUE (pottery type/color) stands for a fragile yet cherished attitude toward one's heritage.

DELICATESSEN portrays ethnic karmic connections.

DELIRIUM suggests a loss of all control.

DELIVERY PEOPLE pertain to one's delivery or presentation to others in life; may also indicate a forthcoming message or event.

DELIVERY ROOM See birthing center.

DELPHINIUM See larkspur.

DELTA (shape) See triangle.

DELTA (shoreline configuration) relates to the discarded elements of one's spiritual search.

DELUGE See flood.

DELUSION comes to reveal a false belief; perhaps an instance of fooling oneself or creating a false belief so as not to be forced to face a reality.

DEMENTIA See insanity.

DEMERIT connotes negative behavior or karmic debt.

DEMITASSE (cup) pertains to the need for a small portion of motivation or energy to get one back on track. Suggests one needs nothing more than a little push.

DEMO (music) refers to a sampling of one's perspective, how one's life song is sung; a taste of one's attitude.

DEMOCRACY implies a relationship, situation, or condition that benefits everyone; a tendency to focus concerns on the disadvantaged and middle class; empathy.

DEMOCRAT See left wing.

DEMOGRAPHICS advises of the wisdom of knowing those with whom one associates; having background information on an issue.

DEMOLITION denotes the absolute destruction of something. Who was doing the demolition? What was being demolished?

DEMOLITION CREW characterizes the life aspect (or those associated with it) that brings about a destruction of something in the dreamer's life.

DEMOLITION DERBY usually represents congenial, lighthearted competition, yet may also signify a destructive type depending on the related dream elements.

DEMOLITION EXPERT will point to someone who is experienced in ways to eliminate something. This is a dreamscape symbol that has the duality of positive and negative interpretations. Demolishing a negative element would be a positive symbol. Demolishing a positive aspect would be a negative one. Recall what the demolition expert was proficient in destroying.

DEMON will always characterize any aspect that plagues one's life or mind. Normally a negative connotation would be associated with a demon; however, someone who is a procrastinator could be plagued by the subconscious nagging of the urgings to get moving.

DEMONSTRATION is a symbol that usually brings a visually explanatory message for the dreamer. It may show how to accomplish something.

DEMOTION advises of a need to watch one's arrogance of heightened perception of self-worth. This dreamscape element will come to cut down an overblown perception.

DEMULCENT will refer to a soothing aspect that may be needed in one's life.

DEN (animal) refers to our natural instincts; gut feelings; intuitiveness.

DEN (room) symbolizes the quality and frequency of one's personal enrichment or restorative time.

DENALI (mountain) represents strength and power of the spirit.

DENIM (fabric) alludes to long-lasting; an aspect that endures.

DENIZEN See inhabitant.

DENMARK symbolizes a tolerance/acceptance for another's unique individuality.

DEN MOTHER characterizes a woman in one's life who is nurturing of many others.

DENOUNCE corresponds to an open condemnation, denial, or accusation.

DENSE exemplifies thick or compact. This is usually meant to advise one to clear out or give air to some life aspect.

DENT connotes a life aspect or action that has made a small difference or effect on something.

DENTAL EXAM advises a closer look at one's manner of speech; perhaps a less harsh manner is indicated.

DENTAL FLOSS warns against making innuendos or voicing assumptions.

DENTAL HYGIENIST characterizes an individual in one's life who continues to remind or guide others away from making assumptions.

DENTAL TECHNICIAN portrays one who helps others to express themselves appropriately.

DENTIFRICE See toothpaste.

DENTIST represents one who works to help others articulate their thoughts.

DENTISTRY (study of) indicates a desire to help others express themselves.

DENTURE denotes a new manner of beautiful speech. This would also include the voicing of new, enlightening perspectives.

DEODORANT implies a cover-up; or an attempt to avoid offending another.

DEPARTMENT STORE connotes an aspect that offers a variety of opportunities.

DEPENDENT pertains to anyone who looks to another for support.

DEPILATORY alludes to an aspect or agent that has the capability of drastically negating another's thoughts or perspectives.

DEPORTATION refers to the permanent physical removal of someone from one's life.

DEPORTMENT will usually reveal one's inner emotional or psychological state.

DEPOSIT (initial payment) marks firm intentions.

DEPOSIT (money account) portrays asset accumulation. This will refer to finances unless silver was deposited.

DEPOSIT (security) pertains to some type of assurance given; a promise; an insuring factor.

DEPOT reflects a directional or course change.

DEPRECIATION advises of something that has reached a state of lessening value.

DEPRESSION (economic) forewarns of a need to watch finances.

DEPRESSION (low point in path) indicates a low point or an aspect that has sunk below the normal level.

DEPRESSION (mental) warns against a perception of hopelessness or loss of acceptance.

DEPRESSURIZE advises of a need to reduce personal pressures and stress levels.

DEPRIVATION may indicate a need to live without something or it may refer to something one is willfully leaving out of life.

DEPROGRAMMING is a strong advisement to counteract some negative aspect in one's life.

DEPTH CHARGE stands for a negative life aspect that will destroy one's spiritual foundation.

DEPTH FINDER indicates the depth of one's spirituality.

DEPTH PERCEPTION denotes analytic ability; capable of extensive reasoning and logical thought; unless the depth perception was shallow.

DEPTH SOUNDER See depth finder.

DEPUTY characterizes one's chosen assistant or associate.

DERAILMENT pertains to going off track in life. May point to an attitude or a recent perceptual leaning regarding an issue.

DERBY (hat) suggests out-dated ideas; old fashioned.

DERBY (race) denotes a competitive personality or aspect.

DERELICT (person) characterizes a need to be motivated, usually through a new perspective of self-worth.

DERELICT (remiss) warns against neglecting responsibilities.

DERMABRASION See exfoliant (skin).

DERMATITIS stands for life's irritating aspects; annoyances that get under the skin.

DERMATOLOGY (study of) characterizes those who are interested in understanding the hows, whys, and cures of other people's reactions to certain life factors. This could also indicate a psychologist, psychiatrist, or some type of counselor.

DERRICK represents valuable resources, particularly material ones.

DERRINGER exemplifies a source of hidden power.

DESCENDING (directional motion) implies a downward or lowering move and could refer to several aspects in one's life, depending on surrounding associative symbols.

DESCRAMBLER (electronic device) symbolizes an inherent ability to understand others; a natural capacity for seeing psychological ploys of others.

DESECRATION signifies spiritual disrespect or apathy.

DESEGREGATION represents an integration of perceptions, attitudes, or concepts; usually this is an advisory message.

DESENSITIZED warns of apathy or emotional indifference; insensitivity; hardened heart.

DESERT (forsake) See abandon.

DESERT (hot, sandy region) connotes a life stage or condition whereby one needs a reserve of strength and perseverance.

DESERTED (devoid of human habitation) stands for a call for self-reliance and ingenuity.

DESIGN (pattern) portrays an array of specific meanings for each dreamer. For generalized interpretations, refer to the name of specific pattern types.

DESIGNATED DRIVER means a person of responsibility. May refer to an individual who is leading others.

DESIGNER characterizes an individual who creates specific situations or conditions in one's life. Could be a cautionary reminder that you're letting someone else design your path or perspectives.

DESIGNER DRUG warns against using self-styled crutches in life.

DESIGNER SHOES caution against walking a path designed or initiated by another. Each person needs to be their own path stylist.

DESK denotes type, quantity, and quality of work being done. This usually applies to individualized efforts given to a life path or advancement.

DESK PAD suggests care/attention given to one's work.

DESKTOP PUBLISHING portrays personalized construction of one's precisely delivered communications.

DESPAIR illustrates a lack of faith or acceptance.

DESPERADO specifically refers to one reacting to a desperate condition or situation.

DESSERT means the ingestion of something sweet after a meal. This is different from eating a sweet anytime. In this context, dessert refers to the rewards received in life for one's efforts applied to one's path; a rewarding benefit from the ingestion of new information or thought spent on an idea or problem.

DESSERT SPOON relates to special rewards.

DESTINY exemplifies life aspects that cannot be altered.

DESTITUTION indicates a complete lack of basic foundations.

DESTROYER (ship) warns of a life aspect that has the capability of destroying one's spirituality.

DESTRUCTION typifies any life aspect that causes great harm. What was destroyed? Who did the damage?

DETAIL PERSON (pharmaceutical) warns of an individual who would attempt to convince others of utilizing their specific resource of help. There are *many* options.

DETAINEE defines one held against one's will. This may refer to any number of aspects, even self-confinement; denial.

DETECTIVE characterizes one who has a high interest in understanding the facts and the sequential process of development.

DETENTION CENTER/HOME signifies a situational condition that is confining; restrictions or self-denial due to efforts to correct a certain behavior.

DETERGENT advises of a need to clean something in one's life. This will usually refer to one's outward presentation to others, the affectations used for public display.

DETERRENT points the way to avoid an undesirable situation.

DETONATE comes as an extreme warning that some aspect in one's life has reached an explosive stage.

DETOUR will usually come as an advisement that one needs to take a side track off the main path in order to learn something important. It reminds us that one-mindedness can be a detriment if we're not fluidly open enough to recognize when elements along the way are important enough to spend time on.

DETOXIFY advises of a great need to get rid of personally damaging or harmful aspects that are associated with one's life.

DEUCE (devil) pertains to a situation that characterizes a perfect example of something bad; epitomizes the worst of something.

DEUCE (wild card) refers to unexpected options and/or outcomes; the existence of many possibilities.

DEVELOPER (chemical) represents a life aspect that has the ability to bring something to completion; capable of bringing through the sequential stages leading to conclusion; turning a negative into a positive.

DEVELOPER (land) typifies misuse of one's resources.

DEVIL characterizes an individual or life aspect that is extremely negative and personally harmful.

DEVIL'S ADVOCATE illustrates self-examination. This means that there is a reason in one's life to examine motives or attitudes.

DEVIL'S-FOOD CAKE connotes rewards or joys one feels unworthy of receiving or enjoying; unjustified guilt.

DEVOTEE characterizes an unrealistic and fanatical attraction to something. This is a warning message.

DEW symbolizes a light spiritual touch.

DEWCLAW connotes an extraneous aspect. This may refer to an attitude, belief, or emotion that is unnecessary for one to hold onto.

DEW POINT refers to the stage in one's life where spiritual factors begin to be integrated into daily living.

DEWY-EYED suggests sentimentality; may indicate a naivety.

DIABETES alludes to an imbalance in one's life.

DIABLO See devil.

DIADEM See crown.

DIAGNOSIS points to the specific cause of something.

DIAGNOSTICIAN refers to an individual who has the capability and knowledge to help others pinpoint the source of their problems.

DIAGONAL (direction/pattern) connotes an attitude, perspective, or path that is slanted.

DIAGRAM advises of the need for clarification before comprehension is attained.

DIAL portrays an indication of level or quantity. This may refer to several aspects and will be clarified by surrounding dreamscape facets.

DIAL (sun) See sundial.

DIAL TONE advises of nonresponsiveness from another; one's attempts at communication falling on deaf ears.

DIALYSIS implies a need for certain aspects of one's life to be separated from others.

DIAMOND exemplifies perfection. Was the dream diamond truly perfect? Did it have color instead of being perfectly white and clear?

DIAMONDBACK RATTLESNAKE See snake.

DIAMOND IN THE ROUGH alludes to hidden quality and value.

DIAMOND MINE depicts a source of wealth, usually not in reference to monetary aspects.

DIAMOND RING suggests a desire for a perfect relationship.

DIANA (Lady Diana Spencer) See Princess Diana.

DIANA (Roman mythology) characterizes women's wisdom; moonlight and its bright symbology of knowledge.

DIAPER exemplifies an effort to control something in one's life.

DIAPER RASH refers to a life element causing irritation. May also point to a need to get moving, get motivated.

DIAPHANOUS (fabric/essence) suggests a delicate life aspect.

DIARRHEA defines an aspect in one's life that is difficult to control.

DIARY connotes personal life accounts; importance of remembering.

DIATRIBE implies the act of routine complaining. May indicate excessive verbiage.

DICE (cut into small cubes) denotes a need to break down ideas so the components can be easily digested or understood.

DICE (game pieces) pertain to changeability; the many probabilities for each outcome.

DICHOTOMY signifies opposing attitudes regarding one idea; a seeming contradiction.

DICKENS (Charles) portrays old-fashioned morals that are still viable.

DICKINSON (Emily) characterizes the beauty of heartfelt expressions.

DICTATOR pinpoints a manipulative personality.

DICTIONARY illustrates a need to clarify misunderstandings or misconceptions. Was a specific entry word highlighted?

DIE See death.

DIE CUT (model) stands for the original from which replicas are formed. This symbol warns against a desire or tendency to imitate others. A die may also indicate a situation that cannot be altered.

DIENER (lab assistant) characterizes an individual who has the capability and knowledge to properly clean up the remaining aspects of a concluded situation or condition.

DIE-OFF comes to remind us to accept the natural order of life.

DIESEL FUEL represents a source of energy/motivation which produces negative ramifications.

DIET usually advises of a need to shed excessive aspects in one's life. This may refer to attitudes, beliefs, negative emotions, superficial elements, etc.

DIETETIC (foods/drinks) represent aspects that assist one in getting rid of the excessive or harmful facets of self.

DIET FAD stands for the current popular ideology.

DIETICIAN characterizes a person in one's life who has the knowledge to assist in bringing about a healthful state. This may also include mental health.

DIFFUSER connotes a lessening of intensity; an aspect that serves to disperse effects rather than condense them; a softening element.

DIGGING (act of) denotes a search; a deeper search. May also point to the act of trying to hide something depending on whether something was being put into the ground or being taken out.

DIGIT See toe; specific finger.

DIGITAL ENHANCEMENT reveals aspects of an individual/issue/element which have been added for the purpose of making the subject more appealing.

DIGITALIS refers to an aspect that will ease heart trouble; usually implies emotional pain.

DIGITAL PHOTOGRAPHY sheds a pall of skepticism over what is seen; things may not be as true as presented.

DIGITAL WATCH suggests a precise time; no question regarding what time it is in respect to one's path. Also, this time presentation may have a specific meaning for the dreamer.

DIGNITARY is associated with individuals specific to the dreamer who are perceived as highly respected.

DIGRESSION warns of not staying mentally focused; a tendency to easily get off track.

DIKE See dam.

DILAPIDATED portrays a well-worn aspect that may still be viable.

DILATED (pupils) suggests a need to see more clearly.

DILEMMA illustrates the presence of a problematical situation that is difficult to resolve; extremely difficult decision.

DILL implies an added aspect to something.

DILL PICKLE connotes a slight problem entering one's life.

DILUTE means a softened or lessened situation.

DIM advises of a situation that lacks clarity or sharp definition.

DIME represents basic needs; life necessities.

DIME BAG stands for a cheap form of temporary escapism.

DIME NOVEL alludes to unnecessary information; intellectual waste of time.

DIME STORE See variety store.

DIMMER SWITCH may advise one to tone down an attitude of anxiety or excitement or it may suggest adding energy and light to something in the dreamer's life.

DIMPLE (skin) indicates individuality.

DINER (eatery) represents commonly used aspects of nourishment that are recognized and utilized by many. This nourishment may be emotional or psychological.

DINER (person) characterizes one who is in the process of nourishing self. This will usually refer to some type of personal nourishment other than physical.

DINETTE SET connotes informal or common aspects that are used to nourish one.

DINGBAT (symbol) portrays an opportunity for self-expression.

DINGHY applies to small spiritual securities; the spiritual comforts we fall back on in life.

DINING CAR corresponds with a need to attend to inner nourishment while attending to one's life journey; a reminder to not be so centered on purpose that energizing aspects are ignored.

DINING ROOM usually typifies a more concentrated and enjoyable manner of being nourished. Surrounding details will clarify which life aspect is being fed.

DINNER connotes one's main source of nourishment.

DINNER DANCE suggests both the joyful and nourishing benefits of a healthful aspect.

DINNER JACKET See tuxedo.

DINNERWARE portrays one's personal perspective toward nourishing oneself.

DINOSAUR exemplifies outdated concepts; primitive thought.

DIORAMA pertains to a visual example of something; a touchable and completely comprehensible presentation.

DIP (depression) suggests a temporary diversion from the norm.

DIP (food) connotes a personal choice.

DIPHTHERIA symbolizes the potential vulnerability of one's emotional state.

DIPLOMA alludes to presumed knowledge or an acquired stage of same.

DIPLOMAT characterizes an individual who is tactful.

DIPLOMATIC IMMUNITY pertains to special benefits for those who use tactful methods of communication.

DIPLOMATIC POUCH stands for private and privileged information.

DIPSTICK (oil) will usually represent an advisement that one's emotional state is about to experience friction from situational stress and one needs to reinforce one's defenses by increasing acceptance and/or tolerance.

DIRECT CURRENT (DC) warns against perceiving only one option or opportunity.

DIRECT DEPOSIT signifies the quickest way to receive a return on one's efforts.

DIRECT LIGHTING will point to a specific life element that's highlighted to attract one's attention to it.

DIRECT MAIL/MARKETING connotes a sales pitch from someone. This may not refer to an actual purchase but could pertain to a situation where convincing will be attempted.

DIRECTOR characterizes the act of controlling; manipulating.

DIRECTORY advises of a need to contact someone.

DIRECTORY ASSISTANCE suggests communication made possible through a middle person or intermediary.

DIRGE portrays the possibility of a great sorrow coming; precedes the end of something.

DIRIGIBLE (balloon) comes to reveal unstable or irrational thinking.

DIRNDL connotes simplicity.

DIRT may indicate hard work or it might refer to an unclean or marred aspect; surrounding details will clarify this intent.

DIRT BIKE implies an attempt to speed over life's rougher roads.

DIRT FARMER stands for perseverance; great efforts.

DIRT-POOR may not refer to a monetary connotation but rather emotional and spiritual riches that are somehow lacking.

DIRT ROAD applies to personally chosen paths in life which present a few additional obstacles and take greater energy to traverse than the paved roads.

DIRTY usually means inattentiveness or lack of morals, ethics.

DIRTY BOMB refers to ulterior motives; an agenda that would negatively affect the most people.

DIRTY LINEN denotes misdeeds and the hidden facts of same.

DIRTY OLD MAN warns against growth that never makes a priority of spirituality; a life immersed in physical gratifications.

DIRTY POOL exemplifies a lack of scruples; underhandedness.

DIRTY VEHICLE advises of a need to cleanse an aspect of self.

DISABILITY INSURANCE represents preplanning/provisions made regarding the insuring of one's continuing path progression in the event of a misstep/mishap.

DISABLED (mechanical/electrical) means

something that's impaired or not functional. Most often this infers that it has been purposely compromised.

DISABLED (person) refers to tenacity; inner strength.

DISADVANTAGED applies to a lack of a basic need or quality.

DISAGREEMENT connotes conflict. May even be within self.

DISAPPEARANCE illustrates an unexpected loss or departure.

DISAPPOINTMENT warns against having expectations.

DISARM refers to an action that neutralizes a negative aspect.

DISASSEMBLE usually signifies a need to look at the parts of an issue, idea, or situation. It may also refer to a confused state of mind that's scattered.

DISASTER (AREA) implies a devastating event or great emotional distress.

DISAVOW stands for a disclaimer of responsibility or prior knowledge; repudiation.

DISBAND means a separation from associates.

DISBURSEMENT indicates the sharing of one's talents; the expending of personal efforts to aid others.

DISCARD connotes the act of getting rid of an unusable aspect; a rejection.

DISCARNATE refers to a hidden life aspect or something the dreamer isn't seeing.

DISC BRAKE illustrates pressure applied for the purpose of slowing or halting further progression.

DISCIPLE characterizes an advocate; a devoted supporter.

DISC JOCKEY represents the spreading or acceptance of selected ideas.

DISCLAIMER points to an effort to avoid culpability/responsibility.

DISCLOSURE STATEMENT stands for honesty; a chance to recognize/reveal any known negatives related to an issue.

DISCO (dance/music) suggests a personal joy or blessing that is unique to the individual.

DISCOLORED signifies an emotion altered by an outside factor.

DISCONNECTED (electrical plug) warns of mental aberrations or scattered thought process.

DISCONNECTED (phone) refers to a severance of communication; no longer a flow of communication.

DISCONTINUED denotes a termination; no longer participating in an action.

DISCOUNT (disregard) means a choice to not believe or accept something.

DISCOUNT (reduce) represents an opportunity to chose a different path leading to the same end.

DISCOVERY signifies a perceptual discernment.

DISCOVERY CHANNEL denotes the opportunity for expanding one's knowledge base and proves that it's more accessible than one formerly thought.

DISCREPANCY connotes an inconsistency; a question of credibility.

DISCRIMINATION usually points to intolerance; a lack of acceptance.

DISCUS THROWER characterizes a competitive nature.

DISEASE exemplifies a state lacking well-being. This may indicate a mental, physical, or spiritual aspect. See specific disease.

DISEMBARK portrays a grounded condition or state.

DISEMBODY See discarnate.

DISENGAGE alludes to an act of releasing something; a break from a life aspect.

DISFIGURED pertains to a specialized life purpose.

DISGUISE warns of hypocrisy and may reveal one's true nature or intention.

DISH refers to a presentation of something. What was on the dish? What color was it? Its condition?

DISH ANTENNA See satellite dish.

DISHARMONIOUS (sound) portrays a vibrational misalignment.

DISHCLOTH implies the clarity of something presented. Will usually mean that a cleaning-up is advised.

DISHEVELED stands for priorities placed on higher aspects, such as intellectual pursuit or spirituality; an attitude that doesn't focus on appearances.

DISHONORABLE DISCHARGE advises of grave admonishments from one's Higher Self.

DISHPAN pertains to one's habit of communicating clearly. May also signify a need to clean up loose ends.

DISHPAN HANDS indicate concerned efforts to communicate well or one who is almost obsessive about tying up loose ends.

DISHWASHER infers a tendency to let others clean up after oneself.

DISHWATER denotes helpful aspects one utilizes to ensure clear communication.

DISINFECTANT advises of a need to maintain efforts toward countering negative aspects that could contaminate one's mental, emotional, or spiritual well-being.

DISINFORMATION connotes the act of willfully misleading others.

DISINHERIT warns against the voluntary decision to leave nothing behind. We should all make some difference through our existence.

DISINTEGRATION defines absolute finality.

DISJOINTED stands for a lack of continuity.

DISK (computer program) See computer program.

DISK (computer/writable) signifies an easy way to make a permanent record of something.

DISK (computer/re-writable) denotes saved information that can be altered or improved; an easy way to work with an ongoing project or situation.

DISK (shape) relates to extended paths or issues that will never be truly resolved.

DISLOCATION connotes a conceptual or emotional lack of alignment.

DISMAL SWAMP warns of a mental or emotional state of self-generated hopelessness.

DISMANTLE may indicate a need to take something apart and give it a closer look or it may warn of behavior which will tear a situation/relationship apart.

DISMISSAL may stand for the shedding of a particular element of an issue or it can point to denial/lack of acceptance.

DISMOUNT refers to a return to congeniality; warns against arrogance.

DISNEYESQUE (atmosphere) warns of an overly optimistic viewpoint.

DISNEYFICATION reveals a tendency to put an unrealistic spin on situations.

DISNEYLAND warns against unrealistic perceptions or goals.

DISOBEDIENCE will usually point to an expression of one's individuality.

DISORDERLY CONDUCT like the symbol of civil disobedience, it can refer to one's right to express objections, or it can come as an advisement to get a better handle on one's behavior.

DISORGANIZED calls for a need to get one's life in order; set priorities; take one thing at a time. May refer to one's thoughts.

DISORIENTATION advises of one's lack of direction or place; confusion.

DISPATCHER characterizes one's Higher Self.

DISPENSARY See pharmacy.

DISPENSATION comes as a grave warning for those who believe they are above the law.

DISPENSER indicates a life aspect that provides opportunities.

DISPLACED HOMEMAKER stands for an inability to make new beginnings or adjust to a new situation.

DISPLAY applies to the act of visual communication; showing something to others. What was displayed? Was it old or new?

DISPOSAL (garbage) advises of the wisdom of completely letting go of a closure's residual aspects.

DISPROPORTIONATE means unbalanced; perceptual irregularity.

DISQUALIFY means an aspect eliminated from one's life; ejected; excluded. May point to an attitude or perception that isn't relevant. Could even refer to an individual who isn't qualified to participate in a situation.

DISROBE alludes to a removal of all extraneous aspects of self; honesty, the real self.

DISSECT signifies the act of or need to thoroughly analyze or examine something in one's life. As an opposing interpretation, this symbol can also point to a need to stop dissecting everything in one's life.

DISSENT stands for an objection or disagreement and one's right to express it.

DISSERTATION See thesis.

DISSIDENT characterizes a disagreeing activist; one who strongly opposes an idea or perception.

DISSOLVE denotes a changed or terminated life aspect.

DISTEMPER refers to excessive irritability; impatience; lack of acceptance.

DISTILLERY is in reference to condensing conceptual ideas down to the basic facts or components; simplification.

DISTORTION depicts a perspective made unclear by slanted personal attitudes.

DISTRACTION emphasizes the fact that the dreamer is allowing diversions to interfere with advancement or focusing attention on one's purpose.

DISTRESS SALE points to the ongoing value of imperfections. Comes in a dream to caution against discounting the value of something just because it's not in mint or brand-new condition.

DISTRESS SIGNAL is always a call for help. The dreamer may be calling for this help or one's Higher Self may be attempting to awaken the dreamer to this end.

DISTRIBUTOR (engine) represents proportionate utilization of one's energies.

DISTRIBUTOR (person/outlet) symbolizes a specialized source.

DISTRICT ATTORNEY characterizes one's Higher Self; one's conscience.

DISTRICT OF COLUMBIA suggests a need for awareness; one's conscience.

DITCH warns of an off-course direction and marks a potential danger.

DITTY BAG denotes emergency measures of preparedness.

DIURETIC implies a life aspect that will aid one in ridding self of negatives.

DIVA points to a woman who excels in her specialty and is usually admired for such attainment.

DIVAN See couch.

DIVE signifies a head-long plunge into something.

DIVE (into water) pertains to a plunging into spiritual concepts.

DIVE (through air) refers to plunging through thoughts; not taking the time to analyze quickly formed opinions; impulsive judgments.

DIVE-BOMB portrays an obsession with a specific goal or target.

DIVERGENCE means a veering from one's normal or customary character, attitude, or path.

DIVERSION cautions one to remain focused.

DIVIDEND pertains to benefits gained from energy expended.

DIVIDER See partition.

DIVINE ESSENCE characterizes the idea of the Supreme Being and comes in dreams to either commend or advise.

DIVING BELL alludes to a fear of losing one's grounded aspects during a spiritual search.

DIVING BOARD relates to a spiritual search that needs a motivational impetus.

DIVING SUIT implies spiritual insulation.

DIVINING ROD See dowsing rod.

DIVISION (math sign) indicates a reduction of something into lesser aspects. Surrounding dream symbols will clarify this for the dreamer.

DIVORCE applies to a clear separation of self from some formerly associative factor.

DIVORCE CERTIFICATE points to proof that one has severed a relationship or perspective.

DIZZY stands for confusion; lack of balance or comprehension. May refer to a hectic (dizzying) pace taken through something.

DNA indicates individualism; a one-of-a-kind uniqueness.

DNA MARKER refers to a specific element of one's personality or perception.

DNA TEST reminds us to keep doing self-exams for defective or harmful attitudes.

DOBERMAN PINSCHER (dog breed) connotes a friend or associate who represents a law-abiding factor in one's life.

DOCENT See tour guide.

DOCK See pier.

DOCKET See date book.

DOCTOR characterizes those in one's life

who are capable of bringing about healing aspects. For specific type of healing aspect, see specific ailment or disease.

DOCTOR JEKYLL (and Mr. Hyde) characterizes an individual's hidden aspects; the duality of an inner, true self and one's outward appearance. Also see Jekyll and Hyde.

DOCTRINE represents a principle; a belief system.

DOCUMENT (paper) signifies something recorded or official.

DOCUMENT (verify) pertains to proof of something; a validation.

DODGEM CARS See bumper car.

DODO (bird) connotes ignorance; a fear of knowledge and the responsibility that attends it.

DOE stands for a source for perpetuating innocence.

DOG always refers to one's friends and close associates. See specific breed.

DOGBANE (botanical) represents the value of special relationships; friendship.

DOG BED signifies one's closest friend(s); the people the dreamer is in bed with—not literally, of course.

DOG BISCUIT refers to the many small joys (treats) of a friendship.

DOG BONE usually signifies a conflict with a friend or close associate; a bone to pick with a friend.

DOG BRUSH will reveal a tendency (or need) to alter the course of a friend's opinion or perspective.

DOGCATCHER cautions against the manipulations of one's friends. May warn of a situation where one has captured a friend's loyalty. Friends need to be free or they're not really friends.

DOG CHEW exemplifies a trusting friend; being able to have someone to talk to; loyalty.

DOG COLLAR warns against forced friendships or relationships; possessiveness.

DOG DAYS symbolize a lack of motivation; inaction; failing friendship.

DOG-EARED (page) relates to information one should take note of.

DOGFIGHT portrays a serious conflict between friends.

DOGGIE BAG denotes the nourishing benefits of friends.

DOGHOUSE represents personal trouble with a friend.

DOG LEASH warns against an overbearing attitude toward friends; points to a manipulative and domineering attitude taken with friends.

DOG PADDLE (swim style) alludes to a spiritual search accompanied by friends.

DOGSLED signifies a spiritual path that follows that of a friend.

DOG TAG (animal's) represents one's strong ties to friends. May point to a cautionary message revealing a necessity to check the loyalty of friends. Once suspicion is confirmed, the *reason* for such lessening in loyalty needs to be identified.

DOG TAG (military) denotes a friend's allegiance to another.

DOG WALKER suggests more attention given to friends.

DOGWOOD (tree) typifies beautiful friendship beginnings.

DOILY refers to protective elements in one's life.

DO-IT-YOURSELF (book/project) means

self-reliance/sufficiency. Points to something one must accomplish alone.

DOLDRUMS warn of a lack of motivation; a slump period; a call to draw on reserves.

DOLL characterizes a message to re-evaluate relationship motives.

DOLLAR See money.

DOLLAR SIGN defines some type of beneficial effect. May also indicate a cost or expense for the dreamer. Surrounding dreamscape elements will clarify this.

DOLL-FACE indicates a presentation of innocence but is rarely a truism.

DOLLHOUSE is a message to return to reality.

DOLLY (wheeled tool) represents a life aspect that serves as a support of help; a life factor that eases our way.

DOLPHIN reflects spiritual companionship.

DOMAIN NAME stands for one's ultimate identity uniqueness; that which separates one from all others.

DOMAIN SQUATTER will reveal an individual who collects and hoards what others want/need, then sells at exorbitant prices.

DOME (shape) denotes balance; a well-rounded perspective.

DOMESTIC DISTURBANCE reveals a problem with a relationship.

DOMESTIC DIVA/GOD will indicate an individual who is skilled at efficiently keeping the foundational aspects of one's life in order.

DOMINO stands for one aspect of a questionable situation.

DONALD DUCK (character) indicates poor planning; one who always seems to have one's plans foiled.

DONATION signifies an offering; thoughtfulness; generosity. Recall what was donated; money would refer to finances; clothing would point to giving goodness; wigs would mean the sharing of one's thoughts; etc.

DONKEY emphasizes independence, perhaps stubbornness.

DONOR (blood) typifies a compassionate individual who freely gives of self.

DONOR (organ) reveals a generous heart; someone willing to freely give of self. See transplant (specific organ).

DONOR CARD (organ) verifies one's generous heart and goodness.

DON QUIXOTE characterizes an unrealistic optimism; a fear of facing negatives or accepting bad endings.

DONUT See doughnut.

DOODLING may be representative of unconscious thoughts or may indicate a warning against idleness.

DOOMSAYER won't normally equate to pessimism or fearful perceptions, rather this symbol will appear as an attention-getting messenger for the dreamer advising of a destructive course.

DOOMSDAY CLOCK will usually be directly associated with the dreamer rather than an overall worldly intent. It refers to the amount of time until a major event happens in one's life. Something is on a fatal course. What time was shown on the clock?

DOOR indicates a life factor that one must experience or pass through to achieve advancement or progression along one's path.

DOORBELL comes as an attention-getting symbol that calls one to an important experience or opportunity.

DOORKEEPER characterizes an individual who must be communicated with before an opportunity can be taken advantage of.

DOORKNOB refers to access to advancement or opportunity.

DOORMAN characterizes one who is ready to open doors for the dreamer as long as the dreamer is deserving or well-prepared.

DOORMAT may indicate a respect for and appreciation of opportunities or it may warn against a poor self-image. Surrounding dreamscape details will clarify this meaning.

DOOR PRIZE indicates extra benefits gained by taking opportunities.

DOORSTEP points to steps or aspects leading to new opportunities.

DOORSTOP comes to suggest we keep doors open.

DOPE See narcotic.

DOPPELGANGER warns against imaginary or self-created fears.

DOPPLER RADAR (weather) will on rare occasions be associated with climate changes but most often refers to the mood of a situation or relationship.

DORMANT refers to underlying emotions or attitudes which affect behavior.

DORMER signifies an acute conscious awareness.

DORMITORY pertains to a subconscious fear of being alone.

DOSAGE points to a proper amount of something.

DOSSIER typifies extensive "background" information.

DOT (pattern) See polka dots.

DOT-COM COMPANY See web retailer.

DOTING warns against an overbearing, smothering behavior.

DOTTED LINE suggests a need for an agreement; indicates a time to own up to an attitude or participation in something.

DOTTED SWISS (fabric/pattern) suggests uniformity; equality.

DOUBLE AGENT characterizes hypocrisy or willful deception.

DOUBLE-BARRELED symbolizes twofold aspects to an issue; one element serving two purposes.

DOUBLE BILLING refers to exaggerations of claiming multiple efforts expended which were only performed once.

DOUBLE BOILER indicates increased mental activity. Depending on surrounding dreamscape factors, this may refer to boiling emotions or situations.

DOUBLE BOOKED is usually a call to slow down, schedule is too full.

DOUBLE CHIN signifies melancholia; self-pity.

DOUBLE-CROSS warns of a betrayal; ulterior motives; personal agenda.

DOUBLE-DEALING reveals duplicity.

DOUBLE-DECKER means twice the amount of something.

DOUBLE DIPPING denotes the questionable act of receiving two benefits generated by the same source.

DOUBLE DUTY represents the multiple uses brought about by a single effort.

DOUBLE-EDGED signifies an aspect which has two interpretations or purposes.

DOUBLE-EDGED SWORD See sword (double-edged).

DOUBLE EXPOSURE stands for an unclear picture, the mixing of issues.

DOUBLE-FACED (two-faced) pinpoints a betrayer or hypocrite.

DOUBLE FEATURE advises of two important facets to one aspect.

DOUBLE-HEADER connotes an event, relationship, or situation that will generate two major benefits.

DOUBLE HELIX defines the living components of reality. This symbol will come as an advisement to attend to priorities.

DOUBLE-JOINTED advises against being impulsive or hasty.

DOUBLE-PANE (window) indicates a filtering or insulating process being done in regard to one's perspectives.

DOUBLE-PARKED advises against being impulsive or hasty.

DOUBLE-SIZED refers to twice the amount of something.

DOUBLE-SPACED is a call to slow down and understand more; clarity is needed.

DOUBLE STAR See binary star.

DOUBLE TAKE advises of the need for a second look at something.

DOUBLE TALK warns against making excuses. May indicate a tendency to talk in circles, going around the main issue; verbal avoidance.

DOUBLE TIME indicates a need to make up for lost time.

DOUBLE VISION usually defines heightened perception.

DOUBLOON will refer to something of extreme value.

DOUBTING THOMAS signifies skepticism. May point to a lack of faith; needing proof of everything.

DOUGH emphasizes the beginnings of specific aspects coming together; a period that precedes ultimate physical manifestation.

DOUGHNUT pertains to idle time.

DOUGLAS FIR (tree/wood) indicates one's cherished convictions or philosophy.

DOVE defines a peaceful nature or condition.

DOVECOTE typifies a contentment with self and surroundings.

DOVETAIL stands for a harmonious relationship.

DOWAGER implies riches gained through wisdom. These riches are not necessarily financial.

DOWAGER'S HUMP portrays a life filled with extensive intellectual pursuits and great personal efforts applied to obtaining wisdom.

DOWEL suggests a connective aspect.

DOWN (direction) represents a return to the basics; a fundamental level.

DOWNBURST See microburst.

DOWN CARD represents a questionable, unknown element which could be either a benefit or a detriment; a risk.

DOWN DRAFT applies to a decline in one's mental or emotional state.

DOWNGRADE pertains to a lowering of value or condition.

DOWNHILL may refer to a worsening condition or it may refer to a less stressful or problematical phase where one can coast for a time. Surrounding dreamscape facets will clarify which meaning is intended.

D

DOWNHILL RACER (skiing) signifies an apathetic approach to spiritual issues.

DOWN-HOME (atmosphere/behavior) equates to honest character; simple, straightforward expressiveness without any trace of ulterior motives or agendas.

DOWNLINK symbolizes inspiration; insights received from one's Higher Self or from a Universal Consciousness.

DOWNLOAD implies the gaining of information from another.

DOWN PAYMENT denotes proof of intent; good intentions.

DOWNPOUR (rain) suggests an influx of incoming information, usually relating to spiritual or ethical aspects.

DOWNSHIFT advises of a need to slow one's pace.

DOWNSIZE cautions one to lessen the scope of something. This could refer to goals, expectations, impressions, area of study, etc.

DOWN SLOPE (wind current) denotes little energies expended on thought. May point to a situation where heavy thought isn't required.

DOWN SPOUT reminds us to utilize all aspects of spirituality in our daily lives.

DOWNSTAGE points to an issue or element in one's life which requires attention; an up-front aspect needing to be more closely looked at.

DOWNSTAIRS represents a ground-floor or lower level element which must be experienced or covered before upward advancement can be achieved.

DOWNSTREAM suggests we review our spiritual beliefs. This usually comes because of a need to thoroughly understand our spiritual foundations before searching deeper or further.

DOWNTIME usually is a call to rest. This is a cautionary message for one who is working or searching too intently.

DOWNTOWN indicates the center or foundational basis of something. This symbol may be advising of a need to return to one's center.

DOWNTREND equates to waning interest.

DOWNWIND connotes a tendency to follow the crowd or general attitude.

DOWNY (texture) naturally means a softness of some type. Depending on the related dream elements, this could be referring to a soft personality such as emotional sensitivity or having a tendency to give others a great measure of leeway, or it could be an advisement to toughen up.

DOWRY designates bought aspects. This could refer to friendships, benefits, favors, employment, loyalty, etc.

DOWSER characterizes one who utilizes spiritual gifts.

DOWSING ROD applies to a spiritual talent or opportunity.

DOZE illustrates a restful pause, often needed to refresh self. This could also come as an advisement to stay more aware.

DRACULA characterizes an infatuation with the overdramatized negative aspects of power. May reveal a draining or tedious type of personality.

DRACULA CAPE warns of delving into the dark side of esoteric aspects.

DRAFT (air) represents an interference

in one's life. May signify a specific thought that keeps returning.

DRAFT (conscription) warns of a forced attendance or attitude; coerced loyalty.

DRAFT (drawn liquid) implies one's act of drawing on inner reserves of energy; fortitude.

DRAFT (money) refers to solid intentions.

DRAFT (outline) connotes beginning plans.

DRAFT (pulling) signifies hard work; great efforts expended.

DRAFTING BOARD advises one to sketch out plans. This would represent a certain need to do this before any actual action is taken.

DRAG (clothing) generally refers to one's desire to understand another by walking in his/her shoes (dressing alike) or it could be suggesting an outward cover-up of one's true character.

DRAG (pull along) may refer to perseverance or it may warn against a tendency to brood or complain about one's problems.

DRAG (pulling force) pertains to hampering factors that impede one's progress.

DRAG (race) connotes dangerous competition; a fearsome competitor.

DRAG (weighted implement) signifies the act of smoothing out; passing through life and leaving a smoother trail for those who follow the same path.

DRAGNET warns against spiritual gullibility; arbitrarily collecting and absorbing *every* aspect found in the spiritual pool.

DRAGON characterizes one's self-generated fears.

DRAGONFLY denotes a strong, positive spiritual force or aspect.

DRAG STRIP indicates a fast lane or a detrimental path where one lines up with vicious competitors.

DRAIN (empty) warns of an energy- or emotionally depleting aspect.

DRAINAGE DITCH represents the containment or channeling of excess elements.

DRAIN BOARD (dishes) refers to an element which funnels unnecessary aspects away from the main issue.

DRAINPIPE symbolizes a need to discard spiritual excesses or unnecessary aspects from one's life.

DRAMA QUEEN See histrionics.

DRAMATIZATION is usually a message for the dreamer. Take note of any symbolism acted out in the dreamscape drama.

DRAPERY See curtain.

DRAW See sketch.

DRAW (select) pertains to choices in life. May point to the fact that some things just happen in life and aren't connected to karma or luck.

DRAWBRIDGE alludes to self-generated barriers and their selective use.

DRAWER stands for organization.

DRAWING connotes creative expression of inner aspects.

DRAWING BOARD suggests plans, planning; perhaps a need to refigure something.

DRAWKNIFE represents personal efforts applied to something.

DRAWL alludes to a communication hesitancy.

DRAWSTRING typifies personal choices and the presence of leeway in respect to how one follows up on those choices.

DREADLOCKS indicate intellectual analyzation. The quality and accuracy of that analyzation depends on the condition of the locks.

DREAM (hope) implies strong aspirations or optimism.

DREAM (imagine) connotes wishful thinking.

DREAM ANALYSIS symbolizes an attempt to understand the clues, messages, and insights our subconscious or Higher Self holds.

DREAMBOAT equates to one's idea of a perfect, most desirable element, issue, or goal.

DREAM BOOK signifies a source holding the keys to understanding and demystifying one's subconscious messages.

DREAM-CATCHER signifies a desire to be shielded from the cause of one's fears. This isn't necessarily a good sign because fears need to be faced and dealt with in order for them to stop being fears.

DREAM DICTIONARY stands for an opportunity to better understand oneself and one's life situations/relationships.

DREAMER may appear in a dreamscape for one of two reasons. Depending on the surrounding related elements, this symbol may equate to one's unique independent thought which stretches into the realm of being visionary, or it can infer the opposite—that one is thinking in an unrealistic manner, perhaps being overly optimistic.

DREAM MERCHANT reveals an individual who has a tendency to encourage beliefs in unrealistic goals.

DREAMWALKER characterizes a spiritually wise individual whose quiet behavior reflects acceptance.

DREAMY (atmosphere) suggests a reality shift. These sometimes come to advise one to shift perspective just a bit in order to see reality clearer.

DREARY (atmosphere) implies a downcast emotional state.

DREDGE applies to the act of scraping the bottom of some issue. This usually is a warning to leave well enough alone. Depending on surrounding dreamscape facets, this dream symbol may actually be *advising* you to scrape the bottom.

DRENCH indicates a saturation point. This will infer an issue that holds no more new information.

DRESS stands for feminine aspects.

DRESSAGE pertains to the ability to manage one's life.

DRESS CODE denotes manipulation; placing restrictions on expressions of individuality.

DRESSER signifies compartmentalized aspects of self.

DRESSING (sauces) will correspond to one's tastes, how one makes life elements more to their liking.

DRESSING ROOM relates to the intentional affectations people display for others; may also refer to the trying-on of new ideas/perspectives; giving a look at new ideas.

DRESSING TABLE See vanity table.

DRESSMAKER See seamstress.

DRESS REHEARSAL connotes a need to take life seriously.

DRESS SHIELDS symbolize an attempt to present a cool image to others, never wanting to let people see you sweat.

DRESS SHOES come as a warning to stop trying to impress others—be yourself.

DRESS UP (playacting) cautions against the attempt or desire to be someone other than self.

DRIBBLE (ball) implies a marking-time stage in life; an interim.

DRIBBLE (trickle) indicates a state of consistency; a slow-paced advancement allowing full absorption of lessons.

DRIED FLOWERS exemplify a need to preserve one's natural talents through continual utilization.

DRIED FLOWERS (decoration) point to one's appreciation of natural gifts and the comfort they give when one surrounds self with their beauty.

DRIED FLOWERS (herbal use) signify extended utilization of one's natural talents.

DRIED FLOWERS (in field/garden) warn of one's natural talents going to waste on the vine.

DRIED FLOWERS (memento) come to reinforce the importance of remembering the personal significance of another's natural talents.

DRIED FRUIT represents preserved talents; a move to extend the benefits of a good thing.

DRIFTER characterizes a search for self.

DRIFT FENCE See snow fence.

DRIFTING comes as an advisement to let one know that one is veering off course. This may apply to one's life path, an attitude, or leaning in the wrong direction.

DRIFTWOOD suggests the smoothness of acceptance brought on by the continual washing of a spiritual faith.

DRILL (practice) illustrates the importance of routine utilization of one's talents; learning and becoming proficient through use.

DRILL (tool) denotes thoroughness in aspects of learning.

DRILL BIT exemplifies the wide variety of learning tools available.

DRILL INSTRUCTOR characterizes unavoidable learning experiences.

DRILL PRESS typifies those life aspects that improve the accuracy/efficiency of the learning process.

DRILL TEAM stands for flawless learning skills.

DRINKING FOUNTAIN indicates a source of basic nourishment. Recall its condition.

DRIP represents a saturation point; overflow; a need for some type of containment.

DRIP-DRY suggests a natural method of letting things take their course.

DRIP-FEED See intravenous feeding.

DRIP IRRIGATION represents slow feeding; nourishment in the form of new information taken at a measured pace.

DRIPLESS (spout) stands for an element which safeguards against wastefulness.

DRIP PAINTING (art form) signifies wild expression of thoughts; uncontrolled emotions; letting the ramifications of one's actions land where they may.

DRIP PAN connotes a life facet that serves as a safeguard; a containment factor.

DRIPPINGS relate to leftover aspects of something that could be useful in other ways.

DRIVE-BY SHOOTING warns of collateral damage done by one's explosive reactions.

DRIVE-IN See fast food.

DRIVE-IN (movie) represents an extra effort applied to some aspect in the dreamer's life.

DRIVER'S LICENSE denotes one's true identity and comes in dreams to remind us to remain true to that identity. This symbol may also point to one's right to proceed on a particular course.

DRIVER'S SEAT represents the one in control. This can be a revealing dream.

DRIVE THRU (window) refers to convenience; a quick aid for accomplishing something.

DRIVEWAY pertains to a region of approach; specific approachability.

DRIVING RANGE suggests the practicing of one's methods for taking long shots.

DRIVING SCHOOL indicates a need to review or learn better methods of managing one's way through life.

DRIVING TIME points to the time it will take for getting from one point in one's progression to another.

DRIVING UNDER THE INFLUENCE (DUI) cautions against needing reality-altering elements as a crutch to help one get through life.

DRIVING WHILE INTOXICATED (DWI) warns of making one's way through life without being in touch with it; lacking courage or belief in oneself.

DRIZZLE signifies a state of gentle spirituality; a peaceful and accepting manner of spiritual intake.

DRONE (bee) alludes to work done without thought applied. This won't refer to those things we instinctually do but rather the things we do that *should* have more thought behind them.

DRONE (monotone sound) usually comes as an advisement for the dreamer to stop tuning out certain things in life. This symbol warns against a tendency to have selective hearing.

DROOLING reflects a lack of control over one's desires.

DROP (fall from grasp) symbolizes the need to get a handle or grip on something.

DROP (liquid measure) means a minute amount. Surrounding details of the dream will clarify this meaning.

DROP (location) relates to a specific locale associated in some way with the dreamer.

DROP BOX stands for an element of convenience for transferring something out of one's hands.

DROP CEILING suggests hidden thoughts.

DROP CLOTH indicates preparedness; a safeguard; protective measure.

DROP IN stands for the unexpected.

DROP LEAF (table) suggests provisions made for expansion; realizing the possibility of needing to expand one's thinking or plans.

DROP-OFF (clifflike) advises of an abrupt decline or decrease in something. Cautions one to proceed slowly and watch footing.

DROP-OFF (lake/river bottom) pertains to a spiritual pitfall.

DROP OUT exemplifies the act of withdrawing from something. This may come as an advisement to do so or as a prompting to stay with it and keep going.

DROPPER portrays a life aspect that serves to regulate the controlled measurement or quantity of something; a controlling aspect.

DROP ZONE stands for the target perimeter of an issue one is in conflict over.

DROUGHT warns of self-generated spiritual starvation.

DROWNING is a strong advisement to come up for spiritual air instead of oversaturating self with a flood of spiritual research.

DROWSY is a call to awareness; a wake-up call to be attentive.

DRUDGERY is a dream aspect that comes to remind us that all our efforts are worthwhile, no matter how tedious or boring.

DRUG DEALER characterizes an extremely negative individual in one's life who has the ability to manipulate, control, and make one a dependent.

DRUGGIST See pharmacist.

DRUG REACTION See allergy.

DRUGS (illegal substance abuse) reveals a lack of self-confidence; dependency; escapism.

DRUGS (prescribed) point to those aspects in one's life that serve as aids in keeping one aligned.

DRUG STORE See pharmacy.

DRUID represents esoteric spiritual aspects.

DRUM (container) See barrel.

DRUM (musical instrument) pertains to the core of one's heart center; deepest emotions.

DRUM (steel) refers to lightheartedness.

DRUMBEAT is a call to the way of nature; natural, heart-moving inner aspects.

DRUM MAJORETTE relates to boastfulness. This reveals one who advertises everything they feel. May be a call for sympathy.

DRUMMER characterizes self-confidence and contentedness. May point to one who blazes her own path.

DRUM ROLL comes as an attention-getting symbol indicating a precursor to something about to appear in one's life.

DRUMSTICK (food) refers to personal efforts leading to nourishment.

DRUMSTICK (music) represents an aid for soul expression and journeying within.

DRUNK (state) warns of overindulgence; an escape from reality and one's responsibility to same.

DRY BED (creek/lake) indicates a spiritual belief that has lost its viability. May point to one's loss of spiritual interest.

DRY CLEANER comes as a strong advisement to give more care to the removal of negative factors from one's life.

DRY DOCK suggests a temporary rest from one's spiritual search or learning. This would indicate an overload or a need to absorb more.

DRYER (clothes/hair) infers a need for more seriousness and maturity.

DRY FARMING points to a conservative perspective.

DRY HOLE indicates a situation or personal attempt that came up empty. May refer to an idea that's not viable.

DRY ICE represents a stage of spiritual cooling; a decline in interest.

DRY KILN advises of a need to absorb and fully comprehend that which one has attempted to learn; a seasoning time.

DRY MOP See dust mop.

DRY ROT warns of the danger of prolonging a negative period in one's life; motivation is urged for the purpose of expunging the negative that's spreading.

DRY RUN refers to practice; a need to test something out.

DRY SOCKET indicates a negative effect resulting from one's verbiage.

DRY SPELL stands for a phase of little activity regarding a certain aspect of one's life. This may be perceived as a bad thing, but it's usually a necessity for further progression.

DRYWALL symbolizes hidden personality aspects.

DUAL CITIZENSHIP suggests dual allegiance; loyalty to more than one individual or issue.

DUAL CONTROLS stands for tandem control; decision-making done in an equitable manner with another. Depending on the related dreamscape elements, this symbol may also reveal a fight for control.

DUCK (bird) pertains to spiritual vulnerability; questionable inner strength.

DUCK (evade) is a sign of awareness; watchfulness.

DUCK (fabric) portrays a self-absorbed personality.

DUCKBOARD suggests protective measures in the way of maintaining an awareness of life elements touched by negatives.

DUCKBILL See platypus.

DUCK BLIND warns of deception; ulterior motive; sneakiness.

DUCKING STOOL advises of unjust and unwarranted conclusions; assumptions and false judgments.

DUCKLING suggests a spiritual novice; one who is just setting foot on a new spiritual path.

DUCK SOUP means something easily accomplished.

DUCKTAIL (hair style) symbolizes a middle-of-the-road attitude.

DUCT represents a connection or passageway that leads to a source that calms (cools) or urges (heats up) one's attitude, pace, or interest.

DUCT TAPE calls for a need to make repairs in regard to one's attitude.

DUDE characterizes an over-concern for outward appearances.

DUDE RANCH connotes an attempt to soften and round out one's stern and sharp personality elements.

DUEL advises of the strong possibility that an outcome or effect will turn out with severe consequences.

DUET typifies a situation that involves two individuals. This in itself may be a very revealing aspect for the dreamer.

DUFFLE BAG suggests a transition stage.

DUGOUT implies a temporary withdrawal from some aspect in the dreamer's life.

DULCIMER stands for inner contentedness.

DULL (finish) is a call to awareness and motivation; lack of clarity.

DUMBBELLS apply to self-strengthening aspects.

DUMBWAITER portrays personal resources; self-reliance.

DUMDUM BULLET defines powerful defenses; an awareness of one's protective preparedness and strength of same. On the opposite side of this coin, the symbol can point to a powerfully deep-seated attitude which could be highly explosive.

DUMMY characterizes voluntary ignorance; a willful state devoid of personal responsibility or independence.

DUMP See landfill.

DUMPLING signifies a nourishing aspect or one that relates to a sweet reward or benefit.

DUMP TRUCK portrays the act of actually dumping something from one's life.

DUNCE CAP connotes foolish thinking; a need to reason and apply a greater amount of intelligence and logic.

DUNE comes as a warning to stop shifting thoughts or attitudes.

DUNE BUGGY symbolizes an attempt to override and obtain control over one's shifting thoughts or attitudes. In some instances, this symbol could point to a manner of traveling through life that doesn't keep one on solid ground.

DUNG BEETLE reminds us that everything in life has meaning and purpose.

DUNGEON pertains to self-induced states of negativity; self-imposed denial or restraint.

DUPLEX indicates a double aspect to something.

DUSK represents a calming period; a time of inner ease.

DUST symbolizes unnecessary aspects of one's life that intrude.

DUST BOWL warns of an extremely unproductive stage in one's life; lacking any nutrient quality.

DUST BUNNY stands for an accumulation of extraneous life aspects that are interfering with and affecting the more important elements; a buildup of irritations.

DUST CLOTH stands for an element which will clear away extraneous aspects of an issue or attitude.

DUST COVER (of book) signifies measures that protect against an intrusion from negative or unnecessary aspects.

DUST DEVIL cautions against mental vacillations and confusion.

DUSTER (coat) refers to actions taken to prevent extraneous factors from taking one's attention from the important aspects.

DUSTING POWDER refers to the utilization of small opportunities that help us personally feel better.

DUST JACKET See dust cover.

DUST MOP stands for one's active efforts to keep one's path and purpose free of distractions.

DUST MOTE defines an existing distraction.

DUSTPAN connotes the collecting and willful disposal of one's distracting factors. This means that one is focused on one's life path or purpose and refuses to be sidetracked.

DUST RUFFLE signifies an attempt to keep extraneous elements from contaminating pure ideas/intentions.

DUST STORM warns of an inundation of distracting elements that confuse an issue or attitude.

DUSTY MILLER (botanical) suggests an increased practice of unconditional behavior.

DUTCH DOOR points to the presence of two ways a certain opportunity can be accessed.

DUTCH OVEN denotes solid and sure methods of obtaining nourishment. This nourishment can be emotional, physical, mental, or spiritual.

DUTCH TREAT reminds us of individual responsibility.

DUTY-FREE pertains to life aspects that bring extra benefits.

DVD (digital video disc) See movie.

DVD PLAYER See video player.

DWARF characterizes the existence of power regardless of size.

DYE signifies misrepresentations; alterations.

DYED-IN-THE-WOOL advises of an unyielding personality or attitude.

DYING forewarns of the death of one's high ideals or an actual physical demise.

DYNAMITE indicates an explosive aspect to something. May refer to a sudden revelation.

DYNAMO See generator.

DYSENTERY indicates a mental state that lacks the ability to absorb or retain information.

DYSLEXIA stands for impaired perception, usually reversing or transposing the main aspects of an issue or idea.

DYSPHORIA reveals a lack of acceptance; high anxiety or expectation; restlessness.

DYSPNEA cautions of a need to slow one's pace for the purpose of breathing more deeply and more freely; a need for breathing room.

E

EAGLE defines the self-confidence of intellectual freedom to pursue unconventional concepts or issues.

EAGLE SCOUT characterizes one who was presumably trained in ethical standards.

EAR symbolizes the quality of auditory reception; how well one listens and, consequently, processes and responds.

EARACHE represents the result of listening to too much verbiage that is unnecessary or extraneous.

EARDROPS advise of measures needed to repair some damage caused by what one has heard or listened to.

EARDRUM connotes how well one listens in respect to comprehending with the application of logic and reason.

EAR LOBE indicates the quality and quantity of one's receptiveness to verbal communication.

EARLY WARNING SYSTEM stands for an individual's inner awareness; their perceptual watchfulness.

EARMARK emphasizes a distinctive characteristic or something that has been set aside for a specific purpose; allocated.

EARMUFF refers to a closed mind; hearing only what one wants to.

EARNEST MONEY stands for a serious intention; putting one's money where the mouth is.

EARPHONE portrays increased perception and/or attention given.

EARPIECE stands for hearing what others can't. This doesn't mean hearing voices but rather being in-tune with one's Higher Self, one's inner guidance.

EAR PIERCINGS refer to behavior which obstructs hearing (perceptual) clarity.

EARPLUG warns of a closed mind, not even hearing what one wants to.

EARRING pertains to the dressing up of what is heard; hearing and embellishing or exaggerating the statements heard.

EARSPLITTING (sound) applies to that which causes a strongly disruptive response within one's being. May point to an alarm calling attention to something the dreamer needs to hear.

EARTH symbolizes humankind's physical side; the three-dimensional touchable aspects of our world.

EARTH-BERMED stands for a solid foundation that has to be monitored for a possible accumulation of outdated, destructive (mold) elements.

EARTH DAY is a symbol that comes as an advisement to bring one's perception or attitude back down to earth.

EARTHENWARE (pottery) illustrates an awareness of reality; a down-to-earth state of being.

EARTH MOTHER signifies the warm and flowing essence of love within all living things; absolute compassion and innocence.

EARTH MOVER denotes overcoming obstacles.

EARTHQUAKE exemplifies dangerously shaky foundations or beliefs. Could forewarn of an earth-shattering situation on the horizon.

EARTHQUAKE INSURANCE stands for foresight; a belief in possibilities.

EARTHQUAKE SCALE See Richter scale.

EARTH-SHATTERING (event) See earthquake.

EARTH STATION pertains to inner awareness; intuition; a cognizant link to one's Higher Self.

EARTH TONES (colors) represent a down-to-earth perspective/character; one not impressed by societal dazzle.

EARTHWORM indicates life aspects that serve to enrich one's foundations. May also point to an interference; a forcing of one's way into something.

EARWAX warns of self-generated misconceptions due to personal selectiveness.

EASEL alludes to a life aspect that is capable of supporting one's future goals or plans.

EASEMENT exemplifies a *passage* opportunity; a way to something.

EASEMENT (conservation) stands for protecting/securing each aspect of one's progression before moving on.

EASEMENT (ingress/egress) denotes one's right to pass through another's space.

EASEMENT (power line) points to an acceptance of motivational elements.

EAST (direction) marks beginnings.

EASTER signifies victory; triumph over life's problems.

EASTER BASKET connotes optimism; hope for a positive outcome.

EASTER BUNNY characterizes an individual or specific life aspect that one believes will resolve difficulties.

EASTER EGG portrays a colored or decorated perception.

EASTER EGG HUNT marks a search for a more pleasing or acceptable reality.

EASTER ISLAND typifies those solid, worldly aspects that stand to point the way to reality.

EASTER LILY See lily.

EASY CHAIR implies a relaxed attitude.

EASY STREET defines a desire for an easier life. May point to a phase that is less stressful and things will go right for a time.

EATING portrays the consumption or absorption of something, usually perceptions or ideas.

EAVES symbolize protective aspects.

EAVESDROP denotes information of which others are cognizant.

EAVES TROUGH illustrates a directed flow of something away from self.

EBB TIDE denotes a time of lessening spiritual involvement or interest.

EBONICS refers to speaking one's own type of language. Implies that someone is in their own little world and isn't communicating well.

EBONY (color) See black.

EBONY (wood) implies an enduring, ongoing puzzlement.

E-BOOK refers to a widely known story or block of information that's readily available to everyone.

ECCENTRIC alludes to the freedom that stems from separating the "I" from self, whereby one exercises intellectual pursuits and special interests without regard to public opinion.

ECHELON refers to degrees or levels of importance; priority designations.

ECHINACEA (flower) represents intense healing forces geared to reinforce one's fortitude.

ECHO stands for a repeated message for the dreamer.

ÉCLAIR relates to a lack of self-control.

ECLAMPSIA warns of a hazardous path chosen.

ECLECTIC applies to the utilization of many varied aspects; using any available resource; the expression of one's unique totality.

ECLIPSE (lunar) pertains to an awareness of true existential Reality.

ECLIPSE (solar) advises of a need to reaffirm spiritual beliefs.

ECOHAZARD stands for an attitude, idea, perception which presents a potentially disruptive element for one's basic foundational beliefs/qualities.

ECOLOGY (study of) calls attention to one's environmental responsibility.

ECONOMIC PLAN reflects thought given to how one can best utilize skills/talents.

ECONOMICS (study of) usually comes as a personal message to reassess one's current distribution of talents.

ECONOMIST characterizes one who is skilled in weighing the pros and cons of a situation or plan; one who analyses the cost of efforts expended against the benefits.

ECOTERRORISM/IST stands for an action/ individual that destroys the natural talents of oneself or others.

ECTOPIC PREGNANCY warns of the danger of forcing new beginnings before one has reached the appropriate time and place along one's path. Groundwork needs to be done before one can put plans into action.

ECTOPLASM denotes a misplaced focus on spiritualism. May also point to a nebulous element in one's life; something that can't quite be pinned down and identified.

ECUMENICAL COUNCIL stands for religious interference/control.

ECZEMA connotes an attitude that needs to be overcome.

EDDY warns of an off-course spiritual situation where one is caught in a distracting current.

EDELWEISS represents courage; tenacity.

EDEMA warns of too much focus being done on a specific spiritual aspect.

EDEN connotes an unrealistic life perspective.

EDGER (lawn tool) cautions against attempting to control the natural order of things; wanting to always trim things to fit one's personal perspective of how it should look or be.

EDITING signifies a need to choose appropriate words or phrasing when attempting to define one's thoughts and ideas.

EDITOR characterizes one who gets to the point. May also refer to someone who alters another's words.

EDITORIAL denotes an expression of personal opinion.

EDUCATIONAL PROGRAMMING (television) comes in dreamscapes to reveal a subject matter one has a need to be more informed about.

EEL alludes to spiritual vacillation.

EERIE (atmosphere) suggests a feeling of trepidation; anxiety; deep sense of expectation. A sense of dreamscape eeriness may also accompany the unexplained residual feeling which comes from a contactee experience.

EFFERVESCENT suggests high excitement over something.

EFFICIENCY APARTMENT emphasizes a prioritized personality.

EFFICIENCY EXPERT characterizes one who defines priorities for others. This is not always a positive dream symbol because people need to define their own priorities.

EFFIGY warns of energies being misdirected in a negative manner.

EGALITARIAN reflects an perspective of equality; generally a nonracist/nonsexist attitude.

EGG implies beginning perceptions; the formation of new ideas.

EGGBEATER (utensil) warns of attempting to form concepts from scrambled idea fragments.

EGG CARTON stands for the source of a multitude of new ideas. The key here is to recall the carton's condition and whether it was full or empty. Broken eggs inside?

EGGCUP refers to an organized concept.

EGGHEAD (skull shape) stands for an intellectual, a deep thinker.

EGGNOG symbolizes a rich or nourishing concept, plan, or idea.

EGG ON FACE stands for embarrassment over being wrong or misjudging.

EGGPLANT implies ideas that incorporate spiritual aspects.

EGG ROLL stands for several individual aspects that are enveloped by a larger, all-encompassing one.

EGG SHAPE See oval.

EGGSHELL warns of a fragile or precarious belief, attitude, or situation. This may not be a negative symbol but rather one that necessitates close attention and care in the way of management.

EGG TIMER advises of the wisdom to closely monitor a specific concept or situation.

EGG TOOTH alludes to one's level of developed preparedness to begin a new path or direction.

EGG WHITE defines the extraneous aspects of a situation, belief, or perception.

EGG YOLK defines the basic foundation of an idea or perception.

EGOCENTRIC marks a self-absorbed individual or situation.

EGRET typifies a spiritual sign; a spiritually related message.

EGYPTIAN COTTON (fabric) symbolizes the desirable character traits brought on by the inner beauty of fortitude/perseverance.

EGYPTOLOGY (study of) exemplifies a high interest in enigmatic aspects of life; a subconscious yearning to discover human beginnings.

EIFFEL TOWER stands for a sign/reminder of a city's past achievement.

EIDERDOWN See downy.

EIGHT pertains to balanced thought. This most often comes to warn the dreamer of unclear or distorted thinking.

EIGHT BALL signifies a problematic situation or relationship. This may even refer to one's own thought process.

EIGHTEEN-WHEELER See semitrailer.

EIGHT-TRACK TAPE suggests old messages that are still relevant.

EIGHTY-SIX (86) comes as a strong suggestion to reject some personally harmful aspect in one's life.

EINSTEIN (Albert) characterizes the high responsibility of directing one's knowledge in appropriate manners; positive use of intelligence.

EJECTION SEAT implies the preparedness of planning with precautionary measures in place. May point to a need to remove oneself from a situation or relationship as quickly as possible.

ELAND represents innocence and gentleness associated with strength.

ELASTIC denotes a giving or flexible relationship or situation.

ELBOW signifies personal space affording comfortable distance from others.

ELBOW GREASE illustrates personal effort applied to something.

ELBOWROOM implies a need for greater personal space from others; more distance is required.

ELDER pertains to one possessing experience and wisdom.

ELDERBERRY symbolizes naturally occurring opportunities that are too frequently overlooked.

ELECAMPANE (botanical) stands for a healing life aspect.

ELECTION connotes a firm decision.

ELECTION DAY pinpoints a specific time to make a firm decision.

ELECTIVE COURSE represents optional information; an opportunity to make a choice about which one wishes to expand a knowledge base.

ELECTIVE SURGERY refers to a desire to improve oneself. This symbol rarely has to do with cosmetic surgery but rather relates to wishing to rid oneself of a negative trait or habit.

ELECTRICAL STORM suggests an impending conflict, possibly within oneself.

ELECTRIC BLANKET See heating blanket.

ELECTRIC BLUE (color) suggests a vivid and energetic expression of one's spirituality.

ELECTRIC CHAIR warns of the finality of one's actions; unavoidable retribution.

ELECTRIC EYE See photoelectric cell.

ELECTRIC FIELD represents a surrounding vibrational space that emits perceptual impulses; one's intuitive perception.

ELECTRIC GUITAR cautions of a self-serving need to gain attention.

ELECTRICIAN characterizes one's personal thought process and the tendency to get others wired in a like manner. May point to an individual skilled in motivating others.

ELECTRICITY applies to a source of energy/power, usually that which serves as a powerful impetus of motivation.

ELECTRIC OUTLET See outlet (electrical).

ELECTRIC RAZOR connotes a personal urgency to shed certain thoughts or concepts.

ELECTRIC SHOCK will usually represent a need for one to be jolted into awareness. This symbol hints at a tendency to fence sit.

ELECTRIC TOOTHBRUSH See toothbrush.

ELECTROCARDIOGRAPH advises of an immediate need for self-analyzation in respect to the *expression of one's emotions*; implies misdirected attitudes.

ELECTROCUTION warns against the desire for power. This can infer many types of power such as knowledge, wealth, leadership, etc.

ELECTROENCEPHALOGRAPH advises of an immediate need for self-analyzation in respect to one's *process of thought;* implies the use of disassociative or aberrant thinking.

ELECTROLYSIS signifies the destruction of personally rejected ideas.

ELECTRONIC BANKING suggests a more efficient method of managing one's talents.

ELECTRONIC FETAL MONITOR advises of a serious need to closely watch the developing aspects leading to one's new path or beginning.

ELECTRONIC MAIL (e-mail) signifies perceptual impressions; readily available information within one's personal surround.

ELECTROPLATING symbolizes a determined effort to ensure the protection or concealment of something.

ELEMENT (of nature) denotes the four facets of life: mental, physical, emotional, and spiritual. See the specific elements of air, earth, fire, and water.

ELEMENTARY SCHOOL illustrates the specific developmental stage that one is at in life.

ELEPHANT stands for a generous and gregarious nature.

ELEPHANT GUN signifies a potentially huge emotional explosion/conflict.

ELEVATOR connotes an easy way up (or down); advancing (or falling behind) with little effort applied.

ELEVATOR MUSIC refers to soothing elements along one's path.

ELEVATOR SHOES allude to a poor self-image; an attempt to present self in a brighter light or higher station; trying to appear taller or bigger than you are.

ELEVEN signifies misplaced values.

ELEVENTH HOUR comes as a message of fair warning that one's time is running out to take advantage of the last chance to accomplishing something.

ELF characterizes proof of something one is skeptical of or doubts. This symbol eradicates doubt with proof.

ELF OWL denotes cleverness; inventive and analytical thought.

ELF SHOES signify a path traveled with an intellectual awareness of reality's true nature. Points to an understanding and acceptance of possibilities.

ELITISM/IST reflects snobbery; a habit of class separation.

ELIXIR represents an imagined cure-all to life's problems.

ELK denotes integrity.

ELM (tree) warns of escapism and comes to advise one to face life with greater inner strength.

ELOPING connotes strong individuality.

ELYSIAN FIELDS means an after-life paradise, but in dreams it equates to an emotional state of high satisfaction (paradise) following an accomplishment having extended effects.

E-MAIL See electronic mail.

E-MAIL SHORTHAND denotes a need to convey something quickly, not be wordy; getting right to the point.

EMBALM advises of a need to preserve something in one's life.

EMBARGO implies the act of disassociation; a refusal to deal with or communicate with another.

EMBARRASSMENT typifies an ill-at-ease state. This can be a telling symbol when combined with surrounding dreamscape facets.

EMBASSY portrays some type of help or assistance for the dreamer.

EMBEDDED refers to a hidden or absorbed element; camouflaged.

EMBELLISHMENT may not refer to exaggerations but rather the addition of elements which better clarify, explain, or describe an issue.

EMBER emphasizes the present existence of some life left in something in the dreamer's life. This could be an attitude, emotion, perception, relationship tie, etc.

EMBEZZLE warns against taking or claiming something that belongs to another.

EMBLEM comes as a message for the dreamer. It usually attempts to call attention to whatever the emblem represents, for this will have a specific meaning to each dreamer.

EMBOLISM indicates a self-induced path obstruction.

EMBOSSED is a symbol of emphasis on something. It comes to draw attention.

EMBRACE implies a closeness; a special connection.

EMBROIDERY (needlework) depicts exaggerations; a tendency to embellish.

EMBROIDERY FLOSS refers to the wide choice of embellishments at one's disposal. What's important is to recall the displayed colors.

EMBRYO illustrates the beginning stage of a new direction or belief.

EMBRYOLOGY (study of) represents an interest in the many methods of generating new beginnings and the development of same.

EMCEE See master of ceremonies.

EMERALD (gemstone/color) signifies the presence and quality of one's specialized talent to heal others.

EMERALD CUT (shape) suggests a generous portion; generosity; giving.

EMERGENCY BRAKE advises of a critical need to stop something the dreamer is doing.

EMERGENCY MEDICAL TECHNICIAN (EMT) characterizes someone in the dreamer's life who has the ability to give immediate help or some type of needed assistance.

EMERGENCY ROOM comes as a strong warning. Surrounding dreamscape facets will clarify this for the dreamer.

EMERGI-CENTER signifies a source providing solutions to minor problems.

EMERITA (title) will reveal one who retains the honor and respect of others.

EMERY BOARD See nail file.

EMINENT DOMAIN comes in dreams to remind us that others can easily steal away our most precious possessions through the means of legal manipulation.

EMISSARY cautions against having others speak for you or do your work.

EMISSION CONTROL stands for an effort to monitor behavior for the purpose of cutting down on negative aspects having the potential to harm others.

EMMY (award) is a warning message. No one in life should receive an award for acting. This is an advisement to start being yourself.

EMOLLIENT (lanolin, etc.) refers to any personal element one uses to soften or smooth life's rough aspects.

EMPATHY usually is an advisement to better understand another's situation or response.

EMPHYSEMA warns of dishonesty.

EMPIRE usually refers to a specific individual's extent of power or control.

EMPLOYEE HANDBOOK symbolizes the working perimeters one is expected to adhere to.

EMPLOYMENT AGENCY directly suggests a change in the manner one works. This may not relate to one's type of employment but could pertain to how one goes about laboring along one's path.

EMPRESS denotes a matriarchal position.

EMPTY connotes a lack or void.

EMPTY-HANDED brings the message of nothing given, nothing received.

EMPTY NEST underscores the time frame allotted for oneself. This is not a self-serving message but rather comes as a sign of encouragement and motivation to rediscover the beautiful individuality of one's own inner essence.

EMU indicates multiple benefits from an unexpected source.

EMULSION portrays the reinforcing message that, although some life aspects cannot completely blend together, they can coexist in a peaceful and pleasing manner.

ENAMEL represents a condition of heavy coating; a thick veneer to one's outward presentation.

ENAMELWARE represents a simple, yet tried and true manner of accomplishing a goal or seeing something through to its conclusion.

ENCAMPMENT See campground.

ENCAPSULATE portrays self-devised enclosure of self; emotional distancing.

ENCEPHALITIS warns of distorted thoughts due to unchecked anger.

ENCHANTED emphasizes acute vibrational perception.

ENCHANTRESS characterizes one who has the talent to communicate the beauty of multifrequency perceptions to others.

ENCHILADA typifies life aspects that serve to provide one or more of an individual's preferred methods of relaxation; manner of experiencing enjoyment.

ENCORE represents a need to repeat something. Surrounding dreamscape facets will usually clarify what this is.

ENCOUNTER GROUP advises of a need to talk something through with others.

ENCROACHMENT alludes to some type of infringement being done.

ENCYCLOPEDIA emphasizes a need to gain a greater depth of knowledge on some aspect in the dreamer's life.

END (of something) clearly means just that. As simple as this interpretation is, it can relate to just about anything in the dreamer's life and the surrounding details will help to clarify this.

ENDANGER warns of the current time frame that is approaching, some type of hazardous or personally compromising situation.

ENDANGERED SPECIES won't refer to an actual animal, instead, it'll equate to the word "endangered" and relate to a relationship, situation, or even one's integrity that's heading for serious trouble, perhaps because of an intended decision or planned behavior.

ENDEARMENTS come to make one aware of another's personal perception of a relationship.

ENDIVE connotes learning experiences that are somewhat bittersweet.

ENDLESS defines a condition or aspect that has no limit; immortal; boundless.

ENDNOTE refers to a concluding explanation; afterthought.

ENDOCRINOLOGY (study of) alludes to a deep interest in understanding the powerful functions and applications of our energy centers (chakras) and the flow of that energy (chi). This, therefore, refers not only to the physical energy flow through the body but will also signify a free-flowing attitude, perspective, or behavior and the possible erroneous attitudes that may be blocking that flow.

ENDORSEMENT applies to one's personal approval of something.

ENDOWMENT stands for an unexpected

opportunity that has been freely presented or gifted.

END PAPER portrays the final stage of an issue; a concluding symbol.

END TABLE suggests convenience; something close at hand.

END ZONE relates to a point of rest beyond the goal; the place in one's path where personal efforts are rewarded.

ENEMA advises of a situation that requires assistance in helping one shed extraneous life aspects. Usually this refers to erroneous attitudes or perspectives. May indicate some behavioral negatives that aren't productive.

ENEMY informs the dreamer of negative aspects or associations in her life.

ENERGY AUDIT is a call to assess one's use of personal energy. This infers a change in disbursement is required.

ENGAGEMENT (appointment) See appointment.

ENGAGEMENT (ring) See ring (jewelry).

ENGAGEMENT (wedding) See betrothal.

ENGELMANN SPRUCE (tree/wood) signifies fortitude; perseverance.

ENGINE denotes aspects of the heart (physical or emotional).

ENGINEER characterizes one who is adept at complex planning.

ENGINEER (architectural) See architect.

ENGINEER (electrical) characterizes one who is proficient at tracing another's thought processes and redirecting them to provide greater clarity and simplicity.

ENGINEER (train) See train engineer.

ENGLAND represents a good friend. Also

suggests a tendency to adhere to social mores.

ENGLISH FOXHOUND (dog breed) denotes fortitude; focus on a goal.

ENGLISH GARDEN signifies an abundance of blessings.

ENGLISH LAVENDER suggests a quiet dignity.

ENGLISH MUFFIN infers a beginning to a two-fold purpose.

ENGLISH SADDLE typifies control of one's path.

ENGLISH SETTER (dog breed) symbolizes a friend's loyalty.

ENGLISH SHEEPDOG (dog breed) See Old English sheepdog.

ENGLISH WALNUT represents a richly nourishing aspect in one's life.

ENGORGED See gorge (eating).

ENGRAVE denotes something that's unalterable.

ENIGMA defines confoundments. These may be solvable, depending on the extent of effort applied to contemplating them.

ENLARGEMENT calls attention to something the dreamer needs to be made more aware of.

ENLIST suggests a need to join something, perhaps be an activist for a specific issue or to openly express a belief or perspective.

ENOLA GAY (Hiroshima bomber) refers to the possibility of a very bad choice being made in the offing, yet one has the chance to circumvent it.

ENROLL See register (enroll).

ENSEMBLE will symbolize all the elements of an aspect, perhaps all the members of a group involved in a particular issue or plan.

ENSNARE suggests underhandedness.

ENTERPRISE ZONE points to choices that benefit others instead of solely self.

ENTERTAINMENT usually comes as a specific message for each dreamer. Perhaps one needs more relaxation time, maybe less. What form of entertainment was being shown?

ENTITLEMENT PROGRAM corresponds with additional assistance needed or given to a specific individual, group, or issue.

ENTOURAGE See ensemble.

ENTRAILS See viscera.

ENTRANCEWAY represents choices. We all have a choice whether or not to pass through any entrance.

ENTRAPMENT reveals underhanded behavior. Recall who was entrapping whom.

ENTREE symbolizes the main issue or concept.

ENTRENCHED signifies a hunkered-down mode; full involvement.

ENTREPRENEUR characterizes an enterprising individual.

ENTRY FORM points to the intent to participate in something; may indicate a bid to take advantage of a possible opportunity.

ENTRY-LEVEL denotes a beginning stage. This usually points out the real level one is currently at.

ENVELOPE signifies a communication. What color was it? Who was it from? To? Was it empty?

ENVIRONMENTALIST exemplifies one who possesses inner balance and harmony.

ENVOY See messenger.

ENZYME relates to an aspect in one's life that acts as a motivating catalyst.

EPAULET implies a haughty personality; pomposity; presumptuousness.

EPIC denotes an issue that is vastly detailed or complex.

EPICENTER reveals the source of great pressure. This will normally refer to an issue, relationship, or situation but may also point to an idea, plan, or individual.

EPIDEMIC cautions of a concept or attitude that is widely held.

EPIGRAM usually comes as an important message for the dreamer and is unique to her individual life situation.

EPILEPSY typifies dream symbols that represent one's involuntary perceptions, the experience and response to same.

EPILOGUE indicates the final words on something; concluding statement.

EPIPHANY pertains to a sudden enlightening event; a shuddering revelation. This most often is not spiritually related but will be associated with a solution to a problem, the right attitude or perspective finally dawning, or some other brilliant inspiration that brings clarification.

EPITAPH comes as a message that summarizes or reveals hidden elements of one's life.

EPOCH symbolizes a specific span of time. This will be unique to each dreamer.

EPOXY warns of a need to secure some type of connecting elements in one's life.

EPSOM SALTS pertains to an aspect in one's life that produces a calming effect. Perhaps the dream symbol is advising of a need to gain a greater measure of calm, serenity.

EQUAL OPPORTUNITY applies to a nondiscriminatory situation or relationship; may advise this attitude.

EQUATION relates to a relative balance; a comparable aspect.

EQUATOR denotes a central point; basic premise.

EQUILIBRIUM equates to balance. This may refer to mental, emotional, physical, or spiritual aspects for the dreamer.

EQUINE See horse.

EQUIPMENT stands for life aspects that serve as tools or even opportunities one can utilize.

EQUITY stands for the accumulated value one has earned from efforts expended.

ERASER portrays chances to reverse or eradicate something. May indicate indecision.

ERECTILE DYSFUNCTION will sometimes equate to the body itself but will most often indicate an ineffective attitude or course of action.

ERMINE cautions against altering self for others; advises of the wisdom of being yourself.

EROSION cautions of a need to give more supportive efforts to some aspect in one's life; something is being worn away. This could point to trust, perseverance, love, etc.

EROTICA exemplifies the baser aspects of life; may warn of a situation where one is too engrossed in physical aspects, especially that of pleasing oneself.

ERRAND reminds us of the importance of attending to responsibilities no matter how small.

ERROR CODE comes to reveal a misstep or a wrong move; may refer to a recently formed attitude or decision.

ERROR TRAPPING (software) advises of a need to be more aware, watchful for wrong thinking; suggests one's careful behavior.

ERUPTION forewarns of a serious confrontation or exposure of something.

ESCALATOR cautions against laziness; taking the easy way that uses little energy.

ESCAPE advises of a way out of something.

ESCAPE ARTIST characterizes one who has a tendency to always cover one's options; never being manipulated or controlled. This may also refer to one who refuses to face or accept personal responsibility; avoidance, maybe even denial.

ESCARPMENT signifies a resulting condition or situation caused by a lack of foresight or planning.

ESCORT characterizes a close associate in one's life.

ESCORT SERVICE points to an individual who provides another with a *temporary* associate or support aide.

ESCROW represents safeguards; protected or guaranteed elements.

E-SIGNATURE symbolizes the ease and convenience of giving signed approval.

ESKIMO DOG (dog breed) stands for a friend's endurance. This suggests a friend who can handle sharing your burdens.

ESOPHAGUS denotes level of gullibility. Recall surrounding dreamscape facets and health or condition of the esophagus shown.

ESOTERICA represents conceptual aspects in one's life that require deeper contemplation.

ESPIONAGE advises of some type of pre-tension existing in one's life; ulterior motives; a separate agenda.

ESPRESSO illustrates rich and nourishing spiritual concepts; conceptual depth. Also suggests strengthened energies; reinforced motivation or perseverance.

ESSAY alludes to an expression of one's opinion. This usually advises one to be more open about personal attitudes.

ESSENE characterizes a true visionary messenger who is quietly cognizant of the true aspects comprising reality, including All-Life interrelationships.

ESSENTIAL OIL will point to that which is a priority in one's life; that which is essential.

ESTATE connotes the whole of one's assets. This may be all-inclusive of the four aspects of life: emotional, mental, physical, and spiritual.

ESTATE SALE points to a betrayal of self—one's individuality. It indicates a selling of self; loss of self-esteem and integrity.

ESTATE TAX indicates that someone is taking something from you that they've no right to have.

ESTIMATE represents approximations; that which cannot be pinpointed or predicted as an absolute.

ESTUARY pertains to the point in time where several spiritual concepts converge; the stage when the dreamer relates several spiritual ideas in an interconnective manner.

ETCH suggests firm opinions and attitudes.

ETHER (anesthetic) warns of total apathy or a stage in one's life where selective awareness is utilized. This is a warning message.

ETHER (space) stands for higher dimensional aspects to reality; possibilities yet undreamed.

ETHEREAL denotes spiritual or true Reality aspects that are associated with one's life.

ETHERNET LINE (computer) signifies communication between associates. May be advising of an urgency to make some type of immediate connection to someone within one's circle. This symbol may also refer to one's intuition or psychic connection to a close relationship.

ETHNOLOGY (study of) indicates a high interest in those different from the dreamer.

ETHOLOGY (study of) alludes to a high personal interest in the interrelatedness of all life.

ETIOLOGY (study of) illustrates a high interest in origins; a desire to understand how things began.

ETIQUETTE signifies a concern for social attitudes; politeness. This could also advise against an overconcern regarding what others think.

ETYMOLOGY (study of) denotes a high interest in language, specifically how a certain communication was passed from one to another.

EUCALYPTUS illustrates a life aspect that has the capability of nourishing through healing.

EUCHARIST See Holy Communion.

EULOGY reminds us to focus on the good points of another instead of any negative characteristics.

EUNUCH alludes to one uninterested in the physical aspects of life. May point to some type of inadequacy or ineffectiveness.

EUPHORIA typifies a state of absolute joy and serenity. Depending on surrounding dreamscape facets, this may or may not be a positive sign. May indicate overoptimism.

EUROPE signifies diversity of ideas/perspectives/traditions.

EUTHANASIA signifies deep compassion.

EVACUATION warns of a situation or relationship from which the dreamer should withdraw.

EVALUATION suggests a need for self-examination in respect to one's actions, beliefs, motives, or attitudes.

EVANGELIST characterizes a zealous personality; one who is strongly impassioned and may have a tendency toward coercion or guilt-tripping.

EVAPORATED MILK signifies a life aspect that is capable of providing the dreamer with a highly concentrated dose of nourishment. This may be emotional, mental, physical, or spiritual.

EVAPORATION represents the absorption of spiritual ideals.

EVASIVENESS cautions against avoiding reality or responsibility.

EVE defines a counter to the theory of evolution. Represents a flaw in a generally accepted idea or perspective.

EVENING denotes a rest period; a call from one's labors.

EVENING GOWN refers to extravagance; a tendency to maintain efforts even in respect to relaxation phases.

EVENING STAR signifies a guiding aspect in one's life; a light in the dark.

EVENSONG symbolizes an appreciation for life's beauty and joys experienced each day; an expression of gratefulness; prayer of appreciation for one's blessings.

EVER-BEARING will point to an element/behavior/characteristic that will produce ongoing benefits or positive ramifications.

EVEREST (Mount) will signify a considerable challenge.

EVERGLADES connotes spiritual sluggishness; mired or tangled spiritual aspects in one's life.

EVERGREENS See conifer.

EVICTION NOTICE comes as a serious advisement to get out of a situation.

EVIDENCE denotes validation or proof.

EVIDENCE TABLE (courtroom) points to multiple verifying elements.

EVIL may not refer to absolute negative aspects; it could be saying only that one believes or *thinks* a person, concept, or thing is evil.

EVIL EYE makes one's personal fears known to the conscious mind. Reveals a superstitious nature.

EVOLUTIONISM cautions one to take a closer look at the periodic consistency of a concept, situation, or issue to be aware of subtle changes.

EXACTO KNIFE points to precision; a need to proceed carefully.

EXAGGERATION warns against embellishments or advises of a situation in one's life where this is present.

EXALT is a message to remember that all people are equal and nobody should be exalted above another.

EXAMINATION usually calls for one to analyze self. This could be one's emotions, mental processes, spiritual beliefs, or physical condition. Surrounding dream aspects will clarify which one is intended.

EXAMPLE most often comes from one's Higher Self as a communication to the conscious aspect of the dreamer.

EXASPERATION advises one to accept more; be more accepting instead of getting so annoyed; patience.

EXCALIBUR symbolizes something one has a singular right to.

EXCAVATION suggests a need for the dreamer to dig deeper into something that requires further understanding. This dream facet reveals the existence of hidden elements to an issue that need to be exposed.

EXCELSIOR exemplifies a protective aspect in one's life; a need to protect something important to the dreamer.

EXCEPTIONS come in dreams to remind us that life is diverse and not everything neatly fits into a general rule.

EXCERPT will refer to sampling of an idea; getting an impression of what something is about.

EXCESS BAGGAGE naturally symbolizes a need to get rid of unnecessary elements in one's life. This most often points to harmful attitudes such as grudges.

EXCHANGE (merchandise return) refers to a need to replace an inappropriate or wrong attitude/idea with a correct one.

EXCHANGE RATE implies karmic balance.

EXCHANGE STUDENT characterizes one who takes advantage of learning from an alternate perspective.

EXCLAMATION POINT indicates a clear message of great importance attached to something in the dreamer's life; an attempt to get the dreamer's focused attention.

EXCLUSIONIST characterizes a separatist; bigot.

EXCOMMUNICATION represents judgment; spiritual judgment through arrogance.

EXCREMENT alludes to extraneous life aspects that one has successfully shed.

EXCURSION refers to a leisurely side trip taken for the purpose of learning more about the lay of the land surrounding one's path.

EXCUSE cautions against not taking personal responsibility.

EXECUTIONER may come as a warning against paranoia or it may actually refer to an individual or event in one's life that is capable of bringing personal disaster. Lastly, is the executioner you? This would warn against a tendency toward self-persecution or playing at being the judge of everyone.

EXECUTIVE characterizes seniority related to a specific area.

EXECUTIVE (suite/office) denotes a place of seniority or expertise.

EXECUTIVE ORDER will usually be a message from one's conscience or Higher Self.

EXECUTIVE PRIVILEGE denotes one's right to privacy. This doesn't necessarily equate to secrecy but relates more to the idea of one not having to divulge everything to everyone.

EXECUTIVE SESSION comes in a dream as an advisement to do some soul-searching.

EXECUTRIX points to an individual who has the right/ability to sort matters out and/or disburse benefits and reconcile debts.

EXEMPTION may equate to some form of immunity from responsibility or culpability.

EXERCISE EQUIPMENT suggests a need literally exercise something. This may refer to one's mind or body. It may be pointing to a need to exercise one's right or individuality.

EXFOLIANT (foliage) warns of an element capable of destroying any benefit to something.

EXFOLIANT (skin) suggests one shed all remnants of former affectations; an advisement to keep one's face (presentation) free of old attitudes.

EXHAUST (vehicle) refers to a lack of energy; a run-down condition. This may also indicate some type of finality experienced in one's life.

EXHAUST FAN represents an attempt to keep attitudes/perspectives refreshed, free of negative or excessively damaging elements.

EXHAUSTION pretty much explains itself. It reveals one's state of overdoing, perhaps beating one's head against a wall and needing to pursue an alternative course of action or perspective.

EXHAUST PIPE refers to withheld emotions, opinions, or energy. This is an advisement to release pent-up aspects of oneself.

EXHIBITION emphasizes one's overall general perceptions; what one is aware of looking at.

EXHIBITIONIST warns against the tendency/need to focus attention on oneself.

EXHUMATION comes as a call to re-examine something in one's life; go back and take another look at something that was missed.

EXILE most often refers to a self-induced state of aloneness.

EXIT (sign) points to a way out of something.

EXIT POLL cautions against a desire to know what others think of something.

EXODUS won't normally refer to a literal departure but rather equate to a flight from responsibility or a refusal to face reality.

EXORCISM characterizes a personally concerted effort to rid self of certain life aspects that don't necessarily have to be negatives.

EXOTIC suggests eccentricity; perhaps a pointed way to advise one to let more of one's individuality be expressed.

EXPANSION signifies growth.

EXPANSION BRIDGE pertains to a way to get to the other side. This symbol comes as encouragement for those believing life's current problems are insurmountable.

EXPANSION JOINT symbolizes possible variations to one's plans and the action taken to accommodate them.

EXPATRIATE will signify a full departure from a former ideology or loyalty.

EXPECTATION warns against being impatient and calls for acceptance.

EXPECTORANT denotes a life aspect that helps one to release negative emotions, attitudes, or energies.

EXPEDITION typifies a dreamscape symbol that defines a search or quest.

EXPEL represents a rejection or denial of a formerly held attitude.

EXPENDABLE signifies a nonessential element.

EXPENSE ACCOUNT pertains to the amount of one's personal talents, opportunities, or tools available for a goal's utilization.

EXPERIMENT stands for personal attempts made; trials; first starts.

EXPERT characterizes an adept; one who has specific knowledge and the corresponding experience to go with it.

EXPERT WITNESS refers to someone who has knowledge of a particular issue. This symbol may come as an advisement to consult a knowledgeable individual.

EXPIRATION DATE will usually be a personal indicator for the dreamer that reminds her/him of how much time is left to accomplish a certain thing.

EXPLANATIONS come to clarify a specific aspect for the dreamer.

EXPLETIVE denotes emphasis placed on something to which the dreamer will personally relate to.

EXPLOITATION reveals deception or manipulation being done.

EXPLORATORY SURGERY points to an attempt (or need) to get to the bottom of what's causing a particular negative in one's life. This will usually relate to a negative attitude or a perspective one knows one shouldn't have.

EXPLORER characterizes a free-thinker; one who follows one's interests or curiosity; a seeker of knowledge.

EXPLOSION forewarns of an emotional event.

EXPLOSIVE refers to a life aspect that has the potential of creating a devastating effect in one's life.

EXPONENT will refer to additional elements associated with an issue.

EXPORTS refer to those personal talents we give to others; the sharing of one's abilities.

EXPOSE forewarns of some type of public exposure being done in one's future. May hint of a betrayer in one's midst.

EXPOSITION stands for a display of available options or improved ways of doing things. This symbol will come to encourage a dreamer who previously thought she/he had exhausted all options.

EXPOSURE (weather hazard) warns against becoming too involved in a current situation/issue/relationship; the timing isn't right for such full-blown involvement.

EXPOSURE METER denotes one's tendency to monitor self.

EXPRESS (travel conveyance) will usually indicate an urgent need to get somewhere; to not procrastinate any longer.

EXPRESS DELIVERY/MAIL caution to instigate a communication as soon as possible.

EXPRESSWAY exemplifies a fast lane; quickest way to a destination.

EXPULSION forewarns of disastrous results coming if one doesn't alter current behavior.

EXTENDED CARE (facility) points out the fact that an issue isn't quite concluded yet, a bit more attention is required.

EXTENDED FAMILY refers to close relationships.

EXTENDED FORECAST will usually be an advisement to look ahead, keep one's eyes on the greater picture for more effective planning.

EXTENSION (cord) suggests a greater use of one's personal energies and/or efforts; the dreamer could be doing more.

EXTENSION (hair) See hair extensions.

EXTENSION (ladder) comes as an advisement that one could be reaching higher.

EXTENSION (more time) refers to a deadline reprieve; more time allotted.

EXTENSION (school) points to further learning needed.

EXTERMINATOR (infestation) characterizes an individual who is capable of helping to rid one's life of negative or unwanted aspects.

EXTINCT indicates a life aspect that no longer exists. This symbol usually comes as a warning to those who are attempting to hold onto something that has gone from their lives.

EXTINGUISHER (fire) See fire extinguisher.

EXTORTION is a negative symbol referring to the wrong use of information; betrayal.

EXTRACT (a concentrate) illustrates basic aspects of an issue or idea.

EXTRAPOLATE cautions of attempts to extend one's knowledge for the sake of others.

EXTRASENSORY PERCEPTION (ESP) is a misnomer because there is nothing extra about it; however, if one has this event in a dreamscape it usually will be an attempt to normalize this talent or related event for the dreamer; demystify.

EXTRATERRESTRIAL See alien (other world being).

EXTRAVAGANCE comes as a warning against same.

EXTRAVAGANZA relates to fabulousness;

E

going all out to present the biggest and best ever display of something.

EXTREME MAKE-OVER signifies a caution against trying to be something you're not; an advisement to like your own beingness; a warning to stop placing appearances at the top of your priority list.

EXTREME UNCTION is a forewarning of someone's death probability.

EXTREMIST will indicate an overreaction; one who jumps to conclusions and acts on them.

EXTRICATION advises of a need to remove self from a harmful situation, relationship, or belief system.

EYE defines one's personal perceptual characteristics. See below:

Bleeding eyes indicate an empathetic nature.

Blinking eyes refer to a lack of seriousness.

Cloudy eyes denote a lack of clarity.

Colored eyes have unique meanings. Refer to specific color.

Darting eyes signify a vacillating perspective.

Dull eyes stand for a lack of interest or ability to comprehend.

Feline eyes portray an acute awareness; watchfulness.

Glass eyes refer to a heightened ability to perceive vibrational images through an extended awareness of true Reality.

Hawk eyes connote a far-reaching perceptive ability.

Hooded eyes represent a calculating approach to perceptions.

Large eyes pertain to a broad-scope perceptual skill.

Misty eyes characterize perceptions affected by emotions/sensitivity.

Owl eyes relate to an ability to perceive what others overlook.

Protruding eyes point to gullibility, an amazement at everything.

Slanted eyes warn of perceptions affected by personal opinions/skepticism.

Small eyes define a small perceptual scope; short-ranged.

Squinty eyes represent self-imposed perceptual selectiveness/suspicion.

Staring eyes indicate judgmental perceptions.

Starry eyes symbolize unrealistic perceptions; too optimistic.

Unfocused eyes allude to undefined perceptions; disinterest.

EYEBALL (out of head) advises of watchers around one.

EYE BANK advises of a need for one to view something through the eyes of another and suggests a current state of misinterpretation going on.

EYE BATH See eyecup.

EYEBRIGHT (botanical) stands for a life aspect that can bring perceptual clarity.

EYEBROW reveals the manner in which one's personal perceptions are shielded from others.

EYEBROW PENCIL applies to aspects used to hide or reshape one's personal perspectives.

EYE CANDY refers to a sweet deal or idea as perceived by the dreamer's eye.

EYE CHART suggests a need to check one's personal perceptions for clarity and accuracy. This infers that one isn't perceiving something accurately.

EYE CONTACT represents a personal perceptual connection with another.

EYECUP indicates a negative aspect has infiltrated one's perception.

EYEDROPPER (for eye medicine) connotes a need to add another factor to one's perceptual viewpoint to gain greater clarity.

EYEDROPPER (general use) refers to an aid for using a small amount of something. This could be associated with just about anything, so the dreamer will need to recall other dreamscape elements that were associated with the dropper.

EYE GLASSES See glasses (eye).

EYEHOOK infers secured perceptions; those that one is unwilling to alter.

EYELASH signifies protection of one's opinions or perceptions.

EYELASH CURLER warns against willingly and purposely altering one's perceptions.

EYELET LACE stands for simplicity, yet not to be equated with simple-minded.

EYELID relates to aspects utilized during the perceptual process. What condition were the dream eyelids? Were they infected? Clean? Closed?

EYE LIFT comes as an advisement to open up one's eyes; droopy or lazy attitude/perspective.

EYELINER defines a tendency to emphasize perceptions by outlining them to others.

EYE PATCH stands for a willful slant to one's perspective of reality.

EYEPIECE See glasses (eye).

EYE-SERVICE indicates a lack of integrity and personal responsibility; can't be trusted unless being watched.

EYE SHADOW pertains to colored perceptions; enhanced.

EYE SOCKET See socket (eye).

EYES-ONLY (clearance level) reveals information that is only available to the dreamer and no one else.

EYESORE warns of hurtful personal perceptions.

EYESTRAIN represents a habit of straining one's perceptions. This indicates a tendency to make more of something than there is; wanting to read more into something.

EYE SURGERY (elective corrective) stands for a personal effort made to perceive more clearly.

EYE TEST indicates a need to see something clearer, usually points to a problem with one's perspective.

EYE VIEW will represent one's unique perception of a situation or issue.

EYEWASH exemplifies a life aspect that clarifies one's perceptual ability by washing negative attitudes from it.

EYEWITNESS indicates verification of one's perception of something; truth to an issue.

F

FABLE symbolizes truths clothed in a story line or experience.

FABRIC denotes a particular type of personality or varying traits. See specific fabric types.

FABRIC/SEWING SHOP will point to the varied options available to express one's creativity in dealing with a wide range of situations. Every situation in life will have an ideal approach to use when trying to deal with it. See specific fabric types for additional clarity.

FABRIC SOFTENER refers to a need to soften one's harsh or judgmental personality.

FACADE (building) represents a false front; phoniness; possibly hypocritical.

FACE (characteristics) reveals one's true personality.

Distorted face indicates the presence of some mental aberrations.

Flushed face warns of an explosive personality or it may point to withheld emotions.

Heavy makeup denotes hypocrisy or a false front.

No face stands for a conformist; no sense of individuality.

Oversized face represents egotism/arrogance.

Pale complexion characterizes an introvert.

Protruding nose refers to an interfering nature.

Red cheeks depict a shy personality.

Round face suggests avarice/greed.

Scarred face indicates perseverance.

Square face denotes an adamantly opinionated nature.

Thin/gaunt face implies a reserved personality.

Two faces allude to a hypocritical nature.

Undersized face represents an introvert or one who thinks small.

Unremarkable face applies to a conformist.

FACE BRICK suggests a show of strength which may not be sincere.

FACE CARD indicates a personal message revealing how one is currently acting in life.

FACE CLOTH See washcloth.

FACE-DOWN (position) represents hidden aspects.

FACELESS points to someone who's unreadable; a tendency to withhold a show of expression or any clue to what one is thinking/feeling. This symbol may also indicate a desire to keep one's distance from others.

FACE-LIFT symbolizes a focus on the self; possible hypocrisy; a dissatisfaction with one's natural beingness.

FACEMASK See mask.

FACE-OFF indicates a confrontation.

FACET (gemstone) stands for one of the many concurrently existing aspects of self.

FACE-TO-FACE stands for the wisdom of having a physical encounter to communicate instead of through the many electronic faceless methods.

FACE VALUE implies initially perceived value of something; value without anything extraneous associated with it.

FACILITATOR will point to one who motivates. This symbol may be pointing to oneself.

FACT-FINDING suggests a need to do some in-depth research or gather more information on something. This indicates a lack of full facts.

FACT OF LIFE connotes an event or life aspect that one cannot avoid facing.

FACTORY represents the manner in which one arranges or assembles path aspects that lead to goals.

FACULTY See schoolteacher.

FACULTY (natural ability) defines those talents or intellectual factors that are available for one's constant use in life.

FAD DIET stands for reaching for popular attitudes instead of using plain logic and common sense.

FADE illustrates a lessening of something in the dreamer's life. This could be a positive or negative sign depending on the surrounding dreamscape elements.

FADE IN forewarns of a specific event or personal attitude beginning to enter one's life.

FADE OUT pertains to something in one's life that is losing strength or interest.

FAD FASHIONS symbolize a desire to fit in; a reluctance to externalize one's unique individuality.

FAERIE See fairy.

FAIL-SAFE illustrates one's self-preservation aspects. This may refer to emotions, mental faculties, spiritual factors, or one's physical immune system.

FAILURE signifies a call for acceptance and perseverance; a message to make further attempts.

FAINT denotes a lack of inner strength. May also reveal a reaction to an unexpected shock.

FAIRGROUND stands for a fair ground to work within; a good atmosphere that is conducive to success.

FAIR-HAIRED indicates an even temper.

FAIR-MARKET VALUE signifies that one's opinion/attitude is a generally correct one.

FAIR WEATHER alludes to a time without any problems; a span of time when one's life appears to be going well.

FAIRY represents the intellect's far conceptual reach through reality.

FAIRY GODMOTHER characterizes the reward of a brilliant spiritual revelation through one's personal efforts of reaching and stretching intellectual reason out past the imaginary limits of reality.

FAIRYLAND equates to the delicate and nebulously fine spiritual aspects that can only be discovered by one who believes in possibilities.

FAIRY LAMP signifies a suggestion to look at something with more delicacy. This means a need to pull back from an aggressive approach.

FAIRY RING symbolizes concepts of the true Reality that cannot yet be proven through currently known laws of physics. This symbol refers to elements of life that are still misunderstood.

FAIRY STONE represents the natural oddities representing elements of true Reality which tend to continually prick at our curiosity. See Stonehenge.

FAIRY TALE represents hidden lessons.

FAITH HEALER is a warning to go within for one's strength and inner healing.

FAKE HAIR See wig.

FAKE NAILS See false nails.

FAKIR symbolizes the power within each of us.

FALCON defines our personal relationship with the higher spiritual forces.

FALCONER is one who recognizes, understands, and quietly accepts a connection with higher spiritual forces.

FALLACY comes as a caution to check the facts of something in one's life.

FALL BACK may represent a forced move made for the purpose of stepping back to get a better perspective of an issue.

FALL DOWN represents a misstep; a failed attempt one needs to get up and recover from.

FALL GUY characterizes one who is falsely blamed; a scapegoat.

FALLING exemplifies one's fear of failure or the unknown; a lack of self-confidence.

FALLING-OUT underscores the fact that one has had a considerable disagreement with another, but the relationship can recover if both parties aren't stubborn.

FALLING STAR applies to personal disappointments.

FALLOPIAN TUBE indicates the initial aspect that could lead to a new beginning.

FALL OUT connotes a possible future disassociation from someone in the dreamer's life. May also represent destructive ramifications from a confrontation or a particular behavior.

FALLOUT advises of forthcoming repercussions.

FALLOW (color/field) symbolizes an unproductive condition or state.

FALSE ALARM alludes to one's false fears; imagined fears.

FALSE ARREST refers to a situation indicating false blame. This is a revealing dream fragment.

FALSE BOTTOM indicates incomplete conclusions; more to be discovered, possible secrets.

FALSE EYELASHES warn of misplaced confidence placed in one's belief that one's attitudes and opinions are remaining private.

FALSE FRONT (building) See facade.

FALSE ID represents a false public persona.

FALSE IMPRISONMENT warns of a serious error in judgment.

FALSE NAILS represent a false sense of security.

FALSE NEGATIVE (test result) stands for a wrongly accused innocent individual.

FALSE POSITIVE (test result) symbolizes a negative element mistaken for being positive.

FALSE PREGNANCY naturally stands for a false start after trying for a new beginning or path.

FALSE PRETENSE advises of a deception or manipulation.

FALSE START suggests a need to go back and begin again, only this time, not be so impatient.

FALSE TEETH See denture.

FAME usually comes as a precognitive symbol.

FAMILY connotes close associations that are supposed to be unified.

FAMILY NAME calls attention to one's heritage or family core.

FAMILY PLANNING pertains to personal responsibility for one's future.

FAMILY ROOM symbolizes congeniality.

FAMILY TREE will most often reveal one's true spiritual heritage, that is, a record of one's past lives.

FAMISHED cautions of an aspect in the dreamer's life that is being starved. Surrounding details usually clarify what this means.

FAN (mechanical) indicates a need for a cooling-off period. This implies a rest period or a need to pull back, ease up.

FAN (paper) suggests a gentle acceptance for a necessary heated-up phase.

FAN (person) characterizes common interests and a sense of support for another.

FANATIC warns of a lack of applying wisdom to one's perceptions.

FAN BELT signifies an important life aspect that keeps other life factors going; a motivating element.

FAN DANCE symbolizes enticements.

FANDANGO (dance) stands for a fiery relationship.

FANFARE comes in a dream to emphasize something important.

FANG represents vicious and cutting speech.

FAN MAIL most often reveals how one is behaving, the condition of one's own behavioral characteristics. This represents how others perceive the dreamer. Recall what the fan mail said.

FANNY PACK represents a tendency to keep personal issues close; reluctance to reveal too much about oneself.

FANTASIA portrays the diversity of one's options for expressing spirituality.

FANTASY LAND cautions of a need to return to reality.

FAN WINDOW signifies a safe/protective way to let in the light without exposing oneself to possible negatives.

FARAWAY (perspective) indicates a life stage that is approaching a personal attitude of losing faith and motivation.

FARCE indicates exaggerated perceptions.

FARM denotes an atmosphere rich in character/spiritual nourishment and a back-to-basics perspective.

FARMER characterizes one who cultivates spiritual and/or simplistic aspects; one who understands the importance of the basics.

FARMER'S MARKET illustrates a nourishing opportunity. This nourishment is usually related to spiritual or corporal factors depending on other dreamscape elements.

FARM HAND points to an individual who is capable of helping one nourish and appreciate another's natural talents.

FARMHOUSE pertains to home and family life. The condition of this dreamscape house will be revealing.

FARMLAND represents the nourishment of one's natural talents and inherent goodness. Recall if the farmland was fallow or fertile. What was growing on it?

FARRIER applies to a serene personality.

FARROWING HOUSE cautions against starting too many projects at the same time.

FARSIGHTED reveals a perception that sees the forest but not the individual trees; a need to understand the elements making up the whole.

FASHION DESIGNER warns against dictating another's lifestyle or manner of path progression.

FASHION PLATE warns against latching onto the latest popular attitudes or beliefs.

FASHION SHOW signifies popular perspectives; what others are buying.

FAST (food abstinence) usually stands for efforts to purify oneself; shed negatives.

FAST BALL advises of a need to sharpen one's personal awareness. This symbol may forewarn of something coming into the dreamer's life that wasn't foreseen.

FAST FOOD suggests nourishment. This doesn't necessarily indicate unhealthy types of nourishment as much as an indication that one requires quick nourishment of some type.

FAST FORWARD can mean one of two things. It can come as an advisement to give more long-range leeway to plans or it can point to denial, not having acceptance or fortitude to face current issues.

FASTIDIOUSNESS will usually indicate a tendency toward painstaking attention to detail.

FAST LANE is a call to personal responsibility.

FAST-TALK warns against making excuses.

FAST TRACK is an advisement that the fastest way is not always the most productive means of achievement.

FAT See grease.

FAT (people) See obesity.

FAT (shape) connotes a fullness; usually overabundance in reference to excesses.

FATALISM is a direct call to use one's free will and assume the responsibilities resulting from same.

FAT CAT characterizes one who has abundant resources. This may not be a negative symbol as the term often can imply.

FAT FARM reveals a need to shed extraneous attitudes/perspectives one is carrying around.

FATHER doesn't necessarily refer to one's biological relationship, for this symbol usually represents a fatherly individual to whom the dreamer personally relates in life.

FATHER'S DAY alludes to the importance of giving recognition to the individual in the dreamer's life who is closely associated with fatherly confidence and advice.

FATHOM connotes puzzlement in one's life. Most often, this is a spiritual type of puzzlement.

FATHOMLESS advises of concepts that are far over one's head.

FATIGUE is a call to re-energize oneself and usually indicates energy ill spent due to a weakened condition.

FATIGUES See combat fatigues.

FAUCET implies the control one has. Usually this is associated with spiritual aspects and implies control used to selectively turn one's spiritual behavior on and off.

FAULT LINE advises of negatives generated by self; one's own faults.

FAUST comes as a reminder that power and knowledge are nothing unless accompanied by the wisdom of the soul.

FAUX (false) points to an imitation; a replication. This symbol carries polarity. The positive intent would be associated with imitations that save lives such as faux fur coats. The negative intent would be related to an advisement to stop presenting false fronts (two-faced).

FAVOR represents generosity of spirit.

FAWN characterizes an emotionally sensitive nature; innocence.

FAX (machine) pertains to a need for a speedy communication. This would indicate a situation or relationship that could be saved by an immediate communication.

FBI AGENT represents one who has an analytic nature; one who has a tendency to check background details.

FEAR signifies one's personal insecurities; a lack of self-confidence. See below for the meaning of the fear of:

Accidents (Dystychiphobia) signifies one's inability to focus on the moment.

Ageing (Gerascophobia) represents a subconscious demeaning perspective of the elderly; a lack of appreciation for life stages; emphasis placed on youthful appearance.

Alcohol (Methyphobia) denotes doubts regarding one's grip on self-control.

Aloneness (Autophobia) refers to a dissatisfaction of one's beingness. May require the presence of others to give one validation.

Amnesia (Amnesiphobia) relates to an insecurity of one's identity; fearful of losing the sense of self.

Amputees (Apotemnophobia) shows that one perceives one's beingness solely identified and related to a wholeness of body.

Animals (Zoophobia) shows a misunderstanding regarding the interrelatedness of all living things.

Ants (Myrmecophobia) refers to an inability or reluctance to cooperate with others.

Asymmetrical things (Asymmetriphobia) indicates an inability to accept anything veering from the norm.

Atomic explosions (Nucleomituphobia) denotes strong empathetic sensitivity toward all living things. May display an uneasiness about others having such destructive control.

Attack (Scelerophobia) relates to an insecurity regarding one's personal defenses.

Automobiles (Motorphobia) signifies some type of uneasiness regarding one's physical self-characteristics, attributes, presentation.

Bad men/burglars (Scelerophobia) relates to a sense of vulnerability.

Bacteria (Bacillophobia) characterizes a dread of being affected by others in some way.

Baldness (Peladophobia) implies trepidation of losing the ability to think clearly.

Bathing (Bathophobia) infers concern over exposing oneself to life's negatives.

Beards (Pogonophobia) points to suspicion over what someone may be hiding.

Bed, going to (Clinophobia) reflects a fear of dying before certain goals are accomplished.

Bees (Apiphobia) signifies insecurities toward teamwork.

Beggars (Hobophobia) indicates a disquieting feeling when faced with another's desperation; wanting to avoid feeling helpless to improve another's situation.

Birds (Ornithophobia) reveals an inability to deal with the various personalities of others.

Black color (Melanophobia) denotes a shrinking from problems and everything one can't immediately understand.

Blindness (Scotomaphobia) refers to a dread of losing one's sharp perceptive skills.

Blood (Hemophobia) relates to apprehension over losing one's motivation, inner strength, or perseverance.

Blushing (Erythrophobia) points to a lack of self-confidence; fear of embarrassment.

Body odor (Bromidrosiphobia) suggests a dread of offending others and diminishing their opinion of self.

Bogeyman (Bogyphobia) indicates a desire to avoid everyone who causes any type of uneasiness or trepidation.

Books (Bibliophobia) connotes an attempt to shield oneself against any information that may invalidate one's perception, belief, or attitude.

Brain disease (Meningitophobia) illustrates a terror of losing one's sense of reason and logic.

Bridges, crossing (Gephyrophobia) denotes trepidation over being cut off from those one is connected to in life.

Buildings, high (Batophobia) refers to an apprehension over having one's feet so far off the ground; a fear of being forced into a situation where one doesn't feel grounded.

Bullets (Ballistophobia) signifies a fear of losing one's grip on self-control; angst over possible emotional explosions or situations that could bring them on.

Bulls (Taurophobia) refers to anxiety over losing one's open-mindedness; a fear of becoming opinionated.

Buried alive, being (Taphephobia) signifies a fear that a pending plan or situation will be buried before it has a chance to prove itself viable.

Cancer (Carcinomaphobia) relates to a fear of a great negative aspect coming into one's life. May also signify a lack of acceptance; inability to deal with problems.

Cats (Ailurophobia) denotes a near panic in regard to possibilities of losing one's independence.

Cemeteries (Coimetrophobia) usually means a fear of having secrets exposed.

Changes (Metathesiophobia) points to rigidity.

Changes, making (Tropophobia) indicates unadaptability.

Chemicals (Chemophobia) denotes a fear of confusion, a mixing of various negative elements that may pose difficulties or great problems.

Chickens (Alektorophobia) alludes to anxiety; fear of being near anything that may elicit anxiety or stressful moments.

Childbirth/pregnancy (Tocophobia) means trepidation over starting anything new, especially brand new beginnings. This may also relate to new ideas.

Children (Pedophobia) stands for an inability to relate to youth; a fear of releasing the child within.

Choking (Pnigophobia) suggests a fear one will misspeak or have to eat one's words at some point. Denotes an extremely verbally cautious tendency.

Churches (Ecclesiophobia) pertains to a tendency to avoid anything remotely connected to religion or spiritual issues.

Clocks (Chronomentrophobia) reveals a time-stressed individual who is almost anal about keeping to scheduled appointments. Usually signifies a type A personality.

Clothes (Vestiophobia) relates to someone who puts a priority on external appearances. This is associated to one who fears her clothing may not present the best possible first impression.

Clouds (Nephophobia) represents an inclination to feel anxiety over anything that one perceives as being a threat to attitudes, perception, or beliefs.

Clowns (Coulrophobia) represents distress for those who are socially reserved and fear the exposure of their lighter side.

Coitus (Coitophobia) won't necessarily refer exclusively to a sexual meaning. It will most often directly point to the issue of getting close to another; fear of having a close relationship that could grow into the kind of intimacy where confidentialities are shared.

Cold (Frigophobia) equates to a worry about losing one's sensitivities.

Cold, extreme, including frost and ice (Cryophobia) applies to a fear of becoming apathetic.

Colors (Chromophobia) reflects an introvert who has a fear of expressing individuality; a fear of standing out.

Comets (Cometophobia) portrays having qualms about experiencing epiphanies or some type of spiritual awakening.

Computers (Computerphobia) indicates one's comfortable position with what they know and points to a fear of having to learn new things or expand their current base of knowledge.

Confined places (Claustrophobia) refers to a fear of being closed in or getting in situations where one is put in "tight" circumstances.

Constipation (Coprastasophobia) applies to the alarming sense of being unable to express oneself.

Contagious, being (Tapinophobia) is associated with the ego, wanting to be liked. This is a fear of being separated or isolated by others.

Cooking (Mageirocophobia) stands for an aversion to having to plan things. This relates to a follower rather than a leader.

Crowds (Demophobia) characterizes a retiring or introverted personality. This shows trepidation over situations where a possibility exists for one to be judged or criticized.

Crucifixes/crosses (Staurophobia) denotes an aversion to "looking back" or being reminded of the sacrifices made in life.

Crystals/glass (Crystallophobia) implies a reluctance to look at one's overall spirituality or spiritual behavior.

Dampness/moisture (Hygrophobia) infers a distasteful attitude toward the slightest indication of anything spiritual.

Dancing (Chorophobia) pertains to a dislike of showing emotions.

Dark (Nyctophobia) stands for an abhorrence of anything one can't see. This usually directly relates to a suspiciousness of another's intentions or ulterior motives.

Dawn (Eosophobia) connotes a fear of starting new things.

Daylight (Phengophobia) signifies a dread of exposure; of light illuminating an issue.

Death/corpses (Necrophobia) refers to an attempt to deny reality. Depicts a fear of having to accept one's mortality; a misunderstanding of true Reality and the essence of oneself.

Decisions, making (Decidophobia) points to a lack of self-confidence; fear of taking a responsible position.

Deformity (Dysmorphophobia) alludes to an inability to see potential in everyone. Signifies a skewed perspective in regard to another's value as a productive individual. May indicate a fear of a situation where one is forced to face another's strength of character.

Demons/goblins (Demonophobia) infers an inability to deal with life's negatives. This could also point to a fear of having to engage in a conflict with one's demons in order to overcome them.

Dentists (Dentophobia) connotes an anxiety over being criticized for one's expressed attitudes or perspectives. This means a fear of someone trying to alter or change one's mind.

Dependency on others (Soteriophobia) suggests not only a fear of losing one's independence but also one's high impression of one's self-sufficiency. This borders on the idea that the dreamer doesn't need anyone.

Depths See fear (bathing).

Dining (Deipnophobia) displays self-consciousness.

Dirt (Mysophobia) portrays angst over anything that isn't straightforward or black and white. This means an attempt to avoid anything not cut and dried or perfectly clean.

Disease/illness (Pathophobia) indicates a mind-set of perfection; a fear of any negatives or problems in one's life.

Dizziness (Dinophobia) refers to a fear of being confused or involved in any type of complex situation or relationship.

Doctors (Iatrophobia) alludes to an aversion to anyone who may offer suggestions. This denotes an arrogant personality who knows the best way to do everything. May also point to a fear of learning something is wrong.

Doctrine deviation (Hereiophobia) suggests a fear of discovering flaws in one's perception of belief.

Dogs (Cynophobia) will reflect a tendency to distrust people, especially friends.

Dolls (Pediophobia) denote a disquietude regarding the motives of others. This may pertain to a tendency to look at another's motives with a suspicious eye.

Double vision (Diplophobia) applies to a fear of losing one's ability to see things clearly.

Drafts (Aerophobia) signifies a fear of one's perspective, attitude, or conclusion being disturbed by the entrance of new angles or aspects.

Dreams (Oneirophobia) stands for apprehension over revealed truths.

Drugs (Pharmacophobia) symbolizes a reluctance to accept help from outside sources; may indicate an unrealistic attitude of being able to handle things oneself.

Dryness (Xerophobia) implies a need to keep hitches out of one's life. A desire to avoid any forms of slow or declining phases; a need to keep things well-oiled.

Dust (Amathophobia) typifies one who must remain active and on top of things.

Electricity (Electrophobia) represents a dislike and distrust for any type of control from a source other than one's own.

Empty rooms (Kenophobia) suggest a lack of creativity. Reflects one's own lack of vision.

England/anything English (Anglophobia) will be a dream symbol revealing a basic attitude of ethnic intolerance.

Everything (Panophobia) denotes severe insecurity; paranoia.

Evil spirits (Demonophobia) points to weak self-confidence; lacking inner strength.

Eyes (Ommatophobia) relates to an introvert with severe insecurities.

Fabrics, specific (Textophobia) reveals a fear of a specific type of personality.

Failure/defeat (Kakorrhaphiophobia) comes from a goal-oriented individual who is an overachiever and can't face the humiliation of an unsuccessful outcome.

Fat, becoming (Obesophobia) reveals a fear of losing control.

Fatigue (Kopophobia) suggests a belief that one's endurance is unsurpassed.

Fear (Phobophobia) signifies a self-assured individual who panics at the thought of showing distress, anxiety, or apprehension over anything. This points to someone who believes her/his feathers can't be ruffled.

Fever (Pyrexiophobia) characterizes an individual who dreads showing emotionalism; someone taking pride in routine displays of inner strength.

Figure 8 (Octophobia) indicates a fear of having irrational or distorted thoughts; one who boasts of always being rational.

Filth (Rhypophobia) symbolizes a loathing for anything having negatives associated with it; a fear of being contaminated by another's characteristics or attitudes that the dreamer perceives as being negative traits.

Fire (Pyrophobia) exemplifies an abhorrence of emotional outbursts or a situation that looks like it may develop into a heated confrontation.

Firearms (Hoplophobia) alludes to a tendency to avoid conflict, even if it will harmlessly come to resolution.

Fish (Ichthyophobia) usually stems from a revulsion of anything associated with religious or spiritual aspects.

Flavors/taste (Geumophobia) applies to someone who is most comfortable with mundane and bland elements of life. This would also be someone who prefers not to experience new things.

Floods (Antlophobia) relates to a fear of being spiritually inundated.

Flowers (Anthophobia) signifies a denial of one's inherent talents.

Flying (Aerophobia) equates to a fear

of having and/or expressing unique thoughts.

Fog (Nebulaphobia) reveals anxiety over obscure or undefined ideas, relationships, or other situations.

Food (Cibophobia) typifies one who is fearful of nourishing a particular aspect of self or one's life.

Forests (Hylophobia) denotes a strong reluctance to acknowledge one's abilities or natural skills.

Freedom (Eleutherophobia) signifies insecurities; a hesitancy to go it alone.

Friday 13th (Paraskavedekatriaphobia) characterizes a deeply superstitious nature.

Frogs/toads See fear (toads/frogs).

Fur/animal skin (Doraphobia) exemplifies a fear of exposing one's self-centeredness.

Gaiety (Cherophobia) pertains to the belief that something bad will happen to detract from joy felt.

Garlic (Alliumphobia) points to a belief that one must acknowledge the negative elements in life if one needs to utilize protective measures against them. Therefore, one fears the idea of protective measures.

Gays/lesbians (Homophobia) signifies a general aversion to inherent human diversity or traits opposite from those of self.

Germs (Microphobia) applies to a dread of contaminating self. This usually pertains to personal perspectives defining social status.

Ghosts (Phasmophobia) indicates a fear of certain elements of one's past returning for the purpose of demanding closure.

God/religion (Theophobia) reveals an aversion to the idea of divinity and all its related elements.

Gold (Aurophobia) refers to a lack of trust regarding wealth. This lack of trust may be associated with self—an inability to handle finances.

Good news (Euphobia) characterizes a pessimist; suggests a belief that all good news has a down side.

Gravity (Barophobia) applies to a fear of reaching one's limitations.

Hair (Chaetophobia) illustrates concern over another's thoughts.

Halloween (Samhainophobia) signifies dread of discovering the hidden aspects of another person's character.

Heart attack (Angionophobia) represents an attempt to escape emotional shock.

Heart disease (Cardiophobia) alludes to a fear of being emotionally hurt.

Heat (Thermophobia) refers to an evasive move to avoid being faced with motivational elements. This points to procrastination.

Heaven (Uranophobia) portrays spiritual denial.

Heights (Acrophobia) indicates a lack of self-confidence; reluctance to advance due to fear of failure; may point to being intimidated by lofty plans or new challenges.

Hell (Hadephobia) usually represents a fear of depression.

Horses (Hippophobia) refers to one's wild nature and the fear of letting others see it.

Hospitals (Nosocomephobia) denotes rejuvenation and the fear of not being the same afterward.

Houses (Domatophobia) applies to an apprehension over losing one's safe and secure refuge. This apprehension turns into an actual fear of what is most prized.

Human beings (Anthropophobia) signifies a distrust of worldly aspects.

Hurricanes/tornadoes (Lilapsophobia) relates to an aversion to fanaticism and the chance one may be drawn into it.

Hypnotized, being (Hypnophobia) implies distress caused by the possibility of being made to do something foolish or being humiliated.

Ideas (Ideophobia) stands for an inability to process new information. May also point to a disinterest in doing so.

Ignored, being (Athazagoraphobia) comes to underscore one's sense of self and avoiding situations where that sense could be eroded.

Imperfection (Atelophobia) infers unrealistic expectations and the fear of them not materializing. This converts to a denial of reality.

Infection (Molysomophobia) refers to an effort to avoid negative elements in one's life that are believed to bring harmful ramifications.

Infinity (Apeirophobia) reflects an insistence on closure for everything. This implies an individual's tendency to fear anything that could remain in an ongoing state.

Injections (Trypanophobia) signifies a fear of anything new or different invading one's personal space.

Injury (Traumatophobia) alludes to concern over some type of harm breaking through one's sense of strong protection.

Insanity (Lyssophobia) signifies a fear of losing one's grip on reality.

Insects (Entomophobia) relates to an inability to deal with life's little irritations.

Jumping (Catapedaphobia) pertains to a fear of becoming impatient.

Knowledge (Epistemophobia) denotes a reluctance to shoulder the responsibility that knowledge brings.

Laughter (Gelophobia) applies to a reluctance to express joy due to the possibility that it will be balanced by grief or hardship.

Lawsuits (Liticaphobia) depicts angst over a possible demand of retribution.

Learning (Sophophobia) stands for a fear of discovering if one is advancing or falling behind.

Light (Photophobia) reveals anxiety over having clear perception without the shadows of one's many attitudes.

Lightning/thunder (Astraphobia) alludes to a reluctance to experience spiritual aspects, such as epiphanies, visions, insights.

Long waits (Macrophobia) refers to an evasion of experiencing impatience, anxiety, stressful situations.

Love, falling or being in (Philophobia) characterizes one who panics at the thought of a broken relationship or being abandoned; therefore, one fears being in love.

Machinery (Mechanophobia) infers a desire to avoid assistance. This means a tendency to rely on one's own energy or ingenuity to accomplish goals.

Magic (Rhabdophobia) indicates an aversion to all things one doesn't understand or can't figure out by applying logic to it.

Marriage (Gamophobia) denotes a fear of close relationships.

Meat (Carnophobia) implies an aversion to accepting basic premises, opting instead for convoluted ideas that are interwoven with personal perspectives.

Medicine (Pharmacophobia) refers to a lack of trust.

Memories (Mnemophobia) denotes a hesitancy to delve into the past. Perhaps there have been traumatic events one is fearful of revisiting. A fear of memories points to someone who lives for the present and only faces forward to the future.

Men (Androphobia) is most often a female phobia and it usually stems from distrust.

Menstruation (Menophobia) can be generated from a religious source because various religions believe a menstruating woman is unclean and others believe the menstrual blood holds great, fearsome power. A dream displaying this type of fear will point to someone who holds antiquated and false beliefs.

Metal (Metallophobia) signifies an attempt to avoid any negative life elements that one could feel threatened or contaminated by.

Mice (Musophobia) refers to worry over something invading and upsetting one's set and secure routine.

Mirrors (Catoptrophobia) signifies apprehension over facing (knowing) oneself.

Money, touching (Chrematophobia) implies an attempt to avoid responsibility. The thinking behind this is that if one doesn't touch something one isn't responsible for it.

Monsters (Teratophobia) illustrates anxiety around whatever one perceives as having power over oneself.

Moon (Selenophobia) applies to trep-

idation over spiritual or psychic aspects that have esoteric elements. May also symbolize a fear of woman power.

Mother-in-law (Pentheraphobia) shows a lack of self-confidence. This fear is associated with anything that may represent a powerful overbearing individual.

Moths (Mottephobia) stands for a fear of being drawn into spiritual beliefs that could ultimately cause harm.

Moving (Tropophobia) portrays a severe insecurity over leaving one's comfortable and familiar surroundings. This indicates a fear of new places, experiences, and starting over.

Music (Musicophobia) represents a desire to shield oneself from being emotionally affected.

Myths (Mythophobia) exemplifies an avoidance of hearing stories that hit home. This applies to a fear of suddenly hearing the truth about something.

Narrowness (Anginophobia) depicts a need for personal space.

Needles/pins (Belonephobia) points to a pessimist. This is because this points to a fear based on the *negative* aspect (being pricked) of the object instead of the *positive* (a tool used for repair) side of it.

New things (Cenophobia) alludes to an aversion to putting the familiar aside.

Night (Nyctophobia) pertains to an over-active imagination. This usually points to an individual who envisions things going bump in the night.

Noise (Acoustiphobia) pertains to a low stress tolerance. This signifies someone who is easily irritated by simple distractions.

Nosebleeds (Epistaxiophobia) relates to a fear of routine being interrupted.

Northern/Southern Lights (Auroraphobia) denotes trepidation over experiencing or being touched by uncommon spiritual events in one's life.

Old people (Gerontophobia) signifies dread over being faced with one's mortality or the idea of ageing.

Open spaces (Agoraphobia) represents insecurities; greatly stressed by the feeling of being exposed, out there.

Opposite sex (Sexophobia) relates to a yin-yang imbalance; a condition of being out of touch with one's opposite gender characteristics.

Outer space (Spacephobia) relates to trepidation over feeling helpless, weightless.

Overworking (Ponophobia) suggests a fear of becoming an A-type personality.

Pain (Algophobia) indicates a dread of being hurt in life. This doesn't solely relate to physical pain but is usually associated with heartache.

Paper (Papyrophobia) is usually connected to the printed word and pertains to a fear of reading something one doesn't understand or is reluctant to know.

People (Anthropophobia) may indicate an introvert or pertain to an aversion to germs.

Performing/being on stage (Topophobia) infers panic over being watched and then judged. This reflects a deep-seated feeling of inferiority.

Philosophy (Philosophobia) stands for a fear of learning the root causes of one's own behaviors.

Photographs/photographers (no term) connotes a personal fear or intolerance of knowledge or aspects of enlightenment. May point to an inferiority complex.

Plants (Botanophobia) reveals a fear of utilizing one's natural talents and not measuring up to expectations.

Pleasure (Hedonophobia) suggests that one believes she isn't deserving of the more enjoyable elements of life.

Poetry (Metrophobia) represents an anxiety over the possibility of unexpectedly hearing or reading hidden messages that hit home. This relates to an overscrupulous conscience.

Pointed objects (Aichmophobia) implies a fear of having to get to the point. This reveals a tendency to avoid issues.

Poisons (Iophobia) suggests angst over being close to a certain element in life that could cause serious harm.

Politicians (Politicophobia) denotes distrust.

Pope (Papaphobia) exemplifies a fear of spiritual domination.

Poverty (Peniaphobia) applies to a fear of recognizing some element of one's beingness that's severely lacking.

Precipices (Cremnophobia) denotes anxiety over the possibility of being pulled into making wrong decisions; a fear of being coerced or manipulated.

Progress (Prosophobia) portrays trepidation over the possibility of failure or an inability to keep up.

Punishment (Poinephobia) pertains to a fear of doing something wrong. This suggests anxiety over the possibility of failure.

Purple (Porphyrophobia) indicates a

deep anxiety over gaining spiritual enlightenment or wisdom.

Radiation (Radiophobia) portrays a fear of the possibility of being the recipient of harming effects caused by outside sources.

Railways (Siderodromophobia) infers an aversion to paths, decisions, or situations that have no alternative course.

Rain (Ombrophobia) could be tied in to the fear of getting wet. This typifies anxiety over the possibility of new or enlightening aspects affecting one's solid belief system.

Red See fear (blushing).

Relatives (Syngenesophobia) denotes an aversion to others knowing everything about oneself.

Religious ceremonies (Teleophobia) reveals a loathing for anything related to structured spirituality.

Reptiles (Herpetophobia) indicates an abhorrence for all things one doesn't understand.

Responsibility (Hypengyophobia) suggests anxiety over failure.

Ridicule (Katagelophobia) reflects feelings of inferiority; a fear of being criticized.

Ruins (Atephobia) indicates a sense of dread over witnessing evidence of a social or cultural decline. This is associated with a fear of impermanence.

Rust See fear (poisons).

Sacred objects (Hierophobia) alludes to a sense of awe and its corresponding feeling of being unworthy.

Safe place, leaving See fear (open spaces).

Saints (Hagiophobia) relates to feelings of inadequacy.

Satan (Satanophobia) indicates a fear of being touched by evil or negative influences.

School, going to (Didaskaleinophobia) portrays a lack of understanding one's potential.

Sea (Thalassophobia) implies a fear of being overwhelmed by spiritual aspects.

Sermons (Homilophobia) relates to a dislike for being lectured to.

Shadows (Sciophobia) may indicate paranoia or a suspiciousness of anything that isn't black and white.

Sharp instruments (Aichmophobia) refers to a reluctance to get near anything that has the possibility of having duality, meaning possibly negative or harmful aspects to it. This would usually point to a pessimist who only perceives the negative side of things.

Shellfish (Ostraconophobia) denotes a fear of spiritual overload.

Sin (Hamartophobia) typifies an over-scrupulous conscience.

Single, staying (Anuptaphobia) reflects a low self-esteem; a lack of self-confidence.

Sitting still (Cathisophobia) usually points to a type-A personality, but may be associated with someone who fears being someone's target.

Skin infested with mites (Acarophobia) reveals an illusion of persecution; a false belief that one is always being attacked; paranoia; a suspicious nature.

Sleep (Somniphobia) illustrates a dread of dying. This may also portray angst over being surprised or caught unawares.

Slime (Blennophobia) applies to a

fear of being involved with a distasteful situation that has to be dealt with.

Smells (Olfactophobia) stands for a dislike for being affected by external sources.

Snakes (Ophidiophobia) pertains to an aversion for facing things that one doesn't understand.

Snow (Chionophobia) signifies an attempt to avoid being touched by spiritual elements.

Social inferiority (Social phobia) refers to a belief that everyone's better than you. This indicates an inferiority complex.

Solitude See fear (aloneness).

Sourness (Acerophobia) represents a tendency to avoid anything in life that has the possibility of causing a bitterness; a desire to evade hard-to-take situations.

Speaking aloud (Phonophobia) alludes to a fear of saying something wrong or being criticized for speaking one's mind.

Speed (Tachophobia) will reveal someone who has to take things slowly in order to remain focused.

Spiders (Arachnophobia) stands for a fear of being caught in sticky situations or being manipulated by someone's ulterior motive.

Stairs (Climacophobia) signifies a fear of moving in a direction that's vertical to one's comfortable course; being afraid of advancing or backsliding.

Stars (Siderophobia) depicts an aversion to any reminders that one needs to keep vigilant in respect to one's spiritual behavior.

Stealing (Cleptophobia) indicates a fear of wanting to achieve goals without expending energy to that end; a sense of undeserving.

Strangers (Xenophobia) stands for distrust.

Streets, crossing (Agiophobia) refers to a fear of having to get to the other side of something; a reluctance to alter a course.

Strings (Linonophobia) signifies great anxiety over having to start something new; fearful of entanglements.

Stuttering (Psellismophobia) depicts trepidation over the possibility of being humiliated while expressing one's opinion.

Sunshine (Heliophobia) may reveal a suspicious nature, fear of something which causes shadows (questionable aspects).

Surgery (Tomophobia) represents anxiety over losing control. May also be associated with a fear of dying.

Swallowing (Phagophobia) stands for a fear of becoming gullible.

Symbols (Symbolophobia) applies to a great dislike for anything that isn't spelled out; a tendency to shy away from obscure ideas.

Symmetry (Symmetrophobia) refers to a suspicion over anything that appears to be precisely balanced; seeming perfection is suspect.

Technology (Technophobia) signifies a distrust of advancements.

Telephones (Telephonophobia) infers an aversion for communicating with a faceless person; avoidance of situations where one can't read another's body language.

Test-taking (Testophobia) connotes anxiety regarding possible failure; trepidation regarding one's ability or competence.

Theaters (Theatrophobia) stands for a fear of any situation that could distract one from focused attention.

Thinking (Phronemophobia) reveals a lack of faith in one's thought process.

Thunderstorms (Astraphobia) applies to a fear that one's spiritual or ethical misbehavior will be discovered.

Time (Chronophobia) exemplifies anxiety over meeting deadlines or keeping to schedules.

Toads/frogs (Bufonophobia) signifies panic over the possibility of becoming mentally impaired.

Tombstones (Placophobia) reveals a fear of facing one's mortality; of the possibility of one's death date being revealed.

Touching/being touched (Aphephobia) indicates an aversion to the possibility of being contaminated in some way from another.

Trains See fear (railways).

Travel (Hodophobia) relates to a deep anxiety over being away from one's secure ground. This points to a fear of being in unfamiliar territory.

Trees (Dendrophobia) denotes apprehension over the effectiveness or quality of one's natural talents.

Ugliness (Cacophobia) applies to a strong desire to perceive everything as though viewed through rose-colored glasses. This is an inability to face reality as it is.

Untidiness (Ataxiophobia) points to one who detests disorder. Life must be orderly, efficient, and well structured.

Vaccination/vaccines (Vaccinophobia) signifies distrust; a conscious choice to avoid protective measures because of suspicion.

Vegetables (Lachanophobia) reflects an inclination to discount basic facts in lieu of sticking to one's own perception.

Vehicles, riding in (Amaxophobia) points to distrust of another's judgment.

Venereal disease (Cypridophobia) relates to a fear of close relationships.

Ventriloquist's dummies/wax likeness (Automatonophobia) stands for a disquietude regarding unnatural or artificial sources.

Vertigo See fear (dizziness).

Vomiting (Emetophobia) pertains to a fear of accepting/ingesting harmful ideas.

Walking (Basiphobia) alludes to a dread of having to go it alone; fear of being independent.

War See fear (injury).

Wasps (Spheksophobia) alludes to a fear of being stung by someone; ongoing suspicion that friendships or plans will backfire.

Water (Hydrophobia) reveals someone who has great trepidation regarding all things religious or spiritual.

Weakness (Asthenophobia) will reveal an egotistical individual who is fearful of displays of frailty.

Wealth (Plutophobia) points to the perspective that wealth causes the world's ills.

Weight gain See fear (fat, becoming).

White color (Leukophobia) denotes a fear that one's imperfections might show.

Wind (Ancraophobia) suggests trepidation over showing emotions, especially strong ones.

Witches/witchcraft (Wiccaphobia) indicates a fear of those of whom one has little knowledge.

Women, beautiful (Venustaphobia) reveals intimidation; fear of being perceived as beneath others, not acceptable in another's eyes.

Woods See fear (forests).

Worms (Scoleciphobia) signifies a fear that one's orderly and comfortable life will be interfered with. This is a tendency to look at everything with suspicion.

Wrinkles, getting (Rhytiphobia) reflects a fear of appearing old. This signifies jumbled priorities.

Writing (Graphophobia) reveals an inhibition to express oneself outwardly.

Wrongdoing (Peccatiphobia) denotes a fear of reprisals.

X-rays See fear (radiation).

Yellow color (Xanthophobia) denotes a fear of being perceived as cowardly and having no inner strength.

FEARLESS may allude to carelessness; a lack of giving due respect to dangerous life aspects.

FEASIBILITY ANALYSIS represents the wisdom of taking a cautionary look at the viability of a plan.

FEAST connotes great satisfaction or personal pleasure.

FEAST DAYS (saints') brings attention to a particular saint's attributes and advises the importance of utilizing those qualities in our own lives.

FEAT designates a great step that is forthcoming and will be successfully achieved. This symbol comes as encouragement for one who is anxious about accomplishing this deed.

FEATHER stands for a free-spirited thinker; applies to an open and expanding intellect; deep wisdom.

FEATHER (in hair) points to an epiphany; some type of bright idea or realization.

FEATHER (in hat) signifies an accomplishment.

FEATHER BED suggests a down-to-earth perspective regarding one's personal attainment of wisdom.

FEATHER DUSTER denotes the use of wisdom to make determining decisions; discerning intellect.

FEATHER HEADDRESS implies an arrogance for one's great intellect.

FEATHERWEIGHT signifies the presence of intellect and wisdom regardless of size.

FEATURE (main item) draws attention to an important life aspect that one may be overlooking or ignoring.

FEATURE (physical human characteristics) See specific type.

FEBRUARY usually connotes a time to begin the formulation of new plans.

FEDERAL BUILDINGS represent major issues in one's life. The symbolic interpretation for this dreamscape factor will hinge on which type of federal building was shown.

FEDERAL CASE warns of serious ramifications associated with one's behavior.

FEDERAL RESERVE SYSTEM cautions of a situation that is slipping out of one's control.

FEDERATION portrays a unified group of individuals.

FEDORA relates to underhandedness.

FEE alludes to some type of cost attached to something. Surrounding aspects will clarify what this specifically refers to.

FEEBLE-MINDED advises of a self-generated condition of psychological escapism for the purpose of avoiding personal responsibility.

FEEBLENESS warns of a dependency.

FEEDBACK suggests a need to listen to one's own words. Give more attention to what one says.

FEEDBAG illustrates a need for motivation.

FEEDER (any type) applies to a supportive life factor.

FEEDING TUBE warns against an idea being force-fed.

FEEDLOT (cattle) indicates a situation or relationship that is being deceptively nurtured; congeniality for the sake of self-motivations.

FEED STORE (ranch) stands for a desire to nourish and care for all life forms and the efforts expended toward achieving that goal.

FEELER See antenna.

FEELING (tactile motion) connotes a cautious approach.

FEET indicate how one travels one's path; recall condition.

FELDSPAR stands for communications; a need to transmit ideas better.

FELINE See cat.

FELINE DISTEMPER See distemper.

FELON will stand for bad past behavior, not necessarily a current negative factor.

FELT (fabric) implies a softened attitude through the compression of comprehensive factors; acceptance by way of overlooking the more personally viewed negatives.

FEMALE represents intellect coupled with compassion.

FEMINIST characterizes equality regardless of separatist characteristics or attitudes

FEMME FATALE pertains to alluring life aspects.

FENCE denotes self-generated barriers; one's personal distance.

FENCE-MENDING comes in dreams to advise of the wisdom of mending relationships, correcting misunderstandings.

FENCE-SITTING implies indecision.

FENCING (material) denotes that which one utilizes to create personal barriers, perhaps even from self.

FENCING (sporting art) refers to the act of being evasive or keeping others at bay.

FENDER portrays one's personal guard; protective factors.

FENDER BENDER stands for a minor altercation; small conflict, perhaps within oneself.

FENG SHUI stands for a desire to achieve harmony through another's idea of it instead of making adjustments according to how you feel about your own rearrangement ideas.

FENNEL connotes a need for emotional calming.

FENUGREEK defines an attitude that serves to aid acceptance.

FERAL (characteristic) will most often refer to an expression of deep passion/fervor. This is not a sexual reference but rather one that reaches to the core of one's beingness. An example would be a feral love of nature.

FERMENTATION usually refers to a state of in-depth analyzation; contemplation; extensive research.

FERN defines fruitful corporal acts. Check condition of the dreamscape fern to determine the precise quality of these acts.

FEROCIOUS (behavior) will most often imply a deeply passionate attitude attached to a specific life aspect. An example would be a mother's protective response toward a defenseless child.

FERRET typifies attitudes or responses tempered with a sense of humor; may also indicate a need to do some further investigative work.

FERRIS WHEEL emphasizes a circling in place; lack of advancement or development.

FERRY represents opportunities to utilize spirituality in life.

FERTILITY CLINIC reveals a need to understand why one isn't motivated to put energy into starting a new beginning.

FERTILIZER exemplifies a need to rejuvenate or nourish a life aspect that could refer to one's mental, emotional, physical, or spiritual facet.

FERVOR See passion.

FESTER advises one to release pent-up emotions.

FESTIVAL represents a cause for celebration. Recall what type of festival it was.

FESTOON defines a joyous state of being.

FETAL DISTRESS warns of dangerous aspects related to new beginnings.

FETAL MONITOR indicates a close watch on the progress of one's new path.

FETAL POSITION means a severe lack of self-confidence; fear of facing reality or one's personal responsibilities. May indicate how one's new path is lining up.

FETID (odor) reveals an issue with one or more elements which aren't quite acceptable.

FETISH See charm.

FETUS characterizes a new life; new beginning.

FEUD indicates a state of altercation; an ongoing conflict.

FEUDALISM warns of a domineering personality or situation.

FEUDAL LORD points to a manipulative and controlling individual; ulterior motives.

FEVER usually refers to fanaticism. This dreamscape symbol may also indicate a self-generated negative state that one must internally fight to overcome.

FEVER BLISTER See canker sore.

FEVERFEW (botanical) indicates a means to overcome one's psychological negatives and bring about an inner balance; open chi channels.

FEZ (hat) connotes a thought process that is affected by specific perspectives or belief systems.

FIASCO advises of a situation or relationship that will have so many negative aspects that it will go wrong from the time of its inception.

FIBERBOARD represents the coming together of diverse aspects for the purpose of blending into a new creation; the result of utilizing one's diversified talents and knowledge.

FIBER-FILL applies to padding being done; exaggerations.

FIBER GLASS connotes dual aspects to something in the dreamer's life. Surrounding dreamscape facets will clarify; will point to an aspect that is highly useful but must be handled carefully to avoid negative effects.

FIBER OPTICS characterize the subtle sensory facets of one's perceptive reception.

FIBER OPTICS LIGHTS relate to enlightenment, the insights from the light.

FIBRILLATION (heart) pertains to instinctual responses.

FICKLE stands for an undisciplined personality; unpredictability.

FICTION implies an imaginative scenario; perhaps inventiveness.

FIDDLE See fidget.

FIDDLE See violin.

FIDDLER CRAB cautions against spiritual gullibility.

FIDGET denotes restlessness; impatience; anxiety; lack of acceptance.

FIELD suggests openness; opportunities.

FIELD DAY signifies a state of great enjoyment or opportunity; a time of high activity.

FIELD GLASSES See binoculars.

FIELD GOAL exemplifies achievements or levels of success that are less than the expected goal.

FIELD GUIDE (book) points to a need/desire to identify or find the source of a specific aspect in one's life. What type of field guide was it?

FIELD HOSPITAL cautions one to monitor self throughout the process of traveling life's more difficult path stages.

FIELD MOUSE portrays the observers we seldom become aware of.

FIELD RATIONS represent the essential elements needed to perform a specific job or achieve a particular goal.

FIELDSTONE connotes that which provides building aspects as opportunities are taken advantage of.

FIELDSTRIP (disassemble) implies preparedness.

FIELDSTRIP (leaving no trace) advises to be thorough; leave no trace or loose ends.

FIELDTEST suggests the need for a dry run of something the dreamer is planning. This could indicate a need for further planning or a switch to an alternate plan.

FIELD TRIP relates to the possible need for hands-on learning experiences. This may indicate a need for one to personally experience what another is going through in order to adequately understand it.

FIELDWORK symbolizes knowledge gained through actual experience.

FIEND is a warning sign that most often will relate to someone with whom the dreamer is directly associated.

FIERY usually connotes an emotionally impetuous personality; often experiencing emotional outbursts.

FIESTA alludes to a joyous inner celebration. What was the fiesta for? This gives greater clarity to the symbol.

FIFTH AMENDMENT represents a decision to keep personal matters a private affair.

FIFTH AVENUE defines the uppity manner by which one presents self to others.

FIFTH WHEEL indicates an unnecessary element; may point to feelings of not belonging or not being welcomed.

FIFTH WHEEL See spare tire.

FIFTH WHEEL (RV) See recreational vehicle.

FIG refers to a triviality. Depending on related dreamscape aspects, a fig can point to inner nourishment for fortifying self-confidence.

FIGHT warns of aggressive opposition.

FIGHTER (pilot) characterizes an aggressive personality; one who is used to expertly maneuvering around and through conflict.

FIGHTER (sport) See box (sport).

FIGHT SONG represents a motivational method. This won't necessarily refer to an intended conflict but rather a way of maintaining inner strength.

FIG LEAF pertains to a concern over trivialities. May point to a tendency to hide certain aspects of one's life.

FIGUREHEAD (on ship bow) represents strength to go forward, usually regarding a spiritual path or spiritually independent thought.

FIGURE SKATING See ice skate.

FIGURINE (statuette) comes as a warning message for the dreamer. This usually is a call to pay attention to what the figurine *represents*.

FIGWORT (botanical) suggests priorities, a recognition of what's really important.

FILAMENT advises of fragile relationships.

FILBERT (nut) See hazelnut.

FILE (claim) implies an act of exposing or making something public.

FILE (line) signifies a need to recognize one's place in life. This could indicate an arrogant personality or a call for more patience and acceptance.

FILE (sort) is a call to put one's life or priorities in order.

FILE (tool) suggests a need to smooth over some type of roughness. Could refer to one's manner of expression or severity of opinion.

FILE CABINET defines stored information. This is usually within self.

FILE CLERK characterizes efficiency.

FILET MIGNON portrays some type of life aspect that is choice for the dreamer; a highly desirable aspect.

FILIBUSTER warns of an obstruction to one's goals; a delay of time spent on an irrelevant issue.

FILIGREE means entanglements; complexities that were not foreseen.

FILL DIRT See backfill.

FILLET (knife) signifies a means of getting to the meat of an issue.

FILLING (food) depicts a main idea or issue.

FILLING (tooth) refers to an active effort to remove negative aspects from one's speech. This does not single out obscenities but is most often meant to relate to one's expression of overopinionated attitudes or hurtful expressions.

FILM (coating) See translucent.

FILM (photo) advises of a need to be sharply aware of a specific life aspect and remember it. Surrounding details will clarify what this is.

FILM CLIP represents a sampling; getting a taste for what something is like.

FILM CRITIC characterizes one who doesn't hesitate to voice opinions.

FILTER denotes a need for personal discernment; keeping the main issues uncluttered.

FILTER (camera) See lens.

FIN (any type) represents a life factor that serves as a directional or motivational force.

FINAL CUT (film) signifies the achievement of an acceptable outcome or plan.

FINALE means a conclusion; a dramatic ending.

FINALIST denotes success.

FINANCE COMPANY illustrates a life factor that serves to provide a means to a goal.

FINANCE OFFICER characterizes one who can open up opportunities to fulfill one's goal.

FINCH denotes emotional maturity.

FINDER'S FEE represents the price for having others uncover or provide opportunities for you.

FINDINGS (artisan supplies) stands for options for expressing one's creativity.

FINE ART refers to talented skill. This could pertain to any type of skill, such as communication, analyzation, discernment, etc.

FINE PRINT advises one to be aware of details. Reveals the presence of extenuating aspects.

FINE-SPUN refers to intricate and delicate details.

FINE-TOOTHED COMB is a call to triple-check facts and conduct in-depth research.

FINE-TUNE represents an attempt to make something as good as it can be; make the last, final improvements.

FINGER usually represents various types of behavior.

FINGER (burned) signifies interference into another's affairs.

FINGER (in pie) denotes meddling or having to be involved in multiple issues or affairs.

FINGER (raising) symbolizes a cautionary advisement.

FINGER BOWL suggests an attempt to disassociate self from something in the dreamer's life; washing one's hands.

FINGER FOOD denotes a casual/easy manner of gaining needed information.

FINGERNAIL connotes the quality of one's personal efforts; the condition will clarify this better.

FINGERNAIL (false/acrylic) points to shifting energy and responsibility to others.

FINGER PAINTING indicates an immature manner of expressing self.

FINGER-POINTING suggests a tendency to identify a guilty party or may point to an effort to shift responsibility.

FINGERPRINT (visible) reveals the fact that someone is/was present or involved with an issue.

FINGERPRINTED (being) suggests an advisement to be true to oneself, one's uniqueness of identity.

FINGER PUPPET indicates an attempt to hide behind excuses.

FINGERS (crossed) indicate hope.

FINISHING NAIL represents a concealed final touch to something.

FINISHING SCHOOL doesn't normally stand for fine social mores but rather spiritually based attributes such as kindness, compassion, understanding, forgiveness, unconditional love, etc.

FINISH LINE marks the stage when one's goals are attained. What was the dreamscape distance to this line?

FINLAND denotes a hardy character.

FIORD defines the narrow and often dangerous rites of passage through one's spiritual life.

FIRE means extreme emotional intensity.

FIRE AGATE (gemstone) stands for confusion.

FIRE ALARM warns of dangers stemming from intense emotions.

FIRE ANT cautions of a relationship, situation, or personal attitude that could end up stinging you.

FIREARM See gun.

FIREBALL means an uncontrollable, unstoppable ramification to one's explosive emotional expressions.

FIREBIRD stands for the proper utilization of emotional intensity.

FIREBOAT denotes personal safeguards against spiritual fanaticism.

FIREBRAND characterizes an individual who has tendencies toward stirring emotions that are directed toward revolt; one who riles others.

FIREBREAK stands for stopgap methods one utilizes to control overemotional states.

FIREBRICK represents an individual or situation that remains unaffected by another's emotional outbursts or tirades.

FIRE BRIGADE suggests several individuals involved in trying to solve a problem or avert a potentially explosive situation.

FIREBUG See arsonist.

FIRE CHIEF characterizes an individual who is experienced at helping to get one's emotions under control.

FIRECRACKER indicates a means of channeling one's intense emotions in a controlled manner.

FIRE DOOR portrays personal efforts utilized to protect self from the intense emotionalism of others.

FIRE DRILL signifies the importance of practicing emotional control and being prepared to face life's unexpected events.

FIRE-EATER pertains to one who effectively absorbs intense emotional expressions; being unaffected while dealing with another's emotionalism.

FIRE ENGINE alludes to life aspects that have the capability to control another's emotional explosiveness.

FIRE ESCAPE indicates one's personal methods of avoiding or escaping from intense emotional situations or events.

FIRE EXTINGUISHER suggests the existence of a specific method to calm another's emotionalism.

FIREFIGHTER represents emotional self-control.

FIREFLY defines times of intensely emotional spiritual illumination.

FIRE HOSE represents behavior or an element capable of stopping a situation from getting out of control.

FIRE HYDRANT applies to an aid in calming emotionally distraught individuals or an emotionally intense situation.

FIRE IRONS See andiron.

FIRELIGHT symbolizes emotionalism that has the ability to affect many others.

FIRE LINE See firebreak.

FIRE PIT See campfire.

FIREPLACE denotes emotional warmth; heart warmth.

FIREPLACE SCREEN stands for an attempt to keep damaging/negative elements from disrupting one's congenial/serene attitudes/feelings.

FIREPOWER represents one's level of emotional effectiveness on others.

FIREPROOF exemplifies a state or condition of being totally unaffected by another's intense emotional displays. This may also point to apathy.

FIRE SALE suggests salvageable elements; all the pieces are not lost and there are benefits still viable.

FIRE SCREEN connotes means of emotional protection; methods whereby one guards self from personally displaying emotional outbursts or guards self from the tirades of others.

FIRE STATION refers to a preparedness for an emotional emergency; an immediate motivational need.

FIRESTONE denotes a life aspect that can emotionally motivate one.

FIRESTORM warns of an extended state or time of intensive emotional outbursts or displays.

FIRE THORN (botanical) stands for a need to fortify one's inner strength to deal with forthcoming difficulties.

FIRE TOWER emphasizes a state of personal awareness regarding one's emotions and the expression of same.

FIRETRAP connotes an atmosphere which easily generates emotional explosiveness.

FIREWALL indicates an emotional barrier.

FIREWALL (computer) refers to self-protective measures put in place in order to avoid emotional confrontations.

FIREWALL (vehicle) pertains to one's attention given to preventive measures against certain damaging or explosive life elements.

FIREWEED (botanical/flower) stands for a need to improve one's perception of possible negatives; points to a need for caution.

FIREWOOD See cordwood.

FIREWORKS forewarn of an explosive situation or relationship.

FIRING LINE illustrates a position of personal responsibility for one's emotional reactive control.

FIRING SQUAD characterizes an individual who could bring devastating ramifications; may refer to a call to openly admit personal responsibility.

FIRMAMENT represents the unimagined expanse of true Reality.

FIRST AID KIT advises of an urgent need to patch up or heal the harmful effects one's actions have caused. This may even refer to a quick-fix healing of self.

FIRST BASE suggests success in accomplishing the first phase of a goal.

FIRST-BORN characterizes one's initial achievement of a new beginning that leads to additional ones.

FIRST CLASS defines optimum quality or mode of operation.

FIRST-DEGREE BURN indicates a lesson learned through a lack of awareness.

FIRST DOWN (football) denotes a first chance or opportunity.

FIRST EDITION refers to the initial dissemination of specific information.

FIRST LADY characterizes a woman who epitomizes something specific.

FIRST NAME usually has a unique meaning for each dreamer. Most often the surrounding dreamscape details will clarify this.

FIRST OFFENDER usually points to a second chance.

FISH (card game) connotes intermittent cooperation from others.

FISH (marine life) symbolizes spiritual aspects in one's life. See specific types of marine life.

FISH BOWL stands for transparencies of character; a lack of privacy or confidentiality.

FISHER (animal) denotes honesty.

FISHEYE means spiritual perceptiveness.

FISH FRY suggests the act of taking care of matters.

FISH HATCHERY denotes a spiritual birthing; developing spiritual beliefs or ideas.

FISHHOOK warns of a lazy or faulty spiritual search. We shouldn't attempt to snag any spiritual concept that happens by.

FISHING represents an unorganized or undisciplined spiritual search.

FISHING LINE refers to a length or measure of spiritual search/inquiry.

FISHING LURE warns of an arrogantly lazy approach to one's spiritual search. An expectation of spiritual information coming to one without having to put out energy to go in search of it.

FISHING ROD signifies a life aspect that has the capability of assisting in one's personal spiritual search, yet the method lacks selectiveness or discrimination.

FISHING TRIP symbolizes an intent to gain further information regarding a particular issue.

FISH MARKET defines the quality and extent of one's personal spiritual belief system. Recall the amount of fish available and their condition. What types were being offered?

FISHNET cautions of a personal lack of spiritual discernment; a tendency to gather up all spiritual concepts without being discriminating in respect to the truths.

FISH OIL stands for a highly beneficial element or characteristic.

FISHPOND illustrates spiritual opportunities.

FISH STORY alludes to spiritual elaborations; exaggerations.

FISHTAIL usually refers to a backlash reaction to some spiritual facet in the dreamer's life.

FISH TANK See aquarium.

FISHY (odor) reveals suspicion; a questionable sense to something.

FISSION portrays the multifaceted individualities of the self soul.

FISSURE warns of a crack or deep separation beginning to form within a specific aspect in one's life. Surrounding details will serve to clarify this symbol.

FIST cautions of building internal emotions.

FISTFIGHT warns against the utilization of negative resolutions.

FIT (child's) See tantrum.

FITNESS CENTER See health club.

FITTING (clothing) denotes an attempt to keep one's public persona aligned with one's true character.

FIVE signifies change.

FIVE O'CLOCK SHADOW (beard) represents overwork; time to take a break.

FIVE-STAR (rating) defines the highest quality.

FIX (drug) stands for dependency; lack of responsibility; fear of facing reality.

FIX (mend/repair) reflects a desire to correct or repair a situation or relationship.

FIXATION warns against an obsessive nature.

FIXATIVE See preservative.

FIXED INCOME stands for one being limited to what one can work with.

FIXER-UPPER points to a deal, as long as one is willing to put some personal effort into improvements.

FIZZ signifies activity, usually mental.

FLACCID means a loss of resilience; lack of motivation or energy.

FLAG symbolizes loyalty to a cause.

FLAG BEARER represents one's outward expression of loyalty.

FLAG DAY comes as a call for a show of loyalty.

FLAG PERSON (construction) comes as a warning message. What type of flag was the dream person waving? Was it a traffic caution to slow down? Stop?

FLAGPOLE alludes to opportunities to prove one's loyalties.

FLAGSHIP advises of precedent-setting individuals or events.

FLAGSTONE denotes specific life aspects that serve to pave one's way along one's path.

FLAIL reflects a tendency to blame others; strike out; retaliate.

FLAK JACKET See bulletproof vest.

FLAMBÉ connotes an intensely nutritional aspect. This will not infer dietary nutrition but rather an emotional factor for the dreamer.

FLAMBOYANT refers to an elaborately shown personality; one who must outdo others; a need to stand out in a crowd. However, this symbol may also point to one who is incredibly optimistic and can't control overwhelming feelings of joy or cheer.

FLAME signifies great intensity, usually connected to the emotions.

FLAMENCO (dance style) represents an outward expression of intense emotions.

FLAMETHROWER warns against directing uncontrolled emotions at others.

FLAMINGO is an advisement to keep both feet on the ground. This may indicate a perspective that lacks reality and needs grounding.

FLAMMABLE (objects) implies a life aspect that has the potential to become explosive.

FLANNEL (fabric) relates to levelheadedness; down to earth.

FLAPJACK See pancake.

FLAPPER denotes a frivolous nature.

FLARE See torch.

FLASH (of light) most often comes as an attention-getting message and may accompany some type of powerful words of wisdom.

FLASHBACK always reveals an important event or fact for the dreamer to remember.

FLASH BULB suggests a need to add more light to something; a need to look closer.

FLASH CARD indicates that which must be remembered or utilized on a consistent basis.

FLASH DRIVE (computer) refers to the ease of gaining/transferring information; a speedy manner of memory retrieval; may come as a reminder to keep certain information on the front burner.

FLASHER (exposing) characterizes someone who has negative motivations and uses negative impact attention-getting methods.

FLASHER (warning light) comes as some type of warning that will be clarified by surrounding dreamscape details. What was the flasher light associated with? Was it night or day?

FLASH FLOOD warns of an overload of spiritual intake. May indicate a fanatic.

FLASHLIGHT advises of a need to better illumine a specific aspect in one's life; more light (knowledge) needs to be gained.

FLASH POINT forewarns of the approaching stage where a situation or relationship will come into serious trouble.

FLASK implies convenience. This would refer to a condition whereby an important factor to the dreamer is readily available; close at hand.

FLAT (bland) represents a lack of emotional expression.

FLAT (level ground) means a span of obstacle-free pathway.

FLAT (living quarters) See apartment.

FLAT (musical notes) refers to false joy; unenthusiastic; disinterest.

FLAT (shape) denotes little substance; perhaps an emptiness.

FLATBED (truck) pertains to a life factor that constitutes a heavy load for the dreamer to carry.

FLATBOAT cautions against carrying too heavy a spiritual load; spread out one's conceptual spiritual intake over time.

FLATBREAD See unleavened.

FLATCAR (train) advises of the danger of taking on philosophical perspectives of others that are narrow-minded or one-track.

FLAT-FOOTED illustrates an uncompromising nature.

FLATIRON See iron (appliances).

FLATLAND See flat (level ground).

FLATLANDER characterizes one who is fearful of taking risks or encountering difficulties in life.

FLAT LINE reveals a dead issue; no reason to keep putting energy into it because there's no chance of it being revived.

FLATTERY warns of ulterior motives.

FLAT TIRE stands for a temporary pause in the progression of one's journey; a minor problem needing immediate attention before going any further.

FLATTOP (hair style) alludes to surface thinking; having no interest in deeper thought.

FLATULENCE relates to a pretentious nature; tediously verbose.

FLATWARE See specific utensil.

FLAVORING represents the addition of personal perspectives to facts; making something more palatable to self.

FLAVORING (artificial) See artificial flavor.

FLAW refers to shortcomings.

FLAWLESS symbolizes a sound aspect.

FLAX (botanical) signifies a life aspect that offers multiple benefits.

FLEA refers to an interference of some type.

FLEABAG (lodging) cautions against misplaced trust.

FLEABANE (plant) pertains to a defense or counter aspect to interfering life elements.

FLEABITE alludes to a temporary inconvenience or annoyance.

FLEA COLLAR implies one's personal immunity to slight setbacks; strength of character.

FLEA MARKET alludes to opportunities, especially unexpected ones.

FLECK comes as an attention-seeking message for one to notice something outstanding in one's life.

FLECKED (pattern) See speckled.

FLEDGLING stands for a beginner; a novice.

FLEECE (fabric) means a comforting aspect but also may indicate fraudulence.

FLESH pertains to one's overall character. Recall its condition.

FLESH WOUND marks a temporary setback.

FLEUR-DE-LIS (pattern) connotes aloofness.

FLEX (connector) implies adaptability.

FLEX (muscles) denotes a challenge.

FLICKER (bird) See woodpecker.

FLIGHT (airline) exemplifies a departure from the norm.

FLIGHT ATTENDANT characterizes someone in the dreamer's life who makes one's life journey easier, especially regarding perspectives and attitudes.

FLIGHT BAG signifies a planned departure from the norm.

FLIGHT PLAN stands for one's intended course or plan of action.

FLIGHT RECORDER See black box.

FLIGHT SCHOOL represents a desire to become well educated about a new direction one is planning to take.

FLIGHT SIMULATOR represents a sharpening of wit and reaction responses to sudden events; an attempt to be prepared for the unexpected.

FLIMFLAM MAN depicts fraudulence; deception; delusions. Who was this symbolic person? You? A business associate?

FLIMSY indicates superficiality.

FLINCH relates to a failure to control responses or reactions.

FLINT signifies a quick response or reaction.

FLINTLOCK See gun.

FLIP-OFF (gesture) points to rudeness; an inability to control knee-jerk reactions.

FLIPPANT relates to disrespect; arrogance.

FLIPPER See fin.

FLIRTING connotes an attempt to approach in a testing manner.

FLOAT See meander.

FLOATERS (eyesight) suggest impaired perspective; reading extraneous elements into something; assumptions.

FLOAT PLANE denotes vacillating thought patterns.

FLOCK cautions against a lack of individualized thought.

FLOCKING (fabric) denotes the a willful addition of emphasis or attention-getting elements to one's surroundings or means of communication.

FLOE (ice) See ice floe.

FLOOD warns of spiritual inundation; drowning in unprocessed spiritual information.

FLOODGATE pertains to personal controls that appropriately regulate one's spiritual intake.

FLOOD INSURANCE stands for spiritual preparedness; an open mind in respect to spiritual possibilities; a guard against spiritual overload or inundation.

FLOODLIGHT applies to an acute awareness.

FLOOD PLAIN warns of potentially dangerous ground. This usually refers to one's thought process or a specific situation.

FLOOD WALL portrays personal safeguards that shield one from being overcome by too much information; an awareness of one's intellectual capabilities; personal informational-intake regulation.

FLOOR pertains to one's moral, ethical, or spiritual foundations.

FLOOR DUTY (real estate) stands for providing another with availability and opportunity to be assisted.

FLOOR JOISTS signify the main basic philosophical concepts our character is based on. These would be ethics, morals, and sense of rightness.

FLOOR LAMP suggests a light over one's shoulder, not in a spiritual context, but more for the purpose of seeing things more clearly.

FLOOR MANAGER See floorwalker.

FLOOR PLAN constitutes thought planning.

FLOOR SAMPLE/MODEL stands for multiple opportunities.

FLOOR SHOW cautions of misplaced priorities.

FLOORWALKER signifies the wisdom of frequently checking one's personal foundational ethics against current actions.

FLOPHOUSE See fleabag.

FLOPPY means indecision; a lack of firm attitudes or strong ideals. May also point to an attitude of acceptance, a whatever attitude.

FLOPPY DISK relates to one's stored information; personal knowledge; memory bank.

FLORAL See flower.

FLORIDA signifies rewards following hard work, the upside after achievements/goals have been attained.

FLORIDA KEYS point to one's reach into new spiritual waters; the stretching of one's spiritual quest/curiosity.

FLORIST characterizes one with a multitude of natural talents. What was the condition of the flowers? What type of flowers were featured?

FLOSS See dental floss.

FLOTSAM denotes erroneous spiritual concepts.

FLOUNDER warns of spiritual faltering or vacillation.

FLOUR advises of a need to increase one's

efforts; one of the main basic elements of a plan or issue.

FLOUR MILL See gristmill.

FLOW CHART details one's best method of progression along one's path.

FLOWER pertains to one's natural and inherent talents that should beautifully blossom as they're utilized. See specific flower type.

FLOWER (dried) See dried flowers.

FLOWER CHILD See hippie.

FLOWER GIRL represents the utilization of one's budding natural talents.

FLOWERPOT signifies the conscious caring and personal cultivation of one's natural abilities and talents.

FLOW METER advises one to better regulate energies or emotions.

FLU See virus.

FLUE See air vent.

FLUFF refers to a lack of substance.

FLUME denotes a quick way to spiritual resources.

FLUNK means a failure of some type.

FLUORESCENT LAMP symbolizes one's inner light.

FLUORIDE relates to misconceptions; a tight-fisted grip on old false ideas.

FLUORITE (gemstone) provides protective forces against external negativity; defenses against life irritations.

FLUOROCARBONS connote life aspects that are dangerous.

FLUSHABLE suggests a disposable element; an advisement that something is safe to rid oneself of.

FLUSHED (complexion) implies embar-

rassment or guilt; may indicate repressed emotions.

FLUTE applies to personal power.

FLUTED (pattern) usually denotes a gregarious personality; may also point to an idea that is open to interpretation.

FLUTIST refers to a balanced and centered individual.

FLUTTER implies perplexity.

FLUX (welding) symbolizes instability; a need for a better flow of communication/information.

FLY (bait) suggests unfair/unscrupulous methods of achieving ends; using personal knowledge of someone to draw him/her to you.

FLY (insect) illustrates a life aspect that has the capability of becoming a harmful interference.

FLYBLOWN signifies corruption; a contaminated element.

FLYBY pertains to a need for close observance of something in the dreamer's life.

FLY-BY-NIGHT constitutes something in the dreamer's life that is unscrupulous and deceptive.

FLY-CASTING warns of intermittent spiritual fishing done.

FLYCATCHER (bird) denotes a positive element in one's life.

FLYER See handbill.

FLY-FISHING points to teasing or tempting with bait for the purpose of achieving a goal or drawing another to oneself.

FLYING (in plane) pertains to beginning awareness; may indicate spiritual aspects.

FLYING (w/o plane) points to an attained high level of awareness.

FLYING COLORS signifies a sense of achievement; an overwhelming triumph; success.

FLYING DUTCHMAN warns of spiritual imaginings.

FLYING FISH symbolizes spiritual application; an expanded potentiality for the expression of one's spiritual gifts.

FLYING PIG suggests a belief that something has a nil chance of becoming reality.

FLYING SAUCER See unidentified flying object.

FLYING SQUIRREL connotes the hidden aspects of self.

FLY-ON-THE-WALL reveals the presence of a (or a need to) spy; a desire to know what's happening or how another is reacting.

FLY-OVER represents an attempt to get an overall picture of an issue or situation before one actually takes action to become involved.

FLYPAPER portrays personal awareness.

FLY SHEET See handbill.

FLY SWATTER indicates an opportunity to personally deal with some of life's irritations or interferences.

FLYWHEEL reveals a need to stay on an even keel and not fluctuate between overwork/overenthusiasm and underachievement/disinterest.

FOAL characterizes new beginnings.

FOAM (rubber) pertains to exaggerations; something that's being padded for extra importance or weight.

FOAM (sea) symbolizes spiritual confusion.

FOAM (soap) See bubble bath.

FOAMY (consistency) refers to a life aspect that serves to soften or insulate.

FOCAL POINT will usually zero in on the main element of an issue. It advises where to place one's attention and energy.

FOCUS GROUP represents an unhealthy interest in what others think, an over-concern for the public's opinion—usually regarding one's appearance, behavior, or personal opinion/attitudes. This dream element points to a need for approval.

FODDER typifies useless information; lacking substance or quality.

FOE See enemy.

FOG warns of spiritual obscurity; unclear spiritual perception.

FOGHORN is always a spiritual warning. Surrounding details should clarify this for the dreamer.

FOG LIGHTS (vehicle) means an ability to see through pretenses.

FOIL See aluminum foil.

FOLDER usually represents information.

FOLDING CHAIR signifies a temporary situation, one in which one's position provides for the option of movement.

FOLDING DOOR represents opportunity; ease of entering/exiting a situation.

FOLIAGE connotes natural abilities.

FOLK ART suggests an honest, open expression of self.

FOLK DANCE defines a healthy, comfortable perspective of self.

FOLKLORE constitutes the preservation of the spirit of truths.

FOLK MEDICINE pertains to a natural, inner healing capability.

FOLK SINGER characterizes one who keeps tradition alive.

FOLKTALE See folklore.

FOLLIES (stage) refer to a beginning venue to start using one's talents.

FOLLOWING warns of a lack of self-confidence or individual thought.

FOLLOW-UP advises of a need to recheck something or make a second communication with another individual.

FOLLY indicates a lack of reasoning and logic; impulsiveness; recklessness.

FONDUE signifies warm emotional responses; congeniality.

FONT (receptacle) means abundance.

FONT (type style) emphasizes one's individual character.

FOOD always connotes some type of nourishment. This nourishment rarely has a direct relation to the physical body.

FOOD BANK represents inner strength; stored nourishment, energy.

FOOD CHAIN advises one to do deeper thinking about how everything is interrelated, how one act of behavior can affect so many different elements.

FOOD COLORING See artificial coloring.

FOOD COURT represents a source of multiple opportunities for emotional nourishment.

FOOD FAD suggests the acceptance of certain concepts because others are believing them.

FOOD INTOLERANCE refers to an idea that one can't accept.

FOO DOG (Chinese image/statue) suggests one's personal defense mechanisms; may reveal a need for them to be strengthened.

FOOD POISONING warns of nourishment obtained from contaminated sources. This would indicate a situation where one is absorbing false concepts, misconceptions, delusions, slanted perceptions, etc.

FOOD PROCESSOR indicates one's personal manner of processing information. Recall what was in the processor. Was it operational? What color was the contents?

FOOD SERVICE cautions against being handed any type of nourishment offered rather then personally choosing for self.

FOOD STAMPS emphasize the fact that everyone is entitled to emotional, mental, and spiritual nourishment.

FOOL warns against willfully avoiding knowledge and the intellectual processing of same.

FOOLPROOF defines solidness; no possibility for error.

FOOL'S CAP relates to foolhardiness and associated ramifications.

FOOL'S GOLD warns against jumping to conclusions; not thinking things out; lacking appropriate knowledge; needing discernment.

FOOSBALL (game) hints at lighthearted competition hinging on one's skill level.

FOOT signifies one's journey along one's path and the type of behavior used to progress.

FOOTAGE (film) denotes solid proof; verification.

FOOT-AND-MOUTH DISEASE signifies the negative tendency to say hurtful things to (or about) others.

FOOTBALL relates to winning through force and deception. Who were the players?

FOOTBALL PLAYER alludes to one who uses aggressiveness and complex maneuvers to attain goals.

FOOT BATH denotes an attempt to ease the aches of traveling one's path.

FOOTBOARD (vehicle) See running board.

FOOTBRIDGE connotes the connective aspects to one's life path.

FOOT-DRAGGING warns against a reluctance to continue along one's life path; a possible inner fear causing this procrastination.

FOOTGEAR See shoe; specific types.

FOOTHILLS point out a life aspect that presents a slight upward climb; a time when more energies are needed for advancement.

FOOTHOLD defines a grip on something; the attainment of a secure position.

FOOT IN DOOR naturally represents the first step in a new direction or entry into a new situation.

FOOT IN GRAVE indicates a strong advisement to back away from something and stop being involved in a dangerous situation or behavior.

FOOTINGS (construction) signify the foundational basis for an idea's development to build on.

FOOTLESS suggests the need for an alternate way of achieving one's goals. This symbol isn't a negative one, it comes to reveal the presence of an alternative direction/method.

FOOTLIGHTS warn against willfully spotlighting one's individual path for the arrogant purpose of leadership.

FOOTLOCKER will reveal one's personal priorities in life; keeping one's most important and basic elements close by.

FOOTLOOSE signifies acceptance.

FOOTMAN refers to someone who can guide your steps and help to prevent faltering moves.

FOOT MASSAGE like a foot bath, points to a tiredness regarding traveling one's path and the efforts to accept the tribulations by working to soothe each trouble spot and gain the fortitude to keep going.

FOOTNOTE advises of the wisdom to check informational sources.

FOOTPATH represents one's individualized and unique life path that, when walked, presents specialized opportunities for one's particular advancement.

FOOTPRINTS denote trace markings of those who have gone before us or those marks in life we leave behind.

FOOTRACE warns against a competing attitude.

FOOTREST advises of a need for a pause time; a resting period from walking one's path; a need to re-energize self.

FOOT SOLDIER characterizes one who walks one's path as a warrior.

FOOTSORE is a warning. Your walk along your life path has been too full of attempts to force goals. There is a need to ease up and allow events to unfold naturally.

FOOT STAMPING signifies an inability to compromise; a tendency to always need to get one's way.

FOOTSTOOL is a dream symbol that comes as an advisement to slow down as your life path is traveled. Perhaps you need to assimilate deeper meanings of lessons being presented.

FOOTWEAR signifies the manner in which one's path is traveled. See specific footwear terms for more in-depth explanations.

FOOTWORK connotes how one reacts to events and opportunities encountered along life's diverse pathways.

FORAGING pertains to efforts actively applied to taking advantage of every benefit, trial, and opportunity presented in life.

FORBIDDEN CITY portrays a fear of knowledge and attending responsibility of same.

FORBIDDEN FRUIT stands for those truths of reality that exist for our discovery, but we're fearful of admitting knowledge of them.

FORCED MARCH illustrates a life situation that needs focused attention yet shouldn't be forced into a conclusion.

FORCE-FEED warns against forcing opinions or concepts on others. Who was being fed? Who was doing the feeding?

FORCE FIELD means a barrier. This could be a self-created psychological barrier, a barrier caused by fear, or a personal field of one's energy or protection. Surrounding details will clarify this intent.

FORCE MAJEURE signifies an unavoidable cause of failure.

FORCEPS warns against forcing a spiritual rebirth.

FOREARM alludes to defense attitudes or preparations.

FOREBODING (atmosphere) comes as a warning sign and advises one to be acutely aware of surroundings and developing events.

FORECAST (weather) applies to the utilization of one's senses to perceive developing aspects to a relationship, event, or condition.

FORECLOSURE forewarns of an upcoming failure or some aspect in the dreamer's life that will not be fulfilled.

FOREFATHER See ancestor.

FOREFINGER See index finger.

FOREFRONT (of dreamscape) represents the most pressing or important aspect. Most often denotes the present time frame.

FOREGONE CONCLUSION alludes to conclusions believed to be inevitable; however, this belief may not prove to be an actuality.

FOREGROUND See forefront.

FOREHEAD indicates a clue to how one perceives life aspects.

> **Broad forehead** applies to an open mind.

> **Narrow forehead** denotes narrow thinking.

> **Pitted forehead** relates to ingrained opinions; one-mindedness.

> **Scarred forehead** stands for lessons learned through previous misconceptions.

> **Slanted forehead** depicts biased or prejudiced perceptual handicap.

> **Wrinkled forehead** would mean one who worries or is overly skeptical.

FOREIGN connotes new and different ideas.

FOREIGN AID signifies assistance coming from an unexpected source.

FOREIGN CORRESPONDENT characterizes a connective line to different ideas; one's personal receptivity to such.

FOREIGNER is associated with a different perspective or idea.

FOREIGN EXCHANGE pertains to the sharing of new ideas.

FOREIGN MINISTER characterizes an individual who presents new and innovative concepts to others.

FOREIGN MISSION typifies spiritual work one does outside the scope of one's own specific path.

FOREIGN POLICY will be unique to each dreamer in that it represents one's own personal perspective toward innovative or foreign ideas; may also point to a lack of understanding or ability to communicate with others.

FOREMAN characterizes one who has the knowledge and experience to guide another.

FORENSIC MEDICINE emphasizes a need to examine all aspects of a situation, relationship, or event before forming an intelligent conclusion.

FOREPLAY alludes to preparations made for something; getting into the right frame of mind.

FORERUNNER represents prerequisite research; something appearing before the main event.

FORESIGHT usually advises of a need to increase one's awareness and perceptive abilities.

FOREST signifies one's individualized attitudes in relation to natural talents; may also refer to how one utilizes corporal deeds. Recall condition of this forest.

FOREST FIRE cautions one against the popular belief that one's inherent talents can be exhausted through overuse.

FOREST RANGER characterizes one's conscience, specifically related to spiritual aspects.

FORESTRY (study of) represents a concentrated effort to uncover ways to use one's talents for the purpose of aiding others.

FORETELL See prediction.

FOREWARNING almost always comes to reveal a near-future event/ramification/outcome.

FORFEIT pertains to a life aspect which needs to be abandoned or given up.

FORGE (mold) connotes a standard of something which may not be right for everyone.

FORGERY naturally stands for a false representation; may indicate a statement or behavior accredited to the wrong person.

FORGET-ME-NOTS advise of a very specific need to remember someone or something important. Usually surrounding details will clarify this.

FORK (in road) defines a choice in one's direction.

FORK (utensil) denotes a repressed personality.

FORKED TONGUE reveals double-talk.

FORK LIFT connotes life aspects that have the capability to ease one's burdens or paths.

FORMALDEHYDE represents a need to preserve some facet of the dreamer's life.

FORMALWEAR stands for high-minded attitudes.

FORMLESS (shape) constitutes a lack of definition to one's opinions, attitudes, and perspectives; an unclear or vacillating viewpoint.

FORM LETTER signifies a group of people or a situation of considerable size; a situation common to many.

FORMULA (infant) signifies the nourishing of a new beginning.

FORMULA (mathematical) comes in dreams to offer possible solutions.

FOR-PROFIT cautions against a tendency toward self-interest as one's prime motivational force.

FORSAKEN refers to a life aspect that must be given up. This may also indicate a self-generated psychological ploy for sympathy or attention if it refers directly to the dreamer's beingness.

FOR SALE BY OWNER denotes the choice to accomplish a goal without the aid of others.

FORSWEAR connotes denials.

FORSYTHIA signifies confidence in one's new beginning; a bright outlook for the immediate future or one's newly chosen direction.

FORT symbolizes one's personal quality and strength of defense. Depending on surrounding dreamscape details, this symbol can mean one who is an introvert, who desires to remain safe within self, or it can refer to a *need* for self-protective measures.

FORTHRIGHT pertains to open honesty.

FORTITUDE applies to perseverance. Perhaps the dreamer needs this or the word may denote a commendation.

FORT KNOX defines a situation, relationship, or opportunity that has the possibility of bringing great rewards or benefits.

FORTNIGHT comes as a unique time message for the dreamer.

FORTRESS See fort.

FORTUNA (Roman mythology) characterizes a priority placed on material goods; a love of and a striving for riches.

FORTUNE COOKIE illustrates a desire for knowing one's future; anxiety over being the beneficiary of only good aspects in life.

FORTUNE 500 characterizes those with the greatest measure of wealth and the heaviest burden of responsibility.

FORTUNE HUNTER implies one who is extremely materialistic.

FORTUNETELLER characterizes one who lives for the future instead of the moment; a fear of seeking within self.

FORTY-NINER connotes high expectations.

FORUM See town hall/meeting.

FORWARD (direction) advises one to refrain from stopping one's path walk; a need to continue going forward.

FOSSEY (Dian) defines one who strongly believes in convictions and has the fortitude and strength to fight for them; fearless in the face of adversity.

FOSSIL relates to preserved, immutable truths; validations.

FOSTER CARE/HOME reminds us that we must have sisterly love and take personal responsibility to care for anyone needing it; a reminder that we are all members of the human family.

FOUL LINE represents the boundaries that encompass the atmosphere of rightness; to cross this warns of misdeeds done.

FOUL-MOUTHED denotes arrogance and a lack of respect for others.

FOUL ODOR will indicate something that's not right, a bad smell to something.

FOUL PLAY warns of serious misdeeds. Who was doing this foul play?

FOUNDATION (building) connotes the moral, ethical, and spiritual tenets by which one lives.

FOUNDATION (non-profit) indicates a selfless cause.

FOUNDLING comes as a message to consciously attend to personal responsibilities. May also refer to individual thought; unique beliefs or perspectives; innovative thinking.

FOUNDRY alludes to the beginning stage when one is forming perspectives and initial plans.

FOUNTAIN (decorative) means spiritual abundance. Recall its dreamscape condition. Was the water colored? Lighted? How was it constructed, decorated?

FOUNTAIN (drinking) signifies spiritual refreshment.

FOUNTAINHEAD points to something's source. This can be very revealing for the dreamer.

FOUNTAIN PEN suggests quality of writing. What was or about to be written with the pen? Who was picking it up or using it?

FOUR exemplifies reference to the physical body.

FOUR-H CLUB connotes good values instilled early on in life.

FOUR HUNDRED stands for love of self; conceited; egotistic; arbitrarily haughty.

FOUR-LEAF CLOVER denotes an attitude of high expectation without factoring in any probabilities for failure or disappointment.

FOUR-O'CLOCK (flower) stands for a need to strengthen one's self-confidence.

FOUR-PLEX (housing) will refer to the three people closest to the dreamer.

FOUR-POSTER (bed) depicts night fears.

FOURSCORE comes to indicate that the number eighty has some unique meaning specific to the dreamer.

FOURSQUARE See square.

FOUR-STAR (rating) represents excellence

FOURTH DIMENSION alludes to higher knowledge or level of experience.

FOURTH ESTATE See journalist.

FOURTH OF JULY denotes questionable independence; selective freedoms.

FOUR-WHEEL DRIVE signifies the need for greater strength and extra efforts.

FOUR-WHEELING suggests a daring attitude when faced with life's rough roads; confidence one will overcome and persevere; the love of a good challenge.

FOWL See specific type.

FOX connotes cunning; shrewdness.

FOXFIRE portrays an aspect of true Reality.

FOXGLOVE (flower) exemplifies the powerful healing abilities of natural talents.

FOXHOLE See dugout.

FOXHOUND (dog breed) signifies a tendency to gravitate to shrewd and cunning personalities rather than thinking for self.

FOX TROT (dance) indicates tricky maneuvers done regarding a relationship or other situation.

FOXY (appearance) symbolizes a draw, an attraction which may, in reality, be a cover for less desirable traits. This symbol may also come to actually reveal an individual who is clever to the point of being conniving.

FOYER connotes an entrance to something to which the dreamer will personally relate.

FRACAS applies to a conflict.

FRACTAL pertains to one small aspect of the true Reality.

FRACTION denotes one part of something greater; one needs to realize that what is seen or understood is not the whole of it.

FRACTURE (bone) implies a defect; a crack in one's personality or plan; something amiss. Surrounding details will clarify this specific meaning for the dreamer.

FRAGILE is a caution to tread lightly; handle something carefully.

FRAGMENT See fraction.

FRAGMENTATION BOMB forewarns of approaching fallout ramifications.

FRAGRANCE comes with unique interpretations associated with specific scents. Refer to specific scents.

FRAIL (appearance) pertains to a weakened state.

FRAME (picture) reveals individual perception of what is framed in the dream. Recall its condition and color.

FRAME-UP warns of deception; possibility of scapegoat meant here.

FRAMEWORK (construction) denotes one's preparations for beginning a new project or endeavor.

FRANCE refers to the inner strength to fight for one's rights/freedom.

FRANCHISE pertains to the right or granted authority that frees one to pursue a specific endeavor; within one's rights.

FRANGIPANI (flower) signifies a sensitive nature.

FRANK (Anne) characterizes strength of character in the face of adversity.

FRANKENSTEIN stands for self-created monsters in one's life; those out-of-control emotions or attitudes that require containment.

FRANKFURTER See hot dog.

FRANKINCENSE alludes to a biblical age past life.

FRANKLIN (Benjamin) illustrates diversified talents.

FRANTIC usually warns of a lack of acceptance; lack of faith.

FRAT (appearance) suggests rigid opinions and right-wing perspectives. May point to an individual who needs to blend in with the accepted crowd, fearful to allow one's individuality to show (and shine).

FRATERNITY emphasizes male camaraderie; friends sharing a common interest or attitude.

FRAUD advises of a relationship, situation, or specific aspect that is not what it seems; not authentic.

FRAYED (clothing fabric) symbolizes wear and tear, usually associated with one's hardscrabble life which has been persevered through.

FREAK SHOW comes to remind us that compassion and intellectual understanding bring acceptance for that which is different.

FRECKLES usually denote a congenial nature; sunny disposition.

FREE (cost) represents blessings; opportunities.

FREE AGENT reminds us that we are our own mind; the decisions are ours to be responsible for.

FREEBASING See cocaine.

FREEBOOTER See pirate.

FREEBORN comes to encourage one to cherish uniqueness and express independent behavior and thought.

FREE DELIVERY stands for something handed to one without expending cost in the way of energy to obtain it.

FREEDOM FIGHTER characterizes active responses to unjust or oppressive authoritarianism. May reveal an activist.

FREEDOM MARCH connotes organized protests against injustice or oppression.

FREEDOM OF SPEECH comes as message reminding one that one has a right to speak up.

FREEDOM OF THE PRESS reminds us that everyone has a right to express an opinion, even in writing, but since others may not agree, they don't have to read it.

FREEDOM OF THE SEAS defines one's right to explore all spiritual ideologies; spiritual freedom.

FREE ENTERPRISE denotes the following of one's dream with little outside interference.

FREE FALL represents the loss of one's grounding aspects; may also indicate a headlong dive into an issue, situation, or relationship.

FREE-FLOATING cautions of spiritual indecision.

FREE-FOR-ALL usually points to a situation in which the participants are getting out of control.

FREE HAND indicates independence and the following of one's own ideals and perceptions.

FREEHEARTED relates to compassion and emotional generosity.

FREELANCE portrays the utilization of various opportunities.

FREELOADER characterizes a lack of self-responsibility and self-esteem.

FREE LOVE applies to indiscriminate behavior; irresponsibility.

FREE LUNCH connotes an unexpected benefit that presents itself in one's life; a positive aspect that comes without thought or personal effort applied to its manifestation.

FREE RANGE See open-range.

FREE REIN relates to a boundless opportunity; a limitless aspect.

FREE RIDE cautions one against depending on others to carry one along the path.

FREESIA (botanical) refers to an opportunity which won't remain fresh (available) for long.

FREE SPEECH reminds us not to be reticent or fearful of expressing self.

FREE SPIRIT characterizes an unconcern for conventional aspects; the ability to wholly express one's unique individuality.

FREESTANDING indicates independence; not needing supportive aspects.

FREESTYLE symbolizes freedom of personal expression and methodology.

FREETHINKER characterizes one who stretches the mind to explore far-reaching possibilities rather than confining perceptions to conventional concepts based within established popular boundaries.

FREE THROW points to a clear opportunity to take advantage of.

FREE TRADE represents open relationships and communications that are not restricted by any taboo issues.

FREE UNIVERSITY suggests a need to look into unconventional concepts.

FREE VERSE expresses the freedom to speak one's mind regardless of unconventionality.

FREEWAY See expressway.

FREEWHEELING indicates a carefree personality, relationship, or situation. May point to a pride in independence.

FREE WILL comes to remind us of our right to make our own choices in life.

FREEZE-DRIED is one of many dream symbols that implies a need to quickly preserve something in the dreamer's life.

FREEZE-FRAME emphasizes a scene, object, or individual that is important to the dreamer. The surrounding details will clarify this.

FREEZER suggests that something in the dreamer's life needs to be put on ice for a time; a postponement or preservation needed.

FREEZER BURN reveals a situation, idea, plan, or other personal element in one's life has been put on hold for too long.

FREIGHT denotes that which we carry around with us, usually mentally or psychologically.

FREIGHTER pertains to one's personal spiritual baggage.

FREIGHT TRAIN cautions of the negativity and detriment of carrying the excessive beliefs or perspectives of others instead of being more of an independent life traveler.

FRENCH BERET See beret.

FRENCH DOOR represents a life passageway that offers many opportunities for different perspectives.

FRENCH FRY connotes shortcuts; life aspects that have time-saving qualities.

FRENCH HORN implies verbosity; an elaborate way of saying something.

FRENCH KNOT portrays a socially delicate situation.

FRENCH TOAST relates to a life aspect that carries added benefits.

FRENCH TWIST (hair style) suggests knotted/twisted ideas; plans or situations needing straightening out.

FRENCH WINDOW signifies an opportunity to have a broader view or perspective.

FREQUENT FLIER applies to one who routinely has thoughts that are a departure from the norm; high inquisitiveness.

FRESCO denotes ingrained attitudes.

FRESHET pertains to a sudden influx of fresh spiritual ideas.

FRESHMAN indicates one beginning a new phase.

FRESHWATER will usually symbolize a viable spiritual element.

FREUD (Sigmund) comes as a caution when conducting a self-examination of one's motives.

FRIAR See religious figure.

FRICTION TAPE advises to smooth over a situation or relationship; a need to protect a life aspect from sparking or causing a shocking incident.

FRIDAY is the day to address closures; attend to loose ends.

FRIEND usually characterizes loyalty and trust.

FRIGATE (bird) denotes egotism; a need to impress others. May point to a tendency toward greediness; stealing another's thunder or ideas.

FRIGATE (ship) warns of a personal spiritual conflict within self.

FRIGHT (sudden) advises one to maintain awareness; realize that the unexpected is part of reality.

FRIGID indicates a stiff and unemotional personality; a rigid and straitlaced nature.

FRIGID ZONE points to a phase in one's life when it's nearly impossible to communicate with others; a time when other's aren't being receptive to one's behavior, situation, or ideas.

FRILLS stand for extraneous elements; added aspects which dress something up but don't add to its basic value.

FRINGE (on fabric) denotes a border; an aspect that is not well defined or encompassed within a specific conceptual framework.

FRINGE BENEFIT connotes an extra benefit to something; additional rewards or unexpected benefits.

FRISBEE is one of many dreamscape symbols that refers to a good intent at communicating.

FRISK (body search) cautions to be aware of possible concealments.

FRISKINESS reveals lightheartedness; joyful expressions.

FRITTER (food) connotes a breaking-down process; a fragmenting.

FRIVOLOUS means inconsequential; lacking any importance or relevance.

FRIZZY (hair) See fuzzy (hair).

FROCK See smock.

FROG represents an impaired mental or physical condition.

FROGMAN characterizes an unhealthy spiritual attitude or belief system.

FROLIC See friskiness.

FRONT (position) denotes priority.

FRONTAGE ROAD See service road.

FRONT BURNER signifies a current situation that takes priority over others of less importance.

FRONT DESK See receptionist.

FRONT-END LOADER alludes to a need for intensive clarification. The surrounding dreamscape details will clarify this for the dreamer.

FRONTIER characterizes a new and exciting path that holds the promise of multiple discovery opportunities.

FRONTIERSWOMAN pertains to one who is traveling a path of self-discovery.

FRONT-LINE represents the position of action or most exposure.

FRONT MONEY stands for one's intent; a life aspect that reinforces a greater measure of confidence.

FRONT OFFICE applies to responsibility or authority.

FRONT PAGE reflects priority; a place of importance; something to take note of.

FRONT RUNNER constitutes the option most likely to succeed; an option that appears to have the highest probability of being chosen.

FRONT-WHEEL DRIVE advises of a path traveled half-heartedly.

FROST points to a temporarily chilled attitude.

FROSTBITE comes when one reacts in a

willfully unresponsive manner; karmic effects of refusing to respond or communicate.

FROST-FREE suggests open communication or emotions.

FROSTING may indicate a cover-up or it may refer to an aspect that constitutes a final action that makes matters better or worse.

FROST LINE relates to an individual's point of abiding acceptance; the point where one gives up or stops being responsive.

FROSTY (atmosphere) See hoarfrost.

FROTHY refers to mental, emotional, or spiritual confusion.

FROWN infers displeasure or sorrow.

FROZEN FOOD defines nourishing life aspects that are not being utilized or benefited from.

FROZEN LAKE warns of spiritual aspects that are not being utilized.

FRUGAL may commend thrift or advise against it. Thrift in this context refers to the utilization of one's talents or expressions of emotions. Surrounding dream details will clarify this intent.

FRUIT most often points to the nourishing and beneficial effects of using one's talents for the benefit of others. Recall the condition of the dreamscape fruit for further clarification. See specific fruit.

FRUIT BASKET signifies a gift of one's talents; a bountiful benefit received or given.

FRUITCAKE signifies a lack of logic and reason.

FRUIT COCKTAIL constitutes a multitude of benefits.

FRUIT FLY pertains to destructive aspects affecting personal talents.

FRUIT GROWER characterizes one who has a high interest in cultivating talents, abilities, and means of helping others.

FRUITLESS warns of unexercised spirituality.

FRUIT TREE stands for spiritual talents and humanitarian expressions.

FRUIT WOOD signifies the remaining benefit from an element which provided a multitude of them.

FRUSTRATION is a message of acceptance and perseverance.

FRY implies quick conclusions.

FRYING PAN relates to increased activity; a quickening of action.

F-STOP (setting) suggests a need to adjust one's perspective for better clarity.

FUCHSIA (flower & color) represents compassion, love, and humanistic expressions.

FUDGE (confection) applies to hedging; grey areas.

FUEL is associated to one's energy and/or that which nourishes.

FUEL GAUGE comes as an aid in determining the amount of energy one is running on. Did the gauge read empty? Full?

FUEL TANK is associated with our supply of energy and usually pertains to strength of character or perseverance.

FUGITIVE advises to stop running from one's problems or fears. This may even refer to an attempt to escape self.

FUGUE denotes a state of unawareness, possibly a self-willed one.

FUJITA SCALE See wind force scale.

FULL (capacity) represents a condition that has reached its ultimate state.

FULL-BLOODED will not necessarily refer to heritage, as it usually implies "purity" as in a belief system or an individual's intentions.

FULL-BLOWN defines something in the dreamer's life that cannot be developed or advanced beyond its present state.

FULL-BODIED stands for intensity or richness.

FULL-BORE refers to thoroughness; nothing held back; full steam ahead.

FULL CIRCLE denotes completeness; a return to the beginning.

FULL DRESS relates to appropriateness in action and one's presentation.

FULL MOON See moon (full).

FULL-SCALE indicates total effort applied; strong determination.

FULL SERVICE stands for the act of giving one's all.

FULL-SIZE reveals accurate proportions. This may indicate that the dreamer is either exaggerating or belittling something.

FULL SPEED comes as an advisement to slow down.

FULL SWING represents an issue, plan, or situation that's well underway.

FULL TERM points to completeness; the development/achievement of something that won't succeed unless it's given its full measure of time to manifest according to plan.

FULL-TIME advises of a need to devote attention or energy to a specific aspect more than part-time.

FUMBLE relates to a temporary setback; a small glitch.

FUMES mean harmful situations generated from one's lack of controlled response.

FUMIGATION symbolizes full-blown measures to take care of a problem.

FUNCTION KEY (computer keyboard) stands for options at one's fingertips.

FUND-RAISING is associated with the act of helping another; getting others involved.

FUNERAL underscores a state of loss; relates to an acceptance of losing something in one's life.

FUNERAL DIRECTOR characterizes one who helps another through difficult times.

FUNERAL HOME signifies a dying condition and a need to put it to rest.

FUNGICIDE refers to a need to attend to a situation, plan, idea, relationship, etc. that has elements that are becoming a growing problem.

FUNGUS warns against inactivity. This suggests a need for the dreamer to get going regarding a specific life aspect.

FUN HOUSE is an advisement to face one's fears and see them for what they are, maybe even laugh at them.

FUNK (mood) usually refers to a disappointment; an expectation not fulfilled as anticipated.

FUNNEL suggests a need to slow one's intake of knowledge in order to assimilate more; indicates a need for better comprehension.

FUNNEL CLOUD See hurricane; tornado.

FUNNY BONE corresponds to the funny

feelings we get; perceptual sensations which often accompany sudden insights.

FUNNY MONEY See counterfeit.

FUNNY PAPERS See comic book.

FUR (clothing/coat) denote a selfish personality.

FUR BALL refers to an unpleasant issue one needs to resolve.

FURL suggests a need to open or uncover something in one's life.

FURLOUGH See vacation.

FURNACE connotes emotional intensity. Was the furnace blasting? Was it cold?

FURNISHINGS give clue to a dreamscape's atmosphere. How was a room furnished? Did it have a warm or cold feeling to it? Were there any period or ethnic decoration pieces?

FURNITURE alludes to one's character. Was it elaborate? Sparse? Spotless? Lived in?

FURRIER characterizes a self-serving nature.

FURROW See groove; trench.

FUSE (electrical) represents energy level. Was it new? Burned out? What type of fuse was it?

FUSE (explosive) points to an amount of patience or acceptance. Recall length of fuse line for more clarity.

FUSE BOX defines one's level of comprehension and readiness for higher knowledge. The number of good fuses clarifies this message.

FUSELAGE most often symbolizes an individual's capacity for understanding new concepts. Recall size and condition.

FUSION emphasizes a need to incorporate several different aspects into a centrally focused issue. This will be specific to each dreamer.

FUSSY (behavior) defines impatience or anxiety.

FUTILE reveals an unproductive situation, relationship, or effort.

FUTURE is most often a precognitive revelation.

FUTURE SHOCK defines a fear or lack of acceptance for one's path direction.

FUTURIST reveals someone who has an eye for long-range planning or ramifications.

FUTURISTIC (scene) usually corresponds with an individual's personally unique vision or conceived idea of the future. May also be presented as a visual of one's fears.

FUZZ relates to a coating of some type being done; misrepresentation.

FUZZY (fabric/texture) most often refers to a soft touch; compassion and/or understanding.

FUZZY (hair) points to unclear thoughts; lacking clear definition; confusion.

FUZZY (vision) See eye (unfocused).

G

GAB See chatterbox.

GABARDINE (fabric) signifies diligent work effort.

GABLE denotes a differential facet to one's thought process; thought affected by a unique quirk.

GADFLY alludes to a life irritation.

GADGET represents personal aids utilized to implement goals.

GAFF See hook.

GAFFER (lighting tech) characterizes one who sheds light on an issue or situation.

GAG See practical joke.

GAG (over mouth) is a warning against talking too much; gossip; revealing more than one should.

GAG (reflex) pertains to an inability to swallow something; a lack of acceptance; having to deal with a distasteful issue.

GAG ORDER is a message to keep silent about something. Surrounding dream-scape details will clarify this.

GAIETY suggests a lighthearted atmosphere or situation.

GAITERS refer to protective measures taken along one's path.

GALA denotes a celebration; a joyous event or situation.

GALAPAGOS ISLANDS portray perseverance; a long-lasting condition or situation.

GALAXY See cosmos.

GALE cautions against overexerting one's faculties.

GALL (behavior) stands for audacity; a provocation.

GALL (growth) represents a negative element that's growing from within.

GALLBLADDER relates to accumulation of life trials. Recall condition.

GALLEON connotes an esoteric spiritual journey.

GALLERY (art) represents qualities and life aspects one admires.

GALLERY (audience) illustrates those who watch you and listen.

GALLERY (balcony) signifies a clarity of perception.

GALLEY (large rowboat) cautions of a spiritual journey propelled by others rather than self.

GALLEY (narrow kitchen) refers to a narrow assortment of nourishing benefits one chooses to utilize.

GALLEY PROOF advises of a need to check for errors that lead to misconceptions.

GALLOP connotes a bounding speed; a fast-paced advancement.

GALLOWS exemplify a need to complete something, finish it up.

GALLSTONES characterize accepted tribulations; life stressors that have taken their toll.

GALVANIZED stands for motivation; an electrifying spur forward or into awareness.

GAMBLER characterizes those who attempt to beat the odds; taking chances. May point to an optimist, a death grip on hope.

GAMBLING refers to an attempt to win at something; taking advantage of a slim chance.

GAMBLING CASINO relates to risks taken; a big opportunity with small odds of winning.

GAMBREL (roof) corresponds with a thought process that is affected by two differing perspectives.

GAME (amusement) depicts mental stimulation. Depending on which type of game is shown, this symbol may indicate risks taken.

GAME (hunting) See prey.

GAME BOARD reveals moves made in life.

GAMEKEEPER advises of self-serving motives.

GAME LAWS denote the limits of one's predatory nature.

GAME PLAN relates to tactical schemes.

GAME ROOM symbolizes a concerted effort applied to one's mental stimulation. May also stand for a meeting place where plans are devised.

GAME SHOW cautions against a boastful intelligence; a desire to be intellectually superior.

GAME WARDEN suggests a need to be aware of how one's natural talents are used (or not used).

GAMUT connotes an entire scope of something; all-encompassing.

GANDER implies self-imposed ignorance; willful or feigned ignorance.

GANDHI (Mohandas Karamchand) characterizes living spirituality; fighting for spiritual principles.

GANG applies to a group of people. Recall surrounding details to determine if this symbol was a positive or negative one.

GANGLAND (style) represents a harmful, negative method of achieving a goal.

GANGPLANK indicates a way or path.

GANGRENE denotes a self-destructive aspect in one's life.

GANGSTA RAP (music) refers to a brutally honest way of telling how things are; a cynical, often degrading, perspective focused on the dark side of life.

GAP may indicate an opening opportunity or it may refer to a missing aspect in one's life.

GAPE (stare) corresponds to a reaction of awe or astonishment.

GAP-TOOTHED stands for holding back information or the whole story; indicates an individual who doesn't reveal everything, preferring to keep some elements close to the vest.

GARAGE represents a place of rest or stored energy.

GARAGE SALE typifies the act of ridding

self of extraneous aspects; getting down to basics; setting priorities.

GARB See specific clothing types.

GARBAGE defines the useless aspects in one's life; those items one *perceives* as being useless. Recall if there were any specific items featured in the dreamscape garbage. There may have been items that shouldn't have been discarded.

GARBAGE CAN connotes what one chooses to throw away. Again, what was in the garbage can? Was it something that should not have been tossed away so lightly?

GARBAGE COLLECTOR characterizes one's willful accumulation of useless aspects such as negative attitudes, erroneous perceptions or beliefs, or materialistic factors.

GARBLED (speech) denotes perplexity; mental bewilderment; talking about issues one has no clear understanding of.

GARBO (Greta) characterizes solitude and a need for same.

GARDEN constitutes spiritual blessings and talents. What condition was the dream garden in?

GARDEN CLOGS represent a preparedness to nurture one's inherent, natural talents.

GARDENER characterizes one who nurtures humanitarian acts and spiritual attitudes.

GARDENIA implies purity.

GARDENING stands for attention in the way of nourishment and cultivation given to one's humanitarian/spiritual behavior; a cultivation of one's natural gifts.

GARDEN PARTY indicates personal joy taken in one's rewarding benefits brought through humanitarian and spiritual acts.

GARFIELD (comic cat) pertains to self-absorption.

GARGANTUAN (size) illustrates an overwhelming aspect to one's life.

GARGLE indicates an effort to clarify one's communication skills.

GARGOYLE usually represents an attempt to protect one's spirituality. It also may refer to some type of distortion being done in one's life.

GARISH See gaudy.

GARLAND (botanical) symbolizes bountiful spiritual acts; continual utilization of one's humanitarian and/or spiritual gifts.

GARLIC pertains to personal defenses against negative aspects or forces.

GARMENT See specific type.

GARMENT BAG relates to protected characteristics or attitudes; a part of us that is kept protected and hidden.

GARNET (color and stone) refers to intense emotions. (Garnet can be a variety of colors; this interpretation corresponds to the more commonly known color of deep, dark red).

GARNISH (food) stands for enhancing aspects applied to a basic one; adornment; embellishment.

GARNISHMENT (monetary) signifies a forced payment/collection of one's debt to another.

GARRISON See military post.

GARRISON HOUSE (architecture) signifies a top-heavy way of thinking, one's intellect outweighs the emotions.

GARTER symbolizes the act of upholding something.

GARTER SNAKE denotes harmless qualities or aspects that many fear.

GAS constitutes duality; the positive and negative aspects of something.

GAS BURNER pertains to personal responsibility regarding how potentially harmful aspects are utilized in a positive way.

GAS CHAMBER advises to use discernment; suggests increased awareness.

GAS FITTER See pipe fitter.

GAS-GUZZLER (vehicle) warns of using methods of advancement that consume more personal energy than necessary; doing things the hard way.

GASH denotes a temporary setback; a hurtful incident from which one quickly recovers.

GASKET alludes to a need to seal something; a finalization; a need to stop the leakage of something in the dreamer's life.

GAS LEAK See leak (gas).

GASLIGHT signifies a perpetual illumination maintained by one's personal awareness.

GAS LOGS refer to imitations in life; second-best options.

GAS MAIN exemplifies a potential hazard in one's life that is concealed beneath one's path.

GAS MASK cautions one to protect self from potentially harmful situations or relationships.

GASOLINE applies to physical energy.

GASP advises against being caught unaware or off guard.

GAS PEDAL See accelerator.

GAS PUMP relates to a source of energy; a source of motivation.

GAS STATION signifies the source of one's energy or motivational force.

GAS STATION ATTENDANT represents one who attends to another's needs, especially for the purpose of conserving and maintaining another's energy level.

GAS TANK (vehicle) connotes an individual's personal energy level. Recall if the tank was empty or full.

GASTRIC LAVAGE See stomach pump.

GATE pertains to that which must be passed through (experienced) for one to further advance along one's path.

GATECRASHER warns against forcing advancement.

GATED COMMUNITY refers to one's guarded general surroundings; a tendency to be protective or defensive of one's friends. This symbol may also reveal an elitist attitude.

GATE HOUSE symbolizes one's right to experience an event or passage.

GATEKEEPER characterizes one's Higher Self; conscience.

GATEPOST connotes a supporting factor that helps to mark specific events one must experience.

GATHERING (collecting/picking) indicates the act of seeking out and obtaining required specialized information or other aspects vital to one's unique path advancement.

GATLING GUN See machine gun.

GATOR See alligator.

GATORS (leg coverings) refer to protective measures taken to insulate self while traversing a particularly difficult phase of one's path.

GAUCHE implies a lack of tact or sensitivity.

GAUCHO See cowboy.

GAUDY connotes a state of extremes; overemphasis done.

GAUGE depicts quantity. Recall what the dreamscape gauge was measuring.

GAUNTLET (armored glove) relates to one's personal protective methods of not being touched or affected by the negative or hazardous factors that we have to come in contact with in life. This may not be a positive symbol because we become stronger and learn important lessons by being exposed to certain negatives that are in our path.

GAUNTLET (ordeal) illustrates life's tribulations; these are frequently generated by self.

GAUZE (bandage) relates to a temporary setback; a minor injury.

GAUZE (fabric) warns of an ineffective cover-up being done.

GAVEL defines finality; a message from a higher authority.

GAWK connotes rude attention given.

GAY See homosexuality.

GAYFEATHER (botanical) reminds us to gain a greater sense of humor.

GAY PRIDE DAY relates to individuality and everyone's right to celebrate the uniqueness of their beingness.

GAZEBO represents a place or time of respite; a needed rest.

GAZELLE refers to an innocent characteristic; naïveté.

GAZING GLOBE (garden) signifies an appreciation for nature's beauty and efforts to have it reflected in one's behavior.

GAZPACHO suggests mental and emotional nourishment.

GEAR connotes mechanisms used to effect movement; motivational factors, instigators; personally forceful aspects.

GEARBOX See transmission.

GECKO See lizard.

GEEK (appearance) generally points to assumptions regarding another.

GEEK-SPEAK won't necessarily refer solely to techno-talk but will usually be associated with someone who has a tendency to use one-hundred-dollar words.

GEESE defines instincts; inherent characteristics. Depending on surrounding dreamscape details, geese may also warn of one's personal desire to escape problematic issues.

GEIGER COUNTER pertains to an individual's intuitive perceptions.

GEISHA characterizes servitude; a tendency to react or behave in response to the anticipated desires of others. This is usually a warning symbol.

GELATIN implies cohesiveness; aspects that serve to bind.

GELDING signifies a need to control the expression of emotional extremes.

GEMOLOGY (study of) portrays an interest in understanding natural spiritual talents and the varied methodologies of same.

GEMSTONE alludes to personality characteristics and behavioral responses. See specific gem type.

GENDER-BENDER will rarely have a sexual association but rather will refer to a healthy blending of one's yin and yang traits.

GENDER GAP will stand for counterpoint opinions due to a difference in gender perspectives generated from socio-political situations.

GENE will stand for a particular trait that's unique to the dreamer. Recall in what context this symbol was displayed.

GENERAL DELIVERY suggests an unsettled situation.

GENERAL MANAGER characterizes an overseer. This symbol may reveal someone who has the ability to help manage something for the dreamer.

GENERAL PRACTITIONER See physician.

GENERAL STORE connotes a variety of opportunities to choose from.

GENERATION GAP stands for differences in attitudes.

GENERATOR connotes inner sources of energy one falls back on; strength of character.

GENERIC means all-inclusive; common; nonspecific. This would usually be a message to express one's individuality more often.

GENERIC DRUG represents the presence of an alternate; a choice that contains equal value (benefits) yet is less costly in the long run.

GENESIS defines a major new beginning.

GENE-SPLICING warns against mixing concepts; a loss of purity in respect to identity.

GENETIC DISORDER stands for those aspects (or handicaps) one specifically came to work with or overcome.

GENETIC ENGINEERING represents a control over one's behavior; personal responsibility to alter negative behavior generated by psychologically manipulative conduct.

GENETIC MARKER reveals one's susceptibility to something. This could be symbolic or literal, depending on the dreamscape's related elements.

GENETICS (study of) indicates an interest in the historical trail of another's behavior or characteristic expression.

GENETIC SCREENING equates to a self-examination of one's behavior, especially primary motives.

GENIE characterizes false promises and hopes; empty visions of goals or desires quickly obtained; unrealistic perspective.

GENITALIA may suggest a need to be more productive in life or it may warn of some type of negative aspect specific to a physical condition.

GENIUS symbolizes high intelligence. This dream detail may be a warning to use wisdom in connection with intellectual brilliance.

GENOCIDE won't normally point to an issue of racism but rather refer to one's adamant refusal to even broach a subject/issue that is attempting to be excised from one's life.

GENRE implies a specific category of something. This will pinpoint an important factor in the one's life and will be unique to each dreamer.

GENTEEL doesn't necessarily refer to a prudish attitude; it may indicate simple refinement.

GENTIAN denotes simplicity; innocence.

GENTIAN VIOLET (botanical) applies to the healing benefits of inner spiritual convictions.

GENTLEMAN will indicate a good-hearted, respectful man who is comfortable with his own beingness without having to affect exaggerated manly airs.

GENTLEMAN'S/LADY'S AGREEMENT characterizes decency; integrity.

GENTLEWOMAN stands for a woman who has a quiet, genteel nature and doesn't feel the need to accentuate her womanly traits to be noticed or bolster her self-image.

GENUFLECTING indicates respect; giving honor; a recognition of high worth.

GEODE emphasizes the inherent beauty of the living spirit within everyone.

GEODESIC DOME represents the interlocking aspects of life.

GEOGRAPHY (study of) connotes an interest in physical characteristics. This may or may not be a positive dream symbol depending on the surrounding elements.

GEOLOGY (study of) indicates a high interest in understanding humankind's genetic relationship with earth; symbolizes one who takes interest in understanding others.

GEOMAGNETIC STORM See magnetic storm.

GEOMETRIC (patterns) See specific type.

GEOMETRY (study of) refers to a high interest in comprehending the interconnectedness of life.

GEOPHYSICS (study of) signifies an awareness of the true Reality.

GEORGIA signifies a tendency toward a separatist type of independence.

GEOTHERMAL (activity) usually comes as a warning of inner turmoil.

GERANIUM (flower) alludes to optimism.

GERBIL (as pet) depicts life aspects that serve as small comforts.

GERMAN SHEPHERD (dog breed) characterizes a helpful friend or close associate.

GERMANY signifies fortitude and renewal.

GERMICIDE See disinfectant.

GERMINATING applies to a life aspect that has taken hold within one. This could relate to an attitude, belief, emotion, etc.

GERMS signify negative aspects with which one could contaminate self.

GERM WARFARE defines vicious and unconscionable retaliative responses.

GERONIMO characterizes one's familial protective qualities.

GERONTOLOGY (study of) represents a high interest in elders. This will be specific for each dreamer in respect to which quality or characteristic is focused on. May also refer to an interest in the future ramifications of a current issue or plan.

GESTAPO characterizes restraints; factors that severely hamper one's choices, individuality, or ability to freely advance; will also stand for intolerance.

GESTATION PERIOD represents the phase of preparation and development of a new idea or venture.

GETHSEMANE implies abandonment; betrayal.

GEYSER symbolizes one's active outpouring of spiritual and humanitarian talents.

GHETTO stands for tribulations to be overcome.

GHETTO BLASTER See boom box.

GHOST indicates a fear of spiritual matters. Also may refer to recurring episodes of guilt.

GHOST DANCER characterizes a strong spiritual belief; faith in the power of spiritual strength.

GHOST-DANCE SHIRT denotes spiritual protection and one's powerful belief in it.

GHOST STORY implies a possibility; a subject to contemplate.

GHOST TOWN corresponds to a tendency to live in the past; pining over what once was.

GHOSTWRITER cautions against doing another's thinking.

GIANT pertains to one who is idolized or looked up to.

GIANT SEQUOIA relates to ancient truths comprising reality that remain immutable.

GIANT SLALOM (skiing) comes as a warning message to slow down in order to avoid a collision course.

GIANT SQUID stands for the hidden elements (possible dangers) lurking behind certain motivations related to alleged spiritual behavior.

GIARDIA (parasite) stands for the negative effects of an intake of contaminated ideas.

GIBBERISH naturally points to communications or ideas others can't understand; may even refer to one's own confused thoughts.

GIBBET usually warns against an action or personal course that could result in self-destruction; a path toward hanging self.

GIBBON See ape.

GIBLETS refer to utilization; a message to make use of the whole aspect of some-

thing. This carries a specific interpretation for each dreamer.

GIDDINESS won't normally indicate juvenile traits but will usually reveal nervousness, a lack of self-confidence.

GIFT indicates an offering; perhaps an unexpected opportunity.

GIFT CERTIFICATE denotes unconditional assistance from another.

GIFT OF TONGUES See glossolalia.

GIFT SHOP illustrates opportunities for kindness.

GIFT-WRAP denotes personal joy taken when helping others or from expressing acts of kindness.

GIGGLING stands for inner joy. What may be more revealing here is to recall *what* one was giggling over.

GIGOLO characterizes one who takes advantage of others for the purpose of avoiding personal responsibility. Will point to an individual with an ulterior motive of having others support him; dependency.

GILA MONSTER symbolizes cherished ideals.

GILD warns against a personal need to enhance self; represents a poor self-image.

GILL stands for spiritual breathing; the intake of spiritual aspects as one's very breath.

GILT-EDGED (pages) connotes an advisement to note the high quality of value.

GIMLET (drink) See alcoholic beverage.

GIMLET (tool) indicates a personal need to bore into or penetrate something in one's life; search for deeper understanding.

GIMMICK warns against using methods of trickery or manipulation.

GIN (drink) See alcoholic beverage.

GIN (machine) represents a personal aid that assists in advancing toward goals.

GINGER depicts a life aspect that can be used or internalized to aid in obtaining personal acceptance and greater tolerance.

GINGER ALE refers to a soothing factor; a calming aspect.

GINGERBREAD constitutes a nourishing factor that serves to settle temporary emotional upsets.

GINGERBREAD HOUSE warns of a self-induced perspective on one's personal life as being the epitome of sweet perfection. May indicate a tendency to overdo the ornamentation in one's life (excessive affectations).

GINGER JAR denotes a reserve of inner strength.

GINGERSNAP typifies a calm that nourishes and restores one's emotional strength.

GINGIVITIS See gum disease.

GINSENG corresponds with one's overall health; an aspect that has the capability to bring general wellness.

GIRAFFE warns against the habit of meddling in the affairs of others.

GIRDER portrays main support; a life aspect that serves as one's main source of strength.

GIRDLE usually refers to that which surrounds oneself. This will indicate a separate aspect for each dreamer.

GIRL stands for beginning feminine perspectives.

GIRLISH (qualities) signifies a touch of innocence to one's character.

GIRL SCOUT characterizes a female who strives to live according to her moral and spiritual beliefs.

GIRL TALK signifies the freedom to share female confidentialities.

GIVEAWAY defines generosity; materialistic unconcern.

GIVEN NAME most often comes as an important message that indicates a personal importance for the name. Recall what the name was and watch for it to show up during your waking state.

GIZMO See gadget.

GIZZARD corresponds with an aid to acceptance.

GLACIER denotes frozen spirituality; a call to thaw and use one's talents.

GLACIOLOGY (study of) indicates a high interest in understanding people's lack of humanitarian and spiritual responsiveness.

GLADIATOR advises of illogical reasoning for negative behavior.

GLADIOLUS represents an upcoming span of peacefulness in one's life; reminds us to be grateful for our daily blessings.

GLAMORIZED warns against downplaying negative aspects.

GLARING (brightness) is an advisement against jumping to conclusions.

GLASS pertains to a state or condition of fragility.

GLASS BLOWER characterizes subtle, delicate creativity.

GLASS BLOCK (construction material) points to an extremely clouded view of something.

GLASS CEILING indicates the hidden barriers that one must break through.

GLASS CUTTER represents a way to break through perceptual barriers or obstructions interfering with clear vision.

GLASSES (eye) refer to added aspects to one's sight (perceptual ability).

Bifocal glasses See bifocals.

Broken glasses denote an inability to adjust perspectives.

Cracked glasses indicate a fractured viewpoint.

Dirty glasses imply a perspective altered by negative attitudes.

Foggy glasses refer to an unclear perspective.

Granny glasses allude to a narrow view of things.

Greasy glasses signify perception altered by ulterior motives.

Heavily framed glasses denote a seriously obstructed perspective.

Oversized glasses indicate a wide, comprehensive perspective.

Pitted glasses connote a perspective altered by hardships; cynicism.

Rimless glasses define an unobstructed view of things.

Rose-colored glasses apply to an overly optimistic perspective.

Scratched glasses suggest a perspective marred by personally damaging elements.

Scratch-resistant glasses indicate unaffected perspectives.

Shattered glasses pertain to fragmented perspectives.

Smeared glasses pertain to negative attitudes affecting the ability to clearly perceive.

Sunglasses denote a perspective resistant to popular opinion.

Thick glasses refer to major adjustments made to clearly perceive.

Tinted glasses portray a colored or slanted perspective.

GLASS EYE refers to a heightened ability to perceive vibrational images through an extended awareness of true Reality.

GLASS HOUSE reminds us that we are always being observed.

GLASS JAW warns of one's state of vulnerability.

GLASS WOOL is a cautionary symbol; an advisement for one to be more aware; stay watchful.

GLAUCOMA represents a deteriorating perspective; losing one's perspective.

GLAZE (coating) connotes a cover-up of some type. Surrounding details will usually clarify this for the dreamer.

GLAZE (confection) equates to the frosting on the cake; a final word, behavior, or event that tops everything that has gone before.

GLAZED (look) may indicate confusion, a lack of understanding, or a shocked reaction.

GLEE CLUB typifies short periods of contentedness.

GLEN PLAID (pattern) See checker (pattern).

GLIDER (plane) implies a lack of mental focus.

GLIDER (swing) suggest a time of contemplation; restful thought times. In a few instances, a glider may warn against self-generated unawareness.

GLITCH indicates a temporary setback or problem.

GLITTER denotes a fascination.

GLOAMING See twilight.

GLOBAL POSITIONING SYSTEM (GPS) comes as an advisement that one should pay attention to where one is and become focused on the moment. This infers that one is perhaps looking to the future or pining about lost opportunities of the past.

GLOBAL WARMING suggests an alteration of one's general surroundings. This symbol points to a change in the atmosphere around one.

GLOBE portrays earthly matters that need attention. Frequently this will infer a more broad-scope view of something.

GLOCKENSPIEL refers to accuracy. In the dream, were the notes struck right? Were they clear?

GLOOMY (atmosphere) most often is caused by a psychological source. Who was within this gloomy atmosphere? Just yourself?

GLORY See fame.

GLORY HOLE (mining) represents a source of wealth. See mother lode.

GLOSS (finish) suggests a need to shine; wanting something to stand out.

GLOSSARY advises of a need to correct the usage of one's specific terminology that is in error. This dream fragment may also display a word (or words) that is revealing—disclosing the true character of a situation or other individual.

GLOSSOLALIA warns of unintelligible speech; a personal need to be noticed.

GLOSSY symbolizes insincerity.

GLOVE COMPARTMENT indicates readiness to assist others.

GLOVES represent personal service to others. Depending on the style and condition of these gloves, the dreamer can determine if this service is for self or others, begrudging or purely humanitarian.

GLOW (inner) implies inspiration or emotional warmth.

GLOW (light) suggests a radiance of some type; resplendence.

GLOWWORM indicates a light in the darkness.

GLOXINIA (plant) exemplifies deep joy; bright happiness.

GLUE pertains to a sticky situation, condition, or relationship. May also signify an element that is capable of repairing something.

GLUE GUN refers to the tool that one can use to repair a broken relationship or situation.

GLUE SNIFFING denotes an effort/desire to alter one's reality; form of escapism.

GLUTTON characterizes a greedy personality; insatiability.

GLYPH depicts some kind of symbology specific to the dreamer. This glyph will reveal a unique symbolism.

GNARLED warns of a strongly held negative attitude; a twisted idea.

GNAT relates to mental or emotional irritations.

GNAW is an advisement message to get focused and get to the bottom of something in one's life.

GNOME comes in a dream to warn of a need to guard one's beliefs or attitudes.

GNOSTIC will relate to intuitiveness.

GNU See antelope.

GOAL signifies aspirations.

GOALIE GEAR applies to preparation measures taken for the purpose of entering an upcoming conflict that blocks one's way toward advancement.

GOALKEEPER characterizes an individual who keeps one motivated.

GOAL LINE is an advisement to keep one's eye on goals.

GOAL POST is another symbol for one's aspirations or goals. What's important to recall from the dream is the condition of the goal post. Was it upright? Tilting? Falling down? In disrepair? Shiny?

GOAT warns against a voracious intake. This could refer to information, self-consumption, etc.

GOAT CHEESE represents a strong sense of purpose; a wholesome knowing of oneself.

GOATEE indicates a pretentious personality.

GOATFISH stands for spiritual independence; making one's unique spiritual journey.

GOATSBEARD (botanical) suggests a need for discretion.

GO-BACK (computer) signifies an ability to change reality by returning to the time preceding a negative event, thereby literally creating a situation clear of the event and its damaging ramifications. In dreams this symbol represents a desire to take back bad behavior or hurtful words—wishing they'd never happened.

GOBBLE implies a ravenous appetite, usually for information.

GOBLET typifies quiet sophistication.

GOBLIN connotes a spiritual fear.

GOBY (fish) signifies unique spiritual beliefs.

GO-CART advises of a need to re-assess one's direction.

GOD represents the highest authority; ultimate goal. See Divine Essence.

GODCHILD will refer to a spiritual inspiration/insight which becomes a foundational element in one's life.

GODDESS signifies the feminine Divine Essence.

GODFATHER warns us to achieve goals through personal efforts.

GODMOTHER characterizes comforting warmth; welcoming hearth.

GODSEND represents a blessing, windfall, or a manifested need.

GODZILLA corresponds to fears; the fearsome events one is afraid to approach, experience, and get past.

GOGGLE-EYED relates to astonishment; stunned.

GOGGLES are an attempt to better understand something.

GO-GO (dancing) signifies a frantic bid for attention.

GO-GO BOOTS represent a path walked in an attention-seeking manner.

GOITER warns of a current state of perceptual aberration.

GOLD (color) denotes goodness.

GOLD (metal) means financial aspects; facets of one's physical life.

GOLDBRICKER characterizes one who shirks responsibility; ulterior motives. May point to worthless efforts.

GOLD COAST symbolizes affluence, those seeking to be associated with it.

GOLD COIN signifies a valuable aspect. This will usually point to the high value of something else in the dreamer's life; a sign of value.

GOLD DIGGER represents the willful manipulation of others for personal gain; a tendency to use people for selfish purposes.

GOLD DUST usually refers to material benefits gained from one's giving behavior.

GOLDEN AGE constitutes peace and/or prosperity.

GOLDEN BANNER (flower; also wild pea) represents joy; comes to advise of a need to raise/uplift one's emotional outlook.

GOLDEN BOUGH indicates a validation for one's readiness for advanced spiritual concepts/experiences

GOLDEN CALF warns of negative goals and misplaced priorities.

GOLDEN FLAX (botanical) refers to cheerfulness.

GOLDEN GATE BRIDGE represents human potential, vision, and viable possibilities.

GOLDEN GOOSE represents an unlimited source of blessings/benefits.

GOLDEN HANDCUFFS define bribery; manipulation; an attempt to snag one in a Catch-22 situation.

GOLDEN HANDSHAKE stands for an incentive to quit something.

GOLDEN OLDIE represents memories, a spark which sends one back to a youthful time.

GOLDEN PARACHUTE represents a measure taken to protect oneself against a loss of beneficial aspects; assurance of being well compensated.

GOLDEN RETRIEVER (dog breed) denotes loyal companionship.

GOLDENROD (botanical) illustrates a natural talent.

GOLDEN RULE signifies ethical and moral behavior.

GOLDENSEAL (botanical) refers to a healing aspect in one's life.

GOLD FEVER represents unrealistic expectations.

GOLD FIELD indicates an opportunity.

GOLDFISH warns of a spiritually confining situation, belief, or condition.

GOLDFISH BOWL stands for a lack of privacy; the openness of one's plans, attitudes, or ideas.

GOLD FOIL See gild.

GOLDILOCKS connotes irresponsibility; a dependence on others.

GOLD LEAF See gild.

GOLD MEDAL represents the highest achievement attainable.

GOLD MINE denotes a great material benefit; a highly beneficial source.

GOLD PLATE indicates unnecessary extravagance; overdone refinement additions.

GOLD RECORD signifies recognition for one's accomplishment.

GOLD RUSH alludes to material desires; financial priorities.

GOLD SEAL stands for an official approval.

GOLDSMITH characterizes a fascination with manipulating specific aspects of life.

GOLD STAR signifies recognition of superior efforts expended.

GOLDSTONE See aventurine.

GOLD THERAPY See chrysotherapy.

GOLD TOOTH signifies a brazen, pompous attitude regarding one's intellect—the verbal delivery of it.

GOLEM pertains to misused spiritual abilities.

GOLF applies to the easiest path chosen.

GOLF BAG refers to the collection of our perceived tools to achieve certain goals.

GOLF BALL denotes a goal marker; what one aims for as a course marker then follows.

GOLF CAP warns against lazy thought; a lack of seriousness.

GOLF CART represents haughtiness.

GOLF CLUB emphasizes a life aspect that one utilizes to lessen personal efforts needed to achieve a specific goal.

GOLF COURSE typifies a area of one's path that is not taken seriously.

GOLF SHOES imply a path traveled in leisure; excessive complacency.

GOLF WIDOW characterizes one who suffers from another's sense of self-importance.

GOLIATH characterizes an individual or situation that must be overcome in order for advancement to proceed.

GONDOLA (boat) cautions of a lack of spiritual seriousness; a lazy spiritual journey.

GONDOLA (lift) See cable car.

GONDOLIER characterizes an individual who carries others along a spiritual path. This is not a good symbol, for it means one is depending on a leader for spiritual guidance rather than following one's own inner promptings.

GONG is a call to attention. The Higher Self is attempting to bring the dreamer's attention to something important.

GOOD BOOK See bible.

GOOD EGG will refer to an easy-going, agreeable personality.

GOOD FAITH represents trust.

GOOD FRIDAY stands for shared grief; deep empathy.

GOOD NEIGHBOR characterizes a generous, caring, helpful individual.

GOOD NEWS pertains to an encouraging or motivational revelation.

GOOD OLD BOY See old-boy network.

GOOD SAMARITAN defines humanitarian acts.

GOODWILL (organization) points to a generous helping hand.

GOOFY (character) refers to someone who doesn't quite have it all together, yet is a good person just the same.

GOOSE advises of a need for more seriousness in life.

GOOSE BUMPS connote one's immediate reaction to fear.

GOOSE EGG represents some type of mistake made; an unfruitful result.

GOOSE-NECK cautions against excessive curiosity taken to the extent of becoming intrusive.

GOPHER represents multiple tentative starts; a simultaneous digging around done in a surreptitious manner.

GORGE (eating) warns against periods of excessive ingestion, usually refers to intake of specific information.

GORGE (ravine) denotes the narrow and oftentimes rocky stretches of one's unique path.

GORGON characterizes those who are negative or make unproductive relationships.

GORILLA may indicate mental or emotional dysfunctions, but it usually refers to gregariousness. Surrounding dreamscape details will clarify this dual meaning.

GOSHAWK points to a predatory nature; a cut-throat way of reaching goals.

GOSLING implies fledgling instincts; the beginnings of newly formed responses.

GOSPEL applies to a truth as *perceived* by a specific individual.

GOSPEL MUSIC alludes to spiritual joy.

GOSSAMER See fine-spun.

GOSSIPMONGER advises to hold one's tongue and stop spreading hearsay. Recall who was doing the gossiping in the dream.

GOTHIC (attitude/style) refers to an affinity for the unexplained.

GOTHIC (setting) pertains to mystery; esoteric aspects.

GOUGE See chisel.

GOULASH implies full-bodied nourishment of some type, usually not in reference to food.

GOURAMI (fish) represents camaraderie; an intensified sense of spiritual friendship and companionship.

GOURD exemplifies a spiritual opportunity.

GOURMAND characterizes a gluttonous nature.

GOURMET illustrates high quality nourishment of some type; mental, emotional, or spiritual sustenance.

GOVERNESS corresponds to the quality of care given to one's humanitarian aspects.

GOVERNOR will point to the one running the show and, in reality, comes as a reminder that that individual should be oneself.

GRAB warns against impulsiveness.

GRAB BAG advises one to be more discerning, selective.

GRACE PERIOD refers to a time extension given.

GRACKLE (bird) signifies an important message forthcoming; a need to pay particular attention to upcoming communications.

GRADE POINT AVERAGE will come to reveal one's accurate level of understanding, attainment, or general progression.

GRADER (road) connotes a life aspect that has the capability of smoothing something out in one's life.

GRADUATION implies a completion of learning not yet rounded out by experience.

GRADUATION CAP emphasizes information gained through study rather than life experiences; learned perspectives vs. those gained through developed wisdom.

GRADUATION RING See ring (jewelry).

GRAFFITI usually comes as a warning specific to the dreamer. Recall what the graffiti depicted.

GRAFT (botany) connotes an attempt to join forces.

GRAFT (gain) warns against self-gain through unscrupulous methods.

GRAFT (skin) refers to renewal and the efforts expended to accomplish it.

GRAHAM CRACKER implies a positive experience bringing personal satisfaction.

GRAIL See Holy Grail.

GRAIN connotes life aspects that have the capability of bringing emotional, mental, or spiritual nourishment.

GRAIN ELEVATOR symbolizes reserve talents; the capacity for great stores of humanitarian deeds. The hint is to recall what this dreamscape grain elevator looked like. Was it in good shape? Full or empty? Have any mold around it?

GRAINY (image/photo) marks an unclear viewpoint; an unclear perception or attitude. Recall what the photograph or image was of.

GRAMMAR SCHOOL See elementary school.

GRAMMY AWARDS relates to receiving recognition.

GRAMOPHONE signifies old tunes used as excuses; cautions against falling back on the same old tunes for reasons behind one's actions.

GRANARY See grain elevator.

GRAND CANYON exemplifies solid evidence; time-tested, visible effects.

GRANDCHILD characterizes a personal responsibility for nurturing those who follow us.

GRANDEUR represents arrogance; a tendency to be showy.

GRANDFATHER CLAUSE pertains to an exemption of some type given.

GRANDFATHER CLOCK is a message that applies a serious connotation of time for the dreamer.

GRAND FINALE points to a showy conclusion to something.

GRAND JURY comes as a severe warning. Surrounding details will clarify the precise meaning.

GRAND LAMA characterizes high spiritual attainment.

GRAND LARCENY refers to an extremely costly misdeed.

GRAND MAL (seizure) indicates serious repercussions forthcoming.

GRAND MARCH symbolizes vanity, fatuousness.

GRAND MARSHALL characterizes one who has many followers.

GRANDMOTHER stands for a source of women's wisdom; a genteel wise woman.

GRAND OLE OPRY denotes the solidness and enduring nature of tried-and-true ways.

GRANDPARENT characterizes an individual who has the capability of sharing great wisdom.

GRANDPARENTS DAY refers to an advisement to maintain respect and honor for those with great wisdom and experience.

GRAND PIANO corresponds with the great potential of one's personal talents. They key here is the condition of the dreamscape piano. Was it highly polished? Were the ivory keys yellowed? Any of them broken or missing altogether?

GRAND PRIX (race) refers to a dangerous manner of competition—fast, furious, and possibly deadly.

GRAND SLAM defines the best possible outcome.

GRANDSTAND warns against having a self-absorbed tendency to always want to impress others.

GRAND TOUR signifies a recognition of one's limitations.

GRANGE illustrates an interest in nurturing the talents of others.

GRANITE depicts a solid foundation.

GRANITEWARE See enamelware.

GRANNY DRESS signifies an unaffected personality; a confidence in one's genteel nature.

GRANOLA is another dreamscape symbol that applies to inner nourishment of one's emotional, mental, or spiritual aspects.

GRANT applies to some type of life aspect or event that serves to clear one's way toward achieving a goal.

GRANULE illustrates a fragment of a whole; a part of something greater.

GRAPE refers to multiple aspects, the fact that an issue holds many varying facets.

GRAPEFRUIT advises one to shed certain excesses in life.

GRAPE HYACINTH (flower) comes to reveal the presence of one's hidden natural abilities; a need to recognize one's own potential.

GRAPEVINE typifies a life of rumor; the sequential and progressive alteration of facts.

GRAPH See diagram.

GRAPHIC ARTS symbolize a talent for communication clarity; a skill for explaining things.

GRAPHICS connote a need for further explanation; a visual required for complete comprehension.

GRAPHOLOGY (study of) denotes an interest in obtaining insights into others.

GRAPH PAPER usually is a call to figure something out on paper before acting on it.

GRAPPLE (tool) indicates a struggle to hold onto something.

GRASS corresponds to spiritual foundations.

GRASS CLOTH (fabric) will relate to spirituality associated with a specific life element. Was the grass cloth a wallpaper in one's home? Which room? Was it on an office wall? What type of office or business?

GRASSHOPPER signifies a destructive force related to spiritual foundations.

GRASSLAND See prairie; savanna.

GRASSROOTS defines people power; activism generated by common folk.

GRASS SEED pertains to a life aspect that has the capability of taking hold and developing into a spiritual foundation or perspective.

GRATE will indicate a protective measure.

GRATUITY implies thankfulness; a reciprocal response denoting appreciation.

GRAVE symbolizes finality.

GRAVEDIGGER characterizes one on a fatal course; the act of digging one's own grave.

GRAVEL represents loose footing; a need to pay attention to one's path walk.

GRAVEN IMAGE See idol.

GRAVE ROBBER is one who enjoys gaining from the downfall of others.

GRAVESTONE usually reveals one's fatal course; may forewarn of an actual death date.

GRAVEYARD has ominous connotations. Most often advises of a condition or situation where the dreamer is treading on dangerous ground.

GRAVEYARD SHIFT reveals a darkness surrounding one's life and advises of the wisdom of bringing some light in.

GRAVITY defines imagined limitations.

GRAVY represents an easy access to something.

GRAVY BOAT signifies a life aspect that has the capability of providing an easier course.

GRAY corresponds with the physical brain and the mind contained within. In some cases, this color may point directly to a lack of clarity; a gray area.

GRAYBEARD equates to an experienced, conservative personality, usually an elder individual.

GRAY JAY stands for recognizing every opportunity and making the most of each one.

GRAYLING (fish) stands for spiritual commonality; generalized traditional dogma.

GRAY MARKET refers to a slightly unethical way of accomplishing something; slightly unethical behavior on the same vein as telling a little white lie.

GRAZE portrays nonchalance; a skimming of the surface.

GREASE warns of bribes and ulterior motives.

GREASE GUN points to behavior which makes progression or accomplishment easier.

GREASE MONKEY See mechanic.

GREASE PAINT warns of hypocrisy; a false face presented to others.

GREASE PENCIL represents a way to convey a message to a nonreceptive individual.

GREASER (appearance) suggests a liberal, left-wing attitude. May also point to a devil-may-care personality who doesn't let the attitudes of other's interfere with the freedom to express oneself.

GREASY usually calls for increased watchfulness; an issue isn't as assured as assumed.

GREASY SPOON implies questionable aspects in one's life; factors that should be questioned. The surrounding details will assist the dreamer in pinpointing these.

GREAT BARRIER REEF signifies spiritual concepts that are highly cherished and perceived as fragile treasures.

GREATCOAT warns against distancing oneself from others.

GREAT DANE (dog breed) points to a noble friend, one having solid integrity.

GREAT DIVIDE indicates solid strength. Also may point to a type of division in one's life.

GREAT HORNED OWL denotes wisdom.

GREAT LAKES emphasizes a surround of multiple spiritual reserves.

GREAT PLAINS allude to a span of time when one journeys through an unproductive period; a time of neutrality lacking advancement.

GREAT PYRAMID applies to historical ignorance; lacking a true and clear comprehension of reality.

GREAT PYRENEES (dog breed) denotes a friend having great courage.

GREAT SALT LAKE exemplifies an unexpected event.

GREAT SERPENT EARTH MOUND connotes personal verification. The dreamer will understand what this proof relates to. It will be different for everyone.

GREAT SPHINX relates to skepticism.

GREAT WALL OF CHINA warns of a deep rift in a relationship.

GREAT WHITE SHARK will reveal the presence of a possible threat existing in one's life. Sometimes this symbol's related elements will pinpoint this for the dreamer.

GREBE (bird) denotes spiritual goodness.

GREECE represents attained skills; philosophical ideas.

GREED warns against a tendency toward self-interest and self-centeredness.

GREEK GOD (appearance) suggests desirable attributes.

GREEN represents health and growth.

GREENBELT pertains to preservation; realizing something's worth.

GREEN BERET refers to skill in handling oneself.

GREEN CARD gives reassurance regarding one's current project or course of effort.

GREEN DRAGON comes to reveal envious feelings that one doesn't own up to.

GREEN EYES depending on brilliance vs. dullness and depth of color intensity, can refer to healing abilities or jealousy.

GREEN FLAG stands for a go-ahead. It's time to begin something.

GREEN GLASS signifies inferior quality.

GREENGROCER characterizes an individual who has bountiful natural talents, those related to inner goodness and a giving nature.

GREENHORN refers to inexperience.

GREENHOUSE reveals one's current state of spirituality. Recall what condition the greenhouse was in. Was it full of bountiful and healthy botanicals? Empty? Have wilted plants?

GREENHOUSE EFFECT will indicate ramifications of one's negative behavior returning on oneself.

GREEN LIGHT naturally means permission granted; the go-ahead signal.

GREEN LUMBER points to an attempt to build on a plan before the tools themselves are well developed or seasoned.

GREEN ONION stands for a simple and readily available element used to counter a negative; a safe-guard against being affected by negative aspects.

GREEN PARTY/PEACE represents environmental concerns.

GREEN PEPPER represents a controlled temper; a cool thinker.

GREEN POWER equates to an attitude that money is power.

GREENROOM constitutes a waiting period; the pause just before the action begins.

GREEN'S FEE refers to the price paid for taking the easy path.

GREEN SOAP connotes a healing factor, usually emotionally.

GREEN TEA represents a significant benefit.

GREEN THUMB corresponds with a nurturing nature.

GREETING CARD will portray a specific sentiment depending on the type of card it was. This message will carry a different interpretation for everyone.

GREGORIAN CHANTS stand for prayer.

GREMLIN pertains to a temporary problem or hitch in one's plans.

GRENADE signifies an aspect that has the capability of exploding if not carefully handled; a potentially explosive situation or relationship.

GRENADINE typifies a personality smothered in false sweetness.

GRENADINE (fabric) refers to insubstantial thought; cursory thinking without in-depth consideration.

GREYHOUND (dog breed) refers to a fast friend or associate.

GRIDDLE defines a hot situation or relationship. This advises of a need to take a neutral position in order to effect a cooling-down status.

GRIDDLECAKE See pancake.

GRIDLOCK constitutes a deadlocked condition or a Catch-22 situation.

GRIEF depicts a needed release of emotions.

GRIEF COUNSELOR will reveal an individual who understands grief and can offer helpful ways of dealing with it. This symbol may not relate to the literal sense of grief, but more to depression, melancholy, disappointment.

GRIEVANCE COMMITTEE will point to a source for resolving issues of conflict or dispute.

GRIFFIN characterizes strength and intelligence.

GRIFFON (dog breed) refers to a friend who will always listen without judgment.

GRILL (cooking) alludes to a more productive way to accomplish something. This will be defined by surrounding dreamscape details and will mean something different for each dreamer.

GRILLWORK symbolizes effective defenses; protective measures that are strong without being able to be detected by others.

GRIMACE connotes displeasure.

GRIME reveals depression.

GRIM REAPER warns of a potentially dangerous associate, situation, or course.

GRINDER/GRINDSTONE advises of a need to apply greater effort.

GRISTLE constitutes a disbelief; skepticism; something hard to believe.

GRISTMILL corresponds to natural talents and the use of same.

GRIT (granules) illustrates irritations in life.

GRIT (teeth) pertains to negative emotions. May point to stress.

GRITS connote unwilling acceptance.

GRIZZLY BEAR denotes a self-absorbed personality.

GROCERY MARKET represents diet. Recall what was purchased for a better understanding of what this symbol is attempting to convey.

GROGGY warns against a lack of awareness.

GROOM (wedding) See bridegroom.

GROOMER (animal) characterizes a compassionate individual.

GROOVE denotes an old routine; old tendencies or methods.

GROPE alludes to a lack of direction.

GROSBEAK (bird) denotes camaraderie; a deep appreciation of one's friendships.

GROSGRAIN (fabric) signifies a rough personality.

GROSS ANATOMY (study of) suggests a high interest in understanding technicalities and/or the many facets that make up a whole. This may apply to issues or situations.

GROTESQUE reveals a distorted perspective out of touch with reality.

GROTTO reveals a need to take spiritual respite time.

GROUCH implies a need to talk to someone.

GROUND denotes a generally defined beginning point, yet it's really what is underneath (unseen) that must be discovered.

GROUNDBREAKING refers to an effort to discover hidden aspects. For some dreamers this may indicate a beginning.

GROUND CLOTH suggests a protective measure taken.

GROUND COVER defines prolific spiritual or humanitarian qualities that are fruitfully used.

GROUND CREW represents one's emotional support group.

GROUND FLOOR connotes the beginning stage of a project, situation, or course.

GROUND FOG reveals a situation of being too close to an issue to see it clearly.

GROUNDHOG reflects a fear of responsibility; hiding from reality or problems.

GROUNDHOG DAY reveals superstition.

GROUND NOISE See humming.

GROUND OWL stands for ground-level watchfulness. This means not advancing further or higher until all current issues or aspects are well developed.

GROUND RULES allude to moral, ethical, and spiritual guidelines.

GROUNDSEL (botanical) represents joy.

GROUNDSKEEPER See gardener.

GROUND SQUIRREL See prairie dog.

GROUND SWELL stands for a growing perspective or movement; quickly gaining in popularity or support.

GROUND WATER See spring (water).

GROUND WIRE comes as an advisement to get grounded, perhaps one's thoughts/perspectives have begun to run wild.

GROUNDWORK denotes preliminary preparations. May point to an information-gathering stage.

GROUND ZERO signifies a target for destruction. This is usually a serious message for one to cease zeroing in on someone or something with a destructive intent.

GROUPER refers to independence.

GROUP HOME suggests the advisability of working closely with others, perhaps success is dependent on doing so.

GROUPIE is a caution against following others instead of listening to the inner voice that leads self.

GROUP RATE suggests a situation, relationship, or course that will benefit from the participation of several people.

GROUP THERAPY advises of the wisdom of talking through one's problems.

GROUSE connotes a troublesome factor in one's life; a cause for complaint.

GROUT refers to the in-between elements, the connective aspects between main issues.

GROVE pertains to the need to pause and contemplate.

GROVEL alludes to a lack of self-respect and inner strength.

GROWING PAINS are an advisement to slow down; indicates a forcing of development or advancement.

GROWL warns of adversity; a potentially threatening situation or relationship.

GROW LIGHT signifies any aspect that is capable of providing light upon one's path.

GROWTH HORMONE comes as an advisement to grow up; stop the immature behavior. Depending on the related dream elements, this symbol may also warn *against* trying to fit into shoes one isn't ready for; may represent more time needed for one to grow into something or more time for something to develop more fully.

GROWTH RING stands for a specific age; references time that is meaningful to each dreamer.

GRUBS characterize a destructive force present in an early stage of development.

GRUBSTAKE denotes ulterior motives behind the assistance one gives another.

GRUEL reveals an unproductive factor; a false nourishment.

GRUESOME connotes a repulsive reaction; a loathsome and unacceptable aspect in one's life.

GRUMBLE advises one to accept those life aspects that cannot be altered.

GRUNION (fish) signify a lack of independent spiritual thought.

GUANO comes as a reminder to reassess elements assumed to be useless.

GUARANTEE marks verification; reassurance.

GUARD denotes a protective measure or factor.

GUARD DOG will point to a friend who has your best interests in mind; a friend who watches out for you.

GUARD DUTY represents a call to sharpen one's awareness; an approaching phase when one needs to be particularly watchful.

GUARD HAIR indicates one's personal first defenses.

GUARDIAN characterizes an individual who watches out for another. In actuality, we are all guardians of someone.

GUARDIAN ANGEL portrays one's Higher Self; the Inner Voice heeded.

GUARDRAIL refers to a life aspect that keeps one on course; protective measures applied to keeping one from overextending self or overstepping bounds.

GUAVA connotes bountiful spiritual talents.

GUERRILLA reveals a forceful activist; one who aggressively fights a resistance force.

GUESS reveals a lack of knowledge or information; an assumption.

GUEST characterizes a temporary association.

GUEST BOOK comes in dreams to remind us to remember our friends.

GUEST HOUSE represents a personal receptivity to others.

GUEST LIST points to those we need to include in something we're planning.

GUIDE suggests a person who is capable of showing the way.

GUIDEBOOK symbolizes a life aspect that serves to keep one on course.

GUIDED MISSILE reveals a destructive intent. May also point to a goal that one is intently focused on.

GUIDE DOG emphasizes a knowledgeable friend who is capable of assisting another; one who will never steer you wrong; one willing to help you attain personal goals.

GUIDELINES will signify behavioral perimeters.

GUIDEPOST serves to mark one's way.

GUILD denotes a group that shares the same interest. This usually advises the dreamer of the existence of such a group.

GUILE reveals deceit.

GUILLOTINE warns against sticking one's neck out; interference.

GUILT comes to reveal culpability and many times it's the dreamer's.

GUINEA PIG reveals a lack of self-confidence; fear of experience.

GUITAR suggests self-expression.

GULAG connotes a situation or relationship that forces another in some manner.

GULCH stands for a temporary situation when extra efforts are required.

GULF advises of a spiritual gap.

GULL See seagull.

GULLET See esophagus.

GULLIVER characterizes one who has trouble dealing with personal adversity or trials.

GULLY See gulch.

GUM indicates a need to chew something over; a lack of understanding; more thought is required.

GUMBALL exemplifies a difficult to understand concept, idea, or situation.

GUMBO refers to a sustaining nourishment, one that's long-lasting.

GUM DISEASE infers infected (negative) speech. This symbol could infer a tendency to gossip or it could stand for half-truths/exaggerations.

GUMDROP advises of a need to ponder something over. This something is a temporary situation that only requires a bit more thought before it's resolved (dissolved).

GUMSHOE characterizes a stealthy individual or personality.

GUN warns of mental or emotional dysfunctions; erroneous attitudes or perceptions; potential for an emotional outburst, explosion; may also point to one's protective measures.

GUNBOAT pertains to dangerous spiritual attitudes or beliefs; spiritual beliefs or behavior that are headed for conflict, perhaps inner conflict.

GUN CONTROL warns of attempts to gain power or the upper hand over an issue.

GUN DOG represents a friend who is loyal through thick and thin.

GUNFIGHT portrays negative resolutions.

GUNFIRE (hearing) advises of a potentially dangerous situation close to the one doing the hearing.

GUNG HO denotes high enthusiasm and a readiness to act on it; stoked.

GUNMETAL (color) symbolizes a cool, reserved attitude toward spirituality.

GUN MOLL signifies an attraction to power.

GUNNY (fabric) denotes an unsophisticated personality; warm but a little coarse.

GUNNYSACK alludes to one's personal down-to-earth qualities.

GUNPOINT (held at) warns of a forced situation; against one's will; coercion.

GUNPOWDER reveals a highly explosive aspect in one's life. This could refer to a relationship, situation, belief, or psychological state.

GUN RACK stands for possible ongoing conflicts or emotional explosions present in one's life. The key here is to recall if the rack was full or empty.

GUN ROOM defines a personal supply of defensive methods.

GUNRUNNER indicates one who is capable of privately supplying others with protective means. This is not normally a negative dream aspect.

GUNSHOT (sound) will be an attention-getting element pointing to an emotional explosion or an imminent one.

GUN SHOW represents the multitude of choices available for anger management or self-protection; may also be symbolic of the variety of ways an emotional explosion may be forthcoming in the dreamer's life.

GUN-SHY refers to reluctance; hesitancy to take control or make a big step forward.

GUNSLINGER points to an overconfident individual, one who gets pushy/manipulative.

GUNSMITH characterizes an individual who creates protective aspects for others to use.

GUPPY represents a spiritual neophyte.

GURNEY advises of a serious physical condition.

GURU connotes spiritual arrogance; current spiritual fads.

GUSSIED UP usually points to a desire to put one's best foot forward but, depending on the related dreamscape elements, this may also point to an affected public image.

GUST pertains to a sudden emotional outburst; advises a need for greater control.

GUTLESS is an advisement to gain more courage, self-confidence, and stand up for oneself.

GUTSY symbolizes confidence in one's belief; unafraid to speak out or act in an unexpected or unconventional manner.

GUTTER may indicate the preservation of spiritual aspects or it may warn of a lack of spirituality depending on the surrounding dream details.

GUTTURAL (voice) denotes a surprised or stunned reaction.

GUY WIRE stands for a supportive element; a balancing or reinforcing aspect.

GUZZLE warns against impatience; inhaling information instead of digesting it with comprehension.

GYMNASIUM denotes an atmosphere that provides exercise, usually indicating mental exercise.

GYMNAST warns of a conniving personality; one who contorts and twists facts.

GYPSUM represents a gentle faith; secure with one's beliefs.

GYPSY characterizes a free spirit. Depending on surrounding dream elements, this may or may not be a positive sign.

GYPSY MOTH reveals the presence of a possible destructive force.

GYROSCOPE stands for steadfastness; remaining true to one's course.

H

HABERDASHERY relates to the manner in which thoughts are displayed or covered up. Refer to specific hat type for more specific information.

HABIT signifies repetitiveness; action without thought.

HABITAT FOR HUMANITY signifies the unconditional sharing of one's talents.

HACIENDA portrays a relaxed lifestyle where individuals are afforded personal space and privacy.

HACKAMORE denotes control.

HACKBERRY (tree) stands for a need to sharpen analytical thought; heighten discernment.

HACKER (computer) See computer hacker.

HACKLES indicate one's position of defensiveness.

HACKSAW alludes to difficult solutions.

HADDOCK represents traditional spiritual beliefs.

HADES (Greek mythology) characterizes the dark forces (negative influences) and also may connote hell (an extremely difficult time).

HAG signifies old grudges.

HAGGARD portrays a long struggle; exhaustion; tired of continually putting forth the effort without seeing results.

HAGGLE See bargain.

HAIGHT-ASHBURY characterizes an atmosphere that is conducive to free thinking.

HAIL warns of an inundation of hard spiritual issues.

HAIL MARY (prayer) points to a last hope or last ditch effort.

HAIR symbolizes thoughts. Refer to specific hair types, conditions, and colors for specific interpretations.

HAIRBALL connotes a misconception that must be gotten rid of (regurgitated).

HAIRBRUSH advises of a need to clean out and untangle confused thoughts or ideas.

HAIRCLOTH See horsehair (cloth).

HAIR COLORING applies to thoughts colored by personal attitudes. This symbol refers to an attempt to alter one's perspectives.

HAIR CURLERS stand for a desire to alter or dress up an issue or attitude with softening elements.

HAIRCUT symbolizes an attempt to cut away extraneous elements to an issue; a desire to stay focused on the main issue and not have it complicated by non-essential aspects.

HAIRDRESSER represents one who

affects the thoughts of others; persuasiveness.

HAIRDRESSING signifies controlled thoughts.

HAIR DRYER refers to a shielding of one's spirituality; reticence to talk about spiritual matters.

HAIR EXTENSIONS stand for an attempt to appear as a deep thinker.

HAIR GROWTH PRODUCTS indicate efforts to think deeper.

HAIR IMPLANTS represent new ideas stemming from alternative thought.

HAIR LOSS infers a shift to more shallow thinking; perhaps grown less thoughtful/sensitive.

HAIR NET warns of a need to contain one's uncontrollable thoughts.

HAIR PICK stands for intensive thought—picking one's own brain; deep thinking/analyzation/planning.

HAIR PIECE warns of a thought process that is partially in error (false).

HAIRPIN applies to a method of controlling the odd thought.

HAIRPIN CURVE (in road) indicates a tendency to do a lot of backtracking.

HAIR SHIRT denotes self-reproach; guilt.

HAIR-SPLITTING means faultfinding; pettiness.

HAIR SPRAY pertains to stiff thinking; unyielding attitudes.

HAIR STYLE See specific type.

HAIR TRANSPLANT See transplant (hair).

HAIR TRIGGER stands for an explosive temperament.

HALCYON illustrates a peaceful atmosphere.

HALF (of something) implies more to be obtained; one doesn't have the all of it yet.

HALF-AND-HALF connotes a tempered situation or attitude.

HALF-BAKED signifies a premature aspect; an undeveloped idea or plan.

HALF BATH denotes an alternative respite option.

HALF BLOOD constitutes a rightful identity or authority.

HALF BREED See half blood.

HALF-COCKED (gun) means ill prepared. May point to an anxiety to begin a conflict.

HALF DOLLAR depicts a starting point; all is not lost.

HALFHEARTED represents a lack of interest.

HALF-MAST reveals sorrow.

HALF-MOON exemplifies partial illumination of one's path; underscores enough light to be guided by. This would indicate an individual who believes she/he has no guidance.

HALF NOTE implies a quickened pace.

HALF PINT defines a smaller aspect that may be as important or potent as a larger one; something not to be overlooked or viewed as insignificant because of smaller size.

HALF SHELL represents concealed elements; not a whole presentation shown.

HALF-SLIP pertains to something that's partially shielded, usually refers to an aspect of one's personality.

HALFTIME advises of a time of respite; a break to re-energize and regroup.

HALFTONE suggests subtlety; a need to soften harshness.

HALF-TRACK reveals a need to venture into untraveled regions; enter new territory. This refers to knowledge.

HALFWAY HOUSE is an advisement to remove self from an undesirable situation or relationship.

HALIBUT pertains to spiritual nourishment.

HALITOSIS applies to offending language. This isn't usually associated with cussing, but crude or insensitive comments that hurt others; thoughtlessness.

HALL (large room) indicates an important gathering.

HALLEY'S COMET relates to the continual fluctuations of true Reality.

HALLMARK exemplifies a sign of approval.

HALL OF FAME represents narrowly perceived greatness.

HALLOW refers to an individualized idea of what is perceived as sacred.

HALLOWEEN illustrates personal revelations; insights into another's hidden character.

HALLUCINATING may, in reality, be insights into true Reality or it may warn against conscious imaginings that one believes as fact.

HALLWAY suggests a transition.

HALO portrays spiritual enlightenment.

HALTER suggests forwardness of character.

HAM (meat) applies to theatrics; over-emotionalism; dramatics.

HAMBURGER signifies questionable nourishment; an aspect one depends on for support that may not be a positive factor.

HAMLET implies a surround of close associates; one's circle of friends.

HAMMER warns of forced attitudes or beliefs.

HAMMER AND SICKLE relate to a common bond.

HAMMER TOES indicate difficulty walking one's path.

HAMMOCK cautions against laziness.

HAM OPERATOR characterizes one who is able to provide immediate responsive communications; a quickly helpful individual.

HAMPER (clothes) suggests that which needs cleaning up in one's life.

HAM RADIO refers to helpful communications; preparedness; an ability to get through to someone.

HAMSTER See gerbil.

HAND connotes service done for others. Recall condition of same.

HANDBAG See purse (handbag).

HANDBALL depicts personal efforts expended.

HANDBILL represents the personal sharing of ideas; the tendency to broadcast one's thoughts/ideologies/opinions.

HAND-BLOWN signifies personal energy put into creative efforts.

HANDBOOK warns against following a stilted lifestyle; regimentation.

HANDCAR cautions against fanaticism related to following another's life or spiritual path.

HANDCART stands for the carrying of one's personal burdens.

HAND-CLAP See applause.

HANDCLASP represents a unifying force.

HAND COVERING See specific type.

HANDCUFFS reveal restraints. This usually points to a plan that can't be implemented yet or a situation that one can't interfere with; ineffectiveness.

HAND DELIVERY points to a desire to be assured a particular communication has been made.

HAND-DIPPED CANDLES represents personal efforts expended toward gaining independence (or attempting to gain more information—enlightenment—on a subject).

HAND DRILL denotes extensive personal efforts expended for the purpose of getting to the bottom of an issue.

HAND FEED can indicate ideas which are force-fed or the symbol can mean caring enough to insure another is nourished by certain healthful/healing ideas. The related elements to the symbol will clarify which interpretation was intended.

HANDICAPPED indicates subconscious fears that hold one back.

HANDICAPPED ACCESS points to a way to alleviate fears of advancing.

HANDICRAFTS denote creativity generated from personal efforts.

HAND IN COOKIE JAR suggests misbehavior; may indicate nosiness.

HAND IN GLOVE cautions against forming relationships that are too close, too revealing of self, or too interdependent.

HAND IN HAND signifies cooperation; close association.

HAND IN POCKETS suggests reluctance.

HANDKERCHIEF implies preparedness.

HANDLE (door) relates to comprehension.

HANDLE (touch) means getting the feel for something.

HANDLEBAR pertains to personal control; a control of one's direction.

HANDLEBAR MUSTACHE reveals pretentiousness.

HANDLESS suggests a feeling of helplessness.

HANDMADE points to personal efforts; a desire to personally accomplish something.

HANDMAID signifies a female assistant.

HAND-ME-DOWN refers to a highly useful aspect in one's life.

HAND MOWER denotes efforts to personally care for one's appreciated blessings.

HANDOFF applies to an exchange being done; passing of information or benefits.

HANDOUT exemplifies sharing.

HAND OVER FIST suggests a fast pace.

HAND OVER HEART usually implies sincerity.

HANDPICKING means personal choice or decision.

HANDPRINT denotes that which we leave behind; a mark of our identity.

HAND PUPPET represents expressiveness once removed. This means a tendency to attribute the originality of one's ideas to another.

HANDRAIL portrays one's personal means of support along the way.

HANDS DOWN stands for complete agreement; a reinforcing sign.

HANDSHAKE portrays good intentions.

HANDSOME (appearance) suggests an attractive aspect. Recall surrounding details to see if this is true or the opposite is meant. Outward appearance can be deceptive.

HANDS OVER EARS point to a lack of acceptance, not wanting to hear certain things.

HANDS OVER EYES warn against voluntary ignorance.

HANDSPRING relates to a sudden burst of joy or excitement.

HANDSTAND depicts elation; extreme happiness.

HAND-TO-MOUTH connotes a time of great tribulation; desperation; lean times that one must get past. This difficult phase won't always be associated with finances but may point to a time when one is going through a stage of lean spiritual behavior such as apathetic feelings.

HAND TOOLS represent personal efforts geared to one's unique style of creativity.

HAND WARMER suggests a desire to stay prepared for hands-on work.

HAND WASH signifies the giving of special care to something.

HAND WRINGING defines worry; lack of acceptance. Many times this symbol will point to one's ploy for gaining sympathy.

HANDWRITING emphasizes one's inner character. What qualities did it have. Was the writing stilted and stiff looking? Was it a fancy script? Jagged? Unreadable?

HANDWRITING ON WALL reveals a message; forewarning.

HANDYPERSON characterizes an individual who is capable of fixing a multitude of problems; one who may have a variety of solutions.

HANGAR (plane) advises of the need for a time of contemplation; a rest period from research or expending great efforts.

HANGER (clothes) See clothes hanger.

HANGER (picture) See picture hanger.

HANG-GLIDE corresponds with effortless thought; ideas or concepts that come easily.

HANGMAN characterizes one who is capable of posing a dangerous threat to another; someone who could hang you; a betrayer. But was the dreamer the hangman? That points to behavior that will end up hanging oneself; self-defeating.

HANGNAIL denotes a lack of acceptance; worries or anxieties we pick over; fretting.

HANGOUT stands for a place one feels comfortable going to for support.

HANGOVER represents the negative results of irresponsibility.

HANGTAG See price tag.

HANG-UP (phone call) represents a missed communication/message; may indicate a change of mind, a reluctance to make a contact.

HANSEL AND GRETEL characterize loss of direction through misplaced trust; betrayal; placing trust in someone who has ulterior motives.

HANSOM See carriage.

HANUKKAH comes as a reminder for us to rekindle the light in our souls for our spiritual beliefs.

HAPHAZARD advises of a fragmented mind; a lack of orderly thought.

HAPPY HOUR typifies a short period of time when troubles can be set aside.

HARANGUE cautions against sermonizing to others.

HARASSMENT denotes a lack of acceptance; hanging on to irritations; a refusal to let go and let things be.

HARBINGER connotes forerunner; something that comes first.

HARBOR pertains to a spiritual comfort; a spiritually safe place to be; a secure spiritual belief system.

HARBOR LIGHTS represents the lights of inspiration, insights.

HARBOR MASTER characterizes an individual who has the capability to guide others to a spiritually safe place.

HARD (consistency) usually implies a difficult aspect; unyielding; harsh or insensitive.

HARDBALL denotes a tough situation to deal with. May reveal an insensitive person who plays hard to get or manages situations/dealings with a sense of strictly business acumen.

HARD-BOILED defines an insensitive personality.

HARD CANDY represents a lasting benefit; may indicate a particularly sweet idea one needs to mull over.

HARD CASH symbolizes immediately available means to accomplish something.

HARD COPY means a visible, touchable aspect.

HARD-CORE signifies a strong opinion or perspective; one that cannot be changed.

HARDCOVER (book) relates to an enduring quality; lasting.

HARD DISK applies to a wealth of information on a particular subject.

HARD DRIVE points to the mind; the well of knowledge we've retained. This symbol may also refer to one's memory capacity.

HARD-FISTED may indicate determination/fortitude or it could point to ruthlessness.

HARD-HANDED reveals a tyrannical personality.

HARD HAT portrays strong opinions; a thought process that resists new ideas.

HARDHEADED applies to a realistic perspective; shrewdness.

HARDHEARTED reveals an aloof personality; unemotional and insensitive; apathetic.

HARDINESS CHART See zone chart.

HARD LABOR (maternity) signifies great personal efforts applied to changing one's life.

HARD LABOR (penalty) relates to serious ramifications for past or planned behavior.

HARD LANDING portrays a difficult ending; hard work applied to a conclusion or closure.

HARD LINE denotes a firm position or belief; uncompromising.

HARD MONEY points to cash-in-hand; available assets to work with.

HARD NEWS represents important new information.

HARD-NOSED refers to a firm position; a difficult-to-change attitude.

HARD OF HEARING denotes difficulty understanding concepts; may point to willful means of denial.

HARD ROCK (music) signifies a release of stress, pent-up tension.

HARD ROCK MINER characterizes one who expends great personal efforts to advance along a personal path.

HARDSCRABBLE reveals perseverance in the face of extended adversity; managing to advance despite little to work with.

HARD SELL suggests coercion; a pushy, insistent personality.

HARDTACK exemplifies something that's hard to swallow; difficult to accept.

HARDTOP implies thought given to protective methods or aspects.

HARDWARE STORE denotes hard work. May indicate a need for hard work applied to fixing up some aspect in one's life.

HARD WATER signifies the elements of reality which are difficult to soften (make easier to accept).

HARDWIRED is associated with inherent characteristics.

HARDY (plants) will equate to strong character qualities related to endurance.

HARE See rabbit.

HAREBELL (flower) signifies hope, signs of renewal.

HARELIP stands for impaired speech relating to errors in perception or attitude.

HAREM applies to separatism; an attitude based on class or position.

HARLEQUIN (pattern) characterizes one who avoids responsibility; lacks a true view of reality and takes life too lightly.

HARLEQUIN DUCK denotes individuality; a solid sense of self without affectations.

HARLEY DAVIDSON represents pride in one's independence.

HARLOT See prostitute.

HARMONICA corresponds with relaxation; a time for self.

HARMONIZING pertains to efforts applied to obtaining balance.

HARNESS represents control and/or containment.

HARP (musical) implies spiritual peacefulness.

HARP (nag) indicates a lack of acceptance; a tendency to interfere.

HARPIES (mythology) suggest guidance upon death. This death may not be a physical one but refer to elements such as a relationship or situational ending.

HARPOON stands for spiritual selectivity.

HARP SEAL defines innocence; spiritual vulnerability.

HARPSICHORD represents outdated ideas.

HARRIER (bird) See hawk.

HARRIER (plane) See helicopter.

HARROW implies a greatly disturbing incident.

HARVEST portrays the fruits of one's shared gifts.

HARVEST HOME signifies the inner joy felt when one helps others.

HARVEST MOON See moon (harvest).

HASH (food) relates to nourishment comprised of multiple factors.

HASH BROWNS represent an important, basic factor in one's life.

HASHISH See marijuana.

HASH-SLINGER See short-order cook.

HASSOCK See footstool.

HAT corresponds with one's way of thinking; personal inner thoughts. See specific type of hat for further information.

HATBAND reveals added aspects to one's character.

HATBOX signifies altered or changeable perspectives; a tendency to switch attitudes.

HATCH (bird birth) points to the birth of an idea or solution.

HATCHBACK pertains to an open-ended situation or relationship.

HATCH COVER means a way out of something.

HAT-CHECK connotes the holding back of expressing personal opinions or attitudes.

HATCHERY connotes multiple ideas or theories; one who is full of new ideas.

HATCHET pertains to a resentment; a desire to get even; retaliation; irascible and disagreeable personality.

HATCHET JOB stands for an idea or plan that has been ridiculed or picked apart so completely that little remains.

HATCHET MAN characterizes an individual who rarely accepts another's opinion.

HATCHLING denotes a new beginning; a fresh start or brand new plan for one's personal direction.

HAT DANCE represents the joyous feeling of a new love.

HATE CRIME signifies behavior borne of intolerance.

HATE MAIL reveals a lack of acceptance; intolerance; negativity; insensitivity.

HATHOR (Egyptian deity) equates to the ideology of the Mother God.

HATPIN indicates a need to hold on to one's thoughts or attitudes.

HAT RACK advises of the wisdom of hanging up one's presumptions for the purpose of being open and staying objective.

HAT TRICK suggests ulterior motives; intellectual/psychological maneuvering.

HAULING TRAILER warns of excessive weight carried around. This could refer to physical body weight or voluntarily held burdens.

HAUNTING corresponds to self-generated fear. May indicate guilt from past behavior.

HAUTE COUTURE warns against letting others dictate your personal style or method of expression; a loss of individuality.

HAUTE CUISINE implies extravagant methods of nourishment; reaching for nourishment that is highly regarded without realizing that the most beneficial nourishment comes from the simplest and most basic sources.

HAVELOCK pertains to a lack of trust; an attempt to protect one's back.

HAVEN illustrates a life aspect within which one believes one is well protected; may refer to a place within self; a retreat within.

HAVE-NOT characterizes an individual who refuses to recognize her/his own gifts; a lack of acceptance; ignoring one's real riches in deference to materialism.

HAVERSACK portrays a light traveler; one who recognizes the basics as opposed to excessive baggage.

HAVOC pertains to total confusion, usually one's thought process.

HAWAII represents a protective attitude toward one's natural talents; deep respect for natural bounties/blessings.

HAWK characterizes acute perceptions; an ability for quick discernment.

HAWK-EYED stands for heightened awareness.

HAWSER represents a life aspect that keeps one spiritually bound to a specific belief system; spiritual constriction.

HAWTHORN exemplifies unrecognized benefits.

HAWTHORNE (Nathaniel) characterizes ethical and spiritual living.

HAY implies active efforts; work time.

HAY FEVER warns against a reluctance to work; laziness.

HAYFORK connotes a tool that helps us accomplish a goal.

HAYLOFT pertains to the resulting evidence of one's efforts.

HAYMOW refers to efforts expended toward the completion of a specific project.

HAY RIDE reveals an inner joy taken from hard work.

HAYSTACK signifies the completion of one's specific work.

HAYWIRE means the final work to be done before completing something; may also infer something gone completely wrong.

HAZARD LIGHT refers to one's personal ability to sense dangerous situations; forewarning insights.

HAZARDOUS WASTE warns of harmful aspects surrounding the dreamer. This will be different for everyone.

HAZE (atmospheric) alludes to an unclear aspect, usually a lack of clear thought or understanding.

HAZE (harass) stands for a ridiculing personality or situation; amusement at another's expense.

HAZEL (eye color) means a cheery, down-to-earth personality or attitude.

HAZELNUT implies common sense.

HAZING signifies a price paid for certain advancements or desire to be accepted. This symbol also points to a meanness lying just below the surface that comes to the fore at every available opportunity.

HEAD pertains to the thought process.

HEADACHE exemplifies difficulty in processing one's thoughts; a problematical situation needing resolution.

HEADBAND warns against confining one's thoughts; advises expanding and exploring new concepts; a need to express oneself.

HEADBANGER characterizes an individual who has a tendency to easily release stress.

HEADCHEESE signifies the use of life elements having little nourishing value.

HEAD CLEANER (CD, printer, etc.) stands for an advisement to keep thoughts clear of extraneous elements that compromise or confuse an issue.

HEAD COLD signifies a clogged mind; a need to clear one's thoughts.

HEAD COVERING See specific type.

HEADDRESS reveals a uniquely specific and individualistic attachment; corresponds with a certain attitude or association.

HEAD-HUNTING connotes one's search for a specific individual or type of personality; a quest for knowledge.

HEAD IN THE SAND naturally points to denial; a refusal to face reality; escapism.

HEADLESS warns of a thoughtless person; one who has no intellectual pursuits or interests; a lack of personal opinion.

HEADLIGHT denotes logic and reason; a light on the subject. Usually refers to one's eyes and may be associated with one's clarity of perception.

HEADLINER signifies the main event/attraction.

HEADLINES come as important messages. This will carry different meanings for each individual. Recall what the headlines were.

HEADMISTRESS characterizes an individual who helps to guide another's learning process.

HEAD-ON symbolizes a strong will and determination to face reality and/or deal with conflicts.

HEADPHONES stand for focused thought; the blocking out of unimportant audibles.

HEADQUARTERS portray a central source regarding a specific idea.

HEADREST indicates intellectual respite; a time to pause from one's pursuit of knowledge.

HEAD RESTRAINT suggests precautions against the possibility of a backlash.

HEAD ROOM pertains to time and space to think.

HEAD-SCRATCHING indicates puzzlement; a lack of understanding; confusion.

HEADSET signifies an effort to listen well, to thoroughly hear what's being said.

HEAD SHOP corresponds with a source that provides one with tools to escape from problems.

HEADS OR TAILS denotes an opportunity to make a choice.

HEADSTAND indicates the act of doing everything one can (even standing on one's head) to accomplish something.

HEAD START represents an opportunity.

HEADSTONE See gravestone.

HEADSTRONG warns against being obstinate.

HEADS UP represents an advisement to be watchful, aware; a forewarning.

HEAD TABLE symbolizes a position of importance.

HEAD-TO-HEAD denotes an intellectual conflict.

HEAD TRIP signifies mental exhilaration.

HEAD WAITPERSON stands for an experienced coordinator/assistant.

HEADWATERS stand for a spiritual source.

HEADWIND constitutes a counter-force to be overcome along one's path.

HEALER characterizes an individual who is capable of restoring the well-being of others. Was this dreamscape healer you?

HEALTH CLUB/SPA advises of a need to shape up or restore some specific aspect of self.

HEALTH DEPARTMENT will pertain to a specific aspect in one's life that is unhealthy.

HEALTH DEPARTMENT VIOLATION refers to a negative (unhealthy) attitude or behavior that one is aware of.

HEALTH-FOOD STORE represents a choice of multiple tools to maintain personal health. This may refer to mental or emotional health, depending on surrounding dreamscape details.

HEALTH INSPECTOR will most often symbolize one's conscience in respect to watching oneself for unhealthy attitudes or behavior.

HEALTH INSURANCE denotes self-doubt; a lack of faith in one's own healing abilities.

HEALTH MAINTENANCE ORG. (HMO) stands for letting other's dictate which methods are best to heal you. This is a negative symbol that points to one being manipulated.

HEARING AID indicates a lack of attention and awareness; implies one does not listen well or only hears what one wants to hear.

HEARSAY implies questionable information.

HEARSE corresponds with death. This could refer to the death of a relationship, situation, condition, or some other aspect within self. Sometimes this symbol may forewarn of an actual physical demise.

HEART applies to the emotions and their health.

HEARTACHE naturally equates to sorrow, emotional distress.

HEART ATTACK portrays an emotional setback.

HEARTBEATS signify emotional stability. Recall if the beats were steady or irregular. Were they fast or slow?

HEARTBURN connotes emotional pain that can easily be alleviated if one so desires.

HEART DISEASE usually refers to a lack of empathy, but may also indicate emotional stress/damage due to a lack of acceptance.

HEART FAILURE signifies apathy; a lack of emotional sensitivity.

HEARTH refers to homey aspect; warmth and comfort.

HEARTH RUG implies measures used to protect one's personal feelings of comfort and privacy.

HEARTLESS stands for apathy, sternness, insensitivity.

HEART-OF-HEARTS implies confidentiality; open expression of sincerity; what one cherishes most.

HEARTS (card game) implies a manipulation of another's emotions.

HEART-TO-HEART implies confidentiality; open expression of deep sincerity.

HEART TRANSPLANT See transplant (heart).

HEARTWORM warns of an emotionally destructive force in one's life. This may even indicate a self-generated source.

HEAT connotes one's energy.

HEATER represents an element which motivates.

HEAT EXCHANGER pertains to the act of helping to re-energize another or rejuvenate them in some manner.

HEAT EXHAUSTION warns of a depletion of one's energy; a time to rest and recoup.

HEATHEN characterizes spirituality versus the dogmas of organized religions.

HEATHER (botanical) represents a bountiful stage in life.

HEATING BLANKET stands for emotional comfort.

HEATING PAD advises of a need to re-energize self.

HEAT LIGHTNING exemplifies a sudden depletion of one's energy.

HEAT RASH relates to the use of one's energy for self-defeating purposes; an unproductive effort.

HEAT-SEEKER will equate to a desire to have the latest gadgetry; also point to someone who stays on top of issues; keeping current.

HEAT SHIELD signifies a specific method one uses to conserve personal energy; efficient use of one's time and energy.

HEAT STROKE connotes overwork; unregulated energy usage.

HEAT WAVE defines a span of time during one's path walk when extra efforts are required for advancement.

HEAVEN stands for what one perceives as the ultimate state of being.

HEAVY implies an intense or profound burden. Surrounding details will clarify which meaning is intended.

HEAVY CREAM signifies a blessing rich in extended benefits.

HEAVY-DUTY symbolizes strength, endurance.

HEAVY HAND represents a harsh and tyrannical personality.

HEAVY-HEARTED denotes melancholia.

HEAVY METAL (music or metal) warns of an extremely negative aspect one needs to either get rid of or accept and move on; a need to expel building stress.

HEAVYWEIGHT characterizes an intellectual; a highly influential individual.

HECKLE warns against a tendency to irritate another; taunting.

HEDGE exemplifies a habit of circumventing; evading issues or responsibility.

HEDGEHOG See porcupine.

HEDGEROW implies a guiding facet in one's life.

HEDGE TRIMMERS refer to an attempt to reshape one's path.

HEDONISM warns against excessive self-indulgence; a preoccupation with self.

HEEL symbolizes exhaustion.

HEIMLICH MANEUVER advises of a need to get something out of one's system; get an internalized emotion or attitude out in the open.

HEIRESS characterizes one's right to something. This could be a multifaceted symbol in that it may refer to factors such as knowledge, material goods, an employment position, etc. Surrounding dreamscape details will clarify this specific meaning.

HEIRLOOM signifies great personal value.

HEIST See burglar.

HELEN OF TROY represents the factor that has caused great strife in one's life.

HELICOPTER reveals a vacillating mental state; frequent indecision.

HELIOTHERAPY advises of a dark, depressive condition that needs brightening with a recognition of one's blessings.

HELIOTROPE (flower) signifies inherent spiritual talents.

HELIPORT corresponds with a grounding aspect in one's life.

HELIUM indicates a life aspect that has the capability of uplifting attitudes, emotions, or situations.

HELL may illustrate various conditions such as a great tribulation, extremely difficult situation, a dark and depressive state of mind, etc.

HELL-BENT stands for a level of determination verging on obsession.

HELLEBORE (botanical) exemplifies a state of duality.

HELL-RAISING usually refers to the act of stirring things up for the purpose of exposing wrong-doings or misconceptions.

HELM represents control.

HELMET connotes protected or hidden thoughts.

HELMSPERSON will point to one in control. Ideally, this should be the dreamer.

HELPER characterizes one who has the capability to aid another.

HELPER T CELL portrays an agent that has the ability to destroy specific negative aspects in one's life.

HEM stands for something that surrounds; encircles; something one is surrounded by.

HEMATITE pertains to the power and strength of one's life force.

HEMATOLOGY (study of) illustrates a high interest in understanding esoteric concepts.

HEMATOMA warns of a need to release a blockage of one's continuously circulating energy flow within the body. This means that some type of clearing is needed.

HEMISPHERE illustrates half of something. Surrounding dreamscape details will clarify this intention.

HEMLOCK advises of a dangerous factor in one's life.

HEMLOCK SOCIETY stands for thought reflecting a realist.

HEMOPHILIA warns of a dangerously low energy level; some aspect in one's life is draining energy.

HEMOPHOBIA See fear (blood).

HEMORRHAGE represents a sudden outpouring of one's energy. This may indicate a needed course of action for the dreamer.

HEMORRHOID corresponds with a harmful situation in one's life. Usually it relates to anxiety and stress.

HEMOSTAT connotes a stanching factor of one's energy outflow. This may be required or warned against depending on other dream details.

HEMP refers to a strong or powerful factor in one's life.

HEMSTITCH applies to the act of finishing something; a conclusion or closure.

HEN characterizes productivity; efficiency.

HEN-AND-CHICKENS (botanical) applies to a fruitful life factor; bountiful.

HENBANE alludes to something in one's life that possesses duality.

HENCHMAN portrays an individual who is content being an underling; one who gains self-esteem by pleasing another.

HENLEY (clothing style) suggests a casual character trait/attitude; acceptance; an easy-going personality.

HENNA pertains to repressed emotions.

HEPATICA (plant) connotes inner strength.

HEPATITIS A advises of a harmful effect

caused by something to which one has *innocently* exposed self.

HEPATITIS B symbolizes a harmful effect caused by bad blood, bad relationships.

HEPATITIS C reveals a harmful effect caused by something to which one has *willfully* exposed self.

HERALD See messenger.

HERALDRY signifies extreme self-absorption; arrogance.

HERBALIST denotes natural methods and techniques.

HERBARIUM represents a study of the many productive uses for botanicals. This dreamscape symbol would indicate a call for one to utilize personal talents more extensively.

HERB GARDEN connotes a cultivation of one's inherent talents/abilities.

HERBICIDE warns of a destructive force that has the potential to hamper the utilization and growth of one's natural abilities.

HERBIVORE will emphasize a more natural lifestyle; a return to the rejuvenating benefits of nature.

HERBS pertain to a variety of meanings. Non-specific herbs relate to natural talents. See specific type for further information.

HERCULES (Greek/Roman mythology) alludes to great strength. This could be strength of character, and the important revealing factor here is *how* this strength was used.

HERD most always indicates a warning to follow one's own path.

HERDER may not mean one who keeps others in line, it may pertain to a personal need to keep self in line.

HEREAFTER (time) connotes the future.

HEREDITARY depicts an inherent personal aspect that *can* be altered through understanding and will. This would refer to a negative personality characteristic.

HERETIC characterizes a diversion from popular belief systems. This may be a positive symbol in that it represents individuality; a free-thinker.

HERMAPHRODITE symbolizes balance; a wholeness of being and thought.

HERMIT may advise one to open up more and be communicative or it might be indicating a need to retreat and contemplate for a time. Surrounding dreamscape details will clarify which meaning this had for the dreamer.

HERMITAGE stands for a place to gain needed respite, solitude, contemplation. Usually this symbol is advising a need to get back in touch with one's inner self and separate oneself from the current societal stressors.

HERMIT CRAB denotes spiritual reclusiveness.

HERNIA reveals a forced action taken in one's life.

HERO (Greek mythology) defines great devotion and love.

HERO/HEROINE represents courage and perseverance.

HEROD THE GREAT characterizes a fear of being bested; refers to an obsession with self; a fear of someone else perceived as being better or more admired than self.

HERON defines the beauty of spiritual wisdom.

HERO WORSHIP warns against an obsessive admiration of another; advises of a need to follow one's personal path.

HERPES SIMPLEX signifies dormant inherent negative qualities of one's personality that can be activated through a lack of control.

HERRING refers to spiritual bounty.

HERRINGBONE (pattern) signifies order; symmetry.

HERSTORY comes to advise the dreamer to pay closer attention to a female's history. The dreamer will know who this female is in reference to.

HESPERIDES (Greek mythology) applies to the protection of one's spiritual values.

HESTIA (Greek mythology) characterizes one who places a high priority on home and family life.

HETEROSEXISM warns against discriminating against those who are different from self.

HEW refers to personal efforts put forth.

HEX (sign) typifies a method one uses to maintain spiritual protection.

HEXAGON applies to mental, emotional, or spiritual protection.

HEXAGRAM (star) signifies wisdom, particularly spiritual wisdom.

HEYDAY points to a phase in one's life that is highly successful and pleasing.

HIATUS constitutes a break in one's work; a rest period.

HIBACHI represents the utilization of the right tool or method for accomplishing specific jobs.

HIBERNATING indicates escapism; a desire to avoid facing reality for a specific amount of time. This points to a desire to avoid having to deal with a certain situation.

HIBISCUS denotes spirituality.

HICCUP stands for an interruption of some type. Surrounding dream details will relate this to a situation in the dreamer's life.

HICKORY emphasizes the strength and enduring characteristics of one's natural abilities as they are used and developed.

HIDDEN (camera) See camera (hidden).

HIDE-A-BED See Murphy bed.

HIDE-AND-SEEK typifies the games people play in life; manipulation; ulterior motives; hidden agendas.

HIDEOUT may infer a need for sanctuary or it may indicate the act of running away from one's problems. Surrounding dreamscape details will clarify which meaning it has for the dreamer.

HIDEY-HOLE suggests secrets. If the compartment is for a person, the symbol is meant to relate to one hiding from something one should probably face.

HIERARCHY represents stages of development or attainment.

HIEROGLYPH symbolizes spiritual truths that are beyond one's current stage of understanding.

HIEROPHANT characterizes an enlightened individual; one who has the advanced development of knowledge coupled with wisdom.

HIGH pertains to an advanced level or position of prominence.

HIGHBALL See alcoholic beverage.

HIGH BEAM (light) suggests more light be given to an issue in the dreamer's life that she/he is having trouble understanding.

HIGH BLOOD PRESSURE warns of a need to slow down and be more accepting.

HIGHBOY corresponds to efficiency; a tendency to avoid wasting time on unnecessary steps.

HIGHBROW indicates intelligence.

HIGHCHAIR represents an immaturity.

HIGH COUNTRY illustrates a path that presents deeper conceptual ideas for one to learn from.

HIGH COURT See supreme court.

HIGH-DEFINITION TV refers to perceptual clarity, intellectual understanding.

HIGH-DENSITY stands for a concentrated aspect. This will be different for each dreamer as it relates to individualized associations.

HIGH-END (product) usually indicates higher quality/expense, yet it may also refer to a tendency to go for the most expensive brand name for the purpose of bolstering one's ego.

HIGH FASHION See haute couture.

HIGH FINANCE doesn't necessarily refer to money; rather, it usually alludes to a difficult or complex situation in one's life that warrants careful consideration and planning.

HIGH-FIVE represents elation, a success.

HIGHFLIER characterizes an individual who has a tendency to go to extremes; extravagance.

HIGH GEAR portrays a phase of intense activity. This could relate to mental or emotional activity.

HIGH-GRADE pertains to superior quality.

HIGH GROUND reveals a perception of superiority.

HIGH-HAT See top hat.

HIGH HEELS caution against raising self above one's current level of development.

HIGH HOLY DAYS signify a time of great importance for the dreamer, usually spiritual.

HIGH HORSE reveals indignation; a continual complaining; advises acceptance.

HIGHJACK See hijack.

HIGH JUMP means one is attempting to avoid or circumvent an issue or life problem.

HIGHLANDER characterizes an individual who has attained an advanced stage of personal development.

HIGH-LEVEL pertains to an elevated level of knowledge.

HIGH LIFE warns against misplaced priorities; advises a shift in what one places importance on.

HIGHLIGHTER (pen or marking) reveals the necessity of noting and remembering certain ideas that are important to the specific dreamer.

HIGH-NECKED (collar) represents constricted thoughts/attitudes.

HIGH NOON emphasizes a specified time when a critical decision or situation will culminate.

HIGH-OCTANE indicates a powerful aspect in one's life. This could refer to a personal characteristic, relationship, or situation.

HIGH-PITCHED (tone) is a call to immediately increase awareness; a warning.

HIGH-POWERED signifies an ability to make things happen.

HIGH PRESSURE (barometric) refers to better times ahead; clear sailing.

HIGH PRICED signifies something that will exact a cost greater than an alternative.

HIGH PRIESTESS characterizes one who has reached the attainment of knowledge coupled with wisdom.

HIGH PROFILE advises of high visibility. This is a cautionary symbol that reminds that one is being observed by others; behavior is rarely private.

HIGH RELIEF denotes an aspect in one's life that stands out and should be noticed or acted upon.

HIGH-RESOLUTION emphasizes clear, vivid dreams which may reveal an actual out-of-body experience.

HIGH-RISE connotes multilevel aspects to something in the dreamer's life. Surrounding dreamscape details will usually clarify this.

HIGHROAD portrays optimism; frequently warns against taking the easier path.

HIGH ROLLER characterizes an individual who has a tendency to take great risks.

HIGH SCHOOL typifies a symbol that represents a step up in one's level of learning.

HIGH SEAS constitute higher spiritual concepts; a place in one's path where one is ready to spiritually progress.

HIGH SIGN corresponds with good relationships.

HIGH-SPEED is most often an advisement to slow down or do things in a more attentive manner.

HIGH-SPEED (Internet) denotes ready access to information or a lightning-quick mind.

HIGH-SPIRITED usually equates to energetic enthusiasm and courage; may point to a mettlesome personality.

HIGH-STEPPING advises against a tendency to be drawn to the fast life.

HIGH-STRUNG indicates a need for personal restraint. This symbol implies a person who flies off the handle without giving logic and reason to reactions.

HIGH TEA denotes an advisement for one to take time to settle down and contemplate or absorb that which has been experienced.

HIGH TECHNOLOGY refers to advanced knowledge or one's path progression.

HIGH-TENSION WIRE corresponds with intense power. This will directly relate to a certain aspect that is specific to each dreamer.

HIGH TIDE portrays a time of intense spiritual influx in one's life.

HIGH-TOPS (shoes) alludes to preparedness for one's walk through life.

HIGH VOLTAGE (sign) warns of a dangerous situation; may signify the high probability for an upcoming explosive confrontation.

HIGH WATER LINE points to a state of full spiritual behavior.

HIGH WATERS (pants) signify rapid growth, usually associated with progression.

HIGHWAY represents a life path taken by many others.

HIGHWAYMEN characterize individuals who attempt to gain by your life walk; an attempt to take something from your advancement.

HIGHWAY PATROL signifies protective forces present along one's path. May also point to occasional restraints that keep us from speeding too quickly over that path.

HIGHWAY ROBBERY See highwaymen.

HIGH WIRE (act) connotes a questionable leap in one's advancement; a fragile situation where one must maintain acute awareness and step carefully; high risks involved.

HIJACK signifies a situation where one is being robbed of benefits personally acquired along one's path.

HIKE connotes extra efforts applied to advancement.

HILARITY typifies the importance of humor in one's life.

HILL stands for a time when extra efforts are needed.

HILL CLIMB (race) warns against participating in a potentially hazardous competition.

HILLSIDE represents continued efforts.

HILLTOP corresponds with reaching a goal; place of accomplishment.

HINDQUARTER usually refers to concluding aspects; nearing an ending or closure.

HINDSIGHT most often represents the lessons we're supposed to learn from bad choices or experiences.

HINGE alludes to probabilities.

HINT is almost always a clue for the dreamer. These should be recalled.

HINTERLAND See back country.

HIP (anatomy) may refer to relationships or it may be indicating an actual physical aspect.

HIP (rose) See rose hip.

HIP BOOTS See waders.

HIP-HOP (music) refers to a subculture philosophy/camaraderie.

HIP-HUGGERS signify an expressiveness of individuality; a disregard for convention or criticism.

HIPPIE characterizes a diversion from established traditions or ideas; the freedom to express one's individuality and attitudes that differ from the general populace.

HIPPOCRATES characterizes an individual who can discern the difference between truth and superstition.

HIPPOCRATIC OATH denotes a determined path; a pure intention.

HIPPOPOTAMUS typifies spiritual generosity; a continual giving nature.

HIPSTER characterizes one who always looks for the unconventional, new innovations or ideas that are coming from outside the box.

HIRED GUN warns against having others deal with your problems.

HIRED HAND represents one who is reimbursed for the help they give. This would mean there are those in your life from whom you elicit assistance and therefore need to be paid in kind.

HIRING HALL See union hall.

HISTORIAN characterizes one who is interested in understanding how past experiences relate to the present.

HISTORICAL FIGURES hold a personal meaning for each dreamer. This meaning will usually be easily identified.

HISTORICAL NOVEL will have a karmic lesson to teach each dreamer.

HISTORICAL SITE usually has some type of personal connection to the dreamer and comes to reveal something important.

HISTORIC PRESERVATION points to a need/desire to keep a past event or relationship from being altered in any way; a preservation of integrity.

HISTRIONICS stand for a tendency to gain attention or sympathy through over-exaggerated emotional displays

HIT (inhale) indicates a need for additional support; utilizing an assisting aspect.

HIT (strike at) exposes unrestrained emotions; impulsiveness.

HIT-AND-RUN warns against running from responsibility; a refusal to answer for one's actions.

HITCH (snag) implies a temporary setback.

HITCH (tow connector) represents a life aspect that helps path progression; that which provides the start-up action from a setback.

HITCHHIKER characterizes laziness; one who advances along the path by way of another's efforts.

HITCHING POST symbolizes the needed pauses taken during our path progression.

HITLER (Adolf) exemplifies the destructive effects of intensely negative forces; the result of manifested evil. Mirrors the extreme apathy for all others wrought from total self-absorption.

HIT LIST will usually reveal those who are detrimental in one's life. It can also refer to someone else's list which is an extremely informative piece of information for the dreamer.

HIT MAN See hired gun.

HITTER (pot) represents frustration; a lack of acceptance; a perceived need to calm anxiety, mellow out.

HIVE See beehive.

HIVES denote a lack of acceptance; a continued state of active irritation over something.

HOAGIE See submarine sandwich.

HOARDING warns against selfishness; may also indicate a need to save up something. Surrounding dream details will clarify this.

HOARFROST pertains to spiritual beauty.

HOARSENESS implies unclear communications. Could indicate a failure to make one's repetitive communications understood.

HOAX reveals a deception present in one's life. The key is to recall what the hoax was and who generated it for what *reason*. This will not always represent a negative act.

HOBBIT characterizes a gentle and peaceful personality.

HOBBLE reveals perseverance. Also see limp (hobble).

HOBBY relates to manner of relaxation and interest. Each hobby will have its own interpretation. See specific type.

HOBBYHORSE connotes an obsession.

HOBBY SHOP represents vast opportunities for constructive mental diversions in relation to satisfying one's need to rest from intensive researching, work, and study. See specific hobby.

HOBGOBLIN alludes to one's fears.

HOBNAIL (pattern) signifies a rustic, laid-back personality/attitude.

HOCK See pawn (hock).

HOCKEY represents a spiritual game one plays.

HOCKEY HELMET signifies prepared-ness for expected spiritual conflict. This would indicate a situation where one has a strong, almost fanatical, spiritual atti-tude.

HOCKEY PUCK is associated with a spir-itual concept or belief that is controver-sial.

HOCKEY STICK indicates a willful bat-ting of a controversial spiritual concept. This could point to an ongoing debate or continual criticism. It may also indicate a desire to keep pushing it away so one doesn't have to look at it more deeply.

HOCKSHOP See pawnshop.

HOCUS-POCUS usually suggests trickery or an attempt to deceive.

HOD CARRIER characterizes one who is willing to do the hard work and expend great effort to help another.

HODGEPODGE may have positive or negative interpretations. The negative intent would be a warning against believ-ing in completely unrelated ideas that comprise a concept, in other words, inconsistencies and contradictions. The positive meaning would be an underscor-ing of one's accurate conceptual beliefs comprised of divergent aspects that inter-relate.

HOE pertains to personal efforts applied to nurturing one's inherent talents.

HOE-DOWN See square dance.

HOG cautions against a tendency to take on too much at once.

HOGAN signifies a natural way of living; simplicity of life.

HOGBACK indicates a need to do some backtracking to capture missed lessons or incomplete aspects that were overlooked or left behind.

HOIST symbolizes a life factor that has the capability of uplifting the dreamer.

HOLD (of ship) See cargo hold.

HOLD (stop order) refers to a temporary pause in action on an issue or situation.

HOLD BUTTON (phone) implies a tem-porary pause in a communication; put-ting an issue, relationship, etc., off for a short time.

HOLDING PATTERN constitutes a tem-porary period of neutrality; a life pause that precludes further advancement for an indeterminate span of time.

HOLDING TANK corresponds with spiri-tual beliefs one is currently deliberating; a time before a spiritual decision is made.

HOLDOUT characterizes a determined opinion or attitude.

HOLD UP (keep from advancing) defines a delay of some type.

HOLDUP See burglar.

HOLE usually refers to an opening; an opportunity. Rarely will it represent a defect. Surrounding dreamscape details will clarify which interpretation was meant for the dreamer.

HOLIDAY denotes a rest time. This most often infers that one is working or con-centrating too hard.

HOLISTIC may not be relating to health aspects. It usually refers to an advisement to stop fragmenting one's thoughts; a need to think in terms of whole concepts or ideas.

HOLLOW (shallow ravine) See valley.

HOLLOW (space) illustrates a lack of depth; a shallow attitude or concept.

HOLLY corresponds with a fresh spiritual idea or concept.

HOLLYHOCK (flower) implies cheerfulness; a bright outlook; old standby ethics and common sense.

HOLLYWOOD typifies dream symbols that relate to superficiality.

HOLLYWOOD BED pertains to a lack of seriousness.

HOLOCAUST defines a monumentally devastating event.

HOLOGRAM means a false perception of reality.

HOLSTER corresponds with a life aspect that has the capability of providing some type of personal protection.

HOLY COMMUNION reflects what some believe to be their personal connection to a Supreme Essence.

HOLY DAY See high holy days. See specific holy day.

HOLY GRAIL connotes a need for spiritual proof.

HOLY WAR See crusades.

HOLY WATER exemplifies a need for spiritual affectations in order to feel power behind one's beliefs; a lack of faith.

HOMAGE warns against giving this to anyone but the Divine.

HOMBURG (hat) usually indicates hidden thoughts, perspectives.

HOME signifies one's place of comfort and security, where one can shed affectations.

HOME BASE illustrates a personal operational base one works from.

HOMEBODY connotes contentedness; one who has few needs and even fewer wants.

HOMEBOUND stands for a nearly completed goal or path.

HOMEBRED portrays an individual who was raised with family values.

HOME-BREW denotes creativity and inventiveness; self-sufficiency.

HOME BUILDER will normally indicate an individual who is capable/skilled in providing a home base for others.

HOME BUYER represents a desire to be settled; establish roots.

HOME CARE stands for the need to attend to one's own problems before attempting to give help to others.

HOME CENTER (store) suggests attention to oneself is needed; home repair (of oneself) is advised.

HOMECOMING applies to a return to one's roots, beginnings.

HOME COMPUTER stands for the easy availability of information and is probably advising the use of it.

HOME ECONOMICS (class) suggests a need to be more efficient and/or arranging priorities.

HOME ENTERTAINMENT CENTER signifies personal methods of relaxation or information gathering sources.

HOME FRONT will refer to those issues closest to an individual, usually family and friends.

HOME-GIRL refers to a Provincial personality; unsophisticated, yet genteel.

HOMEGROWN suggests an ability to make one's own way in life.

HOME IMPROVEMENT CENTER means a nearly limitless source of opportunities to make improvements in one's life if one is willing to expend the effort.

HOMELAND indicates a sense of one's roots; a strong identity.

HOMELAND SECURITY will indicate measures taken to protect one's home (ideals and perspectives); however, if this is overdone, this symbol will point to a warning against being so overly protective that the rights of others have been compromised.

HOMELESS may not be the negative it appears on the surface. It may pertain to a journeyer, one who continually progresses along a life path.

HOMELESS SHELTER represents a port in the storm; a hospitable respite when one is at wit's end during one's path walk.

HOMELY (appearance) reminds us that beauty is subjective to one's personal perspective.

HOMEMADE suggests resourcefulness.

HOME OFFICE reflects the work one personally does. This symbol represents one's dedication to a purpose.

HOMEOPATHY stresses solutions contained within the problem.

HOME PAGE (Internet) denotes the life elements that are most basic to one. It signifies where one's jumping-off place is.

HOME PLATE represents a specific goal one has.

HOMEROOM portrays one's basic beliefs that are built upon.

HOME RULE pertains to independence; a responsibility to self. In some cases, this symbol may point to one's conscience.

HOME RUN reveals an attainment of a goal; having come full circle.

HOME SCHOOL usually signifies slanted learning; instruction given with a particular perspective slant to it.

HOMESICK emphasizes emotional sensitivity. May also indicate a need to return to one's basic values.

HOMESPUN (fabric) denotes simplicity of character and self-reliance. Will usually indicate a personality without prevarications or ulterior motives.

HOMESTEADER characterizes independence and confidence.

HOMESTRETCH advises of a nearly completed goal.

HOME STUDY illustrates high motivation and an independent search.

HOMEWORK advises of more research or information-gathering needed.

HOMICIDE See murder.

HOMING DEVICE represents a need to get to the core of an issue.

HOMING PIGEON pertains to a tendency to continually return to a specific belief, opinion, or perspective.

HOMINOID represents any being that resembles the human form, a humanoid. Many times, this will have an extraterrestrial connotation.

HOMOGENIZE relates to a lack of diversity.

HOMOPHILE signifies a sympathetic attitude for those who are persecuted by prejudice.

HOMOPHOBIA See fear (gays/lesbians).

HOMO SAPIENS See hominoid.

HOMOSEXUALITY usually signifies a carryover spiritual memory. When attraction to another or a sense of love is expressed on the spirit plane there are no genders to differentiate one spirit from another—love is love.

HONE implies a sharpening aspect in one's life; something that brings a factor into finer definition or proficiency.

HONEY represents sweet benefits generated from one's personal efforts applied.

HONEYCOMB illustrates bountiful benefits or rewards.

HONEYCOMB (pattern) refers to benefits gained through cooperation.

HONEY LOCUST (tree) points to resolutions; getting results.

HONEYMOON indicates a harmonious and loyal relationship; a unique bond that has been forged.

HONEY POT stands for the source of great multiple benefits. Also see mother lode.

HONEYSUCKLE denotes earned graces.

HONKING (horn) defines a warning; a call to attention.

HONKY-TONK (music) signifies an effort to conceal melancholy.

HONORABLE DISCHARGE comes as a commendation for accomplishments or efforts applied; points to an ending to a particular life phase.

HONORABLE MENTION constitutes a commendation from one's Higher Self.

HONORARIUM warns against expecting recompense for gifts voluntarily shared with others.

HONOR ROLL refers to recognition for hard work and achievement.

HONOR SYSTEM reminds one to behave in an honest and trustworthy manner even when no one is watching.

HOOCH See alcoholic beverage.

HOOD (head wear) signals a desire to keep thoughts and attitudes private. May warn of secrets held or ulterior motives.

HOOD (over stove) relates to a method of keeping ramifications down to a minimum.

HOOD (residential) See neighborhood.

HOODLUM characterizes an immature perspective; a self-centered nature; an inability to advance past primal instincts.

HOODOO will most often signify a questionable or extremely unusual way of doing something; an unconventional method.

HOODWINKED reveals a deception.

HOOF implies a difficult situation or pathway.

HOOF-AND-MOUTH DISEASE See foot-and-mouth disease.

HOOK alludes to certainty; security; a secure aspect.

HOOKAH refers to an attempt to cool a heated situation.

HOOKER See prostitute.

HOOKWORM warns of a potentially damaging factor that could easily attach itself to one's life.

HOOP denotes a completed aspect; coming full circle.

HOOP SKIRT signifies a tendency to distance oneself from others; a greater than normal social distance.

HOOTENANNY represents spontaneous joy shared with others.

HOPE CHEST relates to one's dreams and aspirations.

HOPE DIAMOND applies to high hopes in regard to achieving goals.

HOPSCOTCH warns against a tendency to jump to only chosen points along one's path instead of covering all the ground.

HORDE illustrates a great multitude. This could refer to many subjects; therefore, the dreamer will receive clarification through recalling the surrounding details. What was being hoarded?

HOREHOUND (plant) exemplifies that which is capable of clearing and sharpening one's communication skills.

HORIZON signifies one's individual perspective.

HORMONE corresponds with a life factor that directly affects one's mental or emotional responses.

HORMONE REPLACEMENT THERAPY warns against trying to recapture or replace something that's meant to be left in the past; an advisement to remember that nature knows best, nature is natural.

HORN (animal) See antler.

HORN (fog) See foghorn.

HORN (musical instrument) See specific type.

HORN (sound) defines a warning.

HORNBILL (bird) denotes analytical thought.

HORNET indicates the "stinging" events in life.

HORNET'S NEST exposes a troublesome situation or relationship.

HOROSCOPE warns against a tendency to be led through life by what others say.

HORROR reveals one's fears.

HORS D'OEUVRES refer to a sampling or whetting the appetite for what's to come.

HORSE emphasizes a wild nature one must continually keep reined in.

HORSEBACK (riding) suggests a desire to feel/experience every nuance of one's traveled path.

HORSE CHESTNUT (tree) stands for resolve; determination.

HORSEFLY refers to biting remarks.

HORSEHAIR signifies a coarse personality covered with a sleek veneer.

HORSEHAIR (cloth) refers to a sleek appearance, yet has a prickly response when rubbed the wrong way.

HORSELAUGH indicates a disdainful reaction; a jeering or mocking response.

HORSEPLAY denotes lighthearted pranks; a practical joke.

HORSE RACE alludes to a controlled speed; a fast-paced progression that is well controlled by another.

HORSERADISH denotes sharp lessons learned; lessons well remembered.

HORSESHOE represents superstition; a belief in charms.

HORSESHOE CRAB suggests endurance; perseverance through time.

HORSE TRADING implies clever negotiations.

HORSE TRAILER stands for the moving of one's impetuosity to a more acceptable or suitable outlet.

HORSE TRAINER refers to the ability to calm others, help them better handle situations.

HORSEWOMAN characterizes one who isn't fearful of blazing her own course; an eagerness to gallop forward into unknown territory.

HORTICULTURE (study of) stands for a high interest in cultivating people's natural talents.

HOSE (water) reveals a willful direction of one's spiritual expressions. May point to a tendency to chose who will benefit from one's spiritual generosity.

HOSPICE portrays compassion.

HOSPITAL comes as a rejuvenation advisement.

HOST suggests a receivership; means a beneficiary.

HOSTAGE represents a demand for security; a desire to obtain a goal without working for it.

HOSTEL suggests a phase of respite for a beginning journey.

HOSTELRY See hotel.

HOSTESS characterizes generosity; congeniality.

HOT most often refers to an intense condition or emotion.

HOT AIR refers to bluster; tending to exaggerate or lean toward pretentiousness.

HOTBED connotes a highly controversial issue; a source eliciting high emotional responses.

HOT-BLOODED signifies a lack of self-control.

HOT CAKE See pancake.

HOT DOG refers to skill; having something covered.

HOT-DOGGING warns of spiritual irresponsibility.

HOTEL symbolizes a transition stage; a temporary condition.

HOT FLASH pertains to a sudden flash of inspiration, what we prefer to call a power surge.

HOTFOOT advises of a need to slow down.

HOTHEADED applies to a quick temper.

HOTHOUSE reveals an oppressive condition or personality; a forcing of advancement or goals.

HOT LINE stands for an unbroken line of communication; the need to keep communication open.

HOT PANTS suggest impatience; an inability to wait for the right time to actuate plans.

HOT PEPPER refers to an attraction and tolerance for touchy issues.

HOT PLATE advises of a need to keep up efforts regarding a specific situation or relationship.

HOT POTATO points to an extremely touchy aspect that everyone would like to avoid.

HOT ROD represents an individualized manner of speeding one's advancement. This is not a good symbol because it pertains to a disrespect for the law and carelessness; a show-off type of personality.

HOT SAUCE implies a highly charged issue or attitude; a tendency toward spicing things up.

HOT SEAT pertains to a situation where one is deeply involved in an undesirable position.

HOTSHOT characterizes an adept individual; an expert. In some cases, this may point to an aggressive show-off.

HOT-SINK (computer) is associated with an immediate transfer of information.

HOT SPOT portrays a place or situation that is intensely active, usually in a negative way.

HOT SPRING warns of an underlying anger in respect to a spiritual issue.

HOT TODDY See alcoholic beverage.

HOT TUB signifies a need to ease tension.

HOTTY (appearance) See foxy.

HOT WATER denotes a position of great difficulty.

HOT-WATER BAG/BOTTLE advises of a need to "warm up" emotionally.

HOT-WIRE typifies an attempt to advance without having the prerequisite learning experience or knowledge (key).

HOUDINI (Harry) reveals an individual who impresses others through trickery; deception.

HOUNDS TOOTH (pattern) signifies delusions; perceptive illusions.

HOURGLASS reveals how much time is left to accomplish something.

HOUSE stands for the mind. See specific types for additional information.

HOUSE ARREST indicates a need for one to remain in a neutral position; a need to force oneself to stay out of an issue or situation.

HOUSEBOAT symbolizes a spiritual home atmosphere.

HOUSEBOUND refers to disinterest in issues unrelated to one's own, immediate surroundings.

HOUSE BRAND connotes a tendency to stay with what one is accustomed to; a reluctance to expand one's experience or try new things.

HOUSEBREAKING (pet) symbolizes the training of a new friend. This, obviously, isn't a positive symbol in that it constitutes an attempt to inform the friend how you want the relationship to go and this symbolizes manipulation.

HOUSE CALL pertains to an extension of one's generosity in regard to giving service to others.

HOUSE CLEANING implies a need to get rid of extraneous aspects in life that only clutter one's progress or perspective.

HOUSECOAT See bathrobe.

HOUSE DETECTIVE advises one to perform a mental self-examination regarding motives and performance.

HOUSE DOCTOR See house physician.

HOUSEFLY reveals a negative aspect that has invaded one's home life.

HOUSE GUEST characterizes one whom you allow to get close to you; the person you can let your guard down in front of.

HOUSEHOLD EFFECTS (decor) reveal one's personality.

HOUSEHOLD GODDESS refers to spiritual behavior beginning in the home (within oneself).

HOUSEHOLD WORD connotes a commonly held belief; easy recognition.

HOUSEHUSBAND characterizes a recognition of a woman's intellect and worth without it feeling threatening.

HOUSEKEEPER represents an individual who helps to keep one's perspectives in order.

HOUSELIGHTS portray one who has the attention of others.

HOUSEMATE characterizes a close friendship; camaraderie; shared life experiences.

HOUSEMOTHER characterizes a surrogate mother figure; someone who watches over a group of young adults, offers advice, and acts as their sounding board.

HOUSE OF CARDS symbolize precarious and insubstantial foundational traits or perspectives.

HOUSE OF ILL REPUTE refers to a disregard for a negative element in one's life.

HOUSE PAINTER depicts a personal cover-up for a negative element in one's life. May also point to a freshening of some personal aspect or a change in attitude. Recall paint color.

HOUSE PARTY refers to openness; a willingness to let others in.

HOUSE PHYSICIAN stands for yourself. You have the power to heal the negative attitudes and emotions of self.

HOUSE PLANT corresponds with one's openly displayed personality traits. See specific types for additional clarity.

HOUSE PLANT (artificial) reveals a false behavior trait put on for appearances sake.

HOUSE-RAISING reveals a multitude of friends who are willing to help one build strong foundations or assist in expending energy to give aid.

HOUSE SITTER alludes to someone you completely trust.

HOUSE SLIPPERS See slippers.

HOUSE WARES refer to the basic necessities of life.

HOUSEWARMING denotes a desire to be liked.

HOUSEWORK stands for the efforts expended to maintain a clean and comfortable home life.

HOVEL suggests poor life foundations; poor ethical training.

HOVERCRAFT usually represents an out-of-body experience.

HOWITZER See cannon.

HOWLER MONKEY denotes egotism.

HOWLING relates to desolation; despair; loneliness.

HUARACHE See sandal.

HUBCAP applies to the center of something to which the dreamer will readily relate.

HUCKSTER See peddler.

HUDDLE (football) stands for a conference for the purpose of scheming, planning.

HUDDLED indicates a fear of self; lack of self-confidence and responsibility.

HUG connotes a desire to touch others; a desire to be close and convey same.

HULA (dance) signifies body language; communicating through behavior.

HULK (action figure) suggests an unrealistic belief in one's abilities; warns against pushing oneself beyond limits.

HULL (casing) represents a hard personality veneer.

HULL (ship) refers to our spiritual foundations which keep us afloat.

HUM denotes a vibrational shift.

HUMAN signifies an excuse for mistakes or errors made.

HUMAN BEING See hominoid.

HUMANE SOCIETY See animal shelter.

HUMANITARIAN characterizes a compassionate and giving nature.

HUMAN RESOURCE (office/dept.) stands for a source for benefits and opportunity.

HUMAN RIGHTS imply an attempt to define and delineate inherent qualities.

HUMBLE PIE advises one to admit mistakes and take responsibility.

HUMID relates to an atmosphere heavy with spiritual aspects.

HUMIDIFIER is an aspect that increases the level of spirituality.

HUMIDOR reveals a negative factor that depletes an individual or atmosphere of spiritual qualities. This symbol stands for something that *adds* or *preserves* spiritual aspects.

HUMILIATION illustrates a feeling of dishonor or discredit. May indicate an inferiority complex.

HUMILITY usually advises one to give credit for accomplishments, even to self.

HUMMING (earth sound) gives evidence of nature's vibrant life force, it's living essence.

HUMMING (person) usually reveals a secret idea or plan; personal satisfaction.

HUMMINGBIRD warns of frequent indecision; mental vacillation.

HUMMINGBIRD FEEDER indicates a hidden source (psychological) for one's continuing difficulty making decisions.

HUMMUS represents a simple benefit; nutrient.

HUMORIST will usually indicate the tendency to look on the bright side, depending on a sense of humor to get one through, but it may also reveal a tendency to take this attitude too far when important issues aren't taken seriously.

HUMP (in road) indicates a point in one's path where difficulties may arise and extra efforts will be required.

HUMPBACK stands for perseverance in spite of a hard life.

HUMPTY-DUMPTY characterizes a self-created (psychological) condition where one believes one cannot proceed without help.

HUMUS (soil type) stands for a fertile condition or situation.

HUM-VEE relates to tenacity; perseverance; determination.

HUNCH portrays personal insights; psychic impressions. Recall what the hunch was because this will be an important message.

HUNCHBACK reveals one who is burdened with self-imposed psychological barriers and/or obstacles.

HUNGARY signifies a pride in one's ethnic traditions; a strong character.

HUNGER constitutes an inner need; a personal requirement that needs fulfillment before one can proceed along the pathway.

HUNGER STRIKE implies personal activism; a sympathizer.

HUNG JURY relates to indecision, usually within self.

HUNTER may indicate a killing of innocence whereby one obliterates positive attitudes and spiritual truths or it may mean an individual who is searching for something important in life. Surrounding dreamscape details will clarify which meaning is intended.

HUNTER'S GREEN (color) stands for fertile ground; rich and bountiful natural talents.

HUNTER'S MOON See moon (hunter's).

HURDLE pertains to an upcoming difficulty the dreamer must experience.

HURRICANE warns of an emotional dysfunction caused by spiritual inundation. This means one has attempted to learn too many spiritual concepts without taking adequate time to properly absorb and comprehend each idea individually.

HURRICANE LAMP connotes preparedness for properly absorbing spiritual concepts.

HURT See injury.

HUSH MONEY See bribe.

HUSK denotes stripping away the extraneous aspects of an issue; getting down to basics.

HUSKY (dog breed) characterizes a strong friend or associate on whom one can always depend.

HUTCH (furniture) implies that which we display publicly.

HUTCH (rabbit) warns against confining or hiding one's more innocent qualities for fear of ridicule.

HYACINTH (flower) symbolizes the blossoming of a new spiritual gift or talent.

HYBRID portrays a blending of dissimilar aspects to create a new and fresh quality or effect. This symbol touches on the theory behind true Reality.

HYDRA (Greek mythology) characterizes a persistent problem that has many varying aspects connected with it.

HYDRANGEA (botanical) connotes the utilization of one's spiritual talents in a generous and unconditional manner.

HYDRANT See fire hydrant.

HYDRAULIC (system) constitutes an aspect in one's life that is capable of making advancement easier.

HYDROCEPHALUS pertains to an obsessive fascination with spiritual matters, especially the esoteric qualities.

HYDROELECTRIC PLANT symbolizes spiritual energy and the regeneration of same.

HYDROGEN PEROXIDE is a symbol that contains duality, yet it most frequently refers to a healing aspect in one's life.

HYDROPHOBIA See fear (water).

HYDROPLANE See seaplane.

HYDROPONICS signifies nurturing by way of spiritual aspects.

HYDROTHERAPY denotes the use of spiritual elements as healing tools.

HYENA implies a lack of seriousness or a vicious nature. Surrounding dreamscape details will clarify which meaning is inferred.

HYGROMETER will reveal one's level of spirituality or spiritual comprehension. Recall what the instrument read.

HYMNAL denotes personal praise of the Divine and our expressions of spiritual joy.

HYPE warns against excessive promotion of self or something one desires known.

HYPERACTIVITY cautions one to slow down; a need to conserve energy; a need to comprehend more.

HYPERBOLIC CHAMBER stands for a need to adjust how one deals with stress/pressure.

HYPER-DRIVE warns of a type-A personality; one who runs on overdrive; obsessed with achievement.

HYPERLINK signifies identical conceptual elements or attitudes shared by separate individuals or differing philosophies.

HYPERSPACE pertains to a doorway to understanding the components of reality.

HYPERVENTILATING advises of over-emotionalism; overreacting; a need to gain acceptance.

HYPHEN indicates an aspect that serves as a connecting force.

HYPNOPHOBIA See fear (being hypnotized).

HYPNOTIST characterizes a manipulative personality; one who has the capability of easily swaying another.

HYPOCHONDRIA advises one to stop using psychological ploys to gain sympathy.

HYPOCRITE warns against professing beliefs or attitudes one does not honestly hold.

HYPODERMIC NEEDLE/SYRINGE reveals a serious need for one to regain inner balance. This may refer to any physical, mental, or emotional negative condition currently present within self.

HYPOSENSITIVITY is a strong advisement to be more emotionally sensitive to others.

HYPOTHERMIA indicates a "cold" personality; insensitivity; apathy. This is closely related to the symbol of hyposensitivity.

HYPOTHESIS will usually come in dreams as a message that may bring solutions to specific problems.

HYSTERECTOMY represents the removal of problems that have caused difficulties in getting started on a new path.

HYSTERIA warns against losing control of logic and reason.

I

I-BEAM stands for one's main source of support.

IBEX See goat.

IBIS denotes esoteric aspects to spirituality.

ICARUS (Greek mythology) implies unawareness and the hazards it creates; unrealistic goals.

ICBM (missile) pertains to a destructive force in one's life.

ICE signifies frozen spiritual truths, frequently voluntarily frozen by oneself.

ICE AGE represents an extensive span in one's life when spiritual matters are ignored or not held as a priority.

ICE AX connotes an attempt to chip away, regaining one's formerly ignored spirituality.

ICE BAG See ice pack.

ICEBERG applies to spiritual aspects looming on the horizon of one's life. This is an attention-getting message.

ICEBOAT suggests a sailing over one's frozen spirituality; ignoring the fact that one should be integrating spirituality in one's daily behavior.

ICEBOX See refrigerator.

ICEBREAKER (ship) is a warning message which tells one that she/he had better break up the spiritual aspects that

have been frozen before further path progression can be accomplished.

ICE BUCKET portrays a frequency of denying one's spiritual aspects.

ICE CAP relates to a hard spiritual shell one has created; a spiritual hardness that prevents the open giving of one's gifts or talents.

ICE CREAM indicates the intake of spiritual aspects yet one doesn't externalize them.

ICE-CREAM CONE implies spiritual aspects carried around but not shared with others.

ICE-CREAM MAKER illustrates one's personal ability to generate spiritual growth yet rarely externalizes it.

ICE-CREAM PARLOR applies to opportunities to share one's spirituality.

ICE-CREAM SANDWICH connotes spirituality that is hidden by physical or material aspects.

ICE-CREAM SODA implies an effervescence to one's spirituality that is not demonstrated to others.

ICE DANCING (pairs) suggests a relationship in which spirituality isn't freely expressed or openly shared.

ICE FLOE represents intermittent periods of spiritual frigidity; selective spiritual expressiveness.

ICE FISHING stands for a search for or expectation of spiritual insights.

ICEHOUSE corresponds with personality frigidity stemming from the subconscious. These need to be thawed.

ICELAND refers to largeness of character; self-reliance; fortitude.

ICE MAKER/MACHINE symbolizes a frozen spiritual belief that there is but one way to the Divine.

ICE MILK exemplifies a refusal to gain spiritual nourishment; a reluctance to admit to that which one involuntarily gains.

ICE PACK alludes to efforts applied to gaining spirituality yet there remains a small measure of doubt.

ICE PICK corresponds to personal energy put into chipping away at one's spiritual aspects that have been voluntarily hidden from view.

ICE SCRAPER stands for a method or tool for bringing about clearer perception. This symbol suggests a need for same.

ICE SCULPTURE illustrates the futility of trying to keep one's spiritual aspects frozen (hidden) in an unexpressive manner.

ICE SHOW demonstrates the beauty of bringing out one's spiritual aspects and using them for the benefit of others.

ICE SKATE connotes skating over one's frozen spiritual aspects. This is a clear message to unthaw these and begin using them.

ICE STORM represents an inundation of spiritual concepts that one is not yet ready to comprehend.

ICE WATER suggests the intake of spiritual concepts that are a blend of those that are understood and those that need contemplating. This is a good dreamscape fragment.

I CHING depicts a high interest in outcomes and the future; therefore, it also represents a lack of acceptance for *what is*.

ICICLE relates to a state of growing spiritual frigidity that has the capability of becoming so heavy it could fall back on one and cause personally devastating effects. This symbol could also point to an intermittent thawing of a particular spiritual belief—a vacillation.

ICING See frosting.

ICON warns of misplaced adoration.

ICONOCLAST characterizes a spiritually destructive individual.

ICONOGRAPHY exemplifies a call for extensive contemplation.

IDAHO represents pure objectivity; attitudes untouched by personal issues.

IDEALIST stands for one who has high hopes yet lacks a clear perspective of reality.

IDENTICAL TWIN represents one's alter ego.

IDENTIFICATION CARD (ID) portrays that which one presents as an exterior self. Frequently this dream symbol will alter one's identity to reveal the real self.

IDENTITY CRISIS may come in dreams to correspond with crossover past-life personalities that are beginning to break through the consciousness.

IDENTITY THEFT refers to one's power being stolen. This symbol comes as an advisement to step forward and take back your life.

IDIOT usually reveals this characteristic as a message that advises how one is responding to a specific given issue or situation.

IDIOT BOX refers to that which wastes intellectual potential.

IDIOT CARD See cue card.

IDIOT LIGHT will usually reveal some type of guidance for the dreamer.

IDOL corresponds with whom or what one overly admires or is fascinated. This gives a clear look into one's priorities and level of advancement, for no human or material object should be idolized.

IDYLLIC (scene or situation) represents one's hopes.

IGLOO constitutes a cold home life; emotionally unexpressive.

IGNITION KEY pertains to that which is capable of supplying one with proper nutrients that energize.

IGNORANCE is most often a warning to stop refusing to learn new things; a self-induced fear of knowledge.

IGUANA See lizard.

ILLEGAL is a warning of wrong-doing or of plans that are not in spiritual alignment.

ILLEGAL IMMIGRANT stands for one who breaks the law to achieve goals.

ILLEGIBLE (writing) denotes mental confusion; perceptual dysfunction.

ILLEGITIMACY alludes to an attitude/opinion that's in error.

ILL-FITTING (clothing) connotes a free spirit or one who is restricting thoughts and/or expressiveness.

ILLINOIS signifies tolerance; a live and let live attitude.

ILLITERACY warns of a condition of self-induced ignorance.

ILLOGICAL (aspects) indicate confusion or illogical thought present in the waking state.

ILLUMINATED TEXT points to something important the dreamer needs to take a more serious look at.

ILLUMINATI reveal individuals in one's life who are, in reality, unenlightened. Nobody should claim absolute enlightenment.

ILLUMINATION reveals some important factor to which the dreamer should pay particular attention. This is a message.

ILLUSION will usually reveal a falsehood believed by the dreamer in the waking state.

ILLUSIONIST characterizes those who manipulate others or attempt to dazzle with trickery.

ILLUSTRATION connotes a visual message specific to each dreamer. Recall what was illustrated.

IMITATING cautions one to be true to self; advises against emulating others or following in their footsteps.

IMITATION (objects) such as leather and fur convey a preferred aspect for one to utilize; however, if the object is something like food or original art pieces then the message is to avoid these.

IMMACULATE (condition) usually denotes an exact perspective with nothing out of place or focus.

IMMACULATE ASSUMPTION refers to the assumption (belief) that there is a God the Father and a God the Son *without* a God the Mother. This symbol refers to a huge misconception/assumption in one's life.

IMMACULATE CONCEPTION will most often attempt to reveal the accurate reality of this issue: immaculate in respect to being born without the stain of Original Sin. As a dreamscape fragment, this will point to an innocent individual.

IMMATURITY portrays an individual who is not yet ready for the next level of advancement. This could caution one against attempting to gain knowledge one is not properly prepared to absorb.

IMMERSION indicates a totality; a saturation; complete belief.

IMMIGRANT refers to a voluntary choice to dramatically change one's path and set of opportunities.

IMMOBILIZED See paralysis.

IMMORTALITY corresponds with one's spirit, the eternal life of it.

IMMUNITY connotes one's level and strength of personal methods of protection against negative aspects. This may point to a talent for exceptional perceptiveness. This symbol could also refer to innocence, a lack of guilt regarding something in particular.

IMMUNIZATION advises one of a possible negative aspect invading one's life; extra awareness and protective measures are needed.

IMP characterizes a recurring irritation, possibly a person. This indicates a need to address the problem for proper closure.

IMPACTED (tooth) signifies a serious need to extract some negative type of speech. This could refer to the verbalization of a specific attitude that is causing harm to self and others.

IMPACT STUDY points to a need to give a hard look at the possible ramifications of a planned idea or move.

IMPALA See antelope.

IMPASSABLE reveals a need to retrace one's steps. This will refer to a specific situation in the dreamer's life that she/he will readily identify with.

IMPATIENCE calls for one to accept the proper timing of events in life.

IMPATIENS (botanical) signify the frequent moments of joy that come into our lives.

IMPEACHMENT refers to behavior which many object to; a wrongdoing that disqualifies one from maintaining a current position.

IMPERFECTION may remind us that nothing is absolutely perfect in this world or it could reveal an error in one's behavior, situation, or perspective. Recall surrounding dream details for further clarification.

IMPERSONATOR reveals one who is dissatisfied with self.

IMPETIGO emphasizes the need for balancing, most often a physical condition.

IMPLANT (medical, nonspecific) signifies a need to replace a negative in one's life. This may refer to a physical, mental, emotional, or spiritual aspect.

IMPLOSION reveals an inner fragmentation beginning. This is an important warning that indicates a self-destructive course is being set and will be devastating if the withheld negatives are not externalized by facing or openly expressing them.

IMPORT pertains to new ideas.

IMPORT SHOP portrays a multitude of opportunities to take advantage of valuable *foreign* ideas; being open to new experiences.

IMPOSTER characterizes a deceiver.

IMPOTENCY won't normally have a sexual association, usually it refers to generalized ineffectiveness.

IMPOVERISHED usually won't infer a financial meaning but rather address one's emotional or mental aspects.

IMPREGNATE rarely pertains to sexual intercourse. This symbol will allude to one's success at getting through to another for the purpose of helping in some way.

IMPRESSION See imprint.

IMPRESSIONIST (art style) signifies a different way to see something; an alternative viewpoint.

IMPRESSIONIST (entertainer) characterizes an individual who has the capability of mirroring others so they can see themselves as they really are. This would indicate a need to see self clearly.

IMPRIMATUR warns against censorship; a barrier to one's freedom to choose for self.

IMPRINT connotes that which has gone before; a sign of one's passing. This doesn't necessarily have to be the imprint of a foot.

IMPROVISATION relates to an ability to cope; a quick wit.

IMPULSE BUYING denotes a lack of self-control.

INANIMATE OBJECT See specific type.

INARTICULATE corresponds to difficulty expressing oneself.

INAUGURATION underscores one's official beginning of something.

IN-BOX symbolizes receptivity to new ideas.

INBREEDING won't usually have a sexual/genetic connotation, but will most often refer to an incorrect mixing of ideas or perceptions.

INCANTATION typifies one's need for spiritual trappings.

INCENDIARY (device) pertains to an explosive or fiery aspect in one's life.

INCENSE may represent a calmative or it can indicate spiritual embellishments. Surrounding dreamscape details will clarify which meaning was intended.

INCENTIVE points to an element serving as a motivational factor.

INCEST dramatizes the seriousness of a dangerously negative relationship.

INCH implies a small measurement that is usually related to one's amount of progress.

INCHWORM denotes a slow and steady advancement that is progressing in a natural way.

INCINERATOR indicates the complete disposal of selective negatives in one's life.

INCISION symbolizes a need to release a negative attitude or emotion.

INCISOR (tooth) alludes to cutting remarks.

INCLINE See slope.

INCOGNITO reveals a disguised individual. Was this the dreamer?

INCOME rarely corresponds with finances; rather, it pertains to the return benefits generated from the spiritual talents shared with others.

INCOME TAX exemplifies required payments or dues. This usually connotes a karmic aspect.

INCOMPATIBILITY doesn't necessarily refer to a relationship; in fact, it most often will advise of a person's specific belief in something that is not vibrationally aligned with the individual.

INCOMPETENCY cautions against attempting to understand or take on higher concepts for which one isn't ready.

INCOMPREHENSIBLE indicates a concept or situation one isn't prepared enough to tackle.

INCONSISTENCY marks some type of discrepancy in one's life. Surrounding dreamscape details will help clarify what this is.

INCONSOLABLE defines a great need to feel loved. Regardless of why someone is consumed with deep grief, being held by another becomes the greatest healing comfort one can get.

INCONSPICUOUS refers to those subtle aspects in life that we often miss taking note of because of unawareness of our surroundings.

INCONTINENCE will not signify a physical condition in one's waking state but rather it will caution of a need to use more restraint in life.

INCORRIGIBILITY illustrates a strong character; a refusal to be confined or controlled by another.

INCUBATOR denotes special nurturing care one gives to newborn concepts or paths.

INCUBUS warns against transferring aberrant psychological mechanisms to self-created (imagined) manifestations.

INDECENCY connotes a rebellion; a psychological need to shock others.

INDEFINABLE pertains to higher aspects of reality that we have no established terms to correspond with. Sometimes this symbol can refer to that which overwhelms one.

INDELIBLE (ink) symbolizes that which cannot be altered, reversed, or undone.

INDENTURE suggests a need to perform a return service for another. This usually points to some form of debt.

INDEPENDENCE DAY See Fourth of July.

INDESTRUCTIBLE advises of something in one's life that cannot be undone or gotten rid of; enduring strength and longevity.

INDEX CARD indicates a need for organization.

INDEX FINGER usually implies an accusation of some type; also can indicate something to which the dreamer needs to give attention or notice—a pointing finger.

INDIA exemplifies a wealth of spiritual diversity.

INDIA INK stands for a need to get something better defined. This would point to some type of grey area existing in one's life.

INDIAN (American) See American Indian.

INDIAN (East) characterizes one holding ritualistic spiritual beliefs.

INDIANA signifies pacifism, a tendency to take a middle-of-the-road attitude.

INDIAN AGENT refers to a self-serving agenda.

INDIAN BLANKET (botanical) stands for one's inner defenses; strong confidence.

INDIAN CORN connotes survivability; life-giving seed.

INDIAN GIVER portrays an ulterior motive.

INDIAN PAINTBRUSH (botanical) relates to vibrant spiritual energy.

INDIAN PIPE (botanical) suggests an openness to ideas; communication.

INDIAN SUMMER denotes a time of peaceful respite. May also point to extra time given to get something accomplished; a reprieve.

INDIAN WRESTLING See arm wrestling.

INDICTMENT signifies a serious accusation.

INDIGESTION indicates a situation or other aspect that one finds hard to stomach and points to a lack of acceptance.

INDIGO (color) signifies high spirituality.

INDIRECT LIGHTING suggests one look at the entire picture (situation) instead of only focusing on the main issue.

INDISPENSABLE will define that which one believes is essential in life.

INDIVIDUAL RETIREMENT ACCT. (IRA) suggests planning with an eye on the future; long-term planning.

INDOOR-OUTDOOR (carpet) represents a need to balance or bring uniformity to personal aspects that one holds privately (within self) and displays publicly (without).

INDOORS applies to the inner self; that which is private and rarely shown or expressed.

INDUCEMENT alludes to some type of personal motivation entering one's life.

INDUSTRIAL ARTS (study of) denotes a high interest in learning how to utilize spiritual tools (energy) to help others. Also see trade school.

INDUSTRIALIST characterizes one who provides opportunities for others.

INDUSTRIAL PARK exemplifies a location where many energies are combining to generate specific outcomes.

INDUSTRIAL REVOLUTION pertains to a lack of self-reliance; a move that increases quantity and lessens quality.

INDUSTRIAL STRENGTH denotes greater energy or power.

INEDIBLE warns of something that shouldn't be intellectually ingested; a concept or idea that is negative; a preposterous idea.

INELIGIBILITY advises of one's lack of readiness.

INESCAPABLE reminds one to face reality.

INEXPENSIVE See cheap.

INEXPERIENCE underscores one's current level of advancement or personal development. This usually comes to a dreamer when she/he is planning on attempting to undertake research or an experience that is beyond adequate comprehension.

IN EXTREMIS reveals a short measure of time left to make amends, get affairs in order, or change ways.

INFALLIBLE usually comes as a "don't kid yourself" message but can also point to a trustworthy individual.

INFAMOUS reveals a possibly dangerous individual.

INFANT See baby.

INFANTICIDE reveals the willful suppression of one's spirituality through loss of belief or lack of use.

INFANTRY represents those who handle the groundwork, especially related to keeping things running smoothly or handling conflicts.

INFECTION points to the negative effects of a destructive element in one's life. Something needing to be dealt with before it gets worse.

INFERENCE implies forthcoming innuendos; possible new insight.

INFERIORITY COMPLEX represents a serious lack of acceptance in one's life; a failure to feel the loving essence of the Divine within oneself.

INFERTILITY doesn't usually refer to the physical reproductive system, but rather it indicates a lack of spiritual fruitfulness; an absence of spiritual giving.

INFESTATION (insect) connotes a destructive force that has invaded an aspect of one's life. For some specifics, see below.

Insects in air relate to a destructive element connected to one's mental or emotional state.

Insects in attic refer to a destructive factor in one's subconscious.

Insects in basement infer a faulty and harmful foundational belief or attitude.

Insects in garden pertain to a destructive use of one's gifts or skills.

Insects in house point to a destructive element in one's home life.

Insects in kitchen denote the *ingestion* of a harmful attitude or perspective.

Insects in water apply to a destructive aspect to one's spiritual life.

INFIELD connotes within oneself; internal aspects; thought and psychological processes.

INFILTRATION warns of a negative aspect that has entered one's life.

INFINITESIMAL is a symbol that comes to remind us that everything, no matter how small it may seem, has importance in life—there's reason for its existence.

INFINITY (sign) represents continuum, an ongoing situation, conceptual belief, or relationship. This refers to an element which will be present throughout one's life.

INFIRMARY See hospital.

INFLATE emphasizes something blown up, out of proportion; exaggerations and embellishments.

INFLATION (economic) usually comes in a dream to advise the dreamer that he/she is expending too much energy (costly) on something.

INFLUENZA See virus.

INFORM comes as a guiding message and suggests that the dreamer communicate with a particular individual.

INFORMAL (dress/occasion) naturally equates to a casual issue or attitude; congenial.

INFORMANT portrays an individual who possesses information/specific knowledge. This may point to an instance of betrayal.

INFORMATION BOOTH points to a need for more information; the whole story isn't known.

INFORMATION SUPERHIGHWAY See Internet.

INFORMED CONSENT (form) signifies proof of prior knowledge and one's agreement to it.

INGOT signifies materialism as being one's priority in life.

INGROWN (nail) warns of self-imposed grief, stress, or pain.

INHABITANT infers viability of a situation.

INHALATOR See respirator.

INHALER corresponds with an aspect in one's life that has the capability of easing tension or stress.

INHERITANCE defines that which is handed down to another; what another has left behind for us to benefit from.

INHERITANCE TAX denotes strings attached to a benefit, gift, or windfall.

INHIBITION corresponds with one's fears.

INHIBITOR suggests a blocking aspect. This blocking may be voluntarily achieved through denial or even acceptance.

IN-HOUSE will relate to something coming from within oneself, usually an attitude, but can also refer to negatives such as self-defeating behavior.

INHUMANE (treatment) will reveal harsh underlying emotional disturbances.

INITIALS are messages unique to each dreamer because they'll stand for recognized words or names.

INITIATION marks a beginning of something the dreamer will relate to.

INJECTION applies to new aspects entering one's life. Recall what substance was injected to determine if this is a positive or negative message.

INJUNCTION will come as a warning to stop destructive behavior.

INJURY reveals some type of harm done to one. Surrounding dreamscape details will further clarify what this harm is.

INJUSTICE defines a wrong conclusion or judgment made in one's life.

INK pertains to recording or marking so as to solidify or verify.

INKBLOT usually comes as a sign that something in one's life is amiss or not balanced.

INKBLOT TEST See Rorschach test.

INK CARTRIDGE relates to an ongoing readiness to verify beliefs or solidify agreements.

INLAY stands for the attitudes we accumulate in life and incorporate into our overall foundational perspectives.

IN-LINE SKATES See roller skates.

INN connotes a resting place along one's life path.

INNER CIRCLE will indicate privileged information and those who perceive themselves as having a right to it.

INNER SANCTUM is associated with one's innermost thoughts and feelings, those we tend to want to protect from being hurt or made public.

INNER TUBE applies to the state of one's emotional state as the path walk is made. Recall if the inner tube was patched. Was it full of air? Deflated? Torn?

INNING reveals one's advancement on one's path. Recall what inning it was.

INNKEEPER characterizes an individual who is capable of providing rest and comfort to another.

INNOVATION stands for independent thought; perhaps visionary thinking.

INOCULATION See immunization.

INQUEST advises of a need to fully investigate some aspect in one's life. There is something yet to be revealed.

INQUISITION pertains to an invasion of one's privacy. Usually this will be a validating symbol for the dreamer.

INSANITY implies a total loss of reality.

INSATIABILITY advises of an inner void that needs to be filled.

INSCRIPTION comes as a warning or revealing message. Recall what was inscribed.

INSECT See specific type.

INSECTICIDE reveals a need to get rid of negative attitudes/irritations, usually through acceptance or greater tolerance.

INSET stands for an added element.

INSIDE See indoors.

INSIDE INFORMATION most often refers to thoughts and insights that come as inspiration.

INSIDE OUT (clothing) suggests backward perspectives or a tendency to present a public persona which is opposite from one's privately held attitude/character.

INSIDER TRADING refers to ill-gotten gain or benefits.

INSIDE TRACK underscores one's advantageous placement in life; a choice position.

INSIGNIA will reveal one's privately held attitude or sympathies.

INSOLVENCY won't normally equate to finances but rather refer to a quality in which one has become bankrupt.

INSOMNIAC characterizes one who fights acceptance.

INSPECTION OBJECTION reveals a flaw in a plan or idea.

INSPECTOR stands for one's own Higher Self who acts as an advisor and guide.

INSTALLMENT (payment) connotes the gradual balancing of one's karmic debts.

INSTANT MESSAGING suggests a need for immediate communication.

INSTANT REPLAY advises of the wisdom of looking more closely at something a second or third time. This indicates something was overlooked.

INSTRUCTOR See teacher.

INSTRUMENT (musical) See specific type.

INSTRUMENT PANEL portrays the controls one has in life; the opportunities one has to choose from.

INSULATION relates to one's personal quality and level of self-protection.

INSULIN is a substitute for a vital aspect one needs in life. Surrounding details will help to clarify this for the dreamer.

INSURANCE implies protective measures. If a great amount of insurance was shown, that means a lack of faith.

INSURANCE AGENT characterizes one who has a predatory nature and takes advantage of another's lack of faith.

INSURANCE CLAIM stands for a benefit reaped from one's protective methods or an injurious event.

INTAGLIO is a sign that validates humankind's kinship with all intelligent life.

INTEGRATION rarely refers to ethnicity but rather comes as an advisement to combine diverse aspects. This indicates that the dreamer was missing something, not including all possible factors associated with an issue or concept.

INTELLECTUAL characterizes one who has knowledge yet may not have the wisdom to go along with it.

INTELLIGENCE AGENT denotes an invasion of one's privacy. This comes as an advisement to be discerning when opening up to associates or friends.

INTELLIGENCE REPORT offers the dreamer valuable information she/he has been needing.

INTELLIGENCE TEST See aptitude test.

INTENSIVE CARE UNIT (ICU) is a warning to seek immediate help. This may be associated with mental, emotional, or physical aspects.

INTERCEPTION connotes an interference in one's life. Surrounding dreamscape details will clarify this if the dreamer isn't aware of such an event happening in real time.

INTERCHANGE represents a decision regarding an upcoming change of course option.

INTERCOM symbolizes inner communication between one's conscious and Higher Self.

INTERCOURSE (communication) refers to a need to convey or express opinions more.

INTERCOURSE (sexual) points to a need for an intimate conversation. This relates to an honest heart-to-heart talk with someone.

INTEREST (added to debts) signify increased indebtedness.

INTEREST (earned) signifies added benefits gained through the sharing of one's talents.

INTEREST RATE indicates the long-term cost of being in debt. This debt may not relate to finances but could be associated with favors others grant you.

INTERFACING stands for interaction.

INTERGALACTIC implies a beginning phase of understanding reality.

INTERIOR DECORATOR characterizes an individual who continually attempts to change others. This could mean personality, opinions, perceptions, appearance, or beliefs.

INTERMEDIARY See mediator.

INTERMISSION advises of a need for a break from one's work, study, or other type of pursuit.

INTERMITTENT CURRENT suggests indecision; vacillation.

INTERN characterizes an individual who has knowledge and is in the process of gaining applied experience.

INTERNAL AFFAIRS stand for one's conscience.

INTERNAL CLOCK See biological clock.

INTERNATIONAL FLIGHT represents extended thinking; long-range thought.

INTERNATIONAL LAW indicates common sense, logic.

INTERNATIONAL WATERS symbolize spiritual concepts which are so basic that everyone respects them with reflected behavior.

INTERNET denotes information that's easily accessed.

INTERPRETER signifies a need for better understanding; clearer communication.

INTERROGATION points to a need to examine one's own motives or attitudes.

INTERSECTION See interchange.

INTERTWINED points to a thorough involvement or a convoluted issue.

INTERVIEW advises in-depth communication that will reveal more information.

INTIMACY emphasizes a close relationship; a companion; confidante.

INTOXICATED See drunk.

INTRAUTERINE DEVICE (IUD) See birth control (methods).

INTRAVENOUS FEEDING comes to warn of a serious lack in one's life. Most often the dreamer will automatically relate to what this is.

INTRODUCTION advises of a need for new relationships or concepts in one's life.

INTROVERT pertains to quiet acceptance.

INTRUDER connotes an individual who disrupts specific aspects of one's life.

INTUITION corresponds with one's insights or feelings. This symbol comes as a message of validation for the dreamer.

INVALID (person) calls for courage to continue on one's path regardless of adversities.

INVASION warns of a multitude of invasive aspects entering one's life.

INVENTOR characterizes intellectual exploration and creativity.

INVENTORY comes as an advisement to take stock of one's life.

INVERTED suggests a misinterpretation or misunderstanding; one has something backwards or upside down.

INVESTIGATOR advises to do more in-depth research on an issue.

INVESTING doesn't usually refer to finances but rather what one is accepting as truth and into which one is placing all one's energy.

INVISIBLE (being) may denote an actual out-of-body experience or it may indicate that one isn't being effective, possibly being ignored.

INVISIBLE INK stands for hypocrisy; deception.

INVITATION means a request from another. Recall what the invitation was for. Who was it from?

IODINE indicates that which will soothe and heal. Surrounding dreamscape details will clarify this for the dreamer.

IOWA stands for respect for the land; a striving to nurture possibilities.

IPECAC is a severe warning that a highly destructive aspect has entered one's life and there's a need to expel it.

I-POD refers to the ease of changing one's mood. This comes to underscore that one's mood can be altered by oneself through a change in attitude or focusing on the brighter side or one's blessings.

IRELAND relates to undiscovered elements of reality; unproven aspects of reality; the range of reality's wide possibilities.

IRIDESCENT comes as an attention-getting message. Recall what was iridescent.

IRIS (botanical) connotes hope.

IRIS (eye) will reveal one's quality of perception. What color was it? Was it cloudy or clear?

IRISH COFFEE exemplifies a life aspect that has the capability of providing balance.

IRISH LINEN pertains to the fragility of reality.

IRISH SETTER (dog breed) denotes a friend capable of providing guidance, pointing you in the right direction.

IRISH STEW symbolizes basic, foundational nourishment.

IRISH WOLFHOUND (dog breed) stands for a friend possessing strong character.

IRON (appliance) advises of a need to straighten out a relationship, perception, or situation in one's life.

IRON (metal) signifies strength.

IRON AGE represents strength.

IRON CURTAIN won't relate to the former Russian situation but instead reveals one's voluntary separation of self from a life issue; denial or escapism.

IRON HAND depicts an unyielding personality; possibly manipulation.

IRON LUNG is an advisement to be more independent; think for self; make your own decisions.

IRONWOOD (tree/wood) points to complexity; intricate elements to an aspect.

IRONWORKER characterizes a strong personality. Depending on surrounding dreamscape details, this may or may not be a positive sign.

IRRADIATION signifies an altered aspect.

IRRIGATION suggests a need to use more spiritual aspects in one's life.

IRRITATE denotes a lack of acceptance; inability to release negative attitudes.

IRS implies benefits that haven't been personally earned.

IRS AGENT characterizes one who gains from the efforts of others; a leach.

ISIS (Egyptian deity) emphasizes a bountiful aspect in one's life; moving mountains to achieve a goal; a willingness/readiness to do anything for one's love.

ISLAND represents a time to pause during one's spiritual search.

ISOLATION usually connotes a self-induced condition.

ISOMETRICS imply a conflict within self.

ISRAEL represents holding onto one's rights with unyielding tenacity.

ISTHMUS See land bridge.

ITALICS are shown for the purpose of drawing your attention to something important you should be aware of; places emphasis on something.

ITALY refers to emotional expressiveness.

ITCHING means a restlessness; calls for acceptance. May point to some type of irritation in one's life.

ITINERARY implies a planned course. This may not be a positive dream element if there hasn't been time for unexpected events or delays factored in.

IVORY corresponds to the value of one's relationships. Recall what the ivory was shaped as.

IVORY (color) points to treasured or cherished elements.

IVORY TOWER stands for needed solitude; contemplative time. Rarely does this symbol refer to material riches or an arrogant attitude.

IVY (botanical) exemplifies bountiful knowledge; prolific creativity.

IVY LEAGUE denotes intellectual arrogance.

J

JABBERING stands for incoherent communication; confusion.

JABOT represents speech and perceptual affectations; embellishments.

JACK (tool) denotes a life aspect that has the capability of easing one's burdens' lifting some of the weight.

JACKAL illustrates a predatory nature.

JACKBOOT suggests a bully, one who is insensitive/manipulative/domineering.

JACKET See coat.

JACK FROST characterizes one who could put a damper on spirituality.

JACKHAMMER symbolizes an individual's hard shell; a need to break open the hardened barrier behind which one has hidden for too long.

JACK-IN-THE-BOX implies insensitivity; an inability to recognize the more serious aspects of life.

JACK-IN-THE-PULPIT (plant) connotes spiritual expressiveness.

JACKKNIFE indicates impatience.

JACK/JANE-OF-ALL-TRADES relates to versatility.

JACK-O'-LANTERN reveals one's perspective on life. Recall how it was carved. Sad? Angry? Fearful? Scary?

JACK PINE See pine (tree).

JACKPOT emphasizes benefits and rewards received throughout life.

JACKRABBIT See rabbit.

JACK RUSSELL TERRIER (dog breed) represents a devoted friend.

JACKS (game) pertain to the pressure under which one lives. This usually is a self-generated situation.

JACKSON (Andrew) epitomizes racism, genocide, and greed.

JACOB'S LADDER (botanical/flower) stands for a need to heighten perceptual skills; points to a sensitive situation.

JACQUARD (pattern) illustrates a complex situation or idea.

JACUZZI refers to comforting spiritual beliefs that soothe.

JADE (gem) alludes to healing qualities or talents; protective aspects.

JADE (plant) points to perseverance.

JADED connotes weariness; cynicism.

JAGGED (edge) implies a situation left with loose ends.

JAGUAR represents changeability; an altering personality.

JAIL reveals a state of self-confinement.

JAILBREAK defines an escape from a confining aspect in one's life.

JALAPEÑO alludes to a spirited personality.

JALOPY indicates a free thinker.

JAM (food) signifies a troubling situation.

JAM (music) symbolizes a lighthearted mood.

JAMB (door) indicates a situation where one feels closed in.

JAMES (Jesse) portrays an individual who gains from the efforts of others; a lack of personal responsibility.

JAMES (William) corresponds with deep thought.

JAMESTOWN (Virginia) illustrates perseverance.

JAM SESSION (verbal) reveals a need to talk things out.

JANE DOE signifies a repressed personality; one who doesn't express emotions or opinions; a fear of displaying independence.

JANITOR constitutes a need to clean up one's act.

JANUARY pertains to a time of contemplation on one's past path and casting an eye toward the future road.

JAPAN suggests spiritual tranquility.

JAR often represents that which we contain within self.

JARGON indicates concepts or ideas that are beyond one's understanding. This symbol may also point to a tendency to talk above others.

JASMINE (botanical/scent) alludes to a mysterious quality to one's personality.

JASPER denotes a life aspect that has the capability of drawing negativity from the body.

JAUNDICE warns of waning strength.

JAVELIN See spear.

JAW pertains to the level of one's inner strength. Was the jaw strong? Thin?

JAWBREAKER represents that which depletes one's strength in reference to expending too much energy on whole concepts. This suggests a need to break down these concepts into their various aspects so they can be understood one at a time.

JAWS OF LIFE will correspond with a life aspect that can extricate one from a serious problem or situation.

JAY See bluebird; gray jay.

JAYWALKING implies a tendency to cut corners; not always go by the book.

JAZZ applies to perseverance.

JAZZERCISE pertains to willful energy applied to perseverance and/or endurance.

JEANS connote a nonconformist; a relaxed personality.

JEEP See four-wheel drive.

JEFFERSON (Thomas) characterizes a striving for knowledge.

JEKYLL AND HYDE emphasizes a changeable personality; hypocrisy; vacillation. May point to someone who has a tendency to play both sides.

JELL-O implies anxiety; nervousness.

JELLY See jam (food).

JELLYBEANS refer to the small blessings we frequently overlook.

JELLYFISH warns of a lack of firm convictions; using one's stinging defense mechanisms to maintain an air of free-floating irresponsibility.

JELLYROLL connotes a frivolous, impassive personality.

JERKY (meat) represents the nourishment from one's preserved convictions/ideologies.

JERRYBUILT alludes to a lack of integrity. In some cases it may indicate an attempt to work with whatever resources one has.

JERRY CAN relates to one's level of preparedness for life. Recall what the can contained; or was it empty?

JERSEY (fabric) suggests a soft-hearted, soft-spoken personality.

JESTER characterizes a lackadaisical attitude; rarely attending to anything serious.

JESUS symbolizes a high spiritual messenger; one who sacrifices much for a goal.

JESUS FREAK signifies spiritual fanaticism; an intolerance of another's belief system.

JET (color/gem) alludes to a deep mystery; high concepts; pessimism.

JET (high-velocity) applies to a strong force; highly motivated; quick action taken.

JET LAG advises of a need to slow down for the purpose of catching up.

JETLINER corresponds with spiritual advancement, the speed of same.

JETSAM exemplifies the extraneous aspects one needs to get rid of in life.

JET SET characterizes misplaced priorities.

JET SKI warns against racing over or through new spiritual concepts, thereby skimming rather than comprehending the depth of them.

JET STREAM defines popular beliefs or ideas; generally accepted and followed beliefs.

JETTY See pier.

JEWEL See gemstone; specific type.

JEWELER characterizes one who places a high priority on material aspects in life; or may symbolize one interested in fine detail. Surrounding dreamscape aspects will clarify this.

JEWELFISH denotes spirituality being one's most valued priority in life.

JEWELRY (excessive) implies an attention-demanding personality; one who aggrandizes self.

JEWELRY BOX denotes one's collection of riches. Recall if they were more silver (spiritual aspects) or gold (material aspects).

JEWELRY STORE portrays exterior values that one may not necessarily hold within self.

JEZEBEL refers to one who tempts another into wrongdoing; manipulative.

JIG (dance) signifies a moment of elation.

JIG (lure) connotes an unfair advantage.

JIGGER (measurement) depicts a small portion. The key here is to recall what was in the jigger. Sometimes a small amount of a volatile substance will be too much.

JIGGLE suggests an unstable condition.

JIGSAW denotes a need to cut corners; be clear about the shape of a situation.

JIGSAW PUZZLE indicates a problem in one's life and this dreamscape fragment may actually show the dreamer how to put the pieces together.

JILTED indicates a sudden termination of something in one's life.

JIMMY See crowbar.

JIMSONWEED (botanical) emphasizes the duality or polarity of something in one's life; possessing positive and negative aspects, depending on how it's used.

JINGLING (sound) usually is a call to pay attention to something that's presently being ignored. Surrounding dream details will clarify this.

JINX constitutes an excuse. This implies a situation where one refuses to admit responsibility; using a scapegoat.

JITTERBUG (dance) refers to a lack of direction.

JOAN OF ARC characterizes what can be accomplished by acting on one's visions (inspirations).

JOB (employment) reveals the dreamer's opinion of her/his own work.

JOB BENEFITS signify the rewards that come with expending energy on advancing and being productive.

JOBBER points to someone who has a particular skill to help another.

JOB DESCRIPTION refers to knowing everything a specific project or issue will entail.

JOB-HOPPING cautions against instability; undependability.

JOB-HUNTING implies motivation; a desire to be productive.

JOBLESS may indicate a push toward being more productive or it may suggest a need to rest a while. The dream's surrounding details will clarify which interpretation is meant.

JOCKEY (any type) pertains to one who is skilled in maneuvering various aspects into their best position.

JOCK ITCH alludes to problems of a sexual nature; usually these are not physical but rather tend to indicate a psychological source.

JOCKSTRAP connotes a need for psychological counseling (support) in respect to one's sexually related attitudes.

JODHPURS symbolize selective arrogance; a high attitude regarding a specific subject.

JOGGING represents a steadily paced progression.

JOHN See bathroom.

JOHN (male customer) stands for the source of a negativity in one's life. It points to the demand that keeps a negative going.

JOHN DOE See Jane Doe.

JOHNNY APPLESEED portrays one who spreads ideas; plants the seeds of specific concepts or ideas.

JOHN THE BAPTIST emphasizes a forerunner; a messenger.

JOINT (smoke) signifies a personal manner of calming self.

JOINT (union) alludes to some type of bond or link.

JOINT CHIEFS OF STAFF symbolize one's personal Advisor together with one's Higher Self.

JOINT TENANCY (title work) signifies equal ownership and rights of full inheritance. This would mean an idea or issue having equal rights of possession by the originators.

JOINT VENTURE suggests a move to join efforts with another for a specific purpose.

JOKE will usually reveal something important for the dreamer, frequently about self.

JOKER (card) portrays humiliation.

JOLLY ROGER (flag) warns of a dangerous aspect in one's life. This could relate to a situation, relationship, or even self. Because the Jolly Roger (skull & crossbones) is commonly associated with a pirate ship, this symbol is most often connected to a *spiritual* aspect.

JOLT denotes a call to attention and sharper awareness. The dreamer is missing something important in life.

JONSES represent who or what one strives to be equal to or better than; one-upmanship.

JONQUIL (botanical) refers to peacefulness.

JOSHUA TREE stands for a heightened appreciation of one's blessings.

JOSS STICK See incense.

JOURNAL may indicate a need to keep a journal or it may reveal aspects happening in one's life that are being overlooked or not given enough attention to.

JOURNALIST characterizes one who keeps track of events in one's life; could refer to one's Higher Self or those who watch us.

JOURNEY forewarns of an upcoming time of discovery or search.

JOUSTING applies to a personal combative state, frequently within oneself.

JOWLS relate to many difficulties overcome throughout life.

JOY RIDE warns of carelessness; a lack of personal responsibility. In some circumstances, this symbol points to an actual joyful time.

JOYSTICK indicates controlling factors; an opportunity to be in control.

JUDAS (Iscariot) reveals misplaced trust; poor judgment.

JUDGE JUDY characterizes one who gets down to basic issues and doesn't beat around the bush; one who cuts to the chase.

JUDGMENT DAY reminds us that all our life actions and thoughts will be one day reviewed and judged. This symbol comes to advise us to listen more to our conscience.

JUDO See martial arts.

JUG connotes common sense.

JUGGLER characterizes efficiency; organization.

JUGULAR (vein) connotes a vital aspect in one's life; that to which one is most vulnerable.

JUICE represents an easing factor in life.

JUICE HEAD See alcoholic.

JUICER refers to a life aspect that has the capability of producing a calming or easing effect.

JUJITSU See martial arts.

JUJU warns of a psychological aberration, particularly regarding the effects others have on you. This suggests a need to believe in oneself.

JUKE BOX alludes to that which one chooses to listen. This usually comes as a warning to stop being so closed-minded.

JULY denotes a time for self examination; meditation.

JUMBLED denotes mental or emotional confusion.

JUMPER (dress) refers to simplicity.

JUMPER (suicide) See suicide.

JUMPER CABLE See booster cable.

JUMP DRIVE (computer) See USB port.

JUMPING implies impatience with one's path progression or advancement.

JUMPING BEAN typifies restlessness; anxiety.

JUMPING JACK signifies a lack of individualized thought; acting on the direction or thoughts of those around you.

JUMPING MOUSE denotes efficiency; cleverness; mental agility.

JUMPING-OFF PLACE marks a beginning point.

JUMP RING stands for a life element which is used for connective purposes.

JUMP ROPE pertains to being directed by others, perhaps to the point of subservience.

JUMP SEAT warns of gullibility.

JUMP-START stands for a need to be re-energized, motivation. See booster cable.

JUNCO (bird) denotes friendship.

JUNCTION means a joining of forces or may indicate a new option.

JUNCTION BOX (electrical) corresponds with one's mental analytical and reasoning ability.

JUNE denotes a time to review one's relationships.

JUNG (Carl Gustav) characterizes mental reaching to transcend current limitations.

JUNGLE warns of a confused spiritual state; could point to schizophrenia.

JUNGLE FEVER pertains to a continued state of mental and emotional confusion.

JUNGLE GYM warns of a self-generated state of confusion and twisted perspectives.

JUNIPER (botanical) signifies the refreshing aspects of spirituality and the living of same.

JUNK corresponds to the relativity of value.

JUNK ART denotes an altered perspective.

JUNK BOND warns of a high risk.

JUNK COLLECTOR refers to hidden values.

JUNKET signifies a self-serving act; selfishly gaining from ulterior motives of others.

JUNK FOOD warns against putting energy into learning unimportant concepts as they will not be fulfilling.

JUNKIE won't equate to only a drug addiction but any strong habit one should overcome.

JUNK MAIL illustrates insignificance.

JUNKYARD symbolizes unexpected opportunities.

JUNKYARD DOG points to a friend one doesn't fully appreciate.

JUPITER (planet) refers to the Provider in us; caring for oneself and those around us.

JURY pertains to one's Higher Self.

JURY POOL applies to those whose opinions count.

JURY-RIG suggests improvisation.

JUSTICE DEPARTMENT (Federal) See court.

JUSTICE OF THE PEACE stands for rash decisions; impulsiveness.

JUTE (fabric) means a rough type of inner strength.

JUVENILE COURT portrays the law as it applies to a searching beginner; basic or novitiate philosophical concepts.

JUVENILE DELINQUENT characterizes one who rebukes philosophical and spiritual concepts during a beginning stage of discovery.

JUVENILE DETENTION (center) is an advisement to halt immature tendencies to ignore what one knows is right; a need to take time out and think about being more mature.

JUXTAPOSITION advises of a need to compare different aspects. The surrounding dreamscape details will clarify what the dreamer needs to analyze in life.

K

KABALA symbolizes the higher esoteric facets of spiritual truths.

KABUKI (dancer) calls for a more frequent expression of one's emotions, especially by men.

KACHINA (doll/image) corresponds to our ancestral teachers; the Starborn ones.

KADDISH reminds us to remember our dead.

KAISER ROLL suggests big issues that one attempts to take on or ingest.

KALE represents a personal need of some type. The dreamer will usually know what need she/he has.

KALEIDOSCOPE warns of distorted perceptions; vacillating attitudes.

KAMIKAZE characterizes a self-destructive personality.

KANGAROO cautions against overprotectiveness.

KANGAROO COURT constitutes one who is too quick to judge another.

KANGAROO RAT signifies long endurance.

KANSAS suggests the source of an issue—the meat of it.

KANT (Immanuel) illustrates one's ability to reason.

KAPOK (tree/fabric) denotes that which one uses to soften life difficulties.

KARATE See martial arts.

KARAOKE may represent a desire to be heard or it can refer to unrestrained joy (feeling free to sing as though nobody can hear you).

KARLOFF (Boris) indicates an individual the dreamer is uncomfortable with and somewhat fearful or skeptical of.

KARMA stands for making retribution; behavioral balance.

KATYDID See grasshopper.

KAVA represents duality, positive and negative aspects of one thing.

KAYAK connotes a highly personal spiritual path.

KAZOO indicates immaturity.

KEA See parrot.

KEEL signifies the foundational and motivational strength of one's personal spiritual search.

KEELBOAT warns against the carrying of excess spiritual baggage.

KEENING signifies grief; lamenting; pining.

KEEP See tower.

KEEP LEFT (road sign) See road signs.

KEEP RIGHT (road sign) See road signs.

KEEPSAKE applies to respect and honor for one's memories.

KEESHOND (dog breed) denotes a protective friend.

KEG See barrel.

KELLY (Grace Patricia) represents hopes and dreams.

KELP corresponds to spiritual health. Recall the kelp's condition.

KELPIE signifies a playful, joyful spirituality.

KENNEDY (Jacqueline) signifies inner strength.

KENNEDY (John F.) stands for wisdom behind leadership/power.

KENNEDY (Robert F.) exemplifies tenacity.

KENNEL implies a confining relationship.

KENNEL COUGH advises of a negative aspect picked up from a friend.

KENO applies to the taking of slim chances; taking risks.

KENTUCKY suggests efforts to contain one's impulsiveness; wildness streak to one's nature.

KENTUCKY DERBY represents a celebrated fast-paced competition in which many are interested.

KEOGH PLAN See retirement.

KERATIN depicts inner strength; that which generates strength.

KERATOSIS advises one to be more emotionally sensitive to others.

KERCHIEF See handkerchief.

KERNEL pertains to one's inner talents or abilities.

KEROSENE denotes one's ability to energize or motivate others.

KESTREL See falcon.

KETCHUP applies to elaborations; a need to spice something up.

KETTLE advises of something brewing in one's life.

KETTLEDRUM stands for a call to attention. There is something important in the dreamer's life that isn't being noticed.

KEWPIE DOLL represents unrealistic expectations.

KEY denotes a solution to a problematic situation or an inspiration.

KEY (land) See reef.

KEYBOARD (computer) refers the ease of communication access. This indicates someone who believes a certain communication/dialog isn't approachable.

KEYBOARD (musical) pertains to the freedom to play one's own song; indicates a suggestion to follow one's own path.

KEYCARD illustrates one's right to do something; having authority or permission.

KEY CLUB implies separatism; a specific chosen group.

KEYHOLE suggests an opportunity in life. May point to a clue of some type; a small insight.

KEYNOTE (speaker) signifies one who is supposed to be experienced or have higher knowledge regarding a specific issue.

KEYPAD represents options at one's fingertips.

KEY RING refers to an effort keep an important life aspect from being lost.

KEYSTONE defines an aspect in one's life that pulls things together and brings understanding.

KEYSTONE KOPS characterize a ridiculous legal aspect that holds no validity.

KEYWORD See password.

KHAKI (color/fabric) implies a regimented personality.

KIBBUTZ refers to community involvement. This may not mean literally but rather be associated with a general attitude.

KICKBACK warns against expecting recompense or monetary benefit from service given or efforts expended for another.

KICKBALL suggests a tendency to bounce ideas around.

KICKING calls for acceptance; denotes impatience or lack of self-control.

KICKOFF marks a beginning.

KICK PLATE suggests an intent or desire to protect one's record from missteps or mishaps occurring during one's journey through life.

KICKSTAND connotes the stopping and pausing points along one's path.

KID See children; goat.

KIDDIE CAR suggests a childish approach to one's life path or purpose.

KIDDIE RIDE alludes to immature aspects.

KID GLOVE exemplifies gentle treatment, or interaction needing a delicate approach.

KIDNAP cautions against a desire to possess another or another's idea.

KIDNEY represents a cleansing factor, usually refers to mental or emotional aspects.

KIDNEY BEAN pertains to an intake of something that has the capability of cleansing or balancing oneself.

KIDNEY STONE advises of a blocking factor in one's life.

KIDNEY TRANSPLANT See transplant (kidney).

KIELBASA See sausage.

KILLDEER (bird) signifies protectiveness.

KILLER (of anything) warns of a fatally negative facet in one's life. The dreamer will usually already know what this is associated with.

KILLER BEE infers a new danger from a foreign source.

KILLER T CELL means an avenger; something that eradicates a negative facet in one's life.

KILLER WHALE stands for spiritual generosity; magnanimity.

KILLING FROST represents an attitude, behavior, perspective that kills one's spirituality.

KILL MESSAGE (phone) signifies an option to stop a communication; a chance to change one's mind.

KILN denotes personal energy applied to one's advancement.

KILT implies pride in one's ancestral heritage.

KIMONO suggests servitude; inequality; suppression of opinion.

KIN See relative; specific relation type.

KINDERGARTEN denotes a beginning stage of learning or discovery.

KINDLING relates to aspects that exacerbate a condition or situation; something that will make matters more intense.

KINETIC ART alludes to the beauty of moving along one's path; making progress.

KING See royalty.

KING (Martin Luther, Jr.) characterizes courage to speak out against adversity and/or injustice.

KING ARTHUR (of legend) signifies one's destiny.

KINGBIRD denotes aggressiveness.

KING COBRA warns of a major negative existing in one's life; an individual or situation that could be venomous.

KINGDOM pertains to egotism and associated material desires; a personal realm where one proclaims self as ruler.

KINGFISHER (bird) denotes a spiritual curiosity.

KING KONG characterizes an overbearing personality; seemingly insurmountable problems.

KING-OF-THE-HILL (game) translates to a desire to be in control and have that power recognized by others.

KINGPIN corresponds to a major/central player in a relationship or specific situation; the one in absolute control.

KING POST (construction) represents the main support to one's thought process. Depending on the condition of this symbol, it will reveal a strong or weak intellectual strength.

KING-SIZE denotes a revealed measurement or quantity of something in the dreamer's life. This usually points out the fact that this something is much larger than currently being perceived. Surrounding dreamscape details will clarify this.

KING SOLOMON suggests great wealth. This may not refer to material riches, but rather spiritual or moral wealth; great amount of blessings.

KINK implies a problem or setback.

KINNIKINNICK (botanical) symbolizes bountiful and prolific gifts and talents.

KIOSK will reveal important information to the dreamer. This will be specific for each dreamer.

KIRK See church.

KIRK (Captain James T.) characterizes one who has the courage to explore the far reaches of reality . . . go where no one has gone before. This symbol stands for innovative thought, imagination, thinking outside the box.

KIRLIAN PHOTOGRAPHY illustrates one's field of energy. Was it bright and strong? Weak? Flaring? Undulating?

KIRMAN RUG (Persian) emphasizes wisdom and a high interest in knowledge.

KISMET means destiny.

KISS pertains to a show of intention.

KISS OF DEATH connotes a fatal or destructive outcome.

KIT means having all the parts comprising a whole.

KITCHEN refers to the method of food preparation. May also signify a place of planning, a cooking up of ideas. Recall the kitchen's overall condition, color, style, cleanliness.

KITCHEN GARDEN signifies fresh ideas; a tendency toward homegrown (innovative) thought.

KITE represents the effort one expends on reaching for inner understanding of emotional impulses.

KITTEN suggests an innocence of character; may indicate one who is helpless or at another's mercy. Surrounding dream details will clarify which meaning is intended.

KIVA illustrates one's personal manner of meditating. Recall the kiva's condition and occupancy to see if this is a good message or not.

KIWI (bird) signifies protectiveness; a raised observational skill.

KLEPTOMANIAC characterizes uncontrolled impulses.

KLIEG LIGHT is an attention-getting message that advises of a need to get some light on an issue or situation.

KLUTZY points to awkwardness but not necessarily coupled with being inept. May refer to a characteristic comparable to the absent-minded professor who is just too intellectually distracted to pay attention to the small stuff.

KNACK refers to a talent or skill.

KNACKWURST See sausage.

KNAPSACK connotes flexibility; free-spirited.

KNAPWEED (botanical) suggests emotional balance.

KNEADING indicates time and effort given to something in one's life.

KNEE corresponds with adaptability; resiliency.

KNEE BENDS portray continual efforts applied to staying resilient.

KNEECAP See patella.

KNEE-DEEP stands for a situation of being heavily involved.

KNEEHOLE (space) denotes an accommodating situation or relationship.

KNEE-JERK (reaction) symbolizes a first impression or uncontrolled responses.

KNEELING suggests a state of subjugation.

KNEEPAD indicates planning; good preparations done; foresight.

KNEE SOCKS exemplify protective qualities of oneself.

KNICKERS relate to immaturity.

KNIFE reveals a cutting off from some specific element in life.

KNIGHT characterizes an advocate; a champion of a cause or another individual; one who stands up for another.

KNITTING implies planning.

KNITTING NEEDLE warns of manipulation.

KNOB illustrates a means of controlling something; self-motivation.

KNOCKDOWN refers to a destructive event or action. May point to a temporary setback.

KNOCKING usually is an attention-getting message. This means one needs to give more notice or serious attention to something in life that has previously been ignored.

KNOCK-KNEED pertains to a specific difficulty walking one's path. This unique problem will be recognized by the dreamer.

KNOCKOFF stands for an attempt at imitation.

KNOCKOUT means impressive.

KNOCKOUT DROPS connote something that takes one by surprise; completely unexpected.

KNOLL indicates high ground and would suggest an upcoming need for more personal efforts to be expended in one's life.

KNOT represents a problem one needs to untangle.

KNOTHOLE constitutes a natural aspect; one that isn't covered or made perfect; the beauty of certain unique imperfections.

KNOTTY PINE connotes the attractiveness of natural simplicity.

KNOW-IT-ALL displays a lack of wisdom.

KNOWLEDGE is a message in itself. It comes to reveal specific information for the dreamer.

KNOW-NOTHING may know more than the know-it-all. Those who admit they know nothing usually know more than we think.

KNUCKLE may refer to a conflict, frequently within self, or it may be relating to a need to apply self in a more serious manner.

KNUCKLE SANDWICH typifies repercussions forthcoming.

KOALA See bear.

KOAN symbolizes a need for contemplation; deeper analyzation; the exercising of one's thought process.

KOHL See eyeliner.

KOHLRABI implies something in the dreamer's life that's difficult to sort out or understand.

KOKOPELLI (Native American mythology) characterizes an individual who easily compels others; one to whom others are drawn.

KOMONDOR (dog breed) denotes a friend having great inner strength.

KOSHER pertains to the proper manner or process.

KOWTOWING can represent respect or it may indicate a state of subjugation.

KRAKEN (Norwegian legend) portrays spiritual fears.

KRISS KRINGLE See Santa Claus.

KUDZU (botanical) symbolizes a suffocating aspect in one's life.

KU KLUX KLAN denotes an attitude of superiority; separatism; intolerance.

KUMQUAT applies to small needs that are as important as seemingly greater ones.

KUNDALINI illustrates spiritual energy.

KUNG FU See martial arts.

KWANZAA suggests a celebration of one's blessings.

$\mathcal{L}$

LAB COAT signifies an analytical mind; attention to detail and research.

LABEL comes as a unique warning message for each dreamer. Recall what the label said.

LABEL MAKER cautions against a need to label everything and everyone. Some concepts cannot be defined by a single term or be cubby-holed.

LABOR (birth) See hard labor (maternity).

LABORATORY indicates a need for analyzation; self-discovery.

LABOR CAMP points to a situation in which one has made more work for oneself.

LABOR DAY celebrates one's accomplishments gained from personal efforts.

LABOR PAINS stand for the tribulations encountered while making a new start or beginning a new journey.

LABORSAVING (device) won't necessarily mean laziness; it may suggest a more efficient method of doing something. Surrounding dreamscape details will clarify this for the dreamer.

LABOR UNION represents justice in the work place; the maintenance of fair-play while striving for accomplishment.

LABRADOR RETRIEVER (dog breed) signifies a determined friend, one who will always return to offer aid after rebuffs.

LABYRINTH calls for patience and acceptance while one walks a complex path for a time.

LACE (fabric) may denote an aloof or extremely particular personality or it may allude to a sensitive and delicate nature. Recall other dream details for further clarification of this symbol.

LACERATION signifies a temporary setback; a slight injury to one's ego.

LACES/LACING represents means to secure a closure.

LACEWING (insect) symbolizes a method of getting rid of one's life irritations.

LACKEY characterizes a subservient individual.

LACKLUSTER See dull.

LACQUER symbolizes the manner in which something has attempted to be finalized. The key is the quality of the finish. Was it cracked? Shiny? Dull? Rough? Was there a specific color added?

LACTOSE INTOLERANCE indicates emotional sensitivity.

LADDER denotes an opportunity for upward progression to be made.

LADDER-BACK (chair) indicates the need for a rest period before advancing further.

LADIES' MAN reveals a manipulative individual with an overblown self-image.

LADIES' NIGHT OUT comes in a dream to remind us of the importance of friends and taking the time to spend time together.

LADLE signifies generosity; one who is always ready to pour out talents or abilities for others.

LADY depicts real femininity and quiet reserve.

LADYBUG connotes a positive aspect that negates the negative and irritating facets of one's life.

LADYFINGER (confection) refers to a delicate or fragile situation.

LADY GODIVA stands for going the extra mile for one's beliefs; giving of oneself for the betterment of others.

LADY IN WAITING characterizes a supportive associate or friend.

LADY-KILLER implies male arrogance.

LADY LUCK stands for the ideology of an imaginary angelic persona who either smiles and brings blessings or frowns and brings misfortune; a scapegoat.

LADY OF THE LAKE characterizes an individual who holds the key to something; the keeper of the power or knowledge.

LADY'S MANTLE (botanical) refers to refined dignity.

LADY'S-SLIPPER (botanical) portrays a possession of fragile natural talents; those that must be nurtured.

LAGER See alcoholic beverage.

LAGGARD defines an irresponsible personality; a procrastinator.

LAGOON represents spiritual tranquility.

LAID-BACK usually will indicate a state of acceptance.

LAIR connotes the special place one goes to rest and recuperate from the stress and commotion of daily life.

LAKE suggests spiritual aspects in one's life.

LAKEBED indicates spiritual foundations; basic concepts.

LAKE EFFECT corresponds with the effect spiritual aspects have on one's life; spiritual motivation/force.

LAKEFRONT (land) emphasizes a need to be close to one's spiritual beliefs, taking daily comfort in them.

LAMAZE (training) symbolizes good intentions.

LAMB refers to the Divine.

LAMBING GROUND suggests attempts to connect with the Divine Essence.

LAMB'S EARS (botanical) symbolizes our prayers being heard by the Divine Essence.

LAMB'S QUARTER (botanical) represents food for thought.

LAMB'S WOOL See fleece.

LAME defines ineffectiveness.

LAMÉ (fabric) typifies dream symbols pertaining to a flashy personality; a need to be noticed; a love of attention.

LAME DUCK characterizes inconsequential actions; ineffectiveness.

LAMINATION implies a need to preserve something important; protection.

LAMP connotes light required on an aspect of one's life. This could refer to a relationship, an event, a situation, or even self.

LAMPLIGHTER characterizes one who lights the way; brings understanding.

LAMPOON suggests ridiculousness; a sarcastic or humorous attitude toward an issue or individual's behavior.

LAMPSHADE emphasizes a need to tone down the light on something in one's life; control the light's direction; soften the brightness so it's not so harsh and perhaps blinding.

LANCE See spear.

LANCET See scalpel.

LANCET WINDOW suggests a narrow perspective or view of something.

LANDAU See carriage.

LAND BANK refers to an opportunity to obtain the foundational element on which to build.

LAND BRIDGE signifies a path traveled with spirituality being to one's right and left; one who wants one's spiritual beliefs to guide the way.

LAND DEVELOPER See developer (land).

LANDFALL represents the end of one's spiritual searching and the beginning of the related practical application.

LANDFILL reveals one's covered up negative aspects.

LAND GRAB usually denotes greediness, but may also indicate a desire to take advantage of a good opportunity.

LAND GRANT exemplifies an open opportunity capable of fulfilling one's multiple goals.

LANDING GEAR signifies a grounding source. Recall if the gear was down or up. Broken? One wheel down and one stuck?

LANDING STRIP marks one's intended destination; an immediate goal or next stop along one's life path.

LANDLADY will refer to an individual who provides shelter. This may not stand for a physical roof over one's head but rather shelter in the way of comfort, a sounding board, or counsel.

LAND LINE stands for grounded communications, clear and well-understood.

LANDLOCKED denotes a self-generated condition preventing access to higher concepts or advanced knowledge.

LANDMARK comes as a personal message for each dreamer. Recall what the landmark was. What state? Did it represent a specific historical site or time period? Did it pertain to a specific historical individual? In what condition was it?

LAND MINE reminds us to be always aware of the presence of pitfalls and setbacks that are hidden along our life path or spiritual search.

LANDSCAPE in dreams is a major symbol in itself. It sets the scene and often the mood as well. Always recall what the landscape was.

LANDSCAPE GARDENER See gardener.

LANDSLIDE advises of a backsliding condition.

LANE (country) connotes a pleasant phase of one's life journey.

LANE (highway) refers to single-mindedness.

LANE-SWITCHING stands for vacillation; indecision.

LANGUAGE in dreams will add another dimension to the overall symbology. Foreign accents, biblical verbiage, obscenity, specialized terms, etc., all reveal clues to correct interpretation along with the mood or tone of voice.

LANGUAGE BARRIER warns of ineffective communications.

LANGUAGE LABORATORY constitutes a personal effort to understand and fully comprehend higher knowledge.

LANKY usually defines efficiency; sticking to basics without adding anything extraneous.

LANOLIN advises of a need to smooth out or soften some type of roughness or hardness in one's life. This could be associated with insincerity, stubbornness, one-mindedness, etc.

LANTERN refers to more light being required on an issue or situation.

LAP (lick up) pertains to an eagerness to obtain something.

LAP (thighs) refers to a closeness; keeping something close to one.

LAP (track) connotes progression. What was the number of the last lap completed?

LAP BELT See safety belt.

LAPBOARD corresponds with efficient work habits; keeping the process convenient.

LAP DANCE represents the things in life that one wants but are out of reach, they're unobtainable, untouchable.

LAP DOG is a friend or close associate who is overly eager to give assistance. May also point to a sympathetic friend.

LAPEL will reveal one's quantitative ego. A few examples are below.

Clownish lapel portrays immaturity.

Designer lapel signifies arrogance.

Narrow lapel shows one who rarely thinks of self.

No lapel denotes an absence of any egotistical aspects.

Wide lapel indicates a large ego.

LAPEL PIN will reveal a specific sympathy one has for a cause.

LAPIDARY (study of) represents a desire for precision; exactness.

LAPIS LAZULI (gemstone) connotes deep interest or research into high spiritual concepts.

LAP ROBE illustrates a desire to keep good relationships.

LAPSED refers to a voluntary omission of something from one's life.

LAPTOP (computer) reveals a desire to have the convenience of information access at all times.

LAPWING (bird) stands for a spiritual cautiousness.

LARCENY See burglar.

LARCENY (grand) applies to the theft of a major element. This could be associated with the theft of one's identity, livelihood, good name, etc.

LARCH (tree) stands for the fragile state of balance one has caused inherent talents to be in.

LARD indicates a heavy coating; cover-up or embellishment.

LARDER See pantry.

LARGE PRINT (type) will usually come as an attention-getting element which suggests that one has been missing something.

LARIAT signifies an attempt to rope something in; get a handle on it; secure it.

LARK BUNTING (bird) stands for joy; heightened optimism.

LARKSPUR (botanical) implies spiritual talents that are generously shared.

LARVA reveals the beginning stage (gestation) of a negative aspect in one's life, possibly within oneself.

LARYNGITIS pertains to an inability to express oneself adequately, perhaps self-induced for psychological reasons.

LARYNX portrays one's expressiveness; whether or not inner emotions or attitudes are verbalized. Recall the condition of the larynx if a view was provided.

LASAGNA represents a multilevel relationship or situation; could also refer to some type of concept or idea one is absorbing.

LASER denotes consolidation or the condensing of multiple aspects into a single form.

LASER GUN advises of the wisdom to accurately target one's goal.

LASER PRINTER portrays a clear and sharp communication.

LASER SURGERY constitutes a step up from primitive thought or methods.

LASSIE epitomizes a friend's loyalty.

LASSO See lariat.

LAST (enduring) implies a perpetual state; will remain unchanged.

LAST (in line) suggests a need for patience or tolerance.

LAST (position) denotes an end to something.

LAST (say) See last word.

LAST-CALL RETURN stands for a desire or need to return to a conversation; a sign that an issue isn't over.

LAST JUDGMENT comes as a strong warning message that implies one has little time left to bring balance into one's life.

LAST LAUGH signifies one's opinion had been proven; a verification.

LAST MINUTE denotes a state of urgency.

LAST RITES rarely is a forewarning of death; it usually enters dreams as a strong warning to make reconciliations.

LAST STRAW advises one to become involved; take responsible action or intervention.

LAST SUPPER won't have anything to do with Christianity or Jesus, but will reveal the possibility of forthcoming tribulations to bravely face and overcome.

LAST WORD denotes a final opportunity to have one's way.

LAS VEGAS portrays indulgences; excesses; risks taken.

LATCH See lock.

LATCHKEY KID stands for self-reliance learned early in life.

LATE implies a time expectation that is not met or was originally unrealistic.

LATE BLOOMER signifies eventual realizations.

LATE CHARGE comes to advise that there will be a penalty or cost to not accomplishing something on schedule.

LATECOMER characterizes one who is slow to make realizations or decisions.

LATENT symbolizes the hidden aspects of self; those emotions or attitudes that are not openly expressed to others.

LATENT IMAGE reveals the presence of ulterior motives or attitudes.

LATEX See rubber.

LATHE relates to a life aspect that has the capability of accurately shaping or defining one's self-expression or goals.

LATHER applies to confusion; possible frustration or anger.

LATIN (Mass) represents an attraction/preference for religious traditions.

LATITUDE usually represents some form of freedom; no limitations.

LATRINE See bathroom.

LATTICEWORK stands for one's defenses that are not perceived by others.

LAUDANUM See opium.

LAUGHING GAS See nitrous oxide.

LAUGH SIGN (audience) stands for insincerity; manipulated responses.

LAUGHTER applies to a humorous situation or happiness. Recall who was doing the laughing. What was the quality of it? Sarcastic or genuine? What was being laughed at?

LAUGH TRACK reveals false happiness; an exterior presentation/response that differs from one's inner feelings; not insincerity, exactly, but rather an attempt to hide real feelings.

LAUNCH PAD connotes a need to get something off the ground; put something into action.

LAUNCH WINDOW stands for a critical span of time or phase when a particular behavior or beginning moves can be made.

LAUNDROMAT emphasizes some type of cleansing is required. Surrounding dreamscape details will usually clarify what this is.

LAUNDRY alludes to a specific item in one's life that needs cleaning up. Refer to specific clothing items for further clarification.

LAUNDRY LIST comes as a reminder of things to accomplish and not forget about.

LAUREL (tree) exemplifies honor and praise; having the emotional sensitivity to recognize another's good works.

LAVA warns of a personal state of inner turmoil before self-confidence is gained. This symbol calls for a release of these withheld emotions or attitudes so that they can be replaced with inner strength.

LAVATORY See bathroom.

LAVENDER (color/flower/scent) portrays a gentle, comforting spiritual belief; spiritual wisdom and the peace it bestows.

LAW (study of) represents a high interest in societal perimeters. Frequently this symbol will refer to spiritual or moral issues.

LAW BOOK comes in a dream as an advisement to check the legality/rightness of a particular attitude/behavior/plan.

LAWLESSNESS warns of a disregard for authority.

LAWN See grass.

LAWN (fabric) connotes aloofness.

LAWN CHAIR represents an opportunity to gain blessings of leisure from nature; a chance to gain tranquility from easily accessible, natural sources.

LAWN EDGER implies a perfectionist; a tendency to attend to every loose end. May point to a perfectionist who can't stand anything being out of place.

LAWN MOWER (manual) characterizes an individual who expends greater efforts to *avoid* advancement (growth) than the work to attain it would take.

LAWN MOWER (powered) applies to someone who has an *automatic* reaction toward anything leading to one's personal growth and advancement—effortless denial.

LAWSUIT pertains to a demand for retribution; forcing justice or judgment.

LAWYER See attorney.

LAXATIVE advises of a need to rid self of some type of negative aspect.

LAY-AWAY PLAN signifies impatience. It may point to working for what one wants in life.

LAYERED (clothing) doesn't refer to a homeless person, it indicates a preparedness for any eventuality; an eye on possibilities.

LAYERED (haircut) implies one who keeps thoughts trimmed, thereby preventing an accumulation of extraneous, inconsequential factors; sticking to the basics.

LAYING ON OF HANDS represents good intentions.

LAYOFF connotes a forced termination of one's current work or path efforts; involuntary path setback.

LAYOUT (visual arrangement) most often enters a dream as a personal message. It will reveal a specific plan, solution, or condition relating to the dreamer. Was the layout confusing? Was it sharp and vivid? Was it pleasing to the eye?

LAYOVER implies a temporary setback; a delay in one's plans; a need to readjust one's timing.

LAZARUS (biblical) exemplifies the technical capabilities of interdimensionality comprising true Reality.

LAZULITE (gemstone) stands for spiritual awareness.

LAZY EYE stands for an inability to focus on one particular issue; may also refer to the skill of being able to simultaneously see both sides of an issue.

LAZY SUSAN depicts convenience.

LEA See meadow.

LEACH implies a dilution or breaking down of something; suggests that one is too fanatical or zealous and needs tempering.

LEACH (parasite) reveals a dependency on others. Who was the leach on? Who was it associated with?

LEACH FIELD stands for disbursement of residual elements.

LEAD (graphite) See pencil.

LEAD (guide) refers to someone who is capable of showing the way; guidance.

LEAD (lure) warns of being deceived, manipulated.

LEAD (metal) illustrates a potential negative aspect in one's life that could cause harmful effects.

LEAD (possibility) suggests possible options/openings/chances.

LEAD (precede) usually signifies a messenger.

LEAD (primary) will designate a paramount concept, individual, or event.

LEAD (tether) See leash.

LEADER BOARD reveals one's progress; may also point to a situation of competition.

LEAD FOOT is a dreamscape element which reveals recklessness; a need to slow down.

LEAD-FREE signifies an element in one's life which is free of a particular negative one has been concerned about or trying to avoid coming into contact with.

LEAD-IN represents broaching an issue or the beginning moves to reveal a specific attitude.

LEADING INDICATORS will come in a dreamscape to forewarn of certain situations or attitudes that are developing; hints to what's approaching.

LEADING LADY will refer to one who is the main player in a situation; may reveal who holds the reins.

LEADING QUESTION stands for behavior intended to discover information.

LEAD POISONING pertains to the harmful effects of a negative aspect in one's life.

LEAD-TIME suggests a need for more preparation; denotes a time extension required.

LEAD WEIGHT equates to a heavy burden. This may refer to guilt or a current responsibility.

LEAF (botanical) symbolizes natural abilities; natural talents.

LEAF BLOWER comes as an advisement to give greater attention to one's inherent talents. This symbol points to a nonchalant attitude bordering on apathy.

LEAFHOPPER (insect) warns of the presence of one's own attitude or other individual who behaves in a manner which destroys one's efforts; eating away the beneficial results of one's work or good intentions; self-defeating attitudes.

LEAFLET See brochure.

LEAF MOLD represents the creation of a fertile or fruitful condition.

LEAF RAKE See rake (leaf).

LEAGUE (association) pertains to a specific tie to another; having like interests.

LEAGUE (class) reveals a stage one is at. What level was indicated?

LEAGUE (measurement) will correspond with one's level of spiritual attainment; a deeper depth denotes a higher advancement level.

LEAGUE OF NATIONS advises of an ineffective or meaningless title or representation.

LEAK will indicate a loss of whatever the leak is associated with. Was the leak a slow drip or a flowing type? See below for some examples.

> **Alcoholic beverage container leak** reveals an improvement in one's ability to face problems.

> **Gas leak (gasoline)** points to reduced energy; dwindling motivation.

> **Gas leak (natural/propane)** refers to a reduction of supportive elements that powered one's steadily advancing pace.

> **Hydraulic line leak** means that one is doing something to make progress more difficult to achieve; someone is making life harder.

> **Milk carton leak** could indicate a lessening of one's immaturity, or losing some form of nourishment which usually refers to emotional aspects.

> **Oil leak** points to increasing friction, usually associated with one's stress level. May mean friction between the dreamer and another person.

> **Toilet bowl leak** pertains to something the dreamer is doing to hamper the natural release of stress.

> **Water leak** stands for a dwindling of spiritual attitudes/behavior.

LEAK (of information) See informant.

LEAK PROOF connotes a secure condition or status.

LEAN (meat) refers to an absence of extraneous elements. This may pertain to one's lifestyle or belief system.

LEANING (angled stance) reveals a slanted perspective; nonchalance or indifference.

LEANING (dependency) represents a need for some type of support system.

LEANING (propensity) indicates a near-decision.

LEAN TIMES stand for a phase when things are more difficult.

LEAN-TO See shed.

LEAPFROG illustrates competition; continual one-upmanship.

LEAPING implies rapid progression; making great strides in advancement. It may also suggest a need to slow down in order to stop missing important elements that require notice or actual attention.

LEAP SECOND advises one to accept the timing of events unfolding along one's path; don't attempt to speed things up or hold them back.

LEAP YEAR indicates an adjustment to one's personal timing needs to be made. This suggests that one is going too fast or too slow.

LEARNING will validate one's inner questioning as to whether or not one is progressing or acquiring additional knowledge. This symbol denotes an affirmative answer.

LEARNING DISABILITY advises of a learning capability level. It counsels one to cease being frustrated or angry at not being able to understand certain concepts. It emphasizes the importance of operating within one's individual and unique framework.

LEASE represents an extension of time. Recall what the specific time was.

LEASH stands for self-imposed limitations.

LEATHER reveals one's manner of interaction with others. The key is whether this dream leather was soft and supple or hard and brittle.

LEATHER (patent) See patent leather.

LEATHERBACK TURTLE symbolizes eternal spiritual truths.

LEATHERETTE connotes an ability to forge ahead in the face of setbacks or problematical situations; being able to utilize substitutes; creativity.

LEATHER WORK exemplifies one's individualized, uniquely personal manner of relating to others.

LEAVEN See brewer's yeast.

LEAVE OF ABSENCE alludes to a personal need for rest or diversity.

LECHERY reveals an individual who is not spiritually aware or advanced.

LECTERN implies a need to communicate.

LECTURE will be an individualized symbol unique to each dreamer. Recall what the lecture was about. This will have personal meaning.

LEDERHOSEN relates to perseverance.

LEDGE signifies a precarious situation or relationship.

LEDGER displays one's life debits and assets; a behavioral balance sheet.

LEECH signifies a freeloader; one who lacks self-respect and personal responsibility.

LEEK represents a counter force to negativity.

LEERING reveals an ulterior motive.

LEERY means distrust.

LEFT (directional position) characterizes diversification; a shift away from rigid, established perceptions or traditions.

LEFT-BRAIN pertains to a control or dominance over the establishment; a convincing power.

LEFT FIELD connotes new ideas; difficult to accept concepts; may also reveal a perspective that's way off-track.

LEFT-HANDED means ambiguous; perplexing statements or situations; tactless or cryptic.

LEFTOVERS advise one to utilize one's total potential.

LEFT WING points to an open mind; tolerance; liberal perspectives; loves raising one's head to see what's outside the box; tending toward empathy for other's misfortune.

LEG denotes a supportive aspect in one's life. In what condition was this dream symbol? Was it strong or weak?

LEGACY constitutes that which we leave behind for others to benefit from or that which has been left for us by others.

LEGAL AID implies everyone's inherent right to justice.

LEGAL AIDE characterizes a person who is capable of helping another get justice.

LEGALESE stands for a form of communication which one can't follow/understand without further explanations.

LEGAL HOLIDAY See specific holiday.

LEGAL PAD indicates a need to make notes regarding a negative situation in one's life; note the chain of events.

LEGEND (myth) relates to basic facts or underlying truths; referencing an actual event.

LEGEND (symbol code) will usually reveal a key to solving some life problem; could provide an inspirational idea.

LEGGINGS refer to self-protective measures one uses.

LEGION portrays a multitude.

LEGIONNAIRE connotes an individual who belongs to a large group; someone who has a strong backing.

LEGIONNAIRES' DISEASE indicates the presence of a hidden, potentially harmful negative aspect in one's life.

LEGISLATOR pertains to one who places restrictions on others.

LEGITIMIZE illustrates an act that rectifies wrongdoings; something brought into balance once again.

LEG ROOM stands for a need for space; alludes to a pressure or stressed state.

LEGUME See pea.

LEG WARMERS emphasize a personal concern and efforts taken to insure one's progression isn't hampered.

LEGWORK corresponds with research; a need for gathering more information.

LEISTER See spear.

LEISURE (time) usually exemplifies the importance of taking mental and physical rest time from one's work or path advancement.

LEISURE WEAR connotes an informal situation or relationship.

LEMMING warns against a tendency to be the follower of another rather than traveling a personal path; a lack of individuality and/or personal thought.

LEMON (color/fruit) constitutes bitterness or indicates a state of perpetual troubles.

LEMON DROP signifies thought applied to a currently troublesome issue/situation.

LEMON LAW connotes a life aspect that has the capability to break one's stream of consistent troubles.

LEMON OIL stands for an attempt to cover up one's troubles (making something smell better); denial; diversionary tactics.

LEMON VERBENA (botanical) signifies a natural talent/skill which attracts others.

LEMONWOOD represents an element with multi-use aspects.

LEMUR illustrates enigmatic aspects; difficult to understand situations or concepts; indistinct, ghostly facets in one's life.

LEMURIA See Atlantis.

LEND represents helpfulness or assistance given to another.

LENGTHEN connotes an extension of some type being done or required.

LENIENT exemplifies forgiveness; making allowances.

LENS signifies personal perception. The key is to recall the condition of the dream lens. Was it cracked? Clean or dirty? Was there a coloration to it? If so, what color?

LENS COVER advises of a state of blindness; perceptual aberrations.

LENT warns against setting aside an official or traditionally designated time for self-examination. This should be a *daily* exercise.

LENTILS allude to time-tested aspects that emotionally or spiritually nourish.

LEOPARD symbolizes a resistance to change.

LEOTARD connotes perseverance; inner strength; a second skin.

LEPER pertains to strength of character; tenacity in spite of adversities.

LEPRECHAUN typifies hidden facets of spiritual development; wisdom.

LESBIAN won't usually have a sexual connotation but rather reveal a close camaraderie between women friends; may also point to a feministic perspective.

LESION pertains to a life irritation that one has allowed to get under the skin; a lack of acceptance.

LESSON PLAN represents a tendency toward systematic learning; taking one step at a time.

LESSONS come as a specific message for each dreamer. The lesson needs to be taken to heart.

LETDOWN signifies a disappointment; advises against expectations.

LETHAL denotes a highly dangerous aspect in one's life.

LETHARGY most often reveals a depressive state; lack of motivation or faith.

LETTER implies correspondence needed. Frequently this will serve as a personal message for the dreamer.

LETTER (varsity) pertains to an individual accomplishment.

LETTER BOMB exemplifies a devastating communication or revelation.

LETTERBOX See mailbox.

LETTER CARRIER refers to an individual who conveys a message; a messenger.

LETTERHEAD connotes a message that

points out importance for the dreamer. What did the dreamscape letterhead say? Was the lettering a specific color? Style of type?

LETTER OF CREDIT reveals one's level of responsibility. Was the letter a good or bad report?

LETTER OF INTENT signifies an insured or sealed promise; guaranteeing one's intention or an agreement.

LETTUCE represents the need to clear up a misunderstanding in one's life.

LEVEE connotes the purposeful directing of one's spiritual path.

LEVEL (ground) corresponds with a time frame when one's life path is relatively smooth.

LEVEL (tool) denotes stability and balance; a desire for same.

LEVER corresponds with an advantage.

LEVIATHAN relates to a great size or amount. Surrounding dreamscape details will clarify what this refers to.

LEWDNESS reveals a lack of spiritual development; a preoccupation with the physical world.

LEWIS (Meriwether) characterizes fortitude.

LEY LINE portrays a field or course of flowing energy and refers to a path lit with high energy and good probabilities for success.

LHASA pertains to high spiritual aspects; acquired deep spiritual wisdom.

LHASA APSO (dog breed) denotes a friend who can give support.

LIAISON indicates a connecting aspect. Surrounding dreamscape details will clarify this for the dreamer.

LIBERAL characterizes a free-thinker; not confined by limitation or tradition.

LIBERAL ARTS symbolizes extensive general knowledge.

LIBERATION defines a state of freedom; release from limitations. Often one needs to liberate self.

LIBERTY BELL stands for our civil liberties. This symbol will mean something different for each dreamer.

LIBIDO as a dream symbol usually denotes personal motivation; one's mental and emotional strength.

LIBRARIAN corresponds with an individual who has the capability of guiding one's direction for gaining deeper knowledge.

LIBRARY relates to a multitude of opportunities to extend one's knowledge.

LIBRARY CARD represents the easy availability of information without personal cost.

LIBRARY EDITION (book) will usually point to a popular title/subject matter and the dream symbol may be pointing out an issue which is common knowledge.

LIBRARY OF CONGRESS refers to a wealth of information; a source for further learning or research; the acknowledgment of one's sole right to claim ownership of an original idea.

LIBRARY TABLE suggests that more research/study is required.

LICE reveal an unhealthy state of being.

LICENSE (any type) emphasizes one's credentials/permission/entitlement or legal right.

LICHEN refers to a fertile atmosphere; a bountiful condition.

LICORICE connotes mobility; a motivational factor.

LID (cover) applies to a limit marker; a cap on quantity.

LID (quantity) implies something that's within legal bounds.

LIE (untruth) reveals hidden facets of an individual; a concealed aspect of self.

LIE DETECTOR See polygraph.

LIE-IN (protest) denotes efforts expended toward personal activism; a vehement protest.

LIEN represents a spiritual debt to be paid before further advancement can be accomplished.

LIEUTENANT GOVERNOR will usually point to the possibility of tandem power; an individual who has a strong possibility of being in control.

LIFEBLOOD refers to one's driving force.

LIFEBOAT stands for something that spiritually rescues or saves one.

LIFEGUARD characterizes a savior-type individual in one's life; someone who can rescue a situation or provide a way out of a troublesome problem.

LIFE INSURANCE advises of a state of fear; a lack of faith.

LIFE JACKET See life preserver.

LIFELESS portrays a lack of spirit; motivation; loss of energy or will.

LIFE LINE signifies a life aspect that keeps one grounded; a facet that gives hope or acceptance.

LIFE PRESERVER corresponds with a second chance.

LIFE RAFT implies a spiritual belief that keeps one afloat.

LIFESAVER (candy) will literally make an implication of something needed to save a

situation or reputation. It will denote a life-saving aspect for the dreamer. Note the color.

LIFE-SUPPORT SYSTEM emphasizes an essential supporting factor in one's life.

LIFE TENANT signifies a permanent relationship.

LIFTOFF denotes an activated beginning.

LIFT TRUCK symbolizes a work/time-saving element in one's life.

LIGAMENT defines an essential bond or connection in one's life.

LIGHT refers to good perception; added information; understanding.

LIGHT (weight) implies simplicity; general knowledge; easily understood or learned.

LIGHT BULB stands for a new thought; inspiration; sudden awareness.

LIGHT DUTY comes in dreams as an advisement to cut back on the level of efforts expended. This symbol may also refer to stressors and indicate the need for more acceptance.

LIGHTENING (color) This symbol can be referring to several aspects in one's life. It can be associated with hair lightening which would be a call to lighten up on one's thoughts and attitudes, or it could refer to workload or behavior which would be depicted by various activities such as repainting one's office or home walls with a lighter color.

LIGHTER pertains to illuminating factors in one's life; motivators.

LIGHTER FLUID As with any incendiary type of symbol, this equates to a flammable element in one's life which has the potential to spark an emotional or situational explosion. This, naturally, calls for extreme caution.

LIGHT-FOOTED indicates a cautious progression; a reluctance to interfere in another's life; awareness.

LIGHTHEADED can refer to a state of being overwhelmed or it may indicate a frivolous personality who has no handle on reality or responsibility.

LIGHTHEARTED reveals a state of acceptance in one's heart.

LIGHTHOUSE connotes spiritual guidance through wisdom.

LIGHT INFANTRY stands for a problem which doesn't require a heavy-duty solution.

LIGHT METER See exposure meter.

LIGHT-MINDED stands for a lack of seriousness; one who focuses on frivolous issues.

LIGHTNING signifies a connection with spiritual forces; may indicate a forthcoming moment of inspiration or an epiphany.

LIGHTNING ROD implies a desire to connect with spiritual forces; an active attempt to open communication with the Divine.

LIGHT PLANE represents cursory thoughts applied to an issue.

LIGHT PROOF warns of a self-imposed state of ignorance.

LIGHTSHIP emphasizes a life aspect that serves to warn one away from destructive or grossly misleading spiritual ideas.

LIGHT SHOW sheds light on that which one should give attention to or something one should avoid. This is a call to attention or a warning, depending on other clarifying dream details.

LIGHT TABLE points to an aspect in one's life that is capable of shedding light on issues or attitudes which are below the surface.

LIGHT THERAPY designates the power of knowledge, acceptance, and tolerance.

LIGHTWEIGHT (person) characterizes one who is ineffective or of lesser importance.

LIGHT-YEAR defines a great distance removed from something; a long, long time away; sometime in the far, distant future.

LIKENESS applies to false appearance; something that appears like another.

LILAC (botanical/color/scent) represents spiritual purity.

LILITH (Hebrew folklore) characterizes an independent and free-thinking woman.

LILLIPUTIAN pertains to something of little consequence; trivial; may also reveal an inferiority complex.

LILY (flower) stands for innocence and purity; a new birth.

LILY OF THE VALLEY (botanical/scent) connotes a delicate naïveté; a lack of worldly experience.

LILY PADS indicate the fruits of spiritual work and expression, especially if they've bloomed.

LIMBER emphasizes tenacity; resourcefulness; acceptance.

LIMBO (religious dogma) connotes a state of inactivity; ineffectiveness; inaction. It may also pertain to a phase when one remains in neutral until opinions or perceptions are well formed.

LIMBO (dance) suggests a need to go the extra mile, bend over backwards.

LIME (color/fruit/scent) illustrates a negative emotion; bitterness.

LIME (mineral) See quicklime.

LIMEADE symbolizes the ingestion of a bitter aspect; having to accept a negative element.

LIMELIGHT may reveal one's attitude of superiority or it may point out someone to whom one should listen. Surrounding dream details will clarify which meaning this symbol was giving.

LIMERICK (verse) although often frivolous, will usually bring a personal message.

LIMESTONE corresponds with a foundation type of belief or attitude.

LIMIT implies boundaries or restrictions.

LIMIT (speed) See road signs.

LIMITED EDITION typifies something of higher value.

LIMITLESS relates to total freedom; permission to go or reach as far as possible.

LIMIT SWITCH represents the same as a safety valve—it prevents something from exceeding its limits.

LIMOUSINE alludes to an obsession with appearances; a preoccupation with self.

LIMP (flimsy) reveals a lack of inner strength; a defeatist.

LIMP (hobble) denotes perseverance.

LIMPET refers to one who receives inner strength and nourishment from spiritual aspects.

LINCOLN (Abraham) represents integrity.

LINCOLN (Memorial) symbolizes all that one can be proud of in a people or nation.

LINEAGE stands for an alignment of some type. Surrounding dreamscape details will clarify this for the dreamer.

LINEAR stands for an alignment of some type. May possibly point to a time when no advancement is being made, usually for a reason.

LINEAR PERSPECTIVE reveals a false perspective of time and distance. This indicates that the dreamer has a fear that a goal will take a long time to accomplish.

LINEBACKER pertains to one's backup or secondary defenses.

LINE DANCE warns against a tendency toward having to stay in step with everyone else. This comes to advise of the need for independent thought.

LINEMAN characterizes an individual in one's life who has the capability to restore another's strength or reconnecting a line of communication.

LINEN (bed sheets) signifies one's moral/ethical behavior.

LINEN (fabric) usually indicates a rigid personality.

LINEN CLOSET represents ethical and tolerant behavior. Was the closet full of fresh linen or empty?

LINE OF CREDIT See credit line (monetary).

LINE OF FIRE will usually come as a warning that one is in the way of another's conflict and may get hurt if one doesn't remove oneself from the issue.

LINE OF SCRIMMAGE marks a conflict demarcation between differing perspectives, attitudes, or opinions.

LINER See lining.

LINER (ocean) See cruise.

LINEUP connotes those associated with one another in some way.

LINGER may refer to a delay or it may indicate a persistent nature.

LINGERIE See underwear.

LINGUIST characterizes an individual who has exceptional communication skills.

LINIMENT portrays that which soothes life's more difficult times.

LINING signifies an insulating or protective shield.

LINK corresponds with a connective factor in one's life. This will directly refer to a specific aspect in the dreamer's life.

LINOLEUM suggests a hardness to one's current life. The dreamer will recognize what this refers to.

LINSEED OIL alludes to protective characteristics one uses.

LINSEY-WOOLSEY (fabric) See homespun.

LINT advises one to get actively involved in ridding self of stagnating extraneous life aspects such as attitudes, opinions, and narrow perspectives.

LINTEL reveals the strength or rightness of one's new direction. Did the lintel appear sturdy or thin and weak? Was anything decorating it?

LION relates to a braggart. May also imply strength of character.

LIONFISH denotes spiritual arrogance; self-righteousness.

LIONHEARTED exemplifies a courageous individual or action.

LIP See mouth.

LIP BALM relates to an attempt or desire to keep one's communications from being harsh.

LIPOSUCTION reveals the fact that one requires assistance in getting rid of the extraneous aspects in life.

LIP READING typifies hidden meanings in what others say.

LIP SERVICE denotes false intentions.

LIPSTICK will denote inner personality traits. Was it a deep, dark color or a light shade? Tending toward brown?

LIP-SYNCHING signifies a tendency to imitate the words or perspectives of others; a lack of individualized thought.

LIQUEFACTION (of soil) warns one is not on firm ground.

LIQUEUR See alcoholic beverage.

LIQUID See specific type.

LIQUIDATE suggests a need to unload superficial aspects in one's life. This may refer to emotional, mental, spiritual, or materialistic factors.

LIQUOR See alcoholic beverage.

LISP reveals an inability to verbalize one's thoughts accurately.

LIST advises of a need to remember details; infers forgetfulness.

LIST (ship movement) denotes spiritual imbalance; a spiritually precarious position in the form of an attitude, perspective, or belief.

LISTENING DEVICE signifies an intent to spy; things aren't as private/secret as one thought.

LISTENING POST stands for an intent to listen well; may point to an equivalent of spying, being overly nosey.

LISTLESS may denote a lack of motivation or it may indicate a state of apathy.

LIST PRICE usually represents something placed at the highest price according to what the market will bear. This is an advisement that that something, though having value, can be gotten at a far lesser price.

LITANY suggests remembrance; may warn against an unforgiving nature.

LITERATI suggest those who are perceived as intellectuals, yet may not have an ounce of logic or common sense.

LITERATURE will reveal an important message for each dreamer. Recall what type of literature was represented.

LITHE connotes tenacity; endurance and perseverance.

LITHOGRAPH alludes to an ability to keep different aspects separate in life.

LITMUS PAPER will refer to a life aspect that has the capability of gauging honesty or the rightness of something.

LITMUS TEST indicates an act of verification; concluding proof.

LITTER (bed) implies laziness or a disinterest in physical comforts.

LITTER (offspring) portrays multiple new ideas.

LITTER (refuse) pertains to mental or emotional confusion.

LITTERBAG signifies orderly thought processes; a recognition/discernment regarding the value of ideas.

LITTERBUG refers to an individual who broadcasts meaningless ideas.

LITTLE (size) will denote a small amount of something, but usually will also indicate greater importance.

LITTLE DIPPER reminds us that small spiritual works should be a continual aspect in our lives.

LITTLE FINGER relates to the smaller aspects of self that help to create the whole character.

LITTLE RED RIDING HOOD characterizes misplaced trust; misjudgment.

LITTLE THEATER connotes experimental methods of manipulation.

LITTLE TOE pertains to a personal aspect that adds to one's stability or the creation of proper balance in one's life.

LITURGY cautions against spiritual formality.

LIVE-IN denotes a surface association with someone; may extend the meaning to also include a personal relationship.

LIVELIHOOD won't necessarily correspond to one's awake-state career. This symbol will usually reveal a hidden aspect of one's character.

LIVER illustrates fortitude.

LIVER DISEASE warns against giving up, losing motivation or faith.

LIVER SPOT represents hard work and hardships one has endured through life.

LIVER TRANSPLANT See transplant (liver).

LIVERWURST denotes a life factor that serves to energize or motivate others.

LIVESTOCK See specific type.

LIVE WIRE reveals erratic, uncontrolled energies.

LIVING FOSSIL represents an enduring element.

LIVING ROOM depicts one's attitudes toward daily life. Recall the color, how it was decorated and furnished. Was it tidy or cluttered?

LIVING WILL signifies an understanding of death or a futile situation.

LIZARD connotes a lack of scruples.

LLAMA will correspond to one who has the capability of easing another's burden.

LOADING ZONE signifies a point in one's

life when extra responsibilities become a priority to attend to.

LOAD LIMIT/LINE will usually refer to the amount of stress or work one can take on.

LOAF (lazy) pertains to disinterest.

LOAF (shape) usually implies a type of inner benefit or nourishment.

LOAFERS (shoes) represent a lack of direction.

LOAM depicts a fertile situation or condition; bountiful ground one is currently on.

LOAN applies to a temporary stopgap solution.

LOAN COMMITMENT refers to a promise to give aid.

LOAN OFFICER characterizes one who is capable of helping with another's problem; one who can provide another with the resources to attain a goal.

LOAN SHARK reveals self-gain through negative methods.

LOATHING defines a personal aversion. This may reveal another's inner attitude that is not externalized in a public manner.

LOBBY (persuade) is an attempt to sway one's opinion.

LOBBY (room) refers to neutral ground.

LOBELIA (botanical/scent) stands for an emotionally calming aspect.

LOBSTER advises of a tendency to grab at any new idea or concept. This symbol is a call for discernment.

LOBSTER POT denotes a controlling factor that curbs one's tendency to accept fad ideologies.

LOCAL ANESTHETIC See anesthetic (local).

LOCAL COLOR adds important clues to each individual's dream. Recall all the facets that were represented.

LOCH NESS MONSTER stands for possibilities.

LOCK emphasizes a secure aspect. Depending on surrounding dreamscape details, this symbol may reveal a need to unlock something.

LOCK (hair) stands for personally treasured aspects of another.

LOCK (water) signifies an adjustment to one's spiritual level.

LOCKBOX (Realtor's) applies to the fact that only certain individuals with the code can gain access to something.

LOCK-DOWN equates to confinement, usually for one's own safety.

LOCKED (interest rate) signifies a guaranteed position.

LOCKED (Website) means a protected, safe communication.

LOCKER relates to one's private aspects.

LOCKER ROOM symbolizes an opportunity to alter (change) one's attitude/opinion/behavior.

LOCKET corresponds to cherished relationships.

LOCKJAW See tetanus.

LOCKSMITH characterizes one who can solve problems. This person should be you. Every problem contains its own solution key.

LOCOMOTIVE See train.

LOCOWEED exemplifies a life factor that generates mental or emotional confusion brought on by experiencing aspects in life having the duality of positive and negative elements.

LOCUST warns against something in one's life that has the potential to destroy spiritual belief systems.

LODE symbolizes a bountiful aspect or supply.

LODESTAR defines a guiding force or light.

LODESTONE indicates a strong attraction; a compelling force or drive.

LODGE refers to a safe haven.

LODGED implies a temporarily immovable situation; a time of inaction or neutrality.

LODGEPOLE PINE connotes that which one can build on or with; aspects that serve as building blocks or forces; tenacity generated from spiritual convictions.

LODGER See live-in.

LOFT denotes high-minded attitudes.

LOG See journal; logbook.

LOG (wood) suggests potential opportunity.

LOGANBERRY See blackberry (fruit).

LOGBOOK advises of a need to keep a record of events.

LOGGER See lumberjack.

LOGGERHEAD TURTLE denotes spiritual narrow-mindedness.

LOGISTICS indicate a need to give attention to planning detail.

LOGJAM reveals mental or emotional confusion in association with spiritual beliefs.

LOGO will be a sign having diverse interpretations for each dreamer.

LOG ON (Internet) signifies an intention to communicate with someone or do research.

LOGOS stands for the word of the Divine Essence.

LOINCLOTH represents a basic need.

LOITERING implies a lack of purpose; apathy.

LOLLIPOP See sucker (candy).

LONELY usually indicates a lack of companionship and, in some cases, may point to having a perspective few others share or are willing to accept.

LONELY-HEARTS CLUB signifies a lack of companionship; a reaching out. This symbol may also reveal a bid for sympathy; wanting a "pity party."

LONE RANGER applies to a desire to work individually.

LONE WOLF characterizes one who works best alone; one who walks a uniquely individualized path.

LONG (length) connotes a great measure of time or distance in association with a particular aspect in one's life.

LONG ARM reveals an individual or issue which has a long reach—it can affect many and have multiple ramifications.

LONGBOW pertains to directness; honesty.

LONG DISTANCE (call) advises of a need to reconnect with someone the dreamer has been out of touch with.

LONG DISTANCE (runner) signifies endurance, determination.

LONG DIVISION refers to something which takes a bit longer time to figure out.

LONGEVITY reveals a lasting element in one's life.

LONG FACE signifies either sadness or disappointment.

LONG HAIR illustrates analytical thought; mental exploration; complex contemplation.

LONG HAUL relates to determination.

LONG HOUSE portrays an accommodating nature; acceptance of others.

LONGITUDE denotes a measure of acceptance or patience.

LONG JOHNS illustrate preparedness.

LONG JOHN SILVER characterizes manipulative arrogance.

LONG JUMP reveals an advancement; a great progression.

LONG-RANGE pertains to something that will cause extended or multiple resulting effects.

LONG RUN (play) simply means extreme popularity. The key here is to recall the title of the play, that's what will be the clue to the symbol's intent.

LONG RUN (time) refers to benefits reaped after an extended amount of time; a plan which will take a longer period of time to manifest its rewards.

LONGSHOREMEN illustrate the use of one's spiritual aspects. Were goods being shipped out? Incoming? Busy dock? Empty?

LONG SHOT typifies the taking of a great chance; a small probability of success.

LONG SUIT corresponds with one's best quality; greatest talent.

LONG-TERM emphasizes a commitment.

LONG-WINDED stands for redundancy; repetitiveness; a tendency to prolong one's point.

LOOFAH (sponge) indicates a need to perceive with greater depth.

LOOK-A-LIKE portrays one who imitates you; may reveal one's alter-ego.

LOOKING (behind you) reveals a sense of insecurity or paranoia; may point to distrust.

LOOKING (down) implies defeat or embarrassment.

LOOKING (in) denotes in-depth thought or deeper curiosity.

LOOKING (out) refers to awareness.

LOOKING (over) exemplifies discernment.

LOOKING (past) indicates a far-reaching perspective.

LOOKING (under) symbolizes perceptual depth.

LOOKING (up) signifies acceptance and progression.

LOOKING GLASS See mirror.

LOOKOUT represents watchfulness; a personal awareness.

LOOM connotes multiple elements that are woven into a whole issue or aspect.

LOON denotes mental or emotional confusion or convoluted thought processes.

LOOPHOLE implies a conniving nature.

LOOSE usually refers to extra room or leeway.

LOOSE CANNON illustrates unpredictability; irresponsibility; untrustworthy.

LOOSE CLOTHING signifies an open mind; open to new ideas.

LOOSE END corresponds to something that is left unfinished.

LOOT refers to a multitude of valuables. Recall surrounding dream details to determine whether or not this symbol was a positive one.

LOOTER indicates a lack of positive, individual resourcefulness; gaining from the efforts of others.

LOPE refers to a steady progression or advancement.

LOPSIDED typifies a dream symbol that means slanted opinions or perceptions.

LORE See folklore.

LORELEI (German legend) symbolizes false spiritual lures.

LOSER alludes to a temporary setback; may refer to a lack of foresight or insight.

LOST alludes to a state of despondency; a time of self-doubt and insecurity.

LOT (land) represents one's chosen destiny. Recall surrounding dream details for further clarity.

LOTHARIO characterizes a manipulative personality; ulterior motives; a deceiver.

LOTION denotes a soothing aspect; a factor that smoothes out a rough situation or relationship.

LOTTERY connotes a tendency to take chances that have little potential for success.

LOTTERY TICKET stands for a possibility, but a long shot.

LOTUS (botanical) pertains to spiritual sacredness.

LOTUS-EATER (Greek mythology) reveals a spiritually unaware individual; an inability to perceive reality; lacking personal responsibility.

LOUD (sound) may be a call to attention or it may indicate unawareness.

LOUDMOUTH indicates one who must be the center of attention in order to feel any measure of self-worth.

LOUDSPEAKER emphasizes a message unique to each dreamer. What words came over the dream loudspeaker?

LOUISIANA suggests one's uniquely uncommon characteristics and the celebration of them.

LOUNGE (room) relates to a designated time to pause or relax.

LOUNGE CHAIR usually points to a lack of motivation.

LOUNGEWEAR stands for a relaxed attitude; an easy-going personality.

LOUPE suggests a need for closer inspection; deeper analyzation.

LOURDES connotes misinterpretation; false perception; illusion.

LOUSE See lice.

LOUSEWORT (botanical) reveals self-created problems; suggests greater acceptance and perseverance.

LOUVER See shutter (window).

LOVE corresponds to feelings of great fondness; cherished.

LOVE BEADS suggest independent thought; individuality.

LOVEBIRD stands for companionship; an appreciation of others.

LOVE CHILD rarely points to an actual child but rather indicates a new beginning or idea brought on by or shared with another.

LOVE FEAST/FEST signifies a celebration of camaraderie.

LOVE-IN refers to a lighthearted gathering of those sharing the same sense of freedom toward self-expression.

LOVE KNOT points to one's symbol of affection for another.

LOVE-LIES-BLEEDING (botanical) designates a state of being heartbroken.

LOVELOCK (hair) points to love's mementos; the remembrance of a cherished relationship.

LOVELORN symbolizes the empty feeling which comes from a sense/perception of not being loved or appreciated.

LOVE NEST stands for a specific place, situation, or element of one's life where a very special relationship exists.

LOVE POTION not only stands for a strong desire to be loved but also a willingness to go to any lengths to achieve that goal; a forced/manipulated attraction.

LOVERS denote our loving nature. Recall what the lovers were doing for further clarification. Were they fighting? Snuggling? Strolling along a shoreline?

LOVERS' LANE advises of a time and place for the expression of affection.

LOVERS' LEAP points to a despair or great disappointment stemming from an unsuccessful close relationship.

LOVE SEAT signifies a situation or condition directly associated with two specific individuals. This symbol won't usually refer to the idea of love, but will be more likely pointing to a close situational relationship with another.

LOVESICK warns of a lack of emotional control; loss of awareness and focus.

LOVE SONG will indicate one's expressed depth of affection.

LOVING CUP signifies one's token of affection/high esteem.

LOW-BALL symbolizes an underestimation.

LOW BEAM (light) usually calls for the need of more light on a subject; greater perspective is required for an accurate view.

LOWBORN denotes humility.

LOWBOY exemplifies a multitude of extenuating factors existing just out of one's current perceptual view.

LOWBROW characterizes an individual with a tendency to avoid intellectual issues/pursuits.

LOW-BUDGET signifies an attained goal which was fairly easy to manifest, especially in respect to few resources or little energy involved.

LOW-DENSITY connotes conceptual simplicity.

LOWERCLASSMAN See underclassmen.

LOWER WORLD (mythology) See underworld.

LOW FREQUENCY indicates easily understood ideas.

LOW GEAR refers to a slow pace or progression.

LOW-KEY symbolizes a private individual; humility; one who tends to keep out of the public eye; a possible introvert.

LOWLAND denotes a relatively level path or phase of one's development.

LOW-LEVEL implies basics; beginning phase.

LOWLIFE reveals an unethical or immoral character.

LOW PRESSURE indicates increased emotional tension.

LOW PROFILE See low-key.

LOW ROAD refers to deceitfulness.

LOW TIDE stands for a time for spiritual discoveries to be made.

LOZENGE calls for a need to correct one's manner of speech.

LUBRICANT indicates an irritated or rough situation or characteristic that requires smoothing to prevent further friction.

LUCID DREAMING represents the awareness of a situation and ability to interact with it or have some control.

LUCIFER See devil.

LUCITE connotes the preservation of integrity. This could refer to keeping one's beliefs unadulterated.

LUCKY CHARM See charm.

LUGE relates to "going down a slippery slope" and will indicate a situation/relationship or other element such as recent behavior as being destructive, sliding downhill fast.

LUGGAGE stands for extraneous aspects one carries about.

LUG NUT alludes to extra strong protection or assurances.

LUKEWARM connotes a lack of enthusiasm.

LULLABY indicates something that tends to lull one into a sense of false security.

LUMBER pertains to any type of tool or building aspect that serves as a driving force for one's advancement or path progression.

LUMBERING (gait) won't necessarily refer to laziness or a lack of motivation, it usually commends perseverance and tenacity.

LUMBERJACK emphasizes a spiritually destructive force.

LUMBER MILL relates to the shaping of opportunities.

LUMBERYARD connotes the current existence of dormant talents and abilities in one's life. This is a call to activate them.

LUMINARIA represents spiritual celebration.

LUMINESCENCE will come in dreamscapes as an attention-getting element. Recall what was luminescent.

LUMPECTOMY stands for a need to rid oneself of a possible negative in one's life.

LUMPINESS denotes multiple inconsistencies.

LUMP SUM suggests an abundance of something the dreamer will recognize.

LUNACY may not indicate craziness, it may well reveal a mental state of reality comprehension. Be careful to recall all surrounding dreamscape fragments that have a bearing on this symbol.

LUNA MOTH alludes to spiritual insights.

LUNAR RAINBOW refers to those inner knowings that one is subtly aware of, yet remain just out of clear focus—they're not quite within reach of one's full comprehension.

LUNATIC FRINGE warns of an ideology or path that's nearing extremism.

LUNCH BOX may come in a dreamscape to represent something as simple as an advisement to cut financial corners or it can indicate a temporary phase when one should be getting as much done as possible (working through lunch).

LUNCHROOM implies a need to take time out from one's daily efforts to revitalize oneself.

LUNG connotes sustaining qualities; one's ability to take in and sort out the positive from the negative. Recall condition of the lung if it was shown.

LUNG TRANSPLANT See transplant (lung).

LUNGWORT (botanical) portrays perseverance.

LUPINE (botanical/flower) stands for longevity brought on by maintaining inner balance.

LUPUS (disease) stands for repression.

LURE (fishing) warns of spiritual fads; misguided spiritual beliefs.

LURKING indicates a stealthy nature; underhandedness.

LUSHNESS denotes fertile ground to work from; multiple opportunities.

LUST constitutes a severe craving, not necessarily a sexual connotation.

LUSTER exemplifies a gentle inner beauty shining through, rather than a blinding brilliance.

LUTE portrays inner tranquility.

LUTHER (Martin) represents the separation of spiritual from materialistic aspects.

LUXURY doesn't necessarily refer to physical pleasure or material riches; it frequently relates to the inner feeling of comfort stemming from spiritual or moral fiber.

LUXURY TAX reminds us that some types of nonessentials can carry hidden costs.

LYCRA See elastic.

LYE corresponds to that which has the potential to negate negative forces or efforts.

LYME DISEASE warns of internalizing personal irritations; a lack of acceptance.

LYMPH NODE represents personal defense mechanisms.

LYMPHOMA reveals an inability to defend self, usually self-generated by controlling psychological manipulations.

LYNCHING signifies guilt, usually self-guilt.

LYNX denotes cleverness; an acute observational skill.

LYRE denotes harmony.

LYREBIRD emphasizes one's state of inner harmony; being at peace.

LYRETAIL (fish) denotes spiritual verbosity; superfluous spiritual facets; spiritual fluff.

LYRICIST characterizes an individual who possesses strong emotions; an ability to express beautiful feelings.

LYSINE (amino acid) represents a counter to a viral-like negative in one's life which could personally affect one's healthy perspective.

LYSOL See disinfectant.

M

MA'AT (Egyptian goddess) stands for justice and righteousness.

MACABRE relates to some personally unspeakable deed or situation; an appalling and abhorrent act or personality.

MACADAM See pavement.

MACADAMIA NUT alludes to quality inner nourishment and deepened emotional receptivity.

MACARONI See pasta.

MACAROON denotes a beneficial outcome generated by a rough time.

MACAW See parrot.

MACBETH characterizes personal gain through serious misdeeds.

MACE (club) relates to aggressiveness.

MACE (spice) See nutmeg.

MACE (spray) signifies one's personal defenses against external negative forces or influences.

MACHETE denotes a forcing of one's advancement of enlightenment.

MACHIAVELLIAN exemplifies an attitude of using whatever means available to reach a goal or gain control; unethical and immoral methods of advancement.

MACHINE GUN reveals a continual state of anger.

MACHINERY refers to personally devised instrumentations that one uses to hasten or ease a path advancement.

MACHINE SHOP pertains to the creation of examples, models, or molds. Recall what condition the templates were in. What color? Shape? Were they defective in any way?

MACHINIST characterizes those who set the example and are looked to for guidance.

MACHISMO portrays arrogance and male superiority; an exaggerated sense of masculinity; an attitude of false power and ability.

MACHU PICCHU symbolizes ancient knowledge.

MACKEREL infers an unexpected event or development.

MACKEREL SKY suggests distinctive thoughts; recognition of issues being separate; awareness to the possibility of something altering.

MACKINAW (blanket) denotes emotional warmth/comfort derived from camaraderie.

MACKINAW (boat) pertains to a fresh spiritual search.

MACKINAW (coat) suggests personal security; confidence.

MACKINAW BRIDGE reveals the presence of a connecting option bridging a wide gap in one's life. This symbol lets the dreamer know that the possibility for making this desired connection is available.

MACKINAW ISLAND stands for a return to more simple ways; a respite from life's hectic and complex world.

MACKINTOSH denotes personal methods of protecting self from spiritual fads; spiritual discrimination.

MACRAMÉ represents twisted truths or convoluted ideas; complicated issues.

MACROBIOTICS cautions against extreme measures and advises one to temper the tendency to focus on one aspect; suggests wide diversification.

MACROCOSM implies the entirety of something. This will be associated with a specific facet of each dreamer's awake state consciousness.

MACRO LENS signifies a need for closer inspection or research.

MAD may not refer to craziness or anger, it often indicates a great difficulty or embroiled situation.

MADAM (brothel) connotes an individual who gains from the efforts of others.

MADAME (title) See lady.

MADCAP refers to one who appears recklessly adventurous; a reluctance to pay attention to warnings or possible dangers.

MAD COW DISEASE reveals the danger of ingesting (accepting) negative ideas which were never viable from the outset.

MADD (Mothers Against Drunk Driving) illustrates the powerful effects of working together for a united purpose.

MADE IN USA (label) See union label.

MADEIRA See wine.

MADE-TO-ORDER See custom-built.

MAD HATTER characterizes one who has confusing thoughts; disassociative ideas; impulsive behavior.

MADHOUSE denotes great confusion or intense activity; pressure and stress.

MADISON AVENUE applies to advertising; a need to share or broadcast one's ideas.

MAD MONEY corresponds with extra assets not designated for necessities. This usually refers to assets available for long-shot possibilities.

MADRAS (pattern) portrays a casual attitude or personality; laid-back.

MADRIGAL denotes a shared opinion or idea.

MAELSTROM warns of mental or emotional confusion; an inability to focus thoughts or single out ideas.

MAESTRO characterizes one who is capable of leading groups. Recall if the sounds created were harmonious or discordant.

MAFIA exemplifies manipulation for self-gain; strong-arm control methods.

MAGAZINE will connote a different message for each dreamer depending on the type of magazine presented in the dream. Recall if it was illuminated or shadowed. What color was dominant?

MAGAZINE RACK indicates multiple opportunities for gaining information.

MAG CARD See magnetic card.

MAGDALENE (Mary) stands for a misunderstood personality; a false public opinion or impression of an individual. Also equates to spiritual companionship and unconditional love.

MAGENTA (color) infers spiritual zeal.

MAGGOT reveals a self-serving personality who gains from the efforts of others.

MAGI apply to those who have attained spiritual knowledge and wisdom; spiritual awareness.

MAGIC may refer to an illusion or it may stand for something in one's life that is difficult to figure out or understand.

MAGIC BULLET illustrates a solid solution.

MAGIC CARPET connotes a quick and secure method of enhancing or speeding the attainment of one's goal.

MAGICIAN characterizes false prophets and manipulative personalities who easily gain control and confidence of others.

MAGIC LANTERN denotes a need to examine something further; take a closer look at.

MAGIC MIRROR signifies one's true reflection of one's inner self.

MAGIC SHOP advises of multiple methods of trickery and illusion available for unscrupulous people to use; methods of deceit.

MAGIC SQUARE verifies one's ideas or conclusions.

MAGIC TRICKS usually refer to ulterior motives; manipulative behavior.

MAGISTRATE denotes an official authority.

MAGMA warns of internalized negative attitudes or emotions. These will need to be released.

MAGNA CARTA represents a guarantee of one's basic rights.

MAGNESIUM denotes a clarified perspective; enlightenment.

MAGNET reveals a compulsive nature; obsessive behavior.

MAGNETIC CARD represents access. This access can refer to information or a literal passkey allowing one entry.

MAGNETIC FIELD denotes a strong allure; an enticement or captivation.

MAGNETIC NORTH (MN) emphasizes the greatest intensity of something; strongest draw, force, or quality.

MAGNETIC RESONANCE IMAGING (MRI) relates to a need for close analyzation.

MAGNETIC STORM reveals a disruptive force or aspect in one's thought process; great mental and emotional confusion.

MAGNET SCHOOL pertains to an opportunity to gain from learning from an extensive source of higher knowledge; special focus on higher learning.

MAGNIFICAT reminds us to be aware and appreciative of our connection with the Divine.

MAGNIFYING GLASS connotes closer inspection; deeper understanding.

MAGNITUDE (measurement) will indicate intensity or extent of something relevant to the dreamer. This could refer to a personal attribute, quality, knowledge, effectiveness, involvement, etc.

MAGNOLIA represents a fragile or delicate aspect in one's life.

MAGNUM (measurement) denotes a significant amount.

MAGNUM OPUS symbolizes greatness of creativity; a monumental work.

MAGPIE (bird) alludes to the absorption of insignificant or useless concepts.

MAGUS portrays one who has attained high wisdom.

MAHARANI suggests a dignified person; a lady.

MAHARISHI constitutes a spiritual teacher, usually someone associated with the dreamer.

MAHATMA defines a spiritually enlightened individual who lives beliefs.

MAHJONG (game) implies a right combination is required. This will be a hint to a problem-solving resolution.

MAHOGANY (color/wood) portrays an inner warmth of character.

MAID See servant.

MAIDENHAIR FERN denotes delicate natural talents.

MAIDEN VOYAGE signifies the initial practice of a new spiritual belief.

MAID OF HONOR points out a placement position of a secondary importance.

MAIL (armor) illustrates the quality and strength of one's personal protective methods.

MAIL (postal) connotes communication forthcoming or needing to be sent.

MAILBOX refers to communication.

MAIL CALL advises of a forthcoming message or communication.

MAIL CARRIER characterizes one who is capable of bringing or sending a message.

MAIL DROP points to secrets or privy information.

MAILER See envelope.

MAILING TUBE stands for a desire/effort to keep something in good condition, maintain its integrity.

MAILLOT (fabric) implies honesty; no hidden aspects.

MAIL-ORDER CATALOG relates to multiple opportunities that are readily available and easy to take advantage of.

MAIL-ORDER HOUSE will denote an opportunity source.

MAIL PEOPLE See postal worker.

MAIL POUCH/PACKET stands for many different communications needed to be made.

MAIL ROOM alludes to discernment in communicating ideas to the right people.

MAIMED denotes a temporary difficulty to overcome. The key here is "overcome."

MAIN COURSE represents the central idea of an issue.

MAIN DRAG warns against walking a road traveled by most everyone. This calls for individuality and personal decisions.

MAINE points to strong independence and fortitude; a strong character.

MAINFRAME emphasizes the brain aspect; the main source of knowledge or information; an intelligent leader or guide.

MAINLAND will usually represent a grounded state; one's home base.

MAINLINING won't always infer hard drug use. This symbol will most often refer to a method or practice of absorbing conceptual information via the most efficient means; a tendency to recognize and accept the main truths of an issue or subject.

MAINSPRING relates to that which has the power; the energizing factor.

MAINSTAY symbolizes a main supporting facet; an anchoring idea or quality; the source of motivation.

MAINSTREAM illustrates a widely accepted idea; beliefs held by the majority; commonality.

MAINTENANCE (work) advises of a need to attend to some aspect of one's life, perhaps an emotional or mental facet of oneself.

MAITRE D' connotes a person in charge; the head person.

MAIZE See corn.

MAIZE (color) pertains to a lighthearted disposition; optimism.

MAJOLICA (design) suggests celebratory gaiety.

MAJOR-DOMO signifies a preferred assistant.

MAJORETTE See drum majorette.

MAJORITY illustrates the greater amount.

MAJORITY RULE applies to control held by those comprising the highest percentage of common belief or attitude, though it may not be the right belief or attitude.

MAJOR LEAGUE suggests a higher position acquired through greater experience and knowledge.

MAKE-BELIEVE may refer to innocent daydreaming or it may indicate a psychological condition of living false illusions; attempting to personally alter the truth to a fact or existing reality.

MAKE OVER pertains to an attempt to change self. This may be a positive or negative message, depending on the dream's surrounding details.

MAKER'S MARK is a sign identifying the maker (originator) of something creative. This symbol will come as an advisement to be sure one knows the true source of a particular piece of information.

MAKESHIFT reveals clear innovativeness; self-reliance.

MAKEUP (cosmetics) may expose a false front one creates or it may indicate a need to address opportunities to enhance one's self-image.

MALABSORPTION DISEASE reveals discernment; an inability to tolerate ideas one doesn't believe in.

MALACHITE typifies healing qualities or forces.

MALAISE indicates an uneasiness or sense of disturbance in one's life; a disquieting sense; often forewarns of an impending disruption.

MALAMUTE (dog breed) alludes to a friend or associate who has the capability to ease one's burden or quicken progression along a life path.

MALARIA usually equates to an obsession; fanaticism.

MALAYSIA suggests being underappreciated.

MALE CHAUVINIST See chauvinist.

MALE MENOPAUSE See mid-life crisis.

MALEVOLENCE reveals the existence of multiple negative qualities or forces.

MALFUNCTIONS denote faulty functioning. This could refer to one's emotional, mental, spiritual, or physical aspects. This might also point to one's plans.

MALICE stands for a desire for revenge; intent to harm.

MALIGNANCY reveals a harmful negative existing in one's life or within self. This usually won't be associated with a physical cancer.

MALIGNING reveals a slanderous personality; malicious defamation of another.

MALL (shopping) pertains to multiple opportunities available to one.

MALLARD applies to strong spiritual beginnings.

MALLEABLE symbolizes resiliency; a flexible personality.

MALLET signifies a life aspect utilized for the purpose of getting something started; an instigating agent.

MALLOW (botanical) stands for broad scope natural talents.

MALNUTRITION warns of a seriously imbalanced perspective or behavior.

MALPRACTICE refers to impropriety or negligence.

MALPRACTICE INSURANCE points to the possibility of negligence; a preparedness against making a mistake.

MALT (ale) See alcoholic beverage.

MALTED MILK implies a needed nourishing aspect that has to be enhanced to make it palatable.

MALTESE (dog breed) represents close companionship.

MALTESE CROSS indicates a specialized spiritual belief based on an ancient sect.

MALTESE CROSS (botanical) symbolizes the practice of general spirituality rather than one based in a currently recognized religion.

MAMBA (snake) denotes a swift retaliation.

MAMBO (dance) suggests fast moves done with another; may point to ulterior motives or moving ahead too fast.

MAMMAL will be associated with behavioral elements. See specific type.

MAMMOGRAM advises of a need to examine one's recent expressions of compassion or emotional sensitivity. This also may refer to a physiological condition.

MAMMOTH (animal) corresponds with an overbearing and/or manipulating individual in one's life.

MAMMOTH (size) reveals a true proportion of a situation or action; emphasizes totality.

MANACLE refers to limitations or restrictions; most often these are self-generated.

MANAGER characterizes one who organizes; an overseer.

MANATEE connotes spiritual largess; being generous with one's talents.

MANCHESTER TERRIER (dog breed) constitutes a friend or associate who protects one from negative personalities.

MANDALA is a spiritual sign that is meant to inspire or remind one of the beauty of spiritual expression (behavior).

MANDARIN (collar) denotes personal restrictions; chosen limitations.

MANDARIN (duck) represents brilliant spiritual insights.

MANDARIN (orange) See tangerine.

MANDATE symbolizes a command or action that must be followed, usually ordered by self as a means of insuring one stays on track.

MANDOLIN See lute.

MANDRAKE (botanical) indicates a negative aspect in one's life.

MANDRILL See baboon.

MANE relates to cleverness.

MANGE alludes to the harmful irritations affecting a friend or associate. If the dreamer has the mange condition in the dream, it has been caused by a friend or associate.

MANGER (feed trough) See corn crib.

MANGLE (machine) denotes a need to iron out something in one's life.

MANGLED See mutilated.

MANGO pertains to a hardened exterior personality covering a sweet inner sensitivity.

MANGROVE illustrates spiritual bounties.

MANGY (appearance) indicates a rough life that has been endured.

MANHATTAN stands for a wide range of diverse opportunities, yet are costly to reach and maintain.

MANHATTAN PROJECT warns of a misuse of intelligence.

MANHOLE symbolizes self-generated setbacks and pitfalls.

MANHUNT suggests that there is someone you need to find; a need to seek out and locate someone who will be important in your life.

MANIAC denotes a loss of reason and logic; a psychologically dysfunctional individual.

MANIC-DEPRESSIVE (illness) pertains to a vacillation between extremes.

MANICOTTI See pasta.

MANICURIST will indicate an individual who has the capability of cleaning up the reputation of others.

MANIFEST DESTINY constitutes an attitude of racial superiority.

MANIFOLD suggests the existence of multiple outlets or solutions.

MANILA PAPER depicts strong, firm communications.

MANIPULATION reveals a desire to control situations or others; frequently one allows self to be manipulated in order to avoid personal responsibility.

MANITOU represents a positive spiritual force.

MANNA exemplifies spiritual nourishment.

MANNEQUIN warns against apathy, unconcern whether or not one is being controlled or manipulated.

MAN-OF-WAR (jellyfish) stands for spiritual intolerance.

MANOR/MANSION emphasizes a pretentious personality.

MANSARD (roof style) suggests a tendency to look at things from several angles.

MANSLAUGHTER warns against a tendency to be unaware; a devastating effect of being unaware.

MANTA RAY characterizes attractive spiritual aspects that may prove to be dangerous.

MANTEL pinpoints one's priorities in life. Mantels are traditionally a place of distinction in the home and usually display items of pride or personal interest.

MANTILLA connotes emotional sensitivity.

MANTIS See praying mantis.

MANTLE (head wear) typifies a subconscious attempt to cloak one's inner feelings.

MANTRA portrays one's personal method of spiritual or psychological reinforcement.

MANUAL serves as a reference one relies on to double check path progression; analyzation of one's direction.

MANUFACTURED HOME See mobile home.

MANURE (stable) represents a fertile situation or condition; an aspect ready for development.

MANUSCRIPT will most often connote an individual's private thoughts or detailed future plans. Recall who wrote the dream manuscript and what it was about. This can be an extremely revealing symbol about you or someone you know.

MANX (cat breed) denotes simplicity of character; unpretentiousness.

MANZANITA denotes a life factor that is capable of cleansing. This dream symbol will signify the need for some type of cleansing to be done in the dreamer's life.

MAP comes as a personal directional message that will serve to guide one's path or supply other information pertinent to the dreamer's personal questioning.

MAPLE (tree) portrays current benefits or gifts that one hasn't yet recognized or acknowledged. Points to a need to recognize/appreciate the benefits (fruits) of one's labors.

MAPLE SYRUP is a reminder to be appreciative of our needs that have been provided for in life.

MAPMAKER See cartographer.

MARABOU relates to personality affectations displayed for the benefit of others; being overdramatic.

MARACAS are likened to the meaning of ceremonial rattles; they constitute a clearing out effort; a recognition of negative forces and the resulting act of attempting to repel or dispel them.

MARANTA illustrates nourishing provisions that exist for the dreamer to currently take advantage of.

MARASCHINO CHERRY defines a desired goal; an attainment; the perfect effect or result of something strived for.

MARATHON implies great efforts expended on an achievement.

MARAUDING See raid.

MARBLE (stone) refers to a lasting effort or aspect; enduring.

MARBLE CAKE pertains to an achieved goal that will hold its strength and form for a long time.

MARBLED (pattern) suggests an ever-changing (evolving) pattern; an ability to integrate ideas.

MARBLES (game) applies to immature competitiveness.

MARCASITE (gemstone) refers to multiple spiritual elements and comes in dreamscapes to enhance our recognition of the many spiritual opportunities we have to utilize goodness.

MARCH (month) signifies a time to begin activating initial steps toward one's desired goal.

MARCHING alludes to strength of one's belief. Recall who was doing the marching and the manner of marching. Proud? Weary?

MARCHING ORDERS stands for a time for one to leave something behind; an end.

MARDI GRAS suggests it's time for one to openly express happiness or experience lighthearted freedom.

MARGARINE implies an effective substitute is available for the dreamer to use. This type of symbol will be personally recognized by each dreamer.

MARGARITA See alcoholic beverage.

MARGIN stands for limitations; staying within specified perimeters.

MARGINAL denotes a questionable factor in one's life.

MARIACHI (music) connotes carefree joy.

MARIE ANTOINETTE characterizes insensitivity; arrogance; indulgent in excesses.

MARIGOLD (botanical) comes as a sign of encouragement.

MARIJUANA is an indication to cut down on stressful situations; a need for emotional balance.

MARINA relates to spiritual associates or friends; spiritual camaraderie.

MARINARA (sauce) implies a spicy aspect to a situation; the addition of an interesting facet.

MARINATE symbolizes a need to let something rest for a time; a need to absorb all details or aspects of something.

MARINE LIFE See specific types.

MARINER characterizes one who is on a spiritual search or quest.

MARIONETTE is likened to a person who lacks personal responsibility or thought; no expression of individuality; lacking self-confidence.

MARIPOSA LILY represents hope.

MARITIME LAW relates to the rules/concepts associated with one's particular religious/spiritual belief system.

MARJORAM alludes to a delicate aspect; a fragile situation.

MARKDOWN (price) indicates that something one needs in life is just as valuable but now is more accessible.

MARKER (pen) denotes a need to note or emphasize something. Recall what was being written or singled out with the marker. Who was using the marker?

MARKER (sign) will usually designate a personal message for each dreamer.

MARKER (token) represents an asset owned.

MARKET (sell) refers to an attempt to convince others of something's benefit or value.

MARKET (shop) relates to available opportunities; choices.

MARKET ANALYSIS suggests research should be done.

MARKET RESEARCH calls for a comparison; a hard look at priorities.

MARKET VALUE in dreams will usually reveal what something is really worth; will rarely indicate an inflated value.

MARKSWOMAN characterizes an individual who has the skill of being on target most of the time.

MARKUP points to an inflated value.

MARLIN (fish) corresponds with spiritual focus; centered spiritual attention.

MARMALADE See preserves.

MARMOSET See monkey.

MARMOT signifies insecurities; a lack of self-confidence.

MAROON (color) relates to having spiritual depth; insights.

MAROONED reveals a self-imposed state of remoteness; willful distancing from others.

MARQUEE almost always brings an important message for the dreamer. Recall what the marquee said.

MARQUETRY (pattern) denotes intricate details; an attention to fine and complex concepts or situations; an interconnecting of ideas or concepts.

MARQUISE (shape) connotes duality; perhaps even a Catch-22 situation.

MARQUISETTE (fabric) typifies a transparent personality or situation.

MARRIAGE See wedding.

MARRIAGE LICENSE suggests one's plans to commit to someone or something in the near future.

MARROW See bone marrow.

MARS (planet) refers to the warrior within; inner strength; fortitude.

MARSEILLE (fabric) pertains to an emphasis needed. Recall what the raised area of the fabric was shaped like.

MARSH constitutes spiritually saturated ground one is walking on.

MARSHAL characterizes authority, usually one's Higher Self; one's conscience.

MARSH ELDER (botanical) alludes to gifts of the spirit; spiritual talents.

MARSH GAS connotes heavy spiritual contemplation; fermenting ideas.

MARSH MALLOW (botanical) relates to an abundance of spiritual gifts.

MARSH MARIGOLD (botanical) brings spiritual encouragement.

MARTEN symbolizes inquisitiveness; curiosity.

MARTIAL ARTS represent multiple opportunities and methods of defense.

MARTIAL LAW emphasizes the importance of order in one's life.

MARTIAN brings a subconscious subject or fear to the forefront.

MARTIN See swallow (bird).

MARTINI See alcoholic beverage.

MARTIN LUTHER KING DAY reminds us of the importance of tolerance and equality; encourages us to celebrate the striving for rights.

MARTYR characterizes one's psychological belief of being persecuted; paranoia.

MARY JANE See marijuana.

MARYLAND suggests separatist attitudes combined with qualities of perseverance.

MARZIPAN (confection) denotes an unrecognized benefit or reward; a positive aspect in disguise.

MASCARA applies to an emphasis expressed or required.

MASCOT portrays a supporter; one who provides encouragement.

MASH (drink) suggests an easy-going personality.

MASH (pulpy mixture) represents an incomprehensible concept or situation.

MASHED exemplifies a destroyed factor in one's life; something that is not capable of being reconstituted.

MASHER (man) characterizes a lack of respect for women; selfish ulterior motives.

MASK connotes hypocrisy; may reveal one's true character that is kept hidden.

MASKING TAPE pertains to an attention to detail; an ability to keep differing aspects separate.

MASOCHISM reveals a self-abusive individual.

MASON indicates a person with strong foundational beliefs.

MASON-DIXON LINE denotes a firm difference of opinion; a strong line one won't cross.

MASON JAR relates a message to preserve something important in one's life.

MASONRY reflects solid work; strong foundations.

MASQUERADE illustrates deceit. Recall who you or someone you recognized was dressed as. This is usually a very revealing message.

MASSACHUSETTS signifies a strong sense of righteousness and a willingness to stand up for it.

MASSACRE represents a grave misdeed done or forthcoming.

MASSAGE suggests a need to work out an internalized problem or negative.

MASSAGE PARLOR may warn of ulterior motives or healthful benefits depending on the other dreamscape aspects.

MASSEUSE depicts one who is capable of easing one's withheld stress.

MASS-MARKET implies something that is widely known or available.

MASS PRODUCTION pertains to something produced in a great quantity and without any personal touches.

MAST See pole.

MASTABA advises of the wisdom of preserving and protecting truths.

MASTECTOMY reveals a fear of heart pain.

MASTER connotes proficiency or one who holds control.

MASTER BUILDER characterizes a skilled planner; one who can spot flaws in another's plans or method of operation.

MASTER KEY See passkey.

MASTERMIND refers to a highly intelligent person; one capable of complex analyzation or planning.

MASTER OF CEREMONIES will point to the person who directs operations or ensures efficiency. May point to a manipulative individual.

MASTERPIECE pertains to excellence; near perfection.

MASTER PLAN stands for big plans; all of the elements associated with a specific goal have been taken into consideration; a long-range plan.

MASTER'S DEGREE emphasizes higher learning; greater efforts applied to gaining knowledge or expertise.

MASTHEAD will reveal a name or purpose. This constitutes a personal message for each dreamer.

MASTIFF (dog breed) refers to a friend's gentleness; an even-keel personality.

MASTODON signifies an overwhelming situation or idea.

MASTURBATION reveals a subconscious desire to rid self of repressed emotions, attitudes, or other types of psychologically damaging factors such as pent up stressors.

MAT (pad) denotes an insulating quality or a means of protection.

MAT (tangle) signifies confusion.

MATADOR connotes a tempting of fate; seeking admiration through foolhardy means; false bravery.

MATCH (contest) implies competitiveness.

MATCH (lighter) will indicate a potentially explosive aspect in one's life.

MATCH (pair/likeness) suggests compatibility; equality.

MATCHLESS constitutes a lack of energy or motivation; an inability to incite interest.

MATCHMAKER pertains to a person who is capable of organization, brining things together.

MATCH POINT symbolizes a winning effort.

MATCH UP represents comparable, nearly equal skills or levels of development.

MATERIALISM reveals misplaced priorities.

MATERNITY WARD exemplifies a prime time to begin a new direction or new belief; fertile ground for nurturing new ideas.

MATHEMATICIAN will indicate a person in one's life who can offer solutions; one who can figure things out.

MATHEMATICS (study of) illustrates a high interest in analyzation, discovering interconnectedness.

MATINEE indicates a suggestion to take time out from one's workday to alleviate stressful situations.

MATRIARCH signifies a woman of wisdom who is chosen to lead others. In some cases, this symbol may point to a manipulated family member.

MATRICULATE connotes one who is accepted.

MATRIX portrays an identified pattern to something in one's life.

MATRON characterizes an experienced female elder.

MATTE (finish) suggests subtlety; refinement; avoidance of flashiness.

MATTE (frame) portrays individual traits or preferences; will reveal clues into one's hidden qualities.

MATTRESS will reveal one's manner and quality of rest. Recall the condition and color of the dream mattress. Hard or soft? Lumpy? What size was it?

MATTRESS PAD represents a personal interest in the quality of one's rest; rejuvenation is important.

MAUL (attack) defines an overwhelming aspect in one's life.

MAUSOLEUM typifies buried memories or thoughts; hurtful memories locked away in the mind's dark vault.

MAUVE (color) implies a spiritual lightheartedness.

MAVERICK characterizes an open nonconformist; one who takes joy in living life her way.

MAXIMALIST symbolizes a person who advocates taking an issue to its full extension; a tendency to maximize opportunities or talents.

MAXIMUM SECURITY signifies a need for heightened guardedness or secrecy. May also point to a situation or path holding many restrictions or operating limitations.

MAY (month) relates to the time to experience spiritual joy; rejoice in one's beliefs.

MAYANS warn of the devastating effects of a people being spiritually influenced by a dark, negative force; the dark side of spiritual power.

MAY DAY suggests a time of new birth celebration; rejoice in Grandmother Earth's blossoming gifts to humankind.

MAYDAY (signal) connotes a severe warning message for the dreamer.

Surrounding dreamscape details will pinpoint this warning.

MAYFLOWER (ship) stands for opportunities and how one takes advantage of them. This symbol is a type of advisement to use opportunities in positive ways. Opportunities can soon turn against one if they're used in any kind of negative manner.

MAYONNAISE relates to the use of positive aspects to aid in attaining a nourishing aspect of a goal in life.

MAYOR usually represents one's Higher Self or conscience.

MAZE may illustrate a type of mental or emotional confusion, but it most often corresponds with the unnecessarily complex manner one is going about a life path.

MAZURKA connotes the outward expression of great joy.

MC JOB stands for beginning opportunities; an entry level starting point.

MEAD See alcoholic beverage.

MEAD (Margaret) pertains to knowledge gained through observation.

MEADOW represents inner tranquility.

MEADOWLARK (bird) stands for inner joy; a deep appreciation of blessings; optimism.

MEADOW RUE (botanical) refers to a freedom to let one's individuality show.

MEADOWSWEET (botanical) stands for the serenity brought on by tolerance/ acceptance.

MEAL (grain) applies to coarse lessons that provide nourishment.

MEALS ON WHEELS represents the presence of people around you who are more than willing to give support.

MEAL TICKET reveals a dependency on others to provide for self.

MEALWORM warns of a dangerously negative factor that has infiltrated that from which one is taking nourishment.

MEANDER (stream) means an aimless spiritual path.

MEASLES warn of the act of internalizing negative feelings.

MEASURING CUP/SPOON comes as an advisement to give attention to the importance of keeping the right balance of input into an issue. This means a balance of give and take, a balance of positive reinforcement and critical assessment.

MEAT refers to solid basics, highly nourishing elements.

MEAT AND POTATOES connote a preference for the basics or prime factors of an issue.

MEATBALLS indicate irrationality; times one loses sight of reason.

MEAT CLEAVER See cleaver.

MEAT HOOK denotes an aggressive nature; intrusiveness.

MEAT LOAF represents the combining of basic ideas or elements.

MEAT-PACKING HOUSE illustrates the quality of foundational concepts of basic ideas one ingests. Recall the condition of the place. Was it clean? Were there rodents or bugs?

MEAT TENDERIZER alludes to one's special need to soften the hard or tough facts one wants to believe, make them more palatable.

MECCA signifies a greatly desired goal or attainment.

MECHANIC characterizes one who is capable of repairing a dysfunction or negative in another's life.

MECHANICAL pertains to a lack of thought or personal input. This symbol could also stand for a lack of emotional responsiveness.

MEDAL is a sign of encouragement or commendation from one's Higher Self or conscience.

MEDALLION stands for a self-confirming sign; verification.

MEDAL OF HONOR pertains to personal benefits; inner joy as a result of ethical or spiritual behavior.

MEDDLESOME applies to an interference by another; perhaps it was by the dreamer.

MEDEVAC advises of an immediate need for emotional or psychological help.

MEDIA CENTER signifies a source of information.

MEDIA EVENT defines a gravely important situation or issue needing one's attention.

MEDIAN STRIP represents a guideline along one's path; a protective measure that lets one know when one is making a reversal or backsliding.

MEDIATOR signifies an urgent need for assistance with a personal relationship.

MEDIC characterizes an individual in one's life who has the knowledge and skill to repair a negative aspect within another.

MEDICAID stands for a means of assistance that has questionable elements.

MEDICAL BUILDING emphasizes a need for some type of personal care or healing.

MEDICAL EXAMINER (ME) characterizes one who is capable of pinpointing the source or cause of a problem or failure.

MEDICAL RECORDS refer to one's history of behavior and whether or not it was always healthy.

MEDICARE applies to a dependence on others to protect you against future negative aspects.

MEDICATION connotes external solutions rather than working from within.

MEDICINE BALL denotes efforts given to strengthening one's inner self.

MEDICINE BUNDLE corresponds to one's personal inner power.

MEDICINE CHEST will reveal what one needs to cure an ill or it will display an excess that one is ingesting. Recall surrounding dream details for clarification.

MEDICINE SHOW reveals false cures or solutions.

MEDICINE WOMAN characterizes one who has the knowledge and skill to heal.

MEDIEVAL (time period) usually denotes a lack of intellectual reasoning; however, it may also refer to a past life experience, depending on surrounding details.

MEDITATION will advise one to be passive. This comes when one has been too active in something, perhaps being too intrusive in another's affairs or diligent to the point of being obsessive.

MEDIUM (amount) implies average; middle-of-the road; neutral.

MEDIUM (art form) alludes to quality or manner of self-expression. See specific form such as ink, oil paint, etc.

MEDIUM (psychic) connotes the connective link between the conscious mind and one's Higher Self.

MEDLEY (music) signifies a harmonic blend of ideas.

MEDUSA (Greek mythology) comes as a strong warning to straighten up one's thoughts before they become dangerous.

MEERKAT denotes cooperation; commitment; community minded.

MEERSCHAUM (pipe) illustrates an analytical mind; reason and wisdom.

MEETING suggests a need for open communication.

MEETINGHOUSE pertains to a coming together; shared ideas; a camaraderie.

MEGADOSE signifies an extraordinary amount of something. This symbol can come as a warning regarding too much or it can come as an advisement that more is needed.

MEGALITH pertains to ancient truths that remain valid today.

MEGALOMANIA warns of misplaced priorities; a lack of enlightenment; a focus on self.

MEGAPHONE can be an advisement that one is not being heard or it can indicate a message unique to each dreamer depending on who is using the object. It's particularly important to recall what was said through the megaphone.

MEGAVITAMIN will normally indicate a need for motivation.

ME GENERATION will warn against arrogance, selfishness, and apathy.

MELANCHOLIA denotes a lack of acceptance; self pity.

MELANOMA See malignancy.

MELBA TOAST implies a strong character.

MELD See merger.

MELLOW relates to a state of acceptance.

MELODRAMA represents gross exaggerations; emotional manipulation.

MELODY may bring a message via a recognized title of the tune or it could connote a harmonic aspect in one's life. Surrounding dreamscape details will distinguish between the two meanings.

MELON symbolizes inner nourishment obtained through personal efforts.

MELTDOWN reveals an absolute failure or collapse of something in one's life.

MELTING may refer to a need for some type of softening to be done or it may indicate a loss of definition (uniqueness or purity). Surrounding dream facets will clarify which meaning was intended.

MELTING POT will usually advise of the negative situation caused by blurring or stirring or confusing concepts or issues.

MEMENTO reminds us what should be kept as important aspects in life.

MEMOIR comes as a prompting to record one's life events and remember same. By doing this, one usually has some type of revelation.

MEMORABILIA will define a specific interest; may refer to a past life.

MEMORANDUM (memo) is a call to remember something important; may be a new revelation for the dreamer.

MEMORIAL brings a special message for each dreamer. Who or what was the memorial for?

MEMORIAL DAY may pinpoint a specific time, event, or individual associated with the dreamer and be prompting one not to forget that facet of one's past. This symbol may also signify a need to give personal attention to courage.

MEMORIZING stands for a need to learn or remember something important.

MENACE reveals a harmful aspect in one's life. Recall who or what the menace was. Was it yourself?

MENAGERIE denotes a great assortment of something. Usually this refers to benefits gained from a wide search; using multiple sources.

MENDICANT implies efforts expended for others.

MENDING (sewing) typifies an interest in repairing torn or broken relationships. May refer to the repair of one's less than stellar behavior.

MENHIR See megalith.

MENIAL (work) symbolizes acceptance and humility; an understanding that some advancements can't be accomplished unless the small elements are attended to.

MEN IN BLACK point directly to those holding huge secrets and devote all their energies and go to great lengths to keep them from becoming public; those with ulterior motives and secret agendas.

MENOPAUSE defines a life or path change. This symbol could well reveal that a key element in one's life has stopped being effective and advises of a total acceptance of that loss rather than trying to replace it or keep it active.

MENORAH reminds us of our beginnings; eternal spirits temporarily borrowing humanoid forms. May also come as an advisement to keep our inner lights shining in respect to blessings bestowed.

MENSA equates to intellectual brilliance but not necessarily common sense.

MENSTRUATION can have a variety of meanings depending on the surrounding related elements. It could point to a phase of fertileness. It may indicate an unfruitful situation, relationship, or path. It might indicate a time when one is in one's power. And, for some, it spells relief.

MENSWEAR (clothing department) signifies characteristics of the male perspective, his choices of expression, the yang.

MENTAL BREAKDOWN denotes a lack of acceptance; an inability to cope with reality.

MENTAL HOSPITAL See psychiatric hospital.

MENTALIST reveals deception.

MENTAL TELEPATHY See telepathy.

MENTHOL (flavor) connotes a fresh or refreshing aspect.

MENTOR usually identifies someone in your life who has the knowledge and wisdom of guiding you.

MENU emphasizes one's multiple opportunities to gain inner nourishment.

MERCENARY portrays one who would do anything for personal gain or the pure adventure of it. This may reveal someone who will take care of a problem for a price.

MERCHANDISE suggests choices available. The type of merchandise will bring a different message to each dreamer.

MERCHANT will denote a person who can offer choices to another.

MERCURY (element) implies a fluctuating situation; vacillation.

MERCURY (planet) depicts an impossibility.

MERCURY (Roman mythology) characterizes a messenger in one's life.

MERCURY-VAPOR LAMP calls for special

illumination required on a subject. The dreamer will make this association.

MERCY comes as a message to use same. This is a call for compassion, empathy.

MERCY KILLING See euthanasia.

MERGANSER See duck (bird).

MERGER refers to a blending; a bringing together; compromise.

MERGING LANE See acceleration lane; road signs.

MERINGUE (confection) reveals a deceptive surface appearance or cover; a fluffy presentation or representation of a more serious issue.

MERIT BADGE stands for recognition of accomplishments. The refining element with this symbol is if the dream presented it as a commendation or as a caution to not wear one's accomplishments for the purpose of boasting.

MERIT PAY represents the earning of additional karmic assets.

MERLIN (bird) See falcon.

MERLIN (of legend) characterizes the active manifestation of one's spiritual talents and the use of same for the benefit of others.

MERLOT See wine.

MERMAID reveals a state of spiritual confusion; indecision as to what the truth is; may also represent a denial of reality; a refusal to believe in anything existing outside the traditional box.

MERRY-GO-ROUND illustrates a lack of forward progress; no intellectual or searching advancement made. Also see carousel.

MESA connotes high spiritual truths.

MESCAL BUTTON See peyote.

MESH suggests a need to be more congenial, compatible.

MESMER (Franz) characterizes a person in one's life who has an ability to convince others of her/his viewpoint. May also point to ulterior motives, manipulation.

MESMERIZED warns of a lack of awareness; usually a conscious move to avoid personal responsibility for one's beliefs or path.

MESQUITE defines the possession of extremely potent spiritual power; exceptional strength of spiritual knowledge and wisdom.

MESS (condition) alludes to a state of near-total confusion. This most often refers to mental and emotional factors.

MESSAGE brings a revelation or some type of epiphany.

MESSENGER will reveal a person in one's life who will provide a solution, answer, or important clue to something.

MESSIAH corresponds with someone in the dreamer's life who will prevent his/her personal failure or loss of direction; will point to someone who saves the day.

MESS KIT symbolizes the tools we use in life to gain inner nourishment, gain knowledge, or attain a measure of forward progression.

METAL See specific type.

METALLIC (finish) denotes a lustrous appearance that may or may not reflect that which is inside or beneath.

METALLURGY (study of) represents a high interest in learning the various benefits and faults of using differing tools to accomplish life goals.

METAL ROOF indicates an effort to safeguard the home-front aspects in one's life, protect it from damaging outside influences.

METAL SCULPTURE stands for a lasting image. What was the sculpture of?

METAMORPHOSIS suggests a complete change. This could refer to a situation, relationship, belief, or an aspect within self, such as perspective or attitude.

METAPHYSICS (study of) represents a desire to understand the underlying principles of causation.

METASTASIS means something has spread, widened in scope.

METATE suggests a more basic, simpler way of accomplishing something.

METEOR represents an influx of enlightenment or inner awareness.

METEOROLOGIST characterizes one who is highly interested in understanding converging factors that can affect conditions or situations.

METEOR SHOWER will warn of an inundation of spiritual ideas. This is a caution to be discerning.

METER (gauge) denotes the level of one's progress.

Electric meter will indicate knowledge. A low reading will advise more in-depth study or research is required.

Gas meter alludes to one's energy level.

Water meter implies spiritual aspects.

METHAMPHETAMINE connotes a need to either slow down or re-energize self.

METHANE See marsh gas.

METHODICAL connotes efficiency; organization skills.

METHUSELAH (biblical) applies to a great age; a time-tested aspect.

METRONOME calls for a need to pace oneself. Recall if it had been going fast or slow. Was it still?

METROPLEX implies a high concentration of societal involvement; may be indicating an advisement to give more attention to social servicing behavior.

MEXICAN HAIRLESS (dog breed) points to the strong determination/fortitude of a meek appearing friend.

MEXICO suggests a readiness for expressing emotions, opinions. This may come as an advisement to express oneself more openly or it could be suggesting a need to hold one's tongue.

MEZUZAH symbolizes an external sign of one's spiritual beliefs and the faith in the personal protection it has the potential to provide.

MEZZANINE stands for a mid-level positioning.

MIA (missing in action) corresponds to one who has lost the way. This symbol could also refer to apathy.

MIASMA warns of a dangerously negative atmosphere.

MICA relates to the shiny bits and pieces of joyful moments we experience while making our life journey.

MICE See mouse (rodent).

MICHENER (James) stands for in-depth research and background material.

MICHIGAN suggests an abundance of fresh spiritual ideas/inspirations.

MICKEY MOUSE (character) connotes acceptance of life's little irritations; an ability to utilize humor as a means of dealing with small problems.

MICRO (size) will indicate a very small measurement. Surrounding dreamscape details will clarify what this symbol is associated with.

MICROCHIP refers to the source of a great amount of information.

MICROCHIP ID (in pets) alludes to a loyal friend who will always come back to one's side.

MICROBE will correspond with something that has entered one's life unnoticed. Other dream fragments will clarify whether or not this is a positive facet.

MICROBIOLOGY (study of) pertains to one who is highly analytical and interested in knowing one's enemies.

MICROBURST warns of an unexpected surge of knowledge or incoming information; an inundation. May also refer to a sudden emotional outburst.

MICROCOSM signifies a small example or replica of a larger comparable.

MICROFICHE (machine) portrays a method of consolidating information.

MICROFILM illustrates the mind; memory.

MICROORGANISM See microbe.

MICROPHONE suggests a need for one to be heard.

MICROSCOPE calls for an advisement for one to look at something much closer; more analyzation is needed.

MICROSURGERY implies a delicate maneuver; a fragile move; great care required in order to avoid a wrong move.

MICROWAVE OVEN emphasizes an efficient and quick conclusion is needed.

MICROWAVE TOWER stands for secretive or confidential communications.

This would refer to a quiet one-on-one transference.

MIDAIR pertains to an unfinished aspect; something hanging in limbo.

MIDAS TOUCH alludes to a record of success; an ability to conclude efforts in a positive manner.

MIDDAY (time) See noon.

MIDDLE (position) points out neutrality; may imply a lack of opinion or decision-making ability.

MIDDLE-AGED will exemplify a considerable level of experience but not enough to have gained deep wisdom.

MIDDLE AGES (time period) represent a time when one will begin to become more aware.

MIDDLE CLASS denotes average.

MIDDLE FINGER indicates centeredness; a balancing element.

MIDDLEMAN characterizes someone who is acting as a go-between in one's life. This may be an advisement to communicate directly instead of through another.

MIDDLE-OF-THE-ROAD applies to indecision; fear of taking a stand.

MIDDLE SCHOOL represents a stage or level of one's current advancement; mediocre experience and/or knowledge.

MIDDLEWEIGHT refers to one's level of effectiveness or influence. This symbol connotes an average amount of both.

MIDDY BLOUSE suggests a beginning spiritual search; a novice stage of spiritual knowledge.

MIDFIELD signifies an advancement position that places one halfway to one's goals.

MIDGET emphasizes a caution to never correlate power or knowledge with size; larger never means more or greater.

MIDLIFE CRISIS indicates a lack of acceptance; an inability to recognize the Divine Force within oneself.

MIDNIGHT refers to intense spiritual energy.

MIDNIGHT BLUE (color) signifies mystery; an enigmatic personality or aspect.

MIDNIGHT SUN reveals the brilliance of spiritual forces or influences that are not always evident during one's darker times.

MIDSTREAM cautions not to stop efforts before something has been concluded or accomplished.

MIDSUMMER EVE suggests a time for celebration or the expression of joy. There are times in life when positive events come unrecognized and we need to be more aware and appreciative of these small blessings.

MIDTERMS call for a time to stop and analyze oneself; double-checking to make sure we've retained and learned from lessons we've experienced along our path so far. Depending on the dreamscape's related elements, midterms may also point to the halfway point of achieving one's goals.

MIDTOWN represents a level phase in one's life where few ups and downs will be experienced.

MIDWAY (carnival) denotes misplaced priorities; an inability to have a mature perspective of reality. May point to ulterior motives or the possibility of being duped.

MIDWIFE characterizes an individual in your life who has the knowledge and skill to assist in bringing about a new path or rebirth.

MIDWINTER See winter solstice.

MIGHTY MOUSE (character) cautions against misjudgments; applies to an admonishment against forming solid opinions from first impressions or exterior appearances.

MIGRAINE indicates a state of intense pressure; great stress usually caused by oneself through a lack of acceptance or tolerance.

MIGRANT WORKER represents resourcefulness; efforts applied to advancement or path progression.

MIGRATION (animals) may suggest an actual, physical relocation or it may caution against conceptual or perceptual vacillation.

MIGRATION (birds) stands for a vacillating spiritual belief; indecision as to what one actually believes.

MIKE See microphone.

MILD (flavor) signifies something that's readily accepted; palatable.

MILD (weather) connotes amiability; easily accepted; lacking extremes.

MILDEW illustrates inattention; a lack of awareness; letting something go for too long without giving it proper attention.

MILE MARKER/POST reveals one's current location along one's life path.

MILESTONE signifies an event that marks a great accomplishment or turning point.

MILITANT won't necessarily denote aggression, it may indicate activism related to righteousness; standing up for one's rights or beliefs.

MILITARY alludes to controlling factors in one's life.

MILITARY CAP represents regimentation; an inability to think for oneself.

MILITARY INTELLIGENCE connotes ulterior motives for gaining information. This symbol may point to something in one's life that's a contradiction in terms.

MILITARY OFFICER stands for arrogance; a love of power.

MILITARY POLICE (MP) pertains to an active and correct conscience; the policing of oneself.

MILITARY POST indicates a domineering personality or situation.

MILITIA refers to self-defense; one's personal, inner protective measures.

MILK connotes immaturity; or it may apply to some type of essential nourishment. Recall dream details for more clarity.

MILK (chocolate) alludes to a sweetened perspective; sugar-coating being done.

MILK (goat) points to a perspective cluttered with extraneous elements.

MILK (soy) refers to a perspective generated by self-serving aspects.

MILK GLASS alludes to an immature perspective; an inability to see things clearly.

MILKING pertains to taking fullest advantage of something. This may or may not be a positive symbol if one is taking advantage of others.

MILK OF MAGNESIA indicates a stressful situation or condition; advises more acceptance.

MILK RUN indicates multiple aspects to give attention to.

MILK SHAKE implies willful immaturity and the enjoyment of same.

MILK TOOTH symbolizes first experiences; beginning lessons in life.

MILK TRUCK connotes actual dairy products because any *vehicle* symbol directly stands for one's physical body. This will advise of an actual increase or decrease in one's dairy requirement. A truck driving away indicates reduction in dairy foods.

MILKWEED (botanical) See silkweed.

MILL corresponds with a need to grind or break down something into more manageable or visible parts. This symbol advises one to look more closely at the parts that comprise a large whole (situation).

MILLBOARD See hardcover.

MILL BOND points to additional funds or energy needed to achieve something.

MILLENNIUM is a time marker that comes to dispel fear and anxiety.

MILLET typifies a filler aspect; unimportant elements or issues on which one expends efforts, funds, or time.

MILLINER characterizes a person who easily influences others.

MILLINERY (shop) connotes a source for diversity of ideas.

MILLING points to an effort to reshape or redefine something.

MILLIONAIRE characterizes an individual possessing great resources yet, with that, comes great responsibility to act on opportunities to perform acts of goodness.

MILLIPEDE relates to acceptance; an ability to overcome small setbacks.

MILLPOND defines spiritual benefits; an abundance of spiritual gifts.

MILLSTONE connotes a great burden.

MILLSTREAM defines a motivating factor; a source of energy.

MILL WHEEL represents one's continuing efforts to spiritually advance.

MILLWRIGHT characterizes an ability to put things in motion; having knowledge, skill, and motivation.

MILT implies an active aspect; a factor that's capable of joining with another to create a new idea or issue.

MIME represents honesty; visible attitudes and character.

MIMEOGRAPH applies to imitation; the utilization of a master image to duplicate its characteristics. This is usually not a positive symbol.

MIMIC is a caution to return to one's own individuality.

MIMOSA (botanical/scent) denotes a delicate innocence of character; a fragile yet strong nature.

MINARET depicts a method of gaining another's attention.

MINCE signifies a halting manner or progression.

MINCEMEAT alludes to the destruction of something in one's life.

MIND connotes one's thought process.

MIND-BOGGLING implies a lack of comprehension; an inability to understand.

MIND-EXPANDING relates to an experience or learning event that results in greater understanding or new revelations.

MINDLESS signifies an inability to think for self or comprehend information.

MIND READING See telepathy.

MINDSET reveals a set opinion, perception, or attitude that one refuses to alter.

MIND'S EYE defines mental visual insights; mental images.

MINE (earth) represents truths and natural talents that exist for one's self-discovery.

MINE (explosive) reveals negative aspects waiting along one's path.

MINE DETECTOR signifies one's inner sense or awareness to perceive upcoming troubles.

MINEFIELD symbolizes a setup or condition of entrapment existing in one's path.

MINER characterizes a spiritual searcher.

MINERAL See specific type.

MINERAL BLOCK implies essential life aspects; necessary basics.

MINERALOGY (study of) pertains to an interest in natural talents and their practical application in the world.

MINERAL OIL connotes a soothing aspect; a factor that eases rough phases in life.

MINERAL RIGHTS point to the rightful owner/person through which multiple blessings/benefits come.

MINERAL WATER illustrates essentials in life; that which is basic and without extraneous facets.

MINER'S HAT typifies light shed on ideas, concepts, or perceptions.

MINESHAFT represents in-depth research; digging down further and further for the more hidden aspects of something.

MINESTRONE corresponds with diverse information or conglomerate issues.

MINE SWEEPER stands for heightened awareness; an inner knowing.

MINGLING suggests a need to experience diversity; a caution against being an ideological separatist.

MINIATURE will usually refer to compact knowledge; a great amount of information or power located within an unexpected source.

MINIATURE GOLF suggests a trial run; a practice experience before the real thing is attempted.

MINI-MART stands for convenience; multiple opportunities showing up along one's path.

MINIMUM SECURITY denotes a situation or path that holds few restrictions or operating limitations. Could also indicate little need for secrecy.

MINIMUM WAGE won't necessarily indicate a negative aspect; it most often underscores a benefit (though small) to an effort one expends.

MINISERIES connotes sequential stages to one's current experience, search, or path progression.

MINISTER See religious figure.

MINIVAN denotes a moderate amount of personal effort needs to be expended to accomplish something satisfactorily.

MINI-WHITES See amphetamine.

MINK (animal) pertains to cleverness.

MINK OIL emphasizes a softening aspect in one's life; a factor that is capable of easing experiences that are tough to get through.

MINNESOTA signifies a hardiness of character.

MINNOW reveals spiritual insecurity.

MINOR (youth) indicates a more immature and inexperienced aspect or perspective.

MINOR LEAGUE defines a secondary factor; one that isn't perceived as a priority level issue.

MINOTAUR (Greek mythology) constitutes a demanding personality or situation.

MINSTREL signifies a person who tends to bring a measure of joy or lightheartedness into another's life.

MINT (botanical) See specific type such as catnip, horehound, lavender, etc.

MINT (money) denotes a high value on something.

MINT JULEP See alcoholic beverage.

MINT MARK refers to an originating source.

MINUET pertains to a fragile relationship or situation, one where people need to carefully watch their step, their every move.

MINUTE represents a small measure of time. Recall surrounding dream aspects for further clarification and associative factors.

MINUTE HAND signifies the passing of time; will advise of the importance of mere minutes.

MINUTEMAN characterizes an individual who can be depended on for support.

MIRACLE corresponds to the normal working of true Reality.

MIRACLE DRUG will stand for a solid solution.

MIRACLE WORKER portrays a person who provides solutions to difficult problems; one capable of making things happen.

MIRAGE connotes misperceptions; illusions; delusional behavior.

MIRANDIZE (reading one's rights) points to knowledge of one's rights. This symbol rarely points to a wrongdoing but rather the recognition of an intent to do so.

MIRED pertains to the condition of being overwhelmed; bogged down.

MIRROR stands for self-perception; a call for self-examination.

Broken mirror (piece[s] missing) stands for an incomplete picture of self. This would mean that one is only looking at certain attributes or faults rather than seeing the whole person.

Ceiling mirror signifies a tendency to have to look up to see oneself, giving a diminutive perception.

Clouded mirror implies a lack of clear perception of oneself.

Colored mirror denotes a colored perception. Refer to the specific color for further clarification.

Compact mirror refers to a minimized viewpoint and could indicate a perception of inferiority.

Cracked mirror typifies a faulty self-image.

Floor-to-ceiling mirror indicates a clear viewpoint of one's wholeness.

Foggy mirror points to an unclear, indistinct self-impression; no clear understanding of oneself.

Magnifying mirror represents an egotistical view of oneself.

Pitted mirror relates to irregularities with one's self-image.

Rear-view mirror signifies a perception of oneself as judged from hindsight. This usually is a deprecating perspective.

Reflection in window glass pertains to sudden insights into one's true personality.

Slanted mirror suggests a biased viewpoint.

Warped mirror implies an unbalanced perspective.

Wavy mirror points to indecision about oneself, a vacillating perception.

MIRROR IMAGE usually personifies an alter ego; one's hidden self.

MIRROR WRITING signifies backward communications; a need to be straightforward.

MISCARRIAGE denotes the shedding of an erroneous spiritual belief.

MISCHIEF-MAKER spells trouble; reveals a problematical individual in one's life.

MISCOMMUNICATION reveals the need to recommunicate with someone to correct a misunderstanding.

MISCONCEPTION advises of an idea or attitude held in error. This is a wonderful message symbol that keeps you on track.

MISDEAL alludes to deceit.

MISDEMEANOR will warn of an offense one did. This type of symbol is in direct relation to one's conscience.

MISDIAGNOSIS advises of a wrong cause or source attributed to an event in one's life.

MISDIAL depicts a situation where one communicates information to the wrong party.

MISER represents deep insecurities; may indicate selfishness.

MISERY implies a lack of acceptance; could reveal self-induced state.

MISFILED connotes a need for heightened awareness; concentrated attention required.

MISFIRE usually advises of a blessing that kept one from making a mistake or serious error in judgment.

MISFIT won't necessarily indicate a negative connotation. This symbol will usually denote individual expressiveness; following one's own drumming.

MISMATCHED reveals incompatibility; unsuitability.

MISOGAMY points to a hatred of forming close relationships/associations.

MISOGYNY reveals resentment or prejudiced attitude toward women; a male elitist.

MISPLACED alludes to there being a reason for temporarily being without something.

MISPRINT may indicate unawareness or it might pertain to a message for the dreamer, depending on how the misprint was made.

MISQUOTE warns of a lack of concern for accuracy.

MISSAL See prayer book.

MISSILE reveals a harmful negative aimed at one's experience. This could even be generated by self to another.

MISSING LINK illustrates a hidden factor that brings sense to a puzzling issue.

MISSING TIME may refer to forgetfulness/denial or it may be associated with the more important aspect of an abductee's implanted amnesia.

MISSION (church) will pertain to a specific work one needs to do; may point one in the right direction for one's life purpose.

MISSIONARY corresponds to a person with a purpose. We are all missionaries in life. This symbol simply underscores it for the dreamer as a reminder.

MISSION CONTROL will represent one's Higher Self, one's conscience.

MISSION IMPOSSIBLE represents those things we *think* we can't do; proving our potential.

MISSISSIPPI suggests a resistance to change.

MISSOURI signifies a tendency toward skepticism.

MIST constitutes a spiritual atmosphere; may reveal a highly spiritual aura around someone. Recall if there was a color to the mist.

MISTAKE will almost always indicate the presence of an error one has made in life. It usually comes as a good sign to reveal a misstep in thought and can be corrected.

MISTLETOE (botanical) represents good intentions.

MISTRESS characterizes one who breaks up partnerships.

MISTRIAL implies faulty procedure followed or a failure to agree on something. Surrounding dream details will point to which meaning the dream had.

MISTY-EYED connotes an effort to control one's emotions; sensitivity.

MITE (amount) suggests a very small measure of something; an insignificant aspect.

MITE (insect) infers small irritations in life.

MITER BOX corresponds with a need for precision; exactness.

MITTEN symbolizes a restrictive factor; a limiting condition.

M

MIXED BLESSING denotes an element having both positive and negative aspects.

MIXED DRINK See alcoholic beverage.

MIXED MARRIAGE portrays higher advancement; nondiscriminatory attitudes.

MIXER (appliance) See blender; cement mixer.

MIXER (music) represents one who recognizes a multitude of nuances and is capable of blending them to create a new/unique perspective.

MIX-UP reveals a lack of adequate communication.

MOANING indicates a regretful realization of transgressions; may also infer sorrow or a lack of acceptance.

MOAT constitutes spiritual distance; the use of spiritual beliefs as protective or defensive measures.

MOB (of people) signifies a group of people with like attitudes or intentions; may not infer a negative connotation.

MOBILE HOME represents a temporary position on one's life path; good chance of relocation or moving forward.

MOBILE TELEPHONE See cellular telephone.

MOB MENTALITY warns of losing one's rationale/sense of reason; a loss of ethics and/or morals.

MOBSTER See mafia.

MOCCASIN illustrates a high level of awareness while cautiously progressing along one's life path.

MOCHA (flavor) suggests a high quality; a richness.

MOCKERY indicates a feeling of humiliation; may indicate personal embarrassment.

MOCKINGBIRD denotes a lack of individualized expression.

MOCK ORANGE (botanical) connotes contentedness.

MOCKUP See model (prototype).

MODEL (example) points to a quality that's considered the ideal.

MODEL (professional) will reveal someone who works to sell something to another.

MODEL (prototype) portrays an intended plan.

MODEL (toys) denote a smaller version of something larger; an imitation on a lesser scale.

MODEM relates to an opportunity to choose a variety of communication methods for a situation.

MODERN refers to a current time frame or method.

MODERN DANCE pertains to an ability to freely express oneself.

MODERNIZE implies an updated aspect; making something current.

MODESTY stands for awareness; a considerate, respectful, and refined personality.

MODIFICATIONS exemplify an effort expended on improving something; alterations, usually for the better.

MOGUL characterizes a powerful and influential individual.

MOGUL (skiing) refers to the bumps along one's spiritual path.

MOHAIR (fabric) emphasizes an irritating or heated situation.

MOHAWK (hair style) reveals a person with a single train of thought; an inability to refocus or redirect an attitude or perspective.

MOIRÉ (fabric) depicts a rough exterior personality; a lack of expressive sensitivity.

MOISTURIZER (beauty product) refers to a need to express more compassion and overall sensitivity.

MOJO stands for one's inner power; the magic combination of enchanting elements; charisma and charm.

MOLAR (tooth) represents an ability to process ideas. Recall the condition of the molar for further clarification of this intended meaning.

MOLASSES defines a factor in one's life capable of providing needed energy or motivation.

MOLD (growth) See fungus.

MOLD (shape) cautions against the choice of imitation rather than individual creativity.

MOLDING (carpentry) signifies finishing touches.

MOLE (blemish) reflects a distinguishing characteristic; individuality; uniqueness.

MOLE (informant) See informant.

MOLE (rodent) indicates a lack of communication; fearing reality.

MOLECULE denotes the smallest aspect of something. This refers to the importance of looking at every facet making up an issue or situation as being important.

MOLEHILL pertains to a lack of acceptance; a tendency to exaggerate a situation that would be better left alone.

MOLESKIN (fabric) alludes to a gentle and tolerant personality.

MOLL See gun moll.

MOLLIE (fish) denotes traditional spiritual beliefs.

MOLLUSK warns against hiding from problems; withdrawal.

MOLOTOV COCKTAIL stands for a potentially explosive situation or attitude building.

MOLTEN implies an embroiled emotion or situation; one needing cooling.

MOLTING signifies the shedding of negatives or excesses; letting go of the past.

MOM-AND-POP (store) represents a homelike atmosphere with associative attitudes of understanding and acceptance.

MOMENT OF TRUTH will relate to a revelation or it may indicate a need for introspection or open communication.

MONARCH (butterfly) connotes perseverance; going the distance.

MONARCH (ruler) won't necessarily depict the meaning of ruler but will usually indicate one's inner power and strength. In some cases, this symbol may carry the negative significance of someone who tries to rule every relationship and situation.

MONASTERY pertains to privacy in respect to one's spiritual beliefs.

MONASTICISM applies to a desire to lead a purely private life and forsake societal involvement and material trappings.

MONDAY suggests the time to review one's motivations and strengthen them for the purpose of actively going forward.

MONDAY MORNING QUARTERBACK cautions against claiming false foreknowledge or wisdom; seeing through the lens of hindsight.

MONEY stands for riches; wealth.

Coins stand for *blessings* we rarely count; *opportunities* rarely recognized.

Found money implies a *sudden realization* of one's talents or blessings.

Gold signifies *physical* wealth.

Newly minted money represents new or forthcoming wealth.

Old money signifies *inherent* talents meant to be freely used to benefit others.

Paper money refers to *opportunities* to *share* wealth.

Rare money signifies an *exceptional form* of wealth one needs to fully utilize for the benefit of others.

Silver denotes *spiritual* wealth.

Uncirculated money comes as a warning against being *miserly* with talents.

MONEYBAG symbolizes a quantity of wealth.

Empty bag connotes poverty.

Full bag portrays an abundance.

Torn bag reveals a situation where one is allowing some form of wealth to waste away. This may point to excessive spending or a loss of understanding the value of one's wealth.

MONEYCHANGER represents a conversion of one's assets; altering form such as turning it into a gift or shared talent.

MONEYLENDER characterizes a person who shares wealth for self-serving reasons; ulterior motives.

MONEY ORDER connotes guaranteed payment; an assurance that an asset or benefit is a positive and valid one.

MONEY ROLL indicates an abundance of personal assets; these may refer to monetary, mental, or emotional wealth. A money roll will not signify a spiritual factor.

MONEY TREE pertains to riches gifted to another.

MONGOLIA stands for a stalwart and forthright character.

MONGOOSE represents a quick wit and sharp awareness in respect to perceiving deception.

MONGREL (mix-breed) will define a compound aspect of a situation. This means that something has manifested through diverse means and factors.

MONITOR (computer screen) reveals a method of viewing or keeping an eye on something. This will point to a means of access one previously thought nonexistent.

MONITOR (person/overseer) relates to observation and usually comes in dreams to advise of a need for closer attention or observation to be done.

MONK will characterize an individual who chooses to forgo materialism in lieu of devoting a life to spiritual good works and contemplation.

MONKEY indicates intelligence hiding behind immaturity or a lack of individuality.

MONKEY BARS relate to contorted maneuvers to emulate others.

MONKEY-FLOWER (botanical) illustrates a carefree attitude.

MONKEYSHINES pertain to mischievous behavior. This behavior may be negative or acceptable depending on surrounding dream details.

MONKEY WRENCH usually warns of a disruptive aspect in one's life, perhaps even one's own behavior.

MONKSHOOD (botanical) See wolfsbane.

MONOCHROMATIC (one color throughout

dream) indicates an overall perspective or personality aspect that "colors" one's life. Recall what color washed the dreamscape then refer to the specific color.

MONOCLE denotes a singular mental focus; an inability to open self to a broader scope or greater availability to new ideas.

MONOGAMY may not refer to a marriage or partnership, but most often will correspond with one's belief system or focus of attention.

MONOGRAM represents important initials that will have a specific meaning for each dreamer. Many times a monogram will turn out to be an acronym. Recall what the letters were.

MONOLITH signifies a particular facet of one's life that is perceived as being a great goal or burden.

MONOLOGUE will usually symbolize a discussion one needs to have with oneself; something needs to be talked out or analyzed.

MONOMANIA indicates a destructive fanaticism.

MONOPLANE refers to assurance and fortitude.

MONOPLEGIA reveals a self-generated mental or emotional handicap.

MONOPOLY (corporate) signals a fear of competition.

MONOPOLY (game) alludes to misplaced priorities; a tendency to want it all.

MONORAIL applies to one-mindedness; an inability or refusal to veer from one's course. This is usually a negative symbol, for there are many times we need to take a sidetracking detour to learn an important life lesson.

MONOTHEISM points the Way.

MONOTONE signifies inexpressiveness; it calls for more outward expression of feelings.

MONOTONY suggests an expansion of one's horizons or goals.

MONROE (Marilyn) implies a draw toward physical aspects. This will usually indicate an overinterest in the physical facets of life that will result in an imbalanced character.

MONSOON reveals an inundation of spiritual information; one is attempting to seek out and assimilate a wide diversity of spiritual concepts too quickly.

MONSTER will always stand for a fear one has.

MONSTRANCE depicts that which one reveres. This is a revealing symbol that will point out whether or not what we revere is spiritually correct.

MONTAGE (art form) indicates a state of thought.

> **Related montage visuals** denote a wholeness to one's perspective.

> **Unrelated montage visuals** will warn of a disconnective or disassociative thought process.

MONTANA refers to an abundance of wealth (natural talents and spiritual).

MONTANE (zone) See mountain.

MONTESSORI METHOD pertains to a freedom to explore oneself and one's leanings; an expression of abilities.

MONTEZUMA II represents an advisement to preserve one's higher ideals, ethnicity, or best qualities.

MONTH denotes a time frame and will usually have a specific meaning for each dreamer. See specific month.

MONUMENT alludes to individual loyalties.

> Beautiful monument is a correct placement of one's loyalty.

> Decrepit monument reveals misplaced loyalty.

MOODINESS cautions one to accept more in life; an inability to reconcile events.

MOOD LIGHTING pertains to a ground laying set-up for a specific intention.

MOOD MUSIC is a dreamscape element which serves to set the general tone.

MOOD RING alludes to an attempt to monitor one's emotional responses.

MOOD SWINGS signify indecision; vacillation.

MOON corresponds with spiritual wisdom/gifts and their application.

> Crescent moon points to a sliver of one's glimpse at high wisdom regarding a spiritual epiphany or an understanding of reality. This refers to having nothing more than an undefined hint (fleeting thought) of inspiration.

> Eclipsed moon stands for forgotten wisdom.

> First quarter moon denotes a turning point.

> Full moon refers to a period of strong magnetic pull; a time of heightened interest in something; a time when efforts could be most effective.

> Harvest moon denotes the time to benefit from one's spiritual works; a time to reap the bounties that return to one through selfless giving.

> Hunter's moon relates to the time to be on the watch for new spiritual issues to enteer one's life. This symbol calls for increased awareness lest an important aspect pass unnoticed.

> Last quarter moon signifies a winding down period.

> New moon alludes to hidden spiritual concepts/wisdom that will be revealed.

MOONBEAM comes to shed a revealing or awakening light on one's spiritual talent. This will usually be a call for more active use of one's spiritual wisdom and talent.

MOONBOW See lunar rainbow.

MOON-EYED reveals a sense of wonder or amazement.

MOON-FACED connotes an emotional openness.

MOONFLOWER VINE will refer to the moon opening up the vine blossoms and clearly exemplifies the bountiful spreading of a singular spiritual deed. Also it can stand for the blossoming of wisdom.

MOONLIGHT signifies the light of spiritual knowledge and talent use.

MOON LUTE See samisen.

MOONQUAKE refers to an attention-getting attempt to help one recognize a need to reconnect with one's inner knowledge; an advisement to remember an important issue.

MOONRISE reveals a rising spiritual talent/wisdom within one; a developing gift or insight.

MOON ROCK points to a forgotten or denied spiritual concept.

MOON ROOF suggests a need to stay open-minded; points to possible current skepticism.

MOONSCAPE suggests that one has entered new spiritual territory where discoveries and perhaps inspirational epiphanies will be experienced.

MOONSHINE See alcoholic beverage.

MOONSTONE (gemstone) empowers one's spiritual talents; strengthens abilities.

MOONSTRUCK will caution against a tendency to be over zealous to the point of negating one's spiritual efforts or effectiveness. This symbol often points to one reacting in an overwhelming way to wisdom gained through a dramatic moment of inspiration.

MOONWALK (dance move) comes in dreams to point out that one only appears to be falling behind, that some backward moves are required for greater (more beneficial) advancement.

MOOR See anchor

MOOR (fish) stands for esoteric aspects of spiritual concepts and their demystification.

MOOR (landscape) means a stage in one's life where one allows self to become bogged down by spiritual concepts that are too heavy or deep to currently comprehend.

MOOSE implies a spiritual burden.

MOP suggests a cleanup is required in one's life. This will refer to a uniquely individualized factor in each dreamer's life.

MOPED denotes the use of energizing thoughts; positive thinking.

MORAINE relates to a stage in one's life when a seemingly excess of burdens is presented.

MORALIST may be a positive or negative symbol, depending on the dream moralist's behavior.

MORASS relates to an overwhelming aspect in one's life.

MORATORIUM comes to advise one stop a certain behavior or cut out a specific element in one's life. Surrounding related aspects will clarify what this in connection with.

MORAY EEL warns against spiritual over-exuberance; spiritual aggressiveness.

MORBIDITY (behavior) points to a loss of inner strength; cynicism.

MOREL See mushroom.

MORGAN (horse breed) denotes dependability; trustworthy.

MORGANITE (gemstone) points to indecision and calls for a need for clarity of thought and quicker decision-making.

MORGUE will connote futility; a dead-end or an unproductive aspect.

MORNING (time) illustrates a new beginning; a fresh start.

MORNING-AFTER PILL points to reconsiderations; a stop-gap prevention move.

MORNING-GLORY (botanical) calls for spiritual expression.

MORNING SICKNESS implies an inner anxiety to make a new beginning; doubts.

MORNING STAR defines encouragement. Mornings can be extremely difficult emotional times of day and the star shines to give support.

MOROCCO (leather) signifies a gentle emotional expressiveness.

MOROSE See melancholia.

MORPHINE See narcotic.

MORSE CODE suggests communication misunderstanding or a lack of comprehension.

MORSEL indicates a small amount. This may appear to be a negative symbol, yet a morsel is still something that may be just a beginning.

MORTALITY (rate) emphasizes a measure of viability. Recall surrounding dream detail to determine what this symbol referred to.

MORTAR See cement.

MORTAR AND PESTLE suggest a need to take something to a finer consistency; look at the finer aspects of an issue.

MORTARBOARD stands for advancement; the gaining of greater information/learning and now it's time to put it into action.

MORTGAGE pertains to an extended or long-lived debt; a karmic responsibility.

MORTGAGE BROKER characterizes someone who may be able to realize one's goals—for a price.

MORTICIAN See funeral director.

MORTUARY See funeral home.

MOSAIC (art form/pattern) symbolizes the many beautiful aspects that create a whole. This will have uniquely revealing meanings for some dreamers.

MOSAIC VISION signifies an ability to immediately perceive all elements of an aspect.

MOSES (biblical) characterizes a messenger; one who has the capability of overcoming adversity through perseverance.

MOSQUITO refers to mild set-backs or temporary irritations that can be disruptive forces.

MOSQUITO NET refers to an awareness that offsets or deflects the minor irritations that can disrupt one's focused attention.

MOSS denotes vitality.

MOSS GREEN (color) represents an energetic personality or phase.

MOSS ROCK portrays determination and fortitude.

MOSS ROSE (botanical) symbolizes the beauty of optimism, energetic motivation.

MOTE (size) corresponds to the presence or existence of something in one's life. This usually refers to an idea, emotion, or belief that is still alive.

MOTEL will allude to some form of transitional phase in one's life.

MOTH constitutes a destructive belief; one that will appear to lead into the light yet will result in eventual harm.

MOTHBALL connotes a preventive measure applied to protecting one's direction from false trails.

MOTH-EATEN represents the results of a destructive negative in one's life.

MOTHER characterizes a nurturing aspect; may represent personal real time associations.

MOTHERBOARD signifies the main source of information.

MOTHER EARTH symbolizes one's natural blessings/bounties.

MOTHERGOD stands for a source of deep empathy and a giving nature.

MOTHER GOOSE pertains to immaturity.

MOTHER HEN suggests interference; overly protective; a doting personality; may also indicate pessimism.

MOTHER-IN-LAW depicts added responsibility in life.

MOTHERLAND won't normally signify a

birth country, but will refer to one's nurturing when young; the moral training and sense of home comfort one remembers.

MOTHER LODE stands for the most bountiful source of something.

MOTHER NATURE stands for plenty, bountiful gifts. This symbol may also point to events outside one's personal control.

MOTHER-OF-PEARL symbolizes the best aspect.

MOTHER'S DAY pertains to honor and respect for the one who gave us a new beginning and nurtured us.

MOTHER SHIP represents a source of spirituality; one's sense of spiritual home.

MOTHER SUPERIOR (head nun) See religious figure.

MOTHER TERESA characterizes a selfless personality; compassion; one who gives aid.

MOTHER TONGUE represents an advisement to return to one's own level of understanding. This would denote an attempt to learn that which is far too complex.

MOTHER WIT symbolizes age-old, dependable wisdom.

MOTHERWORT (plant) stands for a solution (cure) for problems associated with a new path/direction.

MOTHPROOF applies to the individualized protective measures one uses to safeguard against misdirection. Also see mothball.

MOTIF will reveal a dominating ideology, usually the one prevalent in one's life.

MOTION SENSOR stands for one's awareness level. Recall if the sensor was operating, turned off, or in disrepair.

MOTION SICKNESS reveals psychological restrictions placed on oneself to prevent development or path advancement; a fear of advancing; lacking self-confidence or reliance.

MOTIVATIONAL SEMINAR may indicate low motivation. Recall what the seminar was motivating.

MOTOR refers to a life aspect that can provide additional energy or motivation; an impelling force.

MOTORCADE denotes emphasis. The surrounding dream details will reveal the precise meaning for each dreamer.

MOTOR COURT See motel.

MOTORCYCLE applies to the freedom to follow one's unique path and the activation of same.

MOTOR HOME reveals a transitional sense of illness or lack of direction.

MOTOR MOUTH points to one who talks a lot yet has little of value to convey.

MOTOR POOL indicates a sharing of lessons learned along one's life journey; a sharing of experiences.

MOTOR SCOOTER signifies a phase of moving away from immature thought/attitudes.

MOTTLED (pattern) denotes thought vacillation; indecision.

MOTTO will sometimes reveal one's basic attitude, yet it most often will come as a message that defines what one's perspective *should* be.

MOUND (earth) exemplifies hidden aspects that one hasn't perceived.

MOUND BUILDER characterizes one who cherishes truth and strives to protect and preserve it.

MOUNTAIN refers to a major obstacle to overcome in life.

MOUNTAIN BIKE represents personal effort expended while taking the rougher road.

MOUNTAIN BLUEBIRD typifies encouragement as one struggles to overcome life's burdens or obstacles.

MOUNTAIN CLIMBING stresses personal efforts expended toward reaching goals.

MOUNTAIN FOLK suggest down-home attitudes and an appreciation of nature's beneficial, tranquil qualities.

MOUNTAIN GOAT connotes a determined effort to persevere; tenacity.

MOUNTAIN LION See cougar.

MOUNTAIN MAN characterizes self-sufficiency and fortitude.

MOUNTAIN RANGE relates to a major block one needs to overcome and conquer, this oftentimes being a self-generated restriction.

MOUNTAIN SICKNESS See altitude sickness.

MOUNTAINSIDE pertains to an insight into what one must encounter and overcome in the immediate future.

MOUNTAINTOP See summit.

MOUNT EVEREST represents the presence of a challenge in one's life.

MOUNT RUSHMORE represents spiritual desecration; spiritual apathy.

MOURNING See grief.

MOURNING DOVE calls for a greater expression of compassion or sympathetic attitudes.

MOUSE (computer) corresponds to precise control and the need for same.

MOUSE (rodent) connotes a negative aspect that has infiltrated one's life.

MOUSE PAD (computer) indicates an aid in maintaining a controlled communication or search.

MOUSE-EAR (botanical) suggests a need to listen better. Be quiet as a mouse and hear the things you've been missing.

MOUSER (cat/dog/snake) portrays a deterrent to a negative influence.

MOUSETRAP defines an attempt to rid one's life of destructive aspects.

MOUSSE (food) applies to superficial factors in one's life.

MOUSSE (hair dressing) warns against a lack of mental focus on important aspects.

MOUSTACHE illustrates a tendency to ineffectively express one's thoughts.

MOUSY (appearance) pertains to a timid or introverted personality.

MOUTH represents the manner in which one speaks or communicates.

MOUTHFUL calls for a need for the mind to be focused when communicating with others. Saying a mouthful can sometimes be hazardous to one's health.

MOUTH ORGAN See harmonica.

MOUTHPIECE suggests the advisement to speak for oneself.

MOUTHWASH comes to warn against harmful or abusive language.

MOUTH-WATERING alludes to a desire to be satisfied with a certain communication.

MOUTON (fabric) reveals a deception.

MOVIE indicates a personal message for the dreamer. Recall what the movie was about. Was it fiction? Real?

MOVIE PRODUCER characterizes one who has the capability to bring clarity to a situation through vivid visuals. This, in essence, will show any false perspectives one may have had.

MOVIE STAR may indicate hypocrisy or it might represent a glamorized or unreal perspective of life.

MOVIE THEATER connotes a possible unrealistic perspective and an attempt to clarify it.

MOVING See relocation.

MOVING SIDEWALK symbolizes an effortless phase of one's life journey.

MOVING VAN suggests a change of perspective or surrounding.

MOWING warns against cutting one's abilities or talents.

MOZZARELLA denotes an abundance of nourishing factors in one's life.

MUCILAGE See adhesive.

MUCK signifies a confused mind or situation.

MUCKRAKER characterizes an individual who is focused on the negatives in another's life.

MUCUS implies a protective agent in one's life. However, an excessive amount in a dream may point to a complex situation one is involved in.

MUD may represent perceptual distortion or it may indicate a healing factor in one's life. Recall surrounding dream details for further clarity.

MUD DAUBER See mud wasp.

MUDDLE-HEADED corresponds to mental confusion; an inability to do things right.

MUD FLAPS See splash guard.

MUD FLOW pertains to an inundation of confusing aspects in one's life.

MUDGUARD See splash guard.

MUD PUPPY See salamander.

MUD ROOM alludes to negative attitudes brought into the home.

MUDSLIDE See mud flow.

MUDSLINGING warns against defiling another's reputation or character.

MUD TURTLE reveals a state of near-constant confusion that is usually self-generated.

MUD WASP pertains to an individual in one's life who has a tendency to interfere and confuse issues.

MUD WRESTLING signifies a display of fun-loving competition; exaggerated conflict resolution for the sake of show.

MUEZZIN suggests a call to prayer.

MUFF connotes a tendency to avoid involvement.

MUFFIN represents small security factors in one's life.

MUFFLER (clothing) stands for an advisement to use more communicative discretion.

MUFFLER (exhaust) infers a quieting of intended or possible outbursts.

MUG (cup) corresponds with a strong character. Recall if the mug had any words on it. This will give further interpretation to the symbol.

MUGGER characterizes one who gains through the efforts of others.

MUGGY See humid.

MUG SHOT will reveal something important to each dreamer. Who was the photograph of? What was it in reference to? Was it yourself?

M

MUKLUKS stand for efforts applied to the prevention of losing sight of one's spirituality.

MULBERRY (tree) represents joy.

MULCH defines a fertile atmosphere; the right timing.

MULE may symbolize stubbornness, yet it usually indicates independence; a reluctance to be influenced; a combination of differing elements.

MULE DEER See deer.

MULESKINNER characterizes an extremely influential personality.

MULL (spice) implies a maturity is needed; more development.

MULL (think) See contemplation.

MULLEIN (botanical) symbolizes a healing aspect in one's life.

MULLION (window) defines multiple perspectives to an issue.

MULTIDIMENSIONAL (visuals) will denote multilayered factors to whatever is being presented. This is a valuable insight.

MULTIPLE-CHOICE refers to the many opportunities available.

MULTIPLE PERSONALITY will reveal inner thoughts or attitudes.

MULTIPLEX (movie theater) refers to multiple unrealistic perspectives.

MULTIPLICATION SIGN applies to the possibility of increasing something; opportunity to develop or advance.

MUM See chrysanthemum.

MUMBLE denotes a fear of expressing one's opinion or emotion.

MUMBO JUMBO pertains to illogical and irrational thought.

MUMMY exemplifies an unyielding personality; lacking open-mindedness.

MUMPS represent an inability to express emotional responses.

MUNCHING indicates an advisement to chew information; mentally process information better.

MUNCHKIN characterizes an animated personality; one who has an exuberance for life.

MUNDANE points out the balancing factors in life; a necessary counter to high spiritual levels.

MUNG BEAN See bean sprouts.

MUNITION See ammunition.

MURAL will reveal a specialized message for each dreamer. Recall what the mural depicted.

MURDER will usually represent a symbolic death. This may refer to a relationship, plan, or other type of current situation.

MURKY denotes a lack of clarity; a confused issue or situation.

MURMUR (low sound) suggests a call to attention; the dreamer needs to listen better and give greater attention to something in life.

MURPHY BED illustrates an efficient method; ingenuity.

MURPHY'S LAW implies a pessimistic outlook.

MUSCATEL See alcoholic beverage.

MUSCLE signifies effort applied. This symbol will reveal the quality of effort by displaying the condition of the muscle.

MUSCLE-BOUND warns against arrogance; self-love.

MUSCLE CRAMP/SPASM signifies a hitch with one's plans or behavior.

MUSCULAR DYSTROPHY pertains to an inability to motivate self.

MUSE See contemplation.

MUSE (Greek mythology) characterizes a source of one's inspiration.

MUSEUM relates to antiquated concepts.

MUSH See porridge.

MUSH (consistency) connotes unclear thoughts; confusion.

MUSHROOM represents a benefit resulting from a seemingly negative factor.

MUSHY (texture) points to inconsistency; an idea that's not based on firm elements; soft thinking.

MUSIC will indicate a harmonic or discordant state depending on the type of music presented.

MUSICAL CHAIRS (game) defines a stagnant phase of one's path; a lack of forward movement; going in circles.

MUSIC BOX suggests melancholia.

MUSIC HALL denotes an interest and appreciation for harmony in one's life.

MUSICIAN indicates spiritual harmony within oneself.

MUSIC OF THE SPHERES defines spiritual balance and inner peace.

MUSIC SHOP reveals the state of one's spiritual awareness. Recall what type of music was being perused. Who was doing the looking? What kind of music did the shop specialize in?

MUSIC VIDEO will connote how one applies harmonious inner aspects to life. What type of video was presented? Was it wild or gentle?

MUSK (scent) connotes a down-to-earth personality; one close to the earth; possessing primal (basic) spiritual beliefs without superficiality.

MUSKEG See bog.

MUSKETEER exemplifies a guarding aspect in one's life; a protective characteristic.

MUSKRAT signifies a repulsive attitude; an aversion.

MUSLIN (fabric) indicates simplicity; homespun wisdom and common sense.

MUSSEL refers to spiritual protectiveness, perhaps bordering on reclusiveness.

MUSTACHE See moustache.

MUSTANG reveals a wild type of individual freedom verging on recklessness.

MUSTARD (botanical) signifies a desire to enhance life events; exaggerations.

MUSTARD GAS warns against a highly dangerous aspect in one's life; a factor that could suffocate freedoms or beliefs.

MUSTARD PLASTER denotes a need to address negative factors in life that repress freedoms; a need for breathing room; fresh air is required.

MUSTARD SEED will most often indicate a new idea and the planting of same.

MUSTY indicates a need for fresh air (getting away from stale ideas).

MUTANT/MUTATION will indicate an altered perspective or character.

MUTE may call for silence.

MUTILATED refers to something destroyed beyond recognition; the destruction of integrity.

MUTINEER illustrates rebellion or the need for some. Surrounding dreamscape details will clarify which meaning this has for the dreamer.

MUTT (dog) represents a friend who will remain loyal.

MUTTER indicates insecurity; a lack of acceptance.

MUTTON See lamb.

MUTTONCHOPS (sideburns) imply spiritual verbosity.

MUTUAL FUNDS denote speculation.

MUUMUU relates to a carefree attitude. This could possibly refer to a tendency to hide behind appearances.

MUZAK alludes to subliminal communicative methods.

MUZZLE (device) connotes a restraint on communication or insights.

MUZZLE (gun barrel) pertains to aggressive communication.

MUZZLE (snout) suggests sensory insights.

MUZZLE LOADER applies to antiquated communication methods; ineffective contacts.

MYNA (bird) depicts congeniality.

MYOPIA (nearsightedness) emphasizes a lack of long-range perspective.

MYRRH defines spiritual insights and wisdom.

MYRTLE (botanical) refers to gentleness.

MYSTERY will correspond to a puzzlement in one's waking life and will usually contain demystifying factors.

MYSTERY (novel/movie) suggests a fascination with suspense and an interest in untangling convoluted situations.

MYSTIC (person) points to an overemphasis on the paranormal facets of spirituality and reality.

MYSTICAL (atmosphere) usually symbolizes the experiencing of an epiphany or an entry into one of the planes of true Reality. This symbol may also indicate a journey of the Higher Self.

MYTHICAL CHARACTER will constitute a wide variety of interpretations. Refer to specific character.

MYTHOLOGY (study of) stands for an interest in delving through the extraneous to discover the root of a truth.

N

NACHO connotes a wide range of personal expression.

NADIR (directional position) represents a beneath or under position. This could refer to a less advanced or developed aspect.

NAG (bother) may correspond with one's conscience. Recall surrounding dream details for clarification.

NAG (horse) pertains to weariness.

NAIL (finger/toe) See fingernail.

NAIL (metal) represents a need for attachments; connections.

NAIL BED will reveal one's state of health; may also refer to emotional health.

NAIL BITING stands for a lack of acceptance; anxiety and worry; lack of faith.

NAILBRUSH refers to a need to change one's ways; clean up dirty methods and tactics.

NAIL CLIPPERS illustrate an advisement to cut down and temper one's aggressive or rough behavioral tendencies.

NAIL ENAMEL See nail polish.

NAIL FILE comes as an advisement to smooth out one's rough edges in reference to dealing with others.

NAIL GUN alludes to making quick and easy connections.

NAIL HEAD will pertain to the basic aspect of an issue.

NAIL POLISH can reveal one's underlying personality or character. Recall depth of color and condition of polish.

NAIL SCISSORS See nail clippers.

NAÏVETÉ characterizes an innocent or uninformed person.

NAKEDNESS connotes an open heart; nothing to hide; no agendas or ulterior motives.

NAME(S) will have special meaning for each dreamer. The dream name may not correspond to an individual's awake-state name but will most frequently be the name of someone the Higher Self is attempting to draw attention to.

NAME BRAND usually indicates a preferred choice for the dreamer. It may also signify a brand to avoid, depending on how it's presented.

NAME-CALLING can portray an individual's true attitude toward another.

NAME-DROPPING is a suggestion for the dreamer. This will indicate someone or something to connect with or avoid. Recall surrounding dream details for this clarification.

NAMELESS connotes a lack of ego.

NAMEPLATE pertains to an identity, a

desire for same; implies a desire to be recognized.

NAMESAKE will indicate a respected or admired individual.

NAME TAG not only displays one's identity, it shows a willingness to do so. This symbol refers to mixing and meeting new contacts.

NANNY See babysitter.

NAP (fabric) can suggest a directional move. Recall if the nap was straight up or slanted to the right or left.

NAP (sleep) indicates a need for rejuvenating respite. Some dream intentions will point to an advisement to *stop* sleeping on the job.

NAPALM denotes an explosive aspect in one's life.

NAPHTHA connotes a versatile factor.

NAPKIN (table) applies to one's personal level and quality of preparedness in life. Recall color, fabric, and condition to gain deeper meaning.

NARC characterizes a person who exposes the secrets of others; one who can't be trusted with confidences; betrayer.

NARCISSUS (botanical) illustrates the dangers of egotism. The narcissus has narcotic properties.

NARCISSUS (Greek mythology) warns against self-centeredness.

NARCOLEPSY (sleepiness) denotes escapism; denial.

NARCOSIS warns against a self-induced state of apathy.

NARCOTIC defines an escape from reality associated with a lack of acceptance and personal responsibility. May also refer to

an aspect that lessens pain of a hurtful life situation.

NARRATIVE most often infers a dream as a message. Recall what the narrative was about and who was giving it.

NARROW (width) denotes a course or aspect with little room for error.

NARROW GAUGE (railway) represents a straight and very narrow path. This isn't necessarily a positive dreamscape fragment to manifest, for few true paths follow such a set course as a railway because there's no allotment for necessary detours.

NARROW-MINDEDNESS cautions one to expand intellectual explorations and inner perceptions.

NASDAQ relates to a source of specific information that may be valuable to the dreamer.

NASTURTIUM (botanical) refers to natural talents that, when utilized for the benefit of others, nourish self.

NATIONAL DEBT corresponds with a major obligation or responsibility in one's life.

NATIONAL GUARD pertains to a massive upheaval forthcoming in life.

NATIONAL MONUMENT will most often bring an important message specific to the dreamer. Check for personal associations with the presented monument. See specific monument.

NATIONAL PARK SERVICE refers to those who work to preserve inherent abilities/bounties.

NATIONAL RIFLE ASSOC. (NRA) stands for one's rights to protect and defend oneself. This symbol may appear in the dreams of someone who is reluctant to stand up for her/his rights.

NATIONAL WEATHER SERVICE signifies those who watch over us. This symbol can even refer to one's own intuitiveness.

NATIVE (indigenous) will symbolize one's right to something that may currently be denied.

NATIVE AMERICAN See American Indian.

NATURAL CHILDBIRTH (unplanned emergency birth) signifies a premature manifestation of a goal or new life.

NATURAL FOOD (no additives) indicates a pure aspect; one having no affecting factors, such as a basic idea or attitude.

NATURAL GAS alludes to potentially explosive factors in one's life. This is a symbol pointing to something that carries the potential for great negatives in spite of its useful benefits.

NATURAL HISTORY (study of) denotes a high interest in the human bond with all living things.

NATURAL HISTORY MUSEUM reflects a call to/desire for getting in touch with our bonded relationship with all of life.

NATURALIST will most often reveal a spiritually enlightened individual.

NATURAL RESOURCES represent inherent characteristics and talents, our personal natural gifts.

NATURAL SCIENCE (study of) denotes a high interest in discovering the extent of true Reality; an extended and reaching search.

NATURAL SELECTION alludes to the power of inner strength; perseverance.

NATURE TRAIL connotes a life path chosen for the value of its multiple lessons.

NATUROPATHY symbolizes synergic solutions; the application or utilization of inherent healing qualities within self or nature.

NAUGAHYDE (fabric) See leatherette.

NAUSEA warns of an inability to accept or absorb a disagreeable facet in one's life. This symbol will sometimes advise one of the wisdom to overlook more in life.

NAUTILUS (shell) defines the multidimensional interconnectedness of spiritual aspects and true Reality.

NAVEL (anatomy) relates to a strong bond with another.

NAVIGATION (instrumentation) refers to the personal methods or tools we each use to make our way in life. These will usually refer to the use of awareness, intellect, inner drive, reflection on lessons gained from hindsight, etc.

NAVIGATOR characterizes one who has planned out a set course in life.

NAVY BASE connotes one's personal spiritual protective/defensive methods.

NAVY BLUE (color) stands for rigid religious beliefs.

NAVY YARD suggests spiritual repair work that needs to be done.

NAYSAYER reveals a pessimistic or cynical attitude. May also imply contrariness.

NAZI exemplifies one who desires to have control over others; a megalomaniac who is apathetic to the rights of others.

NEANDERTHAL will not necessarily mean primitive but usually refers to a willful state of ignorance.

NEAR BEER indicates a factor in one's life that verges on being negative; getting close to being a potentially destructive aspect.

NEAR MISS denotes an off-center or unfocused direction; a path that will lead one off-course.

NEARSIGHTED See myopia.

NEBRASKA suggests a stewardship of one's natural gifts/bounties.

NEBULA pertains to an obscure idea.

NECK reveals a person's inquisitiveness; curiosity.

Broken neck indicates the result of sticking one's neck out where it didn't belong.

Long neck refers to high curiosity and imagination.

No neck suggests an absence of curiosity to the extent of having no imagination or interest in thinking outside the box.

Rubberneck points to a nosy individual, one loving gossip.

Short neck represents a mild amount of interest.

Stiff neck reflects set ways and attitudes.

NECK ACHE stands for a self-generated block to one's desire to gain further knowledge on a specific subject; frustration over trying to solve a problem or figure out solutions.

NECK AND NECK connotes competitiveness.

NECK BRACE points to efforts to support or bolster one's inquisitiveness; perseverance in regard to pursuing an issue.

NECKERCHIEF alludes to perseverance; extended personal efforts.

NECKLACE emphasizes a type of personal interest or attraction; may reveal inner traits.

NECK OF THE WOODS See neighborhood.

NECKTIE warns against willfully choking off or smothering intellectual pursuits or inquisitiveness over something.

NECROMANCY signifies interdimensional communication; ease of multilevel communication or perception.

NECROPHILIA comes as a message to focus on aspects of one's life rather than dwelling on the past.

NECROPHOBIA See fear (death/corpses).

NECTAR corresponds with that which is sweetest in life; attained goals; fruitful relationships or concluding situations.

NECTARINE relates to a fresh idea or perspective.

NEEDLE (medical) See hypodermic needle.

NEEDLE (sewing) pertains to an aspect in life that has the potential to be used for repair or connective purposes.

NEEDLECRAFT (hobby) refers to a cleverness for finding solutions; an attention to details others tend to miss.

NEEDLE-NOSE (pliers) See pliers (needle-nose).

NEEDLEPOINT illustrates fortitude. Recall what type of needlepoint was presented. Who was doing it? What was the needlepoint image of?

NEEDLE THREADER represents a desire/attempt to use every aid possible to get to the main issue (eye) of a problem or situation.

NEEDY emphasizes available opportunities. Some neediness is perceived rather than being actual. In this case, the symbol stands for a bid for sympathy.

NE'ER-DO-WELL implies unrecognized direction and associative lack of motivation.

NEGATIVISM signifies a pessimistic outlook; a cynic.

NEGLIGEE See nightgown.

NEGOTIATIONS indicate a desire for compromise.

NEIGHBOR will pinpoint someone who exists within close proximity to another, not necessarily an associate or friend.

NEIGHBORHOOD refers to a cultural or economic indicator that will have a revealing effect on additional dream aspects. A neighborhood can expose one's inner attitudes or opinion, desires or fears.

NEIGHBORHOOD CRIME WATCH See road signs.

NEMESIS (Greek mythology) corresponds with guilt; karmic justice forthcoming for misdeeds done. May also point to an ongoing irritation, anxiety, problem, or fear.

NEON (fish) will pertain to a spiritual light for one to pay attention to.

NEOPHYTE See novice.

NEOPRENE defines a willful avoidance of spiritual aspects in one's life.

NEPHRITE (gemstone) symbolizes a healing aspect in one's life which sustains self-healing capabilities.

NEPOTISM warns against preferential treatment or behavior.

NEPTUNE (planet) refers to one's inherent natural abilities; spiritual gifts.

NEPTUNE (Roman mythology) See Poseidon.

NERVE will correspond with a specific type of emotional sensitivity. Recall surrounding dreamscape details for further clarity.

NERVE BLOCK usually refers to a self-generated, psychological blocking being done; selective sensitivity.

NERVE CENTER signifies the source (hub) of one's motivational force. Depending on related dreamscape elements, this symbol may also point to one's sensitivities, the panel of buttons people can push.

NERVE DAMAGE suggests a self-generated disability caused by not reconciling a past event.

NERVE GAS connotes a desire to control others through emotional manipulation. Recall who possessed the gas or where it came from.

NERVE-RACKING indicates an inability to overlook life irritations; a need for acceptance to generate inner tranquility.

NERVOUS BREAKDOWN signifies a need for inner strength and acceptance.

NEST denotes a security factor and will imply insecurity.

NEST EGG symbolizes preparedness; efficient planning.

NESTING refers to foresight; insights that hint at needed preparations.

NESTLE exemplifies a comfortable situation; a feeling of security.

NESTLING See fledgling.

NET alludes to entrapments; method of catching another or not allowing anything to get by you.

NET (Internet) See Internet.

NET INCOME suggests the benefits/assets left after one subtracts the output elements. This symbol is advising one to weigh the pros and cons of a situation or plan.

NETTING (mosquito) constitutes some form of protective measure; an insurance-type of aspect.

NETTLE (botanical) suggests some form of major annoyance in one's life.

NETWORKING signifies a chain of information-sharing; reveals a situation that is no longer private.

NEUROLOGIST characterizes one who has a high interest in determining causal psychological factors that prevent others from utilizing full potential.

NEUROLOGY (study of) depicts a desire to understand the self-generated restraints used by others.

NEUROSIS defines a lack of acceptance resulting in a loss of inner peace.

NEUROTIC characterizes multiple inner fears; lack of trust and acceptance.

NEUTER denotes a cause or source barring effectiveness.

NEUTRAL (gear) typifies a situation that lacks any developmental aspects; a stage of nonmovement; no opinion or desire to express same.

NEUTRAL GROUND/ZONE defines a phase, situation, or condition that is without opposing factors; a time or place allowing for peace regardless of differing attitudes.

NEUTRALIZED signifies a negation of power.

NEVADA signifies character/attitude extremes.

NEVER-NEVER LAND represents a fear of growing up; an inability to face the world and attending responsibilities of maturity.

NEW AGE equates to a blend of physics and spirituality. The symbol points to a realization and utilization of elements related to true Reality.

NEW BLOOD (people) indicates a need for new and fresh ideas and perspectives.

NEWBORN will correspond with a new life, path, belief, or other type of personal discovery.

NEWEL (post) constitutes a main supportive aspect in one's life. This could refer to an emotional, mental, or spiritual issue.

NEWFOUNDLAND (dog breed) refers to a friend having great fortitude; a staunch friend.

NEW HAMPSHIRE suggests a tolerance for the expression of individuality.

NEW JERSEY refers to personal resourcefulness.

NEWLYWED relates to a new relationship that has been forged.

NEW MEXICO signifies a pride of one's ethnicity/inherent traits.

NEW MOON See moon (new).

NEWSCAST/FLASH will almost always bring important information to light that is relevant to the dreamer.

NEWS CONFERENCE See press conference.

NEWSLETTER comes as a message specific to each dreamer. Its purpose is to keep one up to date on an aspect in one's life.

NEWSPAPER represents an awareness within oneself.

NEWSPRINT (paper type) implies widespread information.

NEWS RELEASE pertains to a special announcement message the dreamer needs to note. This symbol comes as a major personal message and should always be taken seriously.

NEWSSTAND indicates the opportunity for readily available information. This would usually refer to someone (possibly the dreamer) who believes he/she has little access to new ideas or information.

NEWT See salamander.

NEWTON (Isaac) pertains to the simplicity of true Reality and the revealing messages nature has to teach us.

NEW WAVE (fashion/music) signifies the expression of innovative, controversial, or unique personal perspectives; a freedom of bold expression without concern of ridicule.

NEW YEAR'S DAY always stands for the first day of a new beginning, unless that particular day marks something of importance unique to the dreamer.

NEW YEAR'S EVE connotes the approach of a whole new set of opportunities that are just around the corner.

NEW YEAR'S RESOLUTION sets one up for disappointment and self-deprecating situations. This symbol in a dream will come to infer that a general plan is wise, but a solid resolution is not reasonable nor, in the end, a productive promise to self.

NEW YORK stands for diversity; an acceptance of another's uniqueness.

NEW ZEALAND suggests pastoral respite.

NEXT DAY DELIVERY reveals an urgent document or communication.

NIAGARA FALLS connotes a powerful spiritual renewal.

NIBBLE signifies a manner of taking in new information through discretion (nibbling).

NICHE will symbolize a designated proper place for something. This may refer to a deed, verbal expression of an emotion or opinion, or one's life purpose;

the best possible place or position for alignment or success.

NICK (dent/mark) alludes to a small setback or disappointment; may refer to marks of experience gained along the way.

NICKEL (coin) connotes the presence of a means that has the capability of gaining power to accomplish a goal in one's life.

NICKEL (metal) implies a replacement method or means to utilize in place of a formerly planned approach.

NICKEL-AND-DIME denotes an insignificant amount that has the potential of growing into an impressive volume.

NICKNAME will reveal an important characteristic or hidden aspect of someone.

NIGHT corresponds to the preferred time to explore hidden aspects of self or spiritual matters.

NIGHT BLINDNESS warns of a self-induced ignorance.

NIGHTCAP (drink) infers the existence of unresolved problems.

NIGHTCLUB pertains to missed opportunities for gaining deeper understanding.

NIGHT COURT represents the time for self-analyzation.

NIGHT CRAWLER (worm) typifies a personal incentive to actively delve into enriching spiritual concepts that are generally considered high intellectual aspects.

NIGHTGOWN denotes an appropriate preparedness for one's planned activity.

NIGHTHAWK connotes extreme high awareness.

NIGHTINGALE (bird) relates to one's outward expression of spiritual joy.

NIGHTINGALE (Florence) exemplifies the power of determination and its resulting manifestations.

NIGHT-LIGHT represents a small measure of anxiety; a subconscious lack of self-confidence.

NIGHTMARE emphasizes one's inner fears.

NIGHT OWL characterizes a natural knowing of the most effectively powerful timing to engage in self-discovery or intellectual contemplation.

NIGHTRIDER warns of underhandedness; hidden aggression.

NIGHT SCHOOL advises of a need for immediate learning. There is something in the dreamer's life that must be quickly learned.

NIGHT SHIFT denotes a suggestion for one to apply self during the quiet night hours. This comes as a message for those claiming they have no time for advancing or developing through learning or study. This may even refer to a proper meditative time for the dreamer.

NIGHTSPOT See nightclub.

NIGHTSTAND/TABLE comes to visually display an important item (aspect) one needs to further development or understanding.

NIGHT STICK See billy club.

NIGHT SWEATS usually stand for our fears and anxieties that we keep hidden during the daytime hours. Also see menopause.

NIGHT TERROR relates to vulnerability; a deeply subconscious susceptibility to awake-state subliminal suggestive impressions.

NIGHT WATCHPERSON characterizes one's personal defenses; protective measures.

NIKE (Greek mythology) symbolizes great inner strength and strong determination to carry something through to a successful conclusion.

NILE (river) pertains to spiritual life.

NILE CROCODILE represents a potentially destructive spiritual force.

NIMBLENESS stands for tenacity; an ability to bounce back after a setback or disappointment.

NINE (number) implies a productive path.

NINE-ELEVEN (9-11 date) stands for a catastrophic event that shocks us to the bone; the appearance of a Phoenix Days event.

NINON (fabric) portrays a delicate aspect to one's personality; a specifically fragile sensitivity.

NIRVANA signifies a mental/emotional state of euphoria. This is not a positive dreamscape fragment, for it infers that the dreamer is living in a fantasy world and not within acceptance of daily reality. This usually indicates one living in one's own world.

NIT-PICKING frequently comes from one's own conscience to reveal a criticizing tendency.

NITROGLYCERIN emphasizes the existence of a highly explosive personality, situation, relationship, or belief system.

NITROUS OXIDE corresponds with a psychological mechanism one utilizes to ease the pains and disappointments in life.

NOAH (biblical) characterizes strong faith and behavior related to same.

NOBEL NOMINEE points to recognition

for great efforts applied and resulting successes.

NOBEL PRIZE pertains to recognition by higher forces for efforts expended toward others; symbolizes a great achievement.

NOBILITY implies a tendency to make class distinctions; an arrogance.

NO CALL LIST exemplifies those who don't want to waste their time on insignificant or undesirable aspects.

NOCTURNE alludes to a tranquil state of inner peace.

NOD (of head) suggests recognition or agreement.

NODDING OFF either denotes a need for respite from overwork or it points to an inability to remain aware due to disinterest or boredom.

NODULE represents an irregularity. Recall surrounding dreamscape details for further clarity.

NO-FAULT comes as a message to discount blame or judgment.

NO-HITTER underscores a successful endeavor that carried no setbacks or problems with it.

NOISE MAKER represents an issue made of something. This may infer that one needs to bring an issue to another's attention or it may warn to leave something alone instead of making an issue of it. This meaning will be clear after surrounding dream details are looked at.

NOISE POLLUTION advises of a need for one to sort through information or communications for the purpose of gleaning the important basic ideas.

NOMAD connotes the freedom to follow one's own chosen path.

NOM DE PLUME See pseudonym.

NOMINATION will reveal the best qualified person; the person of choice.

NONCHALANCE may not necessarily mean apathy or indifference; it may indicate an attitude or opinion that's reserved until further knowledge has been obtained.

NONCONFORMIST applies to a freethinker; one unafraid of expressing individualism.

NONFICTION will most often reveal the truth to a matter.

NONSENSE may not be nonsense in a dream; it frequently represents something the dreamer has not sorted out yet and has the potential to reveal solutions.

NONSTICK (surface) will symbolize an aspect in one's life that has the potential of easing one's way.

NOODLE See pasta.

NOON will pinpoint a preferred time designation associated with something one is planning. Each dreamer will associate various events with this time-related symbol. It may also point to a midway point of something.

NOOSE forewarns of harmful or disastrous outcomes if a current path is followed.

NOR'EASTER refers to a temporary emotional upset; a phase of emotional distress which can't be avoided.

NORFOLK ISLAND PINE stands for a heightened sensitivity to others.

NORFOLK TERRIER (dog breed) signifies a sympathetic friend, one eager to listen and offer comfort.

NORTH (direction) denotes a direction that may need to be taken. North indicates an above or higher position.

NORTH AMERICA signifies perseverance and free-expression of individuality.

NORTH CAROLINA signifies the beauty of one's natural blessings and the need to recognize/appreciate them.

NORTH DAKOTA represents one's roots and their traditions.

NORTHERN LIGHTS See aurora borealis.

NORTH KOREA currently represents suppression.

NORTH POLE comes as a directional advisement to obtain balance. North will indicate higher conceptual aspects to focus on.

NORTHWEST PASSAGE signifies guidance for one's spiritual search. The surrounding dreamscape details will make this more clear for the dreamer.

NORWAY stands for resilience; courage.

NORWEGIAN ELKHOUND (dog breed) denotes a friend's loyalty.

NOSE (anatomy) corresponds to a person's sense of direction; instincts; ability to recognize insights.

Broken nose points to a wrong direction taken or an error in judgment.

Large nose corresponds with a lack of discretionary analyzation; an inability to differentiate important elements from the insignificant ones.

No nose reveals no sense of direction or lack of instinct.

Small nose portrays a mild ability for accurate discernment.

NOSEBLEED implies an interfering nature.

NOSE CANDY See cocaine.

NOSE CONE pertains to a planned path that is efficiently austere; a direct methodology.

NOSE DIVE depicts a headlong immersion into something. This may be a positive or negative symbol, depending on surrounding dreamscape aspects that will clarify the intended meaning.

NOSEGAY (small bouquet) connotes a small yet extremely meaningful act that serves to encourage or comfort another.

NOSE JOB See rhinoplasty.

NOSEPIECE relates to protective measures one uses as one advances along a chosen path.

NOSE SPRAY stands for a need for breathing room; suggests a personally suffocating situation.

NO-SHOW emphasizes a reluctance to participate. Recall associative dream details to pinpoint what this refers to.

NOSINESS comes to caution against interfering in another's life.

NOSTALGIA corresponds with one's memories. These always come as a message to either remember something in one's past or to accept and go on in life.

NOSTRADAMUS (Michel) advises of the wisdom of sharing that which one knows; stands for strength of one's convictions in spite of opposition or humiliation.

NOTARY PUBLIC constitutes a personal verification of one's chosen direction; a validating nod of approval.

NOTATIONS See note.

NOTCH usually indicates taking note of or marking one's advancing steps in life.

NOTE pinpoints a matter of importance that one needs to give attention to or make note of. This will come as a personal message for each dreamer.

NOTEBOOK suggests a need to recall details or keep a record of something.

NOTICE is an attention-getting symbol. Recall what the notice pertained to. This will be important.

NOTORIOUS will reveal an individual's hidden negative aspects.

NOUGAT (confection) alludes to a positive aspect or event that presents a measure of complexity to work through.

NOUVEAU RICHE warns against an attitude of arrogance regarding one's possessions, material wealth, or talent gifts. Points to a great responsibility in regard to how one's wealth is managed—generously or miserly.

NOVEL illustrates personal, sometimes hidden, interests one uses as an escape mechanism. Recall what type of novel it was. Mystery? Romance? War story? Gory? Erotica?

NOVELTY indicates a passing fancy; a temporary fad that usually pertains to a new and fascinating idea that proves to bare little substance when thoroughly analyzed.

NOVEMBER is a time to count one's blessings; appreciate the positive elements in one's life.

NOVICE reveals a lack of experiential or knowledgeable background; a beginner.

NOVOCAIN warns of a state of self-induced apathy; a *purposeful* avoidance of *selective* life aspects.

NOZZLE pertains to one's personal mode of delivery; how one interacts with others. Recall the condition of the nozzle and if it was working properly. What was coming out of it? Was this substance hazardous? Clear? What color?

NUANCE connotes a subtle suggestion; a fear of openly expressing an opinion or personal attitude; innuendo.

NUCLEAR FAMILY characterizes those closest to the dreamer.

NUCLEAR-FREE ZONE represents a personal desire for harmony and peaceful conditions in one's life.

NUCLEAR POWER PLANT stands for a high-risk option.

NUCLEAR REACTOR defines a potentially contaminating negative facet in one's life.

NUCLEAR WINTER illustrates the devastating outcome of one's current behavior or path; a destruction of one's current condition and relationships.

NUCLEUS comes as a strong advisement to get to the core of an issue or concept. This would indicate a wasteful involvement with superficial facets instead of focusing on the basic premise.

NUDE See nakedness.

NUDGE symbolizes a push from one's Higher Self.

NUDIST COLONY portrays honesty among one's associates.

NUGGET applies to a small treasure found in one's life; an extremely valuable piece of information.

NUISANCE may exemplify one's own conscience; one's Higher Self.

NULLIFIED will pinpoint an unproductive aspect, thereby saving the dreamer time and effort expended on a path or purpose that is superficial and unproductive to a goal.

NUMBERS are extremely meaningful dream symbols and have a multitude of diverse meanings. See specific number. See below for numbers in specific places.

N

Numbers circled on a calendar will define an important day having special significance for the dreamer.

Numbers in a bank book reveal a forthcoming change in the dreamer's status of wealth. Wealth does not specifically refer to money but also to natural talents and spiritual gifts. Recall the bank book's condition and color.

Numbers in an airport terminal come as strong warnings. These may be attempting to warn you "away" from a specific flight number or they could be advising you to take the represented flight number. The dream details will clarify which meaning is intended.

Numbers in or over water refer to the dreamer's spirituality.

Numbers in the sky connote a spiritual communication forthcoming.

Numbers on a book can reveal if the information provided within its pages is productive to one's knowledge base or pertinent to one's life.

Numbers on a house indicate a special association between the person residing there and the dreamer. It may also reveal a numerical interpretation for your own dwelling.

Numbers on a license plate usually warn of an upcoming vehicular accident involving the dreamer (or someone close to the dreamer) *and* the vehicle presented in the dream.

Numbers on a lottery ticket usually suggest a forthcoming change in financial status. This is not necessarily a positive dream fragment. Recall the condition and color of the dream ticket.

Numbers on a mile marker can reveal how far one still has to go to attain a goal.

Numbers on an infant will signify a purpose in life.

Numbers on a timepiece (all the same) call for a need to slow down. It's vitally important to recall the number that appeared on the timepiece. This will clarify the meaning further.

Numbers on a timepiece (out of sequence) imply that your life is out of order, your timing is off.

Numbers on a tombstone (dates) point to a death date. This date may refer to a physical death or a termination of something personally valuable. Usually the surrounding dream details will clarify this information.

Numbers on a wall emphasize a fact that should be obvious to the dreamer; reveals what one's course will manifest in the end.

Numbers on billboards will be directly associated with whatever the sign is displaying.

Numbers on grocery items come as a suggestion to increase or decrease the ingestion of the food presented. Diet dreams should never be ignored.

Numbers on medication advise of a need to increase, decrease, or stop taking the medication altogether.

Numbers on people's foreheads reveal one's true mental or spiritual state of being.

Numbers on playing cards will indicate the manner in which one lives life (plays the hand dealt).

Numbers over people's hearts emphasize their true emotional state or attitude.

Numbers surrounded in black will be a forewarning symbol often referring to a death of some type.

NUMBERS GAME refers to a slim chance one has taken or is thinking of taking in life; risks.

NUMBNESS warns of a self-induced state of emotional or mental selectivity; a willful ignorance or insensitivity.

NUMEROLOGY (study of) cautions against basing one's overall opinions or perceptions on a singular set of narrow guidelines.

NUN characterizes the incorporation of spiritual facets throughout the fabric of one's daily life.

NURSE portrays a compassionate and selfless personality, one capable of healing others.

NURSEMAID characterizes a caregiver. This symbol usually reveals an unruly, incompetent, or reckless individual who needs routine watching over.

NURSERY (botanical) represents the concentrated nurturing of one's natural talents and spiritual gifts.

NURSERY (infant) pertains to the special care given to one's new beginnings.

NURSERY RHYME can reveal an important message specific to the dreamer.

NURSERY SCHOOL pertains to the learning stages of a novice or beginning seeker.

NURSE'S AIDE will denote a person willing to help another.

NURSE'S CAP indicates one whose thought process is tightly woven with compassion and healing.

NURSE SHOES reveal one who willingly gives assistance to others while walking her/his personal life path.

NURSING HOME represents one's perspective toward those who are more experienced and have more knowledge. Recall the condition of the home. Who was residing there?

NUT (food/tool) indicates a lack of logic and reason; in essence, someone who is a literal nut case.

NUTCRACKER will exemplify a need for resolutions and/or solutions.

NUTHATCH (bird) portrays an ability to discover solutions.

NUTMEG connotes an inherent, natural essence of self; an inborn ability.

NUTRITIONIST alludes to one who has the potential to advise others of what their life is lacking; providing what is needed for advancement.

NUTS AND BOLTS signify the basics of an issue.

NUTSHELL relates to self-devised shells one uses for self-protection. This symbol may also indicate a need to consolidate one's beliefs or perspectives into a basic, simple form. Recall surrounding dreamscape details to determine which interpretation your dream intended.

NUZZLE corresponds to emotional expressions of love and companionship.

NYLON (fabric) implies some form of disassociative personality trait; a personal desire to distance self from others or certain situations.

NYMPH (Greek mythology) symbolizes a person who takes great inner joy from being close to nature; one possessing multiple natural (nature) qualities.

O

OAK (tree) denotes an unyielding personality; a lack of sensitivity; rigidness.

OAR represents great personal efforts and suffering endured while on one's spiritual path.

OASIS pertains to rejuvenating respite phases.

OAT See grain.

OATH relates to promises that must be kept, even those to self.

OATMEAL signifies a life aspect that personally comforts and nourishes.

OBEDIENCE TRAINING (dog) isn't usually a good symbol, for it implies manipulation either of a friend or from a friend.

OBEDIENT PLANT (botanical) suggests a need to stop ignoring one's conscience.

OBELISK denotes an important factor for the dreamer. Dreamscape shapes such as obelisks refer to spiritual conceptual truths.

OBESITY represents an overindulgence of some type; an inability to deny oneself; lack of self-control. This symbol may also point to a love/hate conflict within oneself.

OBI connotes personal encumbrances; superficial or extraneous beliefs, attitudes, or perspectives we carry around.

OBITUARY comes as a warning of a forthcoming death that may be emotional in respect to a relationship rather than an actual physical event. Recall surrounding dreamscape details for clarity. Was there a specific name presented? A date? Cause of death?

OBJECTIONS will reveal an individual's true opinion. An objection in a dream can also be a message from one's Higher Self.

OBJET D'ART will usually represent a personal message unique to each dreamer. This piece of art will symbolize something important in one's life.

OBLIVION means a state of mind that is devoid of emotion, purpose, or humanitarian aspects.

OBLONG (shape) alludes to the act of stretching out one's efforts unnecessarily; extraneous work one believes is part of one's path.

OBSCENITY won't necessarily denote a negative sign; it may present itself as a means of emphasis or revelation of an individual's hidden attitudes.

OBSERVATORY implies deeper knowledge and higher awareness needed.

OBSESSION will stress an overemphasis applied to a specific issue. This is a warning symbol.

OBSIDIAN (gemstone) expresses the beauty of the more esoteric spiritual concepts and gifts and the protection of them; denotes strengthened empowerment.

OBSOLESCENCE refers to outdated information, attitudes, or manner of doing something.

OBSTACLE COURSE indicates a life path containing difficult situations to overcome. This course could be self-generated and not necessarily an imperative factor of reality.

OBSTETRICIAN characterizes a person who has the knowledge and ability to bring forth a new life or awakening in others.

OCCULT means hidden or little understood aspects; therefore, this symbol will refer to something in one's life that needs to be looked at harder and given deeper contemplative time.

OCCUPATIONAL DISEASE indicates a suggestion to alter one's life course or change a harmful situation.

OCCUPATIONAL HAZARD refers to a seriously harmful main element associated with one's current or chosen course.

OCCUPATIONAL THERAPY implies a need to discover, learn, and apply enhanced methods and skills directed toward one's life path and/or manner of communication.

OCEAN alludes to spiritual facets in one's life.

OCEANFRONT See lakefront.

OCEANOGRAPHY (study of) relates to a high interest in diverse spiritual concepts.

OCELOT denotes patience.

OCTOBER represents a uniting time; sealing relationships; reaffirming personal bonds. This also stands for a time to reap (appreciate) the blessings of home and family.

OCTOPUS warns of spiritual flailing; a situation where one is randomly reaching out in all directions for whatever spiritual idea one can grab onto.

ODD JOBS can bring significant learning experiences and usually come in dreams to represent this message.

ODDS will reveal probabilities for success in relation to something the dreamer is anticipating doing or is concerned about.

ODDS AND ENDS symbolize remnant aspects that need to be attended to.

ODDS-MAKER characterizes a person who has a knack for sensing probabilities.

ODOMETER displays the amount of progression or advancement one has made in life.

> **High mileage** indicates a great deal of ground has been covered.

> **Low mileage** will suggest a need to get going.

ODORS provide important pieces of information that can reveal a negative or positive quality to something.

> **Floral scent** will relate to the specific flower. See specific flower species.

> **Food smell** refers to the meaning of that specific food item.

> **Fresh scent** alludes to a fresh idea.

> **Repulsive odor** indicates an aversion.

> **Sea scent** will relate to a spiritual element.

> **Sewer odor** implies an extremely negative connotation.

ODYSSEY will represent a life path full of self-discovery.

OFF (position) defines a condition or

state of affairs. This symbol may indicate a need to turn something *on*.

OFFAL pertains to waste aspects on which one shouldn't be expending personal efforts or attention.

OFF AND ON connotes a vacillation; an intermittent effort or attention.

OFFBEAT most often signifies thoughts/ideas that are considered outside the box.

OFF-BRAND represents a cheaper alternative; a substitute that may work just as well as one demanding more energy output.

OFF-BROADWAY signifies an experimental attempt or move; the testing of an idea.

OFF-COLOR will point to something that's been compromised by an affecting attitude; perhaps a judgment or opinion that's biased or affected by personal perspective.

OFFERING represents good intentions.

OFFICE always pertains to work or personal efforts applied.

OFFICE BOY characterizes one who expends efforts to help another achieve a purpose/goal.

OFFICE MANAGER characterizes one who has the capability to guide another through a more efficient manner of work or effort.

OFFICE SUPPLY STORE implies the wide variety of tools available to accomplish a goal.

OFF-KEY illustrates a lack of harmony, perhaps even within self; being *off* regarding course or perspective.

OFF-LIMITS comes as a severe warning; one is trespassing where one shouldn't be.

OFF-LINE signifies a break from research, communication, or intellectual expansion due to either a voluntary choice or from one's connection being interrupted.

OFF-PEAK See off-season.

OFF RAMP represents a choice or opportunity to get off the fast track for a time.

OFF-ROAD VEHICLE See four-wheel drive.

OFF-SEASON signifies a time when a certain activity is not generally carried out, yet this symbol may suggest that the off-season is the preferred time to accomplish something the dreamer is contemplating. Surrounding details will clarify which message was intended.

OFFSHOOT exemplifies a resulting manifestation generated by something one has said or done; a ramification.

OFFSHORE directs one toward a spiritual aspect.

OFFSHORE DRILLING relates to efforts given in search of deeper spiritual meaning.

OFFSPRING signifies aspects of ourselves or those qualitative elements that we leave behind.

OFF-THE-BOOKS reveals hidden assets or an attempt to keep something secret.

OFF-THE-CUFF refers to spontaneity; instinctual reactions; impulsiveness.

OFF-THE-RACK/SHELF alludes to something that is easily accessible.

OFF-THE-RECORD signifies a secret or information that is not for general information.

OFF-THE-WALL represents shocking behavior; totally unexpected and perhaps irrational.

OFF-TRACK BETTING constitutes a chance taken without being aware of all the associative factors involved.

OFF-WHITE (color) will indicate an affecting facet to something; not quite pure or the whole truth.

OGLE applies to a lack of respect and acceptable behavior.

OGRE stands for an inability to accept life; a poor self-image.

OHIO signifies quiet opinions; a tendency toward silent acceptance.

OIL indicates a lack of abrasiveness or friction; that which soothes and eases; an element essential to keeping things going smoothly.

OILCAN signifies a means to lessen life irritations and rough relationships.

OILCLOTH (fabric) typically denotes a need for more healthful eating habits, not what one eats but rather the manner of eating. Generally, we eat on the go too much and portions are far too large. We eat when we're upset and when angry.

OIL COLOR (art medium) See oil paint.

OIL FIELD indicates a poor choice of opportunities, one that carries multiple negative side effects.

OIL PAINT (art medium) signifies an inherent gift of creativity that comes easily to one.

OIL PAN defines efficiency; an ability to cover all aspects of an issue.

OIL REFINERY comes as a message to refine one's crude qualities; indicates a need to soften or control insensitive expressiveness.

OIL SLICK warns of a need to proceed cautiously, with high awareness.

OIL SPILL points to dangerous behavior which suffocates one's spirituality.

OILSTONE See whetstone.

OIL TANKER represents a method of protecting one's spirituality from being contaminated by dangerously negative elements.

OIL WELL corresponds to a great opportunity that must be carefully planned out in order to optimize its potential for good.

OINTMENT signifies a healing or emotionally soothing element in one's life. What type of ointment was shown? Who was offering or using it?

OKLAHOMA symbolizes a strong sense of self, not in a self-centered way, but a strong feel for one's individuality.

OKTOBERFEST relates to a reason to rejoice; a time to celebrate one's home, family, and closest friends. This is a revealing symbol that usually points out a positive element in one's life that may not be recognized for the benefits/blessings it brings.

OLD-BOY NETWORK stands for the adage: It's not *what* you know, it's *who* you know. This usually reveals a situation in which those outside a certain circle of individuals are shut out and not afforded the same advancing opportunities as those within the circle. This will have a very specific meaning for each dreamer.

OLD COUNTRY pertains to long-held traditions and where one's heart might still lie. Also could point to the existence of certain underlying loyalties.

OLD ENGLISH SHEEPDOG (dog breed) signifies a loyal, faithful friend, one who can be counted on.

OLD FAITHFUL (geyser) denotes trust and dependability.

OLD FARMER'S ALMANAC stands for wisdom from nature; a natural, inherent wisdom.

OLD-FASHIONED HATS represent outdated ideas or attitudes that could be related to good old common sense or ideas/attitudes that are behind the times.

OLD-FASHIONED SHOES warn of an out-dated way of accomplishing a goal; a path traveled via antiquated methods.

OLD FOLKS See elder.

OLD GROWTH (forest) indicates perspectives/ideas that have endured and passed the test of time.

OLD GUARD suggests a reluctance to alter attitudes or perspectives.

OLD HAND characterizes gained experience.

OLD HAT connotes an old-fashioned idea; something that has been around for a long time and is generally well known.

OLD MAID (card game) implies an anxiety or fear of age; may refer to a fear of having to care for an elder. This may also stand for a woman's independence. Surrounding dreamscape fragments will clarify which meaning was intended.

OLD MASTERS (artists) characterize those whose creative achievements of individuality have left valuable contributions in their wake.

OLD MONEY See money (old).

OLD SCHOOL alludes to strong, traditional perspectives that aren't currently applicable.

OLD SHOE will stand for someone with a lot of experience at something.

OLD TESTAMENT comes as an advisement to readjust one's thinking on something. The dreamer will have a knowing of what this issue is.

OLD-TIMER will characterize one who knows the history/tales; one who's experienced.

OLD WEST (setting) signifies a secret wish for adventure in a less complicated world.

OLD WIVES' TALE will reveal a piece of truth the dreamer will recognize.

OLEANDER (botanical) reminds us that appearances can be deceiving; an appearance of something in one's life that seems to be good or be a blessing may, in actually, ultimately prove harmful.

OLEO See margarine.

OLIVE/OLIVE OIL applies to a positive, beneficial element in one's life.

OLIVE BRANCH naturally signifies a peace offering; a desire to terminate conflict and go forward.

OLIVE GREEN (color) symbolizes waning natural talents. There's usually an underlying reason why one's inherent gifts are losing strength. This symbol will advise of the wisdom of spending time to examine one's perspectives.

OLYMPIC GAMES indicate a desire to be recognized as being the ultimate best at something.

OLYMPIC POOL signifies an opportunity to immerse oneself in the whole of a spiritual concept.

OLYMPIC TRAINING CENTER represents great efforts to prove oneself, not to others but more to self.

OMBUDSPERSON characterizes an individual who has the ability to act as an intermediary; one who can investigate a complaint or suspicion.

OMEGA (Greek letter) will emphasize the end element of something in the dreamer's experience.

OMELET connotes multiple aspects connected to something with which the dreamer is directly associated. May signify a mixing up or blending of elements regarding a perspective, relationship, situation, event, etc.

OMEN comes as a sign. Recall surrounding dreamscape details to determine whether or not this is a positive or negative indication. Generally, an omen is commonly perceived as a bad sign, but that's certainly not all-inclusive of the term.

OMISSION will reveal an important message for the dreamer. It will pinpoint an aspect that has been left out of one's perspective or conclusion.

OMNIVORE characterizes a need to take in all elements available regarding a particular issue.

ON (position) symbolizes a current state of affairs regarding one's personal life. This symbol may indicate a right *on* perspective or it may warn of a need to turn an attitude or emotion *off*. Surrounding dreamscape factors will clarify which is intended.

ONE (number) stands for the Divine Essence or an extremely high spiritual source.

ONE-ARMED BANDIT See slot machine.

ONE-HANDED refers to the success of one's personal efforts. This suggests something done with ease.

ONE-LINER will usually reveal a sarcasm, how one really feels. However a dreamscape one-liner can also reveal a succinct idea or truth.

ONE-NIGHT STAND signifies a one-time event or experience that carries no commitment.

ONE-SHOT underscores an opportunity that won't be repeated; the need to be successful the first time an attempt is made.

ONE-SIDED illustrates a biased presentation or perspective.

ONE-SIZE-FITS-ALL refers to an element open to everyone; equality; a lack of preferential treatment or availability.

ONE-WAY (sign) comes as a reminder that there is no turning back/around or reversing direction once begun. This is a call to follow through and keep going forward.

ONE-WOMAN SHOW applies to an action one must accomplish alone. Often this type of dream symbol will underscore the need for the dreamer to stop depending on others to help her along. This signifies a call to be independent in behavior or thought.

ONION points to an element in one's life that, although bringing tears, will end up being a healing factor.

ONION SKIN relates to fragile truths; healing factors.

ONLINE SHOPPING suggests ultimate convenience for obtaining one's needs. This won't necessarily be associated with goods but rather symbolically point to a reminder that certain things are more easily attained or accomplished than one realizes.

ONLOOKER may exemplify Those-Who-Watch. This may even refer to one's Higher Self or conscience. Someone is always watching us.

ON-RAMP reminds us of the presence of

multiple opportunities to begin a new path or direction.

ONTOLOGY (study of) reveals a high interest in gaining an understanding of the connectedness between true Reality and self.

ONYX (gemstone) defines an attraction to high wisdom; often signifies compassion and emotional sensitivity.

OOZE (exude) will indicate an element one can no longer contain or hide.

OPAL (gem/color) symbolizes truths from many sources.

OPAQUE warns of negativity; an inability to see the light or clarity; dark ideas or nature.

OP ART (art form) stands for a simplistic manner of expression.

OPEC corresponds to a controlling power; an element or individual possessing the control.

OPEN (position) denotes a state of affairs. This may indicate a need to *close* something, such as one's mouth or wallet. It may also refer to an informational fact that allows the dreamer to see how *open* something is. This meaning will be different for each dreamer.

OPEN-AND-SHUT refers to a simple or basic aspect that has no complexities associated with it.

OPEN ARMS naturally points to acceptance; an invitation; a sign of receptivity or support.

OPEN BAR suggests benefits without cost.

OPEN BOOK represents clarity, nothing hidden.

OPEN CALL denotes an unrestricted opportunity.

OPEN DOOR signifies accessibility; ease of attainment.

OPEN-END connotes a life aspect having no limits or restrictions; great potential or possibilities.

OPENER (device) points out an element in one's life that is capable of serving as an access tool used to accomplish a goal or desire.

OPEN-FACED (sandwich) suggests a concentrated effort of awareness for information gained or about to be ingested.

OPEN-HANDED signifies generosity; willingness to give aid.

OPEN-HEART SURGERY comes as a strong advisement to correct damaging emotions generated by psychological dysfunctions.

OPEN HOUSE signifies a forthright personality; straightforwardness.

OPEN MARRIAGE is a strong warning against acting deceptively; an inability to feel and exercise loyalty or respect.

OPEN-MINDED suggests an intellectual perception, one primed for gaining wisdom through attained knowledge.

OPEN-MOUTHED infers a mental state of expectation or narrow perspectives.

OPEN-RANGE (cattle grazing) reveals unrestricted possibilities; opportunities everywhere.

OPEN SEASON implies a time of accessibility, not necessarily for positive purposes.

OPEN SESAME will denote a key one has been looking for; a solution or means to accomplish something.

OPEN STOCK represents current availability; something one can still take advantage of.

OPEN WINDOW indicates a clear view of something. This will be understood to the individual dreamer.

OPERA connotes a mature perspective.

OPERA GLASSES relate to attentiveness; an interest in understanding situational events.

OPERA HOUSE typifies a replay of events, indicating a need to better understand a recent situation. May also refer to a counter-productive element in one's life.

OPERATING ROOM stands for the tools and conditions that are right for correcting a negative within self or another.

OPERATION (medical) advises of a need to correct a dysfunctional element or negative aspect in one's life. Recall what type of operation the dream displayed. Who was being operated on? Who was the surgeon? In what condition was the operating room?

OPERATOR (any type) will stand for one who has operational capability and knowledge of a specific element or ability. May point to the one who's in control.

OPHTHALMOLOGIST characterizes a person who has the insight and ability to straighten out another's altered perspective.

OPIUM corresponds to that which one voluntarily allows to dull one's senses, intelligence, reasoning, or perspective.

OPOSSUM denotes backward or inverted views; a caution to stop turning things around to suit self.

OPPONENT refers to an adversary or competitor.

OPPORTUNIST may not infer a negative connotation; it may well indicate a need to begin taking advantage of opportunities presented along the dreamer's path.

OPTICAL ILLUSION points out an element in life that is not perceived with accuracy; a false view. This symbol reveals the fact that things are not as they appear.

OPTIMIST characterizes one who has a tendency to look on the bright side of things; having a great measure of hope. This may or may not be a positive symbol. Recall surrounding dreamscape details for greater clarity.

OPTION presents itself as a dream symbol to reveal opportunities or alternative choices one has in life.

ORACLE usually reveals a forthcoming event in one's life. Yet this same symbol can also warn against being obsessed with the future or one's drive to know.

ORAL TRADITION reminds us of the importance of preserving truths.

ORANGE (color) represents our physical and mental energies.

ORANGE (fruit) portrays the nourishing benefits of using our inner energies/resources to help others.

ORANGEADE denotes aid given/received.

ORANGE OIL stands for a source for cleaning and freshening our energies.

ORANGE PEEL refers to personal efforts which have been expended to aid others.

ORANGE STICK (manicure) comes as a warning to clean up one's behavior and/or manner of interacting with others; utilize more honest and straightforward methods.

ORANGUTAN See ape.

ORATION will reveal an important aspect for the dreamer; will emphasize something the dreamer has been wanting to know.

ORB (shape) See sphere.

ORBIT advises of an unproductive course, one that's going around and around without advancing toward a concluding goal or destination.

ORCA See whale.

ORCHARD almost always symbolizes an individual's inherent talents. For further clarification, recall what condition the orchard was in. Was it fruitful? Diseased? Infested with insects or drought? Flooded?

ORCHESTRA refers to group harmony.

ORCHESTRA PIT stands for a place for harmony. This symbol suggests that there are some instances in life when disharmony is advised for the purpose of clearing up a misunderstanding or correcting a situation. There are times when we opt for harmony (keeping our mouths shut) in order to not upset the apple cart. This dream symbol is sending the message that harmony shouldn't be pulled out of the orchestra pit to cover up a situation that needs confrontation.

ORCHID (botanical) signifies a fragile talent or benefit that must be carefully maintained. This symbol is also associated with feminine traits and perspectives.

ORDINANCE will most often underscore a proper manner of behavior.

ORDNANCE (munitions) defines the tools or means one has available to defend or protect self in life.

OREGANO alludes to an added emphasis placed on an issue; an enhancement.

OREGON signifies spiritual abundance/fertility.

ORGAN (anatomical) See specific type.

ORGAN (musical) pertains to a complex aspect associated with an issue.

ORGAN DONOR See donor (organ).

ORGANDY (fabric) portrays a stiff personality; insensitivity.

ORGAN GRINDER suggests a need for contemplation.

ORGAN TRANSPLANT See transplant (specific organ).

ORGANZA (fabric) reveals a hardened underlying personality.

ORGY warns of an inability to control self. This won't necessarily have a sexual connotation but rather one associated with impulsiveness or self-indulgence. The dreamer will make the correct association.

ORIEL See bay (window).

ORIGAMI symbolizes a tendency to reconfigure events; a warning against altering facts or rearranging them to suit self. As a positive intent, this symbol points to ingenuity; something carrying great potential.

ORIOLE (bird) relates to a helpful element in one's life, yet possesses a potential to generate a negative effect if used incorrectly.

ORNAMENT will indicate the presence of an embellishment or extraneous aspect in one's life. May hint at a specific attitude.

ORNITHOLOGY (study of) refers to a high interest in learning the various psychological mechanisms one's associates use.

ORPHAN See foundling.

ORRISROOT will suggest a stabilizing element in one's life.

ORTHODONTIST characterizes a person who has the ability and knowledge to help another communicate more effectively.

ORTHODOX connotes an adherence to strict basic beliefs or attitudes; firm convictions.

ORTHOPEDIST exemplifies an individual

who can redirect another's path toward a straight course.

OSCILLATING (motion) denotes instability; a continual variation.

OSIRIS (Egyptian mythology) characterizes renewal; a rebirth. This underscores the idea that all is not lost, the pieces can be picked up.

OSMOSIS emphasizes understanding; comprehension.

OSPREY See hawk.

OSTEOPOROSIS indicates a failing of one's inner strength; waning motivation or sense of purpose.

OSTRICH connotes subconscious denials; an inability or refusal to face responsibilities and/or reality.

OTOSCOPE represents a need to analyze the cause of one's unbalanced perspectives.

OTTER implies the recognition of inner joy generated by spirituality.

OTTOMAN See footstool.

OUIJA BOARD comes as a severe warning to look within for answers instead of turning to a dependency on others.

OUTBACK See back country.

OUTBOARD MOTOR relates to spiritual motivational factors.

OUTBREAK suggests a return or exacerbation of an element in one's life, usually a negative aspect that has suddenly increased.

OUTBUILDING See accessory building.

OUTBURST (vocal) stands for an emotional expression of feelings which may have a positive or negative connotation depending on the related dream details. It is important here to recall who said what.

OUTCAST pertains to an individual who doesn't follow the crowd; one who thinks for self. In rare instances, this symbol may indicate a guilt or persecution complex for being different.

OUTCROPPING is an attention-getting symbol. This attempts to draw the dreamer's attention to something important in life.

OUTDATED may not be a negative symbol, for it may apply to a long-held truth that few currently believe. Recall surrounding dream details for further clarification.

OUTDOORSWOMAN characterizes a recognition of one's inherent bond with natural forces.

OUTER SPACE represents deeper knowledge; a reach for greater understanding of true Reality.

OUTGROWTH alludes to a resulting effect or manifestation.

OUTGUNNED connotes a failed attempt to better another. This may pertain to aspects of skill, intelligence, or accomplishment.

OUTHOUSE illustrates a need to rid self of wasteful or unessential elements in one's life.

OUTLANDER characterizes a person who stands out as being clearly different from those around her/him. This usually reveals a free-thinker, one unafraid to openly express unique and individualistic perspectives or ideas.

OUTLAW will indicate one who behaves in an unlawful manner; the lawful aspect can refer to ethical, moral, or spiritual elements.

OUTLET exemplifies an opportunity to release negative or retained aspects that restrict one's freedom or health.

OUTLET (electrical) provides one with an available source of energy or empowerment.

OUTLET (store) stands for possibilities.

OUTLINE signifies a need for planning; suggests deep thought be applied before action is taken.

OUTNUMBERED implies that your plan, idea, or behavior is not shared by the majority. This is not necessarily a negative symbol. It may denote innovativeness and individuality.

OUT-OF-BODY presented in a dreamscape usually corresponds with a true experiential event. It also may reveal a need to look at something from a different perspective.

OUT-OF-BOUNDS stands for exceeding a limitation or restrictive barrier and may commend one for doing so.

OUT-OF-DATE suggests one of two things. It may point to an outdated perspective or way of doing things, or it may advise that something has expired (too late to do anything about).

OUT OF FOCUS reveals a blurred perspective.

OUT OF POCKET portrays determined personal effort; using one's own resources to accomplish something.

OUT OF PRINT means that something is no longer readily available; a growing rarity.

OUT OF ROUND reveals something that's amiss, has become misshapen.

OUT OF STEP usually points to individuality and the gumption to resist coercion to get in step with the crowd.

OUT OF SYNC represents a current attitude which causes a shift away from being aligned with a relationship, issue, or situation.

OUT-OF-THE-WAY usually means that one needs to go out of one's way to gain an important lesson or discover a solution/key to something.

OUT-OF-TOWNER will most often point to someone who isn't familiar with a particular issue.

OUTPATIENT illustrates a negative condition within the dreamer that can only be healed by oneself.

OUTPOST connotes resting points along one's right path. This assures the dreamer that, although the path may be far distant from others, there have been those who've gone before and the dreamer is not alone.

OUTRAGE comes as a message to gain a greater measure of acceptance and intellectual reasoning.

OUTRANKED will usually underscore one's rightness that has externally been overridden by another who is perceived as being more knowledgeable or experienced. This symbol comes as a personal verification message.

OUTSIDE signifies an external position or source.

OUTSIDE CHANCE indicates the existence of a slim probability for something to manifest.

OUTSMARTED implies one didn't consider all aspects of an issue or situation. This is actually an experiential learning symbol.

OUTSOURCING stands for profit placed before all else.

OUTSPOKEN marks a candid, uninhibited communication; basic honesty.

OUTTAKE (blooper) usually illustrates one's mistakes. This can be a personally revealing dream symbol.

OUTWARD BOUND suggests a time or condition ripe for self-discovery.

OVAL (shape) usually represents something which is a bit off kilter but may also indicate a contentedness. The symbol's related dream elements will determine which meaning was intended.

OVATION comes as a personal commendation or sign of recognition from one's Higher Self.

OVEN signals a method to gain completion or accomplishment. Recall the condition of the oven. Was it on? What was in it?

OVEN CLEANER will denote an attempt or desire to insure one's methods are untainted.

OVENPROOF relates to precautions taken while applying methods towards manifesting one's goals.

OVER (direction) pertains to a need to pass or climb over a difficult element blocking one's path. This will call for determination.

OVERALLS See coveralls.

OVERBALANCED connotes overcompensation.

OVERBID signifies a lost opportunity due to an underestimate of its value.

OVERBITE represents the withholding of select thoughts.

OVERBLOWN alludes to an exaggeration.

OVERBOARD warns of spiritual impulsiveness.

OVERBOOKED symbolizes a lack of foresight, planning.

OVER-BRED means elements which have been used so often that they've lost their effectiveness; an idea or aspect which has so many diluted elements to it that it's not viable.

OVER BUDGET reveals bad planning; something costing more than expected.

OVERBUILT points to extravagance.

OVERCAST (sky) suggests mental or emotional cloudiness; a lack of perceptual clarity.

OVERCHARGED is a symbol that converts a karmic overpayment from a balanced status to an asset position.

OVERCOAT exemplifies a personal state of self-protection. Will sometimes refer to a cover-up of some type.

OVERDONE reveals excess; extraneous aspects added.

OVERDOSE pertains to an excess. This will help the dreamer determine the proper amount of something required.

OVERDRAFT corresponds to impatience; one is too anxious and jumping ahead of oneself.

OVERDRAWN doesn't usually refer to finances but rather points to overextending oneself in regard to energy output or possibly promises which can't be kept.

OVERDRESSED suggests exaggerations; a tendency to read/perceive more into something than is warranted.

OVERDRIVE advises one to slow the pace. Going too fast and expending too much energy causes a loss of valuable lessons that are not noted.

OVERDUE usually indicates procrastination. May also mean something a long time in coming.

OVEREXPOSURE signifies redundancy; overkill; beating an issue to death.

OVERFEED signifies the ingestion of too much information; may also refer to a pushy personality.

OVERFILLED (glass/bowl) reveals one's inability to comprehend all that is taken in; much will be missed. This symbol is likened to the message of biting off more than one can chew.

OVERFLOW emphasizes a state of abundance. Recall what was overflowing. Did it have color? Consistency? From what was it flowing?

OVERGRAZED reveals a situation or relationship that gave all it could. It's time to move on.

OVERGROWN will apply to a lack of interest or care given to a personal talent or inherent ability.

OVERHAUL portrays an interest in caring for and maintaining optimum condition of an element in one's life. This could refer to one's physical, mental, emotional, or spiritual aspects.

OVERHANG suggests a protective shield, covering.

OVERHEAD represents the cost of implementing a plan or proposed move. This comes as a suggestion to figure out if the output is going to be worth the result.

OVERHEAD DOOR signifies a selective perspective; choosing what one wants to see and have an opinion of.

OVERHEATED warns of a need to pull back and analyze something in a rational manner; emotions getting out of hand, getting the best of one.

OVERINDULGENCE connotes an excessiveness.

OVERKILL alludes to an exaggeration; an excessive amount of attention or effort applied to something in one's life.

OVERLAP suggests full-coverage; making sure there are no loose ends.

OVERLAY may reveal an ulterior motive or it could represent a protective layer of defensiveness. Recall surrounding dream details for clarification.

OVERLOADED warns against taking on too much; approaching burnout.

OVERLOOKS (scenic) indicate a need for a wider view of an issue. Something is literally being overlooked.

OVERPASS reveals a directional solution to a problematical path obstacle.

OVERPROTECTIVE refers to a fear of letting go; anxiety over spreading one's wings.

OVERQUALIFIED will denote one's inflated opinion of oneself. Every type of work supplies valuable learning experiences.

OVERRATED pertains to an attempt to greatly enhance something.

OVERRIDE suggests an idea/plan that's been superseded by another.

OVERRULED will come as a guiding message from one's Higher Self or even one's own conscience.

OVERSEER usually denotes one's Higher Self or conscience.

OVERSHADOW stands for something/ someone not given proper attention because another aspect/person is more prominent or noticeable. May be an implication that one is vying for competition, or a suffocating/demanding situation is manifesting.

OVER SHIRT alludes to an altered mood; a sense of preserving the essence of oneself from others.

OVERSHOES suggest an attempt to

disassociate one's emotional responses from sensitive issues encountered along one's life path; a lack of bonding sensitivity with the earth.

OVERSHOOT means that one's goal/target was closer than one thought.

OVERSIGHT will naturally point to something that's been left out; an important detail has been forgotten.

OVERSIZED reveals some kind of aspect in the dreamer's life that is too big for her/him at the present time; connotes an issue or concept that one has not yet grown into.

OVERSLEEP warns of unawareness; inattention. This dreamscape element comes as a serious warning to wake up! Be *aware!*

OVER-SOLD suggests a promise which can't be kept; exaggerations made for the purpose of personal gain.

OVERSPEND represents an over-extension of oneself.

OVER-STAFFED indicates an excessive effort applied to an element in one's life.

OVERSTEP will symbolize an attempt to step over the line or cross limits. This is a message from one's Higher Self or conscience.

OVERSTOCKED suggests that it's time to use one's talents to benefit others; time to share.

OVERSTUFFED indicates a lack of acceptance; an inability to take one moment at a time.

OVER-THE-COUNTER (medication) signifies easily obtained remedies for a negative situation or element in one's life; something not requiring a major remedy.

OVERTHROWN implies a missed goal; reaching too far.

OVERTIME points to extra personal efforts needed to accomplish a goal.

OVERTURE stands for an initial move; a tentative testing of the waters; broaching a subject.

OVERTURNED may indicate a need to reverse a decision or choice or it could suggest that one give closer inspection to something—leave nothing unturned.

OVERTURNED (vehicle) See rollover.

OVERVIEW stands for a good perception of the multiple aspects of an issue/situation.

OVERWEIGHT (not obese) will not infer obesity, yet it means that one is carrying excessive burdens and responsibilities; a need to rid oneself of superficial or hampering aspects. This is most often in reference to emotional psychological self-generated mechanisms.

OVERWHELMED may refer to a lack of acceptance of a forcing of knowledge one isn't ready to comprehend.

OVERWORKED comes to emphasize that one can control the level and extent of personal efforts applied to a situation. This symbol will attempt to underscore *who* has the control over this.

OWL characterizes heightened observational skills and developed awareness coupled with sharpened perceptive abilities; wisdom resulting from high spiritual enlightenment.

OWLET will signify one on the correct spiritual path.

OXBLOOD (color) refers to earthy emotions and personality traits.

OXBOW (stream configuration) indicates a meandering spiritual path that is destined to bring enlightenment.

OXEN connotes overwork; suggests a psychological cause.

OXFORD (fabric) suggests a tailored perspective, one designed by personal attitudes; a subjective viewpoint.

OXFORD (shoes) stands for immaturity; a desire to stay youthful and not be subjected to the responsibilities of adulthood.

OXYGEN MASK exemplifies a sense of suffocation; an inability to accept new ideas and the psychological panic they cause within oneself.

OXYGEN TANK suggests one's anticipation of a suffocating situation or encounter; a preparation for an expected claustrophobic reaction.

OXYMORON will reveal a contradiction specific to the dreamer.

OYSTER represents inner fears of anything new or of having to interact with others; social anxiety. Can also indicate wisdom gained from deep introspection.

OZ connotes a willful reluctance to face or accept reality.

OZARKS pertain to basic necessities in life; a personality or lifestyle lacking extraneous elements; understanding and appreciating the value of simple basics.

OZONE LAYER portrays rarely perceived protective elements in one's life and the ignorant unawareness of same; corresponds with the protective manifestations created by the Divine, such as our own spirit essence of the Higher Self, guiding angels, etc.

$\mathcal{P}$

PABLUM is a soft baby food, so it connotes simplistic ideas and easy methods; a fear of difficult situations or tasks; a tendency to keep things as easy as possible for oneself, especially when it comes to spiritual concepts.

PACE CAR will usually guide the dreamer into a proper rate of progression. Depending on the speed of the dream pace car, it will indicate an acceleration or slowing down.

PACEMAKER pertains to a need to regulate one's emotional displays and will most often signify a need to calm routine excitability.

PACESETTER See trendsetter.

PACHYDERM See specific type.

PACIFIER indicates an easier path chosen.

PACIFISM represents a fear of conflict and a tendency to take the most peaceful and less troublesome path.

PACING interprets into anxiety or worry. This symbol comes to underscore the futility of such mental exertion; more acceptance is needed.

PACK (of animals) portrays a multiple of whatever animal is presented in the pack. This will indicate an increase or abundance.

PACKAGE applies to those material goods one perceives as being important in life. What was in the package? Was it gift-wrapped?

PACKAGE DEAL signifies multiple benefits rolled into one element.

PACKAGE TOUR warns against a tendency to see only what others want you to see.

PACK HORSE suggests an opportunity to have our loads lightened; an aspect that can shoulder some of the weight.

PACKING (material) illustrates a need for protection. This implies that something in one's life needs to be handled in a delicate manner.

PACKING HOUSE See meat-packing house.

PACKING UP suggests a forthcoming move. This may not refer to an actual physical relocation but may relate to an employment move or a situational one.

PACK RAT warns of a tendency to collect insignificant or superficial aspects; advises of a return to the important basics.

PACK TRAIN signifies the presence of unnecessary elements in one's life.

PACT signifies a private agreement.

PAD See cushion.

PAD (of paper) See notebook.

PADDING corresponds to the effect of softening or easing something in life. It may also indicate an exaggeration depending on surrounding dreamscape details.

PADDLE See oar.

PADDLE (discipline) See spanking.

PADDLE BOAT (paddle wheel) exemplifies an element that serves as a spiritual impetus; spiritual motivation.

PADDLE WHEEL represents spiritual motivation.

PADDOCK See corral.

PADDY WAGON implies being caught for a misdeed. This will remind one that, in the end, one pays for wrongdoings.

PADLOCK represents hidden elements; aspects we keep hidden.

PADRE See religious figure.

PAGAN will usually symbolize the existence of a spiritual belief that differs from convention. This is not necessarily a negative connotation. Recall surrounding dreamscape details for further clarification.

PAGE (attendant) characterizes a helper; assistant.

PAGE (book) comes to point out something the dreamer should be aware of. Recall what was on the page. What type of book was it in? Color?

PAGEANT refers to active acting out; a demonstration or showing of an idea.

PAGEBOY (hair style) suggests shyness.

PAGE PROOFS signify an opportunity to make changes before the final event.

PAGER See beeper.

PAGODA signifies spiritual misconceptions associated with the Truths as related to the precepts of the Law of One.

PAIL signifies the amount of spirituality one uses in life. What was the pail made of? Was it full or empty? What quality was the content?

PAIN always represents a personally harmful element in one's life. This could be caused by an external source or it may be generated by self.

PAIN IN THE NECK will not be an actual physical indication but rather will refer to a personal irritation usually caused by another individual for whom the dreamer has no tolerance. This suggests a need for greater acceptance.

PAINKILLER See analgesic.

PAINT represents a cover-up of some type being done.

PAINT (artist's) denotes personal tools for self-expression.

PAINTBALL (game) signifies a lighthearted test of skill/survival, yet this symbol may also point to a practice of evasiveness (hunter/prey); could also warn of pseudo war games.

PAINTBRUSH pertains to a desire to alter something in one's life.

PAINTED TURTLE denotes the small joys in life; the little blessings.

PAINTING (picture) will usually contain an important element to which the dreamer needs to give attention.

PAIR may suggest duality or it may infer a close connection between two elements in one's life.

PAISLEY (pattern) signifies an element of true Reality.

PAJAMAS See nightgown.

PALACE See castle.

PALATE corresponds to one's sense of taste in reference to behavior, choices, interaction, perception, etc.

PALAZZO See castle.

PALE (complexion) connotes a dispirited state.

PALEONTOLOGY (study of) represents an inherent curiosity regarding human-kind's beginnings. This will point to an interest in getting to the bottom of things.

PALETTE (art) indicates multiple opportunities to express one's thoughts and/or show one's unique individuality.

PALETTE KNIFE applies to an available tool for combining and harmoniously blending ideas and concepts.

PALL See coffin.

PALL (dull) relates to a waning interest; boring.

PALLADIUM constitutes a personal safeguard; an element of personal protection.

PALLBEARER represents the releasing of personal pain.

PALLET See bed.

PALM (hand) emphasizes revealing qualities of one's character. Recall if the dream palm was soft or calloused. Did it hold something? Was it in a giving or taking position?

PALM (tree) will usually have a spiritual connotation. Recall surrounding dream-scape elements for further clarification. Usually refers to the freedom to feel empowered by convictions.

PALMISTRY typifies irrationality; a lack of acceptance.

PALM PILOT See PDA.

PALM SUNDAY defines an attitude of spiritual reverence.

PALOMINO illustrates a gentle freedom; a quiet appreciation for one's unique individuality.

PALPATE symbolizes the act of giving deeper inspection or attention to an issue.

PALSY will suggest a personally generated impairment of some type. Review personal attitudes or fears.

PALTRY may seem to suggest insignificance, but it usually indicates a personally held perspective of grandeur that is not being realized. This is a caution to lower one's inflated self-image.

PAMPAS GRASS implies a fragile situation or personality, depending on surrounding dreamscape details.

PAMPERED pertains to actions that retard one's growth.

PAMPHLET denotes information specific to the dreamer. Recall what type of pamphlet was presented. What did it say? What design, if any, was on it? Color? Condition?

PAN (cook) represents a tool available to bring something to fruition or completion in life.

PAN (Greek mythology) characterizes a call to return to nature and the appreciation of same.

PANAMA HAT stands for a moderate perspective.

PANATELLA See cigar.

PANCAKE implies a flat quality. This will refer to a personal element in one's life, usually related to self-expression.

PANCREAS connotes a vital aspect in one's life that maintains a balanced perspective.

PANCREATITIS warns of a perception that is in error.

PANDA will reveal a friend with ulterior motives.

PANDEMIC suggests a widespread attitude or condition, usually negative.

PANDEMONIUM emphasizes a state of confusion which usually constitutes an internal mental or emotional state.

PANDER advises one to stop giving in to weaknesses.

PANDORA (Greek mythology) characterizes a person who will eventually cause harm or bring negative elements into one's life.

PANDORA'S BOX (Greek mythology) defines a harmful situation that should be avoided; may also refer to an individual or issue.

PANE (glass) applies to a separation of self from a life element.

PANELING signifies an enhancement of some type; an attempt to improve surrounding conditions.

PANEL TRUCK portrays that which is carried over into the workplace, usually personal attitudes or needed tools. Recall associative dream details for deeper meaning.

PANHANDLE (beg) stands for a state of desperation. Depending on the surrounding elements of the dream, this symbol may warn of laziness.

PANIC ATTACK stands for an overwhelming situation.

PANIC BUTTON represents high anxiety or an extreme state of confusion. It's time to do something.

PANIC HARDWARE (doors/windows) represent an easy way out. Was the dreamscape symbol already in place? Or making a suggestion to put them in place?

PANNIER See basket.

PANORAMA (view) implies a need to obtain a wider perspective of something in one's life.

PANPIPE exemplifies lightheartedness; a cheerful mood.

PANSY (flower) refers to a need to boost one's sense of inner power. This symbol advises one to have more confidence in oneself.

PANTHER suggests caution; a careful approach to something in the dreamer's life.

PANTING symbolizes overexertion or anxiety regarding high expectation; indicates a need for acceptance.

PANTOMIME See mime.

PANTRY stands for a reserve of inner strength. The key here is to recall if the pantry was full or empty. What did it contain?

PANTYHOSE will apply to some type of feminine trait in respect to how a path is traveled. Surrounding dream details will make a clarifying association.

PANTY RAID warns of immaturity; juvenile perspectives.

PAPAYA connotes a need to calm emotions or anxiety.

PAPER most often refers to some type of communication, yet can also have other interpretations depending on the specific type.

PAPERBACK (book) will have a personal meaning for each dreamer. Recall what the book's title was. Did this hold a special meaning for you? What was the book's condition? Where was it found?

PAPERBOY symbolizes delivered information. This may be advising one to seek one's own information instead of receiving only that which someone else deems you should know.

PAPER CLIP suggests a need for attachments; a reminder to keep something secured.

PAPER CUT indicates a careless use of information.

PAPER CUTTER pertains to a need to trim superficial or extraneous elements from a piece of information.

PAPER DOLLS denote choices for the expression of individuality.

PAPERHANGER characterizes a person who attempts to cover up something; one who conceals or attempts to present a better image; may indicate deception.

PAPER MILL relates to the manner in which one processes information. Recall the type of paper being made. Was the mill's operation efficient? Did it require many workers or just a few?

PAPER MONEY See money.

PAPER PLANT (botanical) See papyrus.

PAPER PUSHER signifies an individual who is overly concerned about everything being by the book; one who can't bring oneself to bend the rules or operate in a light grey area.

PAPER SHREDDER See shredder.

PAPER-THIN refers to weakness; having little substance.

PAPER TIGER stands for a false power; lacking authority or strength.

PAPER TRAIL exemplifies evidence one leaves behind.

PAPER WASP See hornet.

PAPERWEIGHT stands for a need to retain important information.

PAPERWORK may indicate unnecessary work associated with an element in one's life.

PAPETERIE represents mental organization; an efficient thought process.

PAPIER-MÂCHÉ portrays what is done with information one receives. Recall what was formed from the paper; this will be the revealing element.

PAPILLON (dog breed) signifies the tenacity of a friend.

PAPRIKA See red pepper.

PAPYRUS corresponds with delicate information that requires careful discernment.

PARABLE emphasizes valuable lessons that need to be learned or recalled.

PARACHUTE reveals psychological rationalizations. Recall the condition and color of the dream parachute. How did it work?

PARADE symbolizes a desire to be recognized; may indicate arrogance.

PARADIGM See example.

PARADISE relates to one's personal perspective of the perfect scenario, condition, or ultimate goal.

PARADOX reveals a situation or concept that appears contradictory.

PARAFFIN signifies a need to preserve or seal something. The dreamer will make the associative connection.

PARAGON characterizes one who has made an ultimate achievement at something; a person who has attained a prime position or status in respect to personal accomplishment.

PARAKEET represents a lack of analytical spiritual thinking.

PARALEGAL characterizes a person who understands the basics of an issue; someone who may be able to point you in the right direction.

PARALLEL BARS signify an equal grip on something in one's life; a firm and balanced grasp of a situation or concept.

PARALYSIS reveals a psychological state of denial; a tendency to be emotionally numb or remain in an immobilized state.

PARAMEDIC defines an individual who is capable of an immediate, knowledgeable response.

PARAMOUR pertains to an intimacy, not necessarily a sexual one.

PARANOIA reveals inner fears. Also see fear.

PARANORMAL (events/abilities) reveals inherent talents or elements of true Reality.

PARAPET refers to awareness; the act of being on the lookout and being prepared.

PARAPHERNALIA connotes personal possessions that are unique or important to an individual.

PARAPLEGIA emphasizes the true essence of an individual; underscores the "mind" as being one's beingness.

PARAPSYCHOLOGY (study of) denotes a high interest in humankind's interconnectedness with true Reality.

PARASAILING implies a spiritually disassociative state; being close to spiritual matters yet not wanting to immerse self in them.

PARASITE alludes to a draining aspect in one's life. This could refer to a physical, mental, emotional, or spiritual element.

PARASOL connotes a frivolous spiritual attitude or belief system.

PARATROOPER usually relates to emotional disturbances.

PARCEL See package.

PARCHED signifies a great inner need. The surrounding dreamscape details will clarify this.

PARCHMENT (paper) illustrates an authoritative message or source. Recall if the paper had writing on it or if it was associated with related aspects of the dream.

PARDON typifies an exoneration; forgiveness intended to negate personal guilt.

PAREGORIC suggests a need for greater acceptance.

PARENT will represent a person to respect and honor. This symbol may have different meanings for each dreamer, depending on individual personal experiences.

PARENTHESIS will usually contain a word that is intended to further explain something.

PARFAIT applies to a variety of spiritual concepts that are combined in a confusing manner.

PARFLECHE portrays basics. This alludes to an individual who sticks with basic necessities or bottom-line concepts.

PARIAH may not indicate a negative aspect. Depending on surrounding dreamscape factors, this symbol may refer to an individual who follows her/his own path.

PARING KNIFE will suggest a need to pare down something in one's life. Associative dream aspects will usually pinpoint this issue.

PARK (grounds) constitutes a place or time of respite.

PARKA connotes responsible reactions.

PARK AVENUE illustrates an egotistical personality; out of touch with reality; misplaced priorities.

PARK BENCH stands for respite along the way; taking moments to appreciate what one has.

PARKING (act of) signifies the defining and securing of a stable state or position, usually temporarily for the purpose of gaining needed information.

PARKING GARAGE/LOT signifies the time or space one allots for ensuring a stable state or position.

PARKING METER will always reveal a specified span of time allotted for one to give time or attention to a particular issue.

PARKS (Rosa) represents the recognition and practicing of one's inherent rights and freedoms regardless of possible repercussions.

PARKWAY connotes a phase of one's path that produces accelerated, trouble-free advancement.

PARLEYED defines an attempt to negotiate a peaceful resolution.

PARLOR alludes to out-dated ideas or characteristics; old-fashioned; stiff personality.

PARODY See sarcasm.

PAROLE represents a time of testing one's integrity; putting one's learned lessons into action.

PAROLEE characterizes a person who needs to carefully watch behavior. This parolee will not necessarily indicate a bad individual but the associative concept that's important for the dreamer is the extreme necessity of watching your Ps and Qs for a time.

PAROLE OFFICER will indicate someone who is devoted to making sure you won't go off track in life; someone responsible for keeping an eye on you. This someone may even be your own Higher Self or conscience.

PARQUETRY (pattern) defines richness in succinct wisdom.

PARQUETRY (woodcraft) reveals an attention to fine detail and associative thought.

PARROT typifies verbosity.

PARRY relates to a defensive position or action taken.

PARSLEY represents unrecognized benefits and nourishing elements in life.

PARSNIP signifies neglected opportunities.

PARSON See religious figure.

PARTICLE BOARD portrays multiple aspects of an issue.

PARTING SHOT implies a last word or the expressing of one's final say on something.

PARTITION exemplifies a separating or disassociative attitude. May point to a need to keep issues separate from each other.

PARTNER relates to someone closely associated with the dreamer.

PARTRIDGE See quail.

PARTY (celebration) will represent a reason for joy, perhaps an unrecognized blessing.

PARTY (political) represents a difference of philosophy.

PARTY LINE (political) stands for basic attitudes one doesn't veer from.

PARTY LINE (telephone) reveals the act of listening in on. This suggests someone is privy to another's behavior or private communications.

PARTY PLANNER characterizes one who is experienced in managing details and pulling them together to create a successful goal.

PARTY POOPER won't necessarily point to an unsocial individual but rather one who doesn't take life frivolously.

PAS DE DEUX corresponds to a collaboration between two individuals. This may be a revealing event for the dreamer.

PASQUEFLOWER (botanical) stands for spiritual inspirations.

PASS (mountain) relates to a way through a difficulty.

PASS (move past) may suggest something missed in life or it may indicate an element that doesn't require attention. Recall surrounding dream details for further clarification.

PASS (sanction) will reveal an acceptance or agreement of something one is planning.

PASS (succeed) indicates a stage or goal that has been accomplished.

PASS (vehicular) comes as an advisement to go around an element in one's way.

PASSAGEWAY will reveal a way through a difficult situation or confusing concept.

PASSBOOK See bankbook.

PASSÉ will infer that something is out-of-date, yet, depending on surrounding dream elements, this may reveal a person's personal opinion rather than actual fact.

PASSED OUT usually indicates overindulgence or overstressed.

PASSENGER portrays movement; actively applying efforts to advance along one's path.

PASSENGER PIGEON connotes beauty destroyed by greed.

PASSENGER TRAIN See train (passenger).

PASSION will not explicitly infer a sexual implication but rather a nearly consuming emotion.

PASSIONFLOWER alludes to the beauty of possessing a positive passion such as empathy, compassion, etc.

PASSION PLAY reveals a person's display of emotional dramatics; an exaggeration for the purpose of attention.

PASSIVE RESISTANCE will advise a peaceful way to resist or express opposition.

PASSIVE RESTRAINT connotes an automatic, usually concealed, method of restraint that's either self-controlled or manipulative.

PASSIVISM suggests a peaceful personality, yet may come as an important advisement to start expending efforts toward a goal.

PASSKEY pertains to advancement opportunities; elements that provide key solutions or inspirations.

PASSOVER signifies the protective elements of innocence or being guiltless.

PASSPORT illustrates one's rite of passage; a readiness for advancement.

PASSWORD denotes aspects in one's life that serve as keys or gateways to prime opportunities.

PAST will sometimes serve as a past example or it will indicate something one should leave behind where it belongs.

PASTA constitutes a substantial or basic element in one's life.

PASTA FORK stands for a desire to stop an issue from becoming a sticky one, prevent it becoming confusing by keeping elements separate.

PASTE (adhesive) indicates a need for temporary cohesiveness. This would infer the need to quickly make attempts at resolving a current problem or negative situation in one's life.

PASTEL (chalk) suggests a person's intent to soften a specific personality trait. Refer to the specific color for further interpretation.

PASTEL (hue) implies a gentleness or soft quality associated with the specific color's individual interpretation. Refer to specific color.

PASTE-UP See layout.

PASTEUR (Louis) characterizes a person who is interested in the basic, pure facts of an issue.

PASTEURIZATION signifies the intent to discount superficial or extraneous elements from an issue or concept. This symbol is not always a positive one.

PASTOR See religious figure.

PASTORAL (setting) portrays a tranquil atmosphere; a harmonic and restful condition.

PASTRAMI exemplifies a condition, concept, or other element that elicits a more than mild emotional response.

PASTRY relates a perception of high value, something sweet. This would be associated with an individual's unique personal perspective and not necessarily be a true indication. Recall what the pastry was and what condition it was in. Was it dripping with honey? Was it stale?

Underbaked? Coated with sugar? Refer to other types of pastry confections listed in this dictionary.

PASTRY SHELL refers to an unexpected and initially unrecognized benefit in one's life.

PASTURE represents one's voluntary usefulness in life. Was someone out in the pasture? Who was in the dream pasture? What were they doing? What condition was the pasture in? Was it full of flowers or weeds? Was it completely barren?

PAT (on back) denotes a sign of encouragement.

PAT (on head) implies a patronizing response.

PATCH (eye) See eye patch.

PATCH (repair) symbolizes a temporary solution.

PATCHOULI (scent) suggests a realist who recognizes that there's a more to life than just what's confined in the proverbial box.

PATCHWORK (pattern) comes to underscore the importance of variety in one's life; pertains to multiple perceptive qualities.

PATE denotes personal energy, possibly inner strength.

PATELLA reflects a vulnerable aspect.

PATENT signifies recognition or the protection of one's innovative ideas.

PATENT LEATHER depicts a personal need for attention.

PATENT OFFICE stands for authoritative recognition.

PATERNITY TEST warns against attempting to circumvent personal responsibility; refers to validating ownership, possession, or rights.

PATH will most often signify a person's individual road or direction.

PATHFINDER characterizes an individual who leads others to their life path. This is a direct warning, for nobody should tell another which path to take in life. This must be a personal decision.

PATHOLOGY (study of) indicates a need to analyze a negative situation that currently exists in one's life.

PATIENCE usually comes as an advisory message.

PATIENT (infirm) implies the need for care or healing. Recall the surrounding dreamscape details for further clarity.

PATINA denotes an overall sensation or impression; a general look to one's appearance and demeanor. Depending on the visual of the patina, the symbol may refer to immaturity or wisdom.

PATIO implies open-mindedness.

PATRIARCH connotes a person acting as a figurehead.

PATRICIAN See nobility.

PATRICIDE illustrates a denial of an inherent part of oneself.

PATRIOT represents loyalty.

PATRIOT ACT suggests a loss of privacy and some associated rights.

PATROL pertains to watchfulness; an acute awareness.

PATROL CAR See squad car.

PATRON characterizes a supportive individual.

PATRON SAINT pertains to a guiding or protective ideal or motivational force.

PATTERNS (designs) indicate multiple characteristics, qualities, and methods through which behavior is expressed. Refer to specific pattern types in this dictionary for individual interpretation.

PATTERNS (sewing) signify the following of another, yet willing to do your own work and perhaps add your own touches.

PATTY SHELL See pastry shell.

PAUL BUNYAN signifies the extent of one's potential.

PAUNCH (stomach) connotes waning awareness and motivation.

PAUPER reveals a person who doesn't recognize the value of personal abilities or worth.

PAVEMENT implies a separation from one's natural bond with earth and inherent natural ability; a barrier preventing sensitivity.

PAVING relates to a desire for an easy life.

PAVLOV (Ivan) exemplifies a conditioned response. This symbol comes to remind one that this type of reaction can be altered through understanding.

PAW (pet's) portrays encouragement and loyalty of a friend.

PAWN (chess) applies to one who is used by another; may also indicate an opinion of oneself.

PAWN (hock) connotes a problematical solution or possible outlet.

PAWNBROKER will signify one who can provide temporary help for another.

PAWNSHOP represents sacrifices made.

PAWN TICKET stands for a way out of a problem; a solution.

PAWPAW (fruit/tree) stands for an awareness of an aspect's subtleties.

PAY-BY-TOUCH (fingerprinting) stands for a price paid for giving up privacy.

PAYCHECK usually represents the value of one's behavior, beliefs, or relationships. Recall what amount the paycheck was for. Was it minimum wage? Was overtime included? Bonus?

PAY DIRT denotes a new element in one's life that has the capability to bring multiple benefits.

PAYLOADER suggests a need for major digging to be done; an advisement to do research or some type of background inspection.

PAYMASTER characterizes those who recognize the value of one's behavior in respect to output.

PAYOLA connotes misdeeds and misplaced priorities; indicates one who would do anything for money; bribery.

PAY-PER-VIEW signifies a price paid for the things we want immediately and can't wait for.

PAY PHONE comes as a reminder to attend to a communication that's been postponed.

PAYROLL usually reveals the value of associates. Recall who was doing the payroll. What were the check amounts?

PDA (personal digital assistant) stands for efficiency and preparedness; a desire to keep information close at hand.

PDF (portable document format) refers to the convenience and efficiency of receiving, processing, and transferring information.

PEA most often symbolizes a small amount of something. Recall what the pea was associated with in the dream.

PEACE CORPS relate to an opportunity to help others.

PEACEKEEPER portrays an individual who attempts to find a peaceful way of resolving conflict. A dream peacekeeper may symbolize one's own Higher Self.

PEACE LILY usually represents a peace offering, a sign of an apology or reconciliatory gesture.

PEACE OFFERING connotes an attempt at reconciliation; an apology.

PEACE PIPE indicates harmonious intentions.

PEACE SIGN stands for a friendly, peaceful greeting.

PEACH constitutes satisfaction; a desired element.

PEACH FUZZ suggests immaturity.

PEACH PIT stands for a healing element.

PEA COAT suggests efforts to weather a spiritual crisis or conflict.

PEACOCK emphasizes arrogance; a priority placed on appearances.

PEACOCK BLUE (color) connotes a healing spiritual energy.

PEAHEN (bird) stands for individuality; confidence in one's personal uniqueness.

PEA JACKET symbolizes efforts applied to spiritual aspects in life.

PEAK LOAD refers to a phase when life stressors are at their height.

PEAL (bells) indicates a call to attention; a need for increased awareness.

PEALE (Norman Vincent) reminds us to help ourselves; stresses our own inner power.

PEANUT will refer to the minor aspects of our life.

PEANUT BRITTLE pertains to a temporarily difficult situation.

PEANUT BUTTER corresponds to a source of energy or motivation; may also reveal a sticky situation.

PEANUT OIL refers to a rich source of nourishment which can imply mental, emotional, physical, or spiritual aspects.

PEANUT SHELLS signify the use of all opportunities presented in one's life; a full experiential awareness.

PEAR represents duality.

PEARL applies to perseverance; spiritually based fortitude.

PEARL (black) stands for fortitude from a negative-based drive.

PEARL (cultured) strength derived from a great expenditure of energy.

PEARL DIVER typifies one who gleans spiritual pearls from searching efforts.

PEARL GRAY represents dignity, classiness of character or behavior.

PEARL HARBOR reminds us to remain aware in life, not let our guard down.

PEARL OYSTER indicates a life aspect that will contain valuable spiritual or motivational elements.

PEASANT connotes simplicity and the value of same.

PEASHOOTER represents a negative aspect (tool) that could cause harm to others. The surrounding dream details will clarify this meaning.

PEA SOUP pertains to a cloudy view; unclear perspective.

PEAT suggests a life factor that has the potential for enriching something.

PEAT BOG See bog.

PEAT MOSS portrays a protective element; a supportive aspect that serves to retain and prolong the effects of multiple nourishing factors.

PEBBLE implies an element of diversity.

PECAN (nut/tree) points to fulfillment following an achievement.

PECCARY See boar.

PECK (pick at) relates to a lack of acceptance; irritable responses.

PECKING ORDER will attempt to remind one of one's place or position. This symbol usually clarifies the cause of an irritating life situation.

PECTIN depicts a desire to solidify some aspect in one's life; a factor that has the potential to manifest a goal or plan.

PECTORAL (necklace) suggests a representation of one's personal protective energy or force.

PEDAL (device) applies to an opportunity to advance or increase motivation.

PEDAL PUSHERS portray a personal preparation for work ahead.

PEDDLER can reveal unexpected opportunities.

PEDESTAL comes as a warning against placing anything or anyone in a highly elevated position.

PEDESTRIANS allude to those around us who are walking their own paths in life, trying to learn through their own experiences.

PEDIATRICIAN characterizes one who has the capability and knowledge to heal or correct beginning problems with one's growth.

PEDICAB represents servitude or arrogance, depending on who was pulling the cab and who was riding in it.

PEDICURE marks an attendance to one's manner of path progression.

PEDIGREE (certificate) refers to a certification of purity; unadulterated. Recall the surrounding dreamscape aspects for clarity here. Usually this symbol will be recognized by the dreamer.

PEDOPHILE warns of someone with a tendency to take advantage of innocence.

PEDOPHOBIA See fear (children).

PEEKABOO (game) warns of game-playing in life; sends a message to stop vacillating or creating personal agendas.

PEEL See paring knife.

PEEL See rind.

PEEL (face) signifies a desire to keep one's public persona as honest as possible.

PEELER (utensil) denotes a need to peel away the surface layer of an aspect in one's life that is lacking clarity or definition; points to the existence of underlying layers to an issue.

PEEPHOLE indicates a hint associated with something the dreamer needs to know; a clue; insight.

PEEPING TOM See voyeur.

PEEP SHOW warns against wasting one's time and energy on superficial life elements; comes as a message to attend to the aspects of one's purpose instead of wasting valuable time.

PEERS may relate to personal associates, acquaintances, or friends, and reveal an indication of associated characteristics; quality and type of one's circle.

PEG represents a marker; indicator; may denote a natural connective element.

PEGASUS (Greek mythology) emphasizes possibilities that are rarely considered.

PEGBOARD represents a method of organization; an opportunity to sort things out and keep an eye on the most important elements of something.

PEG LEG denotes the existence of an alternative.

PEKINESE (dog breed) portrays a self-serving friend, yet will never leave you in the cold or out of the loop.

PELICAN pertains to a spiritual gluttony; possessiveness.

PELLET alludes to an element in one's life that contains multiple aspects.

PELLET STOVE defines an inefficient method of accomplishing something.

PELT (animal skin) will represent an essence bond with the presented animal. See specific animal type in this dictionary.

PELTED stands for an inundation of something in one's life; an overwhelming element.

PELVIS (anatomy) relates to the center or beginning point of one's inner strength.

PEMMICAN signifies an extremely high concentration of one's personal energy or high wisdom.

PEN signifies an intention to write down something that can't be erased.

PEN (enclosure) illustrates confinement, usually self-generated.

PEN (write) exemplifies the recording of something. Surrounding dreamscape details will indicate whether or not something *needs* to be written down.

PENAL CODE will always refer to karmic law.

PENALTY corresponds with a balancing element; a corrective justification.

PENALTY BOX signifies a payment made for a misdeed. Recall who was in the penalty box. What was the infraction?

PENCHANT See predilection.

PENCIL represents an intention that may or may not manifest; tentative plan.

PENCIL SHARPENER denotes diligence—a readiness—to follow through with intentions.

PENDANT will always signify something important. Recall if it contained a gemstone. If so, what was the color, type, and clarity? Was it a specific shape? Form? Silver or gold?

PENDULUM stands for the swinging momentum of life; the ups and downs that can be expected.

PENGUIN suggests spiritual duality. May also indicate a successful effort generated from strong determination.

PENHOLDER implies a need for recording or noting something.

PENICILLIN calls for protective measures to be applied. Surrounding dreamscape details will usually clarify this; if not, the dreamer will most often make the right association.

PENILE AUGMENTATION refers to one's belief that he's not effective; an attempt to improve one's self-image. May point to misplaced priorities and is rarely associated with an actual physical augmentation but relates to a sense of needing a greater type of power, such as being perceived as being influential or close to an A-list personality.

PENILE DYSFUNCTION suggests an inability to carry out one's intent or see things through to their conclusion. Usually this symbol will not be literal but rather refer to plans, goals, resolutions, and the like.

PENITENTIARY denotes an ultimate result or conclusion. This is a dream symbol that stems from one's Higher Self or conscience.

PENKNIFE See pocketknife.

PENLIGHT represents a personally responsible state of awareness.

PEN NAME See pseudonym.

PENNANT (small flag) applies to identity or loyalties. Recall what the pennant represented. What was the color? The condition?

PENNILESS will not refer to monetary aspects but rather emphasize the value of humanitarian or spiritual riches.

PENNSYLVANIA symbolizes a new feeling of liberty, independence.

PENNY See money.

PENNY ANTE suggests a small risk; an element or idea that won't exact a high price if it doesn't succeed.

PENNY ARCADE comes to remind us that we can afford to take a break, take some amusement time and it doesn't have to cost us much in the way of expended energy.

PENNY CANDY points to the small enjoyments we can glean from life; the little things.

PENNY-PINCHING indicates a frugal mind-set. Recall surrounding dream details to determine if this was a caution or advisement.

PENNYROYAL (botanical) will symbolize an element in one's life that eases the effects of irritations; acceptance.

PEN PAL represents companionable relationships that are kept at a distance.

PENSION signifies benefits earned from long-suffering and perseverance.

PENSTEMON (flower) stands for a sensitivity/understanding of life's interconnectedness.

PENTAGON characterizes secretive dealings; ulterior motives.

PENTAGRAM indicates the little things in life that we can't quite figure out; the forever how and why questions we find ourselves wondering about.

PENTHOUSE relates to an attitude of being above others.

PEON indicates a low class. This will represent a personal attitude toward oneself or another.

PEONY (botanical) denotes sensitivity.

PEOPLE portray the more complex human components of dreamscapes. They are more diverse in meaning than any other image; therefore, the dreamer needs to recall multiple elements about the people presented in order to accurately analyze these human facets. Who was the person? Age? Was an occupation presented? What was the person wearing? Any jewelry? Did this person speak to the dreamer? If so, what was said? Refer to specific occupations, clothing, and physical characteristics for further clarification.

PEOPLE MOVER symbolizes a helpful element that will speed one's path when it is going in a general direction for a time.

PEOPLE'S CHOICE AWARDS reveals public opinion; the attitude of the majority.

PEPPER typifies a symbol that indicates a response is needed.

PEPPERCORN often points to a necessary communication forthcoming.

PEPPER MILL calls for finer perceptions or levels of awareness to be used.

PEPPERMINT indicates a cleansing or freshening of one's choice of words; softer manner of communication.

PEPPERONI refers to an interesting or personally provocative idea.

PEPPER SPRAY See mace (spray).

PEP PILL See amphetamine.

PEP RALLY stands for an effort to build enthusiasm for a specific event.

PEP TALK connotes a motivational impetus; a need to boost morale.

PERAMBULATOR See baby carriage.

PERCALE (fabric) alludes to a preferred element, type, or quality.

PERCENT (sign) will reveal a specialized meaning for each dreamer who will make an individualized association.

PERCH See roost.

PERCH (fish) denotes spiritual neutrality; a lack of spiritual direction.

PERCHERON (horse breed) pertains to great personal efforts applied to one's chosen path.

PERCOLATION TEST (soil absorption) refers to a gauge of the amount of spirituality one's foundational aspects contain.

PERCOLATOR (coffee) indicates a state of brewing. Recall surrounding situational presentation. Who was doing the brewing? Did the aroma have a disagreeable or pleasant scent?

PEREGRINE FALCON See falcon.

PERENNIAL (plant) will define a lasting element in one's life.

PERFECTIONIST characterizes an A-type personality, one who is easily frustrated and full of angst. May also point to intolerance and/or impatience.

PERFECT PITCH reveals an attitude, plan, solution, or other element that is right on track; alignment; a harmonic aspect.

PERFORATED will reveal an aspect in one's life that is not complete or is lacking continuity; may indicate a deception of some type.

PERFUME refers to an effort to conceal; a cover-up. May also point to an attempt to feel better about oneself. If the specific scent is known, it may be found elsewhere in this dictionary.

PERIDOT (color/gemstone) denotes a sunny disposition that serves as an uplifting and healing force for others.

PERIL will warn of a forthcoming harmful event.

PERIOD (punctuation mark) implies an end or conclusion to something. Depending on surrounding elements associated with the period, the symbol could be revealing one's *wish* rather than an actuality.

PERIOD (menstrual) See menstruation.

PERIODIC TABLE will usually have a specific chemical element emphasized or highlighted in some manner. This will have a personal indication for the dreamer. Perhaps one needs more iron in one's system. Gold or silver may have specific meaning. Is lead a concern?

PERIPHERY comes as a symbol to draw the dreamer's attention to an aspect in life that's positioned on the outer fringe of one's immediate circle and needs one's greater attention.

PERISCOPE advises one to give more attention to daily life rather than keeping self immersed in spiritual matters. Spirituality needs to be interwoven in daily affairs in the way of one's ongoing behavior, not kept separate.

PERISHABLES will signify a situation or issue that needs immediate attention before it is no longer viable.

PERIWINKLE (color/botanical) represents a fragile talent or inherent ability.

PERIWINKLE (shell) marks a spiritually significant element in one's life.

PERIWINKLE (snail) exemplifies spiritual fortitude.

PERJURY pertains to a falsehood.

PERK TEST stands for a question whether or not a concept, idea, or certain behavior will be generally accepted.

PERMAFROST connotes a frigid personality; one with a cold and unsupportive exterior.

PERMANENT (hair color) symbolizes mental stability; thoughts that are set.

PERMANENT (ink) represents a firm decision, no chance to change one's mind.

PERMISSION usually comes from one's Higher Self or other authoritative source to provide encouragement or motivation.

PERMIT reveals the rightness of a planned move or deed. Recall if the permit was being granted or denied. What was it for? Did it have a specific color?

PERMUTATION See transmutation.

PERNICIOUS always warns of an all-consuming element in one's life; an aspect that can have a fatal effect. May point to an obsession.

PEROXIDE indicates a need to cleanse or heal. This may also refer to a whitewashing or bleaching being done. Recall the surrounding dream details for a distinction here.

PERPETUAL MOTION (device) applies to high energy or some element that has been put into motion and will be difficult to stop.

PERSECUTION most often reveals a personal attitude toward oneself; a paranoid or neurotic thought process.

PERSEPHONE (Greek mythology) reminds us to balance our spiritual and physical lives.

PERSIAN LAMB emphasizes an enduring bond.

PERSIMMON (fruit/tree) indicates a need to clarify resolutions and confoundments; an ongoing puzzlement.

PERSONAL COMPUTER (PC) See computer.

PERSONAL FOUL reminds the dreamer of a willful behavioral misdeed or unfair act against another.

PERSONALITY TEST calls for self-analyzation; introspection into the root causes behind one's behavior and attitudes. This symbol may reveal one's trouble areas in respect to getting along with others.

PERSONNEL (office) may portray a manager of specific records. This could point to a source of benefits or one's personal information. This will be a revealing dream fragment for the dreamer. See also human resource.

PERSPECTIVE (artistic) denotes either how one currently views something or *should* view it. Recall dreamscape details for further clarity.

PERSPIRING alludes to great energy and effort expended. May also refer to embarrassment or a stressful situation.

PERTUSSIS See whooping cough.

PERUSING See reading.

PERVERSION applies to misdirection or misplaced priorities; an advisement to seek professional guidance or direction.

PESSIMISM connotes a lack of acceptance and may also indicate a person who uses this attitude as an escape mechanism to avoid personal responsibility.

PEST (any type) will be different for every dreamer. It's usually a general call to stop being annoyed and take action to resolve a situation or deal with it better.

PESTILENCE will most often correspond with a negative element one brings upon oneself.

PESTLE connotes a life aspect that one has the opportunity to utilize for the purpose of clarifying or understanding a current puzzlement.

PESTO suggests some of the best aspects combined into one element.

PET See specific type.

PETAL (of blossom) will denote a magnified emphasis of the presented flower. Refer to the specific botanical type for greater clarification.

PETER PAN pertains to the power of belief and faith. Emphasizes the importance of a childlike faith and open-mindedness.

PETITE (size) reminds us that size cannot be used for comparison when evaluating potential or power.

PETITION stands for a personal request. The key here is to recall who was petitioning whom and for what purpose.

PETIT POINT (bead/needlework) represents efforts expended on fine detail; an attention to the important little elements.

PETITS FOURS (confection) represent the small aspects in life that serve as benefits or little treats (blessings).

PET NAME will reveal a little-known aspect of an individual.

PET PEEVE advises of a need to gain acceptance in life.

PETREL stands for simplicity; maintaining the essence of one's true character without feeling the need to take on affectations.

PETRI DISH calls for a need to develop or expand a particular aspect in one's life.

PETRIFIED (age) See fossil.

PETRIFIED (fear) See scared.

PETRIFIED FOREST will correspond with one's inherent natural talents that have enduring qualities yet are not used.

PETROLEUM relates to an element in one's life that has multiple aspects and diverse uses. The dreamer will usually make this association.

PETROLEUM JELLY signifies a life element that has the potential for soothing or easing a rough or difficult situation.

PETTICOAT See underwear.

PETTING ZOO advises of a return to more basic, simplistic perspectives and appreciations.

PETTY CASH depicts one's current supply of available resources; usually refers to personal talents or abilities.

PETTY OFFICER characterizes a person who possesses a higher than average level of intelligence, experience, and authority.

PETUNIA (botanical) exemplifies a talent or other personal ability that will proliferate if cared for.

PEW won't necessarily constitute a church or have a religious connotation, it will usually symbolize a concept many sit and listen to or a place where same is done.

PEWTER signifies a simple form of basic spiritual value; a warm and personal embracing quality.

PEYOTE connotes the sacred aspects of personal spiritual attainment.

PHAETON See carriage.

PHANTOM may represent one's fears or it may present a spiritual message. Recall surrounding dreamscape details for clarity.

PHANTOM-LIMB PAIN underscores the reality of one's whole essence.

PHARAOH characterizes spiritual domination. Recall who the dream pharaoh was.

PHARAOH HOUND (dog breed) signifies a dignified, yet faithful, friend.

PHARISEE represents a spiritual hypocrite.

PHARMACIST will correspond with an individual in the dreamer's life who has the potential and knowledge to provide a healing element. This element may relate to spiritual, physical, mental, or emotional ills.

PHARMACY will suggest some type of medication or healing element is needed.

PHASEOUT connotes a waning situation or condition; some element in one's life that should be let go of; may advise greater acceptance.

PHEASANT connotes a spiritual seeking.

PHILADELPHIA EXPERIMENT emphasizes elements of true Reality that are currently doubted or issues generating skepticism.

PHILANTHROPIST characterizes a generous nature; may indicate opportunities to be selfless.

PHILHARMONIC See symphony.

PHILIPPINES stand for hidden hazards.

PHILOSOPHER alludes to one who engages in higher enlightenment through deeper thought and contemplation. May point to a deep thinker.

PHILOSOPHER'S STONE pertains to a magic potion or miracle one hopes to enter one's life in respect to bringing enlightenment or power.

PHLEBOTOMIST relates to a draining personality; one who uses others.

PHLEGM indicates a congested condition, usually within one's mind; confusion.

PHLOX (botanical) denotes cheerfulness and how quickly it can spread to others.

PHOBIA corresponds with one's fears and elements of great anxiety. For specific types of phobias, see fear.

PHOEBE (bird) stands for warm companionship; an enhanced relationship; intensified bond of friendship.

PHOENIX (Egyptian mythology) stands for the quintessential example of a characteristic, ability, or attainment; may also emphasize a powerfully determined personality who bounces back and refuses to be defeated or blocked.

PHONE See telephone.

PHONE BOOK See telephone book.

PHONE BOOTH See telephone booth.

PHONE CARD signifies an invitation to communicate; a connection that doesn't cost anything.

PHONE TAG stands for communication that has bad timing.

PHONICS signifies a general idea of something; an overall understanding without specific knowledge of the individual associated elements.

PHONOGRAPH refers to old information; a need to be updated.

PHONY naturally means a false element; an imitation or deception.

PHOSPHORESCENCE connotes an illuminating (enlightening) element in one's life.

PHOTO See photograph.

PHOTOCOPIER stands for repetitiveness. Recall the condition and color of the dreamscape machine to determine whether or not something actually needs repeating or if this is a warning to *stop* repeating or copying something or someone. Frequently this symbol infers that an individual is *repeating* past mistakes. Who was using the photocopier?

PHOTOELECTRIC CELL (electronic eye) illustrates natural or reflex responses. This may be an advisement to think before acting.

PHOTO FINISH (of race) exemplifies a nearly equal level of ability, knowledge, or development.

PHOTO FINISHING represents the development of one's past efforts of associated elements; a growth through understanding.

PHOTOGRAPH will reveal a message of importance. Recall what or who was in the photo.

PHOTOGRAPHER advises of the wisdom of grasping the moment instead of living for the future or what was.

PHOTOJOURNALISM illustrates the act of learning from one's experiential aspects in life.

PHOTO OPPORTUNITY (Photo Op) suggests opportunities that shouldn't be missed; a need to maintain constant awareness of unexpected experiences in life that carry valuable lessons or insights with them.

PHOTOPHOBIA See fear (light).

PHOTORECEPTOR symbolizes a strong personal desire to expand one's knowledge; a thirst for truth.

PHOTOSENSITIVITY depicts a psychologically based negative response to spiritually related truths or higher knowledge.

PHOTOSYNTHESIS portrays an inherent attraction and personal need for knowledge.

PHOTOTHERAPY denotes a personal recognition of and appreciation for the rich healing value of knowledge.

PHOTOVOLTAIC connotes the mental and emotional energy and motivation one gains from seeking and attaining knowledge.

PHRASE BOOK represents a desire to communicate better and the efforts applied to same.

PHRENOLOGY (study of head shape) comes as a warning that one's current research or learning efforts are focused on a false premise.

PHYLACTERY pertains to a reminder of specific spiritual tenets. The dreamer will make individualized associations here.

PHYSIATRIST See physical therapist.

PHYSICAL EDUCATION (PE) comes in dreams to stress the importance of exercise and hygiene. Recall which aspect was emphasized in the dream to gain specifics for yourself.

PHYSICAL EXAMINATION (health) portrays a need to either have an actual physical exam by a physician or else to seriously engage in introspection.

PHYSICAL SCIENCE (study of) See specific science type.

PHYSICAL THERAPIST signifies some-one in the dreamer's life who has the potential for helping one get back on one's feet.

PHYSICAL THERAPY corresponds to a need to restore normal function of some element of oneself. Recall what was being manipulated or exercised, as this will pinpoint one's area of required improvement.

PHYSICIAN represents a person who has the knowledge and capability to help another overcome a life disability or ill. This won't necessarily be associated with physical ills. Recall what specialty the doctor had, then refer to the specific medical term in this book.

PHYSICIAN'S ASSISTANT (PA) points to an individual who is capable of providing basic diagnostic information; one who can point another in the right direction.

PHYSICIST will characterize someone who attempts to understand nature and reality; a high interest in the interrelatedness of all things.

PHYSIQUE (of people) stands for a multitude of symbolic characteristics and personality traits. Refer to a specific trait.

PIANIST signifies one who desires harmony.

PIANO denotes an opportunity to experience or create a harmonic situation or atmosphere, perhaps even within oneself.

PIAZZA See public square; veranda.

PICADOR warns against an action that will serve to hamper or disable a situation, relationship, or another individual.

PICANTÉ (sauce) denotes a highly interesting (spicy) idea or event.

PICASSO (Pablo) suggests a distorted perspective and/or confused thoughts (a collage).

PICCOLO refers to a higher level; deeper knowledge; more advanced element.

PICK (choose) corresponds with a specific choice one made or is contemplating.

PICK (gather) See gathering.

PICK (tool) corresponds to an aspect that allows one to get at something.

Dental pick relates to self-analyzation for negatives spoken.

Guitar pick indicates a need to carefully express oneself.

Hair pick alludes to straightening out tangled thoughts or confusion.

Ice pick See ice pick.

Lock pick implies a desire to unlock something, solve a problem. Was the lock your own?

Miner's pick See pickax.

Nut pick connotes efforts applied to absorbing nourishing life elements. May also point to an attempt to get through to someone who's thought to be a hard nut to crack.

Toothpick See toothpick.

PICKAX indicates a determination to understand (unearth) something; a desire to get to the bottom of an issue.

PICKEREL represents spiritual greed or arrogance.

PICKET FENCE represents efficiency; tending to live and process information in an orderly manner.

PICKET LINE See protest.

PICKLE alludes to a difficulty that must be faced, accepted, or resolved.

PICKLED See preserves.

PICK-ME-UP will relate to any life aspect that provides an additional surge of energy or motivation for the dreamer. This will, of course, be different for everyone.

PICKPOCKET pertains to a lack of positive resourcefulness or motivation; having no personal responsibility or self-respect; having ulterior motives for getting close to someone.

PICKUP See truck.

PICKUP (person) stands for someone who was helped along the way.

PICKY indicates a firm sense of self. This may not connote any type of negative attitude but will usually be associated with "knowing one's mind."

PICNIC corresponds to an enjoyable respite or a task completed with ease.

PICTOGRAPH will display a message unique to the dreamer. Whatever the pictograph displayed will be important.

PICTORIAL portrays a set of corresponding photographs that will be associated with the dreamer in some way. They may send a clear message or convey a story line to which the dreamer will relate.

PICTURE See photograph; painting.

PICTURE BOOK signifies a need for a simplified or expanded explanation.

PICTURE FRAME (photo) is a revealing dream element that sheds more clarity on whatever the photograph was of. The frame will represent one's attitude toward that picture.

PICTURE HANGER suggests that it's a good idea to place something in full view so it's always in the forefront of one's mind.

PICTURE PUZZLE See jigsaw puzzle.

PICTURE WINDOW presents a wider view. This symbol advises the dreamer to look at something with a wider perspective, less conservatively.

PIE represents a benefit; the sweet fruit of an effort expended.

PIE (shape) reveals three sides to an issue—three people involved or three concepts that are involved. Also see triangle.

PIEBALD (pattern) See spotted.

PIECEMEAL suggests a little at a time, rather than attempting to accomplish something all at once.

PIECE OF CAKE refers to something that's easily accomplished.

PIECEWORK represents benefits gained after each step of the way.

PIE CHART See chart.

PIED PIPER characterizes a person who has a strong magnetic personality and can convince others of almost anything; the following of or susceptibility to these types.

PIE-EYED indicates an emotionally intoxicated condition. This usually refers to a sober mental state rather than a drunken one.

PIER denotes spiritual interest.

PIERCE is differentiated from perforated in that pierce implies a breaking-through type of event; an advancement or discovery.

PIERCINGS (body) See body piercing.

PIE SAFE refers to an attempt to preserve what one has put effort into.

PIETA symbolizes an internalizes spirituality; deep emotional responses to one's spiritual beliefs.

PIETY reveals a person's spiritual state. The surrounding dream details will dis-

close whether or not this is a sincere state.

PIG See hog.

PIGEON connotes gullibility.

PIGEONHOLE implies a tendency to classify others rather than viewing them as unique individuals.

PIGEON-TOED defines an introverted manner of walking one's path; additional difficulties due to personalizing various external elements or events.

PIGGYBACK reveals personal irresponsibility. Recall who was *riding* piggyback and who was *carrying* another.

PIGGY BANK indicates immature goals. May also point to the value of appreciating every benefit or blessing that may be overlooked because it appears too insignificant.

PIGHEADED denotes an obstinate personality.

PIG LATIN refers to a backward way of communicating with others; an inability to clearly express oneself.

PIGMENT See specific color.

PIG-OUT emphasizes avarice; gluttony; greed. This will rarely refer to the physical act of eating.

PIGPEN connotes willful disorder and one's concern over it.

PIGSKIN alludes to a tough attitude, situation, or perspective.

PIGSTY reveals a lack of self-respect.

PIGTAIL See braid.

PIKA applies to quick thinking; mental nimbleness.

PIKE See tollbooth.

PIKE (fish) represents spiritual nourishment.

PILAF (rice) denotes an essential or basic element in one's life.

PILATE (Pontius) exemplifies fear of being bested and/or not liked; a fear of making own decisions; concern about what others think of oneself.

PILE (heap) illustrates a great amount. Depending on what this dreamscape pile contained, it may infer a backup of work to *attend to* or it may signify *unnecessary* efforts in one's life.

PILE (post) will constitute a supportive aspect.

PILE DRIVER indicates a need to express, impress, or make assurances. Something in your life needs reinforcement.

PILEUP (vehicular) alludes to a path journey that follows another too closely; inattention to where one is going and the manner of same.

PILGRIM indicates a searching or the need to discover something important.

PILGRIMAGE symbolizes a necessary journey to gain a significant aspect associated with one's personal search.

PILL represents an agent of personal healing or correction. This may refer to an emotional, mental, spiritual, or physical aspect of oneself. What type of pill was it? Color? Shape?

PILLAGE reveals a lack of over-all respect. One doesn't respect self or others. This symbol indicates a total disregard for authority and order.

PILLAR (exemplary) illustrates a model example of a specific characteristic. This may also warn against revering another.

PILLAR (post) See pile (post).

PILLBOX advises one to carry one's personal inner healing abilities with one.

This symbol implies that one's talents are not always utilized at every opportunity.

PILLORY denotes guilt and self-reproach. This symbol suggests that one shouldn't be too hard on oneself.

PILLOW pertains to an individual's true temperament, state of mind, or level of reasoning. The key here is to recall what the pillow was made of, what color it was; the condition; shape. Did it have any design on it?

PILLOW TALK signifies the revealing of secrets; verbal intimacy.

PILLSBURY DOUGHBOY characterizes personal contentedness; a satisfaction with self and one's position.

PILOT connotes one who had the capability to control one's path direction. The key here is to recall the dream pilot's condition and ability.

PILOT FISH warns against a spiritual path that imitates another's.

PILOTHOUSE See wheelhouse.

PILOT LIGHT stands for one's living spirit; one's true essence.

PILOT WHALE See dolphin.

PIMP denotes a user type of personality; manipulation; ulterior motives.

PIN (bowling) represents a target; something one shoots for; a goal.

PIN (fastener) implies a need for temporary restorative or corrective measures to be taken.

PIÑA COLADA See alcoholic beverage.

PIÑA COLADA (scent) suggests a fresh beginning.

PINAFORE represents honesty and simplicity of character.

PINBALL (game) stands for a striving to better oneself; improve one's success rate through repeated experiences.

PINCERS indicates a tight aspect in one's life. This may refer to another individual, relationship, business deal, personal situation, or belief. Recall *who* was using the pincers? *What* was being pinched?

PINCH will usually represent an attention-getting sign.

PINCH (measurement) signifies an extremely small amount; negligible.

PINCH HITTER pertains to someone who can take over for another at a critical point in time or phase of development.

PIN CURL indicates restricted ideas, an unyielding thought process.

PINCUSHION illustrates one's ability to make allowances and/or devise alternatives.

PINE (scent) denotes a refreshening of one's interconnectedness with nature (basics).

PINE (tree) pertains to natural abilities; one's bonded relationship to nature; inherent talents.

PINEAL EYE constitutes one's inherent knowledge; insights.

PINEAPPLE connotes a fresh aspect of an element in one's life.

PINECONE refers to the seeds of one's natural talents.

PINE NUT stands for the fruits of a person's inherent, natural abilities.

PINE SISKIN (bird) points to fortitude; a heightened sense of self-reliance; enduring drive.

PINE TAR applies to the healing elements of natural talents and gifts.

PING-PONG implies irresponsibility.

PINHEAD connotes ignorance; using a minuscule measure of one's intelligence or reason.

PINHOLE relates to an element without cohesive substance.

PINING alludes to a refusal to accept something in one's life; a great personal loss.

PINK reveals some type of unrecognized weakness that can refer to one's mental or emotional state, physical aspect, or spiritual condition.

PINKEYE represents a personal perspective that is infected with some type of negative or distortion.

PINKIE See little finger.

PINKIE RING See ring (jewelry).

PINKING SHEARS signify an attempt to keep something in one's life from falling apart, unraveling.

PINK LADY See alcoholic beverage.

PINK SLIP connotes an end to one's project or effort. This may be a message from one's Higher Self that indicates futility if one continues expending efforts on a specific phase or aspect.

PIN MONEY represents the reserve resources we keep handy in the event we have need of them.

PINNACLE stands for high points in one's life or spiritual journey.

PINOCCHIO points to exaggerations, fabrications.

PINOCHLE depicts a method of playing out one's life situations through the manner of maneuverability and cleverness.

PIÑON JAY suggests the feeling of inner joy regarding one's acts of goodness.

PINPOINT will define the current existence of something in one's life that may not have been recognized. This is usually a good symbol that gives hope.

PINPRICK represents an attention-getting message. The surrounding dreamscape elements will usually clarify this for the dreamer.

PINS AND NEEDLES most often correspond with a high state of anticipation or anxiety. This is synonymous with expectation which is in direct opposition to acceptance. This is an advisement to gain acceptance in one's life.

PINSTRIPE (pattern) typifies a thought process that finely vacillates between narrowly defined concepts.

PINTO (horse) marks the exercising of multiple experiential freedoms while following one's personal life path.

PINTO BEAN connotes an essential element in one's life.

PINUP won't necessarily indicate an erotic connotation but usually represents that which one admires or is attracted to in life. May also point to a distraction.

PINUP GIRL suggests attractive exterior attributes. This symbol usually comes as a reminder to check priorities because exterior appearances are rarely a reflection of inner character.

PINWHEEL relates to personal tenacity and flexibility to go with the flow and accept whatever comes; a plan that will work no matter which way the wind blows.

PIONEER characterizes an individual who fearlessly forges ahead through unknown territory. This symbol usually pertains to one's life path. May point to perseverance and determination.

PIONEER DAYS (celebration event) comes in dreams to remind us of the work it takes to get anywhere.

PIOUS See piety.

PIPE (conduit) corresponds with connecting aspects; element that has the ability to relate one aspect to another.

PIPE (smoking) indicates an individual's quality of perception. Refer to corncob pipe, Meerschaum, peace pipe, etc.

PIPE BOMB See bomb.

PIPE CARRIER symbolizes highly peaceful individuals; those who keep the sacredness of spirituality.

PIPE CLEANER pertains to a desire to keep one's perceptual thought processes clear of distorting elements and impurities.

PIPE CUTTER correlates to a precise move that results in a precision cut (severance). This is for the purpose of preparing oneself for a new aligned connection.

PIPE DOPE refers to insuring that one's connections to another are well sealed. A double-checking of thought processes that ensure certain ideas hold and are firmly in place.

PIPE DREAM won't have to denote a fantasy or impossible goal; it usually defines a high aspiration that has a high probability of attainment if one's path is carefully traveled.

PIPE FITTER characterizes an individual who has a knack for putting the connecting pieces of a concept or issue together without misinterpretation, error, or misfit parts.

PIPELINE symbolizes the connective link that runs from the past through the present to the future.

PIPE ORGAN See organ (musical).

PIPER See flutist.

PIPESTONE emphasizes the sacred manner in which a spiritual aspect is held within oneself or performed.

PIPE THREADER represents an attempt to make a precise connection.

PIPETTE signifies a careful method; efforts expended toward exactness.

PIPE WRENCH illustrates the effort expended to maintain information integrity.

PIPING (on fabric) applies to an emphasis placed on a specific aspect of one's character. Recall surrounding dreamscape elements to determine which aspect this refers to.

PIPSISSEWA (botanical) refers to naturally occurring opportunities that need to be noted.

PIRANHA reveals a spiritual narrowmindedness; a vicious possessiveness of one's specific beliefs to the point of striking out at those who believe otherwise.

PIRATE characterizes unethical personalities who gain by stealing valuable aspects from others; spiritual greed.

PIRATE (computer) See computer pirate.

PIROGUE See canoe.

PIROUETTE represents inner joy.

PISTACHIO alludes to cheerful generosity; a mildly healing element.

PISTOL See gun.

PISTON represents the energy required to maintain momentum, keep something going.

PIT See kernel; peach pit.

PIT (casino card area) applies to a situation or atmosphere that holds questionable elements; a call to caution when proceeding; situation where every move is being watched.

PIT (deep hole) constitutes a deeply troubling or difficult situation.

PIT (refueling area) connotes a need to reenergize oneself; a break in one's work is suggested.

PIT BOSS characterizes a person who oversees the actions of others; may refer to one's own Higher Self.

PIT BULL (dog breed) suggests aggressiveness.

PITCHER (baseball) portrays an individual in one's life who may attempt to foil another's advancement or success.

PITCHER (container) illustrates that which one views as a source that quenches a thirst or desire. The key is to recall *what* the dream pitcher held. Was it full or empty? Was another person holding it or pouring? What flowed from it? Color?

PITCHFORK See hay fork.

PITCH PIPE represents a life element that will help to keep one on the right track.

PITFALL stands for a major setback or dangerous course leading to great difficulty.

PITH stands for the elemental essence of something.

PITH HELMET implies a tendency or desire to protect one's primal or elementary beliefs.

PIT STOP suggests a time for renewal; respite; time to take a breather.

PITTANCE denotes the existence of some aspect in one's life that was thought gone or nonexistent. This won't necessarily have any reference to finances or a monetary connotation.

PITTED (texture) connotes inner strength; tenacity; experience.

PIT VIPER See snake.

PITY usually refers to self-generated feelings; a method of eliciting sympathy from others; a self-defeating attitude.

PIXIE points to the presence of true Reality's possibilities.

PIZZA indicates multiple opportunities forthcoming.

PLACARD will usually come as a specific message for each dreamer. Recall what the placard said. Did it have colors, a name, or particular design?

PLACATE denotes an effort to soothe or ease a troublesome situation or mood.

PLACEBO exemplifies an aspect that serves as a temporary replacement in one's life. These will be those elements that are phony or false. Frequently these refer to one's mental or psychological excuses for not following one's inner guidance.

PLACE MAT implies a mind for details.

PLACEMENT TEST will come in a dream as an advisement to give attention to where one is on one's path; a self-check.

PLACENTA corresponds to an essential element in one's life; a nourishing aspect.

PLACER (gold) represents a life aspect that has a trace amount of value.

PLACE SETTING connotes an expected response or aspect.

PLAGIARISM portrays an idea that isn't one's own as claimed or presented.

PLAGUE pertains to a serious negative element in one's life that has the potential to be emotionally, mentally, or spiritually fatal.

PLAID (pattern) relates to knowledge stemming from multiple sources.

PLAIN JANE comes in dreams to remind us that appearances can be deceiving.

PLAINS See prairie.

PLAINTIFF reveals the individual who brings a problem to attention; may also represent someone who has an issue with something or a person who's a chronic complainer, perhaps even a pessimist.

PLAIT See braid.

PLAN denotes an intention or method of proceedings.

PLAN B denotes a second choice; the necessity of having to fall back on the alternate plan.

PLANARIAN correlates to an ability to rebound.

PLANCHETTE represents a tool for the subconscious.

PLANE pertains to quality and depth of thoughts. Recall condition, color, speed, etc.

PLANE (tool) illustrates a leveling out or smoothing intent

PLANET refers to an influential element in one's life. See specific planet.

PLANETARIUM denotes a need to expand one's perceptual scope.

PLANK See lumber.

PLANKTON alludes to foundational facts or the basics of something.

PLANT (artificial) See houseplant (artificial).

PLANT (botanical) connotes a natural talent. Refer to various specific plants listed in this dictionary.

PLANT (industrial) refers to one's work efforts. This symbol may not imply one's awake-state place of employment but rather apply to some other type of work the dreamer is involved in.

PLANT (sow) illustrates an attempt to establish or begin some element in one's life; an act of promoting or fostering.

PLANTATION signifies the quality and quantity of one's talents. Recall who was working the plantation? What was planted? What was the condition of the growing vegetation?

PLANTER (container) will relate to a specific quality or personal characteristic of the individual associated with it. What was its color? Was there a special design on it? Was some type of botanical growing in it?

PLANT FOOD See fertilizer.

PLANTING CHART See zone chart.

PLAQUE (decorative) will reveal an important element about someone; will portray a little-known quality or characteristic.

PLAQUE (dental) represents a careless attitude regarding the manner of one's speech; unguarded communications.

PLASMA will represent an essential element to one's existence. This may not refer to a physical aspect, but usually indicates an emotional or mental factor.

PLASMA SCREEN (TV/computer monitor) refers to the newest way of looking at things. Note: each new advancement in viewing technology will mean this.

PLASTER indicates a life aspect that has the capability to smooth out or cover one's mistakes.

PLASTERBOARD connotes an attempt or chance at renewal.

PLASTER CAST (bone) represents a sup-

portive factor that carries one through a healing period.

PLASTER OF PARIS represents a method of imitation or the re-creation of something.

PLASTIC illustrates changeability; lacking high quality.

PLASTIC EXPLOSIVE See bomb.

PLASTIC SURGERY See cosmetic surgery.

PLASTIQUE See bomb.

PLATE (dinner) connotes quality of nourishment in respect to one's personal attitude. This symbol refers to the specific manner or attention given to the absorption of mental, emotional, or spiritual nourishment. Recall what type of plate was presented. Was it made of fine china, earthenware, or paper?

PLATEAU will mark a time to pause and level off during one's journey through life.

PLATE TECTONICS emphasize the fact that an action will cause a reaction; the importance of routinely attending to one's stress level.

PLATFORM See stage.

PLATFORM ROCKER suggests that this is a good time to feel secure in taking a well-deserved break, a rest.

PLATFORM SHOES suggest a desire to appear taller in the eyes of others; a low self-esteem.

PLATING (metal) constitutes a presentation of higher value that conceals an element of lesser value beneath it.

PLATINUM (metal) represents a life aspect that possesses multiple opportunities.

PLATINUM BLOND pertains to a shallow thought process.

PLATITUDE illustrates a lack of original thought; superficial responses.

PLAT MAP signifies a broader perspective of how something sets in relationship to other, surrounding elements.

PLATONIC (philosophy/relationship) denotes an intellectual focus on spiritual concepts rather than on the physical elements of life.

PLATOON represents a group of people with a like intent or purpose.

PLATTER (serving) connotes something easily obtained or attained.

PLATY (fish) symbolizes traditional spiritual beliefs; suggests a need for spiritual expansion.

PLATYPUS signifies an ability to incorporate spiritual elements such as beliefs and talents into one's daily life.

PLAY (drama) will usually correlate to something going on in one's awake state. This symbol comes to emphasize or clarify a situation.

PLAYBACK connotes something one needs to listen to again; hear what one said or how it was said.

PLAYBILL portrays a visual (poster) that serves as an attention-getting message. This symbol will attempt to draw one's attention to something one is missing in life.

PLAY BOOK See script; plan.

PLAY BOOK (sports) correlates to the different moves one has available.

PLAYBOY will point to an individual who doesn't take life or responsibility seriously, usually extremely self-centered.

PLAYER refers to someone who is actively participating in something, usually involved in a specific situation; one with like sympathies or attitudes.

PLAYER PIANO stands for an element that requires the least amount of energy output; something that is nearly self-contained and takes care of itself.

PLAYGROUND suggests childlike traits or attitudes.

PLAYHOUSE See theater.

PLAYHOUSE (child's) represents early formulation of interactive relationship.

PLAYING CARD See card (playing).

PLAYMATE (child's) represents behavioral characteristics formulated by those we interacted with at an early age.

PLAY MONEY suggests an unrealistic perception of value; perhaps excessive spending habits.

PLAY-OFF stands for a final chance at something.

PLAYPEN refers to a babyish manner of behavior.

PLAYROOM (child's) suggest opportunities for early interaction with others; opportunities for developing character.

PLAY THERAPY (child's) indicates a need to discover current psychological problems which are rooted in one's childhood experience.

PLAZA connotes a wide area. This symbol tells the dreamer that she/he currently has a lot of room to accomplish something.

PLEA See petition.

PLEA-BARGAIN indicates a desire to escape blame or responsibility.

PLEAT portrays rigid and sharply defined attitudes.

PLEBEIAN will refer to commonality; the general public in regard to an attitude or segment of people.

PLEDGE indicates a promise. Recall what was promised. To whom was the promise made? To oneself?

PLEURISY results from an intake of a negative idea or concept.

PLEURISY ROOT (botanical) relates to a life aspect that has the potential to negate negative ideas or attitudes. This will refer to something that causes a turnaround in respect to a harmful idea.

PLEXIGLAS connotes a strong substitute.

PLIABLE may allude to acceptance or an easily manipulative personality. Recall surrounding dreamscape details for clarification.

PLIERS refer to a situation where one attempts to pry something out before it's ready to come naturally. This is a clear warning not to "force" things in life.

PLIERS (needle-nose) stands for an attempt to grab hold of a fine detail.

PLODDING usually denotes perseverance; slow but still steady.

PLOT (cemetery) will most often come as a mortality reminder. This reminder is most often necessitated by an awake-state life of misdeeds or a lost course.

PLOT (land) See lot.

PLOT (plan out) pertains to thought given or required.

PLOT (scheme) corresponds to a devious nature.

PLOT (story line) signifies a synopsis of what is transpiring in one's awake-state life. It gives a vivid look at one's attitudes or lifestyle.

PLOVER (bird) stands for discernment; sharp observational skills.

PLOW stands for a determination and perseverance to plow through difficulties encountered in life.

PLOW-BACK stands for a covering-up act or behavior; an attempt to bury; possibly denial.

PLOWBOY implies a down-to-earth personality who clearly perceives the right directions to take.

PLUCKING symbolizes resourcefulness.

PLUG applies to voluntary holds or stoppages.

PLUG (hair) stands for new ideas or solutions that have come from a different issue.

PLUGGED IN represents attention/awareness, not necessarily participation.

PLUM denotes an element of high quality as perceived by the dreamer. This may not necessarily be a true perspective.

PLUMAGE corresponds to the quality or health of an idea. Recall the condition of the bird's plumage. What kind of bird was it? Refer to the specific type in this dictionary.

PLUMB (weight) represents a balancing or equalizing element; a straightening out.

PLUMBER characterizes the presence of a negative situation; may indicate a physical dysfunction or disease.

PLUMBER'S SNAKE alludes to that which is capable of removing problematical elements.

PLUMB LINE connotes an attempt to keep an element in one's life straight and true.

PLUM PUDDING signifies satisfaction, usually resulting from a success or accomplishment.

PLUNDER See pillage.

PLUNGER represents a need to unclog something in one's life. Most often the dreamer will make this association.

PLURAL MARRIAGE See polygamy.

PLUS (sign) See addition (symbol).

PLUS SIZE (clothing) reminds us that bigger or more isn't always better. Size can't be a gauge in estimating worth or potential.

PLUSH (fabric texture) represents a pleasing or emotionally fulfilling element.

PLUTO (planet) indicates a healing element in one's life.

PLUTONIUM refers to a life element with a highly dangerous potential.

PLYWOOD connotes an aspect that has multiple uses and resulting benefits. Each dreamer will make this association.

PNEUMONIA represents a negative element that is causing a suffocating effect; a lack of breathing room.

POACHED (cook) pertains to bringing something to fruition through gentle methods.

POACHED (stolen) applies to something obtained through ill-gotten methods.

POACHER corresponds to stealth and dishonesty.

POCAHONTAS symbolizes intercession.

POCKET (billiards) signifies moves along one's path; advancement increments.

POCKET (clothing) suggests something owned and hidden; possession.

POCKET (position) represents a closed-in or blocked position; may indicate a Catch-22 situation.

POCKETBOOK See purse (handbag).

POCKETBOOK (book) See paperback.

POCKET CALCULATOR exemplifies efficiency; preparedness.

POCKET DOOR represents full availability; a welcoming or totally acceptable attitude.

POCKET GOPHER points to lack of trust; insecurity. May also point to a hidden or behind-the-scenes presence.

POCKETKNIFE pertains to experience and the lessons gained.

POCKET MONEY indicates a state of readiness; a tendency to maintain provisional elements in one's life.

POCKET PC See PDA.

POCKMARK (skin) typifies a life fraught with difficulties or negative aspects; a hard life.

POD (group) symbolizes spiritual life.

POD (seed) refers to sources of knowledge or opportunities for same.

PODIUM pertains to a life factor that aids in communicating with others.

POE (Edgar Allen) characterizes a melancholy to a morbid range of ideas that stem from deep thought.

POEM will usually serve as a message for the dreamer who will make the necessary association.

POET(ESS) relates to the lyrical aspect of oneself which expresses inner thoughts and emotional elements associated with one's life.

POETIC LICENSE portrays conceptual development of expansion.

POGO STICK warns against attempting to advance along one's life path in an emotionally detached manner.

POINSETTIA illustrates spiritual celebration; an externalized spiritual expression of oneself.

POINT (advice) symbolizes suggestions from one's Higher Self.

POINT (bottom line/crux) reveals the essential idea or basic premise.

POINT (finger) will indicate an accusation or serve as a directional motion to draw one's attention to something. Recall surrounding dream details to determine which meaning was intended.

POINT (land) represents an extension into spiritual aspects.

POINT (phase) emphasizes attention or focus on a particular phase of one's life or path.

POINT (purpose) connotes a need to focus on the reason for something.

POINT (sharp end) suggests clarity.

POINT (verge) corresponds to a need to make an important decision.

POINTBLANK emphasizes an in-your-face immediate and direct element one needs to deal with; no beating around that bush.

POINTE (ballet shoes) calls for a need to increase awareness and keep on your toes.

POINTELLE (fabric) denotes a fragile-appearing personality, yet the individual may not be as delicate as initially assumed.

POINTER (any type) will call one's attention to something important in one's life.

POINTER (dog breed) stands for a friend who can be counted on to always point you in the right direction. A friend who has the mental clarity to give good advice.

POINT OF NO RETURN clearly signifies a point in one's life where there is no turning back; no chance to alter events or correct same.

POINT OF VIEW See perspective.

POINT PERSON represents a forerunner; a messenger; one who checks out conditions before others follow.

POISON will warn of an element in one's life that has the potential to cause great harm or a fatal effect if one doesn't proceed with acute awareness and be extremely careful.

POISON IVY (botanical) will denote semi-hidden hazards present on one's path.

POISON-PEN LETTER See hate mail.

POKE (jab) will either come as an attention-getting symbol or it will signify a testing type of inquisitiveness.

POKE (sack) See bag.

POKER (live card game) implies ulterior motives; stealthy behavior.

POKER (tool) See andiron.

POKER (video card game) suggests an opportunity to make choice moves.

POKER FACE indicates a strong business sense; an ability to keep plans or secrets confidential; closed-mouthed.

POKEWEED (botanical) refers to a plan possessing a negative premise.

POKEY See jail.

POKY (slow) may not imply procrastination but rather this symbol usually alludes to an extremely careful and cautious manner of approach or progression.

POLAND stands for a hearty character and a loyalty to one's traditions/roots.

POLAR BEAR relates to spiritual aloofness or an overbearing spiritual attitude. In some cases, this symbol may point to the hidden aspects of oneself and points to a need to look at one's subconscious motives.

POLAR CAP alludes to spiritual frigidity; no interest in spiritual matters.

POLARITY pertains to a personality that exhibits extremes.

POLAROID (camera/photo) represents a need to immediately focus one's attention or memory on something that will be depicted in the photograph or scene.

POLAR REGIONS portray a cold and frozen spiritual attitude; one that isn't exercised or shared.

POLE (any type) pertains to a helpful aspect in one's life. The dreamer will make this personal association.

POLECAT See skunk.

POLE VAULT warns against leaping over important elements in one's life that need to be fully experienced.

POLICE come in dreams as an advisement to self-analyze one's actions; needed introspection. Police can often be associated with one's Higher Self (self-policing).

POLICE CAR See squad car.

POLICE DOG indicates a watchful and guiding friend.

POLICE STATE is an advisement to be more aware of that which is transpiring around oneself.

POLICE STATION refers to restraints; will suggest that someone is always watching you. Were you in the station? What were you doing? Were you the captain? In jail? Reporting a crime or being arrested?

POLIOMYELITIS illustrates a negative aspect that has hampered one's ability to develop or advance as planned; calls for an alternate plan.

POLISH defines a final finish applied to something. The dreamer will identify what this is.

POLITICIAN signifies a self-serving and hypocritical personality; a double-talker.

POLKA (dance type) portrays a lively and cheerful attitude.

POLKA DOTS (pattern) corresponds to indecision.

POLL See survey (poll).

POLLEN indicates elements in one's life that enhance positive aspects.

POLLIWOG See tadpole.

POLLUTION characterizes the negative elements that adversely affect one's quality of life or advancement. The key here is to recall if there was a specific individual causing such affectations. Was it someone you know? Was it yourself? Do you need to change some of your ways? Pollution can also be verbally disseminated.

POLLYANNA implies blind optimism; an inability to accurately perceive reality.

POLO constitutes haughtiness; a presumptive personality.

POLO (Marco) characterizes adventuresome discovery time; a period when one should strike out and experience one's unique path.

POLO SHIRT suggests self-importance.

POLTERGEIST represents misunderstood spiritual concepts and their resulting self-generated fears.

POLYCHROMATIC (multiple colors) corresponds to a Bohemian or eccentric personality; the freedom to openly express oneself.

POLYDACTYL (extra toes/fingers) stands for a heightened ability to efficiently accomplish goals.

POLYESTER (fabric) suggests a lack of originality; rarely expressed individualism; middle-of-the-road position or attitude.

POLYGAMY applies to arrogance and lack of respect for others.

POLYGRAPH will naturally indicate that a question of honesty or integrity is present. The key here is to recall who was hooked up to the machine and who was giving the test.

POLYP (marine) See coral.

POLYP (medical) denotes the growth or extension of a specific aspect of oneself. Recall if it was a positive or negative growth.

POLYURETHANE (varnish) illustrates an attempt or desire to preserve a successful conclusion or finish to an accomplishment.

POMADE (on hair) represents a fear of one's thoughts being affected or changed by others.

POMANDER reflects a tendency to surround self with positive elements and personally uplifting or beneficial aspects. If the dream pomander was being gifted to another, this then represents a desire for others to be surrounded by same.

POMEGRANATE refers to justice; wisdom; rectifying mistakes.

POMERANIAN (dog breed) signifies heightened awareness in a friend. Depending on surrounding dreamscape

aspects, this symbol may also point to a friend's feeling of companionable affection.

POMPADOUR (hair style) indicates an opinionated personality.

POMPON (decoration) connotes a cheerful personality. May refer to a reason to celebrate.

POMPON (flower) See boutonniere.

PONCE DE LEON (Juan) characterizes a dysfunctional perception of reality and the folly that results.

PONCHO See serape.

POND symbolizes a spiritual source in the midst of daily life. Recall the pond's condition and health to determine if this source is a positive or negative one.

PONTIFF See pope.

PONTOON suggests a lackadaisical spiritual attitude.

PONTOON BRIDGE refers to a bridging or way over troubling spiritual issues.

PONY See horse.

PONY EXPRESS typifies a mode of communication that travels from person to person; a word-of-mouth dissemination.

PONYTAIL reflects an accepting attitude; an ability to rebound.

POODLE (dog breed) indicates a dependable friend.

POOH-BAH signifies an ineffective person who believes he/she carries great authority.

POOL relates to one's quality and quantity of goodness; level of humanitarian interaction with others.

POOL (game) suggests cleverness combined with the skill to accomplish a goal.

POOLROOM corresponds with a scheming atmosphere; plotting and planning occurring. The key here is to recall the condition of the room and those within it. Who was there? Do these elements lead to a determination of dirty dealings or healthy competition?

POOL TABLE refers to the issue or subject of one's plans.

POOPER-SCOOPER portrays respectful assistance given to a friend; picking up after a friend's mistakes.

POOR usually refers to a condition of a specific element in one's life rather than denoting a monetary aspect.

POOR BOX suggests being generous with our humanitarian acts.

POOR FARM/HOUSE stands for an inability to externalize one's inner wealth; withholding one's humanitarianism.

POP (soda) See soft drink.

POP (sound) usually comes to draw attention to something the dreamer needs to be aware of.

POP ART depicts a clear visual that's intended as a personal message for the dreamer. Recall what was displayed.

POPCORN relates to a specific aspect of an idea; developed and full-blown elements.

POPCORN BALLS stand for a concept containing all its associative aspects.

POPE characterizes religious domination.

POPEYE (the sailor) stands for belief in one's strength.

POPEYED symbolizes an astonishment; a fear.

POPGUN is usually an attention-getting symbol meant to draw attention to a situation having the potential to elicit high emotional responses.

POPLAR (tree) relates to a personal talent that has blossomed in an accelerated manner.

POPLIN (fabric) suggests a domineering personality.

POPPER (appetizer) represents a taste for interesting ideas; a draw to adventurous experiences and opportunities.

POPPER (popcorn) applies to a life element capable of developing ideas.

POPPER (uppers) See stimulant.

POPPY (botanical) pertains to a natural talent having the duality of positive and negative elements, depending on utilization.

POPPY SEEDS stand for assumptions of guilt regarding an innocent party.

POP QUIZ suggests a need to stay informed regarding a particular situation or issue.

POPSICLE stands for personally altered spiritual perspectives that have been adjusted to one's specific taste.

POP-UP (child's book type) points to aspects that are meant to be highlighted or draw one's attention.

POP-UPS (Internet) symbolize the unwanted and irritating pushiness we're inundated with by others throughout our daily lives.

PORCELAIN applies to an extremely delicate situation, relationship, or other aspect such as mental state.

PORCH signifies the extent of one's personally held distance from other people or life aspects.

Enclosed porches suggest a desire to maintain maximum distance.

Open porches denote a forthright and welcoming attitude.

Screened-in porches stand for a hesitant or cautious attitude.

PORCUPINE stands for a tendency to utilize subconscious defense mechanisms to obtain personal desires and goals. This is usually a strong warning to stop manipulating others. The symbol also means an instinctive responsiveness to bristle and hide from new ideas, relationships, or situations.

PORCUPINE FISH pertains to spiritual defensiveness.

PORCUPINE QUILL illustrates personal defenses.

PORE (minute opening) alludes to the existence of an opening or exit point or opportunity.

PORE (study) depicts intensive research or analyzation.

PORK corresponds with one's efforts applied to work.

PORNOGRAPHY reflects a misplaced priority; wasting valuable time and energy that should be expended elsewhere.

POROUS (surface/texture) correlates to gullibility; easily manipulated.

PORPOISE stands for spiritual guidance; a humanitarian nature.

PORRIDGE signifies an enduring and nourishing life aspect. The surrounding dreamscape details will clarify this association for the dreamer.

PORRINGER See bowl (utensil).

PORT See seaport.

PORT (connector end/receptacle) stands for a correct association made for separate concepts or ideas; a proper sequence of aligned thoughts.

PORT (drink) See wine.

PORTABLE implies efficiency or convenience. May point to an idea or element that can be easily utilized in many areas.

PORTAGE defines a burden of some type, usually effort expended to persevere while taking a spiritual concept over some rough ground to end up in calmer spiritual waters. The dreamer will usually recognize what this individualized element is.

PORTAL pertains to an opening or opportunity; a view into another perspective.

PORT AUTHORITY represents one's right to advance into new path regions; one's right or readiness to pass through.

PORTENT will be a clear sign that forewarns of the potential for danger or a disruptive element of one's life course.

PORTER (hotel) characterizes a helper of some type, one who helps carry the burdens of another.

PORTFOLIO suggests a need to organize an aspect of one's life, perhaps get thoughts or perspectives organized.

PORTHOLE correlates to a spiritual perception, usually a narrow view. Recall if the dream Porthole was clear or cloudy.

PORTICO relates to an elaborate presentation or show of appearances.

PORTMANTEAU See luggage.

PORT OF CALL advises of a need to re-examine one's spiritual beliefs or humanitarian efforts. May exemplify the various advances made while making one's life journey.

PORT OF ENTRY defines a right move in life; underscores the right direction; entering a new phase in life.

PORTRAIT signifies a true revelation of an individual. Recall what type of portrait it was. What was represented? Was it a beautiful representation? Grotesque? A caricature? Dark pigments or soft coloring?

PORTUGAL refers to emotional expressiveness; an ease with which one can openly share feelings.

PORTUGUESE MAN-OF-WAR See jellyfish.

POSE can reflect various meanings depending on the type of posturing that was presented in the dream. An obvious character or attitude revelation will be defined by an exaggerated position.

POSEIDON (Greek mythology) most often signifies a spiritual application regarding one's life course, yet Poseidon may also represent earthly elements that are in turmoil, in conflict with one's spiritual beliefs.

POSH (atmosphere) will denote extravagance and/or arrogance.

POSITION See pose.

POSSE suggests one's assumptions and prejudgments.

POSSET See alcoholic beverage.

POSSUM See opossum.

POSTAGE DUE points to a situation of failed communication because not enough effort was put into it; a weak or half-hearted communication attempt.

POSTAGE METER stands for the cost/value of communicating something.

POSTAGE STAMP refers to the value of communications. Recall what the stamp was on. What was its denomination? To whom was the letter addressed? Was the stamp from a foreign country?

POSTAL ORDER See money order.

POSTAL WORKER reflects those who tend to be efficient and orderly to a stressful/detrimental extent.

POST CARD connotes a brief message or communication.

POSTER will represent a message of some type; may reveal a personal interest or attraction.

POSTGRADUATE stands for advanced research or searching.

POST-HOLE pertains to preliminary preparations being done to apply *supportive* or *separation* efforts toward something. Which purpose the dream intends will usually be recognized by the dreamer.

POST-HOLE DIGGER (tool) refers to one's intention to support or separate oneself from something/someone.

POSTHUMOUS implies that which we leave behind after we're gone; may not necessarily indicate a death but rather something we leave in our wake.

POSTHYPNOTIC SUGGESTION warns of a vulnerable state; easily influenced or manipulated.

POST-ITS (notes) stand for a need to remember something.

POSTMARK will pinpoint a specific date that will be important to the dreamer.

POSTMISTRESS characterizes a person who insures communications are carried out; this symbol may even refer to one's conscience.

POSTMORTEM See autopsy.

POST OFFICE emphasizes a need to communicate with another; may refer to verbal or emotional expression.

POST-OP See recovery room.

POSTPAID indicates a well planned communication.

POSTPARTUM DEPRESSION point to a state of having anxiety and self-doubts after beginning a new direction.

POSTPONE may advise the dreamer to temporarily set something aside or the symbol may indicate a need to *stop* procrastinating.

POSTSCRIPT signifies an afterthought and the need to express it.

POST-SEASON corresponds to recent experiential events.

POST TIME reveals a phase in one's life when chances are about to be taken.

POSTTRAUMATIC STRESS DISORDER exemplifies extremely severe effects remaining from a highly stressful or emotionally impressionable experience.

POSTULANT relates to determined intentions. This symbol may not necessarily have a spiritual connotation.

POSTURE represents a multitude of interpretations. Recall if one was slouching, standing straight (too straight?), bent over, etc. These will depict obvious states of mind, character, or attitude.

POSTWAR reflects a phase that directly follows a difficult time or period of trial, conflict, or stress.

POSY See flower.

POT (any type) will correlate with a container and the dreamer should refer to the specific type of pot presented in the dream.

POT (botanical) See marijuana.

POTABLE relates to an acceptable element in one's life which could refer to an idea, concept, action, plan, or direction.

POTABILITY TEST stands for verification as to whether something is viable/workable or not.

POTATO symbolizes an essential or basic element in one's life; a basic nourishment.

POTATO CHIP portrays alternative forms of a basic need; various methods and manners of obtaining an essential aspect in one's life.

POTATO SKIN relates to the most potent aspect of an issue; the place from which the greater number of benefits will be derived.

POTBELLY (stomach) alludes to an absence of motivation and/or energy.

POTBELLY STOVE denotes a companionable atmosphere; a time for reflection and introspection.

POTHERB See herbs.

POTHOLDER suggests a controlled awareness/guardedness in the face of heated issues or situations.

POTHOLE constitutes a negative element in one's life course that usually can be avoided; a temporary irritation.

POTION will pertain to a positive or negative element that one has to accept in life. Recall the surrounding dreamscape details to determine if this was a good or bad aspect that one has to be aware of and either accept or reject.

POTLATCH indicates an unconditional sharing of one's personal talents or gifts.

POTLUCK suggests the ability to make do with a variety of contributing elements; an appreciation of what others have to offer.

POT OF GOLD (at rainbow's end) stands for unrealistic goals; chasing after dreams or targets that will only prove illusory in the end.

POTPIE connotes multiple benefits contained in one source; various elements contributing to a single nourishing source.

POTPOURRI defines a harmonious blend of elements; a pleasing mix.

POT ROAST signifies a complete aspect; the whole concept or issue that has a nourishing potential.

POTSHERD corresponds to a fact that provides partial validity to a specific concept, idea, or perspective; a fragment aspect of a single issue.

POT SHOT stands for an aggressive or cowardly retaliation.

POTTER characterizes creativity and talents that express one's individuality.

POTTER'S FIELD advises of the wisdom of making a difference in life. This is not implying that one should make a name for oneself, but to leave behind something of value for others to benefit from. This symbol points out the fact that we all should do something beneficial in life.

POTTER'S WHEEL points out a vehicle for one to express creativity and individuality.

POTTERY emphasizes the unique character of individuals. Recall who the pottery belonged to. Were there designs on it? Unique shape? What color? Condition? What was it made of?

POTTING SHED represents a close bond with nature; an appreciation for one's natural gifts or talents.

POTTY-CHAIR implies a need to retrain some negative aspect of oneself. Each dreamer will recognize what this refers to.

POTTY-MOUTH See obscenity.

POUCH See pocket (clothing).

POULTICE will reveal a healing aspect specific to the dreamer. Recall where the poultice was applied. Could you distinguish what it was made of?

POUNCE warns of an unexpected aspect; a surprise revelation.

POUND (animal) See animal shelter.

POUND (weight) will illustrate a quantity of some quality of character or personal deed. This symbol emphasizes the weight something carries.

POUND CAKE reflects a positive element that possesses a concentration of multiple benefits.

POURING (liquid) typifies an act of disseminating information. Recall what the liquid was. Who was pouring it? Did it have color? Odor?

POURING (rain) signifies an inundation of fresh spiritual ideas or insights.

POUT depicts selfishness; an absence of acceptance.

POVERTY will usually represent some type of character quality that's lacking. Also see poor.

POW (prisoner of war) refers to one who has been drawn into a bad situation and is unable to get out of it.

POWDER (consistency) indicates a fine aspect; a sifted element.

POWDER (cosmetic) stands for a desire to put a matte finish on emotions. This means a person's intent to curb enthusiasm or tone down outward emotional displays/reactions.

POWDER (gun) See gunpowder.

POWDER (talcum) See talcum powder.

POWDER HORN portrays a questionable attitude of being ready to enter an altercation or situation where conflict may be possible.

POWDER KEG reveals a potentially explosive situation, relationship, or attitude.

POWDER PUFF typifies a fragile nature or sensitive personality; may also refer to a prime or ideal situation or condition.

POWDER ROOM See bathroom.

POWERHOUSE correlates with a person who possesses the energy and ability to accomplish goals; one who successfully and expediently carries through with plans. This symbol may also point to an overachiever.

POWER MOWER See lawn mower (powered).

POWER OF ATTORNEY pertains to a shift of responsibility or culpability.

POWER PLANT connotes one's inner drive and resulting energy output. The key with this symbol is to recall what condition the power plant was in. Was it operating at optimum level? Shut down? Abandoned? Just being constructed?

POWER PLAY stands for taking opportunity of advantage.

POWER STEERING exemplifies using elements in one's life that make advancement easier; progressing by a less strenuous method. However, this method may not always be the most dependable or the one of choice.

POWER STRIP See extension (cord).

POWWOW signifies a need to communicate; a get-together is suggested.

POX stands for a phase of misfortune; continual bad luck.

PRACTICAL APPLICATION refers to putting knowledge or experience into action.

PRACTICAL JOKE applies to a stress-releasing event. Recall whether or not this joke was harmful. Who was the instigator? Who was the victim? What was the response?

PRACTICAL NURSE relates to a minor personal dysfunction of some type. The surrounding dreamscape elements will clarify what this means.

PRACTICING advises of a need to gain more experience.

PRAIRIE reflects a clear path ahead.

PRAIRIE DOG portrays a communal watchfulness; awareness and attention given to friends and associates within one's circle.

PRAIRIE SCHOONER See covered wagon.

PRAISE correlates with recognition of personal efforts applied to one's life path by a person's Higher Self or spiritual forces.

PRALINE (confection) corresponds to a benefit that one perceives as being sweet and emotionally nourishing.

PRAM See baby carriage.

PRANCING illustrates a lighthearted mood; true contentment or acceptance.

PRANK See practical joke.

PRATTLE reveals mental confusion or an obsession with superficial or insubstantial life aspects.

PRAWN See shrimp.

PRAYER depicts a specific need or desire in one's life. Recall what the prayer's subject was. Who was the prayer directed to? Who was saying it or showing the words?

PRAYER BEADS See rosary.

PRAYER BOOK represents a tendency to have spiritual expectations; a dependency on higher forces to accomplish one's goals.

PRAYER MEETING advises of a state of spiritual weakness; a condition whereby one depends on the spiritual motivation and support of others.

PRAYER SHAWL reflects spiritual humility and respect.

PRAYER WHEEL warns of spiritual inattention; a tendency to place one's responsibility on the Divine rather than recognizing and accepting one's own.

PRAYING MANTIS portrays spiritual hypocrisy; lip-service.

PREACHER See religious figure.

PREAMBLE will define an introductory element that precedes an event or situation; forewarning.

PRE-BUILT suggests partially completed elements; a course of action that already has several aspects in place.

PRECANCEROUS (condition) warns of a highly dangerous situation that has the potential of developing into a hopeless or fatal conclusion.

PRECAST See mold (shape).

PRECAUTIONS reflect heightened awareness; an attention given to probabilities; preparedness.

PRECEPT usually indicates a spiritual, ethical, or moral law.

PRECIOUS STONE See gemstone. Refer to specific type.

PRECIPICE reveals a decision-making moment.

PRECOCIOUSNESS is a dream aspect that comes to advise one of a need to control one's mental energies; too much information or too many elements are being missed due to a racetrack mind.

PRECOGNITION usually underscores an awake-state natural ability.

PRECOOKED refers to having a situation, idea, or other element well researched and prepared before presenting it to others.

PRECUT stands for an efficient manner of accomplishing a goal; having all the elements formulated and ready to fit together.

PREDATOR most often reveals a harmful individual in one's life.

PREDAWN (light) represents beginning insights that are yet to be clearly defined or wholly solidified; the recognition of a yet obscure theory or concept.

PREDECESSOR characterizes a person who attempted to present the same attitude, idea, or plan before you did; one who blazed the same course.

PREDICAMENT will suggest a dilemma or entanglement. This dream may present a potential solution.

PREDICTION may, in fact, come as an actual event. Usually it reveals an outcome associated with the dreamer's current course in life.

PREDILECTION will reveal one's preference or tendency. Recall what this referred to. Was it a positive or negative element?

PRE-EMERGENT TREATMENT (gardening product) stands for actions taken to prevent something from developing.

PREEMIE See premature.

PREEMPTED denotes a temporary interruption of an activity or plan.

PREENING may not infer an arrogant or self-absorbing nature; it usually refers to a cleansing or attention to personal aspects.

PREFABRICATED indicates that certain elements of an issue or situation have been assembled in preparation for the composite completion.

PREFACE will pertain to an introductory communication; an ice-breaking element. May point to a forewarning.

PREFECT indicates a person of moderate authority.

PREFERENTIAL (treatment) refers to partiality. The key here is to determine who gave this treatment and why it was given.

PREFERRED STOCK will indicate a priority.

PREGNANCY signifies an embryonic stage of a specific type of awareness or enlightenment. May point to the beginning formulation of a plan or idea.

PREGNANCY TEST refers to a question as to whether or not this is a good time to start a new venture or beginning.

PREHEAT (oven) alludes to groundwork.

PREHISTORIC (settings/element) constitutes a long-standing aspect.

PREJUDICE applies to a biased opinion or perspective.

PRELATE See religious figure.

PRELIMINARY suggests initial research is required.

PRELUDE portrays an event or situation that precedes the main element.

PREMATURE represents something that is not developed enough to attempt or give greater attention to; the timing isn't right yet.

PREMED (classes) suggests an attempt to gain the basics of a particular issue or situation; learning/discovering the elements leading up to a certain issue.

PREMEDITATED correlates to a life aspect that has been well thought out.

PREMENSTRUAL SYNDROME (PMS) crosses the gender line to reflect a life element that personally affects someone and causes stress.

PREMIER (debut) correlates to the first time something is presented.

PREMIER (person) stands for the prime individual in a situation.

PREMISE pertains to a theory or idea one has.

PREMIUM illustrates a specific type of benefit one gains from participating in a specialized activity.

PREMIX alludes to having all the necessary elements (ingredients) to develop or accomplish a goal.

PREMONITION signifies heightened awareness; an insightful impression.

PRENATAL typifies the phase or time before the actual beginning of a new course.

PREOCCUPIED (mental state) connotes an inability to focus one's attention on the issue at hand.

PRE-OP (surgery) represents the time or phase immediately preceding the activation of a plan or behavior.

PREPAID points to something one has already earned.

PREPARATORY SCHOOL stands for initial research or study.

PREP COOK characterizes one who works behind the scenes.

PREPPY (appearance) implies a specific personal characteristic, usually studious and efficient and, perhaps, needing to be popular.

PREQUALIFY stands for verification of one's ability to perform.

PREREQUISITE indicates a necessary element one needs to obtain before proceeding.

PREROGATIVE depicts a right or personally sanctioned authority to engage in an activity or follow a specific course.

PRESAGE relates to a strong personal insight.

PRESCHOOL applies to basic information; learning essential elements for working with others.

PRESCRIPTION (medical) will come as an advisement indicating what one needs to maintain mental, emotional, or physical health. This symbol may also reveal the best course of action.

PRESEASON depicts a time for preparation; a time to apply energies toward laying groundwork.

PRESENT (gift) represents a benefit or offering. The key to correct interpretation is to recall what the present was and who gave it.

PRESENTATION relates to the exposure or disclosure of something. The dreamer will make the right association as related to his/her life.

PRESERVATIVE will clearly indicate a need to maintain an awareness or memory of a specific aspect in one's life. The surrounding dreamscape factors will clarify what this element is.

PRESERVES reflect a tendency to maintain fundamental elements of an aspect; not losing sight of all of an issue's various factors.

PRESHRUNK alludes to a time-tested element.

PRESIDENT (of a country) characterizes an individual who has the authority and power to lead many. This symbol may not, in actuality, refer to a specific presidential individual and, likewise, may not be a thoroughly positive symbol.

PRESIDENTS' DAY comes as a reminder to honor those who have led many through both hard and good times.

PRESOAK stands for a need to give added attention to an issue before it can be cleansed of negatives.

PRESS (newspaper) See printing press; reporter.

PRESS (squeeze) See cider press.

PRESS (straighten) See iron (appliance).

PRESS AGENT characterizes an individual who speaks for another.

PRESS CARD represents one's right to be somewhere or be privy to certain information.

PRESS CONFERENCE signifies a revealing meeting; providing an explanation or making an announcement.

PRESS JUNKET stands for efforts put into broadcasting information, usually regarding an issue with which one is personally associated.

PRESS KIT indicates the dissemination of background information.

PRESS RELEASE will refer to an announcement of some type. This symbol usually comes to the dreamer as a revelation.

PRESS RUN (book) reflects the extent to which a piece of information has been disseminated.

PRESS SECRETARY will symbolize one who speaks for another.

PRESSURE See stress.

PRESSURE CHAMBER See hyperbolic chamber.

PRESSURE COOKER corresponds to an extremely stressful situation, relationship, or element in one's life; may also apply to an advisement to retain more of the nutrients of the food eaten.

PRESSURE GAUGE comes as an advisement to monitor and stay aware of how you handle stressful situations.

PRESSURE POINT (physiological) will correlate to one's specific area of contention; one's buttons others can push.

PRESSURE SUIT implies the application of a compensating or equalizing aspect to offset the effects of stress.

PRESTIGE pertains to personal distinction or stature among one's peers. This symbol may reveal a perceptual level the dreamer was unaware of or it may indicate a caution to stop inflating one's self-image.

PRETENDER usually denotes a hidden activity or behavior. Recall who the dream presented as the pretender. It also could be oneself and, in that case, the symbol is coming as a message from one's Higher Self for the purpose of telling you to look at what you're doing.

PRETEST suggests attention given to one's qualifications or knowledge.

PRETEXT suggests an ulterior motive; a hidden agenda.

PRETRIAL HEARING exemplifies clarification groundwork aspects.

PRETTY corresponds with a pleasing element.

PRETZEL refers to a twisted perception or thought process. This symbol may signify one's emotional or mental state and relate to a relationship, life situation, or even a specific belief system.

PREVAILING (wind) warns against indecision; mental or emotional vacillation depending on the opinion of others.

PREVIEW defines a sampling of something before a decision is made.

PREWASHED stands for a desire to maintain a state unaffected by impurities or foreign elements.

PREY will reveal a negative situation whereby an individual is the subject of another's negative intent or otherwise a victim. Recall who or what the prey was. More importantly, who was the predator?

PRICE (of something) will usually denote true value. Sometimes this symbol will reveal an exaggerated inflated value or indicate a worth that isn't fully recognized by presenting it as ridiculously inexpensive.

PRICE CUTTING suggests too high a value placed on a life aspect; an inflated perspective of worth.

PRICE FIXING constitutes a misrepresentation of value and worth.

PRICE TAG stands for a cost attached to something one wants or needs. Also see price.

PRICE WAR characterizes a state of competition so strong that the participants may actually lose in the end.

PRICKLY ASH (tree) stands for acceptance and tolerance.

PRICKLY HEAT See heat rash.

PRICKLY PEAR See cactus.

PRIDEFUL means arrogance; a self-absorbed individual.

PRIEST(ESS) See religious figure.

PRIM represents a rigidly formal or puritanical personality.

PRIMA DONNA stands for an egotistical individual; placing self above others; expecting to be admired.

PRIMAL SCREAM warns of being pushed past one's limit/endurance; a phase of ultimate stress.

PRIMAL THERAPY indicates a need to rid oneself of withheld and internalized stress and negative emotions such as anger, frustration, and resentment.

PRIMARY CARE applies to routine maintenance and attention given to one's mental, emotional, and physical condition.

PRIMARY COLOR corresponds to a basic or elemental aspect. This will correlate to the specific color presented in the dream. Refer to that color in this dictionary.

PRIMARY CAUCUS alludes to a gathering of opinions to discover a local, general attitude.

PRIMARY ELECTION signifies efforts to pinpoint or solidify an attitude or direction.

PRIMARY TOOTH See milk tooth.

PRIMAVERA (food) pertains to multiple benefits.

PRIMAVERA (tree) See white mahogany.

PRIME MERIDIAN symbolizes a starting point or point of reference.

PRIME MINISTER characterizes one who carries great responsibility for the welfare of a multitude of people.

PRIME MOVER indicates a motivational force; an element seen as the source of one's motivation.

PRIMER (explosive) will reveal an element in one's life that has the potential to be one of the main ingredients of an explosive situation.

PRIMER (paint) portrays a protective or sealing element. Indicates the idea that the main issue is well protected before additional aspects are built on it. Also see base coat.

PRIMER (text) refers to a need to return to the beginning or foundational aspects of an issue or situation.

PRIME RATE stands for the idea that those with the best record of showing they've been responsible with assets get the best opportunities or breaks.

PRIME RIB represents a choice element in one's life.

PRIME TIME points to the most productive time or phase to achieve optimum effectiveness.

PRIMEVAL reflects a beginning or original element or idea.

PRIMO implies a most desired aspect; excellent condition or situation.

PRIMORDIAL symbolizes the first stage of development for a plan or its progression.

PRIMROSE (botanical/scent) depicts an idea of perfection.

PRIMROSE PATH portrays a life of ease where all desires and goals are successfully attained; an overidealistic goal and course that has a high potential for ending in failure.

PRINCE See royalty.

PRINCE CHARMING pertains to an idealistic perception and overly optimistic goal; unrealistic ideology; an illusionary persona.

PRINCESS See royalty.

PRINCESS DIANA characterizes one having the inner strength to stand up for herself in the face of domineering factors. She stands for inner power.

PRINCIPAL relates to a main person or element.

PRINTER (machine) suggests a finality; one's words imprinted on the fabric of reality.

PRINTING PRESS represents an ability to disseminate information.

PRINTOUT indicates a need for hard copies. This symbolizes proof or verification.

PRINT WHEEL See font (type style).

PRIORESS See religious figure.

PRIORITY MAIL naturally stands for a high priority communication.

PRIORY See monastery.

PRISM refers to an individual advisement to view an element from all angles.

PRISON symbolizes self-imposed restrictions. The key element here is to recall what your role was, if any. Were you the prisoner or guard? Warden?

PRISON GUARD is most often equated to one's Higher Self, the conscience which keeps us in line.

PRISTINE (condition) will usually denote a well cared for element; well preserved, perhaps cherished.

PRIVATE (military) stands for a lesser ranking; less authority, yet prepared for a conflict.

PRIVATE DETECTIVE/INVESTIGATOR correlates to a need for each person to do

her/his own thinking and searching. In some cases, this symbol may reveal a need to watch something more closely.

PRIVATE DRIVE/ROAD See road signs.

PRIVATE ENTERPRISE defines personal resourcefulness; ingenuity; independence.

PRIVATE ENTRANCE represents sole access; may point to unique ideas one has.

PRIVATE EYE See private detective/investigator.

PRIVATE SECTOR signifies minimum restrictions.

PRIVATE SCHOOL refers to individualized thought processes that are more expanded or limited than those of the general public. The type of private school will clarify if these thought processes are pointing to being more expanded or limiting.

PRIVATION See deprivation.

PRIVET HEDGE See hedge.

PRIZE represents specific goals or attainments as personally perceived; an individualistic idea of what a benefit or blessing is.

PRIZEFIGHT warns against engaging in altercations for self-serving purposes.

PRIZE MONEY can stand for the ultimate satisfaction/benefit of achieving a specific goal or it can refer to the carrot that motivates.

PRIZE WINNER portrays an achievement or an unexpected benefit.

PROBABILITY signifies the presence of an alternative element or course.

PROBABLE CAUSE illustrates the existence of a specific motive for doing something.

PROBATE COURT pertains to a source for sorting out elements of a problem.

PROBATION implies a cautionary phase or time; a time to watch one's behavior.

PROBATION OFFICER characterizes those individuals who serve to guide and advise. Use discretion with this, for someone presented as a probation officer may not be right for the dreamer. Recall what she or he wore. Their actions. Colors that were associated with the dream person. In many cases, this symbol can point out a domineering individual in one's life or it can also be associated with one's own conscience.

PROBE means exploration; investigation; research.

PROBLEM will relate to just that—a problem in one's life, yet a dream problem will frequently define the difficulty more clearly and could offer a solution.

PROBOSCIS MONKEY points to self-assuredness.

PROCEDURE most often reveals an efficient course or direction.

PROCESSION symbolizes a chosen life path that follows many others.

PROCESS SERVER will reveal an individual who has the potential to bring bad news or dropping the proverbial bomb in one's lap.

PRO-CHOICE represents a decision that is not hindered by another's personal opinion; the personal freedom/right to make personal choices.

PROCLAMATION will usually reveal a disclosure of some type.

PROCRASTINATION implies an inability to motivate oneself or it may infer the existence of inner fears.

PROCTOLOGIST will constitute an individual who has the knowledge and ability to help you face problems and gain acceptance.

PROD (device) stands for a life element that has the potential to serve as a motivational or energy-building impetus. Recall who was using the prod.

PRODIGY (child) stands for inherent talents, memories, or knowledge from one's accumulative experiential existences.

PRODUCE (edibles) denote nourishing life elements. See specific type.

PRODUCER (film) typifies an individual who has the opportunity and ability to enlighten others; one who displays another's ideas to the public.

PRODUCTION LINE See assembly line.

PROFANITY See obscenity.

PROFESSION signifies multiple interpretations. Check to see if specific type is listed in this dictionary.

PROFESSIONAL refers to an attained level of experience or skill.

PROFESSOR See teacher.

PROFICIENCY represents applied efficiency coupled with skill.

PROFILE (physical) See silhouette.

PROFILE (workup) stands for a composite of one's characteristics.

PROFILER characterizes an individual who has a knack for perceiving another's thought processes and behavioral motivations.

PROFIT signifies benefits from expending one's efforts.

PROFIT AND LOSS (statement) suggests one take a look at one's life balance sheet as far as behavior goes.

PROFITEER characterizes an individual who takes advantage of others or sees self-serving opportunities thought negative means.

PROFIT SHARING denotes a synergistic relationship where everyone benefits from group input.

PROGENY See offspring; children.

PROGNOSIS will reveal a probable outcome.

PROGRAM (any type/source) signifies an individualized message for each dreamer. This dream program will depict one's actions or clarify a situation or course of action.

PROGRAMMED refers to conditioned responses; brain-washed; manipulated and/or influenced.

PROGRAMMER characterizes an individual who has the knowledge and ability to manipulate and/or strongly influence others.

PROGRESS will come as a message of encouragement if the dream depicts an advancement being made.

PROGRESS REPORT See report card.

PROHIBITION represents restrictions placed by others; suppression.

PROJECT (buildings) imply a lack of resources and/or motivation.

PROJECT (venture) will usually symbolize or actually depict a preferred course of action for the dreamer; illustrates what one should be working on.

PROJECTILE portrays the entry of an unexpected element. Recall what was going through the air for further clarity.

PROJECTION BOOTH symbolizes the source of specific information.

PROJECTOR (film) advises of a need to project an idea or attitude to another; a need to externalize and express emotions.

PROLETARIAT signifies the blue collar workers. May point to one who does one's own hard work to get somewhere.

PRO-LIFE alludes to a respect for life but not necessarily for rights.

PROLIFIC correlates with continual productivity.

PROLOGUE reflects an explanatory beginning; an introductory phase of a communication.

PROMENADE pertains to a stage in one's path where a leisure attitude will serve best; a time for acceptance through neutrality.

PROMENADE DECK indicates a time for a spiritual pause; introspection.

PROMISCUITY warns against apathy in regard to oneself; a loss of self-respect.

PROMISE illustrates a personal responsibility to carry something through.

PROMISED LAND most often applies to one's goals or the attainment of purpose.

PROMISSORY NOTE defines one's firm intention of paying a debt back.

PROMONTORY applies to a testing, inquisitive probe into spiritual concepts.

PROMOTER characterizes an individual who supports and promotes another individual or idea for gain. Also see agent.

PROMOTION denotes advancement; progression along one's life path.

PROMPTER See teleprompter.

PRONOUNCEMENT See proclamation.

PROOF OF PURCHASE stands for verification of an action taken.

PROOFREAD comes as a clear warning to be discerning of what is accepted as truth in respect to incoming information.

PROP may indicate a supportive factor or a type of personal crutch. Recall surrounding dreamscape details for clarification.

PROPAGANDA signifies an attempt to indoctrinate others with one's personal beliefs; may indicate falsehoods.

PROPANE exemplifies a life aspect that contains the positive/negative duality aspect. Depending on how the propane was presented in the dream, surrounding factors will clarify its meaning.

PROPANE TRUCK represents a need to eliminate excessive gases from one's system. This doesn't necessarily refer to intestinal gases, but usually indicates other gases within the system. Are you often a braggart? Thinking egotistically? Full of hot air?

PROPELLER signifies forces that have the ability to propel you along your intended path and bring you into a higher level of advancement.

PROPERTY See specific type.

PROPERTY TAX implies a price attached to ownership; dues for what one has. These dues will not refer to a monetary aspect.

PROPHECY stands for a forethought; inspiration; foreknowledge.

PROPHET(ESS) characterizes an astute and wise individual.

PROPORTION comes as a symbol taking multiple forms and usually will reveal proper life priorities. Something may be out of balance in the dreamer's life.

PROPOSITION denotes probability or opportunities. Not all of these will necessarily represent a benefit and this is why this dreamscape fragment is so important. Recall what type of proposition it was. Who did it come from?

PROPRIETRESS emphasizes the rightful owner or originator of something. Surrounding dreamscape details will clarify this.

PROPRIETY stands for respectability; appropriate behavior.

PRORATED pertains to equality; balance.

PROSCIUTTO refers to an involvement in a personally interesting issue.

PROSECUTOR (legal) characterizes higher judgments. May point to one's own guilt and come as a berating symbol.

PROSPECTING represents a search of some kind.

PROSPECTOR characterizes one who is searching for something in life. Recall what was being prospected for. Gold denotes financial gain, while silver will indicate a spiritual element. A lost treasure will point to the expectation of a windfall.

PROSPECTUS indicates a need to research an issue thoroughly before accepting it.

PROSTHESIS denotes a substitute or alternative.

PROSTITUTE won't normally be associated with illicit behavior but rather applies to ill-gotten gains; a loss of self-respect; selling oneself short.

PROSTRATION may refer to a reverential attitude or it may infer a submission.

PROTAGONIST stands for the central figure; an advocate; leader.

PROTECTOR portrays a guarding or method of self-protection one has in place. This could refer to the distance one maintains from others, the tendency to keep private matters close to the vest, or any other behavior that is used to semi-insulate oneself.

PROTÉGÉE is one who has a personal mentor or special teacher.

PROTEIN will symbolize a necessary element in one's life. This usually will point to something other than food.

PROTEST signifies an energetic objection.

PROTOCOL defines the right way to accomplish something; a correct sequence or method of going about an action.

PROTOTYPE illustrates an initial sample of something that will follow; a model example.

PROTRACTOR comes as an advisement to look at all angles; have a balanced view.

PROTRUSION exemplifies a loose end that needs to be handled.

PROVERB typifies an advisement or counsel; will often be enlightening.

PROVIDENTIAL alludes to a fortuitous event or element in one's life.

PROVIDER depicts a patron, care-giver, or contributor.

PROVINCIAL infers an unsophisticated aspect or individual.

PROVING GROUND pertains to one's life; earthly existence.

PROVISO connotes ulterior motives or special provisions.

PROVOCATION emphasizes a need to gain greater acceptance.

PROW (of boat) suggests spiritual priorities; where one is spiritually headed.

PROWLER stands for stealth. Recall who the prowler was.

PROWL CAR See squad car.

PROXY pertains to a loss of input; a state of waning participation.

PRUNE refers to a distasteful or unappealing element.

PRUNING SHEARS relate to a need to cut back on something; trim down excesses.

PSALM reflects inner spiritual thoughts; may indicate a contentedness.

PSEUDONYM may infer a need to protect oneself or it may indicate an alter-ego, depending on the surrounding dreamscape factors.

PSYCHE (Greek mythology) characterizes one's soul.

PSYCHEDELIC (music/pattern) signifies an altered perspective.

PSYCHEDELIC FISH stands for spiritual confusion; a lack of conceptual discernment.

PSYCHIATRIC HOSPITAL may not have a negative connotation, but may represent a need for introspection; self-analyzation.

PSYCHIATRIST characterizes a need to give deeper thought to one's behavior, motivations, or belief systems; a deeper look into oneself is suggested.

PSYCHIC corresponds to one's inherent natural abilities as they relate to the yet undiscovered elements of true Reality.

PSYCHOANALYSIS See psychiatrist.

PSYCHOGENIC reveals a mental or emotional source.

PSYCHOKINESIS stands for repressed emotional energy.

PSYCHOMETRY refers to a heightened receptivity to others.

PSYCHOPATH characterizes an imbalanced perspective.

PSYCHOTHERAPY See psychiatrist.

PSYLLIUM portrays a tendency to take the easy path and suggests a more difficult course.

PTARMIGAN stands for adaptability; a widened scope of one's potential and resources.

PTERODACTYL denotes antiquated thoughts; extinct attitudes.

PUBLIC-ADDRESS SYSTEM See microphone.

PUBLIC ASSISTANCE See welfare.

PUBLIC DEFENDER implies unbiased justice.

PUBLIC DOMAIN applies to an aspect that is open to all; not individually owned.

PUBLIC EYE refers to open exposure.

PUBLIC HOUSING See welfare.

PUBLIC INTEREST symbolizes an issue or element that is of general interest.

PUBLICIST will point to one who disseminates information about you.

PUBLICITY See advertisement.

PUBLIC LIBRARY See library.

PUBLIC OPINION represents the attitude of the majority of the general public. This symbol may be a call to stick to one's own opinion if it differs from many others.

PUBLIC RECORD stands for information that's open to all; not a secret or intending to be.

PUBLIC RELATIONS (PR) constitutes the dissemination of supportive and positive information associated with an individual, group, or situation.

PUBLIC SERVICE alludes to efforts given to help others.

PUBLIC SQUARE represents neutral ground.

PUBLIC TELEVISION symbolizes personal efforts expended toward a goal.

PUBLIC WORKS pertains to general life benefits.

PUBLISHER characterizes one who disseminates information. Recall what type of material was being published.

PUCK (English literature) relates to a mischievous personality.

PUCK (hockey) See hockey puck.

PUCKERED (fabric/texture) denotes a snag or problem associated with an element in one's life.

PUDDING refers to an easy aspect.

PUDDLE represents something that has been left unfinished. This symbol won't necessarily refer to rainwater (spiritual). What type of liquid formed the puddle?

PUDGY (physiology) infers a need to shed some type of excess.

PUEBLO relates to a synergistic relationship.

PUFF See powder puff.

PUFF (of smoke) alludes to the first indicator of forthcoming trouble with an aspect that surrounding dream elements will pinpoint.

PUFFBALL (botanical) symbolizes a healing aspect in one's life.

PUFFER (fish) warns of a potentially dangerous spiritual element that one should defend oneself against.

PUFFIN represents spiritual arrogance.

PUG (dog breed) alludes to a friend who usually guards his/her opinion and rarely shares thoughts.

PUG NOSE portrays a lack of acceptance; a disagreeable nature.

PULITZER PRIZE reveals a prime accomplishment and recognition for it.

PULLEY indicates energy reserves; a supportive or assisting element.

PULLMAN (rail car) can have two meanings; the dreamer will recognize which. One advises of a need to rest along one's journey, to take the time to re-energize oneself and absorb new information. The second warns against sleeping while taking a new path and, therefore, missing important elements.

PULLOVER (clothing) suggests a deception; something pulled over one's eyes.

PULL-TAB depicts an element that has the capability of making it easy to begin or open something.

PULP (food/wood) alludes to leftover elements that still have some value.

PULP FICTION reflects idle intellect; filling one's mind with useless information.

PULPIT signifies preaching; telling others what to do and believe.

PULSAR connotes inspiration.

PULSATION exemplifies steadiness; dependability; continuum.

PULSE (heart) applies to emotional stability. Recall if the dream revealed an actual heart rate.

PULVERIZE See grinder.

PUMA See cougar.

PUMICE STONE suggests that something in one's life needs to be smoothed out.

PUMP implies motivation; that which serves as an impetus.

PUMPERNICKEL See rye.

PUMPING IRON See workout.

PUMPING STATION refers to a source of motivation.

PUMPKIN represents playfulness; a wide range of expressions.

PUMPKINSEED stands for an opportunity to express oneself.

PUN pertains to innuendos.

PUNCH alludes to an unexpected response.

PUNCH (drink) suggests something unexpected; a surprising event.

PUNCH AND JUDY characterize a love/hate relationship.

PUNCH BOWL denotes an aspect that has the potential to contain an unexpected element; a surprise factor.

PUNCHING BAG advises to release pent-up stress or emotions.

PUNCH LINE will reveal a solution or crux of the matter.

PUNCH-OUTS (paper) See cutout (paper).

PUNCH PRESS defines a need to make a strong impression, stance, or statement.

PUNCTUATION MARK See specific type.

PUNCTURE may advise one to make a breakthrough of some kind or it may denote an inconsistency or defect associated with an element of one's life.

PUNGENT symbolizes effectiveness; strong impression.

PUNISHMENT correlates to recompense; may infer personal guilt.

PUNITIVE DAMAGES suggest repayment over and above damages/wrong done; may be a karmic-balancing event.

PUNK ROCKER implies immaturity.

PUNT (boat) corresponds with a gentle yet cautious spiritual journey.

PUNT (football) signifies a lost opportunity; an additional chance to reap benefits from efforts applied.

PUPA reflects a state of transformation.

PUPIL See student.

PUPIL (eye) portrays one's perceptual qualities. Recall this symbol's associative details. What color was the iris surrounding the pupil?

PUPPET reveals an easily manipulated individual.

PUPPETEER points to a manipulator. May reveal the one who's really in charge, the one pulling the strings.

PUPPY will denote a new friendship.

PUPPY LOVE may refer to a budding affection or an immature emotion.

PUPPY MILL warns of insincere friendships; a tendency to form friendships for the purpose of personal gain then discarding them.

PURCHASING POWER will reveal the quantity of one's personal assets. These will not be monetary but rather humanitarian elements.

PUREE See strainer.

PURGATORY reflects reparations; self-analyzation and serious introspection followed by deeds that balance one's negative actions.

PURIST comes as an advisement to attain greater acceptance; one who is overly critical.

PURITAN characterizes a rigid personality; a suspicious nature.

PURPLE constitutes attained spiritual wisdom and enlightenment.

PURPLE CONEFLOWER See echinacea.

PURPLE HEART denotes recognition for one's service to others; courage and bravery.

PURPLE PASSION (botanical) represents intense emotions related to motivation, drive.

PURRING signifies contentedness; satisfaction.

PURSE (handbag) illustrates an opportunity to utilize one's talents.

PURSE (winning award) refers to the payoff benefit for achievement.

PURSER correlates to an individual who holds and protects the valuable assets of others.

PURSE STRINGS symbolize one's assets that are tightly controlled. These don't need to refer to monetary assets, but could represent humanitarian or personal talents. Could point to a tendency toward stinginess.

PURSLANE (botanical) depicts an opportunity to gain inner nourishment; a source of emotional strength.

PURSUIT usually represents a personal quest of some type. If it depicts an actual chasing pursuit, the surrounding details need to be factored in. Who was pursuing whom or what? Were there weapons involved? Was the pursuit public or stealthy?

PURULENT See infection.

PURVEYOR points to one who has the knowledge and ability to access what others need; a supplier.

PUSHING warns of a forcing action in one's life. This indicates a need to gain more acceptance and stop attempting to push things before their time.

PUSHOVER signifies a weak personality; easily manipulated or controlled.

PUSHPIN will usually point to a need to make note of something; keep something on the front burner or in a convenient place where one will be reminded of it.

PUSHY (behavior) represents a nagging or demanding nature.

PUSSYFOOT portrays a timid personality; may also denote a cautious manner of advancement.

PUSSYTOES (botanical/flower) stand for gentleness; a need to soften one's harsher personality elements.

PUSSY WILLOW (botanical) corresponds to bountiful personal talents or gifts.

PUSTULE See infection.

PUT DOWN stands for a taunting attitude that may be generating from oneself; usually reveals a self-deprecating attitude.

PUT OFF can pertain to disgust, yet it most often symbolizes the act of putting something off; procrastination.

PUT-ON typifies an exaggeration; a teasing. Could point to phony affectations.

PUTREFY See decay.

PUTT depicts a cautious move.

PUTTER refers to an individual who idles time; expending mental efforts on insignificant elements.

PUTTY (color/substance) relates to a cor-

rective aspect in one's life. Depending on associated dreamscape aspects, putty can also indicate an easily controlled individual.

PUTTY KNIFE illustrates a method or opportunity to correct a fault or negative element in one's life.

PUZZLE See jigsaw puzzle.

PUZZLE PIECE denotes a part of a solution; one facet of the whole.

PYGMY constitutes unrecognized strength.

PYLON corresponds with a supportive factor in one's life.

PYORRHEA reveals falsehoods; a faulty premise.

PYRAMID pertains to higher wisdom and knowledge.

PYRAMID SCHEME stands for a plan to use others for personal gain; amass benefits by enticing others to do the work.

PYRE (funeral) reveals the misdeeds and negative emotions that one piles up to create one's ultimate downfall.

PYRITE (iron) See fool's gold.

PYROMANIAC characterizes an individual who enjoys making trouble for others; may indicate a person who likes digging up skeletons in the closets of others and exposing them; one who enjoys an explosive and fiery event.

PYROTECHNICS See fireworks.

PYTHON will warn of a suffocating personality or situation.

Q

Q-TIP See cotton swab.

QUACK (sound) represents a swindler; fraudulence.

QUACK GRASS refers to uncharacteristic attitudes; undesirable qualities.

QUADRAPHONIC denotes high awareness.

QUADRIPLEGIC enters dreams to remind us that mental skills can take priority over physical ability.

QUADRUPLET (birth) constitutes a new life or new beginning that has four opportunities or benefits to it.

QUAGMIRE symbolizes a dilemma; a mired situation.

QUAIL stands for fearful thoughts; anxiety; lacking self-reliance. These feelings raise the sense of having to strengthen one's psychological defenses.

QUAINT will not mean old-fashioned but rather a refreshing type of element.

QUAKE See earthquake.

QUAKERS stand for listening to one's inner voice or Divine guidance/inspiration.

QUALIFICATIONS reveal the qualities or skills necessary to accomplish a task or goal.

QUALIFY indicates a need to prove one's skill or knowledge.

QUALITY CONTROLLER characterizes efficiency and a high standard of behavior or productivity.

QUALMS mean doubts; apprehension, perhaps indecision.

QUANTUM LEAP defines a major advancement regarding one's path progression or conceptual knowledge.

QUANTUM MEDITATION means slipping into and participating in the various multidimensional, near-parallel realms of true Reality.

QUANTUM THEORY represents a beginning peek at and step toward understanding true Reality.

QUARANTINE advises of a need to separate oneself from a negative, harmful situation or relationship.

QUARREL means a disagreement. Sometimes the dreamer will be shown to have an internal conflict (quarreling with oneself).

QUARRY (animal) See prey.

QUARRY (pit) symbolizes a mother-lode of knowledge or information; a rich source.

QUARTER (coin) See money.

QUARTER (football) See inning.

QUARTERBACK usually represents an individual who calls the plays or shots in one's life. Was this you or someone else?

QUARTER HORSE alludes to a preferred choice.

QUARTERLY will apply to a specific proportion of time related to an aspect of the dreamer's life.

QUARTERMASTER stands for personal responsibility.

QUARTET will pertain to a harmonic relationship between four individuals.

QUARTZ correlates to spiritual purity of truths. Recall if the dream quartz had color, then incorporate that symbol into the complete meaning.

QUARTZ LAMP See mercury-vapor lamp.

QUASAR stands for a revelation; spiritual insight.

QUATRAIN See poem.

QUAY suggests either the reaping or gifting of benefits/blessings.

QUEASY will reveal guilt or a conscience-stricken mood. May also point to a fear.

QUEEN characterizes a domineering personality.

QUEEN ANNE'S LACE (botanical) will represent an element possessing the duality of positive and negative aspects; may indicate a potentially harmful situation that, initially, looks inviting and attractive.

QUEEN BEE stands for the individual that much activity revolves around. This may or may not be a negative symbol. Surrounding dreamscape factors will clarify it's intent.

QUEEN FOR A DAY connotes a recognition of one's efforts and perseverance.

QUEEN MOTHER will indicate an individual who can exert influence on a leader or other persons of authority.

QUEEN OF HEARTS comes in dreams to point out the importance of the emotional male yang being balanced by his own portion of female yin.

QUEEN OF SPADES represents the key element of a goal.

QUEEN POST represents the female (yin) that serves as a double support for the male (yang).

QUEEN REGENT symbolizes the shouldering of high responsibility for another.

QUEEN-SIZE denotes a larger than average portion.

QUEEN'S PATTERN (silverware, etc.) means a regal bearing without pretension.

QUENCH relates to information obtained or a goal attained.

QUERY LETTER represents an initial presentation of an idea for the purpose of discovering another's possible interest.

QUEST stands for a major goal in life.

QUESTION comes in a dream to pose a self-discovery element; points to an issue or element that one hasn't considered.

QUESTION MARK will suggest a doubt or skepticism.

QUESTIONNAIRE corresponds to a need for the dreamer to spend valuable introspective time; self-analysis is required.

QUETZALCOATL means a spiritual rebirth.

QUEUE implies that one is not alone; there are many others in the same situation.

QUIBBLE portrays a nitpicking attitude; splitting hairs.

QUICHE refers to an unproductive effort; an insignificant aspect.

QUICK BREAD infers a quick fix to a problem that won't necessarily hold or suffice.

QUICK DRAW suggests a tendency to jump to conclusions.

QUICK FIX represents a temporary solution; a stop-gap move.

QUICK-FREEZE signifies an immediate halt to something, perhaps a sudden denial or rejection.

QUICKLIME refers to a highly destructive element in one's life.

QUICK-MIX (food) signifies a short-cut or time-saving procedure.

QUICKSAND signifies a declining situation from which one needs to extract oneself as soon as possible.

QUICK-SET points to a speedy solidification of something; a final decision.

QUICKSILVER See mercury (element).

QUICK STUDY stands for intellectual astuteness; absorption of information or knowledge.

QUICK WIT means swift responses; a lightning intellect.

QUILL stands for protective methods; self-preservation means.

QUILL WORK portrays an attitude of openness in reference to one's inner power/strength.

QUILT pertains to a personal manner of acceptance and inner comfort. The revealing factor here will be to recall if there was a particular design and color on the quilt.

QUILTING BEE stands for the serenity gained from companionship.

QUINCE (fruit) denotes an element in one's life that is effective only when brought into completion.

QUININE signifies that which serves as a healing agent in one's life.

QUINTET will imply an association with five individuals/elements creating a harmonic wholeness.

QUINTUPLET represents a new birth or beginning that will contain five separate aspects to it.

QUIP usually comes as a smart remark that reveals an important element that one has overlooked or voluntarily refused to acknowledge.

QUIRT stands for a motivational factor.

QUIT may come in dreams as an advisement to quit something or it may reveal one who is behaving like a quitter.

QUITCLAIM DEED may *exclude* one from further claim/ownership or it may actually *include* others depending on how the quitclaim read.

QUIVER See tremble.

QUIVER (arrow case) pertains to an intention to be well prepared to be focused on one's goals.

QUIZ will center on questions the dreamer needs to ask self.

QUIZ SHOW usually presents itself in order for the dreamer to gain a proper perspective of knowledge regarding a specific issue.

QUONSET (hut) reflects a temporary situation.

QUORUM corresponds to an issue in one's life that requires the cooperation or agreement of others.

QUOTA warns against attempting to force quantity rather than focusing on quality.

QUOTATION will most often come as a

message or some type of revelation, perhaps the solution to a problem or pointing out a better perspective.

QUOTATION MARKS emphasize the words spoken or written in dreams and serve to make them stand out so the dreamer will recall them.

R

RABBI See religious figure.

RABBIT represents an obsessive preoccupation with mental and/or physical erotic activities. This is a warning. This symbol may also refer to a quiet endurance of one's personal pain. Recall surrounding dreamscape details for clarification.

RABBITBRUSH (botanical) points to the inner strength that comes from having strong personal defenses in place.

RABBIT EARS (antenna) relate to awareness, one's personal antenna.

RABBIT FOOD See salad.

RABBIT HOLE See black hole.

RABBIT'S FOOT denotes a belief in luck rather than in oneself.

RABBLE-ROUSER characterizes a person who incites high emotional responses. This is usually a negative element, yet it can indicate a motivating force in one's life.

RABIES refer to a potentially fatal negative element.

RACCOON illustrates an industrious personality; self-sufficient.

RACE (speed/fast pace) refers to a warning to slow down. This symbol may indicate competitiveness that is blinding, self-serving. A race may suggest that one isn't absorbing all one needs in life because one is going too fast to focus on the important issues.

RACE CAR symbolizes a stressful and hectic work environment.

RACECOURSE exemplifies a designated course that one travels over and over again. This is an advisement to set one's own course and take it at a steady pace.

RACEHORSE illustrates competitiveness; a desire to be better and faster than one's peers; to get ahead of the rest.

RACE RIOT signifies repressed anger and the violent methods of releasing same; a lack of self-responsibility.

RACETRACK usually alludes to the fast track.

RACE WALKING is an attempt to cover up the fact that one is rushing through life without absorbing important aspects or focusing on the minor, yet revealing elements.

RACK See antler.

RACK See shelf.

RACKET See scam.

RACKET (sports) connotes where the responsibility lies. Was the dreamer hitting the ball back into another's area? Was someone else giving the ball to the dreamer? What was the racket's color and condition?

RACKETEER See mafia.

RACONTEUR See storyteller.

RACQUETBALL (sport) corresponds with contemplation; personally accepting an issue to be placed back in one's own hands for further analyzation.

RADAR portrays an acute awareness; intuition; heightened perception.

RADAR DETECTOR represents a perception of another's thoughts, moods or attitudes; insight.

RADIAL SYMMETRY (pattern) signifies an outward radiation from a single source, usually an individual; refers to the importance of giving, sharing one's inherent skills or talents.

RADIANT HEATING signifies an overall warmth of personality one gives off.

RADIATION basically infers a disbursement; far-reaching ramifications. Recall surrounding dream elements to determine if this symbol indicates a positive or negative meaning.

RADIATION SICKNESS reveals negative ramifications spreading far enough to negatively affect innocent parties.

RADIATION SUIT stands for a protective measure against potentially dangerous situations or negative elements that could prove to be toxic to one's mental, emotional, or physical well-being. May point to an insular personality.

RADIATION THERAPY suggests the use of a negative to counter a negative.

RADIATOR (heating unit) is associated with the emotional temperature of home life. Was the radiator broken? Cold? Steaming?

RADIATOR (vehicle) corresponds with one's internal temperature in respect to overheated emotions. Recall what the condition of the radiator was. Was it overflowing? Needing water?

RADIO exemplifies a need to tune into oneself for the purpose of understanding one's motives and responses. May also point an advisement to remain aware of current events.

RADIO COLLAR points to an attempt to keep track of another, possibly intrusiveness; may also indicate a type of stalker personality.

RADIOACTIVITY warns of a potentially dangerous situational atmosphere.

RADIOGRAPH can reveal one's hidden character or it can come in a dream to advise one to be extra watchful.

RADIOLOGIST refers to an individual who is capable of acute perception in regard to the hidden aspects of others.

RADISH signifies an emotionally volatile situation.

RADIUM THERAPY pertains to an attempt to correct or heal a condition through potentially destructive methods.

RADON correlates with forces or elements in daily life that are hidden destroyers.

RAFFIA will suggest a life aspect having the potential to bring multiple uses or solutions.

RAFFLE See lottery.

RAFFLE TICKET stands for a chance taken when an opportunity manifests. May also signify a goal having little potential for success.

RAFT represents spiritual ingenuity as associated with one's path of developed or attained enlightenment.

RAFTER (construction) denotes a supporting element in one's life.

RAG (cloth) relates to a remnant (left-over) factor in one's life that requires attention.

RAGAMUFFIN (child) most often will imply an adventurous or precocious character or attitude.

RAGBAG refers to multiple fragments of a life aspect that needs to be taken care of, finished, or used for a secondary purpose.

RAGE warns of an inability to direct one's energies in a productive manner; emotional immaturity.

RAGGED EDGE stands for something left unfinished in life.

RAGOUT See stew.

RAG PICKER characterizes a person who attempts to utilize leftover aspects; may indicate a resourceful individual who efficiently recycles multiple aspects by recognizing value in things others no longer perceive.

RAGTIME (music) suggests a phase of perseverance through a sense of humor/gaiety; using one's optimism to get through.

RAGWEED (botanical) typifies a life element that has the potential to cause a strong reaction.

RAGWORT (botanical/flower) represents contemplation/introspection.

RAID portrays the possibility of being discovered or caught at something.

RAIL See train.

RAIL FENCE reflects self-devised perimeters one sets.

RAILING See handrail.

RAILROAD constitutes a plan or decision that has been forced into an expedited state without time given to adequate thought. This would be a plan or decision without any options for alternate courses factored in.

RAILROAD CROSSING See train (crossing).

RAILROAD LANTERN refers to markers that light the way along one's chosen path.

RAIMENT See clothing.

RAIN symbolizes a methodical and consistent search for spiritual truth; refreshing insights.

RAIN BARREL shows an awareness of and deep appreciation/respect for one's spiritual beliefs; a cherishing of one's every blessing.

RAINBOW comes as an acknowledgment of one's personal accomplishments or efforts.

RAINBOW TROUT represents a beautiful element of one's spiritual path.

RAIN CHECK connotes postponements; promises to fulfill at a later date; perhaps procrastination. What was the dream rain check for? Who was giving it to whom?

RAINCOAT denotes a personal desire to insulate oneself from spiritual aspects in life.

RAINDROP reflects a singular spiritual element.

RAIN FOREST constitutes spiritual bounties.

RAIN GAUGE will reveal one's level of spirituality; may specifically refer to depth of wisdom or application rather than knowledge.

RAINMAKER characterizes an individual who has a good record of getting results; high rate of success with attempted endeavors. This usually points to spirituality.

RAIN OUT symbolizes a postponement; a temporary delay.

RAINSPOUT marks an attempt to channel one's spiritual aspects into a specific issue or method. This is usually an advisement to use one's spiritual aspects in a broad-scope manner that takes advantage of every opportunity.

RAISIN pertains to a nourishing benefit that manifested from an aspect of another life element.

RAKE (garden) stands for working one's talents for the benefit of others; utilizing them.

RAKE (leaf) implies a need to rake through a current situation or concept; to carefully inspect something. May also refer to the act of gathering up the last remnants of an issue for the purpose of clearing the way for new beginnings.

RALLY defines a supportive attitude; a motivational force.

RAM refers to an argumentative nature or it may be advising one to stop beating one's head against the wall, stop trying to force results.

RAMADAN represents self-denial.

RAMBLING represents a shiftless nature; lack of direction or motivation.

RAMBO characterizes a desire or tendency to force solutions or closures through aggressive means.

RAMBUNCTIOUSNESS reveals a lack of acceptance; anxiety and impatience.

RAMP portrays a life aspect that has the capability of easing one's way.

RAMPAGE See rage.

RAMPART pertains to a means of self-protection.

RAMROD signifies a forcing action.

RAMSHACKLE illustrates something that's been poorly constructed, devised, or executed.

RANCH signifies a domineering personality.

RANCH (house style) relates to efficiency; keeping the aspects of one's life together instead of scattering them.

RANCID emphasizes that some element in one's life has gone sour, turned out bad; a spoiled result.

RAND (Ayn) characterizes the importance of being objective.

RANGE See prairie.

RANGE FINDER symbolizes one's personal priority to follow one's path; keeping an eye to the lay of the land before you.

RANGER (forest) characterizes a person who recognizes and respects natural talents.

RANGER STATION signifies watchfulness; self-restraint.

RANKLE implies an irritation; perhaps an intended aggravated act.

RANSACK corresponds with a thorough search. This may not indicate a negative reference.

RANSOM represents the price of attainment for certain desires or goals.

RANT portrays a lack of self-control.

RAPE reflects a low self-image; a need to continually manipulate others in order to raise self up to a position of power and dominance; the vicious taking of another's inherent right. Regarding land, this symbol points to a wanton clear-cutting, taking everything of value.

RAPIER See sword.

RAP MUSIC infers a failed method of getting one's message across by only presenting it to a select group.

RAPPER (singer) characterizes one who often conveys feelings or messages in an incoherent or angry manner.

RAP SHEET will illustrate one's offenses; a record of misdeeds. This usually comes in dreams to give a visual of one's true behavior.

RAPTURE (emotion) suggests an enthralled sensation or attitude; overcome with captivation.

RAPTURE (event) constitutes a belief that one will be saved from something.

RARE (uncooked) symbolizes an unfinished aspect; something not complete.

RARE (unique) portrays an uncommon element in one's life.

RASCAL characterizes a mischievous nature.

RASH (skin) indicates emotional irritations or psychological difficulties generated by a lack of acceptance.

RASHER See bacon.

RASP (file) indicates a need to smooth out something in one's life.

RASP (sound) exemplifies an inability to accept something; an aspect that grates on one's nerves or sensibilities.

RASPBERRY depicts a distasteful or disagreeable element.

RASPUTIN (Grigori Efimovich) characterizes a manipulative personality; one who uses the impression of attained knowledge to control others and elevate self.

RAT pertains to a "diseased" element in one's life. May reveal a betrayer.

RATCHET (tool) signifies an opportunity to make adjustments in one's life.

RATE OF EXCHANGE suggests the fact that people perceive differing values of things.

RATIO will illustrate priorities. Recall this symbol as accurately as possible, for it may suggest the proper ratio or it may have portrayed your current set of priorities.

RATION comes in dreams to advise of a need to monitor one's use of a specific element; suggests overextension or a need for moderation.

RATIONALE infers a precise reason or excuse for one's behavior. Recall the surrounding dreamscape elements for further clarification.

RAT RACE is a clear message referring to the act of going nowhere fast.

RATTAN depicts a multi-use talent or ability.

RATTLE (ceremonial) represents an aid to getting in touch with one's inner strength and inherent abilities.

RATTLE (toy) will pertain to something one amuses self with and usually indicates insignificance.

RATTLESNAKE comes as a warning; sign of extreme caution.

RATTLETRAP represents a dangerous or unhealthy situation. This is usually associated with one's home life.

RATTRAP See mousetrap.

RAVE constitutes a state of extremely high emotion. Recall dream details to determine if this was a positive or negative symbol.

RAVEN symbolizes watchfulness for and recognition of spiritual falsehoods. Could indicate a spiritual messenger.

RAVENOUS denotes a seemingly insatiable interest in or desire for something.

RAVISHING represents a highly attractive situation, idea, or individual.

RAW usually stands for a basic, unaltered aspect in one's life; something in its natural state.

RAWHIDE may allude to one's inner strength or it may infer a lack of emotional sensitivity.

RAY (of light) comes as a commendation or marks a moment of inspiration.

RAY GUN most often portrays one's own quality of self-protective measures. It may also denote one's spiritual effectiveness with others.

RAYON (fabric) applies to imitation; a synthetic aspect which has no originality.

RAZOR stands for a delicate excising; careful removal of an unwanted element from one's life.

RAZOR BLADE emphasizes the cutting edge of something; symbolizes life's multiple dualities.

RAZOR WIRE stands for one's defenses; a possible attempt to maintain distance.

RAZZLE-DAZZLE points to an overly dramatic attempt to impress, perhaps for the purpose of concealment.

REACTION TIME will reveal one's level of awareness and resulting responses.

READING correlates to the attainment of information. The key here is to recall what was being read.

READY-MADE may suggest a time-saving aspect or it might advise of a need to devise something through one's own ideas or planning.

READY-MIX See premix.

REAL ESTATE pertains to possibilities; opportunities.

REAL ESTATE AGENT characterizes one who is capable of helping another obtain goals.

REAL ESTATE CONTRACT signifies the attainment of a goal.

REAL ESTATE OFFICE refers to a source of potential opportunities for obtaining a goal.

REAL ESTATE SIGN is a marker pointing to an opportunity.

REALISM (art form) stands for a perspective free of extraneous aspects.

REALITY CHECK comes to advise of the need to get real, take of the rose-colored glasses.

REALITY TV reveals the viewer's baser behavioral traits of revenge, voyeurism, a sadistic enjoyment from seeing another's fear and/or backstabbing behavior.

REAM (paper) exemplifies a measure of work. Recall if the paper was filled with print or blank.

REAM (tool) constitutes a need to clear out or broaden as aspect in one's life.

REAP See harvest.

REAR (position) brings a placement mark to some aspect in one's life. Each dreamer will make this specific association.

REAR-ENDED indicates an unexpected event; an attack that comes from behind.

REAR GUARD advises one to watch one's back and not leave self exposed.

REARVIEW MIRROR typifies symbols that advise one to be aware of what's coming up from behind or what's transpiring behind one's back.

REASSIGNMENT will constitute a new direction or purpose.

REASSURANCE comes as a verification or message of encouragement.

REBAR refers to a strong, supportive reinforcement.

REBATE signifies benefits gained through efforts applied.

REBEL characterizes an individual who follows her/his own path; may also denote a continually disagreeable personality. Surrounding dreamscape details will clarify which intent was meant.

REBELLION marks resistance; independent thought; activism.

REBIRTH (spiritual) will not infer a spiritual connotation, yet it signifies a renewal of some type; new inspiration.

REBOUND denotes a return or backlash effect.

REBUILDING See reconstruction.

REBUTTAL refers to a defense of one's personal opinion or attitude.

RECALL usually doesn't imply one's memory but rather it denotes a need to revive a forgotten element in one's life.

RECANT points to a denial; changing one's mind.

RECEDING alludes to a lessening or waning of something. If this was associated with *water,* the intent was associated with spirituality.

RECEDING (hairline) indicates a superficial and apathetic thought process; resting on false assumptions or having less interest in an issue.

RECEIPT stands for evidence or proof.

RECEIVING BLANKET corresponds to one's quality of preparedness for accepting a new direction. The key here is to recall the blanket's condition and color.

RECEIVING DOCK correlates to anticipation or expectation. Recall what was expected to arrive. What type of business was the dock associated with?

RECEIVING LINE will reveal those who claim alliance with another. The key here is claim and may not indicate a true attitude or position. Recall who was the subject of the line.

RECEPTACLE See container.

RECEPTION (electronic) relates to the quality of one's comprehension.

RECEPTION (room) refers to the phase of waiting just prior to a communication. May point to the last chance to change one's mind.

RECEPTION (social) See receiving line.

RECEPTIONIST characterizes an initial contact.

RECESS denotes a period of rest that is being advised.

RECESSION implies a time of losing ground; slipping backward.

RECIPE won't necessarily symbolically relate to the preparation of food but rather will refer to the proper steps and right elements associated with accomplishing a goal.

RECIPIENT will reveal the beneficiary of something that may pertain to an object, benefit, reprimand, praise, or other life aspect. The surrounding dream elements will clarify this.

RECIPROCATION may refer to retaliation or compensation, depending on associated dream elements.

RECITAL connotes the act of taking a close look at what you know and the related application.

RECKLESS exemplifies immaturity; a lack of responsibility.

RECKONING advises of the wisdom to balance one's behavior or character; to appraise one's past deeds and attitudes.

RECLAMATION most often signifies a need to take back one's self-control and/or individuality; to reclaim self and one's inherent rights to choose or make personal decisions.

RECLINER (chair) portrays acceptance; may represent indifference.

RECLUSE characterizes a remote and/or distant personality; may indicate a need to withdraw for a time in order to focus on one's purpose or path.

RECLUSE SPIDER denotes hidden dangers in one's life. Advises increased awareness.

RECOIL points to a knee-jerk response.

RECOLLECT See remembering.

RECOMMENDATION stands for a suggestion. In order to discover if this is a positive or negative symbol, recall what was recommended. For whom and why?

RECOMPENSE means a compensation or reimbursement.

RECONCILIATION denotes an arrangement to settle a disagreement.

RECONDITION suggests a repair or renovation of an element in one's life; implies a current state of further usefulness or viability.

RECONNAISSANCE warns of a need to thoroughly look something over and be aware of all aspects of it before proceeding.

RECONSTITUTE signifies a rejuvenation or re-implementation of an element in one's life.

RECONSTRUCTION denotes the analyzation of a situation, a second look at something's value and the consideration of redeeming that value.

RECONSTRUCTIVE SURGERY suggests a need to change something about oneself, perhaps an attitude or way of looking at things.

RECORD (music) will reveal a message or mood, sometimes even one's character.

RECORD (written) pertains to evidence or historical progression.

RECORDER (musical instrument) See flute.

RECORDER (tape) underscores the need to correctly recall another's words.

RECORDING STUDIO symbolizes the opportunity to preserve one's words or history.

RECOVERY ROOM reflects a state of recovery from an emotional or damaging situational event. This symbol is a sign that things will work out, one will recover.

RECREATIONAL DRUG advises of a need to change one's idea of what constitutes social acceptance; may point to a misplaced motivational method or way of dealing with life.

RECREATIONAL VEHICLE (RV) will usually indicate a time out from one's work; a needed pause for relaxing activities.

RECRUIT characterizes an individual who recently changed her/his way of thinking; one who has begun a new effort.

RECRUITER relates to a person who easily coerces others; a manipulative personality. May point to empty or misleading promises.

RECTANGLE (configuration) represents firm attitudes; set in one's ways.

RECTOR See religious figure.

RECTORY denotes spiritual arrogance; spiritually elevating oneself.

RECUPERATION illustrates a span of time one should devote to regaining mental or emotional strength following a draining event or phase.

RECURRING DREAMS reveal issues that need to be dealt with in life; perhaps an ongoing lack of acceptance in regard to a particular issue.

RECUSE suggests a need to remove oneself from a specific issue, situation, or relationship.

RECYCLING stands for a life aspect's multiple uses; personal resourcefulness.

RED (color) may refer to anger, a fast pace, or danger, depending on the symbol's related aspects.

RED ALERT comes in dreams to bring attention to an urgent situation; a highly hazardous time or destructive behavior.

REDBIRD stands for awareness; heightened observational skills.

RED-BLOODED stands for a robust and hearty constitution; steadfast determination.

REDBUD (tree) stands for a need to bolster one's emotional sensitivity level.

REDCAP See porter.

RED CARPET implies superiority or inferiority, depending on the dream's associated factors.

RED CLOVER (botanical) represents a cleansing element in one's life which brings about inner strength and fortitude.

REDCOAT suggests one's adversary.

RED CROSS emphasizes assistance; immediate help in an emergency situation.

REDECORATING portrays a desire to change and start over; a fresh new beginning. May point to a change in attitude or perspective.

REDEMPTION CENTER (stamps/coupons) stands for an opportunity to restore one's inner peace; balancing out karmic aspects.

REDEYE (eye) comes as a strong warning the dreamer will understand. May point to overwork or an overindulgence.

REDEYE (night travel time) refers to taking advantage of less desirable aspects of an opportunity.

RED-FACED reflects embarrassment; possible guilt.

RED FLAG naturally reveals a warning; perhaps it's time to stop some type of behavior or give up a plan.

RED FOX usually refers to a highly dangerous individual, one to avoid.

RED-HANDED stands for being caught at something.

REDHEADED alludes to a temperamental nature; easily incited.

RED HERRING reveals a superficial diversion; an aspect that diverts one's focused attention.

RED-HOTS (candy) stand for a motivational aspect.

REDIAL (phone button) points to continued efforts made to communicate.

RED INK represents a failing endeavor; an unsuccessful attempt.

RED-LETTER will mark a special event, individual, or idea; points to something to be remembered. Recall what the letter was related to.

RED LIGHT appears as a strong warning to *stop* something. The dreamer will make the correct individualized association.

RED-LIGHT DISTRICT symbolizes a self-serving intention.

REDLINE exemplifies a refusal; rejection; something deleted.

RED MEAT in dreams will not specifically refer to food but rather a highly beneficial element; an aspect providing basic factors.

REDNECK infers a bigoted personality; highly opinionated and narrow-minded.

RED-PENCIL signifies censorship.

RED PEPPER stands for an issue warming up with the potential for becoming hot.

RED RASPBERRY (botanical) points to a cleansing aspect in one's life. This symbol comes to advise of a need to rid oneself of a particular negative element.

RED RIBBON actually represents a second place position, so as a dream symbol it indicates high accomplishment.

REDROOT (botanical) symbolizes perceptual clarity which comes from clearing emotional negatives that block rationale.

RED SNAPPER (fish) stands for spiritual intolerance; a need to raise level of acceptance and tolerance toward the beliefs of others.

RED TAG will indicate a life element which is marked for a particular purpose; may point to a need to remember to return to an issue.

RED TAPE reveals complications.

RED TIDE warns of a dangerous spiritual situation or concept.

REDUCTIONIST characterizes an individual who has the ability to simplify and clarify matters.

REDUNDANCY reveals ignorance; an attempt to impress with one's knowledge.

REDWOOD FOREST stands for inner strength; fortitude.

REED (botanical) symbolizes resiliency.

REEF illustrates spiritual opportunities to attain inner balance.

REEFER See marijuana.

REEL (film) pertains to an opportunity to preserve an important element in one's life.

REEL (fishing) connotes a life factor that has the capability to provide spiritual discoveries.

REFECTORY corresponds to intellectual nourishment.

REFEREE characterizes life's duality; elements that contain positive and negative aspects, depending on use.

REFERENCE BOOK will come as an important message for the dreamer to research an issue more thoroughly.

REFERRAL signifies personal assistance and being directed to its source.

REFERRED PAIN reflects a refusal to acknowledge the specific source of a harmful element in one's life; the creation of a scapegoat.

REFINANCE suggests a move to actively readjust one's life for the purpose of easier management.

REFINERY advises of the wisdom of accepting only pure truths rather than cluttering and confusing issues with inconsequential aspects.

REFINISHING exemplifies a desire to improve something; efforts applied to make something better.

REFLECTION comes in dreams to suggest one reflects on an important factor in one's life.

REFLECTION POOL refers to spiritual contemplation.

REFLECTOR will be a guiding indicator.

REFLEXOLOGY (study of) symbolizes a high interest in understanding the responses of others.

REFORESTATION portrays a renewal of one's natural talents.

REFORM SCHOOL warns of a serious need to change one's behavior or alter slanted perspectives.

REFRESHER COURSE implies a need to keep abreast of new information. The dreamer will understand this individualized intent.

REFRESHMENTS come as an advisement to refresh oneself; a rejuvenation or time to take a breather.

REFRIED BEANS stand for the suggestion to re-analyze something; look at it again.

REFRIGERATOR refers to a calming state; advises one to cool off.

REFUEL naturally means waning energy or motivation and the need to re-energize oneself.

REFUGE represents a protective force or situation.

REFUGEE characterizes a person who has experiential knowledge of a negative life element.

REFUND pertains to a return benefit.

REFURBISH See refinishing.

REGALIA illustrates pretension.

REGATTA warns against participating in spiritual competition.

REGENERATED See reconstitute.

REGGAE (music) represents an individualistic attitude; the sense of being free to express oneself.

REGISTER (enroll) stands for the signing up or voluntary participation in a new venture.

REGISTER (machine) See cash register.

REGISTERED MAIL denotes a solid communication of some type. Recall who sent the mailed article. To whom was it addressed? What was it? Did it have a specific color?

REGISTRAR characterizes one who keeps the records. This will refer to the one who knows personal aspects of another's life.

REGISTRY (bridal) signifies a clear and definitive idea of what one wants in life; may reveal a specific character element.

REGRESSION indicates a backward direction. Recall the dream's surrounding details for more clarity.

REGRETFULNESS usually implies personal guilt.

REGULATIONS connote rules and limitations; may relate to personal guidelines one sets for self.

REGULATOR (device) represents a specific management setting one attempts to maintain for daily behavior; an intent to establish a balanced synchronization based on spiritual goals.

REGURGITATE won't correlate with a physical act of getting sick but rather will correspond to something one needs to bring up or get out of one's system.

REHABILITATION CENTER defines an advisement to change one's ways or it may also represent a personal intent to do so.

REHEARSAL denotes the practicing of one's belief; walking one's talk.

REIMBURSEMENT See refund.

REINCARNATION comes in a dream to remind one of a new beginning and an opportunity to advance self.

REINDEER connotes a tendency to be easily led or controlled.

REINFORCEMENT applies to extra support, strength, or endurance needed.

REINS represent a caution to remember that choices made about one's life can be made only by oneself. Nobody else should be holding the reins of your life.

REINSTATED stands for an acceptance of something that was previously discounted.

REISSUE will usually relate to a popular idea or life aspect.

REJECTION SLIP stands for disapproval; a disaffirmation; a state of disfavor.

REJUVENATION will either symbolize a current state of renewal or it will indicate a need for same, depending on the associated aspects.

REKINDLE exemplifies new life brought into an aspect of one's life.

RELAPSE won't always indicate a negative element in a dream, for it may come to remind one that, sometimes, progression is accomplished only be taking a step or two backward.

RELATIVE (genetic) pertains to those in one's awake state who have some type of elemental association with the dreamer. This dreamscape "relative" may *not* correspond with an *actual* awake-state relation.

RELATIVE HUMIDITY alludes to the depth and quality of spiritual aspects each of us absorbs individually.

RELATIVITY (theory) attempts to emphasize the fact that each individual perceives life elements in a diverse manner.

RELAXANT refers to a need for one to relax one's focused mental or emotional energy. This specific dream symbol warns of a current state of overly centered efforts or concentration that is hampering one's broad-scope comprehension.

RELAY (race) cautions one to not depend on others for personal progression.

RELAY (switch) corresponds to one's inner mechanism that maintains behavioral controls; the application of logic and reason instead of emotional outbursts or knee-jerk responses.

RELEASE OF LIEN points to a zero debt associated with a particular issue; one has paid one's dues regarding something.

RELIC warns against having misplaced spiritual priorities.

RELIEF MAP connotes a need to gain a sharper perspective of one's position in relation to purpose.

RELIEF PITCHER characterizes an individual who has the knowledge and capability to stand in for another; a temporary replacement.

RELIGION (any denomination) symbolizes altered truths or the perspective and application of same; spiritual truths distorted by human ideology and intervention.

RELIGIOUS CEREMONIES stand for man-made affectations and embellishments added to basic tenets.

RELIGIOUS FIGURE will usually come to draw attention to spiritual matters in one's life, not specific religious dogma.

RELINQUISHED portrays a life element one is advised to give up. Most often this suggests acceptance and moving forward.

RELISH (condiment) will refer to something in life that one savors.

RELOAD (ammunition) stands for a reluctance to give something up; a doggedness.

RELOCATION most often foretells of an actual change of one's location.

REMARKS that come from people within dreams will usually reveal their hidden opinions or perspectives.

REMATCH may advise of a need to re-communicate with someone or attempt a second effort.

REMEDIAL (study) depicts a desire to better understand an issue or situation.

REMEDY (any type) reflects a corrective or healing source.

REMEMBERING illustrates a need to recall a specific event or conversation in order to gain further clarity.

REMINISCING pertains to a state of nostalgia; the pleasure derived from retrospection.

REMISSION signifies an abatement of something in one's life; a diminishing or subsiding element. Depending on what this symbol is related to, this could be a negative or positive sign.

REMNANT usually denotes an unnecessary element associated with one's path or purpose, yet it could also refer to a loose end to which one needs to attend.

REMORSE implies personal guilt that one refuses to acknowledge.

REMOTE (location) advises one to engage in deep contemplation.

REMOTE CONTROL (device) reveals a state of control, perhaps even manipulation. It's important to recall *who* had the remote in hand.

REMOTE VIEWING symbolizes a heightened intuitive sense of cognition.

RENAISSANCE (setting) illustrates a fertile atmosphere for renewal and opportunities for enlightenment.

RENAISSANCE FESTIVAL stands for the joy of celebrating new opportunities.

REND (tear) may infer that something in one's life has been split apart or this symbol may reflect a defective element such as a belief system, idea, situation, or relationship.

RENDEZVOUS symbolizes a meeting of some type.

RENDEZVOUS (of mountain men) stands for a joyful celebration of one's self-sufficiency.

RENEGADE characterizes individual thought and behavior; a break from the crowd.

RENEGING warns against ignoring promises made.

RENOUNCE constitutes a denial; a strong rejection.

RENOVATION is an attempt to save or preserve some element in one's life.

RENT (payment) implies an access to an opportunity to accomplish something.

RENTAL (car) stands for an opportunity to further progression.

RENTAL (dwelling) reflects a temporary situation.

RENTAL (equipment shop) signifies a source of opportunities to resolve temporary needs.

RENT CONTROL refers to a cost cap; a specified amount of energy needed to accomplish or maintain something.

RENTER (home) indicates a situation in which one has less responsibility.

RENT STRIKE represents personal power and/or effectiveness.

REORGANIZING denotes an adjustment in priorities.

REPAIR See fix (mend/repair).

REPAIRPERSON characterizes a person in one's life who is capable of solving another's problems.

REPARTEE will reveal an individual's true or hidden thoughts.

REPEAL represents the act of voiding an action; revocation.

REPEATER (antenna) stands for clearer communications.

REPEAT OFFENDER will come as a strong advisement to learn from past mistakes instead of repeating them; behavior that precludes advancement.

REPELLENT (chemical) refers to the use of negative behavior for the purpose of maintaining social distance.

REPENTANT corresponds to self-reproach.

REPERTOIRE correlates to the quality and quantity of one's natural talents; also a plan for how things intend to be played out.

REPERTORY See repository.

REPETITION may indicate the act of repeating one's mistakes or it may stand for a *need* to repeat things until the right lessons are learned.

REPLACEMENT COST refers to the current value of something and the cost it would entail to replace it if it were lost or damaged. This usually refers to a relationship.

REPLAY (audio/video) refers to a need to see or hear something over again. Suggests that something was missed the first time around.

REPLENISHING pertains to a current bountiful state; a desire to maintain full potential or level of energy.

REPLICA See copy; imitating.

REPO MAN stands for an individual who has the capability to take something away from another; warns the dreamer of a possible loss if responsibilities aren't met.

REPORT CARD is a revealing symbol that illustrates the quality and rating of one's current behavior.

REPORTER (newsperson) characterizes an individual who makes the activity of others their priority; exemplifies sensationalism and exaggerations.

REPOSITORY will correlate with a specific type of source within self; a personal store of strength, compassion, patience, etc.

REPOSSESSED portrays the resulting effect of irresponsibility.

REPRESENTATIVE characterizes a person with the authority to speak and act for others; may also point to one who symbolizes a concept, attitude, product, or method.

REPRESSION connotes a self-generated state of limiting controls. May point to denial.

REPRIEVE signifies a temporary suspension of a problematical or distressful situation.

REPRIMAND usually comes from one's own subconscious level of conscience to reflect a misdeed or other negative act.

REPRISAL warns against vindictiveness and a vengeful attitude.

REPRODUCTION stands for an imitation; a copy.

REPRODUCTION COST points to the current value of one's skill or talent. This symbol usually comes to point out someone's worth.

REPROGRAM suggests an attempt to alter something, usually an attitude or perspective.

REPTILE See specific type.

REPUDIATION indicates some type of denial or condemnation.

REPULSIVE corresponds with a life aspect that is personally offensive. This may refer to a situation, event, statement, idea, etc.

REQUIEM forewarns of a dying or quickly declining situation, relationship, or other element in one's life.

REQUIREMENT defines a necessary quality, skill, or perspective one must possess in order to accomplish a select goal.

REQUISITION pertains to a personal request, often a prayer, for the necessary elements to accomplish a goal or purpose.

RERUN (program) indicates a need to learn something that was initially missed.

RESALE VALUE represents the extended long-term value of an action or communication.

RESCHEDULE advises of a more effective time to execute an effort or attempt some type of activity.

RESCIND See repeal.

RESCUE will come to emphasize the saving effect of one's efforts. Recall who was rescued. Who was the rescuer?

RESCUE MISSION will point to a last resort in regard to saving something. This symbol may reveal a need to put greater effort into acceptance or perseverance.

RESEARCH signifies a need to obtain grater knowledge or information on a specific issue.

RESEARCH AND DEVELOPMENT (R & D) points to the need for thorough planning.

RESERVATION (Native American) represents an advisement to relate or make associative connections between true Reality and spiritual aspects. This symbol may also refer to the setting aside or confinement of issues we don't want to face or deal with.

RESERVE (animal) symbolizes the preservation of natural inherent talents.

RESERVIST (military) characterizes personal preparedness; a reserve of inner strength.

RESERVOIR connotes the quality of one's spiritual aspects, specifically natural talents. What condition was the reservoir in? Was the water polluted? Have a color hue to it?

RESHUFFLE suggests a rearrangement of one's priorities or elements of a goal-reaching plan.

RESIDENT See inhabitant.

RESIDENTIAL (setting) depicts a specific background character or atmosphere to one's lifestyle or home life.

RESIDUE alludes to that which is left behind; aftermaths; may refer to something left to attend to.

RESIGNATION stands for a new direction ahead; leaving a former path or issue behind.

RESILIENT defines acceptance. Points to the management of problematical events with less difficulty and more grace than others.

RESIN constitutes a beneficial result.

RESISTANCE (underground) symbolizes courage; a refusal to be forced into something one doesn't believe in or that is morally wrong; civil disobedience.

RESOLUTION pertains to determination; promise; new rule.

RESONANCE denotes lasting strength.

RESORT typifies a strong advisement to obtain some needed rest; a need to get away from current stressors.

RESOURCE indicates an asset one has to use. This is oftentimes not recognized in the awake state.

RESPIRATOR denotes something that helps one breathe easier by filtering out impurities. This symbol infers that there are negative attitudes affecting one from outside sources.

RESPONDENT signifies one who needs to address a problem, often a conflict.

REST AREA will naturally imply a much needed rest from one's work or a stressful situation.

RESTAURANT reveals one's quality of diet. This diet may not refer to physical eating but rather what one fills one's life with as far as beliefs, behavior, type of associates, etc.

RESTAURANT CRITIC will usually symbolize yourself critiquing the quality of what you're filling your life with.

REST HOME See nursing home.

RESTITUTION illustrates compensation; reparation.

RESTLESS LEG SYNDROME stands for a need to pace oneself; may indicate anxiety.

RESTLESSNESS warns of a lack of acceptance; anxiety and/or impatience.

RESTORATION See renovation.

RESTRAINING ORDER stands for an effort to keep one's distance from a negative aspect.

RESTRAINTS define hindrances, usually self-generated.

RESTRICTED AREA may represent some life element that one should avoid until further knowledge, wisdom, or skill has been attained. This symbol may also indicate that from which one voluntarily restricts self; self-control.

RESTROOM See bathroom.

REST STOP See rest area.

RESUME stands for a need to honestly review one's accomplishments and goals. Sometimes a dreamscape resume will reveal a glaring void in a certain area of experiential knowledge.

RESURFACE (appear again) exemplifies

a spiritual concept or other element that has come back into one's life.

RESURFACE See paving.

RESURRECT stands for a renewed interest in something.

RESUSCITATOR defines a life aspect that serves to restore one's motivation, energy, or interest.

RETAIL (store) applies to an opportunity. Recall the type for further clarification.

RETAINER (dental) points to an attempt to maintain one's quality of speech or manner of communication.

RETAINER (monetary) represents intention.

RETAINING WALL correlates with a supportive aspect that serves to hold up or hold back something. May point to denial.

RETALIATION denotes vindictiveness; reprisal.

RETARDANT See restraints.

RETARDATION alludes to a comprehension inability, most often self-imposed.

RETCH pertains to an attempt to rid self of a disagreeable situation or other life element; may reveal a lack of acceptance or evince psychological escapism.

RETENTION POND comes to reveal the importance of something one believes has no value.

RETICENCE denotes a desire to avoid communication; diffidence.

RETINUE infers a belief that one requires a support group in attendance.

RETIREMENT illustrates a finalization; a life stage completion.

RETOOL implies a time to utilize a new set of plans and associated aids. This may

even refer to one's behavior or perspective.

RETOUCHED pertains to final details and the attention given to same. May point to an intent to alter something.

RETRACE advises one to look at something again, closer this time; may infer a need to retrace one's steps.

RETRACTION won't necessarily refer to one's words, it usually suggests a need to pull back or pull something in, such as an unproductive behavioral aspect like being too forward, being tactless, giving incorrect advice, interference, etc.

RETREAD (tire) may denote fortitude or, depending on related dream elements, it might apply to a need to tread over one's former path and backtrack.

RETREAT (military) constitutes an unproductive time to go forward.

RETREAT (respite) stands for a suggested rest; contemplation is called for.

RETRIBUTION corresponds to atonement; may also indicate retaliation, depending on the dream's surrounding aspects.

RETRIEVER (dog breed) characterizes an analytical friend, one who possesses the skill and wisdom to bring back or show you the true psychological motivations for your unproductive behavior.

RETROACTIVE exemplifies an aspect in one's life that is currently affected by one's past.

RETROFIT suggests a need to revise one's perceptions by including new experiential or evidenced elements.

RETROGRADE reflects a move downward and backward. This symbol usually advises one to go back to a former issue and perceive an element from a lower, closer angle.

RETROGRESSION reveals lost ground in respect to one's attained level of behavior, knowledge, or progression.

RETROROCKET stands for a need to slow one's rate of advancement; too much is being missed.

RETURN (merchandise) suggests a change of mind; a rejection.

RETURN ON INVESTMENT will point to a situation whereby one's efforts were either beneficial or detrimental (gain, neutral, or loss).

RETURN RECEIPT (postal) signifies a desire to see something through.

REUNION (class) indicates a suggestion to reconnect with a former associate.

REUNION (family) points to an advisement to reconnect with a family member.

REVELATION brings an insight; sudden understanding.

REVELRY points the dreamer to the cause of the revelry which will reveal an important element that was missed in the awake state.

REVENANT characterizes a return of someone long absent from one's life.

REVENGE is a clear sign that an individual lacks spiritual enlightenment and has attained no acceptance in life.

REVENUE STAMP serves as a verification that one performed an obligation or certain responsibility.

REVERBERATION connotes dissemination.

REVERE cautions against excessive admiration or worship of anyone but the Divine Essence.

REVEREND See religious figure.

REVERIE suggests an advisement to deeply contemplate an element in the dreamer's life. This individualized element will be readily recognized.

REVERSE (gear/direction) may suggest that one needs to go back to learn something or it could connote a retrogressive path or behavior.

REVERSED (clothing or other elements) comes as a severe warning and you need to refer to the specific piece of clothing or element that was reversed in the dreamscape. Such an obvious reversal will indicate a serious dysfunctional aspect in one's life.

REVERSIBLE (clothing/object) usually signifies duality; something has a two-fold purpose or effect.

REVERTER CLAUSE represents the knowledge that a plan has the possibility of needing to start from square one; leaving room for possibilities.

REVIEW is an advisement to become more familiar with a situation, idea, or individual.

REVIEW APPRAISER characterizes an individual who is skilled in verifying value.

REVIEWER (professional) characterizes an individual in one's life who can provide background information or a general overview.

REVISION represents an advisement to reassess one's life, goals, or path direction.

REVITALIZATION PROJECT refers to the strong possibility of giving new life to an old issue, relationship, or situation.

REVIVAL comes as a warning to revitalize an element in one's life; a need to be re-inspired, re-energized, or motivated.

REVOKED is a suggestion to rescind or correct something in one's life.

REVOLUTION may not infer a violent military event but rather stand for a new way or concept. May point to activism or civil disobedience.

REVOLVER (weapon) See gun.

REVOLVING DOOR reveals an unproductive course; repetitive behavior or situations.

REWARD signifies personal benefits derived from positive behavior and good deeds.

REWIND (audio/video) applies to going back to the beginning, but not necessarily replaying the same information. This symbol may advise of a need to retrace one's steps back to the beginning and go down another trail.

REWIRE is a strong advisement to examine one's psychological processes and make correct connections.

RHEOSTAT pertains to the personal control of one's emotional responses.

RHESUS MONKEY vicariously indicates inhumane behavior; arrogance and a lack of compassion.

RHETORICAL QUESTION poses possibilities and impels self-analyzation.

RHEUMATISM See arthritis.

RHINESTONE reflects an effective alternative to a more costly method or course.

RHINOCEROS denotes controlled emotions; the utilization of intellect instead of emotionally instinctual reactions; may denote thick-skinned personality.

RHINOPLASTY stands for an attitude adjustment.

RHIZOME stands for deeply rooted attitudes that affect perspectives.

RHODE ISLAND refers to a spiritual opportunity.

RHUBARB denotes a life aspect that contains dual elements.

RHYME may indicate a juvenile perspective, yet this symbol usually comes in dreams to relay a message.

RHYOLITE stands for protective qualities; enduring traits.

RHYTHM will emphasize the pace at which one is currently progressing. This may also suggest a *proper* pace.

RHYTHM AND BLUES (R & B) represent path progression in spite of difficulties.

RHYTHM METHOD See birth control.

RIB (all types) stand for one's aspects supporting the heart (emotions).

RIBALD pertains to uncouth behavior that reveals a lack of spiritual attainment.

RIBBON symbolizes a positive element in one's life. Recall the fabric and color for more in-depth interpretation.

RIB CAGE infers an emotionally protective element in one's life.

RICE See grain.

RICE PAPER connotes a fragile facet in one's life. The surrounding dreamscape details will clarify what this association is.

RICH (food) relates to bountiful benefits that carry multiple effects.

RICH (wealth) See money.

RICHTER SCALE (earthquake) will illustrate the resulting quantitative effect of an action or event and its level or intensity.

RICKETS reveal a lack of positive reinforcement; a poor self-image.

RICKETY (condition) warns of an unstable and/or precarious situation.

RICOCHET denotes an event that will produce multiple effects. Also may point to something that failed to make its target.

RICOTTA (cheese) portrays a nourishing life aspect that creates recurring benefits.

RIDDLE constitutes a self-devised complexity.

RIDGE relates to a major decision; a potential turning point.

RIDGEPOLE applies to an individual's personal shield or means of protective support.

RIDICULE indicates a serious lack of understanding; reveals an unenlightened personality.

RIDING HABIT suggests an attitude of exaggerated self-worth when making a comparison between self and peers who are traveling the same path.

RIFFRAFF may represent those who most need one's help.

RIFLE (search through) may not infer a negative connotation but rather this symbol usually comes as an advisement to search through one's own possessions, meaning motives and behavioral responses.

RIFLE (weapon) See gun.

RIFLE SCOPE See scope.

RIFT (fissure) relates to a split or fracture present in a relationship, situation, belief system, or the manner of one's perception.

RIGGING typifies supporting elements for a specific aspect in one's life. This symbol will be clarified by the dream's surrounding facets.

RIGHT (direction/position) may represent a supportive role or point to ultra-conservatism. Also see road signs for more directional interpretations.

RIGHT FIELD indicates a tendency to follow generally accepted ideas.

RIGHT-HAND suggests trust and reliability.

RIGHT OF FIRST REFUSAL stands for an individual who must be offered the first option to accept or reject something.

RIGHT OF WAY is self-explanatory. The key here is to recall who had the right of way sign. Did you have to yield? Also see road signs.

RIGHT WING means following a narrowly conservative perspective; fearful of attempting new endeavors or exploring innovative concepts; reluctant to think outside the box or have a willingness to even perceive what's out there; tending toward apathy for the unfortunates in life; self-centered.

RIGID implies an opinionated thought process; not open to alternative ideas.

RIGOR MORTIS symbolizes a dead state; an individual who maintains stiff thinking or conceptual reasoning.

RIME (coating) exemplifies a cold or hidden veneer.

RIND denotes that which harbors fruitful or bountiful aspects. This dreamscape fragment refers to the tough path or exterior that serves as the outlying regions of one's direction of fulfillment.

RING See circus.

RING (crime) See chain gang.

RING (jewelry) generally represents a bond of some type or gives a clue into character.

Anniversary ring is meant to celebrate the time when a specific bond was forged.

Antique ring signifies a very old bond/connection that one cherishes.

Birthstone ring See birthstone.

Bridge ring symbolizes flashiness.

Broken ring reveals a broken bond with someone; lost loyalty.

Celtic Knot ring represents one's complex interconnectedness with another. This deeply involved relationship may be an underlying one that is not readily apparent.

Claddagh ring (Celtic) serves as a sign of one's open heart.

Cocktail ring suggests pretension.

Designer ring reflects personal uniqueness.

Engagement ring refers to one's intent to be forever loyal to another.

Family crest ring indicates pride of one's heritage/bloodline.

Friendship ring refers to a close relationship with another.

Graduation ring signifies a sign of one's former accomplishment.

Infant ring suggests a special bond to a child; may refer to innocence.

Initial ring will point to the initial of someone very important in the wearer's life.

Mother's ring symbolizes an appreciation of one's blessings.

Nose ring infers an in-your-face show of individuality.

Oversized gem usually denotes one's desire to be noticed.

Pinkie ring stands for an attempt to emphasize one's less obvious qualities; rounding out oneself.

Poison/potion ring (secret compartment) represents hidden emotions.

Promise ring indicates a show of intention to cherish a special relationship.

Religious ring points to one's devotion to a specific religious belief system.

Shank too large suggests the bond now includes others.

Shank too small indicates one has outgrown the bond/loyalty.

Signet ring stands for a personal endorsement.

Super Bowl ring stands for a sign of a particular achievement.

Toe ring suggests a free spirit; an independent path.

Undersized gem indicates a protective attitude toward one's bond.

Wedding ring portrays a symbol of one's heartfelt bond of loyalty.

RING (residue) pertains to a need for routine or consistent cleansing through self-analyzation.

RING FINGER alludes to how an individual chooses to present oneself to others; affectations of character.

RINGLEADER points out the instigator or initiator of a plan or idea.

RINGLET (hair) refers to an idea or thought process that turns back on itself or is complex.

RINGMASTER characterizes a person who directs the actions of others; possibly a manipulator; may indicate one who interferes in the lives of others.

RINGSIDE (seats) denotes an onlooker position or perspective; one who prefers watching and waiting instead of participating.

RINGWORM advises one to be more aware of where one walks; going headlong into things without giving adequate investigation, attention, or planning.

RINK (skating) correlates to going around in circles; a lack of advancement.

RINKY-DINK refers to something that can't be trusted or depended upon; insubstantial; inconsequential and of little quality.

RINSE (hair coloring) may relate to an intent to change one's way of thinking or it may reveal hidden perspectives and attitude.

RINSE (water) advises of a need to clarify something; indicates a misunderstanding or misconception.

RIOT signifies deep-seated discontent; demonstrative activism.

RIOT ACT defines a severe warning/chastisement. The dreamer will make the correct individualized association.

RIOT GUN points to an effort to control a situation that's getting out of control.

RIP will reflect a dysfunction or some form of negative element associated with a life issue. Recall surrounding dreamscape details for clarity. This is usually a quickly recognized symbol for the dreamer to understand.

RIPCORD constitutes a life-saving aspect in one's life.

RIPE will point out a matured situation, process, or other element that is ripe for development.

RIPPLE (in water) stands for a continuing spiritual effect.

RIP TIDE warns of a dangerous spiritual belief or path.

RISER signifies a step above; raising oneself to a higher level.

RISK ANALYSIS points to a need to very carefully weigh the pros and cons of something.

RISK FACTOR reveals a life factor that has the potential to be a dangerous or harmful aspect in one's life.

RISQUÉ implies an impropriety; offensive behavior; reveals an unenlightened individual.

RITE (ceremony) corresponds with a self-devised process; a fascination with ceremony.

RITE OF PASSAGE portrays a transitional stage in one's life.

RITUAL pertains to superfluous elements one believes are necessary.

RITZY (setting) may signify sophistication or pretension. Recall the people and action within this setting.

RIVAL may not indicate an enemy but rather someone perceived as an opponent or competitor in the dreamer's eyes.

RIVER corresponds with the spiritual elements running through one's life. Recall its rate of flow, quality, and color.

RIVERBANK symbolizes a close proximity to a spiritual search, aspect, or awakening.

RIVERBED See lakebed.

RIVERBOAT denotes indecision regarding one's direction or leaning in respect to spirituality versus materialism.

RIVER FRONT See lakefront.

RIVER ROCKS signify a spiritual roundedness to one's life.

RIVET exemplifies a secured aspect.

RIVULET refers to a new spiritual idea or insight.

ROACH See marijuana.

ROACH (hair style) represents one-mindedness; rigidly focused ideas.

ROACH (insect) See cockroach.

ROACH CLIP illustrates resourcefulness; a tendency to utilize every element of something.

ROAD will correspond with one's life path either currently or one that is being advised. Recall surrounding dreamscape details for further clarification.

ROADBED depicts the soundness of one's current path. Of what was the road constructed? Did it have a specific color? Level or bumpy? Straight or curvy?

ROADBLOCK comes as a warning advisement that one has yet to attain the experiential depth and knowledge to continue progressing along the current course. This symbol may also indicate a self-generated block due to inner fears.

ROAD GRADER connotes a life aspect that has the potential for smoothing one's way.

ROAD HOG characterizes an individual who isn't focused on her/his path.

ROADHOUSE See motel.

ROAD-KILL stands for collateral damage; the unintentional emotional injuries caused by certain behavior or situational events.

ROAD MAP points out the multiple options available to reach a goal. Sometimes the dream road map will actually give a clear visual that literally leads the way.

ROAD RAGE reveals those under pressure who explode at the first opportunity.

ROADRUNNER (character) denotes impetuosity; advises one to give more thought before rushing forward.

ROAD SHOW refers to points of interest or observation placed along one's path; possible opportunities for expanded learning.

ROADSIDE may indicate a need to pull over and rest while traveling one's path or it may refer to something that should be noticed.

ROAD SIGNS stand for directional path indicators/advisements, or reveal how a path is being traveled. See below for some of the most common road signs.

Arrows (directional) symbolize those life aspects that literally point the way.

Bike Lane sign marks a more casual approach to one's path, an approach with an eye to appreciating every small blessing along the course.

Bridge Icy When Wet sign advises caution when one's path takes them over ground touched by spiritual elements.

Bump sign comes as a forewarning for a bump ahead; a small glitch.

Business District sign is an attempt to draw one back to matters at hand.

Cattle On Road sign cautions us to heighten our awareness on a particular section of our path.

Caution naturally advises increased awareness, watchfulness.

Chains Only sign is a warning of treacherous ground ahead and advises the traveler to take extreme caution.

Construction Zone sign indicates a path that's in the process of being developed and to proceed carefully.

Curve sign warns us to be expecting something akin to a curve ball that's in the immediate offing.

Dead End sign saves us the time and energy of going down an unfruitful path.

Deer X-ing sign tells us that we should be prepared for unexpected events.

Do Not Enter sign comes in an

attempt to keep us from staying off paths that we've no right to enter or aren't aligned with our purpose.

Emergency Vehicles Only sign reveals a section of our path that would be considered an interference or hindrance to others needing immediate help. A path that our presence on would be a detriment to others.

Exit Number signs stand for many opportunities to take different paths.

Falling Rock sign advises us to be prepared for the unexpected.

Forest Service Road sign indicates a path providing additional benefits to gain if one wants to expend extra energy to get to them.

Gas/Food/Lodging sign points to a short detour that provides refreshment, a shot of energy, and respite as we travel our path.

Handicap Parking sign suggests that we should leave certain benefits to those who need them more than we do.

Historical Site sign advises that there's something in our personal history (past) that we need to look at and glean an important element from.

Horse Riders sign cautions us to be aware of and recognize those more vulnerable than ourselves.

Keep Left sign urges us to be a bit more open-minded.

Keep Right sign comes to suggest we be a little more conservative for a time.

Left Lane Closed sign advises us that, at this point in time, there's absolutely no room for an ultraliberal attitude. Suggests a time for strictness.

Loading Zone sign points to a place in one's path where many benefits can be gained.

Load Limit sign warns against taking more than one needs. May also indicate a condition of being overloaded or taking on too much.

Local Traffic Only sign refers to territory which is familiar to a select group who have access to it.

Low Clearance sign advises of a phase for keeping one's head down and not craning one's neck out too far. May infer curiosity or nosiness.

Men Working sign advises a slower pace and higher awareness needed.

Merge Left sign suggests a time to be more conservative and keep a handle on our emotions.

Merge Right sign indicates a phase when more compassion and liberal thought would serve us better.

Neighborhood Crime Watch sign reminds us to police ourselves; this is not a good time to attempt a high-risk act.

No Campfires sign hints that a certain place in one's journey is precariously dry (having little nourishment).

No Hunting sign signifies protection. For some, this will mean a place holding no opportunities.

No Littering sign warns against discarding something that may still have value.

No Loitering comes in dreams as a motivational factor.

No Outlet sign suggests a need to retrace our steps if we go down that road.

No Parking sign tells us that we can't stop at this particular point on our path.

No Passing Zone sign suggests an equal pace; this shouldn't be the time to forge ahead or speed up.

No Public Access sign refers to a path that's not generally open to everyone.

No Services sign signifies a path having no aiding elements, yet may still hold some personal value. Could signify a phase when one must go it alone.

No Stopping In Tunnel sign is a call for perseverance.

No Thru Traffic sign may point to a path leading into a maze or confusion.

No Trespassing sign reveals a path that is not available/open.

No U-Turn sign warns of a point in one's life when there's no turning back; forward is the only direction open at this time.

One Lane Bridge sign signifies a short amount of time when one must go through something without the aid of others.

One-Way sign See one-way (sign).

Pavement Ends sign marks the beginning of a more rough road.

Pedestrian X-ing sign suggests a time when we may have to give way to others; the possibility of concessions or deference.

Private Drive/Road symbolizes those attitudes or personal elements one desires to keep to oneself. These won't necessarily refer to deep, dark secrets, but rather any aspects one feels are special, personally cherished, or not for public knowledge/ disclosure.

Open Range sign See Cattle On Road sign; Deer X-ing sign.

Rest Area sign See rest area.

Restricted Access sign symbolizes a path not open to everyone.

Right Lane Closed sign suggests that, at this time, there's absolutely no room for conservatism or apathy.

Right of Way sign See right of way.

Road Closed sign tells us that a certain path is not open to us, it's not a viable course.

Road Narrows sign suggests a path's phase that holds little room for error.

Road Work Ahead sign comes to prepare us for an upcoming situation demanding greater efforts to get past it.

Rough Pavement sign indicates a short span of minor difficulty to our path. This could simply refer to a rash of irritating situations.

RR X-ing sign See train (crossing).

Runaway Lane sign points to the existence of a net in place in case we get ourselves in trouble. It's a symbol that cautions us against going so fast that we can't stop.

Scenic Overlook sign is a call to stop along the way and appreciate the beauty existing along one's path.

School Bus Zone Next 5 Miles sign suggests the possible need to stop and experience our child within.

School Zone sign points to the wisdom of slowing down and having patience for those less advanced or enlightened than we are.

Service Drive/Road sign signifies a slower-paced method of traveling the same course.

Slippery When Wet sign cautions against carelessly treading over spiritual issues; advises of a time to attend to our footing.

Slow—Children at Play sign comes as a quite literal dreamscape visual. It means the dreamer needs to slow down and have a childlike perspective, take time out for some less serious activities.

Slow Moving Vehicles sign suggests that we have respect and tolerance for those who, for whatever reason, progress at a slower rate.

Soft Shoulder sign indicates a possible mishap if one veers from one's path.

Standing Only sign refers to a time for idling instead of actually turning off one's engine; a time for staying on the same issue, but giving it some contemplation.

Steep Grade sign forewarns of an unavoidable downhill phase to one's path.

Stop sign represents an advisement to stop one's forward progression for a time. Frequently, this comes as a forewarning.

Stop When Flashing sign (lights) act as a yellow stoplight and tells us to be prepared to stop at any time.

Speed Limit will come to advise of the proper pace one will best advance by. Exceeding that pace infers a lack of understanding will occur.

Toll Road sign signals a path that has costs attached to it.

Tourist Info Ahead sign refers to an opportunity to learn more about where one is headed.

Tow-Away Zone sign refers to possible ramifications if one tries nose or back into the wrong issue or situation.

Trucks Entering Highway sign is a reminder to acknowledge and respect our hard-working peers.

Trucks Keep Right sign signifies an easier path to bear when one is surrounded by those working as hard as you are.

Uneven Pavement sign warns of a path that contains a balance of positive and negative elements.

Use Low Gear sign advises us to force ourselves to proceed slower, more cautiously.

Weigh Station sign comes as a reminder to weigh our behavior on the scale of our conscience.

Winding Road sign gives a hint of an upcoming path full of twists and turns. Even though this path takes longer to advance and cover as-the-crow-flies distances, a snaking path will provide more benefits and present more opportunities to learn from than the straight path.

Wrong Way sign will be a wonderfully literal message that keeps the dreamer from wasting valuable time.

Yield sign cautions against an effort to oppose an issue or person, perhaps even one's own conscience; suggests a need to give way to one's better judgment.

ROAD TEST symbolizes one's level of current knowledge and preparedness to safely continue one's life course.

ROADWORK signifies a need to make repairs or adjustments to one's planned course.

ROAMING won't necessarily indicate a loss of direction but rather a seeking for what feels right.

ROAMING (cell phone) stands for a void regarding communication.

ROAMING CHARGES refer to costs involved when one isn't able to communicate with another. These costs won't be associated with money but rather emotions because of the missed timing.

ROAST (cook) represents a developing plan or idea.

ROAST (friendly sarcasm) portrays companionable respect; an ability and freedom to speak one's mind and be honest without ill feelings or repercussions.

ROAST (meat cut) relates to an issue or idea that one intends to develop.

ROASTING PAN stands for a method or opportunity to accomplish something, the *vehicle* through which it can be accomplished.

ROBBERY See burglar.

ROBE (bath) See bathrobe.

ROBE (ceremonial) relates to a desire to present oneself in an aggrandized manner, a need to exaggerate self-importance.

ROBIN emphasizes a rebirth of some type.

ROBIN HOOD characterizes the courage to actively correct a wrong one observes being done; one who goes out on a limb to make a quiet difference; unconditional goodness without any form of publicity.

ROBOT warns one to begin thinking for self.

ROCK refers to the hard, difficult elements or phases in life. May signify loyalty or steadfastness, depending on the surrounding dreamscape elements.

ROCK AND ROLL (music) signifies motivation; a phase of determination to get going and follow one's own unique ideology.

ROCK BOTTOM emphasizes a time to pick oneself up and go forward by looking to the sun; nowhere to go but up.

ROCK CANDY signifies an issue requiring deep contemplation or thorough analyzation.

ROCKEFELLER CENTER refers to cultural and/or extravagant events.

ROCKER See rocking chair.

ROCKET stands for high motivation.

ROCKET ENGINE symbolizes a personal impetus.

ROCK GARDEN corresponds to the acceptance of life's difficulties and the blossoming of personal talents.

ROCK HOUND characterizes a person who recognizes the beauty of opportunities presented by life's difficulties and takes advantage of them.

ROCKING CHAIR pertains to a well-deserved rest period.

ROCKING HORSE may indicate unproductive efforts or deep thought. The dreamer will be given the associated elements to determine which meaning was intended.

ROCK SALT implies a personal effort to break through certain spiritual concepts or searches.

ROCK SHOP correlates with natural talents and how they're utilized for humankind's benefit.

ROCKSLIDE applies to an inundation of temporary difficulties.

ROCKWELL (Norman) characterizes the beauty of simplicity; seeing life without coloring it with personal attitudes or perceptions.

ROCOCO (ornate style) illustrates self-aggrandizement; low self-esteem evidenced by giving off an aura of power.

RODENT See specific type.

RODEO portrays an exhibition of one's power or control over others competing for control.

RODEO CLOWN stands for the taking of risks to save others or one who diverts hazardous elements away from others.

ROGUE characterizes an unprincipled individual.

ROLE-PLAYING illustrates an attempt to understand another's perspective.

ROLLBACK (prices) represents over-shooting a goal and the attempt to pull back for the purpose of gaining lost ground.

ROLL BAR refers to a specific protective measure; a safeguard.

ROLL CALL will reveal important names. Recall the names. For what purpose was the roll called? What did the list represent to the dreamer? Did the dreamer's name belong on the list? Was it deleted?

ROLLER COASTER denotes an unstable path or personality; up and down emotions or vacillating attitudes.

ROLLER SKATES pertains to a desire to skate through life without having to take the responsibility of dealing with distasteful or difficult issues.

ROLLING PIN represents a need to unroll concepts or ideas that one has balled up in one's head.

ROLLOVER (vehicle) may foretell of the possibility of an upcoming vehicular accident, but most often this type of dream event indicates a physiological dysfunction or turn-around with one's health.

ROLL-TOP DESK connotes a need to keep the specific aspects of one's life, work, or plans less public.

ROLODEX implies communication. The key here is to recall if there was a specific name presented.

ROMAINE (lettuce) refers to a light-hearted, perhaps humorous, misunderstanding.

ROMAN CANDLE See fireworks.

ROMAN NUMERALS will give emphasis to the meaning of the number displayed. Refer to specific number for further clarification.

ROMANTICISM (style) relates to empathy; emotional expressiveness.

ROMANTICIZING reveals an inability to perceive reality without attributing overly optimistic or emotionally sensitive qualities to it.

ROMEO AND JULIET forewarn of an unproductive or doomed relationship.

ROOF pertains to one's priorities; highest capping thoughts.

ROOF GARDEN illustrates beautiful, bountiful thoughts. Recall the garden's condition.

ROOFING MATERIAL See shingle.

ROOK (chess piece) portrays a deception in one's life.

ROOKIE characterizes a beginner; one who lacks experience and/or knowledge.

ROOM See specific type.

ROOM AND BOARD corresponds to the two major necessities in life. Recall the dream's details for further information on this symbol.

ROOM DIVIDER suggests a separation of space; a demarcation from one issue to the next.

ROOMING HOUSE relates to an opportunity for self-expression.

ROOMMATE implies companionship; may also allude to suppressed individuality.

ROOM SERVICE won't normally represent servitude but rather the things we can accomplish through simple communication (by lifting up the phone).

ROOM TEMPERATURE would normally represent a comfortable attitude or atmosphere, yet the dreamer needs to recall if the room was cold or too warm to gain the intent here.

ROOST refers to a temporary rest period.

ROOSTER constitutes an awakening of some type.

ROOT (botanical) signifies the existence of a hidden personal talent.

ROOT (hair) depicts an unrealized perception, attitude, or plan.

ROOT BEER See soft drink.

ROOT CANAL symbolizes an urgency to clean out and medicate an infectiously harmful manner of speaking.

ROOT CELLAR exemplifies the opportunity to preserve one's inner talents and bountiful gifts.

ROOT FEEDER stands for the nurturing care given to budding talents or humanitarian aspects.

ROOTING MATERIAL (plants) See vermiculite.

ROOTING VASES represent an effort to perpetuate a good thing. This may refer to any positive element in the dreamer's life and will be different for everyone.

ROOT ROT signifies a bad basic premise; a destructive basic attitude.

ROOTSTALK See rhizome.

ROOTSTOCK refers to the beginnings. This symbol may be pointing to the past origination/source of something.

ROPE alludes to a helpful element in one's life; an aid.

ROPE BURN (on palms) suggests hard efforts expended to accomplish a goal.

ROPE LADDER See ladder.

ROPE TOW See ski lift.

RORSCHACH TEST comes as an advisement to analyze one's perspectives; points to the existence of a different valid way to view something.

ROSARY recommends a time to pray, more specifically, turn to the Divine Essence.

ROSE (botanical/color/scent) portrays strong admiration.

ROSÉ See wine.

ROSEBUD pertains to a beginning or budding attraction; beginning feelings of admiration.

ROSE-COLORED (glasses/lens) See glasses.

ROSE HIP signifies the healing elements of love.

ROSEMARY (botanical) is a sign of remembrance; comes as an advisement to not forget whatever it was related to in the dream.

ROSE QUARTZ represents recognized and cherished spiritual gifts; may refer to new inspirations or deep affections.

ROSETTA STONE portrays a key to understanding a specific personal situation or issue.

ROSETTE (design) signifies a positive attitude/intention.

ROSE WATER indicates an altered element.

ROSE WINDOW connotes a perspective derived from multiple associated aspects. A rose window made of *stained glass* represents the Divine Mother, the Mother God.

ROSEWOOD symbolizes an enduring natural talent or ability.

ROSH HASHANAH indicates a new beginning.

ROSIN warns against slipping off one's course; a preventative against backsliding.

ROSS (Betsy Griscom) emphasizes the importance of symbolism; stands for honorable service.

ROSTER See roll call.

ROSTRUM See podium.

ROT is a symbol possessing duality. This symbol could refer to a humus type of aspect that infers a fertile ground or element, or it could pertain to a rotten, decaying situation, attitude, or other aspect.

ROTATION PLANTING applies to wise planning; the prevention of a depleted condition.

ROTISSERIE connotes a method of developing a plan or goal that insures all aspects are given equal consideration.

ROTOR (device) relates to a balanced perspective.

ROTOTILLER stands for a cultivation of one's natural talents.

ROTTEN See decay.

ROTTWEILER (dog breed) denotes a friend's social selectiveness.

ROTUNDA symbolizes an atmosphere rich in opportunity.

ROUGE suggests an intention to present a healthy state of well-being.

ROUGH (language) indicates a vulgar individual, one who doesn't care about social mores.

ROUGH (physical appearance) may indicate a difficult life or a coarse personality.

ROUGH (sound) denotes a lack of harmony or serenity.

ROUGH (texture) portrays an unfinished state; needs refinement.

ROUGH (waters) stands for a turbulent spiritual path.

ROUGHCAST illustrates a trail or experimental endeavor.

ROUGH CUT pertains to a lack of finesse; crude.

ROUGHHEWN reflects major efforts by one's own hands; self-forged.

ROUGHHOUSING typifies an advisement to release pent-up emotions and/or stress.

ROUGHNECK represents a crude or coarse manner of behavior.

ROUGHSHOD signifies harsh control of others.

ROULETTE (Russian) warns of chances taken that have the potential of causing great harm or having severely adverse effects; risks with stakes that are too high.

ROULETTE (table) stands for questionable chances taken.

ROUND (configuration) most often denotes a completeness; wholeness; coming full circle. Yet it also might indicate a behavior that takes one in circles.

ROUND (boxing) See inning.

ROUND DANCE signifies the full interactive participation of all parties involved.

ROUNDHOUSE suggests a change in one's life course; path options.

ROUND-SHOULDER refers to the weight one carries/has carried; fortitude; perseverance in spite of ongoing stressors.

ROUND TABLE indicates an upcoming conference, the need for same.

ROUND-THE-CLOCK typifies a necessary span of time to fulfill an activity one is planning.

ROUND TRIP implies a return to the beginning or starting point in order to facilitate a closure or completion.

ROUNDUP advises one to gather up personal beliefs instead of allowing them to stray far afield or lie fallow.

ROUSTABOUT characterizes a person possessing multiple talents; diversity.

ROUTE See map.

ROUTER (tool) reveals a way through a current troublesome problem or difficulty.

ROVE See roaming.

ROW (line) connotes the act of setting priorities and getting affairs or elements of an issue in line.

ROWBOAT applies to a vehicle or outlet for one to begin spiritual self-discovery through.

ROW HOUSE suggests a shoulder-to-shoulder relationship; close associations.

ROWING depicts a personal spiritual effort made.

ROWING MACHINE symbolizes efforts to improve or maintain a current situation.

ROYAL BLUE (color) refers to a somewhat uppity/exclusive attitude toward one's spirituality; may indicate self-righteousness.

ROYAL FLUSH (poker) points to a winning hand/idea.

ROYAL PURPLE (color) usually indicates a genteel spirituality; one quietly cherished in a dignified manner.

ROYALTY represents egocentric authority.

RUBBER (material) alludes to an attitude, perspective, or other aspect in one's life that creates a cushioning or buffering effect.

RUBBER BAND emphasizes the extension or stretched limit of an issue or perspective.

RUBBER BULLET See buckshot (rubber).

RUBBER CEMENT See adhesive.

RUBBER CHECK illustrates a groundless or empty factor in one's life.

RUBBERNECK applies to the act of exhibiting unrestrained interest or curiosity.

RUBBER STAMP comes as a personal message that warns, advises, or commends. Recall what the stamp said for further clarity.

RUBBER TREE indicates tolerance and acceptance.

RUBBING (skin) will have several meanings depending on the dream's related elements. Rubbing the skin may indicate an act of soothing, being bothered by an irritation, or ridding self of a distasteful or negative factor by attempting to debride it.

RUBBING ALCOHOL most often indicates a need to settle one's emotions; cool down.

RUBBISH See trash.

RUBBLE refers to the remnants of something. Frequently these leftovers can be put to beneficial use depending on their condition.

RUBDOWN See massage.

RUBY (color/gemstone) refers to life force; motivational energy and fortitude.

RUCKSACK See knapsack.

RUDDER represents the direction and quality of one's spiritual course.

RUDDERLESS warns of a lack of spiritual direction.

RUDDY (complexion) reveals an individual who routinely expends personal efforts toward a goal or assisting others.

RUDENESS portrays a disrespect for others and implies a lack of advancement.

RUDIMENTARY correlates to elemental aspects; the beginning stage or basic idea.

RUFF (collar) signifies an opinionated personality.

RUFFIAN See hoodlum.

RUFFLE (fabric) depicts multiple secondary aspects to an attitude or perspective.

RUG pertains to how one covers something. This will be a revealing dream element that relates to one's character, inner traits, or attitude.

RUG CLEANER applies to an attempt to keep one's personal groundwork or foundational perspectives clear of negatively affecting elements.

RUGGED (terrain) represents a life path that contains difficulties to either accept or overcome.

RUINS (archaeological) may literally infer a ruination of some type or it may indicate a personal revelation, depending on surrounding dreamscape elements. Ruins frequently denote deep wisdom or inspiration.

RULER (measurement) can signify an advisement to attend to a precise rule or personal belief or it can indicate a call to monitor one's utilization of a specific element such as manipulative speech, controlling behavior, gossip, etc.

RULER (person) characterizes an authoritative figure who may imply oneself, that is, one's conscience.

RUM See alcoholic drink.

RUMBA (dance) usually represents a troubled relationship, one in which there's routine aggression then backing down.

RUMBLE SEAT suggests a dissatisfaction with self for not taking control of one's life.

RUMMAGE SALE indicates an opportunity to obtain useful factors in one's life; opportunities.

RUMMY (card game) connotes a suggestion to gather one's facts.

RUMOR makes one responsible for information and the accuracy of same.

RUMPLED (appearance) may not represent a slovenly personality but rather this symbol's most frequent interpretation is that of a persevering individual who is a little worse for wear but maintains motivation and continued effort.

RUN (action) See running.

RUN (for office) See campaign.

RUN (in fabric) represents a flawed perspective or presentation of oneself.

RUN-AROUND represents an inability to attain a focused or centered perspective or position.

RUNAWAY stands for an element in one's life that has escaped one's grasp.

RUNDOWN (condition) can mean various things, but the bottom line for most of them is neglect.

RUNE symbolizes a personal revelation; a key or solution.

RUNG (any type) depicts a connective aspect.

RUNNER See messenger.

RUNNER (rug) suggests an attempt to protect a portion of one's path.

RUNNER-UP represents acknowledgment for efforts expended toward a goal. This will come as a positive symbol which gives encouragement indicating that one only need to put a bit more effort into reaching one's goal.

RUNNING reveals an attempt to escape or

catch up, depending on the dream's related details.

RUNNING BOARD relates to a convenience; a life aspect that serves to assist one along one's way or make progression a bit easier.

RUNNING LIGHT indicates a state of preparedness; anticipatory attitude.

RUNNING MATE represents a companion; an individual who shares one's perspectives or plans.

RUNNING SHOE denotes a need to get going with some aspect in life. This may reveal a state of procrastination that needs to end.

RUNNING START illustrates a position of advantage.

RUNNING TRACK warns of unproductive efforts; going fast and getting nowhere.

RUN-OFF represents ramifications; residual elements to something. May also point to an overabundance.

RUN-THROUGH suggests a trial effort or a need to review all angles of a plan.

RUNWAY (airport) indicates a pathway leading to (or away from) one's purpose. Surrounding details will clarify which interpretation was meant.

RUNWAY (fashion show) stands for a method of displaying something. In some cases, a runway will reveal exhibitionism.

RUPTURE denotes a flaw in a plan or one's thinking. What was ruptured?

RURAL refers to a more open perspective; less affected.

RUSE applies to a cleverly devised scheme; perhaps an ulterior motive.

RUSH HOUR symbolizes a time to act.

RUSHMORE (Mount) warns against the invasion of another's sacredness; a disrespect for another's spiritual belief.

RUSSET (color/fabric) illustrates a rich, earthy perspective; an alignment with reality.

RUSSIA symbolizes perseverance; a strong strength of character; eventual freedom to express individuality.

RUST will advise of a condition of spiritual atrophy.

RUSTIC exemplifies one's down-to-earth perspective and overall reasoning.

RUSTPROOF indicates personal efforts applied to protecting and maintaining one's spiritual state.

RUT (in road) pertains to a self-generated state of neutrality; lacking progression or advancement due to one's own inability to perceive opportunities.

RUTABAGA See turnip.

RUTHLESSNESS signifies a void of sensitivity; lacking moral fiber; ulterior motives.

RUTTING (season) implies a time to plan, start thinking about making new beginnings.

RYE represents rejuvenation.

S

SABBATH See high holy days.

SABBATICAL represents periods of additional learning that are needed. This usually refers to those who consider themselves to be a teacher or leader of some type.

SABER See sword.

SABER RATTLING signifies a threatening intent.

SABLE (color/fur) portrays negativity; a dark mood.

SABOTEUR characterizes a two-faced personality.

SACAJAWEA symbolizes one who possesses the knowledge and capability of providing directional assistance to others.

SACCHARIN implies a tendency to be content with imitations.

SACHEM relates to a person with experiential knowledge and the attained wisdom that accompanies it.

SACHET connotes a cover-up being done; a replacement scent or aspect being utilized.

SACK See bag.

SACKCLOTH (fabric) relates to self-imposed guilt; unnecessary punishment of oneself related to guilt.

SACRAMENT will pertain to any act that one believes will earn grace.

SACRED COW applies to misplaced priorities; or that which one personally perceives as being sacrosanct.

SACRED OBJECTS usually represent something one places faith in.

SACRIFICE may indicate actual awake-state sacrifices one makes for the attainment of spiritual goals or it may have a negative connotation that warns of a potentially dangerous direction or intent.

SACRISTY corresponds with the sacred place within oneself.

SACRUM correlates to the root of emotion.

SAD See melancholia.

SADDLE defines personal control of one's journey through life. Recall the saddle's appearance. Was it plain? Heavily tooled? Worn or new?

SADDLEBAG denotes that which we carry with us on our life journey. Recall the bag's color and condition. Was it full? With what?

SADDLE BLANKET typifies a symbol that gives an indication of what one's attitude is toward one's path.

SADDLER characterizes a person who has the skill to enhance one's journey.

SADDLERY represents aids available to assist one's life journey.

SADDLE SHOE marks a path walked conservatively, with practicality.

SADDLE SOAP exemplifies care given to one's path; personal monitoring and maintenance of its quality.

SADDLE SORE reveals a forced path progression; advises of a need to ease back on one's efforts that have become overly concentrated.

SADISM exposes an underlying obsession with self; apathy toward others; tendency to feel pleasure over another's misfortune.

SAFARI (hunting) represents a life path that follows that of another in which innocent victims are harmed along the way; a ruthlessness.

SAFARI JACKET denotes a predatory nature.

SAFARI TROPHY pertains to someone who has been victimized. Recall where the trophy was. Who did it belong to?

SAFE alludes to an element in one's life that provides personal security of some type.

SAFECRACKER characterizes an individual who has the skill to break through the defenses of others. May also point to someone's skill for problem-solving or identifying the core source of a problem.

SAFE-DEPOSIT BOX stands for a need to keep something from being lost, damaged, or adversely affected by negatives.

SAFE HARBOR stands for an unthreatening attitude or situation.

SAFE HOUSE clearly symbolizes a safe or secure place, situation, direction, or perspective.

SAFEKEEPING stands for efforts expended toward preserving or cherishing something.

SAFETY BELT indicates an opportunity to protect oneself from a possible danger or harmful situation.

SAFETY CIRCUIT relates to personal attention and awareness given to one's thought process; maintaining mental and emotional control; discernment.

SAFETY FILM will pinpoint a potentially hazardous situation in one's life. Recall what specific type of hazard the film was about.

SAFETY GLASS(ES) signifies a right perspective; a protected/guarded one.

SAFETY MATCH illustrates a safeguard that prevents the use of potentially hazardous elements for the wrong purposes.

SAFETY NET suggests insecurity; a lack of self-confidence; a reluctance to take risks.

SAFETY PIN refers to a secure manner of providing a temporary stop-gap action.

SAFETY RAZOR See razor.

SAFETY VALVE exemplifies a personal control over one's emotions.

SAFFRON (color/plant) See orange (color).

SAGA portrays extensive details.

SAGE (botanical) constitutes renewing elements in one's life.

SAGE (person) characterizes an individual possessing high wisdom gained through enlightenment.

SAGE BUNDLE indicates an expression of honor and respect.

SAGGING reveals some type of weakness or weakened condition.

SAGUARO represents a protected spiritual aspect of an individual.

SAIL alludes to an attitude of acceptance.

SAILBOAT relates to a spiritual direction led by destiny.

SAILCLOTH (fabric) correlates to endurance; a strong constitution.

SAILFISH typifies a symbol relating to spiritual destiny.

SAILOR characterizes a spiritual seeker.

SAINT will usually reveal a desired quality, but may also warn against a perspective that one believes self to be a saint. May point to a tendency to look down one's nose on others.

SAINT BERNARD (dog breed) represents a helpful friend.

SAINT CHRISTOPHER characterizes a one who is capable and willing to carry another's burden or serving to uplift them during a stressful phase.

SAINT CHRISTOPHER MEDAL represents faith in one's inner strength.

SAINT ELMO'S FIRE denotes inspiration.

SAINT JOHN'S EVE See Midsummer Eve.

SAINT NICHOLAS See Santa Claus.

SAINT PATRICK'S DAY is a call to turn one's attention to the spirit; stands for a return to spiritual matters.

SAINT VALENTINE'S DAY reminds us that love for others should be one's priority.

SALAD indicates diversity. Recall what the salad's condition was. What type of foods comprised it?

SALAD BAR alludes to choices in life. Recall what was offered. What was taken?

SALAD DRESSING/OIL pertains to the personal manner in which one dresses up or enhances opportunities.

SALAD PLATE may come as an advisement to choose smaller portions of something. This could literally relate to food ingestion or it could be referring to a current revelation that one has too much on one's plate and needs to cut down on activity.

SALAMANDER suggests the blending of spirituality through daily life.

SALAMI depicts an interesting aspect to an issue.

SALARY symbolizes recompense for efforts expended.

SALARY CAP stands for the maximum benefits one can expect to receive from efforts expended.

SALE (reduced price) may represent a good deal or opportunity, yet it also may only appear to be so.

SALESPERSON See clerk.

SALES PROMOTION stands for enticements or incentives.

SALES RALLY refers to the gaining of motivation through the support of others of a like goal.

SALES SLIP See receipt.

SALES TAX pertains to a hidden cost to something obtained.

SALINE SOLUTION implies a need to replace a needed element in one's life.

SALIVA refers to softened speech; thoughtful communication.

SALMON (color/fish) warns against going against a spiritual current; a spiritual search that's somehow in error.

SALMONELLA applies to seriously negative results from ingesting harmful ideas or influences.

SALOME (biblical) characterizes one with ulterior motives.

SALOON portrays a state of unawareness. May also indicate a need to chill out and soothe one's stresses.

SALSA connotes high interest; an exciting and active element in one's life.

SALSIFY (botanical) points to a need to reorganize one's sense of priority; mental focus.

SALT exemplifies gregariousness and dependability.

SALT-AND-PEPPER signifies duality; positive and negative elements.

SALT-AND-PEPPER (hair color) suggests the gaining of wisdom while still learning from experiences.

SALTBOX (architecture) represents a veneer of simplicity.

SALT FLATS signify a phase in one's life when situations, relationships, issues leave one parched for refreshing elements.

SALTINE See cracker (food).

SALT LICK constitutes an attempt to provide others with what they need.

SALT MARSH emphasizes an inundation of spiritual elements; may infer a frequency of overwhelming spiritual aspects.

SALT MINE represents a source for gaining fortitude and grounded thought.

SALT SHAKER relates to an opportunity to cause an enhancement.

SALTWATER represents elemental spiritual truths.

SALTWATER AQUARIUM denotes a personal grasp of the elemental spiritual truths and the cherishing of same.

SALUTE defines an acknowledgment of another; respect; recognition.

SALVAGE (operation) connotes an attempt to save and restore something that would otherwise be lose.

SALVATION ARMY stands for benevolence.

SALVE See ointment.

SALVER See serving tray.

SALVIA (flower) represents hearty sensitivities; strong emotional control.

SALVO symbolizes a bombardment of some type that could elicit either a positive or negative response.

SAMBA (dance) signifies a relationship in which the partners are often at odds.

SAMISEN alludes to a vibratory alignment; balance within.

SAMOVAR See coffee pot.

SAMOYED (dog breed) denotes a friend's gregariousness; a giving, generous, and outgoing personality.

SAMPLE pertains to foreknowledge, knowing what one is getting into.

SAMPLER (stitchery) will imply variety or relay a specific message for the dreamer.

SAMURAI signifies inner strength.

SANATORIUM illustrates a life element that is capable of providing a return to physical, emotional, or mental health.

SANCTIMONIOUS (attitude) reveals false piety.

SANCTION equates to permission; may indicate a behavior aligned with one's Higher Self—one's conscience.

SANCTUARY emphasizes respite; a place of peace. This symbol can refer to emotional, spiritual, or mental peace.

SANCTUM See inner sanctum.

SAND suggests a shifting perspective or attitude.

SANDAL relates to a desire to walk close to the earth, yet the goal hasn't quite been attained yet.

SANDALWOOD (color/scent) implies an unaffected personality.

SANDBAG warns of a spiritual withdrawal—effort to keep the waters of spirituality back.

SANDBANK/BAR represents a spiritual concept that requires contemplation.

SANDBLASTING pertains to an effort to get down to basics; discover the basic, foundational facts or issues.

SANDBOX indicates immaturity of thought and reason.

SAND CASTLE correlates to unrealistic plans; insubstantial ideas; lacking viability.

SAND CHAIR reveals nonchalance bordering on apathy; a tendency to be completely comfortable with one's state of indecision.

SAND CRAB represents the hidden dangers of indecision.

SAND DOLLAR portrays spiritual riches.

SANDER (tool) applies to a life element that has the capability of smoothing over a rough aspect.

SAND FLEA typifies irritations in life, most often one's juvenile/immature relationships.

SANDHILL CRANE suggests a desire to be more decisive.

SAND LILY (botanical) stands for an appreciation of small blessings.

SANDMAN characterizes a need to rest one's mind.

SAND MARTIN (bird) stands for congeniality; gregariousness.

SAND PAINTING illustrates spiritual healing knowledge.

SANDPAPER See sander.

SANDPIPER (bird) connotes spiritual ideas; giving spiritual aspects to one's thought process.

SAND PIT exposes a stage or place along one's life path where indecision will need to be overcome.

SANDSTONE corresponds with a weak foundation; lacking strong basics.

SANDSTORM stands for mental confusion.

SAND TRAP exemplifies problems in life; aspects that are intended to test one's inner strength and problem-solving abilities.

SANDWICH constitutes a boxed in feeling; a situation, relationship, or belief that creates a confining effect.

SANDWICH BOARD will reveal a personal message for the dreamer.

SANDWORT (flower) signifies an attitude of acceptance, a "whatever" attitude.

SANGUINE See ruddy.

SANITATION WORKER See garbage collector.

SANITIZE represents an effort to remove negative aspects from some type of element in one's life. May also point to a cover-up or spin efforts.

SANTA CLAUS characterizes an overly optimistic personality; unrealistic expectations; good intentions.

SANTA'S ELVES symbolize those who would encourage unrealistic expectations or promote false hopes.

SAP represents the life force of nature; inner strength.

SAPLING pertains to the tenuous but persevering nature of newly attained beliefs.

SAPPHIRE (color/gemstone) depicts a fragile spiritual nature.

SAPPHO (Greek poetess) stands for feminine camaraderie and confidences.

SAPSUCKER See woodpecker.

SARCASM may be a positive or negative dreamscape element depending on who said what to whom. Recall the detail for clarity. Just like in the awake-state, revelations often come through sarcasm or side remarks.

SARCOPHAGUS See coffin.

SARDINE advises one to remove oneself from a suffocating situation or belief system; may even refer to a self-generated psychological perspective that is suffocating one.

SARI represents an unaffected personality.

SARONG denotes simplicity.

SARSAPARILLA symbolizes innocence.

SASH See belt.

SASHAY signifies a carefree attitude.

SASQUATCH See Bigfoot.

SASSAFRAS implies well-being.

SATAN See devil.

SATCHEL portrays that which we consider important enough to always carry with us, usually relating to basic ethics and beliefs.

SATEEN (fabric/finish) implies a slick personality; cleverness.

SATELLITE (man-made) reflects an orbiting of the truth instead of reaching and stretching oneself beyond the safe and charted confines of tradition.

SATELLITE (planet) denotes peripheral elements on which one places importance.

SATELLITE DISH suggests a need to be more receptive to others; implies a personal striving for greater receptivity.

SATIN (fabric/finish) reveals an overly optimistic perspective. May also refer to the soft sheen of one's character (as opposed to a need to be glossy).

SATIRE See sarcasm.

SATURATED emphasizes a fullness or a level that has reached capacity. Recall what was saturated. What was the liquid? Water? Blood? Oil?

SATURDAY suggests a time to give personal attention to oneself. This symbol may refer to a wide variety of aspects such as physical, mental, or emotional rest and attention.

SATURDAY NIGHT SPECIAL (gun) warns of highly volatile emotions.

SATURN (planet) implies wisdom and the attainment of same.

SATYR (Greek mythology) characterizes a lack of self control.

SAUCE signifies personal perspectives or character traits that alter basic elements.

SAUCEPAN indicates a desire to affect surrounding elements in a personal manner.

SAUCER relates to protective measures; means of containment.

SAUDI ARABIA signifies power gained through wealth.

SAUERBRATEN See pot roast.

SAUERKRAUT See cabbage.

SAUNA reveals a need for inner cleansing to rid oneself of negative attitudes and emotional impurities that serve as toxins.

SAUSAGE denotes a concise concept; a situation or plan that has been given every conceivable consideration.

SAUTÉ implies a need for contemplation; deep thought.

SAVANNA represents an exposure to personally sensitive concepts or ideas; a clear view.

SAVANT exposes past-life knowledge or talents.

SAVINGS ACCOUNT See bankbook.

SAVINGS BOND portrays foresight; an opportunity.

SAVORY signifies an appealing element in one's life.

SAVVY applies to being well informed; knowledgeable.

SAW represents the capability to cut through a problematical aspect in life.

SAWDUST denotes that which is leftover or left behind after a problem has been resolved.

SAWFISH stands for spiritual discernment; a strengthened ability to cut through superfluous spiritual aspects.

SAW GRASS illustrates a particularly troublesome phase in one's life.

SAWHORSE refers to a life aspect that has the capability of aiding efforts to resolve problems and carry out plans.

SAWMILL constitutes the act of personally identifying the basic factors of a problem.

SAW PALMETTO (tree) stands for personal philosophical concepts; spiritual freedom.

SAW-TOOTHED implies an aggressive approach.

SAW-TOOTHED MOUNTAINS denote a difficult phase of travel; may refer directly to one's intended journey.

SAW-WHET OWL stands for original thought; inventiveness; increased creative inspiration.

SAWYER (Tom) characterizes one who doesn't give logic and reason to the thought process.

SAXIFRAGE (botanical/flower) symbolizes an appreciation of life's more meaningful/memorable moments.

SAXOPHONE alludes to melancholia.

SCAB (worker) advises of an improper substitution or replacement; a wrong alternative.

SCAB (wound) indicates a healing process.

SCABBARD signifies the control of one's emotions.

SCABIES stands for a parasitic (negative) aspect that one has allowed to invade oneself.

SCAFFOLD correlates to the safeguards we personally create to protect us from hurtful emotional events.

SCALD most often identifies a spiritual burn of some type that results from accepting false concepts.

SCALE See climbing.

SCALE (fish) refers to spiritual caution.

SCALE (weight) illustrates balance of some type. Recall the kind of scale to determine this symbol's precise meaning.

What was being weighed? What type of scale was it? Was anything on it?

SCALLOP (fish) portrays the ingestion of harmful spiritual elements.

SCALLOP (pattern) applies to being grounded. This symbol refers to the tendency to return to one's center for the purpose of staying balanced and focused.

SCALP (head) exemplifies one's sensitivity. Recall its condition.

SCALPEL infers a need to excise a negative element from oneself or another.

SCALPER (ticket) refers to personal gain made through unethical means; taking advantage of others.

SCALP LOCK (hair style) represents narrow-mindedness.

SCAM reveals insincerity; ulterior motives.

SCAMPI See shrimp.

SCAM-SPAM (Internet) warns of the possibility of one being drawn into a fraudulent situation or being hoodwinked; this comes as an advisement to be on the watch for ideas or opportunities that sound too good to be valid.

SCAN represents a going over or the need to review something.

SCANDAL SHEET correlates to gossip; sensationalism; comes as an advisement to focus on the important elements in life.

SCANNER (computer) stands for visual input; a need to mentally retain a visual.

SCANNER (merchandise) decodes a hidden message; reveals the cost of something. This will rarely be related to a monetary aspect.

SCANNER (radio frequencies) stands for knowing what's going on behind the scenes.

SCANNER (security) will point to a perceptual awareness or watchfulness for ulterior motives in others.

SCAPEGOAT means an innocent individual; warns of a tendency to place blame on others; lacking personal responsibility.

SCAPULAR (religious) reminds one to maintain personal protection; alludes to the wisdom of watching one's back.

SCAR denotes a former wound.

SCARAB relates to one's inner self; the soul.

SCARECROW signifies a reinforcement of one's personal protection. May also reveal a stern veneer over a soft heart.

SCARED exposes one's inner fears.

SCARF defines an open attitude toward new ideas.

SCARLET See red.

SCARLET FEVER represents the harmful results of accepting a negative idea.

SCAR TISSUE See scar.

SCATTER pertains to a loss of essential elements.

SCATTERBRAINED stands for a loss of emotional or mental focus.

SCATTERGUN See shotgun.

SCAVENGER usually exemplifies resourcefulness, yet whether this symbol is meant to infer a positive or negative message will depend on the related surrounding dreamscape details.

SCENERY plays a major roll in dream interpretation, for the scene of the dreamscape will always reveal important elements that are essential. Refer to specific scenic types and mood settings.

SCENIC EASEMENT points to a need to

have a place of calming respite in one's life; a place or time reserved for rest and rejuvenation.

SCENIC OVERLOOK See road signs.

SCENT has a specific purpose in dreams. Refer to specific scent type.

SCEPTER indicates false authority, often spiritually related.

SCHEDULE signifies regimentation.

SCHEMATIC exemplifies the necessity of detailed and well thought out planning.

SCHEME naturally indicates a plan, but one needs to recall the details to determine if it was for productive and positive purposes.

SCHIZOPHRENIA marks an individual who is not (or has a hard time being) true to oneself.

SCHNAPPS See alcoholic beverage.

SCHNAUZER (dog breed) portrays a friend who watches out for you.

SCHOLAR characterizes a person who possesses knowledge, usually regarding a specific subject.

SCHOLARSHIP stands for an opportunity to attain greater information or knowledge; a chance to learn something without personal costs involved.

SCHOOL may indicate learning or it may refer to the negative aspect of being indoctrinated.

SCHOOL BAG stands for one's preparedness for expanding learning.

SCHOOL BOARD will normally indicate those who determine what others are taught and place perimeters on knowledge. This is not usually a positive dream symbol.

SCHOOLBOOK will reveal the specific area in which the dreamer is lacking adequate knowledge. Naturally the key here is to recall what type of schoolbook it was.

SCHOOL BUS corresponds to the vehicle or way a person can attain additional knowledge.

SCHOOL BUS DRIVER characterizes an individual who can personally lead another to further enlightenment or attained knowledge.

SCHOOL DISTRICT suggests an environment for learning. May also relate to immaturity.

SCHOOLHOUSE (one room) emphasizes general information; the basics.

SCHOOLROOM comes to advise of a situation where there's room for learning more, usually about a specific subject. Recall if there were any decorations or book titles in the schoolroom to indicate what subject needs to be studied.

SCHOOLTEACHER characterizes someone in the dreamer's life who is capable of teaching something important. This will be a specific element unique to the dreamer.

SCHOOLWORK reminds us that we have to continually apply ourselves if we want to learn.

SCHOOL YARD suggests a paced method of study whereby adequate breaks are factored in.

SCIATICA exposes a displaced attitude or perspective; a constant wear on one's nerve.

SICILY symbolizes deep familial bonds.

SCIENCE constitutes expanded knowledge regarding a specific subject. Recall what the subject was.

SCIENCE FAIR points to innovative thinking; ingenuity; possibilities.

SCIENCE FICTION denotes unrealistic attitudes or beliefs; an inability to understand true Reality.

SCIENTIFIC EXPERIMENT will signify a suggestion to move ahead with a particular plan.

SCIENTIFIC JOURNAL comes to advise of the need to do further information gathering regarding specific subject matter.

SCIENTIST characterizes an individual who is highly interested in expanding our knowledge and understanding, yet is caught within self-imposed bounds.

SCIMITAR See sword.

SCISSORS denote a permanent separation. Recall what color they were. Were they used to cut something? What?

SCOFF represents the expression of an opposing opinion.

SCOLD illustrates a reprimand. Recall the dream's surrounding details. Who was doing the scolding? Who was being scolded and what for?

SCOLIOSIS portrays an inability to stand up straight for oneself.

SCONCE will symbolize a life aspect that has the ability to light one's way. Recall if it had a lit candle or bulb. Was it empty? Bright or dark?

SCONE portrays an essential piece of information.

SCOOP (utensil) See ladle.

SCOOP (information) exposes hidden elements to an issue. May point to the first person to reveal specific information.

SCOOTER implies an immature method of gaining information or reaching one's goal.

SCOPE reflects an in-depth look; closer attention given.

SCORCH stands for too much pressure or heat brought to bare.

SCORE (drugs/points) stands for the obtaining of a goal.

SCOREBOARD/CARD connotes an individual's personal balance sheet. Recall what it revealed. What color was it?

SCOREKEEPER represents oneself; responsibility to maintain a balanced perspective.

SCORPION will stand for retaliation.

SCORPION FISH stands for a deadly spiritual element or path.

SCOTLAND suggests a proud heritage.

SCOTTISH TERRIER (dog breed) characterizes a loyal friend who is prepared to defend your honor.

SCOUR depicts deep cleaning. Recall what was being scoured. Who was doing the cleaning?

SCOUT indicates advanced research and exploration needed in one's life before further progression can be accomplished. May point to hidden aspects that need to be ferreted out.

SCOUT LEADER pertains to a person who can serve as a guide along one's life path.

SCRABBLE (game) warns against the tendency to play word games and not communicate in a direct and clear manner.

SCRABBLE (grope) reflects an uncontrolled progression; lack of planning.

SCRAMBLED EGGS represent a mix of new ideas; a confused beginning.

SCRAMBLER (device) emphasizes a need

to be discerning throughout our communications with others.

SCRAP will correspond with a single element in one's life that may or may not be currently relevant.

SCRAPBOOK signifies a personal need to remember accomplishments or events of one's past. Was the scrapbook for a specific event or time? Related to a particular individual?

SCRAPER reveals a need to clear away extraneous elements that cloud or cover basic aspects.

SCRAPHEAP represents that which is of no value. Recall what was in the dreamscape heap.

SCRATCHING implies a personal irritation in one's life.

SCRATCHING POST signifies a need to deal with irritations so one can move on.

SCRATCH 'N' SNIFF will refer to a sampling of something, or provide an additional element about something.

SCRATCHPAD See notebook.

SCRATCH-PROOF portrays an aspect in one's life that is resistant to outside influence.

SCRATCH TEST (for allergy) is an attempt to define the source of one's life irritations.

SCRATCH TEST (for genuineness) represents a watchfulness for imitations.

SCRAWL indicates a communication made in haste.

SCREAM (silent) denotes repressed emotions or unvoiced calls for help.

SCREE refers to a difficult path.

SCREECH OWL will point to a strong warning; a need to raise one's intuitive

sense for the purpose of acute watchfulness.

SCREEN (computer) See monitor (computer screen).

SCREEN (door) exemplifies protected freedom.

SCREEN (strainer) See strainer.

SCREENPLAY represents a proposed plan of action; a speculative idea which envisions the outcome.

SCREEN-SAVER (computer monitor) stands for efforts expended toward preventing one's perception to be overridden by previous first impressions; an effort to reserve opinion based on a first impression until more information is obtained.

SCREEN TEST relates to one's desire to perform a specific task or role and the appropriateness of being the right person.

SCREW (tool) usually refers to an injustice or bad deal.

SCREWDRIVER signifies pressures in life. These may be referring to self-induced pressures or problems. Recall who was holding the tool. Was it being used to *un*screw something? This would mean a *lessening* of pressure.

SCREWDRIVER (drink type) See alcoholic beverage.

SCRIBBLE symbolizes a lack of mental focus.

SCRIBE characterizes the recording of communications.

SCRIM refers to an unclear perspective; foggy viewpoint.

SCRIMMAGE corresponds to a type of struggle.

SCRIMP indicates extreme frugality.

Recall surrounding dreamscape details to determine if this is a positive or negative message and what the scrimping was related to.

SCRIMSHAW See carve.

SCRIPT suggests a need to play by the rules. This infers that an individual is not holding to his/her pre-chosen life path or purpose. Depending on related dream elements, this may also be a call to stop expecting life to follow a predetermined script—be more adaptable to ever-changing circumstances.

SCRIPTURE See bible.

SCRIPTWRITER will represent one who either has control of her/his direction or one who attempts to design a personal reality and expects it to manifest without deviation.

SCROLL See scan.

SCROLL (ancient) emphasizes solid truths.

SCROLLWORK indicates an attention given to detail.

SCROOGE (Ebenezer) reminds us that it's never too late to change for the better.

SCRUB (terrain) alludes to an inactive stage of one's life path.

SCRUB BRUSH connotes a cleansing is required.

SCRUBBY (appearance) may signify a weary soul or it may stand for apathy depending on the dream's related details.

SCRUPULOUS will reveal a conscionable individual.

SCRYING (glass/mirror) stands for an effort/desire to perceive more clearly.

SCUBA DIVER depicts the attainment of spiritual gifts. Recall what the diver was looking at or collecting? Was the water clear, cloudy, colored?

SCUBA GEAR represents aspects that allow one to attain spiritual goals.

SCUDDING connotes a forced progression.

SCUFFED defines wear; perseverance and fortitude.

SCUFFLE refers to an altercation of some type; may even be within oneself.

SCULLCAP (botanical) signifies widening perceptual views to see what's outside the box; new thought and inspiration.

SCULLERY implies a need for cleaning. The dreamer will make the specific correlation.

SCULPTING relates to the act of creating and formulating in a personal manner. May reveal one's individualized perception of something.

SCULPTURE will reveal an important element that the dreamer should give attention to. What was the sculpture of?

SCUM portrays that which lacks value; extraneous elements.

SCURVY defines a lack of inner strength; a weakening of foundational elements.

SCUTTLE See ashcan.

SCUTWORK reminds us that even menial tasks can have beneficial effects.

SCYTHE pertains to cutting through life's excesses or unnecessary aspects.

SEA correlates to life's spiritual aspects.

SEA ANEMONE stands for spiritual diversity.

SEA BISCUIT See hardtack.

SEA BREEZE represents a spiritual sense to something; a hint of spiritual elements.

SEA CHANGE signifies a major change; a sudden and unexpected alteration of course or attitude.

SEA CHEST portrays that which we carry with us on our spiritual search. This symbol could be revealing spiritual *baggage* or *gems* to hold onto. Surrounding dreamscape details will point to which was intended.

SEA CUCUMBER denotes societal spiritual beliefs; traditional dogma; signals a need to distinguish commonly held tenets from actual truth.

SEA FAN connotes spiritual vacillation.

SEAFLOOR refers to spiritual foundations.

SEA FOAM stands for spiritual confusion, a stirring of one's beliefs.

SEAFOOD most often represents spiritual knowledge or nourishment. Recall the condition of the seafood. What type was it?

SEA GREEN (color) refers to behavior touched with light spiritual tones.

SEA GULL pertains to spiritual thoughts and ideals that are utilized in daily behavior.

SEA HORSE relates to an illogical spiritual search or belief and may indicate spiritual beliefs that are more fantasy than reality.

SEAL (animal) portrays the use of spirituality in one's daily life.

SEAL (closure) refers to a need to conclude or seal an aspect in one's life.

SEAL (emblem) will reveal a specific meaning to each dreamer depending on what the emblem was.

SEA-LANE stands for a well used spiritual path. This is usually a warning against following another's belief system rather than sensing one's own.

SEALED BOOK See closed book.

SEALED ORDERS represents knowing what to do when the time comes.

SEA LEGS suggests spiritual comfort; feeling at home with one's personal spiritual beliefs.

SEALER See varnish.

SEA LEVEL pertains to spiritual basic truths.

SEALING WAX defines privacy; confidentiality. Recall who was using the wax. What color was it? Was it impressed with a symbol or initial?

SEA LION See seal.

SEAM (any type) denotes a joining element which may suggest a weak spot.

SEAMLESS indicates unbroken; a complete element.

SEA MONSTER represents a spiritual danger.

SEAMSTRESS characterizes an individual who is capable of bringing various elements together.

SÉANCE exposes misplaced spiritual priorities.

SEA PINK (flower) refers to the little blessings that tend to give us an unexpected uplift.

SEAPLANE symbolizes spiritual thoughts; time spent contemplating spiritual issues.

SEAPORT corresponds to a spiritual transition.

SEAQUAKE warns of spiritually shaky ground; the shaking of one's beliefs.

SEAR See burn (incinerate).

SEARCH AND RESCUE (team) signifies a need to search one's motives and rescue oneself from misconceptions and negative attitudes causing bad behavior.

SEARCH ENGINE (computer) stands for a method or source for opening up a wealth of new information.

SEARCHING relates to a desire or need for specific information.

SEARCHLIGHT See flashlight.

SEARCH PARTY represents the seeking to recoup lost emotions or attitudes.

SEARCH WARRANT portrays an invasion of privacy. Important elements associated with this symbol are the answers to such questions as who was serving the warrant on whom? For what reason?

SEA SALT stands for fortified spiritual aspects/beliefs.

SEASCAPE will reveal the quality of one's personal spiritual search or transition. Was the scene a rough cliff? A tropical and sandy shore? Was it rocky?

SEA SERPENT See sea monster.

SEASHELL defines spiritual gifts and talents. Recall the quality and quantity of the shells. Were they whole? Beautiful or full of barnacles?

SEASICKNESS stands for an individual's state of spiritual confusion; spiritual dizziness or nausea from taking in too much too fast.

SEA SLUG warns of spiritual laziness, or entrapment.

SEA SNAIL denotes a slow and methodical spiritual pace based on one's level of comprehension.

SEA SNAKE See eel.

SEASON See specific type.

SEASONAL AFFECTIVE DISORDER comes to advise of a need to stay on an even emotional keel and not be affected by external shifts in opinion/attitude.

SEASONAL CREEK/STREAM points to a part-time spirituality; a tendency to use spiritual behavior discriminately.

SEASONAL DWELLING represents a dual nature. May also signify the reaping of benefits from more than one aspect.

SEASONING will indicate personal characteristics. Refer to specific type.

SEASON TICKET represents planning ahead for the purpose of not missing elements of personal interest.

SEA SPONGE stands for spiritual overabsorption.

SEA SPRAY applies to spiritual gifts and the opportunity to accept them.

SEA STAR See starfish.

SEAT BELT connotes a protective measure.

SEA TURTLE typifies a cautious spiritual search or path; an enduring path.

SEA URCHIN denotes spiritual immaturity.

SEA WALL refers to self-generated spiritual bounds.

SEAWATER suggests the quenching of a spiritual thirst.

SEAWEED pertains to spiritual indecision; spiritual vacillation.

SEA WORLD suggests a sampling of spiritual concepts.

SEAWORTHY illustrates one's personal preparedness to begin a spiritual quest or search.

SECLUDED most often is an advisement to engage in serious contemplation.

SECOND BASE stands for evidence of progression.

SECOND-CLASS (accommodations) exemplifies an alternative.

SECOND COMING symbolizes expectations made on how we *think* something will occur.

SECOND FIDDLE stands for a supportive role.

SECOND GROWTH (forest) points to rejuvenation.

SECONDHAND defines a useable element or idea.

SECOND HOME See vacation home.

SECOND MORTGAGE may be symbolized by the visual of two mortgage papers on a table or in one's hand. Sometimes the symbol is presented as a house double or shadow. This dream fragment will stand for a good prospect or solid plan.

SECOND-RATE suggests a slightly inferior element.

SECOND SIGHT See clairvoyance.

SECOND WIND implies a re-energized state of being.

SECRET may indicate a revelation for the dreamer.

SECRET AGENT exposes an individual who has ulterior motives.

SECRETARY (furniture type) stands for business, things one needs to routinely take care of.

SECRETARY (person) characterizes an individual who is capable of providing support and assistance.

SECRET BALLOT connotes a personal decision; inner thoughts.

SECRET CEREMONY stands for hidden elements to something; may indicate an ulterior motive.

SECRET POLICE comes as a strong advisement to be more aware of those around you.

SECRET SANTA refers to unconditional giving; one who anonymously gives aid.

SECRET SERVICE signifies a loss of privacy. This symbol may point to someone with ulterior motives who is presenting a false front.

SECRET SOCIETY refers to hidden activities.

SECTION EIGHT warns of undesirable character traits.

SECULARISM indicates spiritual indifference. May point to activities or individuals having no correlation to spiritual aspects.

SECURITIES AND EXCHANGE COMMISSION stands for the maintaining of integrity.

SECURITY BLANKET denotes that which comforts or gives one a sense of security. May point to a crutch of some type.

SECURITY CAMERA reminds us that we're always being watched. This symbol may even be pointing to oneself (conscience).

SECURITY DEPOSIT represents a promise or a safeguard against the possibility of a negative event happening.

SECURITY GUARD characterizes an individual who is capable of providing protection, monitoring; may even be yourself (conscience).

SECURITY RISK stands for a plan or individual who carries a risk; untrustworthy.

SECURITY SYSTEM See alarm system.

SEDATIVE pertains to a calming element in one's life; may indicate a need to gain greater acceptance.

SEDENTARY is an advisement to expend greater efforts.

SEDGEWAY (scooter) stands for traveling over one's path in an attempt to avoid the little bumps in the road.

SEDIMENT represents that which remains or is leftover; nonessential elements.

SEDUCTION warns of a situation that may lure one astray. Though this symbol may be visually presented as a sexual visual in the dream, it will most often have a real-life relation to something in one's awake-state that is acting as a deterrent from central focus; a distraction of some type.

SEED See kernel.

SEEDLING stands for the birthing of new understandings. Recall what type of botanical the seedling was. What was its overall condition?

SEED MONEY stands for an abundance of talent reserved for a specific purpose; a readiness to begin a certain objective.

SEED PEARL symbolizes small imperfections.

SEED PLANT refers to a source for new beginnings/ideas.

SEEING EYE DOG characterizes a friend who has the ability to clarify confusing matters.

SEEPAGE exposes an insecure situation or piece of information. This symbol may also reveal the fact that some form of private information is leaking to another—possible betrayal.

SEERESS indicates an individual who has clear perception of current time situations and sharp instincts for future ramifications.

SEERSUCKER (fabric) alludes to a light-hearted mood.

SEESAW generally relates to the unpredictability of life—the ongoing ups and downs, but may also point to one's tendency to vacillate.

SEETHE warns of a need to release one's pent-up emotions; need for tolerance and acceptance; suggests a cooling off period.

SEE-THROUGH (barrier/fabric) See transparent.

SEGMENTED denotes a multifaceted element in one's life.

SEGREGATION may not infer a racial matter but rather is a symbol that usually advises us to keep diverse issues separate from one another. This dream symbol would imply that the dreamer has been mixing concepts or issues.

SEISMIC LOAD (construction) points to the wisdom of making a plan by factoring in safeguards against the possibility of a tremor/shaking future event.

SEISMOGRAPH constitutes watchfulness; cautions one to be more keenly aware of undercurrents in relationships, business, or personal situations in life.

SEISMOLOGIST emphasizes one's inner sensitivity toward being aware when approaching unstable ground; be watchful of a questionable issue, situation, or relationship.

SEIZE won't usually be a negative symbol, for it most often is an advisement to grasp an opportunity while one can.

SEIZURE warns of a serious adverse reaction; some type of negative aspect that causes an instantaneous response. This symbol may also point to denial.

SELECTIVE SERVICE emphasizes a forced participation.

SELF-ABSORBED warns against placing self as one's priority in life; completely devoted to satisfying oneself.

SELF-ADHESIVE relates to a cohesive aspect that can come only from oneself.

SELF-ANALYSIS reminds us to recheck our motives, perspectives, and behavior for personal affectations.

SELF-APPOINTED cautions against making oneself an authority.

SELF-BASTING refers to an inner awareness for the purpose of maintaining smooth relationships.

SELF-CENTEREDNESS warns against thinking only of self; a love of one's ego; putting oneself first.

SELF-CLEANING portrays a continual monitoring of one's motives and perspectives.

SELF-CONSCIOUSNESS signifies a tendency to feel inferior to one's peers.

SELF-CONTAINED stands for having all the necessary elements of something; may point to one's own sense/state of self-reliance.

SELF-CONTROL reflects a focused individual who has mastered emotional responses and has the inner strength to resist distractions.

SELF-DEFEATING reveals unproductive choices regarding sticking to goals.

SELF-DEFENSE CLASS suggests a way to protect oneself. This may not only refer to physical defenses, but may also represent emotional or spiritual aspects.

SELF-DEPRECATING points to behavior one isn't giving oneself enough credit for.

SELF-DESTRUCTIVE warns against continuing behavior which harms oneself.

SELF-DOUBT implies one's personal lack of confidence in self.

SELF-EMPLOYED characterizes resourcefulness; self-sufficiency.

SELF-EXAMINATION stands for a need to analyze one's perspective or behavior.

SELF-HELP (resources) constitutes a desire to improve oneself. Recall what type of self-help sources were shown.

SELF-IMAGE See mirror.

SELF-INDULGENT comes as an advisement to start considering others.

SELF-INFLICTED exposes the fact that one's troubles were caused by self; self-defeating behavior.

SELF-LIMITING stands for some type of inner fear that prevents one from reaching for further discovery or progression.

SELF-MADE will stand for an individual who reached goals through his/her own efforts and intellect.

SELF-POLLINATION stands for one's ability to generate one's own motivating factors.

SELF-PORTRAIT will reveal how one sees self. This is a very important and revealing dream symbol.

SELF-PROCLAIMED correlates to how one wishes to be known.

SELF-PROPELLED indicates great stores of inner power (energy and motivation).

SELF-PUBLISH relates to personal efforts and determination put into disseminating one's own ideas or perspectives.

SELF-REGULATING signifies behavior guided by one's conscience.

SELF-RESTRAINT stands for one's will power.

SELF-RISING FLOUR suggests a resourceful individual; having knowledge and the associated wisdom; perseverance to rise above adversity.

SELF-SACRIFICE stands for placing others before self; an ability to resist life elements that one knows will be self-defeating or a detriment to goals.

SELF-SEALING signifies an element which, by its very nature, will bring about closure.

SELF-SERVICE represents a call to help self instead of depending on others for same.

SELF-STARTER stands for a well-motivated individual.

SELF-STICK relates to an element having cohesiveness by its very nature.

SELF-SUFFICIENCY refers to a self-reliant personality; creativity and resourcefulness.

SELF-TAUGHT signifies an individual motivated to seek his/her own answers.

SELF-WINDING represents inner strength and motivation to keep going; fortitude.

SELLER'S MARKET symbolizes a lack of opportunities; few choices.

SELLING POINT connotes a convincing aspect; an attractive element.

SELLOUT may indicate a popular issue or concept, or it may represent some type of betrayal.

SELTZER See soda water.

SELVAGE (of fabric) relates to something that will remain intact; will not come apart or undone.

SEMICIRCLE See crescent (shape).

SEMICONSCIOUS exposes a state of half awareness; advises one to be more aware and focused.

SEMIFINAL indicates the stage of progression that has brought one close to the attainment of a goal.

SEMIFORMAL stands for a semi-serious situation or issue, one needing greater than casual notice or attention.

SEMI-GLOSS (finish) denotes a downplayed finish to one's character veneer. This refers to a more refined appearance rather than a glossy, glitzy one.

SEMINAR connotes expanded education; more in-depth information.

SEMINARY pertains to efforts expended for the purpose of gaining deeper spiritual knowledge.

SEMIPRIVATE (room) refers to a situation in which other ears and eyes are present. This symbol comes to reveal a need for circumspection even though one may think one's behavior is unobserved.

SEMIRETIRED will point to one keeping one's hand in things.

SEMISWEET (flavor/taste) symbolizes a dual nature to something; being slightly bitter along with a sense of sweetness.

SEMITRAILER exposes a physical overload; physical stress from overburdening oneself.

SENATE See Congress.

SENATOR characterizes an individual who is in a position to listen to the problems, complaints, and wishes of others and expend efforts to change things for the better.

SENDOFF reflects an expression of encouragement and support. In some cases, a dreamscape sendoff can refer to something the dreamer needs to get rid of.

SENILITY See Alzheimer's Disease.

SENIOR CENTER corresponds to an opportunity to learn from those who have gained experience and knowledge.

SENIOR CITIZEN represents experiential knowledge and wisdom gained.

SENIORITY denotes a higher position; may refer to attained knowledge, experience, or spiritual advancement. May stand for others who have gone before us.

SENSATIONALISM cautions one to readjust priorities.

SENSITIVITY TRAINING comes as an advisement to be more emotionally responsive to others.

SENSORY DEPRIVATION is usually a warning to stop depriving oneself of emotional expression or interaction; insensitivity; possible apathy.

SENTENCING stands for a manner of retribution needed; an advisement to balance out or correct a wrongdoing.

SENTIMENTALITY denotes an open heart; compassion and understanding; emotional receptiveness.

SENTINEL characterizes heightened awareness; watchfulness.

SENTRY See guard.

SEPARATION ANXIETY stands for a need for support; an inability to be independent; fear of independence.

SEPARATIST will not necessarily depict a negative meaning; it may caution one to keep diverse concepts separate instead of combining them erroneously, or this symbol could also come as a personal advisement to stay out of other people's business.

SEPIA (color/photograph) pertains to innocent ignorance; an undeveloped concept or perspective.

SEPTEMBER represents a waning period; a winding down.

SEPTIC TANK/SYSTEM illustrates the complete disposal of the extraneous mental/emotional waste of one's life; ridding oneself of the extra burdens we shouldn't be carrying.

SEPULCHER See mausoleum.

SEQUEL represents a continuation; not the end of something.

SEQUENTIAL signifies a need to take one thing at a time.

SEQUIN portrays a flash to one's personality or character which may directly refer to lights of spiritual attainment.

SEQUOIA See redwood forest.

SERAPE symbolizes personal freedom; a unique life path.

SERENADE stands for an expression of affection. In some cases, this dream symbol may also point to efforts made toward winning over another.

SERENDIPITY pertains to a phase of fortunate events.

SERENITY indicates inner harmony.

SERF See servant.

SERGE (fabric) indicates an unyielding personality.

SERIAL KILLER will usually suggest a self-generated condition whereby one routinely performs in a self-defeating manner; the methodical killing of one's opportunities.

SERIAL NUMBER comes as a numerical message. Recall the sequence then add them together to determine the final number of the message.

SERIES CIRCUIT advises one to deduce in a logical and methodical manner.

SERMON usually brings a personal message for each dreamer. What was the sermon about?

SERPENT See snake.

SERPENTINE (configuration) denotes a winding life path.

SERPENTINE (gemstone) stands for one's duality of character and suggests a need for greater balance to be maintained between the extremes.

SERRATED See saw-toothed.

SERVANT will caution one against being taken advantage of.

SERVICEBERRY (tree) points to opportunity and the awareness of it.

SERVICE CENTER will indicate a source capable of providing repairs or solutions.

SERVICE CHARGE represents an encumbrance connected to a decision or idea; a price associated with something one wants.

SERVICE ELEVATOR/ENTRANCE denotes maintenance/repairs/care being done behind the scenes.

SERVICE MARK is an attempt to define one's purpose.

SERVICE MEDAL stands for recognition for one's efforts expended on a specific project or goal; may indicate a private acknowledgment of unconditional goodness or one's quiet acceptance.

SERVICE ROAD signifies an alternate, slower and less stressful route which leads to the same goal.

SERVICE STATION See gas station.

SERVING TRAY reflects order; efficiency.

SESAME SEED/OIL alludes to a beneficial element in one's life.

SETBACK (from property line) stands for a limit or boundary line marking the extent one can build on; a point to which one can take plans or action.

SET DESIGNER (film/stage) stands for the perceptive ability to create an atmosphere which is appropriately consistent with the mood of events and their participants.

SETI (ET project) represents a method of searching based on an assumption.

SETSCREW suggests an attempt to stabilize an issue/situation.

SETTEE See couch.

SETTLEMENT See colony.

SETTLEMENT (agreement) stands for a need to negotiate and reconcile.

SETTLING CRACKS (in building) represent the seasoning of an idea or situation.

SEVEN signifies a high spiritual attainment.

SEVEN DWARFS stand for the six main energy forces within the body in association with one's activating spiritual development.

SEVEN SEALS represent the stages of spiritual enlightenment.

SEVENTH AVENUE portrays one's outward affectations of aloofness.

SEVENTH HEAVEN depicts a state of extreme happiness.

SEVENTH-INNING STRETCH advises of a need to take time out from overexpending efforts.

SEVER refers to a cutting off or cutting out some type of aspect in one's life.

SEVERANCE PAY exemplifies a benefit or reward for efforts expended toward a former life aspect. May point to a time to move on.

SEWAGE signifies life's basest elements.

SEWAGE TREATMENT PLANT signifies an attempt to salvage a bad situation; efforts expended to improve a bad situation.

SEWER will denote a condition, place, or situation containing highly negative aspects.

SEWING applies to a bringing together; a desire to reconnect; coalesce. This symbol comes when one has severed self from a relationship, belief, or situation with which now requires reconnection.

SEWING MACHINE represents a tool and/or opportunity that can be used to correct a severed situation or relationship that has fallen apart.

SEX is a symbol that correlates with one's manner of communication with others; quality of relationships and type of behavior toward them. Recall what type of sexual presentation was made. Gentle? Violent? Possessive? Deviant?

SEX APPEAL won't necessarily relate to a temptress, for this symbol most often refers to one's personal magnetism; a type of personality that attracts others.

SEX CHANGE reflects an inability to accept and relate to the specific elements one's spirit has chosen to utilize for one's current path progression. This symbol may also reveal a strong recognition with one's prime spirit identity which cannot be overcome by the current life status.

SEXTANT portrays a desire to understand one's personal relationship with spiritual elements.

SEXUAL ASSAULT denotes an irresistible desire for control. This symbol reveals a belief that the only way one can gain control is by forcing it.

SEXUAL DISEASE exposes the result of indiscriminate behavior; lack of responsible discernment and restraint.

SEXUAL HARASSMENT reveals a lack of respect; more importantly, it reveals a lack of spiritual advancement.

SHABBY (appearance) will usually denote weariness.

SHACK (dwelling) exemplifies disinterest in material possessions.

SHACKLES most often refer to self-imposed restrictions, yet also point to restraints or limitations others have imposed on one.

SHAD (fish) denotes spiritual insignificance; superfluous facets.

SHADE See ghost.

SHADE (window) pertains to privacy. May indicate selective perception.

SHADE TREE applies to respite.

SHADOW may pertain to dark (negative) elements or it may represent oneself, depending on the dream's surrounding details.

SHADOW BOX (shelf) displays accumulated affectations and/or specific interests unique to the individual. What objects one places in a shadowbox reveals much about one's character.

SHADOWBOXING reveals a conflict within self.

SHADOW PLAY refers to behind-the-scenes behavior.

SHAFT See mineshaft.

SHAGGY (fabric/hair) represents a disorderly thought process.

SHAKE (shingle) suggests flammable thoughts; ideas capable of inciting others.

SHAKEDOWN refers to a forced method of obtaining something.

SHAKEN-BABY SYNDROME connotes the willful destruction of a new idea or opportunity.

SHAKER (furniture style) stands for simplicity regarding one's needs.

SHAKERS (sect) See Quakers.

SHAKESPEARE (William) reminds us of moral and ethical obligations and the behaviors leading to life tragedies.

SHALE pertains to loose footing; a current state of instability.

SHALLOT See green onion.

SHALLOW signifies surface aspects; a lack of depth.

SHAM (pillow) denotes an empty element; a cover story.

SHAMAN characterizes the higher spiritual abilities and the associated sacredness.

SHAMBLES symbolize ruination; the destruction of something in one's life.

SHAME typifies guilt or humiliation.

SHAMPOO applies to the act of cleansing one's thoughts to get rid of negativity or extraneous elements.

SHAMROCK symbolizes the three aspects of the Divine Essence.

SHANTUNG (fabric) denotes roughly disguised finesse.

SHANTY See shack.

SHANTY (ice fishing) represents an effort to remain diligent at gaining spiritual insights.

SHARD exemplifies a hint, clue, or beginning insight; a fragment of an idea.

SHARECROPPER characterizes the expending of efforts for the good of the whole.

SHAREHOLDER indicates those who have contributed toward something and have invested their resources and confidence.

SHARING portrays selflessness.

SHARK corresponds to religious fanatics; those who try to convert others to their beliefs in a relentless manner.

SHARKSKIN (fabric) relates to a spiritually unethical personality.

SHARPEN See hone.

SHARPSHOOTER suggests a need for discernment and accurate judgments.

SHARP-TONGUED denotes an inability to temper one's words.

SHARP-WITTED signifies astuteness.

SHASTA DAISY (botanical) suggests inner joy from sharing one's natural talents.

SHATTER refers to a totally destroyed element.

SHATTERPROOF GLASS See safety glass.

SHAVER See razor.

SHAVING (hair) stands for a reluctance to reveal thoughts. May also point to an effort to present a veneer of integrity.

SHAVING CREAM denotes an element which helps to soothe an abrasive situation or relationship.

SHAVINGS (metal) represent the harsher aspects of self that have been shed.

SHAVINGS (wood) stands for the formation of a personal method of using one's natural spiritual gifts.

SHAWL alludes to personal ideals, thoughts, and beliefs that are loosely concealed.

SHEAR (shave) relates to a desire to clearly comprehend the basics of an idea or concept.

SHEARLING (fabric) denotes warmth of character.

SHEARS See scissors.

SHEATH represents a cover of some type.

SHED will typify resource reserves; stored energy or inner strength.

SHEDDING (loose hair) refers to the natural course of old ideas falling away.

SHEEN implies an inner beauty.

SHEEP reveals a lack of individuality and/or assertiveness.

SHEEPDOG See Old English sheepdog.

SHEEPSKIN signifies warmth and comfort; may refer to emotional responses/ support.

SHEER (fabric) reveals a transparent personality.

SHEER (steep) emphasizes caution in respect to there being no room for error. Also see steep (vertical).

SHEET (bed) See bedding (clothes or linens).

SHEET LIGHTNING represents a reflection of one's spiritual essence within self; a reminder of such a presence.

SHEET METAL signifies personal strength that is used in all aspects of life.

SHEET MUSIC alludes to the personally composed inner music with which we progress through life; may bring a special message if the sheet music was titled.

SHEETROCK See drywall.

SHELF illustrates stored elements that may need to be set aside for a time; may reveal valuable aspects that need to be preserved.

SHELF LIFE connotes a specified span of time for an element in one's life to be viable.

SHELF ROAD represents a precarious path currently being traveled.

SHELL (bombard) constitutes an inundation.

SHELL (bullet) See ammunition.

SHELL (egg) See eggshell.

SHELL (husk) suggests a need to break through or get at the core of something in one's life.

SHELL (sea) See seashell.

SHELL (structure) signifies an incomplete home life or inner aspect of oneself.

SHELLAC represents a finished issue; a finalization.

SHELLFISH relate to an attempt to absorb as many spiritual aspects as possible.

SHELL GAME applies to evasion; a possible swindle; unethical methods; attempt to confuse.

SHELLPROOF reflects a well-protected self; wise precautions set in place to prevent the entry of unwanted or negative elements; high awareness and discernment.

SHELL-SHOCKED exposes traumatic effects from an experience.

SHELTER See specific type.

SHELTIE (animal breed) See Shetland pony; Shetland sheepdog.

SHEPHERD signifies watchfulness or guardianship.

SHEPHERD'S PIE denotes simple, basic sustenance.

SHEPHERD'S-PURSE (botanical) corresponds to beneficial elements that encourage thoughtfulness.

SHERBET (frozen) applies to a desire to have fewer responsibilities in life.

SHERIFF typifies an authority figure representing the rules or laws.

SHERRY See wine.

SHERWOOD FOREST alludes to a place of safety; respite.

SHETLAND PONY pertains to concealed personal power.

SHETLAND SHEEPDOG (dog breed) depicts protectiveness; watchfulness.

SHIATSU (massage technique) portrays a need for clearing mental and emotional blocks.

SHIELD connotes one's personal form of self-protection that may include mental, emotional, or spiritual elements.

SHIFT (action) signifies an altered perspective, attitude, or pace; also may literally refer to transmission.

SHIFTLESS implies a lack of motivation or energy.

SHIH TZU (dog breed) suggests a non-judgmental friend, close companionship.

SHIM reflects a temporary solution; a stop-gap move.

SHIMMER will most often indicate a spiritual connotation.

SHINER See black eye (bruise).

SHINGLE (roof) symbolizes subconscious defense mechanisms and/or the character of one's thoughts.

SHINGLES (on skin) reveal an emotional

disruption within oneself; internal conflict.

SHIP signifies a method or vehicle that facilitates a spiritual search.

SHIPBUILDER characterizes one who expends efforts to carefully and systematically plan out and manifest one's spiritual search.

SHIPBUILDING stands for the construction of one's spiritual search plan.

SHIPMATE refers to a companion on one's spiritual walk. This points to an individual who shares one's beliefs.

SHIPMENT relates to a forthcoming aspect one is awaiting; may also refer to something one is planning on doing or sending out.

SHIPPING CLERK characterizes an individual who is capable of keeping track of where everything is going, who is getting what. This means the scorekeeper and may even point to oneself and the responsibility to keep one's records balanced.

SHIPWRECK illustrates a spiritual failure or misdirection.

SHIPYARD denotes preparations/intentions to embark on a spiritual journey, perhaps travel over new spiritual waters (new concepts).

SHIRT See blouse.

SHIRTTAIL relates to personal methods used to help others.

SHISH KABOB alludes to multiple nourishing elements in one's life.

SHIVER (tremble) signifies an effort to counter a negative element.

SHOAL exposes spiritual shallowness.

SHOCK ABSORBER emphasizes emotional and intellectual stability.

S

SHOCK-JOCK will stand for someone who blurts out whatever she/he is thinking without consideration for the sensitivities of others. Depending on the related dreamscape elements, this symbol may have a positive connotation; someone who tells it like it is (bottom-line honesty)—and usually this honesty is directed toward someone needing to hear it.

SHOCKPROOF usually indicates a hardened personality, one who expects the worst.

SHOCK WAVE applies to future repercussions expected from a deed done.

SHOE usually indicates how one's path is traveled. Refer to specific type.

SHOE BOX correlates to the multiple personal methods used during one's progression in life; the various types of shoes worn. Recall any wording on the box.

SHOEHORN implies a need to take larger steps toward one's path progression or life goal instead of always trying to stuff oneself into a confined path or manner of walking.

SHOELACE indicates the condition of one's manner of walking a life path. Was the lace untied? Dirty? Too tight? Broken?

SHOEMAKER characterizes an individual who has the capability to guide the life paths of others.

SHOE REPAIR (shop) stands for a source for mending one's path difficulties; someone who can provide motivation and get one back on course.

SHOE-SHINE refers to a desire to impress others with one's method or manner of moving through life. This might point to someone who hints at or boasts that life is easier for him/her.

SHOESTRING denotes meager resources.

SHOETREE signifies an assortment of methods to utilize while walking through the varied phases of one's life path.

SHOJI (paper partition) typifies a thin veneer to one's inner self.

SHOOT (plant) See sprout.

SHOOTING GALLERY (drugs) warns of a situation or relationship where potentially dangerous negative elements are present.

SHOOTING GALLERY (weapons) corresponds to an advisement to give greater attention to one's personal protective/defensive measures.

SHOOTING MATCH indicates an out-of-control disagreement/conflict.

SHOOTING SCRIPT represents one's finalized plan, theory, or decision.

SHOOTING STAR indicates the loss or failing of an important spiritual element; suggests that one has ignored, forgotten, or allowed major spiritual truths to die out. May point to a loss of faith. Depending on related dreamscape elements, this symbol may also point to an appreciation of one's uniqueness.

SHOOTOUT pertains to the resolving of a conflict and won't necessarily infer that this is done in a negative manner.

SHOP (retail) constitutes supply or opportunity. The *type* of shop will be the important element here.

SHOP-AHOLIC signifies one who is continually seeking self-gratification; may point to a tendency toward conflict or resolution avoidance; attempts to replace a void in one's life with continual gifts to oneself.

SHOP DRAWINGS refer to workable plans.

SHOPKEEPER characterizes an individual who provides a service or opportunity for others.

SHOPLIFT See steal.

SHOPPING emphasizes the act of looking for something; searching.

SHOPPING BAG infers expectation; an intent to obtain a need or desire. Were any emblems or words on the bag? What color was it?

SHOPPING CART stands for high expectations.

SHOPPING CENTER See mall.

SHOPPING LIST calls attention to one's need to not forget important elements of an issue or situation. This symbol won't usually stand for things one needs to buy.

SHOP STEWARD characterizes a person who listens to your ideas, complaints, etc. and may have the ability to make changes for the better or bring about a resolution.

SHOPTALK represents a need to attend to one's business at hand; refers to a return to one's life goal or plan.

SHORE (land) will allude to the boundaries of one's spiritual search or direction.

SHORE (support) pertains to a temporary supportive move.

SHORE LEAVE symbolizes a break from one's spiritual search which will provide contemplative time or a required period of respite.

SHORE PATROL reflects one's inner spiritual guidance; conscience.

SHORING (support) reveals efforts made to strengthen or preserve a situation or relationship.

SHORT connotes a concise element; may also indicate a need to expand some aspect in one's life.

SHORTBREAD/CAKE implies a source of energy.

SHORTCHANGED correlates to a debt owed. Recall who was shortchanged.

SHORT CIRCUIT reveals severe misconceptions and/or mental confusion.

SHORTCUT portrays a more efficient method of accomplishing something.

SHORT DIVISION refers to a quick calculation; something that's easy to figure out.

SHORTENING connotes a required aspect of an element; a key ingredient.

SHORTFALL suggests something which was overrated or held in expectations which were unrealistic; disappointment.

SHORT FUSE comes to advise one to be more patient, tolerant.

SHORTHAND (note-taking) signifies resourcefulness; efficiency.

SHORT-HANDED points to a situation where one is forced to work harder.

SHORT LINE reveals a phase of one's path or life that won't be lengthy.

SHORTLIST refers to the top-rated, most desirable choices.

SHORT-LIVED points to a fleeting aspect. This aspect could refer to an emotion, a result of something, a positive/negative result, etc.

SHORT-ORDER COOK characterizes multiple capabilities.

SHORT-PAY (check) denotes an attempt to get away with not paying full value for worth or another's expended efforts. Usually this will refer to a lack of appreciation for another's efforts.

SHORT-RANGE suggests quick benefits, yet they may not be as desirable as those coming after a longer-range plan or greater efforts expended.

SHORT-RUN (time) signifies a plan which reaps early benefits.

SHORT SHORTS See hot pants.

SHORTSIGHTED refers to an inability to perceive the full scope or long range aspects of an issue or plan. Also see myopia.

SHORTSTOP characterizes a versatile individual.

SHORT STORY typifies a specialized message for the dreamer.

SHORT-TERM defines a qualified span of time. Recall what this time was related to.

SHORT-WAVE (radio) See ham radio.

SHORT-WINDED usually points to something said in a concise manner; the main issue packed in a nutshell.

SHOT See ammunition.

SHOT See injection.

SHOT (wounded) exposes an inability to defend oneself; refers to an event that emotionally, mentally, or spiritually injured oneself.

SHOT GLASS points to a small amount of something one ingested. Each dreamer will relate to something different here.

SHOTGUN connotes a life element that has the capability of causing multiple ramifications.

SHOTGUN HOUSE not only stands for commonality, it represents a tendency or preference to be like everyone else; a lack of individuality.

SHOTGUN WEDDING constitutes a forced relationship.

SHOT-PUT (sport) pertains to an attempt to make the most out of one's applied efforts.

SHOULDER (anatomy) will denote the quality and quantity of one's inner strength. Recall if the dream shoulder was slouched, rounded, padded, thick, etc.

SHOULDER (of road) suggests an emergency contingency.

SHOULDER HOLSTER portrays strong defensive/protective measures.

SHOULDER PADS allude to false strength.

SHOUTING will serve as an individual message for each dreamer. Recall who was doing the shouting and what was said.

SHOVE will usually represent a motivational push of some type.

SHOVEL connotes an individual's tendency to overindulge; may refer to the intake or output aspects.

SHOW-AND-TELL comes as a private message for each dreamer. Recall what was shown and told about. Who was doing the showing?

SHOW BILL refers to exaggerations; making a big production of something.

SHOW BIZ signifies a tendency to be in the limelight; a love of an audience.

SHOWBOAT warns of spiritual arrogance; spiritual flaunting.

SHOWCASE depicts what a person values; one's priorities. What was in the dreamscape showcase? Was the glass clear, clouded, or colored? Was the glass cracked?

SHOWDOWN represents the time for confrontation or resolution.

SHOWER (bathing) indicates a need for some type of inner cleansing.

SHOWER (rain) implies a gentle touch of spiritual elements.

SHOWER CURTAIN will expose one's inner negative character aspects. Recall if there were designs on this curtain. What color was it? Was it dirty? Torn?

SHOWER HEAD reflects an individual's strength of intention. Recall what type of shower head it was. Was it a water saver? Was it a massage type? Was it running? If so, was it a hard or gentle spray?

SHOWOFF exposes a personal need for attention.

SHOWPIECE suggests an example of excellence.

SHOW PLACE symbolizes a presentation of perfection to others.

SHOW ROOM will display an array of specific opportunities for the dreamer. Recall what type of show room it was.

SHOWSTOPPER reveals an outstanding performance; implies commendation. May also point to an element that cuts off all adversity or opposing opinion; verification.

SHOW TIME advises of the right time to put an idea into action.

SHOW TUNE corresponds with a specific message for the dreamer. Recall what the tune was.

SHOW WINDOW will usually be an attention-getting venue which literally shows what one needs or points to a solution. The key here isn't the window itself but whatever it featured.

SHRAPNEL denotes those aspects in one's life that leave permanent damage or reminders behind.

SHRED (any type) signifies a fragment of whatever was depicted; refers to remains.

SHREDDER (paper) represents an attempt to hide or get rid of some type of evidence; concealment. May point to efforts at maintaining one's privacy.

SHREW connotes an individual who is never satisfied; a complainer.

SHRIKE (bird) stands for a predatory nature; lacking moral/ethical integrity; vindictiveness.

SHRILL (sound) signifies a harsh message or lesson.

SHRIMP symbolizes the absorption of the more refined spiritual aspects.

SHRIMP BOAT corresponds with a desire to search out and obtain spiritual understanding.

SHRIMP COCKTAIL denotes a tendency to maintain spiritual connotations throughout one's daily interactions.

SHRINE cautions against focusing on singular spiritual facets.

SHRINKING pertains to a waning effect; a diminishing factor. Recall what was shrinking.

SHRINK-WRAP represents an attempt to preserve some aspect in one's life.

SHRIVELED denotes a loss of energy and vitality. This may be a positive sign, depending on the surrounding dream details.

SHROUD exemplifies concealment of one's darker aspects.

SHRUBBERY implies natural talents and the opportunities to use them.

SHRUG points to indecision or nonchalance.

SHUCK See husk.

SHUDDER suggests an inner fear and the recognition of it.

SHUFFLE (cards) connotes an altering of probabilities; changing the possible outcomes.

SHUFFLE (feet) applies to a defeated attitude; may infer weariness.

SHUFFLEBOARD (game) exemplifies congenial competition; friendly contention.

SHUN represents a voluntary disregard for something. Depending on the related elements of the dream, this may be a positive symbol.

SHUNT means an intentional diversion; a setting aside for a time.

SHUTDOWN will most often refer to avoidance; may point to outright denial. This symbol could also come as an advisement to stop some type of attitude or behavior, it needs to be shut down.

SHUT-IN comes as an advisement to go within for the purpose of self-discovery.

SHUTOFF VALVE represents an opportunity to gain needed control. Comes to reveal the presence of a possibility to stop something.

SHUTTER (camera) corresponds to one's personal perspective and how well it's used; awareness; insights.

SHUTTER (window) symbolizes open-mindedness. Recall if the shutters were closed tight or opened wide. What color were they? What was their overall condition?

SHUTTER SPEED reveals one's level of astuteness.

SHUTTLE illustrates intermediate paths and/or directions in life.

SHUTTLE (weaving) pertains to a facilitating element in one's life.

SHYNESS may reveal innocence or a lack of self-esteem.

SHYLOCK characterizes a self-serving individual who takes ruthless advantage of others.

SHYSTER portrays an unscrupulous individual; unethical.

SIAMESE CAT represents sharp perception.

SIAMESE FIGHTING FISH stands for spiritual argumentativeness; points to a tendency to debate concepts and/or the spiritual beliefs of others.

SIAMESE TWIN See conjoined twins.

SIBERIA stands for a remoteness of some type; a distancing; may refer to being far off the mark.

SIBERIAN HUSKY (dog breed) See Husky.

SIBLING won't necessarily represent a close relationship but rather will pertain to someone you are meant to closely interrelate with for a time.

SIBYL (ancient Greek/Roman culture) characterizes an individual possessing strong prophetic abilities.

SICKBAY exposes a spiritual sickness of some type that may be caused by external sources or may be self-generated.

SICK DAY most often comes in dreams to advise of a need to take a well-deserved break.

SICKLE pertains to an opportunity to rid oneself of extraneous aspects; cutting down on the unnecessary elements.

SICK LEAVE represents an extended amount of time or phase in one's life when time is taken for recuperative purposes.

SICK-OUT refers to people who share an attitude of disagreement over the same issue and join together to exhibit a silent protest; a passive expression of protest.

SICK PAY stands for the benefits gained from taking the time off to take care of oneself. This symbol usually comes as an advisement.

SICK PEOPLE illustrate mental dysfunctions or physical diseases. Recall what the illnesses were. Also refer to sick-out.

SICKROOM won't necessarily refer to a literally sick individual, but more often points to the negative elements in one's life (bad feelings) that are withheld or carried around and have the potential to ultimately cause harm.

SIDEARM (pitching style) represents exceptional inner strength.

SIDEBAR corresponds to additional information.

SIDE BET represents an unofficial risk.

SIDEBOARD stands for psychological elements that affect attitudes and opinions.

SIDEBURNS connote a desire to appear intellectual or more mature; may indicate attitudes or ideas that are held off to the side (not openly expressed).

SIDECAR relates to a free ride or an attempt to progress along one's path without applying personal effort.

SIDE CHAIR suggests a secondary position.

SIDE DISH will represent aspects that enhance a main element.

SIDE EFFECTS exemplify multiple ramifications of an action taken.

SIDE-GLANCE symbolizes personal observations; a surreptitious awareness.

SIDEKICK reveals a close companion; an individual who can be counted on.

SIDELINE will illustrate a position of observation; may also indicate an extra activity in association with one's main purpose.

SIDE SHOW refers to those aspects in one's life that are ridiculous or outrageous in respect to one's serious path or purpose.

SIDESTEP correlated to a diversionary tactic; an avoidance of something.

SIDE STREET denotes an off-the-main-track diversion.

SIDE STROKE suggests that one is traveling one's spiritual path and only seeing half of what's there to learn from.

SIDESWIPED stands for a brush with a negative element; a close call.

SIDETRACKED depicts a loss of one's focus on a life goal or issue.

SIDE TRIP symbolizes efforts put into gaining a more rounded impression or experience of something.

SIDEWALK relates to directed paths to follow; implies a need to make one's own course. Recall condition of the dream sidewalk. Was it new? Cracked? Overgrown with weeds?

SIDEWAYS (movement) will usually connote a move to avoid something; an elusive tactic.

SIDEWINDER (snake) represents plans that are secretly held until the actual moment for action. This won't always refer to underhandedness or dirty dealings. Whether this is a positive or negative symbol will depend on the surrounding related elements.

SIDING (on dwelling) signifies an

attempt to alter appearances or efforts expended toward further insulating oneself from something.

SIDING (train track) stands for something that's been set aside for the moment; a temporary postponement.

SIEGE applies to an overwhelming inundation of something in one's life.

SIENNA (color) pertains to an earthiness to one's inner nature.

SIERRA See saw-toothed mountains.

SIESTA See nap (sleep).

SIEVE warns of an inability to manage personal containment; lacking self-control.

SIFT represents extensive research.

SIGH typifies disappointment or weariness.

SIGHTLESS See blind (sightless).

SIGHT-READING points to acute perception and lightning responses.

SIGHTSEEING cautions against superficiality; cursory knowledge.

SIGN will come as a personal message for each dreamer. Recall what the sign said. Was it a directional one? Was it a stop or yield?

SIGNAL (light) is an advisement regarding one's pace through life.

SIGNAL BOARD represents one's instincts; inner knowing/perception; lightning psychic impressions.

SIGNAL PERSON stands for an individual who keeps one on the right track, this could even be one's own conscience or inner sense of direction.

SIGNATURE may indicate authority or provide a specialized message for the dreamer.

SIGNATURE LOAN represents a risk-free benefit.

SIGNET RING See ring (jewelry).

SIGNIFICANT OTHER will always represent the one individual in a person's life who is held closest in one's heart; a lover or cherished individual.

SIGNING IN represents one's readiness to actively participate in something; an intent to expend energy.

SIGNING OFF/OUT signifies one's intention to leave something; one has chosen not to expend more energy on an issue.

SIGNING UP denotes joining something. This may or may not be willingly. The key here is to recall what one was signing up for.

SIGN LANGUAGE reminds us that there are multiple forms of communication that can be effectively used.

SIGN OF THE CROSS (gesture) usually points to a silent prayer but may not refer to the literal act of praying, rather being an outward expression of one's frustration or even hope.

SIGN PAINTER will bring a personal message for each dreamer. Recall what was being painted. What colors were dominant? Who was the painter?

SIGNPOST stands for path markers. These need to be heeded.

SILENCE is an attention-getting dream element that most often advises us to listen to one's conscience.

SILENCER (gun) represents the quiet, silent negative forces that can affect those who don't maintain high personal awareness or become lax.

SILENT ALARM almost always equates to our inner awareness; instinctual warning system and sense of forewarning.

SILENT AUCTION signifies a situation where one is forced to pay a higher price (expend greater efforts) than necessary to insure success or the attainment of a specific goal.

SILENT MONITORING See listening device.

SILENT PARTNER usually stands for one's own conscience; inner guidance.

SILENT TREATMENT won't necessarily be a negative symbol but rather a method of making others think for themselves.

SILHOUETTE constitutes an outline form and cautions one against accepting same as an entirety or whole.

SILICONE represents a multifaceted and versatile tool or opportunity.

SILICONE VALLEY represents the leading edge source for idea development.

SILK (fabric) suggests an inner refinement; a delicate strength.

SILK FLOWERS exemplify lasting beauty. Refer to specific flower type for deeper meaning here.

SILK HAT pertains to a desire to appear successful; extravagance.

SILK-SCREEN denotes replication; may bring a personal message for each dreamer.

SILK TREE indicates sensitivity toward a delicate situation or relationship.

SILKWEED (botanical) will reveal a beneficial element in one's life.

SILKWORM connotes the source of great inner strength.

SILL (geologic) suggests an out-of-character response or it may indicate a need to diverge from one's normal course.

SILL (window) represents the lower confines of one's overall perspective.

SILLINESS doesn't need to infer immaturity, but it may indicate a need to be less serious for a time. This symbol says, "Hey, loosen up! Chill out!"

SILO connotes that which is stored and may refer to an individual's emotional, mental, or intellectual aspects.

SILT relates to spiritual elements that are not germane to one's personal advancement or development.

SILVER (color/metal) stands for the spiritual elements that exist for everyone. The key here is to recall what form the dream silver took and what was being done with it by whom.

SILVER BULLET signifies a final solution; something which is capable of putting an end to a negative element.

SILVER CERTIFICATE represents a highly valuable aspect in one's life; a rarity.

SILVER DOLLAR denotes honesty.

SILVERFISH reveals a damaging element in one's life.

SILVER LINING reveals an unseen or unexpected benefit.

SILVER PLATE suggests a veneer of spiritual elements.

SILVERSMITH characterizes a spiritually ethical individual.

SILVER SPOON symbolizes a lack of experiential learning opportunities.

SILVER-TONGUE implies an influential and persuasive personality.

SILVERWARE relates to utilitarian elements in one's life.

SILVERWARE CHEST corresponds to a

recognition and appreciation for the often unnoticed aids one utilizes throughout life.

SIMMER exemplifies thoughtfulness; contemplation; time expended on logic and rationale. In some dreams, depending on the related elements, this symbol can warn against stewing over something; a need to clear the air and quit fuming.

SIMPLETON See fool.

SIMPLICITY pertains to a firm understanding of correct priorities.

SIMULATION will denote a reproduction or practice effort.

SIMULCAST depicts a multiple venue of communication.

SINCERITY reveals honesty; genuineness.

SINEW symbolizes a staunch character; having stamina.

SING-ALONG relates to shared sentiments.

SINGE See scorch.

SINGER connotes a communicator. Recall the dream's details to determine whether someone is telling what they know or merely gossiping.

SINGLE-HANDED signifies independence; resourcefulness; an ability to perform without the aid of others.

SINGLE-MINDED comes as a suggestion to stop being so focused that one is blind to all else.

SINHALITE (gemstone) refers to depression and calls for one to strive for a brighter outlook.

SINISTER usually stands for a sense of foreboding; ominous sense.

SINK (basin) refers to a life element capable of providing a cleansing opportunity.

SINKHOLE indicates the pitfalls and dangerous regions of one's life path.

SINKING refers to the beginnings of failure or sense of defeat.

SINUS CONGESTION See congestion (sinus).

SIPHON denotes an advisement to rid self of extraneous spiritual elements.

SIREN defines a strong warning. Recall the associated dreamscape elements for further clarity.

SISSY signifies a possible lack of courage, but may also be hiding independence; a determination against being coerced.

SISTER points to a close female relationship.

SISTERHOOD means female camaraderie.

SITAR portrays one's expression of inner feelings.

SITCOM brings a specific meaning to each dreamer. What was the show about and who were the players? What was the main theme of the specific sitcom?

SIT-DOWN expresses an active difference of opinion; a protest; may also point to efforts put into resolving a disagreement or conflict.

SITTING may indicate a lax attitude or it may come as an advisement to take time out.

SITTING DUCK pertains to the act of going out on a limb and placing oneself in a position of exposure.

SITTING ROOM See living room.

SITUATION ROOM represents a call to put efforts into resolving a conflict/disagreement.

SIT-UPS signify an advisement to gain greater tolerance—gut fortitude.

SITZ BATH indicates a call for emotional peace; an advisement to remove oneself from stressful situations.

SIX represents mental, emotional, and spiritual strength.

SIX-PACK See alcoholic beverage.

SIZZLING stands for intense withheld anger.

SKATEBOARD exemplifies an attempt to dodge life's burdens and difficult periods.

SKATING (ice) See ice skate.

SKATING (roller) suggests a desire to skate through life without encountering the tribulations that are meant to be dealt with and overcome.

SKEET (shooting) implies a tendency to shoot down ideas and concepts that are outside one's personal range of perceptual belief.

SKEIN portrays the threads of a theory or situation.

SKELETON may signify the bare bones of an issue or it may allude to personal hidden elements.

SKELETON CREW pertains to the least number of people or elements it will take to get something accomplished.

SKELETON KEY illustrates a life aspect that serves as a key opening multiple opportunities.

SKEPTIC characterizes an individual with a narrow perspective and a mind closed to new, expanded concepts; one having no view to probabilities or possibilities.

SKETCH denotes a tentative outline or trial and error formulation of a new idea.

SKETCHBOOK represents a wealth of new ideas; mental excursions into possibilities.

SKEWER symbolizes a very dangerous or negative element about to appear in one's life. Recall what was on the skewer? Who was holding it?

SKID (tool) refers to something that eases one's burden; something that serves to make advancement/movement easier.

SKIDDING warns of a loss of control; an out-of-control situation.

SKID MARKS reveal a former loss of footing along one's path.

SKID ROW represents a situation or issue in which one has become derelict.

SKIFF See boat.

SKI BOOTS signify an intention to ignore spiritual issues.

SKIING (snow) connotes spiritual indifference; ignoring one's spiritual beliefs or responsibilities as if they were frozen or nonexistent.

SKI JUMP pertains to the avoidance of spiritual aspects in one's life.

SKI LIFT represents material aspects one allows to lift one over spiritual responsibilities.

SKILL emphasizes one's unique talents.

SKILLET See frying pan.

SKIM (read) See scan.

SKIM (remove) indicates the act of selective choosing.

SKI MASK relates to those with shallow thoughts and those who have a tendency to avoid deeper concepts.

SKIM MILK illustrates a nourishing aspect in life that could have been more beneficial.

SKIN (animal) See pelt.

SKIN (human) relates to one's inner strength and general stamina. The condition, texture, and color are important elements to notice.

SKIN DISEASE will suggest a weakened state.

SKIN DIVING exemplifies a serious spiritual search.

SKIN GRAFT portrays an attempt to improve one's stamina.

SKINHEAD suggests intolerance; lacking acceptance of others' individuality.

SKINK See lizard.

SKINNY constitutes a frail and timid personality; denotes a lack of motivation and energized determination.

SKINNY-DIPPING represents an intent to immerse oneself in spiritual concepts; a joyful desire to gain spiritual knowledge.

SKIN TEST See scratch test (for allergy).

SKI PATROL refers to one's conscience.

SKI POLE alludes to personal aids one utilizes for the purpose of avoiding spiritual responsibility.

SKIPPING suggests joy, yet may also pertain to an attitude of indifference.

SKIPPING ROCKS refers to spiritual inattention; a lack of focus on one's spiritual behavior.

SKI RESORT signifies spiritual shallowness; the avoidance of higher concepts.

SKIRMISH infers a minor conflict.

SKI RUN corresponds with a means to swiftly avoid spiritual issues.

SKULL represents the encasement of one's thoughts; the embodiment of a persona's overall thought patterns.

SKULL AND CROSSBONES See Jolly Roger.

SKULLCAP (cap) corresponds to thoughts grounded in spiritual beliefs.

SKUNK connotes a strong desire for justice to prevail in life. Depending on the surrounding dreamscape elements this symbol may also refer to one's self-preservation methods.

SKY reflects the venue for thoughts. Different types of sky will represent specific thought patterns and tendencies. Recall color. Calm or angry? Type of clouds?

SKY BLUE (color) suggests clarity of understanding or presentation.

SKY BOX (arena/stadium) signifies a seemingly privileged viewpoint, yet costly.

SKYCAP See porter.

SKYDIVE corresponds to a dive into a specific thought or issue. This may also warn of uncontrolled thought patterns which could indicate mental instability.

SKYE TERRIER (dog breed) denotes a faithful friend.

SKYJACKING exposes the stealing of another's thoughts or ideas.

SKYLARK (bird) stands for happiness; joy; an optimistic perspective.

SKYLIGHT applies to open-mindedness; a willingness to let the light in. Recall if the skylight was a specific color. What condition was the glass in?

SKYLINE See horizon.

SKY MARSHALL will point to one's own hold/guard on thoughts.

SKYSCRAPER denotes higher thought used throughout one's daily life.

SKYWALK implies the use of one's higher intellect in business dealings.

SKYWRITING comes as a personal message from one's inner self or higher awareness. Be sure to recall what was written. Was the writing done in a color?

SLAB FLOOR suggests a firm opinion or foundation, one without any possibility to be open for debate.

SLACK represents a waning of energy or motivation.

SLALOM relates to a personally devised course set to evade spiritual issues.

SLAM portrays emphasis; force.

SLAM-DUNK indicates assuredness; confidence.

SLANDER pertains to vindictiveness; falsehoods.

SLANG will reveal an aspect of an individual's character.

SLANTED (floor) illustrates an adulterated aspect; a foundational concept/ideal that's affected by one's opinionated perspective.

SLASH See clear cutting.

SLATE (rock) implies a defensive/protective hardness to one's personality.

SLATE (roof) stands for apathy; having no sensitivity involved in thought processes.

SLATE (walkway) refers to a hard, difficult path.

SLAUGHTERHOUSE See meat-packing house.

SLAVE denotes servitude. The key here is to recall who was the slave and what he/she was doing for whom? One could be a slave to one's own desires or habits.

SLAVE DRIVER characterizes a person who demands hard work from others or perhaps only from oneself, depending on the surrounding dreamscape details.

SLEAZY portrays extremely poor taste; may indicate a contemptible element.

SLED connotes a life aspect that allows one to skim through life. This is not a positive dream symbol.

SLED DOG represents a friend who encourages an easy life path, one willing to pull another along.

SLEDGE may refer to a sled type of symbol or it may indicate a helpful aid in life.

SLEDGEHAMMER depicts forcefulness; a severe personality. May also point to an aspect requiring extreme measures.

SLEEKNESS suggests refinement.

SLEEP DEPRIVATION warns of a severe need to cut back on work and/or stressors.

SLEEPER CAR (train) See Pullman (rail car).

SLEEPING correlates with unawareness, possibly by choice.

SLEEPING BEAUTY won't normally be associated with a beautiful woman but rather the beautiful spirit and spiritual truths within everyone which not all of us acknowledge.

SLEEPING BERTH See berth (sleeping).

SLEEPING DOG signifies an unaware friend; may also indicate a friend who doesn't see her/his own potential.

SLEEPING GIANT can be associated with two meanings. It can refer to one's potential that isn't being acknowledged or it can refer to grudges/negative emotions/attitudes that are continually being suppressed and have the potential of one day exploding in a harmful manner.

SLEEPING PILL exemplifies respite from life's stressors.

SLEEPING PORCH represents an opportunity to gain insights when the mind is at rest.

SLEEPING SICKNESS suggests little time spent in full awareness. This symbol warns of possible efforts expended toward denial or avoidance of reality.

SLEEPOVER See slumber party.

SLEEPWALKING may stand for walking through life without awareness or it may indicate a true other-state awareness during the sleep state.

SLEET refers to unrecognized spiritual elements that come one's way.

SLEIGH indicates a means of traveling along one's path without exerting personal effort.

SLEIGH BED (bed style) signifies a desire for one's spirit to reach/travel the heights of true Reality; an acknowledgment of reality's potential and a desire to experience some of its amazing aspects.

SLEIGH BELLS refer to a carefree, non-chalant attitude where a more serious attitude should be given.

SLEIGHT OF HAND reveals deception.

SLEUTH See detective.

SLICE will symbolize a fragment of a greater element in one's life; a sample or piece.

SLICK See slippery.

SLICK (hair) usually points to slippery behavior; may point to slippery thoughts, those which aren't based on solid foundations.

SLICKER See raincoat.

SLIDE (lab) advises of the wisdom to look deeper into some aspect of one's life; a need for analyzation.

SLIDE (playground) warns against a tendency to slide through life without giving attention or awareness to important aspects.

SLIDE RULE alludes to the need to apply reason and logic.

SLIDING SCALE indicates the consideration of all associated aspects of an issue.

SLIME denotes an undesirable element with which one must deal.

SLING pertains to a state of being temporarily handicapped.

SLINGSHOT suggests inadequate measures of self-defense.

SLIPCASE (books) suggests a protective attitude toward one's cherished knowledge; a respect for knowledge.

SLIPCOVER represents an attempt/desire to improve an element in one's life. Depending on the related elements of the dream, this could be associated with one's perspective or aspects of behavior.

SLIP FORM See mold (shape).

SLIP KNOT refers to an option for an out; making alternative plans.

SLIPPERS denote a restful stage of one's path.

SLIPPERY cautions one to watch one's step; be careful of one's footing.

SLIPPERY ELM (tree) represents self-healing/correction.

SLIPPERY SLOPE warns of a worsening situation/behavior.

SLIPSHOD signifies poor quality; carelessness.

SLIPSTITCH points to a repair or fix done without anyone noticing.

SLIVER illustrates a fragment (negative element) which has the potential to pierce and become an irritant.

SLOBBERING exemplifies an inability to communicate one's ideas.

SLOE GIN See alcoholic beverage.

SLOGAN will present a personal message for each dreamer. Recall the exact words of the dream slogan.

SLOOP See sailboat.

SLOPE may represent a slightly more difficult path forthcoming or it may stand for a slanted perspective or path, depending on the related details of the dream

SLOPPY can be one of those relative symbols that will signify different meanings for each dreamer. The surrounding details will be the clarifying factor.

SLOSHING pertains to carelessness; a lack of control or efficient behavior.

SLOTH warns against procrastination.

SLOT CAR stands for a false sense of control.

SLOT MACHINE represents the chances taken in life; the shortcuts attempted.

SLOT TECH (casino) characterizes one who is instrumental in keeping opportunities (or risks) available for another.

SLOTTED SPOON suggests a way to remain focused on the main issue and get rid of the extraneous elements.

SLOUCHING may indicate weariness or laziness depending on the surrounding details.

SLOUCH HAT denotes a lazy mind; an unwillingness to apply mental energy.

SLOW BURN signifies growing frustration/anger.

SLOW COOKER denotes time taken to allow an issue to fully develop.

SLOW MOTION comes as an attention-getting device. This symbol advises one to pay closer attention to whatever action or event has been slowed. This will be a personal message for each dreamer.

SLOWPOKE may not equate to laziness but more to *careful* progression.

SLOW-RELEASE See time-release.

SLUDGE refers to waste in one's life; may depict elements that are extraneous or useless.

SLUG See bullet.

SLUG See snail.

SLUGFEST indicates a loss of control; may point to being drawn into conflict spurred by the negative reactions of those involved; a mob-rule contagion.

SLUICE pertains to the directing of spiritual behavior through one's daily life.

SLUM See skid row.

SLUMBER PARTY represents trust. At no time is one more vulnerable than when asleep. To invite someone to be present while asleep is an act of trust.

SLUM LORD characterizes a person who takes unconscionable advantage of others or another's misfortune.

SLURPING refers to the intake of information in an indiscriminate manner.

SLURRING (words) connotes an inability to communicate accurately.

SLUSH applies to spiritual fallacies and extraneous, frivolous aspects of same.

SLUSH FUND portrays reserve resources.

SMALL merely connotes size and, depending on the associated dreamscape details, may indicate a positive or negative message.

SMALL BUSINESS ADMINISTRATION refers to a source for help with getting a new beginning started.

SMALL CHANGE signifies insignificance.

SMALL POTATOES correspond to ineffectiveness or inconsequential aspects.

SMALLPOX pertains to a negative element that has infiltrated a person's life.

SMALL PRINT See fine print.

SMALL TALK implies an insignificant communication, one geared toward generalities and avoiding the more important issues.

SMALLTIME applies to a minor aspect; of little importance.

SMART CARD signifies memory access. This symbol advises of a need to remember something that one has a tendency to keep forgetting or is in denial of.

SMASHED stands for a destroyed element.

SMEAR (spot) relates to an undefined aspect; something has been compromised or become less clear.

SMEAR CAMPAIGN denotes ruthlessness; slanderous activity.

SMELL applies to the act of testing; discernment.

SMELLING SALTS illustrate a warning to wake up and get focused.

SMELT (fish) depicts small spiritual insights.

SMELTER signifies an attempt to maintain a purity and separation of individual ideas/concepts.

SMIDGEN stands for an amount of something, a very small amount; a trace.

SMILE may suggest friendliness, yet the precise interpretation will depend on the surrounding dreamscape details. This smile may be a disguised or sarcastic one.

SMILEY-FACE (image) usually comes in dreamscapes to remind us to be more lighthearted; more optimism is advised; have a greater sense of humor.

SMITHSONIAN INSTITUTION represents knowledge and the preservation of it; verification of past events and accomplishments.

SMITHY See blacksmith.

SMOCK infers intentions to work; prepared to expend personal efforts.

SMOG relates to distortion; an unclear perception.

SMOKE constitutes a sign that something is amiss and could be close to combustion.

SMOKE BOMB warns of deceit.

SMOKE DETECTOR corresponds with a person's inner awareness or insights that alert and warn of approaching trouble.

SMOKEHOUSE typifies preservation.

SMOKEJUMPER characterizes an individual who is capable of diverting or halting dangerous aspects in the lives of others; one ready and willing to jump into the fray and fight for a resolution.

SMOKE SCREEN relates to defenses or deceptions. Recall the surrounding dream details.

SMOKE SIGNAL connotes a hidden message; a private means of communication.

SMOKESTACK warns of a dangerous or highly negative aspect in one's life.

SMOKETHORN (tree) refers to deepened wisdom of spiritual philosophy.

SMOKEY MIRROR hints at smoke and mirrors. This would suggest an insubstantial element or trickery of some type.

SMOKEY THE BEAR symbolizes acute watchfulness.

SMOKING represents denied or suppressed emotions.

SMOKING GUN stands for evidence; verification; a cause for suspicion.

SMOKING JACKET refers to pretensions.

SMOKY QUARTZ indicates a clouded perception.

SMOLDERING warns of a volatile situation; an explosive element ready to blow.

SMORGASBORD will portray a variety of opportunities.

SMOTHER See suffocate.

SMUDGE (spot) refers to a marred or contaminated element; an unclear issue.

SMUDGE (to clear) signifies an attempt to maintain clarity and rid oneself or others of negativity.

SMUDGE POT/STICK reflects preservation; the clearing out of negativity.

SMUGGLER characterizes deception.

SNACK implies rejuvenation or the re-energizing of oneself.

SNACK BAR typifies choices.

SNAG (clothing) exposes an unexpected problem.

SNAIL stands for a cautious attitude.

SNAKE (nonpoisonous) exemplifies cleverness; proceeding with discernment.

SNAKE (venomous) pertains to swift retaliations or attacks.

SNAKEBITE emphasizes a lack of awareness; caught off guard.

SNAKE CHARMER characterizes a persuasive personality; may indicate manipulation.

SNAKE EYES (dice) points to one who is easily persuaded.

SNAKE OIL pertains to a lack of value; useless.

SNAKE OIL SALESMAN reveals a deceiver.

SNAKE PIT exemplifies a highly dangerous situation, relationship, or belief.

SNAKESKIN implies a swindler; a shiftless personality.

SNAKEWEED (botanical) points to mental sharpness.

SNAP (fastener) represents a quick closure to an event or problem.

SNAPDRAGON (botanical) illustrates secretiveness; an ability to hold one's tongue; integrity.

SNAPPING TURTLE refers to retaliations. May also point to impatience and a lack of tolerance.

SNAPSHOT See photograph.

SNARE portrays some type of setup; a trap.

SNARL warns of an unfriendly attitude; may indicate a type of entanglement.

SNEAKER See tennis shoe.

SNEAK PREVIEW will usually represent personal insights; foresight.

SNEEZE usually stands for an effort to rid oneself of an irritation; may point to the presence of an irritating element in one's life.

SNEEZEWEED represents an irritation in one's life.

SNICKER suggests concealed amusement.

SNIFF See smell.

SNIFTER implies an intention to ignore or divert one's awareness from responsibility or reality.

SNIPER characterizes a person who has a tendency to conceal true intentions; may point to underhandedness or a skill for undercutting (as in an eBay sniper). Also may indicate a tendency to withhold true intentions until the last minute.

SNIPER (eBay auction) characterizes a winner who comes from behind; a player who reveals herself at the very last minute.

SNOB connotes arrogance.

SNOOPY cautions against prying into the affairs of others.

SNOOPWARE See spyware.

SNOOZE See nap (sleep).

SNOOZE ALARM reveals the need for a small amount of additional rest.

SNORING advises that one isn't getting solid rest; indicates a need to improve the quality of respite periods; may warn of an inner restlessness.

SNORKELING pertains to a surface spiritual search or interest. May point to a tentative or cursory look into a new spiritual concept.

SNOW connotes a strong comprehension and grasp of spiritual truths; may also indicate the serenity that can come from one's personally held spiritual beliefs.

SNOWBALL infers a major spiritual concept. Recall who was throwing the snowball at whom.

SNOWBERRY (botanical) stands for sharpened awareness.

SNOWBIRD stands for encouragement; a strong sense of support.

SNOW BLINDNESS exposes spiritual blindness, usually self-imposed.

SNOW BLOWER pertains to an effort to rid oneself and one's surroundings of spiritual elements and/or influences.

SNOW BOARD See slalom.

SNOWBOUND signifies a situation in which one's progression/advancement has been temporarily held up by a problematical spiritual issue.

SNOWCAP portrays a spiritual priority.

SNOW DAY refers to the joyful freedom and uplifting feeling spirituality can bring.

SNOWDRIFT relates to an accumulation of spiritual issues, usually refers to a confusing buildup regarding a specific aspect.

SNOW FENCE warns of an attempt to keep spiritual elements contained and out of one's way.

SNOWFLAKE stands for the multiple shimmering aspects of spiritual truths.

SNOW GLOBE comes as a reminder to include spiritual aspects in our behavior. What scene was in the snow globe? Was the liquid clear or cloudy?

SNOW LINE illustrates a person's attempt to separate spiritual aspects from daily secular elements. This may indicate the hiding of one's beliefs.

SNOW LOAD suggests a preparedness for being able to carry the weight of heavy spiritual thought.

SNOWMAKING connotes the act of

bringing one's personal spiritual beliefs into every aspect of life, which may be a negative act depending on this dream's related details.

SNOWMAN emphasizes a state of spiritual arrogance; spirituality that is selective and temporary.

SNOWMELT represents a thawing of one's frozen spiritual beliefs/behavior; spiritual regeneration/refreshment.

SNOWMOBILE relates to the ease that an individual moves through her/his utilization of spiritual beliefs.

SNOW MONKEY denotes a strong sense of self; assured of one's unique identity.

SNOW-ON-THE-MOUNTAIN (botanical) represents one's developing talents and the awareness of the many ways to put them to use.

SNOWPLOW denotes paths through spiritual difficulties. This refers to complex spiritual concepts that have been plowed through, thereby clearing the way for unobstructed comprehension.

SNOWSCAPE signifies the beauty of spiritual serenity.

SNOWSHED denotes protective measures along one's path which guard against being overwhelmed or suffocated by unexpected spiritual inundations.

SNOWSHOE HARE denotes adaptability; resourcefulness; unique defense methods.

SNOWSHOES represent spiritual respect; softly treading through spiritual elements without being bogged down by them.

SNOWSLIDE See avalanche.

SNOWSTORM warns of a condition of spiritual confusion; an inundation of spir-

itual issues, usually self-generated. Also see blizzard.

SNOWSUIT refers to an insulating effort to shield oneself from spiritual concepts or elements. May also connote a resistant attitude toward blending spirituality with daily life.

SNOW THROWER See snow blower.

SNOW TIRE suggests a desire to comprehend higher spiritual concepts without getting intellectually stuck on them; an attempt to get through the deeper elements.

SNOW WHITE (fairytale character) characterizes an innocent personality; naïveté.

SNOWY OWL stands for hidden knowledge; an expanded intellectual horizon.

SNUFF (extinguish) portrays a desire to end something; a closure.

SNUFF (tobacco) See tobacco.

SNUFF BOX symbolizes a self-imposed need for a psychological aid.

SNUGGLING (alone under the covers or with Teddy bear) suggests insecurity or fears.

SNUGGLING (with another) suggests warm companionship.

SOAK denotes a permeated condition.

SOAP advises of a cleansing of some type.

SOAPBERRY (tree) points to a cleansing element; clearing out negatives.

SOAPBOX pertains to a personal need to sway or convince others of one's own perspective or attitude.

SOAP DISH will be displayed in a dream as a reminder that some element in one's life is in need of cleansing, usually one's hands.

SOAP OPERA relates to an overdramatized situation or event.

SOAPSTONE connotes the creativity that comes after acceptance has been gained.

SOAPWORT (botanical) signifies a need to cleanse away negative attitudes.

SOBRIETY TEST is most often a call from one's conscience to maintain awareness.

SOB SISTER characterizes a woman who has great empathy for others; a woman who has deep compassion and can be counted on as being a sympathetic sounding board.

SOB STORY pertains to a desire or psychological need to obtain sympathy from others; an absorption with self.

SOCCER suggests clever moves; fancy footwork.

SOCIAL (event) alludes to interaction with others.

SOCIAL ANXIETY reveals feelings of inferiority; a need to view oneself in a brighter light.

SOCIAL CLIMBER signifies a psychological need to be better or more successful than one's peers.

SOCIAL ISOLATION equates to intolerance of those different from oneself.

SOCIALITE stands for arrogance; a misplaced perspective of oneself.

SOCIAL REGISTER illustrates those who are self-absorbed.

SOCIAL SECURITY relates to good intentions, but questionable planning.

SOCIAL SERVICE reflects humanitarian intentions.

SOCIAL STUDIES (study of) represents an interest in knowing/understanding the life aspects contributing to another's current situation.

SOCIAL WORK defines a desire to help those less fortunate.

SOCIOLOGY (study of) indicates a personal interest in the behavior of one's peers and their daily conditions.

SOCK See stocking.

SOCKET (electrical) See outlet (electrical).

SOCKET (eye) would infer that the socket is empty and therefore denotes a total lack of physical sight, yet does not exclude perceptual sight or insights. A single empty eye socket would point to a condition of perceiving only half an issue.

SOCKET SET/WRENCH symbolizes resourceful utilization of problem-solving abilities.

SOCRATES emphasizes the fact that most solutions can be found within the problem, answers within the question.

SOD typifies an attempt to recover lost ground.

SODA (drink) See soft drink.

SODA CRACKER See cracker (food).

SODA FOUNTAIN applies to available choices in life.

SODA JERK stands for an individual who is capable of supplying one with multiple options.

SODALITE denotes spiritual wisdom and comprehension.

SODA POP See soft drink.

SODA WATER emphasizes spiritual elation.

SODDEN See soak.

SOD FARM suggests the transference/implanting of new ideas.

SODIUM See salt.

SOFA See couch.

SOFA BED represents duality; multiple opportunities; utilitarian.

SOFT (tactile) signifies gentleness.

SOFT-BOILED suggests an unfinished/undeveloped stage.

SOFT COPY refers to an opportunity for change, to make adjustments/alterations.

SOFT-CORE relates to a tempered approach to something.

SOFT DRINK refers to a tasteful and personally satisfying element.

SOFT FOCUS signifies an attempt to lessen the harshness of an issue; may also indicate a desire to hide the finer details of something.

SOFTHEADED denotes a compliant and commiserative personality.

SOFTHEARTED refers to a highly responsive and compassionate nature.

SOFT LANDING symbolizes a gentle closure to an issue.

SOFT-PEDAL pertains to a willful diminishing of something's value or importance; a somewhat deceptive maneuver.

SOFT ROCK (music) suggests a tempered display of one's emotions or opinions.

SOFT SELL implies subtle enticement; hidden methods of manipulation.

SOFT-SHOE (dancing) represents a routine joy in life; optimism; an appreciation of one's little blessings.

SOFT SHOULDER See road signs.

SOFT SOAP warns of self-serving methods.

SOFT-SPOKEN usually denotes gentleness, yet may infer manipulation or deception.

SOFT SPOT exposes a specific sentimentality.

SOFT TOUCH cautions against being easily manipulated.

SOFTWARE represents multiple opportunities/information sources.

SOFT WATER constitutes groundwork having high potential.

SOGGY See soak.

SOIL corresponds with a person's foundation; ground to build on or progress along.

SOIL CONDITIONER stands for an attempt to create a more favorable medium in which a new idea can take root.

SOIL CONSERVATION typifies a desire to maintain firm and fertile foundations.

SOIL SAMPLE stands for a check of one's basic character traits, whether they're comprised of elements that nourish or drain others.

SOJOURN See journey.

SOLACE reflects some type of comfort that may come from others or be self-generated.

SOLAR See sun.

SOLAR BATTERY portrays inner strength.

SOLAR COLLECTOR represents an energizing/rejuvenating element in one's life.

SOLAR ECLIPSE See eclipse (solar).

SOLAR FLARE implies a disruption or

intensification of personal strength and/or energy level.

SOLARIUM signifies the strong light that infuses a strong spiritual belief system.

SOLAR PANEL connotes an individual's personal capacity for re-energizing oneself. Recall the condition of the solar panel. May also denote an opening of oneself to the Divine Essence.

SOLAR POWER refers to the fact that one is naturally energized through good works; the empowering nature of giving/goodness.

SOLAR PLEXUS stands for the center of one's sensitivity, susceptibility, and power.

SOLAR SYSTEM pertains to a fragment of true Reality.

SOLAR WIND is a call to give heightened awareness to one's subtle insights.

SOLDER/SOLDERING GUN See adhesive.

SOLDIER characterizes a person who upholds the honor and safety of others; fighting for what one believes in. May also indicate a forced participation of a conflict; one who was drawn in.

SOLDIER OF FORTUNE pertains to a self-serving and nondiscriminatory individual.

SOLD OUT signifies a popular issue; may indicate a lost opportunity; a need to reschedule plans.

SOLE (fish) stands for independent spiritual thought; spiritual individuality.

SOLEMNITY may indicate high respect, sacredness, or gravity.

SOLICITOR relates to an individual who acts for or with another.

SOLIDARITY constitutes mutual interest or camaraderie.

SOLITAIRE stands for a state of aloneness; a singular element; may also point to the games one is playing with self—the psychological mind games.

SOLITARY CONFINEMENT exposes a situation of absolute exclusion; may advise that one's state of aloneness has been self-induced.

SOLITUDE advises of a need to contemplate; a need for mental or emotional rest.

SOLO emphasizes the fact that one has acted alone or must proceed along one's path alone.

SOLOMON'S SEAL (botanical) correlates to the strengthening of an individual's inner forces (energies). Also stands for an analytical ability for rationale.

SOLUBLE connotes the capability and possibility of being ended or concluded.

SOLUTION (liquid, unidentified) will denote an answer stemming from multiple sources.

SOLUTION (resolution) will come as a key message and be specific to each dreamer.

SOMBRERO signifies withheld thoughts.

SOMERSAULT portrays complex maneuvers made to accomplish a goal or conclusion.

SOMNAMBULISM See sleepwalking.

SOMNOLENT See drowsy.

SONAR stands for an individual's inner perceptions; insights; heightened awareness.

SONG will pertain to a specific message according to what was sung.

SONG AND DANCE characterizes an elaborate excuse; complex explanation.

SONGBIRD reflects inner joy; personal happiness.

SONG BOOK represents the many choices of perspectives; the many opportunities to view issues/events and react to them.

SONGWRITER characterizes an opportunity to compose and formulate one's own attitude or outlook.

SONIC BARRIER connotes the point at which a person surpasses goals or expectations.

SONIC BOOM signifies the realization that one has reached a goal.

SONNET See poem.

SONOGRAM portrays a visual impression; an insight; vision.

SOOT exemplifies negative elements that have the capacity to contaminate oneself or one's life.

SOOTHING will represent a stress-relieving element.

SOOTHSAYER See seeress.

SOPHIST characterizes a person with a tendency to come up with elaborate arguments.

SOPHISTICATE typifies worldly experience.

SOPRANO relates to excitability; an inability to control emotions.

SORBET See juice.

SORCERER warns against the negative utilization of inherent talents or spiritual gifts.

SORCERER'S APPRENTICE cautions against the desire to learn from misguided individuals or aspire to emulate them.

SORORITY illustrates a group of like-minded women.

SORREL (color) symbolizes an earthiness; naturalness.

SORREL (botanical) suggests a life element that has the capability of providing inner nourishment.

SORROWFUL may denote melancholia, empathy, or regret.

SORORITY stands for female camaraderie. May also refer to a tendency to follow what's popular.

SORTIE refers to an attack that may be instigated by oneself depending on the dreamscape's related details.

SOUFFLÉ reflects a delicate plan; fragile execution of it.

SOUL defines one's vital and prime essence.

SOUL MATE usually points to an individual who one perceives as being the perfect partner/friend.

SOUL SISTER equates to a woman who shares sympathies, love, and a deep kinship with another woman or a man.

SOUND will reveal multiple messages to dreams. Pay close attention to these.

SOUND BARRIER See sonic barrier.

SOUND CARD (computer) represents one's choice to hear all the elements of an issue; may point to one's decision to choose acceptance or denial.

SOUND EFFECTS stand for emphasis; accentuating a thought/idea with added emphases.

SOUNDING corresponds to a probing attempt; a method of discovery.

SOUNDING BOARD symbolizes an advisement to share thoughts and emotions with others.

S

SOUND PROOFING See acoustical (material).

SOUND STAGE denotes a call to be aware of one's actions and words. Recall what type of set was presented. Who was there? Was it a historical period set? Was it lit up or in darkness?

SOUND SYSTEM suggests a desire to understand, in a loud and clear manner, what is said.

SOUNDTRACK will expose a personal message for each dreamer. Recall what type of music was played. What were the words? What film was it from?

SOUP represents a nourishing aspect generated from multiple elements.

SOUP KITCHEN indicates an opportunity to nourish (help) others.

SOUP OF THE DAY signifies an offered choice.

SOUPSPOON suggests an opportunity to help oneself to a beneficial resource.

SOUPY (atmosphere) illustrates an unclear of confusing situation.

SOUR indicates a distasteful situation to endure; a hard-to-take or hard-to-accept situation.

SOURBALL connotes a distasteful situation that one voluntarily accepts and plans to carry through to its conclusion.

SOURCE BOOK reveals multiple opportunities to take advantage of. Was this dream source book associated with a particular subject matter?

SOUR CREAM relates to the duality of having a best case situation yet possessing a somewhat problematical element.

SOURDOUGH implies unlimited benefits stemming from a singular source.

SOURDOUGH STARTER stands for an ongoing, regenerating wealth of benefits.

SOUR GRAPES allude to denial.

SOURWOOD (tree) indicates an increasing level of acceptance.

SOUTH (direction) connotes a lower level or a going back-to-basic message.

SOUTH AMERICA suggests hidden aspects to some bright-appearing benefits.

SOUTH CAROLINA stands for possibilities; the promise of hope.

SOUTH DAKOTA suggests one's homeland; home traditions.

SOUTH KOREA suggests a tenuous position/situation.

SOUTHPAW See left-handed.

SOUTH POLE pertains to basic elements of an issue or concept that are difficult to discover.

SOUVENIR symbolizes a reason to remember a specific event in one's life.

SOVEREIGNTY exemplifies preeminence; autonomy. Stands for total independence.

SOW See hog.

SOW See plant (sow).

SOYBEAN symbolizes a highly nourishing belief.

SOYMILK represents the rich benefits of truth.

SPA See health club.

SPACE See cosmos.

SPACE AGE pertains to a minuscule step toward discovering the aspects of true Reality.

SPACE BAR (keyboard) applies to

intentional spacing; a desire for more room; separation of ideas.

SPACE CADET reveals a lack of mental focus.

SPACECRAFT infers a means or opportunity to intellectually reach toward a beginning comprehension of the true Reality.

SPACED-OUT signifies a willful escape from reality and responsibility; inability to keep one's mind focused; easily distracted.

SPACE HEATER constitutes a desire for personal comfort in respect to one's immediate surround; a fear of being exposed to disagreeable situations.

SPACE NEEDLE (Seattle) signifies a sign/reminder of a former achievement.

SPACE PROBE represents an individual's choice or opportunity to extend a spiritual search to the farthest reaches.

SPACESHIP See spacecraft.

SPACE SHUTTLE reflects the existing freedom to self-discover the reaches of true Reality.

SPACE SICKNESS stands for an inability to comprehend unconventional concepts or think outside the box.

SPACE STATION comes in dreams to reveal the existence of other semiparallel realities existing within the scope of true Reality.

SPACE SUIT portrays a fear of venturing into the farthest reaches of true Reality; a sense one needs protection from discovering the truth.

SPACE WALK represents the tip of humankind's potential.

SPACIOUSNESS applies to unrecognized freedom for self-discovery.

SPADE See shovel.

SPADE (card suit) denotes verification; assurances.

SPAGHETTI exemplifies an ability to absorb complexities.

SPAIN suggests strong traditions.

SPAM (food) refers to a mix of secondary benefits.

SPAM (Internet) See pop-ups.

SPAM BLOCKER (computer) stands for a way to keep out unwanted elements.

SPANDEX See elastic.

SPANISH MOSS corresponds to little-understood aspects of true Reality; a frequently feared concept to delve into.

SPANKING most often comes as a message from one's conscience and suggests a wrongdoing for which one should make reparations.

SPARE PARTS connotes preparedness; resourcefulness.

SPARERIBS typify a need to get down to the bare bones of an issue.

SPARE TIRE pertains to preparations made for possible eventualities encountered along one's life path. In some dreams, this symbol may literally point to being overweight or carrying a load that's too heavy.

SPARK may reflect inspiration or it may warn of a dangerous situation, depending on the surrounding dreamscape details.

SPARKLER emphasizes inner joy generated by insights.

SPARK PLUG represents an aspect in one's life that serves as an impetus toward action or advancement; motivational element.

SPARROW corresponds to a gentle intellectual.

SPARSENESS correlates to frugalness; lacking materialism.

SPASM may not infer a shocking incident, but most often represents an awakening type of reaction.

SPATULA refers to a personal life element that serves as a beneficial aid.

SPEAKEASY defines shared secrecy.

SPEAKER (audio) indicates a need to hear more clearly; indicates a state of inattention, possibly self-generated.

SPEAKER (person) will usually constitute a message for the dreamer. Recall what was said and by whom.

SPEAKERPHONE indicates a personal ease in communicating with others or it may allude to a need to share a conversation.

SPEAKING IN TONGUES See glossolalia.

SPEAR refers to a method of obtaining a desired element or goal.

SPEAR GUN relates to a desire to spear specific spiritual truths for the purpose of clear comprehension.

SPEARMINT (botanical/flavor) signifies a refreshing idea or aspect to an element; insights.

SPECIAL DELIVERY connotes an important message.

SPECIAL EDUCATION stands for a need to gain additional basics.

SPECIAL EFFECTS symbolize emphasis; a need to dramatize for the purpose of greater understanding.

SPECIAL FORCES represents specialized, intensive efforts applied to the accomplishment of a goal. Sometimes special forces directly relate to spiritual forces such as angels.

SPECIAL INTEREST (group) will reveal an individual's concealed intention or attitude.

SPECIAL NEEDS denote just that—it calls attention to an individual or situation needing very special attention, perhaps more tolerance/patience.

SPECIAL OLYMPICS stand for personal capabilities regardless of perceived handicaps.

SPECIAL USE PERMIT (zoning) refers to a temporary or short-term activity.

SPECIFICATIONS pertain to the details of an issue, situation, or relationship.

SPECIMEN will relate to a sample; an example.

SPECKLED (pattern) denotes the existence of multiple elements.

SPECKLEWARE See enamelware.

SPECTATOR reminds us that someone is always watching, even if it's our own conscience.

SPECTER See ghost.

SPECTRUM will symbolize the full extent of something; the gamut or far reaches.

SPECULATION warns against making assumptions.

SPEECH portrays a specific message for each dreamer depending on what was said to whom.

SPEECHLESS may indicate a dumbfounded reaction or it could infer wise discernment, depending on the surrounding dream elements.

SPEECH-READING See lip reading.

SPEECH THERAPY indicates a need to convey thoughts with better clarity.

SPEECH WRITER is a caution to speak for oneself. This symbol points to someone who puts words in another's mouth.

SPEED representations will greatly vary in dreams and will reveal multiple meanings depending on related elements.

SPEEDBOAT warns against speeding through a spiritual search.

SPEED BUMP exposes a need to slow down.

SPEED DIAL suggests an urgency to contact a particular individual. This symbol usually comes as an advisement.

SPEED FREAK characterizes an individual who continually attempts to get the most out of life through overexpending energies.

SPEEDING reveals a cautionary advisement to slow one's pace for the purpose of recognizing realizations that have been formerly missed.

SPEED LIMIT See road signs.

SPEEDOMETER will indicate the speed at which one is progressing through life or it will portray an advisement for one's suggested pace.

SPEED-READING corresponds with a caution to absorb more of what one attempts to learn. This is suggesting that the dreamer is missing something along the way.

SPEED SKATING/WALKING won't normally stand for impatience but rather a tendency toward efficiency; a routine manner of handling situations.

SPEED TRAP comes in dreamscapes to warn of the pitfalls of going too fast along one's life path.

SPEEDWELL (botanical) suggests something in one's life that needs to be overcome.

SPELL (incantation) may not be a negative dream element, but usually comes as a behavioral advisement.

SPELLBOUND connotes a personal fascination of some type and warns against being in a state lacking logic and reason.

SPELLING BEE exposes specific words for emphasis. These words will come as a unique message for each dreamer.

SPELL CHECKER comes to advise that one gets things right (accurate) during communications.

SPELUNKER characterizes a person who delves far into the deeper elements of specific concepts and belief systems to self-discover any hidden aspects that could serve to broaden understanding.

SPENDTHRIFT connotes efficiency; foresight.

SPHAGNUM See peat moss.

SPHERE implies completion.

SPHINX comes as an advisement that one is close to discovering the totality (whole) of an issue.

SPICES represent personal qualities affecting aspects in one's life; an individual's unique perspective and how it affects behavior and experiences.

SPIDER may reveal a conniving individual or it may refer to a unique type of personal defensive measure. Recall the dream's details for clarity of meaning.

SPIDERMAN represents the utilization of personal talents and insights.

SPIDER MONKEY denotes mental acuity, nimbleness.

SPIDER VEINS constitute fortitude; path progression in spite of burdens.

SPIDERWORT (botanical) suggests efforts applied to keeping life elements from becoming confusing/entangled.

SPIEL denotes an effort to persuade.

SPIGOT See faucet.

SPIKE See stake (stick).

SPIKED SHOE symbolizes resentment of one's life problems or burdens.

SPILL-PROOF refers to an idea or plan which has no chance of falling apart.

SPILLWAY represents spiritual excesses or that which is spiritually unnecessary.

SPIN See damage control.

SPINACH alludes to a nourishing life element; a beneficial aspect or opportunity.

SPINAL CORD signifies the strength of one's inner life force.

SPINAL CORD INJURY points to a weakened sense of fortitude.

SPINDLE will denote an important secondary factor connected to a primary element.

SPINDRIFT See sea spray.

SPINE See backbone.

SPINELESS emphasizes a lack of courage or personal responsibility; may also indicate a lack of individuality.

SPINNING WHEEL corresponds with plans; mental maneuvers.

SPIN-OFF signifies a resulting product; a benefit or problem stemming from a primary source.

SPINSTER portrays self-reliance; confidence in oneself.

SPIRAL (configuration) pertains to the interrelated aspects in one's life.

SPIRAL STAIRS stand for a circling path toward advancement; a phase of one's path which involves a return to issues to gain greater understanding.

SPIRE See steeple.

SPIRIT may refer to an entity associated with the dreamer or it may indicate the power and energy of one's own life force.

SPIRIT RAPPING connotes a desire to believe; self-deception.

SPITBALL refers to unethical practices.

SPIT CURL stands for an attempt to gain attention.

SPITTLE See saliva.

SPITTOON signifies a proper place for specific behavior.

SPITZ (dog breed) signifies a companionable friend, one who offers a comfortable feeling to be around.

SPLASH GUARD connotes defense mechanisms; methods of protecting self from negative elements.

SPLEEN reflects hidden emotions.

SPLICE signifies an attempt to join aspects; a bond or linkage.

SPLINT suggests a supportive measure; an attempt to maintain stability during a healing period.

SPLINTER exemplifies the entry of a foreign element or belief; an aspect that doesn't belong; an invasion or defilement. Also see sliver.

SPLIT represents a breach or fragmentation; a separation of some type.

SPLIT-ENDS (hair) stands for quibbling; splitting hairs.

SPLIT-LEVEL (house) warns of an internal conflict.

SPLIT PERSONALITY stands for indecision, vacillation.

SPLIT RAIL (fence) illustrates a self-devised personal perimeter; one's perceptual distance from others.

SPLIT SCREEN (image/visual) comes to advise of a need to look at two issues at once because they may be related.

SPLIT SHIFT implies great personal efforts applied to one's purpose.

SPLIT TICKET (voting) stands for a recognition of the best elements of multiple aspects; a tendency to be savvy enough to recognize people's/situation's best qualities.

SPLURGING suggests self-indulgence; an attempt to comfort or satisfy oneself.

SPOILAGE relates to inattention given a specific issue or life element.

SPOKESPERSON characterizes a liaison. Also see speech writer.

SPONGE relates to absorption and most often pertains to a need to listen and/or comprehend better.

SPONGY (consistency) may infer resiliency or it could indicate a lack of firm strength. Recall the dream's details for clarity.

SPONSOR characterizes a person who takes responsibility for another; the one who enables another to accomplish something.

SPOOK See ghost.

SPOOKED implies timidity; a fearful nature.

SPOOL See spindle.

SPOON typifies that which one spoons out to others or that which one takes in.

SPOONBILL (bird) stands for an opportunistic personality; an awareness of options.

SPOOR alludes to evidence; proof of one's passing.

SPORE constitutes a small element capable of becoming a major aspect in one's life.

SPORTING GOODS STORE refers to tools and equipment for playing the game (getting along in life).

SPORTS symbolize "the game" and will be related to a variety of issues connected to the symbolism of the specific sport. See specific sport.

SPORTS BAR represents support for another's efforts. May indicate an attitude of expectation or amusement to see how another fairs.

SPORTS CAR exemplifies a fast-paced lifestyle and manner of behavior.

SPORTSCAST suggests a personal interest and will reveal one's level of involvement in it.

SPORTS MASSAGE denotes a high interest in staying in the game and a determination behind it.

SPORTS MEDICINE represents a high interest in healing those who sustain personal injuries while progressing along their life paths or who are determined to accomplish their goals.

SPORTS STADIUM applies to a sit and watch attitude; procrastination.

SPORTSWEAR suggests an advisement to don an attitude of acceptance—good sportsmanship.

SPORTSWRITER See sportscast.

SPOT may indicate a defect or marred element in one's life or it can pertain to an attention-getting mark. Recall the dream's related details.

SPOT CHECK connotes a desire to maintain a status quo condition; a monitoring and watchfulness.

SPOTLESS can denote a too-perfect condition or state.

SPOTLIGHT comes as a dreamscape fragment to point out and reveal important aspects for the dreamer to give attention to.

SPOT REMOVER symbolizes an opportunity to remove a negative from one's life or resolve a conflict, perhaps make amends.

SPOTTED (pattern) portrays a hidden personality; vacillation.

SPOTTED FEVER typifies the negativity (illness) brought on by allowing life irritations to "get under the skin" and infect one with feelings of resentment or blame.

SPOTTED OWL stands for inspiration; growing incidences of insightful thought.

SPOT TEST stands for preliminary work done or efforts expended toward discovering a method to resolve a conflict or remove a negative from one's life.

SPOTTING SCOPE stands for taking a closer look at something.

SPOT ZONING stands for favoritism; showing preference. May point to an activity that is out of the ordinary.

SPOUSE will signify a bonded connection to another.

SPOUT exposes an inability to contain information.

SPRAIN corresponds with a temporary setback caused by a lack of awareness.

SPRAY (water) illustrates an exposure to new spiritual concepts.

SPRAY GUN stands for a convenient and effective method of disbursing information.

SPREAD See bedspread.

SPREADER (garden/lawn) relates to the dissemination of information or broadcast nurturing.

SPREADSHEET constitutes an overview, an at-a-glance perspective.

SPRING (metal) represents a tendency to bounce back after some type of adversity or problem has been encountered; tenacity; resiliency.

SPRING (season) defines a time for new beginnings and renewal.

SPRING (water) stands for a well of spirituality within oneself.

SPRING BEAUTY (botanical/flower) signifies optimistic perspectives; renewal.

SPRINGBOARD denotes motivation; an impetus.

SPRING BREAK corresponds to a need to take time out from one's efforts applied to purpose or life path.

SPRING-CLEANING symbolizes the energy put into keeping one's perspective clear of negative or opinionated aspects.

SPRING FEVER portrays inner joy and anticipation for the start of new beginnings.

SPRINGHOUSE pertains to the use of one's spiritual aspects to preserve and maintain the secular aspects of life in peak condition and a positive state.

SPRING TRAINING won't normally relate to physical exercise but rather getting oneself in mental shape to achieve an upcoming goal.

SPRINKLER signifies an attempt to inundate one's life with spiritual aspects; maintaining a spiritual priority with all things.

SPRINTING suggests a paced progression.

SPRITE refers to possibilities.

SPROCKET WHEEL represents a life element capable of maintaining one's forward progression.

SPROUT relates to the birthing of new ideas, especially spiritual concepts or the talents associated with them.

SPUN GLASS See fiber glass.

SPUN SUGAR See cotton candy.

SPUR (boot) reveals aggressiveness; the use of improper motivational methods.

SPUR TRACK cautions against allowing oneself to get sidetracked.

SPUTTERING implies incoherent communication; an inability to clearly communicate.

SPY indicates an untrustworthy individual.

SPYGLASS See binoculars; telescope.

SPYWARE (computer program) points to a method of retrieving another's personal information and getting into his/her private affairs.

SPYWARE DETECTOR/BLOCKER (computer program) stands for a method of knowing if another is invading one's privacy and the way to protect oneself against it.

SQUAD refers to a group of people who have a like interest.

SQUAD CAR symbolizes the mobility (extent) of one's own conscience; an inability to escape one's conscience.

SQUALL represents a temporary state of emotional or mental confusion.

SQUALOR won't necessarily stand for a physical condition but rather it usually pertains to one's state of mind or set of ethics.

SQUARE (configuration) denotes rigidness; narrow-mindedness.

SQUARE DANCE indicates a formulated interaction with others as opposed to one which is spontaneous and more open.

SQUARE KNOT denotes a firm hold.

SQUARE MEAL illustrates well-rounded nourishment; a fulfilling aspect.

SQUARE ONE connotes the beginning point.

SQUARE SHOOTER exemplifies honesty; integrity.

SQUARED TOE (shoes) point to a rigid personality.

SQUASH (crush) refers to the act of ending something rather abruptly.

SQUASH (fruit) implies a source of energy.

SQUASH (game) suggests a competitive situation, possibly even against oneself as efforts at breaking old records or improving oneself are expended.

SQUASH BLOSSOM (jewelry) pertains to inner strength.

SQUATTER stands for an individual who moves in on another's territory; an interloper.

SQUATTER'S RIGHTS reveal an individual's right to be somewhere.

SQUEAKY (sound) relates to a stiff and rigid attitude or situation; stingy.

SQUEAMISHNESS alludes to a lack of courage or self-confidence.

SQUEEGEE connotes a need to gain clearer perceptions.

SQUEEZING signifies pressure.

SQUELCH CONTROL stands for the act of silencing something or making it clearer to understand.

SQUID represents a haphazard spiritual search.

SQUIGGLY (pattern) portrays a complexity.

SQUINT relates to an effort to see something better.

SQUIRM implies an uncomfortable situation.

SQUIRREL refers to the act of hoarding. Depending on the dreamscape's related details, this symbol may indicate a need to reserve something or it may reflect a warning against retaining too much.

SQUIRT GUN alludes to unexpected hits such as responses from others that are uncharacteristic; surprising events.

SQUISHY (consistency) depicts indecision; a lack of solid opinions.

STAB is a symbol containing duality. This could refer to an unexpected retaliation or injury from another, or it might signify an attempt at something.

STABILIZER BAR corresponds to a need to balance some aspect of one's life.

STABLE (barn) will reveal an individual's attitude toward her/his personal inherent abilities. Recall the stable's condition.

STACCATO defines an abruptness of personality.

STACK represents an amount of work to be done.

STADIUM denotes the act of observing; may represent a warning to become more involved. Also pertains to the playing field.

STAFF (people) characterizes those who are ready and willing to assist another.

STAFF (stave) See walking stick.

STAG (deer) implies a self-reliant loner.

STAG (unaccompanied) exemplifies a personal choice to accomplish something by oneself.

STAGE connotes an opportunity or means of expressing self to a multitude of people.

STAGECOACH depicts a plodding manner of progression.

STAGE DOOR JOHNNY will indicate an individual who finds self-esteem by rubbing shoulders with public figures or famous people.

STAGE FRIGHT reveals a fear of expressing oneself.

STAGEHAND characterizes an individual who is capable of assisting another to express feelings or opinions.

STAGE MANAGER will point to an individual who has the ability to pull things together.

STAGE SET See sound stage.

STAGE-STRUCK portrays a fascination and great desire to perform before others; a need to be seen and heard by many.

STAGGER indicates a need for support; unsteadiness.

STAGNANT connotes a lack of vitality; something that has been allowed to go stale.

STAID portrays a quiet dignity.

STAIN (spot) will most often illustrate a negative element in one's life. Recall what was stained. What color was it? What caused the stain?

STAIN (wood) marks an effort to protect one's natural talents. What color was the stain? Was it for interior or exterior use?

STAINED GLASS represents multifaceted elements creating a singular aspect; may denote differential perceptions of various individuals. What did the stained glass depict? Birds? Flowers? What type of design? What were the predominant colors?

STAINLESS STEEL stands for durability; resistant to decay or decline.

STAIRS will pertain to one's ascent or descent in relation to one's life progression or advancement. Recall the type of stairs and the condition of them. Were they a specific color? Lit or darkened? Were there missing steps?

STAKE (bet) indicates a personal interest in something.

STAKE (stick) will denote a marker or a support of some type.

STAKEOUT advises of a need to be acutely watchful of a particular aspect in one's life.

STALACTITE suggests a growing *positive* philosophy or deduction.

STALAGMITE symbolizes a growing *negative* element in one's life, most often from within oneself.

STALE denotes a worn-out issue or attitude; stands for a need to explore new concepts or veer onto a new and different path.

STALEMATE exposes a futile situation; no chance for an altered course or change.

STALKING warns of a silent pursuit, usually of another individual. Recall who was stalking whom for what purpose.

STALL (animal) See stable.

STALL (put off) indicates a temporary postponement of forward progression.

STALLED ENGINE signifies a waning of one's energy or motivation.

STALLION warns of an uncontrolled

strength; a need to contain and direct one's energies.

STAMINA will represent perseverance; fortitude.

STAMMERING indicates an inability to express oneself clearly.

STAMP (foot) relates to emphasis; may denote impatience or anger.

STAMP (label) will reveal a personal message for each dreamer. Recall what was stamped on what object.

STAMP (postage) See postage stamp.

STAMP COLLECTION constitutes a recognition of a specific aspect's value.

STAMPEDE warns against losing self-control and personal direction; refers to the use of emotionalism rather than intellect.

STAMPING GROUND connotes a private and personal comfort zone. Familiarity with a specific element or atmosphere.

STAMP MILL represents intellectual deduction; extracting all informational elements from a singular aspect.

STANDARD (flag) correlates to what one stands for or strongly supports. What type of flag was it? What did it represent to the dreamer?

STANDBY relates to preparedness; readiness. May point to something one is most comfortable with.

STAND-DOWN applies to a withdrawal; a relaxing of immediate plans.

STAND-IN indicates a capable replacement or alternative.

STANDING portrays an adherence to one's convictions.

STANDING ORDER defines a manner of behavior that is practiced until some element alters its effectiveness.

STANDING ROOM may portray a popular concept or attitude, or it may represent an advisement to pursue another course.

STANDOFF See stalemate.

STANDSTILL symbolizes a halt to progression or advancement.

STANLEY CUP See Super Bowl ring.

STAPLE (basics) pertains to basic ethics, humanitarian elements, and spiritual foundational aspects.

STAPLE (fastener) typifies a connective aspect.

STAPLED STOMACH refers to drastic measures to force self-control.

STAPLE GUN relates to a quick fix.

STAR exemplifies truth and the ultimate search for it.

STAR BEING corresponds with the reality of all humankind; the totality of existing intelligence in all forms.

STARBURST (design/pattern) portrays illumination; intellectual enlightenment.

STARCH constitutes firmness. This symbol possesses duality and therefore may indicate a *need* to be *more* firm in one's relationships or it may reveal a method of behavior that is *too* firm.

STAR-CROSSED pertains to ill fortune, multiple difficulties.

STARDUST stands for moments of inspiration or illumined insights.

STARE suggests focused intensity and won't necessarily indicate any type of negative element.

STARFISH signifies spiritual truths.

STARGAZING represents spiritual speculation; intellectual reaching toward a grasp of the true Reality.

STARKNESS portrays the bare elements of an issue.

STARLIGHT connotes a spiritual opportunity to accept the truth.

STARLING (bird) stands for innocence; an enhanced serenity generated by an appreciation of one's individuality.

STARQUAKE will symbolize the shattering of idolization.

STAR SAPPHIRE (gemstone) symbolizes spiritual truths.

STARSHIP signifies the relatedness, the connective bond, between all intelligent species.

STAR-STRUCK warns against allowing oneself to become fascinated with others.

STARTER (bread) See sourdough starter.

STARTER (engine) See ignition key.

STARTER (player) will indicate the individual who is meant to begin something; reveals who should make the first move.

STARTING GATE warns against life competition.

STARTING LINE reflects the beginning point.

STARTLED signifies an unexpected event.

STARVATION implies a serious lack of a nourishing element in one's life; the absence of mental or emotional nourishment.

STAR WARS (film) refers to the ongoing conflict between good and evil and those who chose which side to fight on.

STARWORT (botanical/flower) points to an appreciation of life's blessings and more valuable aspects; recognition of priorities.

STASH stands for hidden elements in

one's life; that which one conceals and hoards.

STATE OF UNION ADDRESS points to a general assessment of one's current condition and progress.

STATEROOM cautions against the tendency to compartmentalize spiritual truths.

STATESWOMAN characterizes a respected person of authority.

STATIC (electricity) warns of a state of mental dysfunction.

STATIC (sound) connotes an interruption in communication that may be self-generated.

STATICE (botanical/flower) stands for tenacity; endurance.

STATION (depot) See depot.

STATION (position) illustrates where one should be and what one should be doing.

STATION (transmitted) implies a frequency; a vibratory rate. Recall what was being said on the radio or TV station.

STATION BREAK refers to a temporary break in communication.

STATIONERY symbolizes a need to communicate with another. May reveal the quality or attitude of that communication. Recall type of stationery. Color? Style?

STATISTICIAN characterizes a person who possesses verifying information.

STATUE presents a specific message for each dreamer. The type of statue will have a unique relation to the dreamer.

STATUE OF LIBERTY emphasizes the ideal of equality and freedom.

STATUESQUE (appearance) pertains to a dignified personality.

STATUS SYMBOL reveals self-absorption; a desire to possess prime material goods. This dream symbol exposes a person who judges one's worth or success by what one owns.

STATUTE will signify a specific law that may relate to ethical, moral, or spiritual aspects.

STAUROLITE (gemstone) represents intellectual complexity.

STEAK connotes high energy; a motivational factor.

STEAKHOUSE signifies a source of encouragement, or aspects which will act as an impetus for action.

STEAK TARTARE comes in a dream to advise against willfully ingesting potentially harmful ideas; risky behavior.

STEAL reveals an unwillingness to expend efforts toward goals; impatience.

STEALTHY implies dishonesty or secretiveness.

STEAM portrays spiritual activity.

STEAM BATH exemplifies being steeped in spiritual endeavors or elements.

STEAMBOAT represents a spiritual search generated by pure spiritual motivations.

STEAM CLEANER refers to a need for a thorough cleanup. The dreamer usually understands what this is in reference to.

STEAM ENGINE denotes spiritual motivations.

STEAMER TRUNK stands for the spiritual tools and elements we carry with us along our life journey.

STEAM IRON relates to the utilization of spirituality to resolve problems.

STEAMROLLER will warn of negative control.

STEAMSHIP signifies a spiritual journey motivated/energized by spiritual elements such as ideals, inspiration, a desire for enlightenment.

STEAM SHOVEL pertains to spiritual work.

STEEL relates to strength.

STEEL DRUMS See drum (steel).

STEEL MILL connotes the many forms that strength can take.

STEEL-TRAP illustrates astute intelligence; a strong and quick mind.

STEEL WOOL symbolizes insensitivity; a strong, yet insensitive nature.

STEEP (soak) exemplifies thoroughness.

STEEP (vertical) will most often stand for a great depth; rich in meaning or philosophical content. This symbol may also represent a difficult or exacting aspect.

STEEPLE suggests a high point to an issue or event.

STEEPLEJACK characterizes an individual who is not afraid to approach high concepts or reach for a comprehension to complexities.

STEER (animal) See cattle.

STEER (guide) connotes directional control. Each individual needs to steer oneself along her/his own life path.

STEERAGE (class) points to the existence of a less costly way to make a spiritual journey.

STEERING COMMITTEE may refer to one's own better judgment or it can relate to being coerced.

STEERING WHEEL stands for control of one's life/destiny. The key to clear interpretation here is to recall what the steering wheel was attached to and whose hands were on it. If no hands were seen, then the symbol is an advisement to place one's own hands on the wheel and stop drifting/wandering.

STEINEM (Gloria) symbolizes the realization of one's self-worth and unlimited potential.

STELE signifies a marker, an impression of something important to the dreamer. This will be different for everyone.

STEM (stalk) represents the supporting factor of an element/issue.

STEM CELL stands for a neutral element that has a multitude of beneficial uses.

STENCH reveals the presence of a serious negative element.

STENCIL denotes an example; a template to follow.

STENOGRAPHER characterizes an individual who remembers another's words; a record of communication.

STEP See stairs.

STEPLADDER signifies the careful taking of one step at a time for cautious life progression and advancement.

STEPPINGSTONE refers to the importance of taking one step at a time.

STEP STOOL represents a small, yet effective aid to progression.

STEREO (equipment) stands for the utilization of one's full potential.

STEREOTYPE pertains to a typecast personality or situation. May warn against a tendency to profile people.

STERILE symbolizes a condition free of negative elements, yet may also point to a tendency to isolate oneself instead of jumping in and getting one's hands dirty.

STERLING portrays the highest quality for a specific characteristic or attitude.

STETHOSCOPE defines a check on one's emotional sensitivity.

STEVEDORE See longshoremen.

STEW stands for anxiety; worry; a confusing complexity.

STEWARDESS See flight attendant.

STICK signifies an opportunity for self-expression that may be a positive or negative element depending on the dreamscape's related details.

STICK-BUILT (construction) refers to a commonly accepted way to do something.

STICKER (gummed) will present a personal message for each dreamer depending on what the sticker symbolized or said.

STICKER (thorn) See thorn.

STICKER PRICE depicts an exaggerated worth.

STICKER SHOCK comes as a call to perform a reality check, for one's goals come at a greater cost (energy) than originally thought.

STICK FIGURE symbolizes the beginning formation of an idea or theory about another.

STICKINESS pertains to a precarious situation or relationship.

STICKLEBACK (fish) stands for spiritual intolerance; advises of a need to relax rigid thought and increase acceptance of other spiritual possibilities.

STIFF portrays rigidness; an unyielding personality.

STIFF-NECKED warns of an inability to easily view all angles; limited perceptual range.

STIFF UPPER LIP alludes to hidden emotions.

STIFLING cautions of a repressive element or situation.

STIGMA relates to a sign or mark revealing a specific quality or characteristic.

STIGMATA stands for a whiner; a persecution complex.

STILE applies to an aid to advancement; also a way to overcome indecision (sitting on the fence).

STILETTO See dagger.

STILETTO HEELS (shoes) indicate strength and/or formidable character behind a seemingly fragile individual.

STILLBIRTH portrays an unproductive beginning; a bad start.

STILL LIFE (painting) will portray an important element for the dreamer to give awake-state attention to. This connotation will be different for each dreamer. Recall what the still life was of.

STIMULANT applies to a motivational factor.

STING (situational backfire) represents an ulterior motive.

STINGER (insect) pertains to a negative rebound response.

STINGRAY exposes a false prophet.

STINGINESS warns against selfishness, greed, and being within a self-absorbed state.

STINK See stench.

STINK BOMB signifies retaliation; a serious rebounding action.

STINKBUG stands for natural talents used in a negative manner.

STINKWEED refers to a concealed negative element in one's life; things look fine on the surface, yet something smells.

STIPEND connotes one's allowable limits.

STIPULATION reveals a condition associated with something.

STIR usually implies that something in one's life is being stirred up and suggests watchfulness.

STIR CRAZY denotes a lack of acceptance and/or patience; a need to look at one's current situation in a different, more creative way.

STIR-FRY calls for a need to insure something is cooked thoroughly, as in fully completed.

STIRRUP denotes an advisement to get a firm foothold.

STITCH (pain) comes as a caution against going too fast or forcing an issue.

STITCH (sewn) indicates the act of pulling something together; an attempt to connect elements.

STOCK See cattle.

STOCK See stock certificate.

STOCK (soup) relates to heartiness; rounded nourishment.

STOCK (supplies) represents preparedness; resourcefulness; forethought. Was the dream stock scanty or plentiful? What type of stock was displayed? Clothing? Food?

STOCKADE See corral.

STOCKBROKER characterizes one who takes risks with another's assets.

STOCK CAR See race car.

STOCK CERTIFICATE relates to a personal interest (stake) in something.

STOCK EXCHANGE signifies great stress.

STOCKING pertains to covering one's footsteps.

STOCKING MASK refers to deception; an attempt to hide oneself.

STOCKING STUFFER stands for those little blessings we're gifted with throughout life.

STOCK MARKET See Wall Street.

STOCKPILE could advise one to *stop* hoarding and share with others. This depends on what was shown to be stockpiled. Also see storage.

STOCKROOM will reveal what one should be retaining and reserving.

STOCKYARD See corral.

STOKE implies a need to rekindle some aspect in one's life. Usually the dreamer will be aware of the individual intent for this symbol.

STOMACH alludes to fortitude.

STOMACHACHE reveals a lack of inner strength or may indicate heightened sensitivity. Could reveal a complainer or something one doesn't have a stomach for.

STOMACH PUMP exposes an attempt to rid oneself of an undesirable life aspect.

STOMP typifies an adverse reaction; an inability to contain emotions.

STONE usually refers to life's smaller irritations.

STONE AGE (setting) connotes a backward or primitive idea, perspective, or manner of behavior.

STONECROP (botanical) stands for destiny and its acceptance.

STONECUTTER See jeweler.

STONE-FACED signifies a desire to conceal responses.

STONEFISH denotes spiritual fanaticism; points out a need for tolerance.

STONE-GROUND pertains to a *natural* method of accomplishing something.

STONEHENGE connotes lost aspects of true Reality.

STONEMASON See bricklayer.

STONEWALL implies delaying tactics.

STONEWARE symbolizes simplicity.

STONEWASHED (color) suggests a lack of strong opinions; an on-the-fence type of perspective; an inability to take a firm stand.

STONEWORK See masonry.

STOOGE characterizes one who is easily manipulated.

STOOL typifies an aid that assists one's advancement or progression. Depending on the type of stool, this could point to a small element providing temporary respite.

STOOP See bent.

STOOP See doorstep.

STOPCOCK See faucet.

STOPLIGHT portrays a temporary halt to one's advancement.

STOPOVER illustrates a need to experience a particular event or communion along one's life path.

STOP PAYMENT (order) constitutes a sudden change in plans.

STOPPER correlates to containment; keeping something from getting away or escaping from one's control.

STOP SIGN See road signs.

STOPWATCH cautions one to pace life according to *acceptance* rather than attempting to *force* matters, thereby making life more complex and difficult.

STORAGE connotes having reserves; preparedness.

STORE See shop.

STOREFRONT pertains to a perception of one's best opportunities that are currently available.

STOREKEEPER characterizes a person who is capable of providing various opportunities.

STORK typifies the approach of a new idea or perception; may denote a new direction.

STORM pertains to a troublesome time; emotional upheavals.

STORM CELLAR signifies one's personal methods of emotional defenses.

STORM CHASER points to an individual who is highly curious and pushes the envelop to get answers.

STORM DOOR relates to one's free will decision to open self to emotional involvement or to remain closed to it.

STORM DRAIN denotes an advisement to *release* one's emotional or psychological burdens and allow them to *flow away* from oneself.

STORM TROOPER characterizes a highly aggressive personality.

STORM WARNING sends an alarm related to a high probability for imminent turmoil in one's life.

STORM WATCH provides a hint that possible trouble lies in one's path. This comes as a wonderful forewarning which should perk the dreamer's awake-state awareness into proceeding more cautiously.

STORM WINDOW represents insulated (protected) perceptions; a desire to maintain personal distance.

STORYBOOK will reveal a personal message for each dreamer. Recall the storybook's title. What was the message of the story? Was someone reading it or handing it to you?

STORYTELLER characterizes one who is interested in preserving the truth.

STOVE denotes an opportunity to complete an aspect in one's life; a means to *cook* it (bring to fruition).

STOVEPIPE connotes an *exit* route for negative elements in one's life.

STOVEPIPE HAT alludes to *tall* thoughts that are unexpressed or purposely suppressed; a need to release or express oneself.

STOWAWAY refers to personal unawareness.

STOWE (Harriet Beecher) represents human rights.

STRADDLE usually applies to indecision; may indicate a desire to remain neutral.

STRAGGLER won't necessarily indicate procrastination, but usually symbolizes one who is cautious and discerning when in a group situation.

STRAIGHT ARROW may portray an upright attitude or it may stand for a closed mind, depending on the related dream details.

STRAIGHT FACE See stone-faced.

STRAIGHT RAZOR suggests a serious and focused personality.

STRAIGHT SHOOTER signifies honesty.

STRAINER implies the need to sift through something; cautions against arbitrarily *taking everything in*; discernment.

STRAITJACKET comes as a strong advisement to *straighten out* one's life, thoughts, emotions, perceptions, or belief systems.

STRAIT-LACED usually refers to an opinionated, unyielding, and overly conservative nature.

STRANGER most often appears in dreams as a messenger. Recall how this stranger made you feel. How was she/he dressed? What was said or done?

STRANGLE HOLD connotes a state of being manipulated; forced or controlled.

STRANGULATION exposes a *choking* condition; a need to free oneself from a suffocating relationship or situation. Who was strangling whom?

STRAP relates to a means of carrying something through life; may indicate a support or burden depending on the surrounding dreamscape details.

STRATEGIST characterizes an individual who is highly capable of thorough planning or analyzation.

STRAW represents an insulating quality.

STRAW BALE HOUSE stands for a well-insulated home life. This means that one desires to keep home a place of soothing respite, separate from the hectic pace and attitudes of the outside workaday world.

STRAWBERRY constitutes a congenial, cheerful nature.

STRAWBERRY MARK See birthmark.

STRAWFLOWER suggests a need for greater openness.

STRAW HAT represents confidence in one's perceptions and beliefs.

STRAW MAN may refer to one who serves as a front for another who wishes to remain in the background or private. Also see scarecrow.

STRAW VOTE denotes an interest in the opinions of others.

STREAK (mark) symbolizes a *touch* of a different element contained in a specific aspect.

STREAK (run naked) pertains to an unexpected event or something presented for its shock value; may even mean a personal *wake-up* call.

STREAKED HAIR warns of false ideas or perspectives mixed in with natural ones.

STREAM applies to the changing course one's spiritual search takes.

STREAMBED connotes the opportunity to discover spiritual riches.

STREAMER correlates to an attention-getting message. It says, "Hey, look over here! Look at this!"

STREAMLINED typifies an element or life aspect, even a belief or perspective, that has been pared down to an efficient form consisting of its basic essence, rid of the extraneous, superfluous elements.

STREET will depict a byway; a course one has an option of traveling. Did the street have a name? Was it lit or dark? Was it deserted or crowded?

STREETCAR See cable car.

STREETLIGHT brightens one's path. Recall if the streetlight focused on a particular shop, dwelling, or individual. Did it light up a sign?

STREET MAP comes to suggest that we need to be sure of our direction.

STREET SMARTS symbolize personal survival skills and pertain to how well one

is prepared to handle difficulties encountered throughout life.

STREETWALKER See prostitute.

STREP THROAT exposes a state of negative communication; indicates a current stage of negativity toward another.

STREPTOMYCIN See antibiotic.

STRESS warns of a mental and emotional state in which the saving quality of acceptance is lacking.

STRESS TEST comes as a personal advisement to check oneself for how one is dealing with troublesome situations.

STRETCHER signifies a warning. Who was on the stretcher? This is a forewarning.

STRETCHING suggests reaching farther; expanding one's mind or perception of possibilities.

STRETCH MARK is a reminder that one has *stretched* his or her potential or perceptions in the past and can do it again.

STREUSEL signifies the *topping* (final touch) to something.

STRIKE (work halt) reveals a personal dissatisfaction with how one's life is progressing; a need for change.

STRIKEBREAKER represents a negative element that temporarily prevents one from changing her/his life course.

STRIKE FORCE refers to one's unfailing determination to reach a goal; a powerful motivation which sets an individual into decisive action.

STRIKEOUT denotes unsuccessful attempts.

STRIKEOVER signifies an indifference toward one's mistakes; no attempt made to cover them correctly.

STRING usually connotes an idea; the

beginning formulation of a new concept or theory.

STRINGER (timber) alludes to a stabilizing factor in one's life.

STRINGER (writer) represents information from differing sources.

STRINGY HAIR warns of ideas that have coalesced into multiple separate issues; a loss of an ability to intellectually perceive the whole picture.

STRIP CENTER suggests convenient opportunities.

STRIPE (pattern) indicates duality; multiple perceptions of one element; unpredictability.

STRIP MINE implies a negative aspect that distorts the quality or inherent integrity of something.

STRIPPED-DOWN relates to the existence of essential elements only.

STRIP-SEARCH comes as a verification that one isn't hiding anything; a call to be more open and forthright.

STROBE LIGHT signifies an attempt to alter reality or see it under a different light.

STROKE (brain) warns of a harmful negative idea or emotion existing within oneself.

STROKE (soothe) reflects sympathy; an effort to comfort oneself or another.

STROKE (sun) See sunstroke.

STROLLER connotes a new birth or new course with which one is content; the feeling of ease that a new attitude brings.

STROLLING signifies acceptance in one's life; the taking of each hour at a time; the understanding that one can't force certain things.

STRONG-ARM (tactics) warns of the harmful effects of attempting to force issues or results.

STRONGBOX suggests a recognition of life's valuable aspects.

STRONGHOLD portrays one's personally protected defenses.

STRONG SUIT reveals an individual's area of strength or talent.

STROP advises of a need to sharpen one's perception.

STRUCTURAL ENGINEER characterizes an individual who has the knowledge to gauge whether or not a plan has foundational merit/strength.

STRUGGLE usually defines an internal conflict; a lack of acceptance.

STRUMMING exemplifies a relaxed attitude; acceptance.

STRUNG-OUT warns of an inability to cope or deal with one life aspect at a time.

STRUT (brace) connotes a supportive element in one's life.

STRUT (stride) exposes arrogance or overconfidence.

STRYCHNINE See poison.

STUBBLE (bristly) represents roughness; incompleteness.

STUBBORN implies determination; strong sense of direction.

STUCCO refers to a lasting finish to something.

STUD (framing) applies to a supportive factor for an idea or plan.

STUD (pin/earring) indicates an altered perspective.

STUD (snow tires) portrays a desire to thoroughly grasp spiritual ideas.

STUDENT connotes one who requires further learning experiences.

STUDENT TEACHER signifies a future teacher who still needs more experience.

STUDENT UNION relates to the need for relaxation times interspersed with efforts applied to learning.

STUD FINDER stands for finding the basic or foundational aspects of an issue.

STUDIO (apartment) stands for one with few needs.

STUDIO (arts) will pertain to one of the arts. Refer to artist, metal sculpture, photographer, etc.

STUDY See library.

STUDY HALL suggests serious efforts are required for researching and discovering all facets of a particular issue or concept.

STUFFED SHIRT reveals a haughty personality.

STUFFING corresponds to a padding or filler element added to something; extraneous aspect; exaggerations.

STUMBLING depicts an attempt to find one's way; an unsure course.

STUMBLING BLOCK denotes a temporary setback.

STUMP (tree) portrays inherent talents or abilities that are denied or willingly left unused.

STUN GUN may indicate the manifestation of an unexpected event that shocks or it could signify a need to temporarily halt current efforts applied to a particular issue.

STUNT DOUBLE (acting) comes as a warning against letting others do your difficult tasks in life. May point to an overblown value of self or a lack of self-confidence (fear of failure).

STUNT FLYING represents one who has a tendency toward flaunting one's ostentatious intellect by using one hundred dollar words. Usually this individual will have little real wisdom behind the show of verbal pretension.

STUPOR implies a state of mental confusion or unawareness.

STURGEON (fish) stands for strong spiritual faith generated from a high level of reason and analytical thought.

STUTTERING symbolizes an inability to communicate one's thoughts.

STY See pigpen.

STY (eye) applies to a negatively affected perception.

STYGIAN (atmosphere) denotes a heavy, negative atmosphere, often self-generated.

STYLUS pertains to precision.

STYPTIC STICK signifies an attempt to resolve a problematical element.

STYROFOAM represents an insulating quality.

STYX RIVER (Greek mythology) comes as a warning to change one's ways or be on the watch for forthcoming dangers.

SUAVE stands for finesse; diplomacy.

SUBCONSCIOUS constitutes hidden issues and aspects of one's awake-state consciousness.

SUBCONTRACTOR characterizes an individual capable of assisting another or carrying a specific portion of another's burden.

SUBCULTURE suggests a differing perspective.

SUBDIVIDED implies a need to break down an idea for the purpose of clarification or analyzation.

SUBDIVISION (residential) See suburb.

SUBDUE refers to the act tempering one's overemotionalism.

SUBFLOOR See plywood.

SUBLET exemplifies the absorption or sharing of another's perspective.

SUBLIMINAL depicts an incomplete thought; hint; partial idea or unformed theory.

SUBMARINE comes as a warning against spiritual hypocrisy.

SUBMARINE SANDWICH reveals an unrecognized benefit in one's life.

SUBMERGED See immersion.

SUBMISSIVENESS refers to a tendency to be easily manipulated. May point to a feeling of inferiority.

SUBORDINATE reveals one's position in relation to a specific life aspect or relationship.

SUBPOENA stands for a need to communicate important information.

SUBSCRIPTION (magazine/newspaper) will expose an individual's attitude, tendency, or personal interest; may even illustrate hidden perspectives or opinions.

SUBSERVIENCE denotes a tendency to defer to others instead of standing up for oneself or feeling free to voice one's own opinions. May point to an underlying desire to please others for the purpose of being well-liked.

SUBSIDY exemplifies some type of assistance given or obtained.

SUBSTANCE ABUSE connotes a lack of self-control; dependency; an inability to face reality or take personal responsibility.

SUBSTANDARD exposes behavior or qualities that do not meet acceptable levels.

SUBSTANTIATE signifies some type of verification.

SUBSTITUTION denotes an alternative.

SUBTERFUGE indicates some type of deception.

SUBTITLE will constitute an explanation or give a clue to what something is about.

SUBTRACTION (symbol) refers to a need to lessen some element in one's life.

SUBURB connotes an intermediate placement or position; a middle of the road yet structured perspective.

SUBVERSION pertains to an attempt to undermine a plan or individual.

SUBWAY stands for an alternate course of action; clever evasiveness; a less obvious manner of getting from point A to point B.

SUCCULENT (plant) connotes a highly desirable aspect or plan that will be successful; an aspect loaded with benefits.

SUCKER (candy) applies to an easily manipulated individual. Depending on other related aspects to the dream, this symbol can also point to a sweet benefit that's long-lasting.

SUCKER (fish) reveals a state of spiritual gullibility whereby even the false or unimportant spiritual issues are eagerly taken in; a lack of spiritual discernment.

SUCKLE depicts a dependence on another.

SUCTION PUMP represents a withdrawal; a pulling back movement.

SUE See lawsuit.

SUEDE (fabric) refers to a naturalness; no false affectations.

SUEDE CLOTH (fabric) represents a sympathetic nature, one that's true and gentle.

SUET stands for multifaceted utilization.

SUFFERANCE suggests gentle acceptance; forbearance.

SUFFOCATE reflects a state of perceived smothering; usually reveals a self-generated condition.

SUFFUSED refers to a thoroughness; interspersed throughout.

SUGAR may exemplify an energizing element or it may allude to a highly desirable aspect in one's life; a sweet benefit or outcome.

SUGAR CANE FIELD suggests a source producing a desirable aspect.

SUGARCOATING warns of an attempt to deceive; trying to alter reality; overly optimistic.

SUGAR DADDY characterizes an individual who retards one's inner growth.

SUGAR GLIDER denotes resourcefulness.

SUGARHOUSE See maple syrup.

SUGAR MAPLE (tree) symbolizes tranquility generated from spiritual wisdom.

SUGAR SUBSTITUTE See artificial sweetener.

SUGGESTION BOX denotes one's ability to make improvements or bring about change.

SUICIDE reveals a loss of inner strength and the perception of being a spiritual facet of the Divine Essence. This symbol may also reveal a self-defeating plan or move.

SUICIDE BOMBER characterizes an individual who is obsessed with destroying another; a willingness to die for one's cause.

SUICIDE WATCH portrays a recognition and attentive monitoring given to an individual who has lost his/her course and strength to persevere.

SUIT pertains to a formality; formal behavior.

SUITCASE See luggage.

SUITE (rooms) implies a temporary state of comfort.

SUITOR relates to heightened attention given another.

SULFUR exemplifies a disagreeable element in one's life.

SULTANA pertains to an expectation of deference; aloofness.

SULTRY portrays a tough or sticky situation.

SUMAC (tree) represents a ready recognition of opportunities.

SUMMARY will reveal a concise message that will mean something specific to the dreamer.

SUMMER (season) illustrates the fruitful time to give heightened attention and nurturing effort to life goals and spiritual journeys.

SUMMER CAMP signifies a recreational, more enjoyable way to spend learning a particular subject.

SUMMERHOUSE See gazebo.

SUMMER KITCHEN denotes a desire to place oneself in a once-removed position; distancing oneself from the core of a heated situation, issue, or relationship.

SUMMER SCHOOL suggests a need for additional information or instruction.

SUMMER SOLSTICE See summer.

SUMMER STOCK stands for phases in life when one has a tendency to don an altered persona; may also point to a temporary time of putting oneself in another's shoes.

SUMMIT stands for high points in one's life or spiritual journey.

SUMMIT CONFERENCE stands for a serious need for an important communication; an advisement to generate a major discussion.

SUMMONS exposes a serious warning for one to answer for erring ways or participate in a process of justice.

SUMMONS SERVER characterizes a conscious awareness of one's wrongdoings; an inability to hide from the truth, or an instrumental element in an attempt to get at the truth.

SUMP PUMP signifies a need to rid oneself of negative or erroneous spiritual beliefs or perceptions.

SUN stands for the Divine Essence.

SUNBAKED suggests a natural way to finalize or develop an idea.

SUNBATHING applies to a desire to absorb the spiritual within oneself.

SUNBEAM pertains to spiritual illumination.

SUN BLOCK denotes an attempt to keep a specified distance from spiritual matters.

SUNBURN forewarns of a state of being spiritually burned by a false concept or perception.

SUNBURST (design) symbolizes the simplicity of the Divine Essence's truths.

SUN DANCE represents inner strength.

SUNDAY connotes a time of reflection on one's behavior, perceptions, and life course.

SUNDAY SCHOOL signifies the deep insights gained from serious reflection and contemplation.

SUN DECK typifies a desire to remain connected with the Divine Essence while on one's spiritual journey.

SUNDIAL comes as a message that advises of *now* being the time to reconnect with the Divine Essence.

SUNDRESS suggests keeping an attitude/perspective befitting the occasion.

SUNFISH refers to the joy taken in one's quiet comfort in personal spirituality.

SUNFLOWER specifically symbolizes spiritual joy.

SUNGLASSES expose an altered perspective that is colored by personal opinions or psychological elements. Recall the color of the lens.

SUN GODDESS characterizes one who has that elated feeling of being spiritually blessed; the uplifting sense brought on by spiritual behavior.

SUNKEN represents a *lowering* direction which usually applies to an attempt to reach *basic* elements or get in touch with oneself by being grounded.

SUNKEN GARDEN signifies efforts to maintain one's inner integrity and remain grounded.

SUN LAMP reflects artificial spirituality.

SUN PORCH refers to an opportunity to let the light in; a matter of choice whether or not an individual sees the light.

SUNRISE pertains to an inner welling of spiritual joy.

SUNROOF stands for a desire to remain connected to the Divine Essence while traversing one's life path.

SUNROOM portrays a home life permeated with spirituality.

SUNSCREEN See sun block.

SUNSET constitutes the most spiritually intense or powerful time.

SUNSPOT connotes heightened spiritual activity.

SUNSTROKE represents a lack in personal spiritual discernment; an inability to control which concepts are accepted.

SUNTAN refers to a routine exposure to spiritual elements.

SUN VISOR See visor cap.

SUPER BOWL denotes a final contest to determine a winner or a final hurdle to determine success.

SUPER BOWL RING signifies the success of a goal.

SUPERFICIAL reveals a fear of becoming involved; a hesitancy to delve into the deeper aspects of true Reality.

SUPERHUMAN (qualities) relate to inner strengths. Depending on the dream's related elements, this symbol can also come to remind one that one shouldn't have such high expectations that they're right off the scale (unrealistic).

SUPERIMPOSED (image) exposes the existence of a dual nature or personality as evidenced by that which one presents to others and that which is kept hidden.

SUPERINTENDENT will usually signify who is in charge. Recall the surrounding dreamscape details to determine *what* this superintendent was in charge of.

SUPERMAN See superhuman.

SUPERMARKET See market (shop).

SUPERNATURAL stands for perceptual and intellectual ignorance of the interrelating elements of true Reality.

SUPERNOVA marks the recognition of a major spiritual insight.

SUPERPOWER pertains to those with the most power and authority, but not necessarily possessing the proper ethics, morals, and spiritual qualities.

SUPER RICH identifies those with the greatest quantity of bountiful assets, thereby revealing those with the greatest spiritual responsibility to help others.

SUPER-SIZE (food portion) denotes a psychological need for abundance. This need stems from a need to ensure one has *enough* of something.

SUPERSONIC denotes a reach or existence beyond popular, generally accepted concepts; into the realm of deeper thought.

SUPERSTAR represents great potential. The key here is to discern *how* this potential is used

SUPERSTITION defines an ignorance of the interacting elements of true Reality.

SUPERSTORE portrays a chance to take advantage of a great range of opportunities.

SUPERSTRUCTURE refers to any idea, perception, plan, or belief developed far beyond its basic elements. These can sometimes become a monster grown unrecognizable.

SUPERTANKER warns against carrying excess burdens or extraneous elements while traversing one's spiritual course.

SUPERVISOR most often connotes oneself (one's conscience).

SUPINE (position) relates to a time of rest, neutrality, or acceptance.

SUPPER pertains to a need to re-energize and nourish oneself.

SUPPLEMENT infers the need for an additional element in one's life.

SUPPLENESS suggests tenacity; an ability to cope with and manage almost any situation.

SUPPLICANT implies a lack of self-confidence and reliance. May point to an overscrupulous conscience, possibly false guilt.

SUPPORT GROUP signifies supportive opportunities; the existence of support or encouragement if one really needs it.

SUPPORT HOSE means a personal recognition that one requires additional support as one travels through life.

SUPPOSITION will not denote an assumption but rather one's deeper thoughts and exploratory reaches into deeper theories and concepts.

SUPPOSITORY suggests that something within oneself is lacking.

SUPREME BEING See Divine Essence.

SUPREME COURT alludes to a need to give researched and contemplative time to a major decision or plan.

SURCHARGE exposes an overwhelming situation.

SURE-FOOTED relates to high confidence; self-reliance.

SURF illustrates spiritual movement, the living essence of it.

SURFBOARD pertains to the participation in a spiritual movement which can be within oneself rather than group-related.

SURGE connotes a sudden increase in activity, energy, or interest.

SURGEON relates to precision and skill.

SURGE PROTECTOR signifies a method of self-monitoring one's energy levels and guarding against *draining* elements or individuals.

SURGICAL SHOE COVERINGS represent a path walked in fear of being touched by any negatives.

SURPLUS STORE represents multiple opportunities.

SURPRISE PARTY stands for a wonderful unexpected blessing.

SURREALISM (art style/atmosphere) represents an altered perspective of reality. May reveal a current phase of one's life when things seem unreal.

SURRENDER usually represents an advisement to accept more rather than having expectations or attempting to force results.

SURREPTITIOUS refers to an action performed without announcement. May also point to deception.

SURROGATE See substitution.

SURROUND SOUND suggests a need to listen better, yet may also point out that one is hearing a specific idea from many sources.

SURTAX suggests a taxing situation, issue; more energy expended on an issue than one was prepared to give.

SURVEILLANCE advises of a need to heighten one's awareness; watchfulness.

SURVEILLANCE CAMERA See camera (hidden).

SURVEILLANCE ROOM refers to eyes on many matters. This could come as an advisement for the dreamer to pay closer

In Your Dreams

attention to details or it could come to reveal that many eyes are watching you.

SURVEY (measure) cautions one to exercise precise planning. May also advise of a need to stay within one's own realm of business.

SURVEY (poll) portrays an interest in the opinion of others.

SURVEYOR relates to an individual who is fragmenting his/her life course; one who draws many lines; a separatist.

SURVIVALIST emphasizes self-reliance; resourcefulness.

SUSPECT marks a questionable individual, plan, or concept.

SUSPENDERS pertain to a supportive element that allows one to hold up under adversity.

SUSPENSE warns against anticipation; advises of the wisdom of maintaining acceptance.

SUSPENSION BRIDGE symbolizes an extended transition period.

SUTTEE exposes a negative self-sacrificing act.

SUTURE correlates to an initial aspect that serves to promote healing.

SVELTE connotes a tendency to keep to the essentials, basics.

SVENGALI reveals an individual who manipulates others for negative purposes.

SWAB pertains to a need to *go over* something; possibly recheck or review.

SWAGGER usually refers to an overly confident attitude; overly self-assured.

SWALLOW (bird) refers to shyness; timidity.

SWALLOW (consume) implies the ingestion of a specific aspect.

SWAMI See yogi.

SWAMP constitutes a weak or confused spiritual foundation.

SWAMP BOAT defines an effort to get through spiritual confusion.

SWAMP FEVER indicates the effects of becoming immersed in spiritual confusion.

SWAMP GAS refers to spiritual gas signifying conceptual waste.

SWAN exemplifies an individual's beautiful and grace-filled spiritual nature; inherent spiritual essence and resulting gifts.

SWAN SONG stands for an end to a specific life stage of direction.

SWAP MEET represents the opportunities to share talents and abilities.

SWARM suggests an overwhelming element in one's life.

SWASHBUCKLER exposes a tendency to dramatize or flaunt.

SWASTIKA (configuration) may not stand for a highly negative element but rather for its original symbology, that of a religious sign of good luck or that one's fortune will be improving.

SWATCH (cloth) portrays a sampling of one's hidden personality or inner character. Recall the type of cloth, design, and color.

SWAYBACK reflects a burdensome phase of life.

SWAYING suggests a tendency to change one's mind; indecision.

SWEAR (cuss) implies an intent to express emphasis.

SWEAR (vow) signifies personal validation.

SWEAT indicates personal effort expended. May also point to expectation and/or great impatience.

SWEATBAND represents an attempt to control one's efforts applied to a specific project or goal. May mean an attempt to gain a greater measure of patience.

SWEAT EQUITY stands for a value of something being assessed by the work one put into it.

SWEATER suggests warmth of character. Recall the style, texture, and color for additional information.

SWEATSHOP warns against forcing efforts, especially the manipulating of another's efforts.

SWEAT SUIT represents an intention of expending effort on an idea or project; a preparedness for forthcoming action.

SWEDEN represents a tolerance for another's individuality.

SWEEPING exemplifies a tendency to maintain a clear path in life.

SWEEPSTAKES See lottery.

SWEET (flavor) most often reflects a desirable element in one's life.

SWEET-AND-SOUR (sauce) marks an element containing the dual aspects of positive and negative factors; pleasing yet somewhat problematical.

SWEET CLOVER (botanical) represents emotional sensitivity.

SWEETENER indicates an attempt to make something more palatable or attractive.

SWEET GRASS denotes a cherishing.

SWEET GRASS BRAID stands for a sign of honoring another.

SWEET GUM (tree) symbolizes an enriching element in one's life and the appreciation of it.

SWEETHEART pertains to an individual for whom one has special affection.

SWEET PEA (botanical) refers to a clinging idea; a solid grasp. Depending on related dreamscape elements, this symbol may also signify fragile relationships or situations.

SWEET POTATO symbolizes an agreeable element in one's life; an essential aspect that is very pleasing.

SWEET TALK See flattery.

SWEET TOOTH correlates to a strong desire for life to contain only desirable aspects; an inability to deal with reality without the urge to sweeten it.

SWELLING See swollen.

SWELTERING represents an inability to deal well with pressure; a hot situation.

SWERVE comes as an advisement to heighten awareness; avoidance and the perceptual awareness to accomplish it.

SWIFT (bird) stands for efficiency; a recognition of inconsequential elements.

SWIG suggests an ability to accept and deal with disagreeable elements.

SWIM FINS stands for impatience to gain spiritual development.

SWIMMER'S EAR warns of receiving negative effects after listening to/accepting questionable spiritual matters.

SWIMMING symbolizes a submersion in one's spiritual search.

SWIMMING CAP reveals an attempt to avoid spiritual issues.

SWIMMING POOL reflects a spiritual search going nowhere; spiritual concepts *treated* with artificial elements.

SWINDLER exposes an individual intent on deception and ulterior motives.

SWINE pertains to excesses indulged in.

SWING (child's) denotes perceptual innocence; an ability to be open to alternative views and broad-scope concepts.

SWING SHIFT advises of a need to experience alternate phases and elements of a specific aspect.

SWIRL (pattern) relates to a convoluted idea, plan, or perspective.

SWISS BANK ACCOUNT stands for an attempt to conceal, usually related to one's assets (talents).

SWITCH (any type) reminds us that we possess the power to make our own decisions; taking personal responsibility. This symbol says, "You can flip the switch if you want to."

SWITCHBACK alludes to retaining past knowledge; infers that one isn't retaining that which has been learned and isn't applying experiential knowledge gained throughout life.

SWITCHBLADE exposes a tendency toward knee-jerk reactions.

SWITCHBOARD signifies an opportunity to make multiple contacts; a means of obtaining expanded information.

SWITCHMAN will signify an individual who is capable of altering one's course in life.

SWITZERLAND suggests neutrality, a tendency to stay out of another's affairs; may also represent the presence of one's fine skill.

SWIVEL CHAIR represents convenience; a means of efficient methodology.

SWIVEL HOOK exemplifies a capability to analyze all angles.

SWIZZLE See alcoholic beverage.

SWIZZLE STICK pertains to a means of blending or coordinating various aspects.

SWOLLEN indicates an expanded element. May point to an excess of something.

SWOON portrays an overwhelming response.

SWORD connotes a self-defensive element; means of protecting one's position.

SWORD (double-edged) stands for something that could backfire.

SWORD DANCE corresponds to the feeling of confidence and self-reliance that one's defensive measures provide.

SWORDFISH apply to spiritual defensiveness.

SWORD GRASS warns of hazardous elements which are present on one's current path.

SYCAMORE (tree) stands for deep emotional responses; admiration.

SYLPH characterizes spiritual grace.

SYLVAN See forest.

SYMBIOSIS exposes a personal need for another individual that may or may not be productive or mutually beneficial.

SYMMETRY portrays balance.

SYMPATHY may reveal a need to *give* compassion to another or it may warn against *drawing* it for self-gratification.

SYMPHONY pertains to coordinated efforts of multiple talents.

SYMPOSIUM illustrates the convergence of ideas.

SYNAGOGUE reflects spiritual associations and the living practice of one's beliefs.

SYNCHRONICITY represents destiny.

SYNCHRONIZED SWIMMING suggests a mimicked spiritual path.

SYNDICATE connotes an affiliation of like-minded individuals with a common goal.

SYNDROME suggests a particular personality aspect generated from various causes; may denote a unique perspective derived from multiple experiential sources.

SYNOPSIS will symbolize a basic idea or elemental facts.

SYNTHESIZER stands for a means of combining various ideas or concepts.

SYNTHETIC (fabric) applies to an artificial aspect; an alternative or substitute.

SYRINGE represents a means of interjection or application.

SYRUP portrays overdramatization; flattery; false sincerity.

SYSTEM MONITORS (Internet) stand for a complete infiltration of one's privacy.

SYSTEMS ANALYST characterizes an individual who is capable of discovering the most efficient course of action or means of reaching a goal.

T

TABASCO represents a highly interesting subject; excitability.

TABBY (cat breed) signifies a gregarious personality, companionable nature.

TABERNACLE denotes sacredness or that which is perceived as such. Recall what was in the tabernacle. Where was it? What color?

TABLE pertains to an element of support and convenience.

TABLEAU will illustrate an important message presented as a scene for the dreamer to view.

TABLECLOTH being fabric will reveal multiple aspects. Recall the condition, type of fabric, design, and color.

TABLELAND See plateau.

TABLE OF CONTENTS portrays the main or basic issues the dreamer currently needs to address in life.

TABLE OF MEASUREMENTS stand for a need to understand that differing issues or aspects can have equal value.

TABLE SALT See salt.

TABLESPOON denotes a larger measure than normal; in reference to some type of life aspect it would indicate an ingredient of considerable importance.

TABLET (ancient) suggests a true element of reality or a timeless truth.

TABLET (pill) See pill.

TABLE TALK connotes surface conversation; containing no deep or heavy material.

TABLEWARE See specific utensil.

TABLOID See newspaper.

TABOO exemplifies a subject or life aspect one fears or avoids.

TABULATE advises one to gather up all elements of an aspect and analyze it in a concise manner.

TACHOMETER indicates speed. Recall if the dreamer was being advised to slow down or increase rate of progression.

TACK (equipment) will relate to essential elements required for a specific purpose.

TACK (nail) pertains to a temporary attachment.

TACK (sewing) signifies a temporary repair measure.

TACKLE (fishing) connotes spiritual accessories that are unnecessary for enlightenment or development.

TACKY (to the touch) implies a sticky situation or poor taste/quality.

TACTICS stand for method of behavior.

TADPOLE correlates to spiritual immaturity; a novitiate seeker.

TAE KWON DO See martial arts.

TAFFETA (fabric) will indicate a stiff personality who appears to be amenable.

TAFFY symbolizes difficulties in life; situations where one needs to pull self up and persevere.

TAG (game) warns against avoiding responsibility or a tendency to place same upon another's shoulders.

TAG See label.

TAGALONG portrays a lack of individual purpose or life course.

TAGGING See graffiti.

TAI CHI relates to self-control generated from spiritual inner peace.

TAIL (end) illustrates a position marking a *last* or final element.

TAIL (follow) denotes a personal special interest in someone.

TAIL (of pet) signifies a friend's attitude. Recall if the tail was wagging, hanging down, held up, etc.

TAIL BONE See coccyx bone.

TAILGATE PICNIC suggests convenience for camaraderie. This is an advisement to take advantage of it.

TAILGATING represents a lack of individuality; comes as a warning to *stop following another* so closely.

TAILLIGHT stands for an aspect (sign) that marks one's presence; making oneself visible or effective.

TAILOR See seamstress.

TAILOR-MADE See custom-built.

TAIL PIPE portrays a means or outlet for negative emotions or attitudes.

TAILSPIN implies total confusion; chasing one's tail; going in circles.

TAIL WIND relates to an element that serves to increase the pace of one's life progression or enhances (speeds) the time it takes to accomplish a goal.

TAINTED indicates some type of contamination. This may refer to an offensive behavior or idea that carries a negative element.

TAKE-OUT (meal) comes as a suggestion to slow down and appreciate life's opportunity for important moments of leisure.

TAKEOVER means overwhelmed; a loss of authority or personal responsibility.

TALCUM POWDER represents a personal means of self-control.

TALENT AGENT will correspond with an individual who tries to control where and when another uses her/his natural abilities/inherent skills. This should be an individual choice.

TALENTS correspond to inherent abilities unique to each individual.

TALENT SCOUT characterizes a person who believes he/she can recognize inherent abilities in others and exploit them.

TALENT SHOW defines the ability one perceives is one's best talent.

TALISMAN connotes misplaced faith; possible superstition; lacking self-confidence.

TALKING STICK indicates who has the authority (or turn) to speak.

TALK RADIO signifies an opportunity to express one's opinion or other type of previously withheld emotion, problem, etc.

TALK SHOW publicizes the opinions or interests of others.

TALL (stature) usually has a psychological symbology rather than a physical one. It will refer to one's attitude of superiority, that of looking down on others.

TALLBOY See highboy.

TALLOW refers to a necessary element needed to attain an enlightened perspective on an issue.

TALLY See scoreboard/card.

TALMUD connotes right living according to a specific belief system.

TALON represents control of one's potential aggressiveness.

TALUS constitutes fragmentation; a breakup into multiple elements.

TAMALE characterizes excitability; high emotions.

TAMARACK (tree) points to spiritual fragility/sensitivity.

TAMBOURINE relates to a festive or joyful situation.

TAME portrays congeniality; neutrality or situational ease.

TAM-O'-SHANTER (hat) indicates perspectives affected by one's ethnicity.

TAMPERING warns of an alteration; intent to change the integrity of something.

TAMPERPROOF denotes a solid plan or idea.

TAN See suntan.

TAN (color) See beige.

TANAGER (bird) stands for cheerfulness; optimism.

TANDEM pertains to a partnership or dual aspects.

TANGERINE (color/fruit) refers to a positive life element that nourishes and refreshes.

TANGLED represents a complexity; a problematical situation; a lack of order.

TANGLED HAIR signifies confused thoughts.

TANGO (dance) stands for the synchronized efforts of two people.

TANK (utility) symbolizes a means to store something.

TANK (military) warns of uncontrolled aggression; a lack of discernment while progressing through life.

TANKARD refers to a great need for personal support or strength.

TANKER TRUCK usually is a type of warning symbol. Recall what the truck was hauling in the tanker.

TANK FARM See storage.

TANK FIGHTER (boxing) reveals an individual who acts out prearranged scenarios; preplanned behavior.

TANK TOP suggests exposed behavior, as in having nothing to hide; out in the open.

TANK TOWN will denote a seemingly unimportant location or stop along one's journey. The idea here is that appearances can be deceiving.

TANNERY applies to a means of preservation.

TANNING BED/BOOTH stands for the willful absorption (acceptance) of spiritual concepts one knows are substitutes for the pure truth.

TANSY (botanical) denotes strengthened insight; a need to boost one's defensive methods.

TANTRUM illustrates a lack of self-control.

TANZANITE (gemstone) represents deep spiritual wisdom and insight.

TAOIST will indicate an individual who

has a tendency to not interfere in things; one who lets life take its course without attempting to alter things.

TAP-DANCE cautions against progressing through life by tapping the resources of others instead of one's own.

TAPE See adhesive tape.

TAPE (audio) See audio cassette.

TAPE (video) See video tape.

TAPE MEASURE advises of a need to gauge limits, affects, responses, etc. before proceeding with a plan; an eye toward possible ramifications.

TAPE RECORDER See recorder (tape).

TAPESTRY (design/fabric) will usually illustrate a visual symbolizing an important message for the dreamer. Try to recall the details of the tapestry if it was a scene; otherwise, this tapestry will signify that *all* interacting elements of a certain aspect should be given consideration.

TAPEWORM warns of the existence of an internal negative consuming self; this will indicate a psychological aberration.

TAPIR pertains to the presence of a personal abnormality one should overcome.

TAPPING (sound) comes in dreams as an attention-getting element. The key here is to recall what the tapping sound was associated with.

TAPROOM See barroom.

TAPROOT represents a foundational element through which offshoots develop.

TAR warns of an element or situation in one's life that has the potential of becoming permanent.

TARANTELLA (dance) represents a passionate relationship. This passion may not always refer to an attraction or love.

TARANTULA applies to a fearful perception.

TAR BABY characterizes a situation from which one cannot extract self.

TARDINESS cautions against procrastination; suggests the possibility that one's actions or response will be too late.

TARGET stands for a goal or focus of attention.

TARGET DATE signifies a time to shoot for regarding achieving a goal or plan.

TARGET SHOOTING exemplifies practice; an attempt to sharpen one's skills.

TARIFF represents a cost attached to the exercising of one's skills or talents.

TARMAC See asphalt.

TARNISHED illustrates an inner or inherent ability left unused.

TAROT CARDS warns of a fascination with the sensationalistic side of spiritual or inherent abilities; impatient to know the future; an inability to take one day at a time.

TARPAPER portrays a personal spiritual defensive method.

TARPAULIN pertains to self-devised defense mechanisms.

TAR PIT forewarns of a pitfall situation about to enter one's life.

TARPON (fish) symbolizes spiritual narrow-mindedness.

TARSIER signifies sharp perceptual skills.

TART (pastry) See pie.

TART (taste) See sour.

TARTAN (pattern) See plaid.

TARTAR (on teeth) points to a buildup of misspoken words or falsehoods.

TARTAR SAUCE symbolizes a personal perspective applied to a specific spiritual belief for the purpose of adding a more tasteful element.

TARZAN characterizes an overblown perspective of self and one's abilities.

TASK FORCE represents a need to combine efforts in order to be effective. This is usually in regard to a specific goal or problem.

TASKMISTRESS will usually refer to the feminine conscience.

TASMANIA signifies a normally sunny disposition due to faith in one's spirituality.

TASMANIAN DEVIL symbolizes fierce vindictiveness; maliciously aggressive behavior.

TASSEL typifies extraneous elements that have been added to a basic aspect.

TASTE BUDS connote personal opinions and perspectives; a fact bearing on relativity and subjectivity.

TASTELESS refers to inappropriateness, uninteresting, or undesirable.

TASTE TESTER usually points to tentative trial sampling of ideas.

TATTERED relates to a worn out or well-used element; may indicate high value if it's well used.

TATTERSALL (pattern) pertains to multiple elements forming a single aspect.

TATTING See lace.

TATTLETALE reveals an informant; an untrustworthy individual.

TATTOO signifies how one perceives self. Recall what the tattoo was. What color and size?

TAUNT See nag (bother).

TAUPE (color) See beige.

TAUT can have opposing meanings depending on the dreamer's life situation. It can point to a situation/issue which is overextended or grossly belabored to the point of having no more elements to consider or explore. Or it can indicate that one still needs to deal with the slack (associated elements) of an issue. This last refers to details remaining.

TAVERN relates to a perceived place or source of respite where one may receive support.

TAX represents an additional responsibility or debt.

TAX COLLECTOR characterizes a freeloader.

TAX CREDIT suggests a break being given; an unexpected return on one's efforts.

TAX DEDUCTION represents a benefit; a counter to the outlay of efforts expended.

TAX EVASION warns against attempting to avoid one's responsibilities.

TAX-EXEMPT stands for a release of a specific responsibility; something having no strings attached.

TAX-FREE signifies a full benefit which doesn't carry an additional cost.

TAX HAVEN denotes a way to keep more of one's resources without having to disburse it to others.

TAXI pertains to a means of assisting one's progress.

TAXI DANCER refers to a lack of companionship; a forced temporary partnership.

TAXIDERMIST suggests shallow beliefs or perspectives.

TAXI DRIVER characterizes an individual who has the capability of carrying others (for a specified distance) along their path.

TAXIMETER symbolizes the personal cost involved in having others transport you along a portion of your journey.

TAX REFUND Since refunds have to be claimed on the following year's return, this symbol points to a false benefit; a benefit with a future cost involved.

TAX RETURN represents one's finances; may portray one's assets.

TAX SHELTER indicates an attempt to avoid responsibility and debts owed.

TEA alludes to healing strength.

TEA BISCUIT indicates light nourishing element in one's life.

TEACHER characterizes specific knowledge and the ability to transfer it.

TEACHER'S PET warns against favoritism displayed in life.

TEACHING HOSPITAL suggests a need to learn healing methods; may refer to self-healing.

TEACUP most often refers to a temporary situation, one which may tend to be over-blown.

TEA GARDEN indicates a source of healing strength, fortitude.

TEAHOUSE signifies a small respite; a healthful break.

TEAKETTLE denotes a specified span of time before an idea or plan is ready to put into action.

TEAKWOOD stands for an enduring perspective/belief that will withstand spiritual negatives.

TEAL (color) symbolizes spiritual beliefs interwoven in daily behavior.

TEA LIGHT (candle) stands for a small, yet safe, illumination; a very good idea.

TEAM refers to those working together for a specific goal.

TEAM OWNER (sports) characterizes one who funds or backs a joint effort.

TEAM PLAYER won't necessarily be a positive dream symbol because it usually points to someone who goes along with the crowd, even if the crowd is wrong.

TEAMWORK signifies cooperative pooling of talents.

TEA PARTY (child's) represents immature or undeveloped social skills.

TEAPOT symbolizes a tool for creating or bringing about healing energies.

TEAR (rip) See rip.

TEAR DOWN points out willful destructive behavior.

TEARDROP (literal or shape) indicates an emotional response that, depending on the dream's surrounding details, may connote sorrow, joy, or empathy.

TEAR GAS implies a means of controlling another.

TEAR-JERKER (movie/story) usually reveals excessive emotionalism.

TEAROOM See teahouse.

TEA ROSE (botanical) signifies a dignified, genteel admiration.

TEAR SHEET corresponds to evidence; verification.

TEAR STRIP points to easy access.

TEASING often symbolizes one's hidden attitude.

TEASPOON portrays a small amount; a small or average measure of something.

TECHNICIAN characterizes one who is capable of figuring out specific things.

TECHNO-GEEK in dreams actually reveals someone more interested in intellectual matters than in societal issues. Contrary to popular assumption, this is not a negative dream symbol.

TECH SUPPORT (computer/programs) characterizes those one can go to for help in utilizing or troubleshooting specific life aids.

TECTONICS (study of) represents a high interest in understanding how certain life aspects are formulated/created and their interaction with other affecting elements; an interest in how things come about.

TEDDY BEAR illustrates a soothing and comforting aspect in one's life.

TEE (golf) will most often point to an irritating element in one's life, something which gets one teed off.

TEENAGER relates to a transitional phase.

TEENYBOPPER stands for immaturity; an inability to face reality or a denial of certain elements of it.

TEETER-TOTTER See seesaw.

TEETH symbolize the manner of an individual's speech which reflects their inner personality.

TEETH CLENCHING/GRINDING reveals efforts to control frustration, anger, or impatience.

TEETHING RING constitutes an attempt to ease one's pain.

TEETH WHITENER stands for efforts expended toward improving one's manner of speech.

TEETOTALER characterizes an individual who claims or believes he/she needs no support in life.

TEFLON stands for a protective shield; relates to self-defense mechanisms.

TELECONFERENCE comes as an advisement to include several others in a communication or to equally include them in a plan or idea.

TELEGRAM will signify a personal message for each dreamer. Recall what the telegram said and who it was from.

TELEGRAPH OPERATOR symbolizes information or messages generated from one's inner perceptual senses.

TELEGRAPH PLANT (botanical) points to the interrelationship between all living things; the psychic bond connecting all life forms.

TELEMARKETING denotes fast-talk; an attempt to sell through impersonal communication.

TELEPATHY signifies insights; a subtle knowing.

TELEPHONE refers to communication. Was the dream phone ringing? Was someone reaching for it as if to call another? Who was using it?

TELEPHONE BOOK pertains to a source of contacts.

TELEPHONE BOOTH exemplifies the availability of opportunities to communicate with others.

TELEPHONE NUMBER may reveal a literal phone number which means something to the dreamer, or the individual digits are meant to be added up to total a number carrying significance.

TELEPHONE OPERATOR characterizes a person capable of assisting one to communicate with others.

TELEPHONE POLE represents a communication element of support.

TELEPHONE TAG See phone tag.

TELEPHONE TRUCK warns of a hearing impairment; one doesn't listen well.

TELEPHOTO LENS See zoom lens.

TELEPROMPTER implies assistance needed to clearly express one's thoughts.

TELESCOPE advises one to look beyond surface presentations.

TELEVISION (watching) See watching television.

TELLER (bank) reveals a person's utilization of personal assets such as wealth, natural abilities, or spiritual gifts. Recall if there was a deposit or withdrawal being made. Was someone in the vault?

TEMBLOR See earthquake.

TEMPER TANTRUM warns against being selfish; a lack of acceptance.

TEMPEST symbolizes a violent emotional outburst/confrontation.

TEMPLATE See die cut.

TEMPLE (site) represents a spiritual element in one's life.

TEMPURA suggests an issue that's been covered up or coated before being exposed or presented to others.

TEN corresponds to closure.

TENANCY IN COMMON represents a shared portion of an idea with no participant having a right to the whole of it.

TENANT See renter.

TEN COMMANDMENTS come to remind one of the simple basics of spiritual behavior.

TENDERFOOT pertains to a lack of experiential knowledge; a beginner setting out to attain a goal.

TENDERIZER denotes an easing factor.

TENDRIL stands for attachments; twining ramifications of certain behavior.

TENEMENT suggests an unsatisfactory situation.

TEN-FOUR represents expressed agreement; confirmation.

TENNESSEE relates to joy felt for blessings.

TENNIS marks a constantly altering element.

TENNIS ELBOW advises of the negative effect of routinely attempting to hit the ball back into another's court.

TENNIS SHOE reflects a need to hold one's ground.

TENOR suggests sincerity; a robust integrity.

TENT reflects a temporary situation; may denote a fragile shelter.

TENTACLE warns of a grasping or flailing for support or firm footing regarding one's life course. Indicates a need to stabilize and ground oneself.

TENURE signifies a well-deserved, lasting benefit/reward for efforts expended.

TEPEE corresponds to a pyramid configuration that centers and condenses one's inner strength.

TEPID (temperature) signifies an attitude bordering on disinterest.

TERMINAL (diagnosis) most often refers to a dead-end situation; having no chance for revitalization.

TERMINAL (travel) signifies opportunities for progress. May indicate a change in direction or goal destination.

TERMINATION will signify the end of something.

TERM INSURANCE refers to a phase of protective coverage which has a time limit.

TERMITE stands for underhandedness; undermining.

TERMITE SHIELD (foundation) signifies an awareness of the possibility of one's plans being undermined and the defensive steps taken to avert such destruction.

TERM PAPER reveals the extent of one's comprehension of a specific subject.

TERN (bird) signifies analytical thought; increased applied reason and logic.

TERRACE See balcony.

TERRA COTTA See pottery.

TERRARIUM portrays a recognition and respect for one's natural abilities.

TERROR See fear.

TERRORIST stands for someone lacking the most basic respect for life.

TERRORIST ATTACK denotes unexpected hostilities.

TESLA (Nikola) characterizes a comprehension of a few elements comprising true Reality.

TEST symbolizes a verification of one's true motivation, knowledge, experiential skill, etc. Often these refer to a self-testing.

TESTATRIX refers to a woman who has left a legacy.

TEST BAN signifies the cessation of an extremely dangerous practice/behavior.

TEST CASE denotes a precedent-setting situation or element in one's life.

TESTDRIVE refers to the testing of a new course or method of traveling that course.

TESTIMONIAL underscores or recommends a specific concept or perspective for the dreamer.

TEST MARKET connotes an attempt to try something out.

TEST PATTERN illustrates the current focus and sharpness of one's present perspective. Recall if the pattern was well defined or blurred.

TEST PILOT refers to self-confidence.

TEST TUBE signifies personal experiments.

TEST-TUBE BABY connotes a personally engineered plan for a new life or direction.

TETANUS reveals a lack of awareness; carelessness.

TETANUS SHOT stands for a diligent level of awareness; preventive measures taken to avoid accidents.

TÊTE-À-TÊTE means a private, face-to-face communication.

TETHER will usually indicate a constraint one needs to break free from.

TETRA (fish) denotes spiritual fragility; advises of a need to strengthen delicate spiritual beliefs or the faith in them.

TEXAS suggests a tendency to have an attitude of superiority; a sense of being a notch better; thinking too big—the big picture—instead of giving attention to the smaller elements which make it up.

TEXTBOOK indicates a specific type of study needed.

TEXTILE See fabric.

TEXT MESSAGING will usually show what the message was and this will be an important specific for each dreamer.

TEXTURE will portray a multitude of meanings. Refer to specific type.

THANKLESS naturally equates to unappreciative, often referring to efforts expended without any acknowledgement.

THANKSGIVING DAY reflects one's thankfulness or gratitude; reminds us to count our daily blessings.

THANK YOU NOTE usually points out a blessing that has been overlooked.

THATCH pertains to natural defenses.

THAW indicates a softening attitude; beginning to express more emotions.

THEATER constitutes a need to *see* more of what transpires around oneself.

THEATER-IN-THE-ROUND symbolizes behavior in full view of everyone; nothing concealed.

THEATRICS points to overdramatizing; exaggerations; tending to greatly overreact.

THEME applies to a specific perspective that will shed light on the dreamer's current puzzlement.

THEME PARK correlates to the manner in which one chooses to relax or find enjoyment.

THEME SONG connotes a particular relationship meaning; may represent some type of personal behavior or psychological element.

THEOLOGIAN denotes deeper spiritual study and a need for same.

THEOSOPHY equates to a philosophical belief in the mystical connection between nature and the Divine Essence; the interrelationship of all living things; the Web of Life.

THERAPIST characterizes an individual who is capable of routinely assisting another to a more balanced attainment.

THERMAL NOISE equates to psychic sensitivity; a heightened awareness of what others rarely perceive.

THERMAL SPRING See hot spring.

THERMOMETER reflects temperament. Recall what degree was presented.

THERMOSTAT suggests personal control in being able to regulate the intensity of a relationship or situation.

THESAURUS indicates a need to choose more appropriate words when communicating with others.

THESIS pertains to thought extension; an advisement to carry one's thoughts further.

THICKENER (additive) stands for an element which gives more substance to an issue, idea, or plan.

THICKET See bush.

THIEF See burglar.

THIMBLE implies a very small amount of something; may also refer to a need to protect oneself.

THIMBLEBERRY (botanical) points to one's attention to details.

THINK TANK advises one to spend time in deep contemplation or analyzation.

THINNER (solvent) signifies an attempt to make a plan or issue more workable.

THIRD BASE refers to progression to the point of almost achieving a goal.

THIRD CLASS represents a commonality; less important.

THIRD DEGREE relates to great intensity.

THIRD EYE stands for insights.

THIRD RAIL refers to the source of energy/power. This suggests that although certain things in life may appear identical, some carry more hidden weight and power than others.

THIRD-RATE symbolizes an acceptable, yet undesirable element or position.

THIRD WORLD represents impoverishment, usually related to one's character.

THIRST signifies an inner need or void; exposes a drive or desire.

THISTLE See thorn.

THISTLEDOWN pertains to a dual nature. The soft side that frequently accompanies a problematical situation.

THISTLE SEEDS (Niger) See birdseed.

TITANIUM symbolizes perseverance and self-confidence.

THOREAU (Henry David) reminds us to not lose sight of the beauty and examples of wisdom that nature freely displays.

THORN relates to the thorny elements in life.

THOROUGHBRED connotes a singular element unaffected by outside influences; a pure aspect.

THRASHER (bird) signifies good communication skills; a sharpened range of language.

THREAD may refer to a connective element or it may indicate a singular, thin idea or chance.

THREADBARE implies a worn out aspect.

THREAT exposes an opposing or interfering element.

THREE symbolizes inner energy and strength; fortitude.

THREE-D GLASSES stand for an attempt to perceive dimensionally, that is, have a well-rounded view of things.

THREE-LEGGED RACE suggests highly coordinated efforts.

THREE-RING CIRCUS exemplifies a ridiculous situation or a confusing chain of events.

THREE STOOGES expose a counterproductive relationship.

THREE-WAY BULB suggests a need for more light on an issue.

THRESHING MACHINE alludes to getting down to basics, essentials.

THRESHOLD stands for a beginning point; poised at the entrance.

THRIFT SHOP relates to resourcefulness; effective management.

THRILLER (book/film) suggests a need for suspense in one's life; a love of living on the edge.

THRILL-SEEKER characterizes an individual who has lost an appreciation of life; a desensitized perspective.

THROAT portrays the inflections in speech; how we often don't realize how our tone of voice sounds to others.

THROAT CULTURE reveals a need to listen to oneself and realize the need to alter the tone in which we speak.

THRONE symbolizes a high position requiring respect and honor. This dream fragment may reflect the true level of an individual or it may represent an arrogant perspective of oneself.

THROTTLE (control) pertains to a means to closure.

THRUSH (bird) stands for spiritual joy; optimism and cheerfulness.

THUG characterizes an individual with no conscience.

THUMB implies a grasp (understanding) or guide.

THUMB (pointing down) obviously indicates disapproval, rejection.

THUMB (pointing up) stands for approval, acceptance; a sign of acknowledgment.

THUMBNAIL will usually indicate a sketchy plan or level of understanding.

THUMB-SUCKING denotes immaturity; being clueless.

THUMBTACK See tack (nail).

THUNDER emphasizes an attention-getting warning related to a specific issue the dreamer will recognize in life.

THUNDERBIRD (design/symbol) applies to inner power/strength.

THUNDERCLOUD reveals an approaching conflict or difficult situation.

THUNDERHEAD represents forthcoming trouble; a problem or altercation brewing.

THUNDERSTRUCK relates to a stunned response to an unexpected event.

THURSDAY is the time to analyze situations and events; give deep thought to one's recent behavior.

THYME (botanical) connotes home life.

TIARA See crown.

TIBET represents persecuted ancient spiritual traditions

TIC (nervous) exposes a subconscious effect or response.

TICK (fabric) connotes a gentle and soft inner nature.

TICK (parasite) exemplifies a negative life element that has the potential to fester beneath one's skin.

TICKER-TAPE PARADE illustrates a major reason for celebration.

TICKET (admission) validates one's right of entry or preparedness.

TICKET (traffic) exposes negative methods of progression along one's life path.

TICKET AGENT will point to the individual who can provide access.

TICKET SCALPER See scalper.

TICKING (sound) emphasizes the passing of time; time may be running out.

TICKSEED (botanical) refers to a need to be more aware, watchful.

TICK-TACK-TOE signifies alignment; implies a need to work at priorities.

TIDAL WAVE forewarns of a spiritually overwhelming state if the current course is not altered.

TIDDLYWINKS refer to a haphazard approach to accomplishing goals.

TIDE reflects spiritual vacillation.

TIDE GATE warns against hoarding spiritual talents; spiritual bounties/gifts which only flow one way, received but rarely given.

TIDE MILL stands for productive behavior flowing from one's spirituality.

TIDE POOL suggests opportunities to experience and appreciate the ever-changing aspects of spiritual beauty.

TIDE TABLES stands for a look at possible/predictable future outcomes.

TIDEWATER represents fluctuating spiritual behavior; inconsistency.

TIE See necktie.

TIE (fasten) pertains to tying up loose ends.

TIE (winners) signify equal skill, talent, or knowledge; may apply to a caution against competitiveness.

TIEBACKS (curtains) stand for a desire to better understand something; wanting to have a better view of things.

TIEBREAKER constitutes a need to prove excellence or superiority.

TIE CLASP/TACK will reveal a hidden aspect of character. Recall the style, color, design, or gemstone.

TIE-DOWNS suggest a need to secure one's position on an issue; have firm attitudes which won't be swayed by the winds of change or affected by pressure from others.

TIE-DYED (pattern) reflects acceptance; implies nonchalance.

TIE-IN (merchandising) represents imitating elements which spin off an original idea.

TIERED (construction/design) signifies various ascending levels to an issue.

TIFFANY GLASS infers comfort within oneself; acceptance; centeredness.

TIGER implies an aggressive nature; emotionally volatile.

TIGER LILY See lily.

TIGER-EYE (stone) connotes awareness; acute perception.

TIGHT See taut.

TIGHT (clothing) exposes self-imposed constrictions; a tendency to restrict oneself and set narrow limits.

TIGHTFISTED warns of selfishness; ego-centered.

TIGHTLIPPED most often reflects a reserved personality rather than being standoffish.

TIGHTROPE signifies a precarious course one is walking. Also see high wire.

TIGHTS exemplify an ability to freely express oneself.

TIGHTWAD will reveal stinginess related to a multitude of elements depending on the symbol's related aspects. This stinginess can refer to emotional support/sensitivity, finances, general helpfulness, etc.

TILE relates to versatility.

TILL (cash drawer) connotes reserves.

TILL (earth) stands for a *freshening* of one's natural talents or gifts; the *turning over* of abilities through utilization.

TILTED (appearance) represents a slanted perspective or foundational premises.

TIMBERLINE represents the demarcation point between being surrounded by opportunities and having to rely on one's own resources.

TIME BOMB warns of an explosive element in one's life.

TIME CAPSULE illustrates the main events and most important aspects of one's life. Recall what was placed within the capsule.

TIME CARD refers to a regimented personality; gives oneself no leeway; makes no alternate plans for other probabilities.

TIME CLOCK comes as an advisement to stop watching the clock.

TIME LINE comes to reveal a history of events regarding a particular issue.

TIME LOCK reminds one of the unalterable amount of time in which something can either be accomplished or happen.

TIME MACHINE is an interesting dreamscape fragment, for it may specify a particular period in time the dreamer needs to give attention to or it may indicate, through a broken mechanism, that one needs to stay focused on the present.

TIME-OUT expresses a break should be taken.

TIMER denotes a stressful situation that has been self-generated through one's obsession with deadlines.

TIME-RELEASE points to a need to pace oneself; a need to experience something or spread out the initialization of a plan over time; spread out one's efforts and not expend them on one life element.

TIME-SHARING represents cooperation; the harmonic sharing of a mutually beneficial aspect or benefit.

TIMETABLE pertains to schedules.

TIMEWORN most often stands for an outdated aspect.

TIME ZONE portrays the fact that time is perceived differently among people; time is relative, nonlinear.

TIMING LIGHT (engine) suggests something amiss or a bit off regarding one's timing for things.

TIN most often connotes an inferior element.

TINCTURE represents a healthful element of which one needs only a small amount. This would indicate something one would benefit from by taking on a routine basis. A healthful element that may not be referring to medicine but rather an attitude like acceptance.

TIN CUP refers to a handout or request for one.

TINDER stands for a highly flammable aspect or situation; a volatile element.

TINDERBOX points to a reasonably sizeable element in one's life that has the potential for igniting.

TINFOIL See aluminum foil.

TIN GOD signifies a perspective of self-importance.

TINHORN refers to a small-time individual who presents oneself as highly influential, experienced, or skillful.

TINKER characterizes an individual who attempts repairs without having the skill.

TINKERBELL emphasizes the importance of having faith in one's potential.

TINKERTOYS provide an opportunity for experimentation.

TINMAN (Wizard of Oz) suggests an appearance of ineffectiveness or insubstantial abilities to manage projects or carry through, yet this is a misconception of one's true character. A Tinman will be someone who keeps his/her cool under fire and doesn't flaunt abilities or intellect.

TINNY (sound) stands for superficiality; having no substance.

TINSEL illustrates glitter without substance; something that appears to have great appeal, yet doesn't really stand up to its glitter.

TINSEL TOWN portrays a place containing little real value.

TINSMITH relates to a specialized skill.

TIN SNIPS signify a life aspect that is capable of making it easier to cut through difficulties.

TINT suggests an issue that's been altered by one's personal attitude/perspective. Recall what color the tint was to get a sharper interpretation.

TIP SHEET represents an aid for lessening risks.

TIPTOE suggests proceeding with caution.

TIRE pertains to one's condition as one progresses through life.

TIRE CHAINS/STUDS represent an attempt to keep a firm hold on one's path.

TIRE IRON See crowbar.

TIRELESS (vehicle) points to an inert phase, perhaps due to a lack of motivation or faith that things will work out or get better.

TIRE TREAD indicates a well prepared and energetic (new treads) outlook toward one's life journey, or a weary and unmotivated (worn) attitude.

TISSUE applies to a life element that has the potential to keep negative aspects from affecting oneself.

TISSUE PAPER represents a nonessential but pleasing added element to an issue.

TISSUE-TYPING suggests a need to keep life elements compatible.

TITANIC (ship) emphasizes spiritual superiority. Folks claimed it was "the ship even God couldn't sink."

TITANIUM symbolizes strength and resistance to corruption.

TITHE relates to *spiritual* support, never financial support.

TITLE (position) will often disclose one's *actual* position in life. In some cases, depending on surrounding dream details, this symbol will reveal how one *thinks* of oneself.

TITLE (vehicle) signifies one's right to be on a particular path.

TITLE COMPANY connotes the verification of purity to an element in one's life; proof that an aspect contains no negatives.

TITLE INSURANCE points to a clean history; an element having no negatives associated with it.

TITLE ROLE stands for the main person involved in an issue or situation.

TITMOUSE (bird) represents ingeniousness; a raised level of analytical skills; increased perception when it comes to spotting opportunities.

TOAD See frog.

TOADSTOOL See mushroom.

TOAST (bread) alludes to a difficult yet nourishing life element.

TOAST (honor) comes as a personal message for each dreamer. Recall who was toasted by whom and what was said.

TOASTER implies a forthcoming disagreement or disagreeable situation.

TOBACCO (native) emphasizes respect and honor.

TOBACCO BRAID constitutes a gift representing honor.

TOBOGGAN See sled.

TODDLER implies one's beginning steps toward a new endeavor, direction, or belief.

TOE refers to an aspect in one's life that contributes to a balanced course.

TOE SHOES (ballet) caution against a tendency to flit through life without setting one's feet firmly on the ground and not taking life seriously.

TOFFEE typifies a difficult aspect to accept.

TOFU alludes to a totally nourishing life element.

TOGA pertains to an incomplete idea.

TOGGLE BOLT stands for a strong issue; one that will hold up under scrutiny.

TOGGLE SWITCH stands for control one may not realize one has; a personal ability to start or stop something, and this may refer to one's own behavior.

TOILET constitutes a need for eliminations. This means any type of negative element present in one's life.

TOKE suggests experimentation; a sampling.

TOKEN symbolizes a sign or indication.

TOLLBOOTH/ROAD applies to a payment required for further advancement along one's chosen course.

TOLL CALL stands for a communication one is willing to expend extra energy on.

TOLL-FREE represents a communication or journey phase having no personal cost associated with it; one of life's little freebies.

TOMAHAWK See hatchet.

TOMATO implies an agreeable or attractive idea.

TOMATO PASTE refers to a good idea that can be used in various forms to fit differing elements.

TOMBOY defines the expression of one's individuality; personal freedom.

TOMBSTONE See gravestone.

TOMB ROBBER See grave robber.

TOMCAT corresponds with indiscriminate behavior.

TOME (huge book) reflects an extensive volume of information.

TOMMYKNOCKER infers serious warning; a forewarning of a dangerous situation or element.

TOM-TOM See drum (musical instrument).

TONE-DEAF won't normally infer a negative connotation but rather will stand for one's unique talent of hearing (perceiving) things in a way that others don't.

TONER See ink cartridge.

TONGS portray an aid in comprehension; something that provides greater understanding; a *grasp* on things.

TONGUE relates to the quality of one's manner of communication.

TONGUE AND GROOVE stands for ideas or plans that fit well together.

TONGUE DEPRESSOR advises silence; indicates gossip.

TONGUE-TIED pertains to a loss for words; inability to respond.

TONGUE TWISTER reflects a difficult idea or concept that one may or may not be able to articulate.

TONIC stands for a helpful or healing element that could be difficult to accept.

TONSILLECTOMY relates to the removal of negative elements that have hampered one's ability to communicate or adequately express oneself.

TOOL symbolizes aids, opportunities, or methods for utilizing personal abilities.

TOOLBAR (computer) represents ease of using available options.

TOOLBOX refers to a readiness to offer one's talents wherever, whenever needed.

TOOL SHED points to a recognition of one's many opportunities to share talents.

TOOTH See teeth.

TOOTHACHE stands for emotional pain from something said or from withholding something which needs to be voiced. The dreamer will understand which was intended.

TOOTHBRUSH suggests a need to clean up one's speech. This may indicate hurtful or thoughtless words.

TOOTH FAERIE exemplifies a lack of reality in one's life; a belief that flattering speech will serve oneself.

TOOTHLESS suggests an inability to express thoughts, opinions.

TOOTHPASTE refers to the attitude, belief, or perspective that will *clean up* one's manner of speech.

TOOTHPICK connotes the presence of a negative aspect *lodged* in one's routine communication style.

TOP (position) usually reflects an above or higher level.

TOP (toy) represents spinning, often out of control.

TOPAZ (gemstone) alludes to optimism.

TOPCOAT represents the final element applied to a situation; the finishing touch for completion.

TOP DOG will usually indicate the individual recognized as having the highest authority, skill, or knowledge; the one in charge or the one to beat.

TOP DOLLAR denotes something which will demand the greatest cost to obtain. This cost won't be in the form of money, but will relate to other life elements such as emotional costs.

TOP-DRAWER refers to a rating of excellence.

TOP GUN portrays the perfection of a skill.

TOP HAT cautions against intellectual arrogance.

TOP-HEAVY reveals the presence of an imbalanced state.

TOPIARY warns against attempting to personally shape one's reality.

TOPKNOT (hair style) represents attitudes tied to a strong basic premise; usually points to being opinionated.

TOPOGRAPHER characterizes an individual who is capable of charting or directing another's course; one who can point out the pitfalls and areas of smooth-going.

TOPOGRAPHICAL MAP stands for a good idea of how the land lays in respect to an intended path.

TOPPING represents the frosting on the cake kind of symbology, thereby indicating a final element for a specific event or issue.

TOP SECRET connotes innermost thoughts and memories.

TOP SHELF represents what one personally considers being the very best quality of a specific element; what one tends to reserve for special occasions or friends.

TOPSOIL refers to surface issues, emotions, or appearances.

TORAH signifies an individual's high spiritual belief system. Refer to the condition and color of the dreamscape Torah. Was it protected or left exposed?

TORCH won't usually refer to a light, rather, it stands for that which we hold close within. This may pertain to negative feelings such as blame, hate, vengeance, or it may apply to positive emotions such as special affection or admiration.

TORCHBEARER will stand for an individual who carries strong feelings toward a cause or former event. Depending on related details, these strong feelings may be positive or negative.

TORNADO symbolizes great inner turmoil.

The tornado connotes emotional or mental problems while the hurricane correlates to spiritual aspects.

TORPEDO pertains to spiritual warfare and will be associated with one's personal life relationships.

TORRENTIAL RAIN constitutes an inundation of spiritual elements in life.

TORRID emphasizes a scorching or passionate emotion and most often comes as a warning.

TORTOISE See turtle.

TORTOISESHELL (pattern) suggests a grounded perspective.

TOSSUP implies a questionable issue; indecision.

TOTAL ECLIPSE characterizes the darkness (ignorance) before the light (illumination).

TOTAL RECALL naturally refers to the memory of all elements of an event. The key here is why such a memory remains so vivid.

TOTE BOARD relates to information at a glance; an overall view of how things are faring.

TOTEM suggests an object of special importance to a person; a heart/soul connection.

TOTEM ANIMAL symbolizes a unique bond shared between an individual and a particular animal which transfers into a comforting sense of good fortune or safety.

TOTEM POLE indicates a correlated spiritual belief system whereby one spiritual aspect is connected to another as though *stacked* in succession.

TOUCAN implies beautiful thoughts.

TOUCHDOWN alludes to being grounded; grasping a fact; gaining understanding.

TOUCH SCREEN signifies ease of control for making things happen; a method of operation having no intermediary or extraneous steps to perform; one-on-one technique.

TOUCHSTONE connotes excellence.

TOUCHUP relates to an improvement; an effort to bring completion or wholeness.

TOUGH LOVE suggests a need to stand one's ground in a relationship.

TOUPEE reflects false thinking.

TOUR constitutes a desire to better familiarize oneself with something specific.

TOUR GUIDE characterizes an individual who is well informed on a particular issue and is prepared to share that guiding knowledge with others.

TOUR GROUP refers to a group of people with a like interest who are desiring to learn more about it together.

TOURIST suggests an effort to learn about a specific issue, concept, or subject.

TOURIST TRAP cautions a seeker to *be aware* and use discernment when searching through chosen issues.

TOURMALINE (gemstone) infers a healing element in one's life.

TOURNAMENT See contest.

TOURNIQUET denotes an effort to staunch further progression of something.

TOUR OF DUTY represents a specific job/work one has promised (or needs) to perform.

TOUSLED (hair) stands for a need to get one's thoughts in order.

TOW pertains to assistance needed or given.

TOW-AWAY ZONE See road signs.

TOWBOAT defines spiritual help; an uplifting or comforting concept.

TOWEL depicts a life aspect capable of absorption. This means an ability to lessen difficulties.

TOWELETTE comes as a reminder to "keep it clean" regarding one's routine behavior. This "clean" refers to comments or other types of unintentional behavior which could be hurtful.

TOWER exemplifies the superconscious aspect of the mind where spiritual talents and gifts await to be awakened and utilized.

TOWER OF BABEL warns of spiritual confusion; double-talk or excessive verbiage confusing spirituality's simplicity.

TOWHEE (bird) stands for common sense.

TOWLINE will represent a saving life aspect; assistance.

TOWN CRIER enters dreams as a messenger who brings a warning of some type. Recall what was cried out.

TOWN HALL/MEETING alludes to a meeting place, more explicitly, a meeting that is needed.

TOWPATH connotes a helpful path or course.

TOW TRUCK signifies an individual who makes it a habit to help others; one who performs unconditional goodness wherever and whenever the need is evident.

TOXIC WASTE refers to residual effects of certain behaviors that remain volatile.

TOXIN See poison.

TOY implies a lack of seriousness or perhaps a serious *toying* with something. Sometimes this symbol is in reference to a childlike nature.

TOY BOX comes in dreams as a suggestion to return to some of one's childlike perceptions or qualities.

TOY SHOP portrays the child within. It often refers to childish behavior, perceptions, or fears. This symbol can also suggest methods adults utilize to *toy* with others.

TRACE (amount) indicates a *hint* of something; a subliminal presence.

TRACE (draw) cautions against attempting to copy another.

TRACER ROUND (bullet) corresponds to an intent to leave evidence of the source which affected something.

TRACING PAPER stands for attempts to copy/imitate something. This dreamscape element comes to remind one to depend on individual creativity.

TRACK (evidence) illustrates a sign of one's passing.

TRACK (follow) infers a search.

TRACK (sports) signifies a circling; lack of progression.

TRACK (train) warns against a rigid path with no capability for diversion or alteration.

TRACKER characterizes a person intent of following another; may denote an intensive search.

TRACKING COOKIES See cookie (tracking, Internet).

TRACKING NUMBER advises of the wisdom to follow a particular concept through various issues.

TRACKING STATION represents heightened awareness, particularly in respect to spiritual insights.

TRACK LIGHTING denotes a highlighted, featured subject/issue.

TRACK RECORD denotes experiential validation.

TRACK SHOE means having a firm footing on one's path; determination.

TRACT HOUSE refers to one's tendency/preference for blending in with the crowd; a fear or dislike for standing out by expressing one's own uniqueness/individuality.

TRACTION signifies a need for patience while a situation is straightened out.

TRACTOR relates to a powerful help; highly effective assistance.

TRADE signifies one's interest; field of endeavor; where efforts are applied.

TRADE AGREEMENT denotes an arrangement in which parties agree to a manner of interaction and the sharing of one another's talents.

TRADE BEADS stand for an exchange of natural talents; helping another in return for her/his former help; give and take.

TRADE-IN points to assets (talents) one can bring to the table.

TRADEMARK illustrates a revelation; exposes true attitudes, beliefs, and intentions of others. Recall the symbols and colors of the trademark.

TRADER characterizes one who possesses a *give and take* attitude; open to options.

TRADE ROUTE will stand for one's method of interacting with others.

TRADE SCHOOL refers to specific instruction that will provide skill to progress along one's chosen life path.

TRADE SECRET correlates to a unique method or ingredient associated with successful operations or progression.

TRADE SHOW stands for a display/presentation of the latest developments regarding a specific issue.

TRADE UNION See union.

TRADE WIND implies thoughts and ideas that follow a common route; a lack of individual thought.

TRADING CARD will usually depict a visual of an important message for the dreamer.

TRADING POST applies to a current need to be giving. This symbol comes when an individual isn't compromising.

TRAFFIC exemplifies traveling activity; stands for the state of one's chosen path. Was the road crowded? Hectic? Gridlocked?

TRAFFIC CONE comes in dreams to represent guidance around a hazard in one's path. This symbol advises one to proceed with caution.

TRAFFIC COURT signifies the costs involved if one loses integrity in respect to one's manner of path progression.

TRAFFIC JAM applies to a setback, a temporary one, appearing along one's path.

TRAFFIC LIGHT marks the rightness of one's path. Did the light show green, yellow (slow down)? Did it indicate a time to turn off onto another road (arrow)?

TRAGEDY (drama) will reveal a situation with dire consequences, indicating a result one may have been unaware of. This usually refers to one's intentions for near-future behavior or an action one plans on taking. This is usually a forewarning.

TRAIL (backward extension) pertains to extended effects; lasting benefits.

TRAIL (drop back) may not be the negative symbol it initially appears to be, for frequently we need to drop back in order to get a better perspective of what's ahead.

TRAIL (path) indicates an individual's unique direction or course.

TRAILBLAZER connotes the courage of one who endeavors to self-discover a new course.

TRAILER (semitruck) See semitrailer.

TRAILER (house type) See mobile home.

TRAIL MIX (food) signifies an opportunity for rejuvenation.

TRAIN warns against following closely behind another who is following a popular tried-and-true course in regard to being safe and well worn.

TRAIN (coal) refers to pulling a line of negative aspects or issues behind one; being burdened with multiple negatives.

TRAIN (crossing) suggests opportunities to avoid the well-worn paths in life; also may come to advise of the wisdom of stopping to let negatives pass by through the use of patience and acceptance.

TRAIN (freight) See freight train.

TRAIN (passenger) reveals a journey that is not unique to the individual, one denoting a follower who seeks safety in numbers or is fearful of expressing individuality.

TRAIN (teach) cautions against indoctrination; being formed into a particular mold.

TRAINEE connotes a follower; beginning learning phase.

TRAIN ENGINEER exemplifies an individual who leads others along the smooth and easy, well-worn path.

TRAINING TABLE cautions against being fed concepts chosen by others.

TRAINING WHEELS stands for an attempt to keep one's balance/perspective while on a learning quest; a careful beginner.

TRAIN WHISTLE comes as a message that warns against separating oneself from others; reminds of humanitarian responsibility.

TRAITOR reveals a lack of loyalty; a betrayer.

TRAM See cable car.

TRAMP/HOBO characterizes a freethinker; a nonconformist.

TRAMPOLINE relates to a tendency to gain insights then discount them.

TRANCE refers to a state of altered or shifted consciousness which opens one to high insights.

TRANQUILIZER will represent any life aspect on which an individual depends for soothing effects; a means for calming.

TRANQUILIZER GUN symbolizes a great need to calm a situation or individual.

TRANSCEIVER directly corresponds to one's open channel within the superconscious mind.

TRANSCRIPT denotes a review of a conversation or communication; verification of what was said.

TRANSFER (ticket) exemplifies a need to alter one's course in life.

TRANSFER STATION (power) signifies the channeling of one's energy or attention into specific areas.

TRANSFORMER comes as a strong suggestion to switch efforts to a different goal or issue.

TRANSFUSION (blood) connotes bad blood is present within; a need to repair bad relations.

TRANSIENT (location/town) denotes a phase of one's path when an extra number of temporary contacts will be made.

TRANSLATOR characterizes an individual capable of bringing understanding or clarifying misunderstood communication.

TRANSLUCENT refers to a nebulous idea, one that is beginning to formulate.

TRANSMISSION means pacing oneself.

TRANSMISSION FLUID pertains to the ease with which one can make transitions or accept changes in life. Did the dream insinuate that one needed to *add* fluid?

TRANSMITTER portrays a need to send a message to another or express an important communication that is being withheld.

TRANSMUTATION depicts some type of transformation needed or currently happening.

TRANSPARENT indicates a lack of deception or ulterior motive; open and honest relationships; nothing hidden.

TRANSPLANT relates to new ground in which to develop; fresh beginning.

TRANSPLANT (hair) signifies new ideas taking root.

TRANSPLANT (heart) stands for a change of heart; greater emotional sensitivity.

TRANSPLANT (kidney) denotes a new, clean perspective.

TRANSPLANT (liver) pertains to renewed energy and motivation.

TRANSPLANT (lung) suggests a new ability to take in (inhale) positive aspects and let go of (exhale) negative elements.

TRANSPORT CAFÉ See truck stop.

TRANSVESTITE exposes an identity crisis; an identification with a past life that still retains strong and overwhelming elements.

TRAP (catch) illustrates the pitfalls that entrap one in life such as arrogance, the ego, materialism, etc.

TRAP (drain) pertains to an opportunity to clean out the negatives in one's life or existing within self.

TRAPDOOR reflects unawareness; possible pitfalls if one isn't watchful.

TRAPEZE reveals an unproductive means of attempting to progress along a life path.

TRAPEZE ARTIST See aerialist.

TRAPPER indicates a resourceful, self-sufficient individual, yet may also reveal a conniving personality.

TRAPSHOOTING typifies a desire to maintain personal skills.

TRASH connotes the useless and extraneous elements in one's life.

TRASH CAN cautions one to throw out the life aspects that are useless; keep oneself unburdened.

TRASH COMPACTOR refers to a need to compress the negatives that are taking up too much space in our lives; to minimize and dispose of our negative attitudes.

TRAUMA TEAM will stand for a critical need to take care of the most obvious and harmful negative elements in one's life.

TRAVEL AGENCY denotes inadequacies.

TRAVEL ALARM defines an attempt to maintain a schedule.

TRAVELER'S CHECKS represent the personal assets (talents) on which one can draw while making life's journey.

TRAVELING SALESPERSON characterizes a person intent on spreading beliefs far and wide. This may indicate a fanatic.

TRAVELOGUE refers to research into different life courses.

TRAVERSE ROD denotes a means of keeping issues open or closed; the choice of doing same.

TRAVOIS suggests a journey is required for path advancement.

TRAWLER warns of a belief that drags on one's overall spirituality.

TREADLE applies to the energy applied to keep one's momentum going.

TREADMILL reveals an unproductive method; a lack of advancement; a neutral position.

TREASURE signifies a personally perceived boon.

TREASURE CHEST represents the expected or awaited-for boon. The key with this symbol is to recall if the chest was full or empty. What was in it?

TREASURE HUNT applies to expectation.

TREASURE ISLAND usually implies a dreamer; not willing to work for one's goals.

TREASURY DEPARTMENT exemplifies the source of one's assets, meaning inherent talents and qualities.

TREATISE comes in dreams to advise of a need to gain full information on an issue.

TREATY relates to agreements that smooth ongoing relationships.

TREE symbolizes life force; living gifts; natural talents.

TREE FARM indicates the cultivation of natural talents and gifts; the propagation of same.

TREE FROG represents an awareness and appreciation of one's bond with nature—the sense of interrelatedness; holding onto one's bond with the Divine Essence through nature with tenacity and an attitude of having a cherished connection.

TREE HOUSE relates to living one's spiritual beliefs through the use of inherent talents and gifts.

TREE HUGGER characterizes an individual who fully appreciates and respects the living essence of all things; one who deeply cherishes the concept of interrelatedness.

TREE OF LIFE (design) represents the interrelatedness of all living things. This will point to a need to realize that the individuality of others doesn't really make them separate, only unique. Also see tree hugger.

TREE TRIMMER characterizes an individual who continually trims and cares for inherent talents and gifts.

TRELLIS correlates with a guiding direction given to one's natural abilities.

TREMBLE reveals a loss of control; instability.

TRENCH denotes perseverance and personal faith in oneself.

TRENCH COAT refers to protective measures one devises to maintain personal strength and fortitude.

TRENCH MOUTH See foot-and-mouth disease.

TREND ANALYSIS stands for efforts put into trying to gauge where popular opinion will be in the near future.

TRENDSETTER characterizes an individual who others follow; one whom others emulate.

TRESPASSING normally refers to the act of getting into another's space or business.

TRESTLE warns of a life path or section of course possessing no grounding factor, no foundation; a tenuous section of one's path.

TRIAD (design/shape) most often symbolizes the Divine Essence plus Its Male and Female Aspects.

TRIAGE advises of a need to establish and maintain priorities; quick decision-making.

TRIAL comes as a suggestion to honestly analyze one's motives and recent behavior.

TRIAL MARRIAGE signifies an effort to test one's compatibility with another before making a long-term commitment.

TRIANGLE (shape) signifies the three Aspects of the Divine Essence.

TRIBESPEOPLE correspond to the universal unit of humankind.

TRIBUNAL pertains to self-judgment.

TRIBUTE denotes an acknowledgment; recognition.

TRICKLE (water flow) is actually a positive sign because it shows that there's enough of one's spirituality left to save and work to increase.

TRICK-OR-TREAT actually refers to the concept of cause and effect—one reaps what one puts out; action bringing like reaction.

TRICKSTER typifies cleverness; a quick wit.

TRIDENT (design) stands for the three Aspects of the Divine Essence.

TRICOLORED reveals three distinct elements to an issue or situation.

TRICORNERED HAT will signify three-dimensional thinking; thought which considers all aspects of an issue.

TRICYCLE won't refer to children, but will be associated with a balanced pathway.

TRIFOCALS emphasize multiple perspectives as utilized to gain a complete comprehension.

TRIFOLD reveals three separate aspects to something.

TRIGGER (any type) indicates the singular element that has the capability to set off multiple responses or ramifications.

TRILEVEL (dwelling) suggests a mind having the a well-integrated perspective or connection between the three mind levels of the conscious, subconscious, and superconscious; one who routinely uses intuition.

TRILITHON pertains to a doorway or entrance; an opportunity for ingress/egress.

TRILLIANT (gem-cut shape) See triangle.

TRILLIUM (botanical) represents those delicate, yet strong, emotional (empathetic) qualities we have; the seemingly fragile attributes which prove to be enduring.

TRILOBITE illustrates a time-tested spiritual concept; a solid truth.

TRILOGY signifies the existence of three aspects creating a whole. Something in the dreamer's life has three different aspects to it.

TRIM (finishing work) represents final touches.

TRIMMINGS (festive) denote expanded benefits from a singular joyful blessing.

TRIM SIZE stands for the elemental, basic shape of a situation or issue.

TRINKET usually refers to personal value applied to a specific object or subject.

TRIP (journey) connotes a forthcoming directional course that will prove productive in providing valuable lessons.

TRIP (set off) cautions against expending too much energy or efforts on a specific issue; an overload is about to happen.

TRIP (stumble) relates to a temporary setback that may serve to provide a beneficial element to one's life.

TRIPE denotes a worthless element; having no value at all.

TRIPLE CROWN stands for three main aspects to a goal/issue/situation which need to be attained/hurdled for success.

TRIPLE THREAT reveals a situation/issue containing three dangerous elements.

TRIPLETS constitute three new beginnings or starts. This doesn't mean a choice between them needs to be made. These three new aspects will usually be very different from each other and will exist simultaneously in one's life.

TRIPLEX will indicate an element consisting of three separate aspects.

TRIPLICATE reminds one that a specific piece of information needs to go to three separate individuals.

TRIPOD suggests a need to steady oneself; a need to get focused without any distortion.

TRIP WIRE warns of an attempt to foil another; a deception.

TRIVIA denotes unimportant aspects to an element.

TROJAN HORSE reveals stealth; deception; underhandedness. This symbol may also point to a manner of getting close to an issue or subject without the intention being broadcast or hinted at beforehand.

TROJANS (Internet) reveals the presence of malicious programs hiding out on one's hard drive for the purpose of stealing or damaging data. This, then, comes as a strong advisement to sharply attend to one's defensive/protective methods, for there's a high probability that privacy has been (or will soon be) invaded.

TROLL represents the skeptical, unbelievable concepts in one's life.

TROLLEY CAR See cable car.

TROLLING warns against accepting spiritual debris.

TROMBONE signifies the deeper elements of an aspect. This indicates the presence of a greater level of complexity in an issue or individual than initially perceived.

TROOP CARRIER represents a suggestion to shift one's defensive measures to another target.

TROPHY (animal) exposes a lack of courage; false power.

TROPHY (award) comes as a sign of accomplishment and serves as motivational encouragement to keep striving.

TROPICAL STORM warns of temporary spiritual confusion/upheaval.

TROPICS suggest stifling spiritual beliefs.

TROUBLESHOOTER characterizes a person capable of discovering the source of a problem and resolving it.

TROUGH (container) usually represents a receptaclelike connotation. This symbol is associated with the need to keep issues separate or elements of an issue together in one place. This suggests that one is mixing issues.

TROUPE stands for a group of people who travel from place to place for the purpose of displaying a specific idea.

TROUSSEAU signifies what one member of a partnership brings to the relationship.

TROUT denotes a spiritual contentedness; a satisfaction with one's spirituality.

TROWEL connotes a personal tool used to smooth over rough times in life.

TRUANT OFFICER represents one's own conscience.

TRUCE constitutes a desire to resolve relationship difficulties.

TRUCK correlates to personal efforts and the energy expended for same.

TRUCKER relates to one who is conscientious regarding closures; one who wants to see things through.

TRUCK STOP portrays a necessary resting phase along one's life path.

TRUE BLUE represents a firm belief, but sometimes leaning toward fanaticism.

TRUE LOVE stands for an enduring devotion and loyalty.

TRUE REALITY stands for all of the knowns and unknowns making up the totality of existence (of the What Is).

TRUFFLE (confection) applies to a personal comfort.

TRUMP CARD will signify the key to a goal or successful conclusion.

TRUMPET (horn) reveals a forthcoming message for the dreamer.

TRUMPET VINE refers to many new (and possibly innovative) ideas which may have been generated through spiritual sources.

TRUMPETER SWAN stands for a refined inner joy generated by the love and appreciation for one's spiritual belief system.

TRUNDLE BED connotes the availability of accommodating a partner or assistant. This may infer a companion or some other type of close associate.

TRUNK (baggage) denotes heavy burdens; excesses perceived as valuable.

TRUNK (tree) applies to inner strength.

TRUNK (vehicle) corresponds with the hidden aspects carried along one's path.

TRUNK LINE relates to the main line of communication one uses.

TRUSTEE reveals a trusted individual.

TRUST FUND represents one's intentions for others.

TRUTH SERUM comes as a strong advisement to be forthright.

TRY ON (clothing) See dressing room.

TRY OUT stands for an attempt to test/gauge one's attained level of development; may also point to a check on one's path progression.

TRYST refers to a secretive meeting.

TSETSE FLY warns of the presence of an undetected element in one's life that has a great potential to slow one down or cause various forms of harm to motivation.

T-SQUARE represents an effort to get something straight; understanding.

TSUNAMI connotes spiritual overkill or a state of being spiritually overwhelmed.

TUBA refers to a full-bodied (strong, yet not aggressive) manner of communication.

TUBAL LIGATION reveals a firm resolve to stop making false starts.

TUBER (botanical) stands for an opportunity for a new life/beginning.

TUBERCULOSIS advises of a need for breathing room; something in one's life is suffocating the very breath out or drowning one with a sense of being overwhelmed.

TUBEROSE suggests pure intentions.

TUBING stands for extensions; a connecting element.

TUBULAR (shape) denotes an extended element to an issue; extenuating circumstances.

TUDOR (architecture style) stands for strong, well-built foundations/defenses.

TUESDAY suggests a need to sharpen one's awareness; attend to sharper perceptions and discernment.

TUGBOAT See towboat.

TUG OF WAR (game) represents an ongoing conflict/disagreement; an unwillingness to give in or concede.

TUITION corresponds to some type of payment due in exchange for the information one desires. Reveals unscrupulous behavior if tuition is demanded for spiritual information.

TULIP (flower) stands for self-confidence; encouragement; motivational factors; may also point to a beautiful beginning.

TUMBLING (gymnastics) suggests an understanding of the possibility of falling down while walking one's path, and having knowledge that softens the fall and allows quicker recovery.

TUMBLEWEED (botanical) portrays shallow aspects of oneself; no roots or firm perspective/opinion.

TUMOR warns of the presence of a negative attitude that has the capability of consuming oneself.

TUNA refers to spiritual generosity.

TUNDRA typifies spiritual aspects yet to be discovered.

TUNE (music) will usually remind one of the lyrics and those will hold specific meaning.

TUNE-UP stands for a need to make internal adjustments and suggests a perception or attitude that's out of alignment or in need of tweaking.

TUNIC See toga.

TUNING FORK suggests that something is not ringing true; a call to make an adjustment.

TUNNEL connotes an alternative route or a way to discovery.

TUNNEL OF LOVE can indicate hidden affections, but may also warn against harboring secret resentments.

TUNNEL VISION advises of the wisdom of widening one's perceptual scope.

TURBAN exposes twisted or convoluted thoughts.

TURBINE exemplifies a source of power; strong motivation.

TURBOCHARGED stands for a burst of energy; may refer to a reserve of energy/perseverance one isn't aware of having.

TURBULENCE (airplane) denotes disturbing thoughts. This symbol may refer to outside influences which negatively disturb a formerly solid belief or idea.

TUREEN suggests bounty.

TURF FARM See sod farm.

TURKEY refers to a hidden intelligence; quiet wisdom behind an unlikely exterior.

TURKEY SHOOT reveals an unfair advantage.

TURKEY TROT (dance) See ragtime.

TURNCOAT stands for a reversed attitude/perspective.

TURNING POINT denotes a realization, a crisis situation, or sudden epiphany which causes one to finally see the light.

TURNIP reflects a reversal; a changed attitude or decision.

TURNKEY indicates completeness; entirety; everything already in place and ready to make one's move.

TURNOVER (employment) denotes a lack of stability; restlessness.

TURNOVER (pastry) implies a desirable benefit.

TURNPIKE See tollbooth.

TURN SIGNAL symbolizes one's intention to alter present course.

TURNSTILE cautions one to focus on a single aspect at a time; a method of slowing one's pace.

TURNTABLE refers to a means of listening. If it's broken, it suggests that one isn't listening well, perhaps forming assumptions or false impressions because of it.

TURPENTINE illustrates a life aspect that is capable of eradicating residual elements.

TURQUOISE (color/stone) defines spiritual health and well-being.

TURRET corresponds to hidden psychological elements.

TURTLE pertains to a fear of facing responsibility or reality. This symbol may also point to a tendency to know when to keep one's nose out of another's business.

TURTLENECK implies a reluctance to expose oneself; lacking self-confidence.

TUSK pertains to natural defense mechanisms.

TUTANKHAMEN stands for the killing effects of jealousy, power, and greed.

TUTOR points out an individual capable and willing to assist another.

TUTTI-FRUTTI (flavor) suggests irrationality.

TUTU (ballet) represents freedom to express inner joy.

TUXEDO signifies a desire to present only one's best side.

TV DINNER usually stands for a relaxed, enjoyable manner of gaining information.

TWEED (fabric/pattern) denotes quiet, dignified intelligence/wisdom.

TWEEZERS relate to a life element capable of extracting an irritating aspect from self or one's life.

TWELFTH-DAY equates to an epiphany.

TWELVE stands for spiritual purpose/motivation.

TWELVE-STEP (program) signifies courageous efforts to get one's life under control and make improvements.

TWIG See kindling.

TWILIGHT corresponds to the magic time, the window, when one is most receptive to higher insights.

TWILIGHT SLEEP denotes a willful state of numbness regarding emotional pain.

TWILIGHT ZONE reflects experiences one has difficulty accepting.

TWILL (fabric) suggests a coarseness to one's character or applies to a current attitude.

TWINBERRY (botanical) See honeysuckle.

TWINE portrays a means of attaching, connecting, or tying something together; closure.

TWIN-ENGINE represents balanced efforts. Recall if both were working properly.

TWINFLOWER (botanical) stands for duality.

TWINKLING refers to the sparkle that accompanies enlightened insights.

TWINS denote the duality of life; the polarity.

TWIN-SIZE stands for singular. This usually points to the idea that one has to go it alone for a time, or already is.

TWISTER See hurricane; tornado.

TWISTING ROAD reflects one's fortitude and perseverance while progressing a burdensome and difficult life path which is currently full of twists and turns.

TWIST TIE denotes a means of closure which avails itself to future re-opening if needed; a closure which may not be permanent.

TWITCH See tic.

TWO represents weakness and vacillation.

TWO CENTS implies a worthless aspect; not worth one's time or energy.

TWO-DIMENSIONAL indicates a perspective lacking depth.

TWO-EDGED connotes the duality of something having ramifications for oneself.

TWO-FACED exposes duplicity.

TWO-FISTED signifies great strength behind resolve.

TWO-HANDED reveals an element weighty enough to require both hands (extra energy); may also point to an element fragile enough to require added awareness or caution in handling it.

TWO-MINUTE WARNING naturally won't relate to football, but will instead be an attention-getting symbol which advises that one's time is nearly up to get something accomplished.

TWO-PLY refers to a double-layered aspect or issue; draws attention to a need to give attention to both aspects.

TWO-STEP (dance) stands for a relationship in which the partners are always in agreement, always having a like perspective/goal.

TWO-WAY STREET alludes to something being available to opposing parties to use or take advantage of.

TYCOON characterizes an individual capable of providing great benefits to others.

TYPECAST warns against prejudgments or placing others in personally perceived categories. Also see profiler.

TYPEWRITER symbolizes preserved ideas.

TYPHOID FEVER warns of the harmful effects of spiritual untruths.

TYPHOON See hurricane.

TYPO pertains to an unintentional error or life mistake.

TYRANNOSAUR corresponds to an overwhelming situation or highly demanding, manipulative individual.

TYRANT stands for an arrogance of one's perceived power or authority and using it ruthlessly.

U

U-BOAT warns of a negative spiritual element in one's life.

U-BOLT represents a strong support.

UDDER alludes to a nourishing factor in one's life.

UFO See unidentified flying object.

UGLY will usually denote a disagreeable aspect as perceived by the dreamer.

UGLY DUCKLING pertains to misconceptions associated with first impressions; assumptions or judgments based solely on appearances.

UKULELE exemplifies a carefree personality.

ULCER warns of stress that has been internalized and the need to alleviate it.

ULTIMATUM connotes a last resort choice.

ULTRALIGHT (airplane) suggests gentle thoughts; kindness.

ULTRAMODERN (style) refers to a lack of cluttering elements; sleek and simple basics.

ULTRASONIC See supersonic.

ULTRASOUND portrays a need to get inside something; take a more thorough look at an issue, event, or other element in one's life.

ULTRAVIOLET FILTER (lens) stands for a tendency/desire to keep spiritual elements out of daily issues.

ULTRAVIOLET LAMP symbolizes an aid to nourish personal growth.

UMBER (color) relates to earthiness; being natural.

UMBILICAL CORD signifies vital connections; a strong bond.

UMBRELLA constitutes skepticism and a willful insulation from spiritual issues.

UMPIRE characterizes a person's conscience; maintaining behavior that is confined within the bounds or rules.

UNABRIDGED pertains to a complete rendition; leaving no elements out.

UNANIMOUS suggests total agreement; no dissension.

UNARMED represents a nonthreatening issue or individual.

UNBALANCED warns of a lack of alignment or an unstable factor that's present in one's life.

UNBEATEN denotes skill; never been defeated.

UNBELIEVER may point to a skeptic or it may simply indicate someone who has yet to seriously look into an issue enough to be convinced.

UNBREAKABLE most often refers to inner strength, yet may relate to a relationship, agreement, or bond of some type.

UNBRIDLED (horse) constitutes an uncontrolled state, but could imply a freedom to express one's individuality.

UNBUTTONED won't infer sloppiness; it most often applies to a personal confidence or comfortable sense of self.

UNCHARTED (course) illustrates an unplanned direction which may, of itself, be specifically planned that way. This indicates someone who desires to let life guide her/him toward self-discoveries.

UNCIVILIZED suggests an absolute disregard for others.

UNCLE comes as an advisement to take personal responsibility and admit to mistakes made in life.

UNCLE SAM corresponds to the fact that no one is completely independent and free of those who make themselves an invasive part of one's life.

UNCLOG typifies the act of ridding oneself of a confusing issue or relationship; reaching the solution to a specific problem.

UNCONCERN speaks of indifference, perhaps apathy.

UNCONDITIONAL represents a lack of strings being attached; a true unrestricted element.

UNCONSCIOUS usually denotes ignorance or unawareness, yet may indicate complete insensitivity.

UNCONTROLLED signifies a lack of direction or planning; may indicate an aspect that has gotten out of hand.

UNCONVENTIONAL frequently comes as personal advice to follow one's own path or ideas. This symbol may also point to something outside the box, meaning unusual, yet workable.

UNCOUTH implies rudeness.

UNCOVERED represents something that has been exposed, revealed.

UNCTION See anointing.

UNCUT stands for an element in its natural state.

UNDECIDED suggests a need to give more thought and analyzation to an issue.

UNDERACHIEVER indicates one's performance/energy output is less than one's capability or potential.

UNDERAGE usually refers to being unprepared.

UNDERBID refers to a failure to understand the true value of something.

UNDERBOSS characterizes an individual having mid-level authority/power.

UNDERBRUSH stands for hidden problems.

UNDERCARRIAGE denotes a supportive or foundational element.

UNDERCLASSMEN/WOMEN characterize those who are less experienced and knowledgeable in one's life.

UNDERCOATING pertains to a protective/defensive measure; an intent to preserve.

UNDERCOVER connotes secretiveness.

UNDERCURRENT stands for a sense of a different attitude.

UNDERCUT reflects the act of undermining; attempting to better another.

UNDERDEVELOPED relates to a lack of full preparedness; needing further growth; immature.

UNDERDOG characterizes an individual perceived as weaker by the dreamer, yet this may come in a dream to advise differently.

UNDERDONE reveals thought/situation needing further energy put into it before it can be fully realized.

UNDERDRESSED stands for a situation/issue which has been misperceived as a low priority.

UNDEREMPLOYED refers to being in a position in which one's full potential can't be utilized.

UNDEREXPOSED (film) signifies an aspect in one's life that requires more time, needs further development.

UNDERFED represents a lack of information; withheld knowledge/nourishment.

UNDERFOOT represents those facets in life to which we need to attend.

UNDERGROUND symbolizes the need for an individual to keep certain elements private. This may also advise the dreamer to get out in the open and contribute one's talents. The surrounding dreamscape details will clarify this.

UNDERGROUND RAILROAD pertains to a secretive endeavor and its manner of operation.

UNDERGROWTH connotes developing aspects to an issue; yet undetected activity.

UNDERHAND applies to unethical practices.

UNDERLINED illustrates emphasis. Recall what was underlined. This will be what the dreamer needs to give attention to.

UNDERNEATH (position) suggests hidden elements to an issue.

UNDERPAID implies a lack of appreciation or recognition of one's experience, skill, or knowledge.

UNDERPASS portrays a way under something; an alternative course.

UNDERPRICED reveals an element worth more than one perceives it to be; selling oneself short.

UNDERRATED signifies an underestimation; lacking an understanding of something's real value or potential.

UNDERSCORE See underlined.

UNDERSHIRT See underwear.

UNDERSIDE suggests a need to look at all aspects (angles) of an issue, even those that are less obvious/visible.

UNDERSTAFFED represents a need for additional resources to accomplish a goal.

UNDERSTUDY refers to an intention of being prepared to take another's place; may also point to an intention to replace another; could infer the practice of emulation. Recall who was studying whom. What was being studied?

UNDERTAKER See funeral director.

UNDER-THE-COUNTER/TABLE represents unethical or secretive dealings.

UNDERTONE See undercurrent.

UNDERTOW warns of negative spiritual beliefs that will eventually pull one under.

UNDERWATER pertains to a state of being submerged in spiritual issues.

UNDERWEAR alludes to a covering up; a fear of exposure.

UNDERWEIGHT symbolizes a lack of recognizing one's own potential/worth.

UNDERWORLD (criminal) stands for the hidden negative elements in one's life.

UNDERWRITER characterizes approval; an endorsement. This may also point to those who weigh risks.

UNDRESSED represents honest intentions. Also see nakedness.

UNDULATING (motion) suggests progression; self-motivation.

UNEARNED INCOME signifies benefits received and acknowledgment given for efforts one never applied; false recognition.

UNEARTH applies to the exposure of something; a new aspect come to light.

UNEARTHLY (atmosphere) may reveal a true Reality experiential event.

UNEDUCATED may either indicate ignorance or it often refers to one progressing through the use of simple logic and common sense.

UNEMPLOYED connotes an unproductive state. This may not infer a negative implication because it could suggest a designated phase when one needs to take a break.

UNEMPLOYMENT COMPENSATION signifies a benefit gained from a time period when one isn't actively applying oneself. This usually refers to the need for rest and a distancing from stressful elements.

UNEVEN (road) stands for bittersweet experiences; the simultaneous occurrences of events carrying the ups and downs of positive and negative elements.

UNFASHIONABLE (clothing) reveals the expression of one's individuality/uniqueness, probably associated with innovative thought which is considered to be well outside the box.

UNFINISHED (condition/state) connotes a call to finish what was begun.

UNFINISHED (furniture) shows opportunities to express creativity/individuality.

UNFOCUSED comes to advise of a need to center one's attention on the issue at hand; may indicate confusion or a lack of understanding.

UNGLUED is a call to regain composure, pull oneself together in order to better deal with or accept a situation.

UNHINGED depicts a lack of control; loss of balance.

UNICORN reflects real possibilities; the reaches of reality.

UNICYCLE denotes self-reliance and resourcefulness; self-sufficiency.

UNIDENTIFIED FLYING OBJECT (UFO) represents the totality of intelligent life; an aspect of true Reality most are still skeptical of and afraid to believe in.

UNIFORM signifies a specific intention or attention to a focused effort. Recall what the uniform represented. Waiter? Security guard or police officer? Delivery person?

UNINHABITED defines self-discovery; an uncharted course or goal.

UNINSTALL points to a dropped belief; may also be associated with a character quality or such elements as lost faith/acceptance.

UNINSURED correlates to high confidence.

UNION portrays a sense of security; having a support group.

UNION HALL corresponds with a desire to utilize one's talents and skills.

UNION LABEL denotes pride in one's work and the appreciation of the work of others.

UNION STEWARD will reveal the presence of someone who you can turn to for help.

UNISEX symbolizes something which is nongender specific, even a perspective.

UNITED KINGDOM signifies an openness to possibilities.

UNITED NATIONS stands for a peaceful relationship or association.

UNITED NATIONS DAY refers to a celebration of cooperation.

UNIVERSE See cosmos.

UNIVERSITY typifies expanded learning.

UNLEAVENED infers fundamental aspects unaffected by extraneous elements.

UNLIMITED points to endless potential/possibilities; sky's the limit.

UNLISTED (phone number) stands for an attempt to maintain privacy.

UNLOAD comes as an advisement for self-analyzation; suggests a need to express oneself.

UNLUCKY pertains to a lack of self-confidence.

UNMANNED will stand for a natural, inherent inner guidance which works without one needing to supply mental input.

UNMASKING symbolizes a need to accurately perceive others; seeing with clarity and through another's facade; getting rid of that which one hides behind.

UNORGANIZED implies a need to be methodical, efficient; alludes to a disoriented thought process.

UNPACKING signifies the act of looking at different aspects; may indicate a need to unload or unburden oneself.

UNPLUGGED reveals a disconnection. This may refer to one's own rationale.

UNPREPARED suggests a lack of planning; no foresight.

UNPROFITABLE comes in a dream as an advisement for the dreamer to think about his/her idea of value and what is being perceived as profitable.

UNQUALIFIED denotes an immature stage in life; needing more experience and knowledge.

UNQUENCHABLE See thirst.

UNRAVELED represents approaching solutions; one is in the process of reaching new understandings. Also see frayed.

UNREADABLE relates to a personal lack of comprehension and may denote concepts or ideas for which one isn't yet ready.

UNRESPONSIVE won't necessarily denote a lack of emotion or communication, it may suggest deep thought.

UNRIPE reveals a situation or plan which needs more effort applied for further development.

UNSANITARY implies an unhealthy condition or situation.

UNSAVORY signifies a distasteful issue or situation.

UNSEASONABLE denotes an out-of-the-ordinary element; may indicate that one has been in expectation as to how or when something would manifest.

UNSEASONED will point to a raw life aspect which hasn't been spiced up or colored according to one's perspective or personal attitude; an objective aspect.

UNSCREWING reflects a lessening of stress and pressure in one's life.

UNSKILLED LABOR refers to work nearly everyone can do. Sometimes this symbol will come to remind us that anyone can volunteer or practice unconditional goodness, there's always something we can do to help another.

UNSOCIABLE usually reveals an introvert or shyness.

UNSOPHISTICATED most often indicates

commonsense wisdom unadulterated by society's mores or elitism.

UNSTEADY exemplifies a lack of self-confidence; on shaky ground.

UNTANGLED refers to straightening out the facts/elements of an issue; applied efforts to finally understand something.

UNVEILING correlates to a discovery of some type.

UNWASHED comes as an advisement to remove the negative elements from some aspect in one's life.

UNWIELDY connotes a cumbersome issue in one's life; difficult to handle.

UPBEAT represents optimism, acceptance.

UPDATE stands for the presence of new information of which one should be aware; a change has occurred.

UPGRADE points to an improvement; a step up in quality; an advancement.

UPHEAVAL constitutes a major disturbance to one's routine; a disturbing event/issue.

UPHILL indicates a phase when extra energy will be needed in order to make advancements.

UPHOLSTERER relates to one who can provide a new outlook or attitude.

UPLINK stands for one's inner knowing; one's connection to the Higher Self or Universal Consciousness.

UPLOAD represents one's transmission of thoughts to another; one's expressed attitude or perspective.

UPPER CRUST typifies arrogance; placing oneself or others into a high-class position.

UPPERCLASSMEN/WOMEN points to

those who have gone before you, have traveled the same path.

UPPITY (attitude) equates to an intractable personality or an inflated sense of self.

UPRIVER reveals a more difficult path; progression which goes against the natural flow.

UPROOTED pertains to a disconnection or disassociation; may refer to personal relationships or a plan or it may connote an actual geographical relocation forthcoming.

UPSCALE denotes an improvement.

UPSIDE DOWN exposes a misconception or idea that isn't perceived correctly.

UPSIDE-DOWN LOAN reveals a situation in which one owes more than the value of something.

UPSLOPE (wind current) advises of a particularly blustery emotional situation in the offing.

UPSTAGE points to a tendency to outdo others. Also see overshadow.

UPSTAIRS stands for a higher level; upward advancement or greater level of information.

UPSWEEP (hair style) shows a tendency for lofty ideas/perspectives; perhaps an overblown self-image.

UP-TO-DATE refers to keeping one's finger on the pulse of events; keeping a close eye on a situation; maintaining full knowledge.

UPTOWN suggests an elitist area of perception/attitude.

UPTREND stands for initial signs of an improving situation; may point to increased acceptance or optimism.

UPWIND stands for exposure; going against the flow.

URANIUM warns of a contaminating aspect in one's life.

URANUS (planet) suggests one attends to philosophical issues.

URBAN BLIGHT points to a situation that's degrading.

URBAN LEGEND refers to a common belief held by a relatively small group of people.

URBAN RENEWAL stands for rejuvenation.

URBAN SPRAWL illustrates a loss of control; the ease by which something gets away from you.

URCHIN (child) pertains to a mischievous immaturity.

URCHIN (sea) portrays spiritual immaturity.

URINE relates to necessary waste; the idea that some elements in one's life are harmful if retained.

URINE SAMPLE advises of the wisdom of testing ourselves for any negative attitudes or perspectives we may be holding.

URN (cremation) refers to the importance of remembering what has been learned by past experiences.

URN (warming) pertains to the need to keep some aspect in your life warm (currently active).

USB PORT (computer) indicates a source for holding a greater amount of information; additional resources for maintaining one's memory capabilities.

USDA symbolizes a protective measure; efforts put into an issue's close inspection for the purpose of insuring that it's a positive aspect.

USER FRIENDLY points to an element which is easy to utilize; compatible with average intellect/skill

USER ID (Internet) represents one's personal validation for the right to proceed.

USHER characterizes an individual capable of guiding another; may represent a counselor, friend, or even oneself.

UTAH suggests a tendency to have an attitude of spiritual superiority

UTILITY CLOSET signifies efficient use of one's energy.

UTILITY COMPANY stands for work and the efforts applied to it.

UTILITY POLE symbolizes a supportive element for communication or motivation depending on whether it was a telephone or power pole.

UTOPIA corresponds to an unrealistic goal or perspective of life.

U-TURN advises of a need to go back or return to a former issue.

$\mathcal{V}$

VACANCY (sign) represents availability; possible opportunity.

VACATION signifies the need to get away; may also denote a warning against being on vacation too long.

VACATION HOME will indicate a desire to maintain one's unique homelike elements in one's idea of a getaway vacation/leisure location; cherishing one's homelife and the fact that one takes great comfort in it.

VACCINE pertains to the awareness of having the foresight to protect oneself from negative elements in one's life.

VACUUM (space) relates to an emptiness, usually a lack of emotion; apathy.

VACUUM CLEANER indicates that a clean up is required. This may refer to a situation, relationship, or even some type of negative within oneself.

VAGABOND characterizes a person who follows her/his own course.

VAGRANT will reveal self-reliance; an independent person.

VALANCE connotes a superficial idea.

VALE See valley.

VALEDICTORIAN signifies a personal opinion.

VALENTINE implies affection.

VALENTINE'S DAY stands for a celebration of those we have affection for. This symbol may come if one isn't expressing their feelings enough.

VALERIAN (botanical) suggests a calming, soothing aspect in one's life and the need for it.

VALET represents servitude.

VALHALLA stands for heroic efforts and its benefits/rewards.

VALIDATION points to approval or acknowledgment; assured fact.

VALLEY won't indicate a low point in life, rather it symbolizes a place (or time) of respite.

VALLEY GIRL suggests immaturity; an inappropriate sense of priority.

VALLEY OF THE KINGS (Egypt) corresponds to undiscovered spiritual aspects of the true Reality.

VALVE portrays control and the regulation of it.

VAMPIRE characterizes an individual who uses others for self-serving purposes; ulterior motives.

VAN alludes to great personal efforts expended.

VANDAL reveals a lack of respect for others; behavior which negatively affect others.

VANGUARD represents a leader or the leading edge.

VANILLA (flavor/scent) indicates renewal.

VANISHING POINT exemplifies a perceived end or finalization, yet the horizon is endless. This reveals the fact that what is seen may not necessarily be fact but simply illusionary.

VANITY CASE portrays enhanced appearances.

VANITY LICENSE PLATE reveals a personal attitude or idea.

VANITY PRESS suggests an arrogant or overblown perspective toward one's own new ideas.

VANITY TABLE comes to point out the importance of taking a good look at ourselves once in awhile.

VAPOR See fumes.

VAPOR BARRIER stands for voluntary separation from spiritual matters; willful denial.

VAPORIZER indicates a review of one's spiritual beliefs; a refresher endeavor. May also point to a need to accept spiritual ideas one seems skeptical or confused about.

VAPOR LOCK represents an obstructed flow of energy current through one's system; a psychological block causing multiple dysfunctions.

VAPOR TRAIL See contrail.

VARIABLE RATE means that sometimes there are situations in which timing plays a key role in determining what our behavior ends up costing us.

VARIABLE STAR warns against depending on the fluctuating opinions of others to control the unique individuality and brightness of one's uniqueness.

VARIANCE (zoning) applies to one's right to be different or do something out of the ordinary.

VARICOSE VEINS reflect a difficult path that has been traversed.

VARIEGATED (colors/pattern) symbolizes a blend of ideas.

VARIETY SHOW connotes ideas derived from multiple sources.

VARIETY STORE represents good accessibility to a multitude of options.

VARNISH relates to a desire to finish an issue. Recall the quality of the varnish work. Was it cracked? Beautiful and smooth?

VARSITY portrays the principal elements or individuals.

VASCULAR DISEASE warns of a harmful condition caused by allowing stressors/ frustrations to build up; a call to release (let go) of grudges and those life aspects one has no control over.

VASE reflects various personality characteristics that aren't always evident. The key here is to recall the condition, color, design, etc.

VASECTOMY represents a behavior or choice which results in ineffectiveness; a new inability to generate new beginnings.

VASELINE See petroleum jelly.

VAT symbolizes a container of great size, meaning a large issue to contain in one's life.

VATICAN exemplifies a specific religious belief rather than a purely spiritual one.

VAUDEVILLE alludes to an attempt to try out one's idea or plan.

VAULT (bank/safe) signifies worth; that which one values. Was the dreamscape vault full of something?

VAULTED CEILING stands for high hopes; great expectations; a soaring intellect.

VEAL pertains to a highly nourishing aspect in one's life.

VECTOR corresponds to a carrier or possibly even a messenger, depending on the surrounding dreamscape details.

VEER may mean an attempt to avoid something or it may indicate a diversion from one's life course.

VEGETABLE OIL portrays a factor that contributes to the completion of something.

VEGETABLES usually stand for essential nutrients. See specific type.

VEGETABLE STEAMER denotes the preserving of important elements.

VEGETARIAN represents a separate opinion or attitude.

VEGETATIVE STATE warns of an attitude of indifference, apathy, and/or unawareness.

VEHICLE correlates to the physiological system. Refer to specific types.

VEHICULAR HOMICIDE comes as a serious warning to halt behavior which is hazardous to self and possibly to others as well. Since the general symbology of a vehicle relates to the physical body, the dreamscape element of vehicular homicide may relate to obesity or another form of destructive habit/addiction one is perpetrating on oneself and, indirectly, harming friends and loved ones.

VEIL emphasizes veiled thoughts; concealment of one's emotions or attitudes; may also point to a nebulous or cloudy idea or issue.

VEIN (blood) relates to a life force element; an essential factor.

VEIN (mineral) reveals the presence of a beneficial aspect in one's life.

VELCRO infers an easy, quick attachment. This may refer to relationships or the acceptance of new ideas.

VELOUR (fabric) symbolizes a warm, compassionate character; may also indicate a quiet dignity or wisdom.

VELUM signifies a wispy veil separating the known from the unknown; a state of near-understanding, but not quite there yet.

VELVET (fabric) denotes a soft and soothing situation, relationship, or state of mind; a very comfortable sense.

VELVET GLOVE reveals a congenial and gentle presentation covering the real characteristics of vindictiveness and ruthlessness.

VELVET PLANT See purple passion.

VENDETTA stands for discord associated with revenge and blame.

VENDING MACHINE refers to easy and convenient access to a want or need.

VENEER signifies a false exterior; a self-designed presentation of oneself.

VENEREAL DISEASE applies to the negative effects of not being aware; careless.

VENETIAN BLINDS relate to selective perception; seeing only what one wants to admit to.

VENETIAN RED (color) signifies suppressed anger/resentment.

VENISON portrays an unethical source from which nourishment is obtained.

VENOM See poison.

VENT represents an opportunity to get rid of negative factors in one's life that will ultimately cause harm if retained.

This usually refers to negative emotions or attitudes.

VENTILATION applies to an attempt to maintain fresh ideas; a method of preventing staleness.

VENTRILOQUIST pertains to a person who tends to speak for another, yet is not necessarily given the authority to do so.

VENTURE CAPITAL exemplifies one element in association with preparing for a goal or new course; reserves backing a new beginning.

VENUS (planet) alludes to dreams and their associated symbology; may refer to a personal dream or desire.

VENUS (Roman mythology) signifies deep affection.

VERANDA represents an opportunity to obtain fresh ideas.

VERBAL ABUSE naturally refers to hurtful comments made from an insensitive personality.

VERBENA (botanical/flower) signifies a need to recognize life's blessings.

VERDANT (setting) reflects an abundance of natural talents/bounties which surround one.

VERDICT pertains to a settled decision.

VERDIGRIS applies to evidence of spiritual affects.

VERIFIER (casino) points to someone capable of providing proof of something.

VERMICULITE illustrates an uplifting and nurturing life factor.

VERMILLION (color) is usually associated with behavior or perspective tainted with a touch of negativity.

VERMIN relates to severe negatives in one's life.

VERMONT refers to an abundance of natural riches/blessings.

VERNAL EQUINOX See spring (season).

VERTIGO reflects dizziness/confusion; an inability to think straight.

VESPERS suggest the wisdom of evening reflection over one's day for the purpose of analyzing behavior and responses.

VEST indicates something that is close to one's heart and therefore protected; may also point to secretiveness or a desire for privacy.

VESTIBULE See foyer.

VESTMENTS stand for outward signs of one's position or belief.

VESTRY denotes a segregation of one's spiritual beliefs from daily life.

VESUVIANITE (mineral) symbolizes mental confusion; indistinct thoughts.

VETERAN will characterize an experienced individual.

VETERAN'S DAY reminds us to remember those who fought against adversity.

VETERINARIAN indicates selflessness; compassion.

VETO comes as a decision-making advisement/suggestion.

VIAGRA stands for the need of an aid in order to be effective.

VIBRATION signifies an insight or indication.

VICAR See religious figure.

VICE SQUAD usually stands for one's own conscience.

VICTORIAN (style) most often represents delicate sensitivities; may indicate/advise of a need to toughen up.

VIDEO CAMERA See camcorder.

VIDEOCONFERENCING symbolizes convenient communication bridging distances.

VIDEO GAME denotes unrealistic scenarios, but also points out an enjoyable manner in which one improves skills.

VIDEO PLAYER (VCR) signifies a method of recalling past events.

VIDEOTAPE refers to the recording (witnessing) of an event and may come as an advisement to remember it.

VIENNA SAUSAGE See hors d'oeuvres.

VIEW FINDER symbolizes a need for clear perception.

VIKING characterizes one on a long spiritual journey.

VIGIL infers perseverance.

VIGILANTE characterizes one set on personal vengeance.

VIGNETTE denotes a small, pleasing reminder of something; a memento.

VILLAGE usually represents a small, close-knit community. This symbol will normally refer to the composite grouping of one's friends and close associates.

VILLAIN reveals a wrongdoer, yet may only represent whomever the dreamer perceives as being in the wrong.

VINE (botanical) relates to far-reaching effects.

VINEGAR connotes a distasteful/bitter life aspect.

VINEYARD exemplifies the fruit of one's efforts. Recall the condition of the dreamscape vineyard.

VINTAGE (age designation) will stand for a specific time frame and perhaps represent out-dated ideas. This symbol may also signify ideas confined to a specific attitude/perspective. Something can be vintage racist or vintage McCarthyism.

VINYL denotes an imitation.

VIOLA (flower) suggests practiced spirituality in the way of behavior.

VIOLATION implies a message from one's conscience.

VIOLET (color/flower) alludes to a healing spiritual element.

VIOLIN represents emotional range of expression.

VIPER (snake) signifies vindictiveness.

VIPER FISH applies to a spiritual skepticism.

VIRGA symbolizes a spiritual thirst or unfulfillment.

VIRGIN almost always refers to an unadulterated idea or perspective.

VIRGINIA represents an appreciation of one's bounties/blessings; an abundance of opportunities to appreciate one's natural blessings.

VIRGIN WOOL signifies an idea or life element which hasn't been affected by opinion or subjected aspects; originality.

VIROLOGY (study of) means an interest in learning how to analyze negative elements which affect the well-being of others.

VIRTUAL MEDITATION stands for meditation which takes one's consciousness into the realms of true Reality where one interacts with others.

VIRTUAL MEMORY relates to an extension of one's surface thought patterns; one's superconscious.

VIRTUAL REALITY constitutes an overactive imagination; an inability to discern clearly.

VIRTUOSO signifies one possessing a masterful talent and skill.

VIRUS will pertain to a dangerous negative element that is contaminating one's life.

VIRUS (computer) See computer virus.

VISA stands for one's right of passage; preparedness to proceed, yet only for a specified span of time.

VISCERA refers to the internal workings or hidden elements of an issue.

VISE (tool) illustrates an advisement to get a firm grip on something; may also indicate building pressure or stress.

VISIONARY characterizes one who has attained deep wisdom through experiential knowledge.

VISION QUEST applies to a desire to know oneself and one's direction.

VISITING NURSE will imply someone who is capable of providing healing assistance or counsel.

VISOR CAP typifies an effort to see more clearly, see past the glare of an initial bright idea or something which seems too good to be true.

VISTA equates to a wide view; a panoramic perspective.

VISUAL AIDS will denote life aspects that bring clarity to one's perception or comprehension.

VISUAL ARTS symbolize creative expressiveness.

VITAL SIGNS are a direct message regarding an individual's state.

VITAMIN corresponds to a specific nutrient. Recall the particulars associated with this dream symbol, for this message could infer that the dreamer needs more of this vitamin or is perhaps ingesting too much.

VIXEN implies a playful cleverness.

VOCATIONAL SCHOOL comes as an advisement to gain greater skill or knowledge in respect to the talents one expects to apply in life.

VOICE ACTIVATED symbolizes a personal, emotional reaction to another individual.

VOICE MAIL See answering machine.

VOICE OF AMERICA normally represents the truth amid a storm of fabrications, yet sometimes it can be the reverse. The related dreamscape details will clarify this or the dreamer will understand and make the connection to a real-time life situation.

VOICE-OVER usually comes as an attention-getting symbol which sends a message from one's Higher Self or conscience.

VOICEPRINT comes to advise of a need to validate oneself. This means that there's a need to know oneself.

VOILE (fabric) suggests the presence of fragile elements to one's character.

VOLCANIC EXPLOSIVITY INDEX stands for a gauge of one's withheld emotional pressure and suggests a need to seek harmless methods of releasing it.

VOLCANO may forewarn of an actual event, yet this symbol most often indicates emotional explosions.

VOLLEYBALL indicates a reluctance to accept responsibility, always batting the ball back into another's space.

VOLTMETER suggests a need to monitor one's energy output. This indicates a vacillation due to selective discrimination.

VOLUNTEER denotes the selfless giving of oneself.

VOMITING See regurgitate.

VOODOO reflects spiritual misunderstanding.

VORTEX exposes an opening of some type; an unconventional course.

VOTING MACHINE defines the right to freely choose or make a personal decision.

VOTIVE CANDLE connotes spiritual comfort.

VOUCHER pertains to validation; reasons behind behavior.

VOW stands for a promise; strong intention; a pledge, often to oneself.

VOYAGER characterizes an individual who is free to follow her/his own spiritual course.

VOYEUR exposes personal inadequacy and a poor self-image. This dream element usually has little to do with sexual implications but rather comes to reveal personalities who are incompetent and dependent upon others in order to feel fulfilled.

VULTURE warns of greedy and aggressive individuals; a user; benefiting from the shortfalls of others.

$\mathcal{W}$

WAD represents an amount or measurement implying a considerable quantity.

WADDLE signifies a personal burden; great weight carried.

WADERS (fishing) refer to a curious interest in spiritual matters yet hesitant to get the feet wet.

WADING stands for testing spiritual waters and getting one's feet wet with new spiritual issues.

WAFER connotes an acceptable form or more utilitarian configuration of a specific life element with which one needs to be associated.

WAFFLE depicts indecision; vacillation; evasiveness.

WAFFLE IRON represents a firm sense of neutrality.

WAFFLE WEAVE (pattern) See honeycomb (pattern).

WAGE See salary.

WAGE EARNER points to one who puts out personal effort to supply needs.

WAGER See bet.

WAGON applies to a helpful aid that eases burdens.

WAGON MASTER characterizes one who leads others along a lengthy journey.

WAGON TRAIN suggests a lack of personal direction or inability to gain confidence in a personal sense of purpose or course.

WAIF characterizes a victim of circumstance; those less fortunate.

WAILING WALL comes in dreams to stress the importance of showing one's feelings; expressing one's emotions/sensitivities.

WAINSCOTING exemplifies a half-truth; an attempt to cover or hide a portion of something.

WAITING LIST illustrates a popular or desirable aspect. What was the waiting list for?

WAITING ROOM symbolizes expectations. Recall what type of room was presented. Was it a delivery room?

WAITPERSON indicates servitude.

WAIVER relates to a voluntary refusal; a decision to decline.

WAKE (death) See funeral.

WAKE (water) implies the effects left behind after one has performed a spiritual deed.

WAKE-UP CALL will symbolize the opening of one's eyes; sudden realization.

WALES denotes goodheartedness; unpretentiousness.

WALKER (appliance) pertains to self-help methods serving one's progression.

WALKIE-TALKIE signifies a need for close communication; a situation in which parties need to stay in contact.

WALKING connotes progression.

WALKING (on air) symbolizes the qualities of acceptance and centeredness that come with spiritual joy.

WALKING (on water) reveals spiritual arrogance.

WALKING PAPERS infer a dismissal; a sign that indicates the end of a particular issue or the dreamer's involvement in it.

WALKING STICK signifies a means of being independent.

WALKING WOUNDED symbolizes perseverance; forward-looking even after experiencing considerable tribulations.

WALKOUT See strike.

WALKOUT applies to defending one's ethics; standing up for beliefs.

WALK-THROUGH stands for an attempt to familiarize oneself with a particular issue or element.

WALK-THROUGH (final inspection) refers to the last chance to make an objection to something.

WALK-UP represents deeper appreciation for extra efforts expended.

WALL may signify various connotations, depending on where the wall was and the surrounding details. Usually a plain wall symbolizes a type of barrier that needs to be dealt with.

WALLABY signifies protectiveness; defensive attitude toward another.

WALLET See purse (handbag).

WALLFLOWER (botanical) reveals a lack of self-confidence. Points to a need to identify and appreciate one's admirable characteristics.

WALL HANGING will represent a multitude of meanings that will provide insight for the dreamer. Recall what the hanging was. What was it made of? What condition and color? Design? Was it straight or lopsided?

WALLOWING relates directly to self-pity or self-indulgence.

WALLPAPER reflects personal characteristics. Recall the design and colors. Condition? Faded or bright?

WALL PLUG See outlet (electrical).

WALL STREET indicates economic elements that may not be solid or dependable.

WALL-TO-WALL represents an abundance.

WALNUT (tree/wood) refers to a utilitarian life element.

WALRUS suggests spiritual righteousness.

WALTZING typifies a lack of seriousness; one is waltzing through life.

WANDERLUST corresponds with one's inner promptings to get going and be on one's way.

WANNA-BE stands for a tendency to emulate or imitate others.

WANT ADS represent opportunities.

WAR portrays an ongoing conflict.

WARBLER (bird) stands for communication simplicity; the conveyance of thoughts with clarity and without complexity.

WAR BONNET reveals an intention to instigate or become involved in an altercation.

WAR BRIDE refers to an action taken before its time.

WAR CHEST signifies resources reserved for a designated purpose.

WAR CORRESPONDENT characterizes an interest in maintaining current information on an opponent.

WAR CRIMES point to a time when one's basest attitudes and behavior is exhibited, usually without prior thought, instinctively; when rage or revenge are acted upon.

WAR CRY signifies instigating acts and/or words.

WARDEN applies to imprisoning elements in life, often self-induced.

WARDROBE reveals particulars regarding an individual's character. Recall the types and colors of the clothing.

WARDROBE MISTRESS characterizes an individual who is expert at perceiving another's out-of-character behavior.

WAREHOUSE exemplifies storage; may infer one's memory.

WAREHOUSE WORKER connotes organizational skills.

WAR GAMES depict a desire to maintain optimum skill and strategy.

WAR HAWK characterizes an aggressive personality who favors the resolution of conflicts through warring means.

WARHEAD exposes a potentially explosive situation, relationship, or other type of life element.

WARLOCK stands for imagined power.

WARLORD pertains to a recognized aggressive personality.

WARM relates to a comfortable perspective of oneself through humanitarian and spiritual acts.

WARM FRONT applies to a forthcoming time of personal peace; a phase consisting of less stress and fewer problematical situations; a time of open and congenial responsiveness.

WARMED-OVER stands for renewed enthusiasm or motivation.

WARMING PAN refers to a life aspect that soothes and comforts.

WARMONGER See war hawk.

WARM-UP SUIT See sweat suit.

WARNING will always denote just that, a warning. Recall the dream's surrounding details for specific information.

WAR PAINT illustrates the intent to engage in some form of conflict.

WARPATH advises that one is proceeding along a course that has the strong probability of ending in an altercation.

WARPED warns of a distorted perspective, attitude, emotion, or belief.

WARP SPEED suggests an immediate need to hasten a closure or conclusion.

WARRANTY refers to validation.

WARREN (rabbit) most often symbolizes the quiet endurance of personal pain.

WARRIOR usually stands for perseverance; personal strength.

WAR ROOM stands for a need to strategize.

WARSHIP signifies a spiritual altercation; ready to defend one's beliefs.

WART pertains to a negative aspect (perhaps emotion or attitude) that one has allowed to grow under one's skin.

WART REMOVER stands for that which is capable of removing/dissolving a negative element one is carrying around.

WASHBOARD alludes to a need to scrub or apply diligent efforts to rid a negative element from one's life.

WASHCLOTH represents a cleansing aspect.

WASHER (seal) connotes a sealing effort; an attempt to confine.

WASHING portrays a desire to be surrounded by positive aspects.

WASHING MACHINE pertains to an aid that is capable of cleansing negative elements from one's life.

WASHINGTON stands for spiritual abundance.

WASHINGTON MONUMENT represents basic rights.

WASHOUT See erosion.

WASHROOM See bathroom.

WASP See hornet.

WASSAIL implies festive attitudes; goodwill.

WASTEBASKET denotes that which is discarded. Recall what was in the dream's wastebasket. Did it really belong there?

WASTELAND signifies a barren or unproductive phase in one's life.

WASTEPAPER reveals unnecessary elements in one's life. It's important to determine what these pieces of paper were. Letters? Plans?

WATCH See clock.

WATCHBAND may reveal how time is personally perceived. Recall what material the band was made of. Gold? Gemstones? Leather or vinyl? What was the color or design?

WATCH CAP (hat) stands for awareness, watchfulness.

WATCH CHAIN stands for efficiency; punctuality.

WATCHDOG defines a friend's alertness; acute awareness.

WATCH FIRE comes as an attention-getting dream fragment. Recall the surrounding details for clarification. Location?

WATCHING TELEVISION will reveal the current quality and state of one's perspectives. A cartoon would represent immaturity; news would represent keeping current with daily events, etc. The key is what one is watching.

WATCH LIST stands for individuals or events to keep aware of.

WATCHMAKER constitutes precision.

WATCHMAN See guard.

WATCHTOWER See lookout.

WATCHWORD See password.

WATER always reflects spiritual aspects.

WATER BALLET portrays spiritual inner joy.

WATER BED reveals a state of sleeping spirituality and advises one to wake up one's spiritual aspects and utilize them.

WATER BLISTER stands for a spiritual burn one has received.

WATER BUFFALO indicates a spiritual arrogance.

WATER CLOSET See bathroom.

WATERCOLOR will reveal a visual (painting) related to a spiritual aspect in one's life. This dreamscape symbol will be different for each dreamer.

WATER COOLER portrays spiritual refreshment.

WATERCRESS suggests spiritual nourishment.

WATERED DOWN reveals waning spiritual strength or interest.

WATERFALL represents a flow of spiritual energy.

WATER FAUCET See faucet.

WATER FILTER pertains to spiritual discernment.

WATERFOWL stands for spiritual thoughts.

WATERFRONT See lakefront.

WATERGATE (historical event) exposes the fact that crime can come from one holding the highest position.

WATER GAUGE See rain gauge.

WATER GUN See squirt gun.

WATER HEATER signifies a need to rejuvenate one's spirituality; expend more energy on spiritual behavior.

WATER HOLE infers a source of spiritual nourishment.

WATERING CAN symbolizes a personal effort to spiritually nourish or affect others.

WATER LILY (botanical) reflects spiritual beauty.

WATER LINE signifies one's level of spirituality. Recall if the line was low or at peak level.

WATER-LOGGED warns of spiritual drowning, an indication of a forced progression whereby spiritual aspects have not been absorbed (comprehended).

WATER MAIN will refer to an individual's spiritual foundation.

WATERMARK denotes originality.

WATERMELON portrays spiritual nutrients.

WATERMELON SEEDS point to seeds of spirituality; aspects that have the potential to regenerate spiritual benefits or rewards.

WATERMELON TOURMALINE (gemstone) points to optimism and its healing benefits.

WATER METER will reveal a person's use of spiritual talents and overall beliefs.

WATER MILL symbolizes the fact that spiritual aspects are the driving force in one's life.

WATER MOCCASIN stands for the presence of a serious negative lying along one's path and the acute awareness needed to step carefully to avoid the encounter/conflict.

WATER PARK symbolizes taking joy in one's spirituality.

WATER PIPE See hookah.

WATERPROOF pertains to spiritual apathy.

WATER PURIFIER refers to an active attempt to filter the intake of spiritual elements; to be spiritually discerning.

WATER-REPELLENT signifies a fear of being touched by spiritual aspects.

WATER RETENTION usually stands for a withholding of one's natural talents; a warning to release one's inherent abilities and share them; practice more spiritual goodness.

WATER RIGHTS come as an important dreamscape symbol verifying one's right to a spiritual belief.

WATERSHED exemplifies a diverted spiritual course; the source of one's spiritual belief system.

WATER-SKIING suggests skimming over spiritual matters.

WATER SNAKE represents spiritual elements that may or may not need avoiding. Recall if the snake was poisonous or otherwise dangerous.

WATER SOFTENER warns of attempting to soften spiritual truths; cautions not to lessen the hard facts.

WATERSPOUT depicts a sudden spiritual insight that's initially a bit confusing.

WATER SPRITE portrays the often unrecognized and unexpected elements of spiritual reality.

WATER TABLE implies a spiritual grounding.

WATERTIGHT denotes spiritual confinement. The key here is to recall if water (spiritual aspect) was kept out or retained.

WATER TOWER implies the presence of spiritual reserves.

WATER WHEEL See water mill.

WATER WINGS portray personal preventive measures taken to ensure against becoming spiritually inundated.

WATER WITCH See dowsing rod.

WATERWORKS connote the amount of spiritual talent one uses.

WATTAGE relates to the quantity and extent of one's inner strength.

WAVE (greeting) pertains to an acknowledgment given to another.

WAVE (water) represents the continually renewing effects of spirituality in one's life.

WAVER implies a hesitation; perhaps indecision.

WAVERING (atmosphere) pertains to an unstable or questionable situation.

WAVY (pattern) represents spirituality.

WAX typifies a pliable personality or plan.

WAXING MOON signifies growing inner strength.

WAX MUSEUM depicts the mask that people present to others (even though it may seem to be an exact replica of themselves).

WAX PAPER connotes an airtight condition.

WAXWING (bird) signifies a gentle wisdom; subtle intelligence.

WAYLAID suggests a pause or temporary halt to one's life progression.

WAY STATION stands for a stopping point or meaningful situation one should experience.

WEAK-KNEED relates to a lack of courage or self-confidence.

WEAKNESS (physical) represents a lack of courage; fear of responsibility.

WEALTH usually relates to inherent, natural abilities; will denote monetary connotations if presented as gold.

WEANED portrays inner growth.

WEAPON won't necessarily indicate a negative meaning, but usually applies to a preparedness to protect oneself from negative elements in life.

WEASEL alludes to a cowardly act; may illustrate evasiveness depending on the surrounding dreamscape details.

WEATHER will bring a multitude of meanings into the overall dreamscape interpretation. Refer to specific type.

WEATHER BALLOON emphasizes one's cautionary tendency to test the air of a situation or relationship.

WEATHER-BEATEN constitutes a difficult life and the fortitude that exists to continue on.

WEATHER BUREAU represents a personal effort to monitor one's own awareness of impending situational changes.

WEATHERCAST denotes a sense for what the mood will be regarding a particular issue or situation; foreknowledge.

WEATHERED correlates with extensive experiential difficulties and the inner strength and power that has been gained.

WEATHER MAP comes as a forecasting of upcoming situational conditions.

WEATHERPROOF See waterproof.

WEATHER RADAR See Doppler radar.

WEATHER STRIPPING symbolizes an attempt to maintain emotional calm; an avoidance of difficulties.

WEATHER VANE cautions against changing opinions or attitudes depending on whatever way the wind blows.

WEATHERWORN See weather-beaten.

WEAVER signifies the totality of true Reality and the multidimensional elements that are woven into it.

WEAVER (bird) stands for the ability to simplify complex concepts or issues.

WEAVING (vehicle) warns of carelessness; a lack of awareness as one travels one's path.

WEAVING LOOM See loom.

WEB See Internet.

WEB (spider) stands for the complexities that one weaves in life.

WEBBING (fabric) exemplifies interrelated aspects to a single element.

WEBCAM reveals a potential invasion of privacy.

WEBMISTRESS characterizes a woman who is skilled at setting up another's personal central communication network.

WEB RETAILER signifies ultimate convenience; minimal effort expended for the purpose of obtaining a goal.

WEB SITE stands for a source of information on a particular issue.

WEDDING usually won't relate to the ceremonial meaning with a religious figure and two betrothed people but rather will signify a joining of some type which will be clarified by the dream's surrounding details.

WEDDING CAKE denotes celebratory sharing.

WEDDING CHAPEL (Las Vegas) suggests a union made in haste with little forethought.

WEDDING PLANNER will be someone who gives careful attention to the preparations or foundations of an impending relationship.

WEDDING RING See ring (jewelry).

WEDGE (shape) stands for interference.

WEDGWOOD BLUE (color) suggests a dignified, gentle spirituality.

WEDNESDAY correlates to a suggested time for re-energizing oneself.

WEED depicts falsehoods; may apply to spiritual ideas that are extraneous and human-devised for the purpose of control.

WEED CUTTER connotes the routine monitoring of one's beliefs and the clearing out of unrelated concepts.

WEED KILLER See herbicide.

WEEKEND usually refers to a time for leisure, time away from stressors.

WEEKEND WARRIOR suggests a temporary obligation.

WEEP HOLES (construction) stand for tempered sorrow/grief. This is a good symbol pointing to one's tendency to often release pent-up emotions so stress/pressure doesn't build up.

WEEPING naturally reflects sorrow. Recall the dream's surrounding details to determine what this sorrow is associated with.

WEEPING WILLOW symbolizes the beauty and sensitivity of nature.

WEEVIL pertains to negative elements that have the potential to destroy one's natural and inherent abilities, these negatives most often being jealousy, egotism, revenge, etc.

WEIGH IN comes in dreams as an advisement to make a decision; express an opinion; time to make a choice.

WEIGH STATION See road signs.

WEIGHTLESSNESS usually reveals a freed spirit experience.

WEIGHT LIFTER characterizes an individual's perceived strength.

WEIGHTS pertain to burdens, some willfully taken on.

WEIMARANER (dog breed) signifies a friend's loyalty.

WEIR symbolizes a spiritual trap, perhaps control or manipulation.

WELCOME MAT means congeniality; one is open to new ideas.

WELCOME WAGON implies one's state of acceptance by others.

WELDING connotes an attempt to make strong connections.

WELFARE applies to situations that may require the assistance or intervention of others.

WELFARE WORK See social service.

WELL (water) relates directly to a spiritual source; may refer to spiritual resources. Recall if the well was full or empty. Was it contaminated? What grew around it?

WELL-DONE (cooked) exemplifies a full conclusion or closure.

WELL DRILLING implies a search. If the driller was looking for *water* this meant a *spiritual* search. If the search was for *oil,* it meant a *financial* search.

WELLHEAD (water) refers to a marker for a spiritual source.

WELLS FARGO TRUCK illustrates a source of bounties, both material and spiritual. Also may refer to the movement of one's assets from one recipient to another.

WELLSPRING signifies an unending source; fountainhead.

WELL TEST (water) denotes a check on the quality of one's own spiritual behavior.

WELSH CORGI (dog breed) symbolizes a companionable friend.

WELSH TERRIER (dog breed) refers to a friend who can be tenacious in helping you stick to goals.

WELT (skin) exposes an injury other than a physical one, such as a business event, an emotional hurt, etc.

WEREWOLF pertains to a dysfunction that alternately varies behavior.

WEST (direction) connotes a near-completed goal.

WEST INDIES refer to uncommon ideas; exotic or eccentric ideas/beliefs.

WEST POINT infers a rigid routine; a need to be more flexible.

WEST VIRGINIA refers to life's simplicities, it's basics.

WET BAR represents an opportunity to soften one's stress.

WET BLANKET suggests a lack of enthusiasm; emotionless.

WETLANDS stand for the richness of spiritual bounties or inherent natural gifts; a wealth of both.

WET NURSE signifies an individual who is capable of providing nourishment, usually of the emotional kind; someone who provides comfort.

WET SUIT portrays a willful distancing from spiritual aspects; an insulating measure.

WHALE corresponds to a person's spiritual generosity or magnanimity; a giving and compassionate individual.

WHALEBOAT symbolizes that which destroys goodness.

WHALEBONE alludes to spiritual strength.

WHALE OIL defines spiritual and humanitarian qualities that are continually used for the benefit of others.

WHALER See whaleboat.

WHARF See pier.

WHEAT signifies some type of nourishing element in one's life. This nourishment usually refers to mental or emotional aspects.

WHEAT GERM suggests a highly potent nourishing aspect.

WHEEL (design) represents completion; full-circle; closure.

WHEELBARROW stands for burdens shouldered. Recall what was in the dream wheelbarrow and who was pushing or using it.

WHEELCHAIR pertains to an inability to stand on one's own feet, yet won't be a negative connotation. This usually infers a temporary setback regarding one's path progression.

WHEELHOUSE stands for the singular control one has over spiritual direction.

WHEELWRIGHT characterizes a person capable of helping another get back on track.

WHEEZING warns of a suffocating situation or relationship; an inability to clearly breathe.

WHETSTONE reflects a life element that will sharpen one's skills or understanding.

WHINING signifies self-pity.

WHIP relates to a motivational source.

WHIPLASH warns against allowing others to push or force progression.

WHIPPET (dog breed) signifies impetuosity, usually related to a friend.

WHIPPING CREAM refers to the frosting on the cake type of meaning; unexpected benefits; additional benefits over and above what was expected or anticipated.

WHIP-POOR-WILL (bird) stands for melancholia.

WHIPSTITCH (sewing) stands for a quick fix; a temporary resolution.

WHIRLIGIG denotes acceptance; a carefree attitude that goes with the flow and takes changes with the perspective of "that's life."

WHIRLPOOL exposes a spiritual

entanglement that could ultimately pull one down.

WHIRLWIND reveals twisted thought; conclusions or assumptions which have been reached too quickly.

WHISKBROOM suggests a need to routinely pick up after oneself. This refers to one's behavior and its effects.

WHISKERS (animal) allude to awareness; acute sensitivity.

WHISKEY See alcoholic beverage.

WHISPERING represents a quiet communication which may have various sources such as another individual, one's inner guidance, or even from the conscience.

WHISTLE most often typifies an attention-getting sound. Recall the surrounding details of the dream for further clarification.

WHISTLE-BLOWER exposes a betrayer; may portray an aspect of oneself which would then signify one's own conscience being the source of this symbol.

WHISTLE STOP emphasizes a message; a need to stop and pay attention to an existing situation.

WHITE applies to purity and goodness; the positive aspects in life.

WHITECAPS represent the positive effects of a highly active spiritual life.

WHITE-COLLAR CRIME refers to negative behavior from those whom we least expect it; negative behavior from those who should know better.

WHITE-COLLAR WORKER signifies confined workspace; confined thought.

WHITE ELEPHANT stands for a rarity; may also point to attitudes or talents that are unique.

WHITE FLAG connotes a peaceful resolution; a capitulation; an end to conflict.

WHITE GLOVES warn against being a perfectionist; expecting too much; selectiveness; nit-picky.

WHITE HAT reveals an individual who is on the right side, has the right attitude.

WHITE HOUSE signifies perceived authority; a tendency to heavily rely on others who act as decision-making advisors.

WHITE KNIGHT corresponds to someone perceived as one's rescuer; one who has the capability to save the day.

WHITE KNUCKLES may indicate fear, anxiety, worry, anger, etc., yet the bottom-line interpretation is perseverance; holding on with all one's strength.

WHITE MAGIC stands for one's inherent gifts used for the benefit of others.

WHITE MAHOGANY (wood) reveals a rare strength of character.

WHITENER See bleach; teeth whitener.

WHITE NOISE warns of a loss of focus, concentration; distracted by irrelevant aspects.

WHITEOUT See blizzard.

WHITE PAGES (phone book) denote the need to contact someone.

WHITE TIE alludes to a formality.

WHITEWASHING exposes a cover-up; deception.

WHITE WATER warns of highly dangerous spiritual paths that could bring harm to those not well prepared or experienced enough to travel through them.

WHITMAN (Walt) characterizes a gentle nature.

WHITTLING relates to a calculated plan for one's life.

WHIZ KID characterizes intellectual attainment, yet may not indicate that this intelligence is accompanied by the wisdom that should go hand in hand with it.

WHOLE GRAIN refers to the whole aspect of a nourishing element.

WHOLESALE represents a deal; getting something for less cost to oneself.

WHOOPING COUGH reveals an inability to deal with reality, life.

WHORLED (pattern) See swirl.

WICK stands for that which generates a type of illumination; a source of revealing information; possibly high insights.

WICKER pertains to ingenuity; resourcefulness.

WICKET See gate.

WIDE-ANGLE LENS connotes an advisement to broaden one's scope of perception.

WIDE-SCREEN stands for an advisement to expand one's perspective.

WIDOW(ER) may not relate to a physical death but rather symbolizes a solitary state. This may refer to reclusiveness, a need to be alone for a time, an independence, or a remote path that has been chosen.

WIDOW'S PEAK (hair) reveals a strong characteristic to one's personality, most often a type of singular ideal.

WIDOW'S WALK defines perpetual awareness. May also refer to a waiting period.

WIG may reveal artificial thoughts as in deception, or it could mean an attempt to alter one's thoughts or correct them.

WILD CARD pertains to a questionable element of an aspect.

WILD DOG exposes an unpredictable friend or close associate.

WILDEBEEST denotes a lack of individuality.

WILDERNESS connotes an unaffected element; untouched, thereby existing in a pure state.

WILD-EYED most often represents fear or great confusion.

WILDFIRE emphasizes a loss of control; something has gotten out of one's hands.

WILDFLOWER generally pertains to the beauty of making free choices in life.

WILDFOWL See specific type.

WILD-GOOSE CHASE signifies an unproductive effort.

WILD MAN stands for a savage personality; violent, erratic behavior.

WILD OATS symbolize immaturity, recklessness, and promiscuity one needs to get out of one's system before real maturity and progression can begin.

WILD WEST (setting) won't stand for wild as much as free to travel one's chosen life course without red tape, restrictions, or limiting confinements.

WILD WOMAN equates to the feminine psyche's connection to the fertile, feral persona of Mother Nature—the Earth Goddess within.

WILDWOODS See wilderness.

WILLIAMSBURG (Virginia) comes in dreams to remind us of the laborious work that the simple life took and to advise us to appreciate how far we've come.

WILL-O'-THE-WISP as opposed to a dictionary definition, this will mean quite the contrary in dream symbology. This little dreamscape fragment stands for subliminal insights or enlightened ideas.

WILLOW pertains to spiritual tenacity.

WILTED See withered.

WINCH implies an uplifting element in one's life that pulls us out of emotionally mired situations.

WIND corresponds to mental activity; the thought process; psychological functioning.

WINDBAG reveals meaningless talk; verbosity; much talk and little substance.

WINDBLOWN alludes to an inundation of ideas; overwhelming concepts.

WINDBREAK indicates a personally devised method of protecting oneself from being overwhelmed or inundated by useless information or gossip-type talk.

WINDBURN reveals the dangerous condition of being burned by allowing oneself to be exposed to negative or harmful ideas.

WIND-CHILL FACTOR warns of ideas that are more dangerous than they appear.

WIND CHIMES symbolize comforting thoughts; perhaps a gentle calling.

WINDFALL pertains to an unexpected benefit or bounty. Also see blow down.

WIND-FORCE SCALE (Beaufort) comes to suggest one keeps an eye on the rate of one's thoughts. Some thinking is done at lightning speed and many important elements are left out.

WIND LOAD represents an awareness of how much one can tolerate emotional issues.

WINDMILL cautions against mental laziness; indicates a lack of individual, original thought.

WINDOW portrays the quality and quantity of personal perception.

WINDOW BOX (curio decor) suggests personal attention given to accurate perception.

WINDOW BOX (flowers) stand for a deep appreciation for nature's beauty/bounty and the efforts expended on surrounding self with it.

WINDOW-DRESSING applies to dressed perceptions; perceptions that one alters according to individual attitudes, qualities, or even the changing seasons.

WINDOW LEDGE may indicate a precarious viewpoint or it may refer to a perception supported by strengthening elements.

WINDOWPANE comes to reveal the accuracy of one's personal perception. Recall the condition, color, and glass type of the dream windowpane. Was it dirty? Cracked? Shattered? Tinted or rippled?

WINDOW SEAT suggests an opportunity to be aware of what's transpiring around one.

WINDOW SHADE warns of a shaded perspective.

WINDOW-SHOPPING implies a search for ideas.

WINDOW WASHER characterizes someone capable of clarifying another's perspective on an issue.

WIND SHEAR reveals a thought or idea that could cut one down if close awareness or monitoring is not maintained.

WINDSHIELD suggests the eyes through which perspectives are formed. Check the condition of the dream windshield. Was it tinted? Slanted? Shielded? Cracked? This symbol is very much like that of a window.

WINDSHIELD WASHER FLUID comes to suggest one doesn't have a clear perspective.

WIND SOCK cautions against a tendency to care about the opinions of others by watching which way the wind blows.

WINDSURFING warns against letting popular opinion direct one's spiritual life path.

WIND TUNNEL exposes mental aberrations and psychological dysfunctions; perceptual inability.

WIND-UP stands for determined motivation; efforts spent on re-energizing oneself.

WINDY signifies a change by way of clearing away negative elements.

WINE denotes fully developed ideas; a healthy, full-bodied element in one's life.

WINE CELLAR stands for a store of ideas. Was the cellar well stocked? Covered with dust? Full of a wide variety of wine types?

WINEGLASS represents a specific new idea that has full potential.

WINEMAKER characterizes the quality of an idea; the formulated potential of it.

WINEPRESS stands for the formulation of good ideas.

WINE TASTING denotes the sampling of new ideas.

WING CHAIR applies to intellectual reaches; high insights.

WING MAN characterizes guided thoughts.

WING NUT pertains to intellectual leverage.

WINGS emphasize personal freedoms.

WING TIP SHOES suggest the donning of dapper airs.

WINK illustrates an unspoken message.

WINNOWING stands for efforts expended on sorting out the facts from associated extraneous elements.

WINTER (season) exemplifies a time to contemplate spiritual beliefs.

WINTERGREEN (botanical) stands for renewal; a wider perspective toward possibilities.

WINTERIZE applies to spiritual preparations.

WINTERKILL reveals the loss of an emotion or attitude due to a devastating event.

WINTER SOLSTICE reflects a time to celebrate the comfort of inner spiritual peace.

WIRE (electric) alludes to the transmission and current of one's inner energy.

WIRE (metal) illustrates a strengthening or supportive factor.

WIRE (send) See telegram.

WIRE BRUSH exemplifies a heavy cleaning or the act of scraping away unwanted elements in one's life.

WIRE CUTTERS caution against severing a supportive element in one's life.

WIRE GLASS refers to perception reinforced by strong opinions.

WIRELESS usually relates to one's connection to another, most often emotional; may also point to intuition.

WIRE SERVICE relates to a source for information-gathering and its dissemination.

WIRETAP reminds us that someone is always listening, even our own conscience.

WIRE TRANSFER (funds) refers to the passing of benefits to another.

WISCONSIN signifies a source of nutrients. These could relate to emotional, intellectual, or psychological needs.

WISDOM TOOTH won't be associated with intellect but rather common sense.

WISECRACK will usually reveal one's true attitude that was heretofore hidden.

WISE WOMAN characterizes attained wisdom carried with quiet dignity.

WISHBONE implies hope.

WISH LIST applies to one's wants, not necessarily the priority needs.

WISPY represents an intuitive feeling; something one can't quite put a finger on.

WISTERIA (botanical) reflects spiritual beauty and grace.

WITCH won't usually denote a negative connotation, for Wicca is a bona fide Nature religion celebrating the seasons, the Divine Essence felt in nature, and the natural gifts inherent in everyone. A witch most often represents an individual who recognizes and uses those natural abilities to help others.

WITCH BALL signifies a protective element used for the purpose of repelling negative elements.

WITCH DOCTOR represents the dual aspects of inherent abilities, whether they're used for negative or positive purposes.

WITCHERY denotes behavior that's not fully understood; unconventional behavior.

WITCH HAZEL (botanical) denotes a healing life aspect.

WITCH-HUNT exposes spiritual and moral immaturity and ignorance.

WITCH'S BREW applies to a blend of various effective elements.

WITHDRAWAL (symptoms) symbolizes yearning for what one needs to deny.

WITHERED suggests a need for refreshing elements in one's life; a spiritual renewal or emotional uplift.

WITHERED (plant) signifies a lack of attention/interest.

WITNESS reminds us that someone is always watching, even our own subconscious; may ultimately pertain to one's conscience.

WITNESS CORNER See cornerstone.

WITNESS STAND connotes the exposure of a formerly hidden deed or thought.

WIZARD refers to arrogant intelligence, often an alleged/contrived intelligence.

WIZARD OF OZ reveals a deception.

WOLF signifies cleverness and evasiveness; will sometimes infer self-interest.

WOLFSBANE (botanical) reflects a dangerous association.

WOLVERINE implies vicious aggressiveness; back-biting; vengeful vindictiveness.

WOMBAT signifies familial associations; learning through example.

WOMEN'S EQUALITY DAY comes as a reminder that we need to see every human being as having equal rights/opportunities.

WOMEN'S WEAR (clothing dept.) stands for the wide range of options a woman can choose from to express her individuality or attitude.

WONDER DRUG represents a powerful healing element or solution.

WONDERLAND usually indicates awareness and the marvels one perceives, but this symbol can also represent wearing those rosy glasses which prevent one from seeing the whole of life.

WONDER WOMAN characterizes one who appears to be able to handle/accomplish anything; emphasizes a woman's inner power and its unlimited potential.

WOOD carries a general meaning related to one's natural talents and inherent characteristics.

WOOD BETONY (botanical) See lousewort.

WOOD-BURNING (craft tool) symbolizes focused creativity; a gently expressed nature.

WOODCARVING typifies creativity through gentleness; acceptance of life.

WOOD CHIPS suggest the common use for mulch; therefore, this symbol refers to an aspect in one's life that preserves spirituality (moisture) and prevents negative aspects (weeds) from infiltrating one's attitude or behavior.

WOOD CHIPPER (machine) suggests an intent to preserve and enrich one's inherent abilities or gifts.

WOODCHUCK See groundhog.

WOODCUT symbolizes a creative way one's natural talents are manifested. What was the woodcut of? How was it utilized?

WOOD DUCK signifies spiritual serenity; deep sense of spiritual peace.

WOOD LILY (botanical) signifies rejuve-

nation caused by an energized sense of determination.

WOOD NYMPH (mythology) represents the undiscovered, hidden ways of nature.

WOODPECKER relates to an effort to rid oneself of negative aspects.

WOODPILE represents preparedness; personal effort expended.

WOOD RAT signifies difficulty recognizing one's priorities. Also see pack rat.

WOOD SHAVINGS denote the residual effects left over after one has used a special talent/skill to accomplish something. If the shavings are cedar wood, then they represent additional benefits—aromatic purposes.

WOODSHED applies to thorough planning.

WOOD SORREL (botanical/flower) represents a rekindled sense of resolve; encouragement.

WOOD SPLITTER connotes an aid for maintaining one's preparedness.

WOOD STAIN refers to one's personal touch to a creation (goal or project). What color/shade was the Stain?

WOODSTOCK (event) suggests free expression.

WOODSWOMAN symbolizes the inherent connection of feral instinct, fertileness, and an inner knowing type of wisdom which women and Mother Nature share in common.

WOODSY OWL comes to remind us of our responsibility to be earth's caregivers.

WOODWORKING refers to utilizing one's inherent talents in creative ways.

WOOL See shearling.

WOOLGATHERING alludes to daydreaming which may or may not be productive thought, depending on the surrounding dream details.

WORD ASSOCIATION signifies those triggers which serve as emotional triggers of the subconscious.

WORD GAMES come as an advisement to speak clearly instead of beating around the bush, making plays on words, or giving out innuendos.

WORD OF HONOR denotes integrity related to promises.

WORD OF MOUTH signifies information passed verbally, but reminds one to consider it may lose some of its original integrity/accuracy.

WORD PROCESSOR relates to the ease of communication that one may be fearing or denying.

WORKAHOLIC comes as a warning to slow down and take time out for oneself/leisure. This is a serious symbol revealing an overworked mental/physical condition.

WORKBENCH represents personal efforts needed to be expended.

WORKBOOK implies more study is required; work to learn more.

WORKERS' COMPENSATION portrays benefits or alternative aspects that enter one's life while temporarily unable to proceed along one's chosen course.

WORKING CAPITAL stands for the talents and personal qualities one has. This symbol will rarely relate to a monetary aspect.

WORKING PAPERS relate to a verification that one is pursuing the right course.

WORKOUT (physical) reveals the need to expend great personal effort toward a specific goal.

WORKROOM represents the quality and quantity of effort one puts into achieving goals.

WORKSHEET signifies a need to figure something out; analyzation is required.

WORKSHOP will generally relate to a hobby or an individualized type of creativity used in an enjoyable manner. It points to the fact that some work can be done in a leisurely manner and actually be enjoyable. What type of workshop was it? Carpentry? Craft? Artsy?

WORK-STUDY PROGRAM refers to learning while doing; putting what one has learned into action while continuing to learn more.

WORLD-CLASS signifies outstanding performance/skill.

WORLD FAMOUS symbolizes an individual, concept, or situation which is familiar to people everywhere.

WORLD HEALTH ORGANIZATION (WHO) equates to those who have the capability and power to affect the health of the masses.

WORLDLY signifies a socially/culturally savvy individual; worldly-wise.

WORLD PREMIERE will relate to the initial introduction of an idea.

WORLD SERIES pertains to competitive efforts applied to aspects unrelated to one's goal or life course.

WORLD'S FAIR attempts to broaden one's perspective and reveal the existence of unlimited opportunities.

WORLD-SHAKING (event) See earthquake.

WORLD-WEARINESS equates to a mood of depression/despair; a disgust, tiredness related to the materialistic, pleasure-seeking, elitist attitudes and dog-eat-dog state of the world. This symbol is a call to shift perspectives to focus on the beauty of the natural world and the simplicity of one's many current blessings.

WORM See earthworm.

WORM (computer) See computer worm.

WORMWOOD illustrates obstructed creativity; an inability to apply oneself due to distractions.

WORRY BEADS come in dreams to advise one to let life take care of itself and have more acceptance for what one can't alter; anxiety, possible obsessing.

WORSTED (fabric) suggests a strong character, yet emotionally warm and sensitive.

WOUND See welt.

WOUNDED KNEE (historical event) reminds us of our right/duty to stand up for our rights.

WOUNDWORT (botanical) equates to a healing element in one's life.

WRAITH can sometimes be a forewarning of one's death, but usually it represents one's unhealthy obsession with dying. This symbol may also be associated with a fear of the death of a relationship, career, goal, or a close friend.

WRANGLER characterizes a confining thought process.

WRAPAROUND DECK signifies complete openness.

WRAPPING PAPER denotes a hidden gift; a surprise, perhaps a new idea soon to dawn or enlightened attitude in the offing.

WRAP-UP stands for concluding efforts applied to a project or goal.

WREATH symbolizes various sentiments depending on what it's made of, the color, and what occasion it relates to. Refer to the specific flower type, color, and occasion such as autumn, Christmas holiday, or funeral, etc.

WRECK (airplane) is associated with ideology, serious/critical damage done to one's perspective or belief system.

WRECK (boat) corresponds to spiritual damage.

WRECK (vehicle) correlates to emotional or physiological damage.

WRECKAGE reveals a destructive end or conclusion.

WRECKING BALL refers to a *purposeful* destructive force or element used to bring about a new beginning; clearing out the old (perhaps bad attitudes) to make way for a fresh start.

WREN symbolizes congeniality; hospitality; a consideration of others.

WRENCH warns against using force to accomplish a goal or closure.

WRESTLER exposes an aggressively manipulative personality. May also point to someone who is currently wrestling with an issue; a time of debating.

WRESTLING stands for an attempt to get one's way; trying to sway another.

WRIGHT BROTHERS characterize innovative thought; thinking outside the box.

WRINGING (fabric) implies an effort to get the most out of a life element. What was being twisted? Color? Did it belong to anyone the dreamer relates to? If so, this points to anger or irritation directed to that individual.

WRINGING (hands) stands for fretting, worry, anxiety.

WRINKLED (clothing) implies indifference to the opinion of others; self-confidence without having to show it.

WRINKLED (skin) exemplifies fortitude gained through expending great personal effort.

WRIST (anatomy) represents tenacity; ability to maneuver effectively.

WRITE PROTECTION symbolizes a safeguard against losing information.

WRITER pertains to a desire to express inner thoughts, ideas, or sensitivities.

WRITER'S BLOCK stands for a temporary absence of inspiration. May point to being at a loss as to where to go from here.

WRITER'S CRAMP comes to advise of the ineffectiveness of trying to force ideas on others; a phase when one needs to let things ride.

WRIT OF EXECUTION stands for verification from one's Higher Self in regard to an intended plan; an authorization to proceed.

WROUGHT IRON pertains to strong ideas or concepts forged from personal creativity.

WULFENITE (mineral) represents an emotionally calming element in one's life that serves to soothe erratic aura activity.

WUNDERKIND signifies early achievement; reaching goals far earlier than normally done.

WYE pertains to a place or phase where paths may cross; possible choices.

WYOMING suggests civil liberties and the free expression of them.

$\mathcal{X}$

XANADU See Camelot.

XENON (headlights) signifies a brighter light shed on issues or one's path.

XENOPHOBIA (fear of strangers) See fear.

XERISCAPING symbolizes giving consideration to the mood/characteristics of a situation and making attempts to work within those limitations; behavior in keeping with the lay of the land.

XMAS See Christmas.

X-RATED reveals a type of negative element in one's life that may have to do with a violent individual. Usually these characteristics are also symbolic.

X-RAY suggests a need to thoroughly analyze something; a look at what lies beneath the surface.

X-RAY TECHNICIAN characterizes an individual who has a tendency to analyze and thoroughly research an issue or concept; having the inherent talent for seeing through people's facades.

XYLOPHONE represents opportunities for an individual to attain balance and personal alignment.

$\mathcal{Y}$

YACHT comes as a sign of spiritual arrogance; a tendency to buy one's spiritual attainment.

YACHT CLUB denotes a desire to associate with only those who are *perceived* as being as spiritually elevated as oneself.

YAK relates to a wild strength; lacking discernment regarding the productive use of inner strength.

YAM See sweet potato.

YAMPA (botanical) symbolizes the wisdom of using diplomacy to manage a delicate situation or relationship.

YANKEE DOODLE characterizes loyalty.

YARD (back) See backyard.

YARD (front) implies that which lies in one's future; may also suggest what one presents to the public.

YARDARM connotes a life element that allows one to be blown along by whatever spiritual wind is blowing.

YARD GOODS See fabric/sewing shop.

YARD SALE denotes multiple opportunities; the possibility of discovering a treasure among another's discards; seeing something of value where others don't.

YARDSTICK indicates a gauge of one's path progression.

YARD WORK stands for personal efforts expended on improving one's surroundings; efforts toward nurturing and beautifying one's behavior.

YARMULKE See skullcap.

YARN pertains to falsehoods or that which could lead to complications. May also point to misunderstandings or plain old gossip.

YARROW (botanical) alludes to a sign of independence.

YAWNING illustrates a lack of interest and suggests getting motivated toward learning and progression.

YEARBOOK alludes to a need to review or remember past relationships or experiences to facilitate learning from current life events.

YEARLING connotes immaturity; a need to grow and learn.

YEA-SAYER indicates a tendency to be agreeable to the point of fearing to express an opposing opinion.

YEAST See brewer's yeast.

YELLOW stands for contentedness; inner peace.

YELLOW ALERT (level) equates to a need for elevated awareness.

YELLOW-BELLIED SAPSUCKER indicates a reticence to speak up; a hesitancy to express individuality.

YELLOW DOG refers to a friend who lacks the courage to express an opposing opinion.

YELLOW-DOG CONTRACT represents coerced loyalty.

YELLOW FEVER exposes a poor self-image; frequently signifies a huge ego that constantly needs stroking from all those around one.

YELLOW JACKET See hornet.

YELLOW JOURNALISM stands for a tendency to fixate on the negative; focusing on one's faults, tragedies, or mistakes.

YELLOW LIGHT is a sign of caution and an advisement to slow one's pace.

YELLOW PAGES (telephone book) reflect a wide range of opportunities that are readily available. Further clarification would come if the phone book was open to a specific category.

YELLOWSTONE (Park) pertains to nature's beauty and bounty reflected inside each of us if we'd only look within.

YELLOW STREAK symbolizes a tendency to be overly cautious to the point of inaction or indecision.

YELLOW WARBLER indicates a habit of claiming innocence; rarely accepting responsibility.

YELLOW WATER LILY refers to a vacillating opinion of one's spiritual beliefs, tending to agree with whomever one is with at the time.

YEOMAN normally indicates a paper-pusher, but in dream symbology it points to one who works behind the scenes.

YES-MAN warns against agreeing with others for the purpose of wanting to be liked or accepted.

YEW (botanical) represents spreading (growing) natural talents; inherent abilities.

YIELD SIGN See road signs.

YIN-YANG reminds us of our duality; female and male aspects within oneself.

YLANG-YLANG (flower) stands for fragile, yet enduring, sensitivities; empathy.

YMCA stands for a source for men to experience wholesome activities and possibly forge good friendships.

YODA characterizes the inner peace that true wisdom brings.

YODELING defines a braggart.

YOGA applies to self discipline; method of attaining inner peace.

YOGI usually implies spiritual showmanship.

YOGURT relates to a type of healthful element in one's life.

YOKE (crossbar) exemplifies a burden.

YOLK (egg) See egg yolk.

YOM KIPPUR (Day of Atonement) comes to advise the dreamer that an apology, restitution, or resolution needs to be made.

YORE (time frame) is presented in dreams for a specific purpose and brings a unique message to each dreamer.

YORKSHIRE PUDDING refers to a lighter substitute for a heavier, more nourishing element.

YORKSHIRE TERRIER (dog breed) stands for heartfelt companionship; a friend's faithful loyalty.

YOSEMITE NATIONAL PARK symbolizes the serenity which nature and its beauty has the potential of instilling.

YOSEMITE SAM (character) represents a

rigid personality, one set in one's ways and resisting change.

YOUNGBLOOD indicates a need for fresh ideas.

YOUTH GROUP represents early indoctrination; affecting perspectives/attitudes through early influencing.

YO-YO denotes an unstable emotional life or a lack of decision-making capabilities; a tendency to vacillate or arbitrarily change course.

YUCCA (botanical) relates to a cleansing element in one's life.

YUKON suggests a hardiness of character.

YULE LOG represents a tendency to uphold tradition; stand on ceremony.

YULETIDE See Christmas.

YUPPIE warns against being materialistic and self-centered.

YURT alludes to simplicity. This may refer to a lifestyle, perspective, or character.

YWCA represents a single source offering women multiple opportunities to participate in wholesome experiences and possibly gain a sense of much-needed camaraderie.

Z

ZANY usually characterizes an individual who behaves in an outrageously unconventional, yet amusing, manner; one who acts on the spur of the moment. This symbol won't normally be a negative element but rather point to the freedom which spontaneity brings.

ZEALOT correlates with fanaticism.

ZEBRA represents the good/evil, right/wrong polarity of various elements in one's life.

ZEN pertains to methods for attaining enlightenment, inner peace, and the activation of naturally inherent abilities.

ZENITH stands for the high point; fulfillment; reaching a goal.

ZEPHYR (light breeze) symbolizes gentle thoughts, insights.

ZEPHYR CLOTH (fabric) refers to optimism, looking on the bright side.

ZEPPELIN See dirigible (balloon).

ZERO (number) reveals an unproductive idea or plan; emptiness; a lack.

ZERO (and below temp.) points to a cold, frigid state of affairs. This may relate to one's attitude or a frozen situation that isn't going anywhere any time soon.

ZERO (on phone pad) represents an option one chooses in hopes of contacting a real person to communicate with.

ZERO GRAVITY comes in dreams to advise of the need to get oneself grounded.

ZERO HOUR equates to the scheduled time to begin a plan or put an idea into motion.

ZERO POPULATION GROWTH actually denotes progress.

ZEST illustrates high interest and motivation; excitement.

ZESTY (flavor) usually points to motivation; a re-energizing element.

ZEUS (Greek mythology) corresponds to a Godhead; one of the Supreme Aspects of the Divine Essence.

ZIEGFELD FOLLIES refer to extravagant ideas having the potential for success.

ZIGZAG (motion/pattern) defines a routinely altered course; may infer vacillating attitudes or perspectives.

ZINC portrays a galvanized issue; a protective/defensive measure.

ZINC GREEN (color) See cobalt (green).

ZINC OINTMENT indicates a healing element.

ZINC OINTMENT relates to a healing element available in one's life.

ZINGER may reveal a hidden attitude exposed through a remark or it may turn out to be a revelation of some type.

ZINNIA (botanical) symbolizes multiple benefits or gifts in one's life that have not yet been recognized.

ZIP CODE will reveal a number message or point to a specific locale that holds particular importance for the dreamer.

ZIP GUN exemplifies ineffective protective/defensive methods.

ZIP-LOCK (bag/closure) will indicate a tight seal, even secrecy.

ZIPPER warns against a tendency to control situations; pertains to an indiscriminate opening and closing of one's receptivity.

ZIRCON (natural) constitutes a grounded and centered individual.

ZITHER illustrates multiple opportunities to express oneself.

ZODIAC comes in dreams as commendations from the highest source.

ZODIACAL LIGHT symbolizes the beginning formulation of an inspirational idea.

ZOMBIE warns against the use of psychological manipulation for any reason.

ZONE CHART (for planting) refers to a gauge of behavior, which type is appropriate for various situations. Some behaviors (or methods) aren't productive if another person isn't the least bit receptive to them. This symbol advises of the wisdom of using appropriate methods for dealing with a situation or individual.

ZONING COMMISSION applies to an attempt to control the activities of others.

ZONING OUT may indicate a willful state of unawareness or it may refer to a much-needed break from mental exertion.

ZOO correlates to the beautiful elements of individuality that are being confined, perhaps even by oneself.

ZOOKEEPER normally characterizes a compassionate personality.

ZOOLOGY (study of) indicates a recognition of life's interconnectedness; an interest in further understanding the interrelated facets of life.

ZOOM LENS symbolizes an opportunity or need to get a closer look or analyze a specific aspect in one's life.

ZOOPHOBIA (fear of animals) See fear.

ZOOT SUIT signifies an overinflated self-image meant to project power.

ZUCCHINI indicates an unrealized benefit or positive element in one's life.

ZWIEBACK applies to an attitude of indifference to the difficulties one needs to face in life.

ZYMOMETER denotes attention given to the development of an idea/plan; keeping a close eye on the timing and condition of a specific progression.

HAMPTON ROADS
PUBLISHING COMPANY, INC.

Thank you for reading *In Your Dreams*. Hampton Roads is proud to publish an extensive collection of Mary Summer Rain's books. Please take a look at the following selection or visit us anytime on the web: www.hrpub.com.

Ruby
A Novel
Mary Summer Rain

When antiques dealer Sadie Brennan is called to her sister's estate outside Chicago, she has no idea she's being pulled into a major mystery. But once she arrives in town, Sadie meets a strange homeless woman named Ruby, and her life truly becomes an odyssey as she seeks to solve the puzzle that is Ruby. In *Ruby*, her first work of fiction in more than a decade, Mary Summer Rain delivers a merry adventure of metaphysical awakening, led by an old woman whose identity and purpose is unclear, but who may be something more than she appears and much more than you've ever imagined.

Paperback • 400 pages • ISBN 1-57174-434-7 • $15.95

Phantoms Afoot
Helping the Spirits Among Us

This updated edition of the fourth book in the classic No-Eyes series includes a new preface and introduction from Mary Summer Rain. A timeless collection of soul-retrieval and "ghost-busting" stories, *Phantoms Afoot* tells the tale of Mary and her late husband's weekend meanderings around the Colorado countryside following stories and folk legends about haunted places. Mary doesn't go to these spots as just another curious tourist, however, she goes to help the ghosts and displaced spirits find their way to the light, thereby releasing them from the hellish state of being trapped between two worlds.

Paperback • 360 pages • ISBN 1-57174-396-0 • $14.95

Spirit Song
The Introduction of No-Eyes

The definitive Mary Summer Rain classic. Mary meets her spiritual mentor, No-Eyes, in the Colorado mountains and begins to deepen her understanding of ancient wisdom, learning to respect the spirit and love the Earth Mother.

Paperback • 160 pages
ISBN 1-878901-61-3 • $12.95

Phoenix Rising
No-Eyes' Vision of the Changes to Come

Book 2 of the No-Eyes series reveals astonishing visions of the Earth's future.

Paperback • 176 pages
ISBN 1-878901-62-1 • $12.95

Dreamwalker
The Path of Sacred Power

Book 3 of the No-Eyes series introduces Brian Many Heart, who teaches Mary about dreamwalkers, those who have moved beyond the desires of this world.

Paperback • 240 pages
ISBN 1-878901-63-X • $14.95

www.hrpub.com   ·   1-800-766-8009

Woodsmoke
Autumn Reflections

A must-have for all Mary Summer Rain fans, *Woodsmoke* is volume 2 of the two-book set *Pinecones and Woodsmoke*. The lyrical and profound passages of *Woodsmoke* evoke the serenity of a true connection with the natural world. *Woodsmoke* is a rare and valuable window into the mind and soul of an extraordinary philosopher and writer, reflecting the ever-evolving nature of her vision. Discover *Woodsmoke* and discover anew the magic of one of the most beloved figures of the New Age movement.

Paperback • 416 pages • ISBN 1-57174-373-1 • $16.95

Pinecones
Autumn Reflections

Volume 1 of *Pinecones and Woodsmoke* is a compendium to savor and share. *Pinecones* is a collection of meditations, verses, parables, and lightning-bolt epiphanies pulled directly from the pages of the woods-walking journals Mary carried for many years.

Paperback • 448 pages
ISBN 1-57174-261-1 • $16.95

Bittersweet

Bittersweet documents the major personal upheavals in Mary's life after the publication of *Soul Sounds*. This edition includes a color photo insert of the people, animals, and places in Mary's life.

Paperback w/ 45 color photos • 248 pages
ISBN 1-57174-032-5 • $12.95

Daybreak
The Dawning Ember

Daybreak features Mary's answers to readers' questions regarding No-Eyes and the earth changes. It also includes a guide to dream symbols and the Phoenix Files, a comprehensive list of hazardous sites around the United States.

Paperback • 624 pages
ISBN 1-878901-14-1 • $14.95

Hampton Roads Publishing Company

... for the evolving human spirit

HAMPTON ROADS PUBLISHING COMPANY publishes books on a variety of subjects, including metaphysics, spirituality, health, visionary fiction, and other related topics.

For a copy of our latest trade catalog, call toll-free, 800-766-8009, or send your name and address to:

HAMPTON ROADS PUBLISHING COMPANY, INC.
1125 STONEY RIDGE ROAD • CHARLOTTESVILLE, VA 22902
e-mail: hrpc@hrpub.com • www.hrpub.com